Timbs John

The Industry, Science, & Art of the Age

Timbs John

The Industry, Science, & Art of the Age

ISBN/EAN: 9783337327811

Printed in Europe, USA, Canada, Australia, Japan

Cover: Foto ©ninafisch / pixelio.de

More available books at **www.hansebooks.com**

The International Exhibition.

THE
INDUSTRY, SCIENCE, & ART OF THE AGE:

OR,

The International Exhibition of 1862

POPULARLY DESCRIBED FROM ITS ORIGIN TO ITS CLOSE;

INCLUDING DETAILS OF THE PRINCIPAL OBJECTS AND ARTICLES
EXHIBITED.

By JOHN TIMBS, F.S.A.

EDITOR OF "THE YEAR-BOOK OF FACTS IN SCIENCE AND ART,"
AUTHOR OF "THINGS NOT GENERALLY KNOWN," ETC.

PRIZE MEDAL OF THE INTERNATIONAL EXHIBITION.

LONDON:
LOCKWOOD & CO., STATIONERS' HALL COURT.
1863.

CONTENTS.

	PAGE
OUR INDUSTRIAL EXHIBITIONS	1
THE GREAT EXHIBITION BUILDING, 1851	7
THE EXHIBITION OPENED	10
RESULTS OF THE EXHIBITION	12
The International Exhibition of 1862	15
LAYING OUT THE BUILDING WORKS	25
PROGRESS OF THE BUILDING	26
THE EXHIBITION BUILDING DESCRIBED	33
THE INTERIOR	37
DECORATION OF THE BUILDING	41
THE EXHIBITION ORGANIZED	51
THE PRIZE MEDAL	57
THE EXHIBITION OPENED	63
PROGRESS OF ART-MANUFACTURES EXEMPLIFIED IN THE EXHIBITION	67
Objects and Articles Exhibited:—	
RAW MATERIALS: MINING, QUARRYING, AND METALLURGY	75
GRAPHITE FROM SIBERIA	82
MINERAL WEALTH OF FRANCE	83
MINERALS OF THE ZOLLVEREIN	84
CHEMICAL SUBSTANCES AND PHARMACEUTICAL PROCESSES	85
COAL-TAR AND LICHEN DYES	90
SUBSTANCES USED FOR FOOD	91
INDIAN PRODUCTS	93
Machinery:—	
RAILWAY PLANT: LOCOMOTIVE ENGINES AND CARRIAGES	97
WHEEL CARRIAGES	98
TRACTION ENGINES	99
MANUFACTURING MACHINES AND TOOLS, AND MACHINERY IN GENERAL	100
STEAM-HAMMERS	101
GWYNNE AND CO'S CENTRIFUGAL PUMPING MACHINERY	102
THE UNIVERSAL JOINER.—FIRE-ENGINES	103
SIEBE'S ICE-MAKING MACHINE	104
LIFE-PRESERVING APPARATUS	104
SUGAR MACHINERY	106
PAPER-MAKING MACHINERY	107
BESLEY'S TYPE-CASTING MACHINE	108
YOUNG'S TYPE-COMPOSING MACHINE	109
BANK-NOTE PRINTING	110
FOLDING, PRESSING, AND STITCHING MACHINE	112
SURFACE DECORATION BY BLOCK-PRINTING	113

CONTENTS.

	PAGE
AGRICULTURAL MACHINES AND IMPLEMENTS	113
CIVIL ENGINEERING, ARCHITECTURE, AND BUILDING CONTRIVANCES:—	
ENGINEERING MODELS	117
CEMENT, AND ARTIFICIAL STONE	120
ARCHITECTURAL PRODUCTIONS	121
CLAY AND METAL PIPE-MAKING	122
NAVAL AND MILITARY MODELS, WEAPONS, AND APPLIANCES:—	
NAVAL AND MILITARY MODELS	123
THE ARMSTRONG AND WHITWORTH GUNS	124
NEW CARTRIDGE	127
MARINE ENGINES	128
PUMPING-ENGINES FOR WATERWORKS	130
GAS ENGINEERING	131
PHILOSOPHICAL INSTRUMENTS	132
PHOTOGRAPHY AND PHOTOGRAPHIC APPARATUS	136
CLOCKS AND WATCHES	137
ELECTRIC TELEGRAPHS AND ELECTRICAL APPARATUS	141
SURGICAL INSTRUMENTS AND APPLIANCES	144
SANITARY APPLIANCES	147
MUSICAL INSTRUMENTS	149
THE PIPING BULLFINCH	151
MISCELLANEOUS MACHINERY:—	
COTTON-SPINNING MACHINERY	152
CARPET-LOOMS	153
WASHING MACHINES	154
FOREIGN MACHINERY	154
AMERICAN MACHINERY	156
SEWING MACHINES	160

Manufactures:—

COTTON FABRICS	162
FLAX AND HEMP	167
SILK AND VELVET	168
WOOLLENS AND WORSTED, AND MIXED FABRICS	169
CARPET MANUFACTURE	169
FOREIGN CARPETS	172
TAPESTRIES OF GOBELINS AND BEAUVAIS	175
FLOOR-CLOTHS	176
PRINTED AND DYED FABRICS	177
LACE-MAKING	180
FURS, FEATHERS, AND HAIR	181
INDIA-RUBBER MANUFACTURES	182
PERREAUX'S PATENT PUMP-VALVES	184
LEATHER, INCLUDING SADDLERY AND HARNESS	185
ARTICLES OF CLOTHING	186
PAPER-MAKING AND STATIONERY	188
PRINTING	191

PREFACE.

THE object of this work is to record, in a compact manner, divested of dry, official detail, the rise, progress, and completion of the Great International Exhibition, held at South Kensington in the present year.

When the vastness of this display, and the multiplicity of its details, are duly considered, it appears desirable to place upon record, in a comprehensive yet tangible form, the leading facts, features, characteristics, and results, of this great industrial, scientific, and artistic collection.

Notwithstanding the multitude of histories, catalogues, synopses, and handbooks, in which this stirring event of our times has been chronicled, it has been deemed advisable so to condense its details as to bring within the grasp of a single volume all the most interesting and important incidents of the Exhibition.

The narrative opens with a brief account of our Industrial Exhibitions, more especially that of the year 1851, and its immediate results. To this succeeds a detailed account of the origin of the recent International Exhibition ; the organization of the plan ; the construction and decoration of the Building at South Kensington ; and the opening ceremonial.

The greater portion of the volume is appropriated to the description of the principal contents of the Collection, in as comprehensive a form as possible, disencumbered of details of ephemeral interest, with the special aim of reviewing the merit and value of the inventions, discoveries, and new facts, which are the first fruits of the Exhibition itself.

In the arrangement of these details, the order of the Official Catalogues has been generally followed. Thus, the first portion relates principally to the British contributions ; but, in some cases, for the sake of more immediate comparison, the Foreign contributions have been placed in juxtaposition with those of our own country. These groups of Objects and Articles occupy more than half of the entire volume.

In the succeeding Section, the contributions from the British Colonies are described; and next are those from Foreign Countries.

Next is the Fine Art Division, wherein the principal treasures of the British and Foreign Picture Galleries, Sculpture and Print collections are glanced at.*

The Declaration of Awards to the Exhibitors is next recorded; and the volume concludes with the Report of the closing ceremony.

As a retrospect of the true glories and peaceful triumphs of the year, this volume addresses itself to a very large number of intelligent readers among the hundreds of thousands who have visited the Exhibition, as well as the still larger proportion who have not enjoyed that advantage. To either class it is hoped the work will be welcome; since no labour has been spared to render it, without infringing upon its permanent and useful character, attractive and entertaining as a volume of recreative reading.

To enhance its value as a permanent and graphic record of the glories of this greatest of the Exhibitions, a beautiful and comprehensive photographic view of the interior, by the London Stereoscopic Company (from negatives specially retained for the purpose), is given as a frontispiece.

* The accompanying Table of Contents will best show the order and succession of the groups of subjects; and the Index at the close of the volume facilitate reference to the special examples.

ERRATA.

Page 72, 3rd line from top, *for* " Man" *read* " Maw."
Page 133, 4th line from top, *for* " Hounslow" *read* " Henslow."
Page 134, 4th line from top, *for* "it is not now shown" *read* "it was not shown."
Page 209, 25th line from top, *for* " constructions" *read* " contrivances."

CONTENTS.

	PAGE
BOOKBINDING	195
EDUCATIONAL WORKS AND APPLIANCES	196
FURNITURE AND UPHOLSTERY	200
MEDIÆVAL ART	205
IRON MANUFACTURES	205
GALVANIZED METALS	212
MALLEABLE CAST-IRON.—IRON PAINTS	213
BIRMINGHAM WARES.—WIRE-WORKING	214
THE HEREFORD SCREEN	215
THE NORWICH GATES.—MEDIÆVAL METAL-WORK	216
WOLVERHAMPTON GOODS.—BEDSTEADS	217
COOKING APPARATUS, RANGES, AND STOVES	217
CHANDELIERS, GASELIERS, AND LAMPS	218
THE BRASS TOY TRADE	219
LOCKS AND SAFES	219
STEEL MANUFACTURES	222
KRUPP'S CAST-STEEL	224
BESSEMER'S STEEL	225
WORKS IN THE PRECIOUS METALS	226
ALUMINIUM ARTICLES	231
JEWELLERY	233
GLASS, FOR DECORATIVE AND HOUSEHOLD PURPOSES:—	
STAINED GLASS	237
HOUSEHOLD AND FANCY GLASS	238
POTTERY	241
THE PROCESS COURT	243
SALVIATI'S MOSAICS	246
SUBSTANCES USED IN MANUFACTURES	248
FIRE-ENGINES	251
COAL IN VARIOUS COUNTRIES OF THE WORLD	252
THE BRITISH COLONIES:—	
JAMAICA	257
TRINIDAD	258
NATAL	258
THE BAHAMAS	260
CEYLON	260
HONG-KONG	260
MALTA, AND THE IONIAN ISLANDS	260
INDIA	262
THE NORTH AMERICAN COLONIES:—	
CANADA	266
NEW BRUNSWICK	267
VANCOUVER ISLAND	268
PRINCE EDWARD'S ISLAND	268
NOVA SCOTIA	268
THE AUSTRALIAN COLONIES:—	
NEW SOUTH WALES	269
QUEENSLAND	271
SOUTH AUSTRALIA	273
WESTERN AUSTRALIA	274

THE AUSTRALIAN COLONIES—continued:— PAGE
   VICTORIA 275
   TASMANIA 278
   NEW ZEALAND 279
   THE SANDWICH ISLANDS 280
FRANCE, AND HER COLONIES 280
   CERAMIC WARE 281
   SILK MANUFACTURES, ETC. 282
   GLASS MANUFACTURE 285
   ONYX MARBLE.—BRONZES 286
   PLATE AND JEWELLERY 287
   FURNITURE, CARRIAGES, ETC. 288
   WINE AND FOOD 289
   MACHINERY 290
   ALGERIA 291
   OTHER FRENCH COLONIES 293
BELGIUM 295
AUSTRIA 296
THE ZOLLVEREIN 300
HUNGARY 303
RUSSIA 304
ITALY 306
SWITZERLAND 308
HOLLAND 309
DENMARK 310
SWEDEN AND NORWAY 311
SPAIN 312
PORTUGAL 313
TURKEY 313
GREECE 315
PERU, COSTA-RICA, AND URUGUAY 316
BRAZIL 317
THE UNITED STATES 317
JAPAN 318
CHINA 320
AFRICA, CENTRAL AND WESTERN 320
MADAGASCAR 321
HAYTI 321
THE EGYPTIAN COURT 321
Fine Art Department 324
   PAINTINGS IN OIL: ENGLISH SCHOOL 324
   ENGLISH WATER-COLOURS 327
   ARCHITECTURE.—DESIGNS AND MODELS . . . 327
   ART-DESIGNS FOR MANUFACTURES 328
   SCULPTURE 330
   ETCHINGS AND ENGRAVINGS 331
FOREIGN PAINTING AND SCULPTURE 333
DECLARATION OF THE AWARDS BY THE JURORS . 338
CLOSE OF THE EXHIBITION 341

VIEW OF THE NAVE FROM THE WESTERN DOME

THE
INTERNATIONAL EXHIBITION
OF 1862.

OUR INDUSTRIAL EXHIBITIONS.

THE origin and history of Exhibitions, National and International, present one of the most remarkable features of the industrial records of Europe, during the last century. In England, these great periodical displays date from about the year when George the Third became King; and, it is worthy of remark, that the parent of these Exhibitions was the Society of Arts, which institution, after a century of varied fortunes, has culminated in the Exhibitions of 1851 and 1862, with a view to the establishment of "Decennial Exhibitions of the Works of Industry and Art." This success has been mainly reached by a *royal road*, which lies in certain directions, though not in that of Geometry. The Society has had Presidents noble and royal: a liberal-minded English Prince, the Duke of Sussex, many years filled the presidential chair, and distributed the Society's annual rewards, and encouraged its exhibitions; but it was reserved for the Duke's successor, the enlightened Prince Consort, to give the *international* form and colour to the Exhibitions of 1851 and 1862, more especially the latter, which must be regarded as an extension of his Royal Highness' portion of the earlier design. Much credit is unquestionably due to the members of the Society of Arts for their unanimous, warm, and steady co-operation in the consummation of these great works : there is, we know, much fickleness and fashion shown in the patronage of public institutions, and the career of the Society of Arts has not been invariably paths of pleasantness or peace: it has languished through times of public indifference, but happily to emerge into the brilliant success which we have already commemorated. "The National Repository," formed at the King's Mews, Charing Cross, in 1828, under the patronage of King George the Fourth, and with a Board of titled persons, and the chairmanship of the eminently practical Dr. Birkbeck,—failed after three exhibitions, and ended its brief existence in a room in Leicester-square. With better success, Practical Science and Polytechnic Exhibitions sprung up; and though their popularity was of forced growth, it undoubtedly prepared the public mind for more systematic displays, with higher recommendation than that of private enterprise.

Meanwhile the Society of Arts held on its more useful course. In 1829, the Secretary read papers on several of the leading industries of the country; and from this date specimens of raw materials, manufactures, and new inventions were frequently collected in the old rooms of the Society's House, in the Adelphi, for the information of the members and the public. There had been for several years Exhibitions held by the Cornwall Polytechnic Society; and these were followed by Trade Exhibitions at Manchester, Leeds, Newcastle-upon-Tyne, Liverpool, Devonport, Derby, and other manufacturing towns.

In 1845, the Exhibition of Manufactures at the Free-Trade Bazaar, held in Covent Garden Theatre, proved a great success: not only as a commercial demonstration in favour of a great political principle and a splendid picture of manufacturing England, but also as a profitable speculation, for the League, in six weeks, cleared by the Exhibition 25,000*l.*, partly by admission-money.

In 1849 was opened at Birmingham a great Exposition of Industry, the most complete of any which had been held in this country. "It filled the entire area of Bingley Hall; and represented very fairly the great variety of manufactures carried on in the neighbourhood of Birmingham. All the most eminent manufacturers contributed something representative of their several industries. A complete set of specimens illustrative of the English plastic arts, was not the least remarkable part of the collection; elaborate samples of electro-plating indicated the future importance of this beautiful process; and the Stafford potteries contributed some splendid wares. The completeness and high character of this Exhibition may be attributed, in the first place, to the stimulus which the adoption of Schools of Design had imparted to the manufacturing arts; and in the second place, to the influence of the splendid French Exhibition of 1844,* as well as the enthusiasm with which the great Free Trade Bazaar, held in Covent Garden Theatre, in 1845, had been received."

Within two years of the acceptance of the Presidency of the Society of Arts by the Prince Consort, the minutes record several exertions for the establishment of a National Exhibition in Eng-

---

* The French Exhibitions, or National Expositions, date from the year 1797, when the first was held in the palace of St. Cloud, near Paris, with the object of reviving the industrial resources of France, which had suffered much during the Revolution. In the same year Napoleon I. commanded to be erected an Exhibition-house in the Champ de Mars; Chaptal, the eminent chemist, and Breguet, the mechanician, taking active parts in the management. This success led the Minister of the Interior to establish similar Exhibitions at various periods, the eleventh of which was held in 1849, and specially reported to the President and Council of the Society of Arts by Mr. M. Digby Wyatt, architect. These several *Expositions* are characterized in the Extra Volume of the *Year-book of Facts*, which reports the Great Exhibition of 1851: such notices extending to seven closely printed pages.

Mr. Blanchard Jerrold also wrote in the *Illustrated London News* an able *précis* of the Industrial Exhibitions of the Continent and the United Kingdom; and Mr. Jerrold is now (1862) publishing an extended History of these several Exhibitions, introductory to a detailed account of the International Exhibition of 1862.

land. In November, 1844, Mr. Francis Whishaw, then Secretary of the Society, "endeavoured to elicit some demonstration of public opinion in favour of a plan he had contemplated."* The same minutes record Mr. Theophilus Richards's efforts as early as 1836, "to get up (at Birmingham) an Exhibition of Industry, including Foreign Manufactures;" and in the same note Mr. George Wallis is referred to as "an early promoter of the plan of National Expositions similar to those on the Continent."

The great success of the French Exposition of 1844 would, however, appear to have more directly stimulated the Society of Arts to the means of realizing a National Exhibition for their own country. A Committee was appointed, and funds were subscribed by them for this purpose, but the attempt failed. In the words of Mr. Scott Russell, then Secretary to the Society of Arts, "the English people were then very imperfectly acquainted with the value of such Exhibitions—their influence on the character as well as the commerce of the nation." They required to be educated for that object; and education had to be provided; Mr. Russell himself generously placing 50*l*. at the disposal of the Council, as prizes for Models and Designs of useful objects, calculated to improve general taste. Other sums were offered, but the progress was slow, and in 1846 scarcely any competitors appeared.

To further this idea, the Council of the Society of Arts at once established a Special Prize Fund, and offered premiums and medals for colours to be used in porcelain, and capable of resisting the action of acids, but not then used in England, and for excellence in combined form and colour. The Society awarded its special prize to Messrs. Minton, for a tea-service in one colour. These and the other prize articles formed the basis of the first exhibition of "Select Specimens of British Manufactures and Decorative Art," which was opened at the Society's House in March, 1847.

Mr. Henry Cole (Felix Summerly), had already commenced the publication of his "Art Manufactures," in which, with the aid of some of our best artists, including Cope, Creswick, Herbert,

* Francis Whishaw, who obtained some distinction as a Civil Engineer and the inventor of various improvements in Telegraphy, was some time Secretary to the Society of Arts, and contributed money as well as labour in originating the Great Exhibition. He was the inventor of the Hydraulic Telegraph, which preceded the Electro Telegraph, and is described in the *Arcana of Science* for 1838. Mr. Whishaw, while resident in Gray's Inn, published a laborious quarto volume of the Statistics of Railways, one of the earliest works upon the subject. He contributed to the Great Exhibition the Telekerephona, or Speaking Telegraph; the Gutta Percha Telephone; Railway Trains Communicator; the Gutta Percha Tube and Lathe-hand, as first made at the Society of Arts in 1845; Subaqueous Insulated Electric Telegraph Conductors; and a Battery Protector. He also wrote for the *Illustrated London News* the most valuable portion of its papers upon the Exhibition of 1851. He considered himself but inadequately remunerated for the assistance he had rendered in the outset of the Exhibition, by the award of one hundred pounds. Mr. Whishaw died in 1856. Although he may have been, by his over-anxious temperament, not well fitted to bear the *mésalliance* so frequent in public societies, Mr. Whishaw was a man of unimpeachable integrity and generous nature.

Horsley, Maclise, Mulready, and Redgrave, as painters; and Bell and Joseph as sculptors; was revived the good old practice of connecting the best art with familiar objects in daily use; to be manufactured in glass, porcelain, *papier-mâché*, carved wood, iron, silver, &c. The invention of a new material named Parian, was a fortunate circumstance; and the Beer-jug, designed by Townsend, and the statuette of Dorothea, from the Marquis of Lansdowne's marble group, by Bell, at Bowood, will be remembered as popular examples. The Bread-platter, also by Bell, carved in wood, was multiplied by many thousands, and thus was created a large and regular demand for this revived article of domestic use. These Art Manufactures were early patronized by the Queen, and from being seen in the apartments of Windsor Castle and Buckingham Palace were soon adopted by the nobility and gentry, and reached the middle classes; they extended to an improved pattern of a Britannia-metal tea-pot.

These proceedings had been duly reported to the Prince President; and towards the close of 1846, a deputation of the Society represented to His Royal Highness the benefit of the extension of the Fine Arts to the various manufactures of the country; in this opinion the Prince coincided, and after speaking of the excellence and solidity of British manufactures generally, added, " to wed mechanical skill to high art is a task worthy of the Society of Arts, and directly in the path of its duty."

In 1847, the Council commenced a series of Exhibitions of Manufactures, a portion of the first collection being appropriated to archæological illustrations of the progress of British pottery and porcelain manufactures from the reign of Elizabeth to the times of Anne, and George I. to that of Wedgwood. Next year the experiment was repeated with such success that the Council determined to hold annual Exhibitions as a means of establishing a quinquennial Exhibition of British Industry, to be held in 1851. Having proceeded thus far, the Council then connected the Schools of Design located in the centres of manufacturing industry, with the proposed Exhibition, for which the Council obtained the promise of the quadrangle of Somerset House, or some other Government ground, as a site for their building.

In 1849, three events proved tributary to the success of the proposed gigantic scheme: the Paris Exposition was the most comprehensive of the series; the Society of Arts Exhibition was of greater excellence than either of its predecessors, the collection consisting chiefly of works in the precious metals;[*] and the Prince President offered two prizes. The third auspicious event was the Birmingham Exhibition already referred to: it was held in the first building erected in England for such a purpose, and was honoured by Prince Albert with a special visit.

[*] A handsome pictorial record of this Exhibition of Ancient and Mediæval Art was published in 1851. It is entitled *Choice Examples of Art Workmanship*, Drawn and Engraved under the Superintendence of Philip de la Motte. The work is now very scarce.

His Royal Highness now consented to take the proposed Great Exhibition under his own personal superintendence. "Now is the time," said this truly liberal-minded Prince, "to prepare for a Great Exhibition, an Exhibition worthy of the greatness of this country ; not merely national in its scope and benefits, but comprehensive of the whole world ; and I offer myself to the public as their leader, if they are willing to assist in the undertaking." His Royal Highness then proposed that the Exhibition should consist of Raw Materials ; Machinery and Mechanical Inventions; Manufactures; Sculpture, and plastic art generally; and the Prince at the same time pointed out the vacant ground in Hyde Park upon which the Great Exhibition building was subsequently erected. At the meeting whereat these details were arranged, Prince Albert gave to the proposed Exhibition that grand feature of universality which ever after formed the chief characteristic of the plan, thus entered in the minute-book :—

"It was a question whether this Exhibition should be exclusively limited to British industry. It was considered that, whilst it appears an error to fix any limitations to the productions of machinery, science, and taste, which are of no country, but belong as a whole to the civilized world, particular advantage to British industry might be derived from placing it in fair competition with that of other nations."

At this meeting, also, a Royal Commission, with his Royal Highness at the head, and the subscription of a fund, were decided on ; and here may be remarked the pre-eminently practical character of the mind of Prince Albert, who, at this single meeting is proved to have proposed the objects of which the Exhibition should consist : the site of the Building ; its comprehensive international plan ; the mode and means of carrying out the great design. Well was it hereafter said, " But for Prince Albert, say what people may of others' part in the affair, we should never have had the Great Exhibition."

Money prizes and medals were then proposed. Her Majesty the Queen headed the subscription with the munificent gift of 1000*l*., and the Prince coutributed 500*l*. The Government promised their aid, but did little more ; for, a great part of the success of the Exhibition was, with truth, attributed to its independence of the Ministry ; "and it may be the boast of our countrymen, that the Exhibition was originated, conducted, and completed independently of any Government aid whatever, except its sanction ;" and when such assistance was attended with expense the cost of it was defrayed from the funds of the Exhibition. (*Mr. H. Cole ; Introduction to the Official Catalogue.*)

We shall not be expected to detail the carrying out of this great plan : suffice it to state, that a contract was entered into by the Society of Arts with Messrs. Munday, to advance funds, and provide the Building, with a proviso that the agreement might be cancelled within a certain time, compensation being made to the contractors. Public meetings were then held in the manufacturing districts, where nearly 5000 persons registered themselves as promoters of the Exhibition; while, in London, Mr. Henry Cole, expressly deputed by Prince Albert to explain his views, addressed the citizens with excellent effect. This example was followed in Westminster, where the Bishop of Oxford eloquently advocated the measure in an address subsequently printed under the title of "The Dignity of Labour," and circulated through the length and breadth of the country. The Royal Commission was then formed; the agreement with Messrs. Munday was cancelled, and the Commissioners undertook the responsibilities; a guarantee fund was formed, the Prince Consort writing down his name for 10,000*l.*; and upon the guarantee deed for 230,000*l.* was borrowed of the Bank of England the sum of 32,500*l.*, which was repaid, with interest, out of the receipts at the doors, after the Exhibition had been open three weeks.

To concentrate the high feeling for the national honour, felt to be bound up with the fortunes of the Exhibition, the Lord Mayor of London (Farncomb) invited the municipal authorities of the United Kingdom at the Mansion House, to meet Prince Albert, as President of the Royal Commission.* At this noble festival, Prince Albert, in responding to the toast of "Success to the Great Exhibition of 1851," declared his views in "a most truthful, most able, most feeling, most religious, and most eloquent statement." In the autumn of the same year, the Lord Mayor of York gave a return banquet to the Lord Mayor of London, for which poor Alexis Soyer prepared his "hundred guinea Dish," to set before the civic kings. At this festival at York, Prince Albert was also present, and in addressing the company, having glanced at the essentially practical nature of the English character, his Royal Highness concluded by saying:—

"Taking this view of the character of our country, I was pleased when I saw the plan of the Exhibition of 1851 undergo its ordeal of doubt, discussion, and even opposition; and I hope that I may now gather from the earnestness with which its execution is pursued, that the nation is convinced that it accords with its interests, and the position which England has taken in the world."

The eloquent appeals made at the banquets at London and York, were re-echoed throughout the country: a vast system of correspondence was undertaken by the Executive Committee; and the local organization begun by the Society of Arts with 65 district committees, was increased by the Royal Commissioners to 297, and about 450 local commissioners were nominated. Two special travelling Commissioners—Dr. Lyon Playfair and Lieut.-Colonel Lloyd—were appointed to communicate with these local committees; and Commissioners were appointed, or committees formed, in eleven British colonies and 30 foreign countries.

* For this measure of patriotic feeling, the Lord Mayor (Farncomb) must ever be gratefully remembered as one of the prime contributors to the *éclat* of the Exhibition, although the commemorative dignity was conferred upon his successor in the civic chair.

THE GREAT EXHIBITION BUILDING, 1851.

The site originally suggested by the Prince Consort having been selected by the Commissioners, with the permission of the Crown, out of the 20 acres of land thus chosen, the Building Committee proposed to cover 16 acres with buildings,—between Rotten-row and the Queen's Drive, in Hyde Park. The plan and arrangement of the buildings were to be determined by public competition, and 233 designs were sent in. The Building Committee selected neither; but under their superintendence, a design was proposed—to consist of a huge structure, mostly of brickwork and avenues of iron columns, and in general unsightliness, resembling a railway-station; to which, upon the suggestion of Mr. Brunel, the engineer, was added a vast central dome, more than 150 feet high, and 200 feet in diameter; the roof and dome to be of iron, and 15 millions of bricks to be used in the construction of the walls. This vastness raised a proportionate degree of opposition: indeed, the public loudly objected to any building in Hyde Park which was not of a light and temporary character. The existence of this feeling led Mr., now Sir Joseph Paxton, to devise a plan for a structure, which was, indeed, a vast expansion of a conservatory design, built by him at Chatsworth, for the flowering of the Victoria lily.

Well do we remember the magic effect of our first sight of the outline of Mr. Paxton's design: it was merely a light outline upon a large surface of bank-post paper, and the instant Mr. Paxton spread out the sheet, we exclaimed—"It is like a fairy palace!" The vast Building in Hyde Park fully realized this idea, though somewhat enthusiastically expressed; and it has ever been a source of gratification to reflect that he who was thus instantly impressed with the graceful character of Mr. Paxton's design was the first to express such an opinion of its novelty and appropriateness in one of the public journals of the next day. How emphatic, too, and, in some degree, prophetic, were the opinions of Professor Cowper.

"I look upon the original idea of Mr. Paxton as one of the most successful efforts of imagination and contrivance, and I consider the way in which Fox and Henderson have made the bold conception *practicable*, one of the most successful and astonishing examples of contrivance, tact, science, industry, perseverance, and engineering skill, the world ever saw; and whatever wonders may hereafter be placed in this Building, *the structure itself will be the greatest wonder of all:*" and so it proved.

The Building was to be chiefly of iron and glass, the contractors, Messrs. Fox, Henderson, and Co., undertaking to construct the whole for 79,800*l*.* It was nearly the length of Portland-place.

* Sir William Cubitt, F.R.S., the eminent Civil Engineer, undertook, at the pressing instance of his coadjutors in the Royal Commission, the superintendence of the construction of the Great Exhibition Building; and his services were recognised by the Queen bestowing upon him Knighthood. Sir William Cubitt's great Railway works will long attest his professional success, which was, in a great degree, to be ascribed to the soundness of his early me_

"I walked out one evening," says Sir Charles Fox, "and there setting out the 1848 feet upon the pavement, found it the same length within a few yards: and then considered that the Great Exhibition Building would be three times the width of the street, and the nave as high as the houses on either side."

Of the origin and construction of this Building a minute description, extending to seventy pages, will be found in the Extra Volume of the *Year-book of Facts*, 1851. We see its plan in the main, in the Crystal Palace at Sydenham, which was mostly built of the Exhibition structure on its removal from Hyde Park. The "Crystal Palace" has, indeed, been adopted as the name of so many similar structures, not only in England and Ireland, but in almost every quarter of the globe, that we shall only briefly describe the outline of the original Building in Hyde Park, and this chiefly for the sake of comparison to be made hereafter.

The *Crystal Palace*, as the building in Hyde Park was appropriately named, from its roof and sides being of glass, was originally devised by Mr. Paxton, as he sat in a carriage upon a railway journey, and was first sketched by him upon a sheet of blotting-paper. It was cruciform in plan, with a transept, nave, and side aisles; and consisted of a framework of wrought and cast iron, firmly braced together, and based upon a foundation of concrete. The general plan was a parallelogram, 1848 feet long, and 408 feet wide; the greatest length running from east to west. There was also a projection on the north side, 48 feet wide, and 936 feet long; the area, from east to west, was divided into 12 avenues, the chief passage was 72 feet wide, and 63 feet high, and occupied the centre. It was flanked on both sides by passages, alternately 24 feet and 48 feet wide, and of 63, 43, and 23 feet high. About the middle of the building, lengthwise, these avenues were crossed at right-angles, by a transept, 72 feet wide, the semicircular roof of which rose 108 feet, so as to preserve three fine old elms; and two other groups of trees on the ground gave rise to open courts, which were inclosed within the building.

The total area roofed over was equal to 18¼ acres, and nearly 294,000 panes of glass were used, the majority of them being 49 by 10 inches. The avenues were formed by rows of hollow cast-iron columns, which acted as supports for the building, as well as rain-water drains. They were placed in lines 24 feet from each other, and rose in one, two, and three tiers to support the roof at the different levels. Between the columns were inserted short pieces, of such a shape as to support the girders in horizontal tiers, at three several levels. 3300 columns were fitted up altogether, and reckoning the different articles of cast and wrought iron which helped to form the building, there were 537,082 separate pieces, representing above 4486 tons. Nearly 2000 yards of gas-pipes

---

chanical experience. He died in 1861. From sameness of name, Sir William has sometimes been confounded with Alderman William Cubitt, Lord Mayor of London in 1860-1, 1861-2, who was at the head of the great *building* firm in Gray's Inn Road, and raised himself from humble life to the above position.

were laid down; the wrought timber used amounted to 265,000 pieces, or more than a million and a third of lineal feet, and the rough timber to nearly 413,000 cubic feet.

The iron girders produced unbroken horizontal lines throughout the building, and formed a lattice-work combining great strength and lightness of appearance. The girders formed the support of the floor of the galleries, which extended the whole length of the palace in four parallel lines, cross-galleries connecting the long lines. The gallery floors consisted of cross-beams, under-trussed, so as to distribute the whole weight brought upon the floor pretty equally upon the eight points at which the ends of the beams rested upon the cast-iron girders. Upon this foundation were fixed the ordinary floor-joists and floor, and the galleries were reached by two double staircases.

The roof was the most novel and interesting part of the Building: it was supported by the upper tier of girders and trusses; in its general formation it was flat, but in detail it consisted of a series of ridges and furrows, of moderate rise and fall. As the roof, girders, and trusses were 24 feet apart lengthwise, they were made to carry the main gutters on their upper edge in the transverse direction of the Building. The space between these was spanned by light wood beams, or rafters, sloping upwards at an inclination of two and a half to one, and contrived so as to support the glass roof, and to carry into the main gutters the rain-water, and the condensed vapour formed under it, at the same time. The total length of the gutters was nearly 24 miles. The advantage of this form of roofing for large areas was its great lightness and economy. The glass of the roof was fixed into the sash-bars, which were grooved to receive it. About 200 miles of sash-bars, and 896,000 square feet of glass were required; and the whole weight of glass used was 400 tons.

The Building was admirably ventilated by metal louvres, the ventilating surface thus obtained being nearly 41,000 square feet, or very nearly one acre. Each story was crowned outside with a cornice, or cresting, and over the columns were fixed flag-staffs.[*]

The half-circular roof of the transept, the most ornamental architectural portion of the Building, is stated to have been designed by Mr. Henderson. It is also claimed for Sir Charles Barry, who proposed similar roofing for the entire Building; but this was abandoned from its great cost, and the transept only was covered with a half-circular roof. This was supported by arched timber ribs, one on the top of every column; between these principal ribs were horizontal timbers supporting minor ribs, and upon these was laid a curved ridge and furrow roof. Along the ridge of the arched roof was a narrow gallery, that workmen might go up to do the necessary repairs; and on both sides of the roof was a wide lead flat, which gave some additional strength to

[*] Abridged from *A Concise History of the International Exhibition of* 1862. By John Hollingshead. Printed for Her Majesty's Commissioners.

resist any tendency in the arched ribs to spread outwards at the springing.

The decoration of the interior, devised by Owen Jones, consisted of the scientific application of the primitive colours, red, blue, and yellow, upon narrow surfaces; it was rapidly executed by 500 painters; its effect was at first much questioned, by persons who understood little about the matter; but it proved charmingly artistic.

The many important additions made to the Building, as originally undertaken by Messrs. Fox and Henderson for 79,800*l.*, raised the cost to 107,780*l.* 7*s.* 6*d.*; and still the contractors were heavy losers by the contract. This was explained by the great speed at which the work had been done, the cost of extra machinery for this purpose leaving no time for economical arrangements. However, as they had punctually completed the Building, the Commissioners paid them the further sum of 35,000*l.*, subject to the proceeds from the sale of the Building, estimated to produce about 33,000*l.*, to which the contractors were entitled; but, as the Building was purchased by the Crystal Palace Company, of Sydenham, for 70,000*l.*, the contractors were thus relieved from all loss.

The ground was broken July 30, 1850; the first column was placed Sept. 26; and the Building was opened May 1, 1851. While the work was in full activity, more than 2000 men were employed on the ground, with four powerful steam-engines.

The vast palace, though covering a million of square feet, gave only half-a-million for the display of goods, besides the vertical space. The whole available space was divided in two: one half was given to England and her colonies, and the other half to foreign countries. The Exhibition, according to the plan laid down by the Prince Consort, had its four great departments: Raw Materials, 4 classes; Machinery, 6 classes; Manufactures, 19 classes; and Fine Arts a class by themselves. The British articles occupied the western half of the Building, geographically arranged; and the foreign articles occupied the eastern half. The foreign and colonial divisions were arranged according to their latitudes, the countries lying nearest to the Equator being placed nearest to the transept.

The Exhibition was opened by Her Majesty on Thursday, May 1, 1851, in the presence of 25,000 spectators. It was a bright morning, and the mass of glass flashed in the sunshine as the semi-state procession passed through the Parks, amidst the acclamations of admiring thousands, to the fairy-like palace of crystal—

> "But yesterday a naked sod,
>   The dandies sneered from Rotten-row,
>   And sauntered o'er it to and fro.
>   And see, 'tis done!
> As though 'twere by a wizard's rod,
>   A blazing arch of lucid glass,
>   Leaps like a fountain from the grass,
>   To meet the sun.

THE EXHIBITION OF 1851 OPENED.

" A quiet green, but few days since,
With cattle browsing in the shade,
And lo! long lines of bright arcade
In order raised;
A palace as for fairy prince,
A rare pavilion, such as man
Saw never since mankind began,
And built and glazed."
May-Day Ode, by W. M. Thackeray;
Times, May, 1851.

The only special preparation in the Building for the ceremony was a carpeted platform and a chair of state for the Queen, placed beneath a canopy, midway in the transept. The Prince Consort, at the head of the Royal Commissioners, read to Her Majesty the Report of the Exhibition proceedings, to which the Queen graciously replied. The Archbishop of Canterbury then implored God's blessing upon the undertaking, and the choir sang the Hallelujah Chorus. A Royal procession was then formed, and on Her Majesty's return to the platform, the Queen declared "the Exhibition opened," which was announced by a flourish of trumpets and the firing of a Royal salute on the north bank of the Serpentine.

The Exhibition remained open 141 days: its foreign exhibitors were 6556, and the exhibitors of the United Kingdom and dependencies, 7382 (exclusive of India), forming a grand total of 13,938. The estimated value of the articles exhibited (excluding the Koh-i-noor diamond) was:—

United Kingdom . . . £1,031,607 4 9
Dependencies of ditto . . 79,901 15 0
Foreign Countries . . . 670,420 11 7

Total . . £1,781,929 11 4

The number of Prize Medals was 2918, and of Council Medals 170, awarded by Juries.

The whole daily admissions by payment amounted to 5,265,429*l.*; by season tickets, 773,766*l.*; together, 6,039,195*l.* Average visitors on each day, 42,831; greatest number present on October 7 —109,915; greatest number at one time in the building, October 7 —93,224. Commissioners' receipts from all sources, to Feb. 29, 1852, including subscriptions, 506,100*l.* 6*s.* 11*d.* Expenditure, 292,794*l.* 11*s.* 3*d.* Balance, 213,305*l.* 15*s.* 8*d.*

The reader who wishes to become familiar with the display of the contents of the Exhibition Building may do so by referring to the section of the *Year-book of Facts*, 1851, entitled, "The Great Exhibition, Geographically Described," pp. 99—120; and the remainder of the volume, entitled "Articles and Objects Exhibited," pp. 124—287.

OTHER EXHIBITIONS.

The success of the Great Exhibition of 1851 naturally led to similar displays all over the world. The Building was removed from Hyde Park to Sydenham, and there forms part of the Crystal Palace, which, however, is larger than its predecessor by 1628 feet, and by nearly one half in cubic contents. Here sculpture is picturesquely grouped with luxuriant exotic vegetation. Groups illustrate the ethnology, zoology, and botany of the Old and New Worlds; and at each end is a vast fountain. In the great transept are the works of French and Italian, German and English, Greek and Roman sculptors; and models of celebrated ancient and modern edifices. Throughout the Building are galleries for the exhibition of objects of industry and fine art; and courts representing the architecture and sculpture of each nation—Egyptian, Greek, Roman Pompeian, Alhambra, Assyrian, Byzantine, and Romanesque; German, English, French, and Italian mediæval; Renaissance, Elizabethan, Italian, &c. The Crystal Palace, loftier than the London Monument, is placed at the head of the Landscape Garden and Park, planned by Sir Joseph Paxton; and here are gigantic fountains, planned and executed by the same master-artist. The several departments of the edifice, to which Picture Galleries have been added, are detailed in a series of admirable guide-books. The Palace was opened by Her Majesty, June 10, 1854. It has cost considerably more than a million of money. To its attractions have been added musical performances upon a scale of grandeur never before attempted: the Commemorations of Handel are entitled to the highest praise.

The more immediate result of the Hyde Park Exhibition was, however, the Cork Exhibition in 1852; and the next year, were Universal Exhibitions in Dublin and New York, both in Buildings of iron and glass. In 1854, followed the Munich Exhibition of the Industry of the whole of Germany. In 1855, the twelfth Exhibition in Paris followed, being the first great French International Exhibition, imitating closely the plan of 1851. In 1857, took place the Manchester Fine Art Exhibition—a collection of ancient and modern pictures, sculpture, and other works of art, never before equalled: the Building was of the Crystal Palace character. In 1861, we had the Dublin Art Exhibition and the Edinburgh Art Treasures' Exhibition, and the Italian National Exhibition at Florence. Besides these, in several of our colonies, small "Crystal Palaces" were erected for exhibitions of industrial art, thus extending the principle to the remotest countries of the civilized world.

In the *Practical Mechanics' Journal* it is judiciously remarked: "We have seen in the preceding brief sketch that the recognition and first development of National Expositions was due to the prescient mind of Napoleon in his early prime; of that great man, who, amidst national hatreds the most bitter, could mark his reverence for Davy, the English chemist, whose chosen companions were such men as Volta, Cuvier, Chaptal, and La Place. The remembrance of this must have recurred to the President of the Republic with justifiable pride, when inaugurating the Exposition of 1849.

"The next great advance, however, was to come from another mind congenial in vigour, and in the thoughtful conception of the true paths that lead to industrial greatness, but in all other respects the happy opposite in attributes to that of Napoleon. To our own lamented Prince Consort belongs the origination of the idea of *International* Exhibitions. France had shown to herself and to Europe what she herself could accomplish, but she had shrunk from permitting other nations to show their achievements, in contrast with and beside her own.

"Perhaps much of the favour with which Prince Albert's proposal was received at length by the people of England arose from the simple courage of the thought; but undoubtedly the immense success which the attempt to carry it out at once attained, as well as the abiding advantages which, as a nation, we have already derived from its results, are due to the idea of international rivalry, as contra-distinguished from merely national display. It ministered not to our insular pride, but proved to us our own comparative shortcomings."

RESULTS OF THE EXHIBITION OF 1851.

It is now time to glance at the financial results of the Exhibition, inasmuch as the disposal of the Surplus or Profit promised to be the nucleus of future important operations. To enable them to apply this money, and keep faith with the subscribers to the original fund, the Royal Commissioners applied to Her Majesty for a Supplemental Charter, which, being granted, empowered them to dispose of the Surplus as they might think fit, and to raise contributions in aid of such Surplus—"to purchase and hold lands in any part of Her Majesty's dominions," and to dispose of them in all respects as they should think fit. They first proposed to provide a home for "the Trade Museum," a collection of articles, valued at 9000*l.*, presented to them by Exhibitors in 1851.* For this purpose they purchased "the Gore House Estate," which Mr. Wilberforce possessed from 1808 to 1821: in 1836, it passed to the Countess of Blessington, who resided here until 1849: in the Great Exhibition year, 1851, the house and grounds were fitted up by Monsieur Soyer as the "Symposium for all Nations:" they were subsequently purchased by the Commissioners for 60,000*l.*, paid out of the Surplus fund of about 186,000*l.* The whole estate comprised about 21 acres, added to which were Gray's Nursery Grounds, Park House, and Grove House, and various market-gardens; the grounds of Cromwell House, and other lands belonging to the Earl of Harrington and the Baron de Villars. Additional funds for these purchases were provided by the Government, who entered into a sort of partnership with the Commissioners, and purchased, in all, 86 acres, for 280,000*l.*, at an average of 3250*l.* an acre. Acts of Parliament were passed, legalizing the plans of the Commissioners, and in accordance various old foot-paths, &c., were stopped, and houses removed.

* A portion of these articles was, for some time, stored in the conservatory adjoining Kensington Palace. It is curious to reflect of what extensive operations they became the nucleus.

They also formed nearly two miles of new roadway, the chief lines of which surrounded the best part of their Estate: namely, the Cromwell-road, the Exhibition-road, and the Prince Albert-road, forming, with the main Kensington-road, four sides of a square.

The object of these purchases of land was to secure a large space to which some of the national exhibitions might be removed, and on which a great art-educational institution might be erected. "A Museum of Manufactures" is proposed in the Commissioners' Second Report: "these localities being recommended for the dryness of the soil, and as the only safe ground for future years amidst the growth of the metropolis." In 1856, it was proposed to remove the National Gallery of Pictures from Charing Cross to this site, which has been named "South Kensington:" the Government, however, lost the Bill in Parliament. Gore House was taken down in 1857. Early in 1858, the Commissioners dissolved partnership with the State; the sums advanced by Government were repaid by the Commissioners, subject to a deduction for the ground and buildings of the South Kensington Museum, now become a Government institution, as a branch of the Department of Science and Art. The Commissioners now became trustees for buying and selling the land, about 12 acres of which they have disposed of very profitably in building leases: lines of lofty and handsome houses have sprung up in a style ornate even to sumptuousness: nevertheless, it was not the object of the Commissioners to become a land company, or to be instrumental in blocking up one of the pleasantest localities in the suburbs with lofty dwelling-houses, shutting out fresh air and a fine prospect. The Commissioners are stated to have nearly doubled their original capital by the above speculation: they next let the upper part of the great centre square, about 22 acres, to the Horticultural Society. "The Commissioners have expended about 50,000*l.* in building arcades in the new Gardens; and the Society have expended an equal amount in terraces, fountains, conservatories, and in laying out the grounds." (*Hollingshead's Concise History,* p. 34.)

This arrangement may be, prospectively, an eligible investment for the Royal Commissioners; but the effect of the Horticultural Society *shouldering* the Exhibition Building, is at present by no means good: that it should be bounded by lines of stately houses is objectionable in proportion to their stateliness—almost effacing the recollection of this being once the finest nursery-grounds round London. Had the entire space been reserved for Exhibition purposes, it would have been more promising for the public than the present realization, which may almost be described as a garden without flowers. The conservatory, of iron and glass, disadvantageously reminds one of the Crystal Palace in Hyde Park.

THE INTERNATIONAL EXHIBITION OF 1862.

The importance of the development of the *International* character of Industrial Exhibitions appears to have been more strongly impressed upon the Society of Arts by the several intermediate displays which have just been enumerated; each of which rendered more obvious the desirability of rendering the Home Exhibition periodical. The period now projected was *decennial*: accordingly, in 1858, the Society first proposed to repeat the Great Exhibition of 1851, the year chosen being 1861. The Commissioners, however, hesitated: they had no funds to meet the expenses of the proposed Exhibition, and they were not satisfied that the scheme would be well supported by manufacturers and the public. The Society of Arts then promised the required information, and their exertions to obtain subscriptions to a proposed guarantee fund of 250,000*l*. Subsequently, owing to the war in Italy, and the disturbed state of the Continent, the proposed Exhibition was deferred until 1862. By the guarantee agreement, in the event of a loss attending the Exhibition, each subscriber was to contribute in rateable proportion to his subscription to liquidate such loss. Earl Granville, the Marquis of Chandos, Mr. Thomas Baring, Mr. Dilke, and Mr. Thomas Fairbairn, consented to be the five Trustees of the Exhibition.

Earl Granville, K.G., "enjoys all the popularity which a very good-natured public man not spoiled by office is sure to acquire." (*Quarterly Review*, No. 223.) His Lordship is Lord President of the Council, and Chairman of the Royal Commission.

The Marquis of Chandos has since succeeded his father as Duke of Buckingham and Chandos. The Marquis some time was Secretary and Manager of the London and North-Western Railway Company.

Mr. Thomas Baring, the capitalist, brother of Sir Francis Baring, sits in Parliament for Huntingdon.

Sir Charles Wentworth Dilke was a Commissioner and member of the Executive Committee of the Great Exhibition of 1851, and at its close is stated to have declined knighthood in recognition of his services. He received his patent of Baronetcy from Her Majesty, at the close of 1861. Mr. Dilke made a collection of all the books and publications respecting the Exhibition of 1851 that he could obtain; and a Catalogue of the collection fills more than a hundred large octavo pages. The books and pamphlets are in the English, Welsh, French, German, Dutch, Swedish, Indian, Spanish, Greek, and Arabic languages. (*Companion to the Almanac*, 1862.) This Catalogue has been printed for private circulation.

Mr. Thomas Fairbairn is the well-known engineer, of Manchester, and brother of Mr. William Fairbairn, F.R.S.

Application was to be made to the Commissioners for a site on the South Kensington estate, and the Trustees were to erect the buildings, temporary or permanent, for the Exhibition, on the express condition that one-third of the sum so expended by them should be employed in erections of a permanent character, suitable for decennial or other exhibitions, and vested in the Society of Arts. The surplus was to be applied to the encouragement of arts, manufactures, and commerce; and in the event of there being a loss which the Society of Arts declined to liquidate, the permanent buildings were to be sold, towards such liquidation. In a more attractive manner, the arrangement has been thus sketched in the *Quarterly Review*, Vol. 112, No. 223 : "The steady-going Society of Arts was now called in, and a very odd triangular arrangement consummated. The Commissioners of 1851 leased to the Society of Arts the desired plot of ground for ninety-nine years, in order that a third body, viz., the Commissioners of 1862, might cover the ground with an additional building. Of this building one part was to be considered temporary, and either to be reckoned the property of the contractors, after a vast royalty had been paid for its use, or else bought out-and-out for a further sum; and the other part was to be held permanent, and to pass for the term of the lease of the Society of Arts, supposing the speculation to be solvent. If the returns were insufficient, this portion was to be pulled down at the close of the Exhibition. The motive power of the whole scheme was a solid phalanx of Englishmen, some of them men of capital, and some men of enterprise, who had from various motives subscribed a deed of guarantee, to the amount of several hundred thousand pounds,* and on the strength of this deed the Bank of England found the money for the immediate undertaking. So there were the Bank that advanced, the subscribers who guaranteed, the New Commission that managed, the Society of Arts that advised and that waited for its windfall, and the Old Commission that sat in its counting-house counting of its money."

The Society of Arts did not fail to back up their advocacy of this second Exhibition. They showed that nearly four millions had been added to the population of Great Britain since the former Exhibition in 1851; that London would contain half a million more persons than it did then. Sir Cusack Roney, an accredited practical authority in railway statistics, showed that the length of railways in England alone would be nearly eleven thousand miles in 1862, compared with six thousand seven hundred and fifty-five in 1851, and that the general system of railway management would be much improved. The Continental managers have now learned to appreciate through-booking, return-tickets, and excursion traffic at reduced rates, which they would not look at a few years back. Many Continental lines have been opened since the year of the Great Exhibition, all more or less converging

* The List of Guarantors was headed by His Royal Highness the Prince Consort, with a subscription of 10,000*l*. The next sum, in amount, was the subscription of his Grace the Duke of Buccleuch, 5000*l*.,—the excellent nobleman whom, through legislatorial blundering, it lately became the business of interested parties to misrepresent as adverse to popular rights.

towards this country, and several others of great importance in shortening existing routes, and putting us in communication with new districts, have been completed during 1859 and 1860. The steam passages between America and Europe have been more than quadrupled, and the fares lowered at least thirty per cent. The chain of railways now joining New York, Boston, Portland, and Quebec, has been tripled since 1851; the distance between London and India has been decreased twenty-five per cent., and between England and Australia fifty per cent.; the time taken for passages to and from our West Indian colonies has been diminished one-third, and we have a well-organized steam communication with South America and Africa, which did not exist in 1851.

Mr. William Hawes next communicated to the Society of Arts these interesting facts, to show in comparison the advantages in 1862 over those in 1851, which, though they do not belong exclusively to the Exhibition, may be incidentally quoted here:

"That the Exhibition fully realized the most sanguine anticipations in showing the state of development of the manufactures of all nations to 1851, and that it gave to the world a more thorough knowledge of the power, and better appreciation of the capabilities, of each nation, is universally admitted. It now remains for the Exbibition of 1862 to show what has been the world's progress from the starting-point so clearly indicated in 1851, not only in the production of works of art, or in the increased beauty of certain manufactures, but in the practical applications of science, invention, and mechanical skill to improve and to cheapen the necessaries of every-day life, and so to raise the social position, by adding to the comforts and enjoyments, of the great bulk of the people."

Mr. Hawes then refers to the jealousy felt in 1851, respecting foreign manufactures, the injury to our home trade, &c., and especially to the alarm and distrust felt at the large number of foreigners which would be brought into England to see the Exhibition.* The following are Mr. Hawes's results:

"The people are better employed, and their social and intellectual condition is improved. Crime, which for years previously to 1851 increased in a ratio beyond that of the population, is now happily decreasing. Railways have been extended from above 6000, to above 10,000 miles. The Electric Telegraph has become universal, and in every direction facilities for communication have been increased. We have repealed the Duties on Soap and Paper, the only manufactures the prosperity of which was then thwarted by excise restrictions. We have abolished all Taxes on the dissemination of Knowledge, and have given increased facilities for the circulation of knowledge by post. We

---

* An instance of this alarm occurred within the Editor's knowledge. A shopkeeper in ———— street, a man of good discernment in his business, as a dealer in Works of Art, was haunted with this apprehension: he was confident that hundreds and thousands of Londoners would be butchered in cold-blood by foreigners, who, unable to obtain lodgings, would prowl about the streets all night, and at a preconcerted signal would overpower the police, and begin the work of slaughter of the Londoners in their beds! . . . The Exhibition came, and a few months after, our alarmist acknowledged himself to have been more deceived in the peaceful result than in all the expericnce of his lifetime.

have repealed the Import Duties, or very nearly so, on Raw Materials, the produce of foreign countries. We have admitted, free of duty, confident in our strength, the manufactures of foreign countries to compete with our own. Old industries have been stimulated and improved. New industries have arisen. In Fine Art, Painting, and Sculpture, it is hardly possible, except in very extraordinary periods, that a marked change can he observed in a single ten years, but this country certainly holds its own as compared with the productions of other countries.

"Photography, hardly known in 1851, has developed itself, and has become an important branch of art and industry, used alike by the artist, the engineer, the architect, the manufacturer, the merchant, and the magistrate. By it fleeting effects of nature are caught, and preserved for the use of the artist; the progress of works is daily recorded, for the information of the engineer; the finest tracery of ancient architecture preserved, in its exact proportions, for the architect; the manufacturer and merchant can transmit to, and receive from their most distant correspondents, exact representations of what they require to be imitated or produced; the soldier, sailor, and civilian on foreign service finds in photographic likenesses, and the facility with which they are renewed, the means of retaining the fondest associations of home and country; and the criminal flying from justice is followed with means of instant identification. This is indeed an international application of art and industry.

"In the preparation of Colours for Printing and Dyeing, most important discoveries have been made by our chemists, to whose researches the manufacturing industry of the country is greatly indebted. The recently-discovered and most beautiful and brilliant colours, called the 'Aniline' series, are produced from coal and its products, and the facility of their application is so great that a complete revolution is taking place in the processes of Dyeing and Printing.

"In the Manufacture of Glass great economy has been introduced; and the process, just perfected, of transferring photographs to glass, and permanently fixing them by the action of fire, will add a new and beautiful style of ornamentation to our houses. The manufacture of Agricultural Implements, and especially the application of steam-power to them, has been so improved and extended, that it is now a highly-important branch of trade: and the exhibition of the improvements which have been made in our spinning, weaving, and winding machinery will afford interesting evidence of our mechanical progress in these branches of industry. Marine Telegraphy, only just accomplished in 1851—the public communication with Dublin having been opened in June, and that with Paris in November, 1852—has now become almost universal, linking together distant countries, and destined ere long to overcome the difficulties of separation by the ocean, be the distance ever so great. In the Manufacture of Iron, improvements have also been made—new bands of ore have been discovered; and day by day we are economizing its production, and a metal between iron and steel is now produced, at one process, which heretofore required two or more processes, alike expensive and difficult. In Artificial Light our sphere of production is enlarged, and light is cheaper, whereby hours are now available for industrial pursuits, and for the acquisition of knowledge by large numbers, which were formerly either unemployed or wasted. In Steam-power, especially that applied to Railroads and to Ocean Steam-navigation, economical appliances have advanced rapidly. The use of Coal for locomotives, in place of coke, and super-heating steam and surface-condensing in ocean steamers, tends to increase the power and economize the cost of these powerful engines of civilization. In Shipbuilding, the past ten years have produced great changes. Our navy and mercantile marine have alike advanced in scientific construction and in mechanical arrangements. In the *Great Eastern* we see the practical application, for the first time, of screw and paddle to the same ship; we have enormous strength in her cellular construction; and we have greater speed, with power smaller in proportion to her size than was ever before attained. In the construction of our *Warrior* and *Black Prince* and other iron-plated ships, we have a combination of wood and iron by which our ships of war may almost bid defiance to whatever may be brought against them, being, both in size and power, far beyond anything which was contemplated in 1851; and machinery is now being constructed, having its origin in the block-machinery at Portsmouth, by which the woodwork required for large boats will be so accurately prepared, that they will be put together in a few hours. In Printing great advances have been made. By the perfection of chromatic printing, views of distant countries, copies of celebrated pictures, most beautifully coloured, have been brought within the reach of almost every class, displacing pictures which neither improved the taste nor gave useful information; and by the application of most expensive and most beautiful machinery to the printing of our daily journals, we have been enabled profitably to meet the increased demand caused by the cheapness of our newspapers. Invention and Mechanical contrivance have thus kept pace with the requirements of intellect and the daily-increasing love of knowledge; and, to crown all, the Gold Discoveries in Australia, but just known in 1851, and following those in California in 1849, have supplied a medium of exchange when it appeared almost indispensable to the full realization of the advantages springing out of the great impetus given to industry during the past ten years.

"But there are two branches of industry not to be overlooked, which did not exist in 1851. The manufacture of Arms of precision, and the voluntary organization of skilled labour to use them, both of which may at first sight appear antagonistic to the progress of art, manufactures, and commerce, but are, in fact, their great protectors. War, a remnant of barbarism, must fortunately be infinitely more difficult, hazardous, and expensive, not only in the preparations for it, but in its results, when arms are constructed of such power that hardly any fortification or ship can resist them. Fortifications and naval architecture now wear a different complexion to what they did before 1851. The manufacture of the Whitworth Rifle and the Armstrong Gun are new industries since 1851. The small gun, directed by high intelligence, throwing a large and destructive missile to a distance beyond any previous belief, becomes a more formidable instrument of warfare than the large forces of olden time, directed only by low intelligence and relying upon brute force for success; and in the perfection of these implements of war, costly though they be, we are as a nation deeply interested; for in so far as we are in advance of all the world in their manufacture and in our knowledge of how to use them, so are we safe from foreign interference. The better armed will rarely be attacked, and still more rarely successfully so, by the worse armed."

It will be seen hereafter that Mr. Hawes's anticipations as regards our Colonies have been realized in a remarkable degree:—

"The effect of the progress we have made since 1851 is also shown by the rapid *increase of our colonial and foreign trades*, and the much greater interest which foreigners now take in England and English manufactures. Then, after a period of great agricultural and commercial distress, we exported but 65,000,000*l*. per annum, now we export 136,000,000*l*. Then India, governed by a separate authority, did not afford facilities for emigration, or to settlements being made by English capitalists. Now that vast dependency, entirely under the government of our Queen, intersected by railways and new roads, and with steamboats traversing her rivers, will become, year by year, more intimately acquainted with, and larger consumers of, our manufactures.

"Then Canada had recently emerged from a period of discontent and difficulty; now, it is one of the most—if not the most—flourishing and rapidly increasing in wealth and population of our colonies, with a system of railways and water communication unsurpassed anywhere; the bridge over the St. Lawrence being one of the greatest triumphs of engineering in the world.

"Our Australian Colonies have not been left behind. The discovery of gold, although for a time it threatened seriously to affect the cultivation of the country, has so stimulated the tide of emigration thereto, that the supply of wool, almost as valuable to us as gold, has been maintained, and industry of all kinds has advanced most rapidly.

"If we look to foreign countries, we find France just entering upon a career of free trade, from which it is all but impossible she can recede, while her people, as a whole, appear more friendly to us than at any former period. Our nearest neighbour and principal foreign competitor in 1851, then prohibited or levied such high duties upon the importation of English manufactures, as all but to exclude them from the country. Now, we have passports abolished, free intercourse encouraged, a low uniform rate of postage established, and a treaty of commerce under which our manufactures are admitted, which must tend, year by year, to increase the commercial transactions between us. Holland, also following our example, has recently opened several of the ports of her East Indian possessions to foreign trade with all countries. Russia, under the guidance of a wise and great sovereign, besides constructing railways and telegraphs, and promoting intercourse between the most distant parts of her vast territories, is emancipating her serfs from bondage, and making a large population at once free and industrious, and therefore larger consumers of the products of the forge and the loom. China is still further open to our industry, and bids fair to be one of our largest and best customers; and it is hardly too much to say that the effect produced in the late war on the minds of the rulers of that nation, by the wonderful power we exhibited with our rifles and Armstrong Guns, had much to do with its early and successful termination; and if so, the entire expense we have incurred in their manufacture will be amply repaid by the great results achieved through their instrumentality in this one short campaign. In Japan, Siam, Madagascar, the Philippine Islands, hitherto almost unknown countries, we find vast populations seeking for our manufactures. Enough has been said to show that if the Exhibition of 1851 was, in the words of our Royal President, 'to form a new starting-point from which all nations were to direct their future exertions,' that of 1862 must still more efficiently perform that function, inasmuch as the basis upon which it rests is broader, the nations interested in the progress of civilisation and commercial freedom more numerous, and the population to be stimulated to exertion enormously larger."*

After the reading of the paper, Earl Granville said :—" With regard to the great undertaking, the feeling concerning the Exhibition which was being manifested in the great centres of trade was most satisfactory. The support which had been accorded in the metropolis was most gratifying. The Colonies were also coming forward with their contributions. He had had a communication with Lord Canning touching the efforts which India was making. Though the funds at the disposal of the authorities were not so large as could be desired, yet he believed India would be worthily represented in the Exhibition. From other countries he had received assurances which, though they differed in degree, were satisfactory. He had lately been in Paris, and he found that a Commission, over which Prince Napoleon presided, had been originated; and he had been informed that the Emperor desired that no expense should be spared in promoting the success of the French portion of the Exhibition. Notwithstanding some feelings of protectionism which might operate on the mass, his (Lord Granville's) opinion was, there was some danger, owing to the great exertions the French were making, that if we did not try to put our right leg foremost, we might not be able to maintain the position which we occupied in the last Exhibition."

The Report of this Meeting has a most melancholy interest; for it was then that the Prince Consort so emphatically and en-

* Mr. Hawes's inferences from these and other details were, that an International Exhibition would amply pay itself in 1861. Lieutenant-Colonel Owen, however, went much further: he prepared some curious railway statistics to show that, *with equal attractiveness*, 7,000,000 country visitors would be as likely to come to London in 1861 as 3,000,000 in 1851, owing simply to the known increase in railway travelling. Granted, according to the improved means of transit; but an important element is left out of the calculation—namely, an increase of money, *pari passu*, to enable the visitors to avail themselves of the railway increase.

couragingly expressed his confidence in the prosperity of the Exhibition, which, unhappily, he did not live to witness.

After some remarks from Mr. Dillon and Sir Thomas Phillips, Prince Albert, among other observations, said:—"*Gentlemen, you will succeed. You are in earnest, and being in earnest, you will succeed.* I can congratulate you on the steps you have taken. You have an able body of managers, with all of whom I am well acquainted, and from my acquaintance I can say that they are thoroughly conversant with all the work you have imposed on them. You have also an able architect—a young officer of engineers—who, as alluded to by Lord Granville, has to-day shown, by the work which has been opened in the Horticultural Gardens, that he is capable of vast designs, novel contrivances, and is possessed of great taste. Gentlemen, Lord Granville and Sir Thomas Phillips have referred to foreign nations. I happen to know that foreign nations look with favour upon this Exhibition, and are prepared to come to measure their strength with yours. I need not repeat the warning and encouragement that Lord Granville has thrown out to the trades of this country,—that they should endeavour to maintain the position they so gloriously took on the last occasion."

The activity of the Society of Arts, doubtless, contributed to the success of the Guarantee Fund, which, on the 8th of June, 1860, was subscribed by 455 persons, to the sum of 308,353*l*.

The Commissioners, in their Fourth Report, informed the Society of Arts that they would grant, rent free, until the 31st of December, 1862, for the purposes of the Exhibition of 1862, the use of the whole of the land on the main square of their Estate lying on the south side of the Horticultural Society's Gardens, estimated at 16 acres ; on the understanding that all the buildings to be erected for the Exhibition, whether permanent or temporary in their character, should be subject to their approval, and that all the temporary buildings should be removed within six months after the close of the Exhibition, if required ; the Trustees of the Exhibition being at liberty, on the other hand, to remove the buildings termed permanent if the Exhibition should be attended with pecuniary loss. They further expressed their readiness to grant to the Society, in recognition of their long-continued services in advancing the interests of the arts and manufactures, and especially in preparing the way for the Great Exhibition of 1851, a lease for ninety-nine years at a moderate ground-rent of those permanent buildings if retained, on condition of not less than the sum of fifty thousand pounds being expended on them by the Trustees, and of their not covering more than one acre of ground ; and also on condition of their being used solely for holding exhibitions and for purposes connected with the promotion of arts and manufactures. "With respect to the Society's application (say the Commissioners), that we should appropriate a portion of our estate for the purpose of future exhibitions analogous to the proposed Exhibition of 1862, we informed them that with the view of meeting their wishes as far as was consistent with our public duty, and at the same time bearing in mind our obligations to our mortgagees, we would undertake, in the event of the payment to us of the sum of ten thousand pounds out of the profits (if any) of the Exhibition of 1862, to reserve for the purposes of another International Exhibition in 1872, to be conducted by such body as might be approved by us, the remainder of the land now proposed to be lent by us for the Exhibition of 1862 that was not covered by the permanent buildings already referred to, such reservation not interfering in any way with the free use by us of that land in the intervening period."

The Society of Arts accepted these terms, and next induced the five gentlemen named in the draft guarantee deed as the proposed Trustees of the Exhibition to accept the trust. Upon their suggestion, the management was then offered to the Commissioners of 1851, within the conditions expressed in the guarantee agreement. This the Commissioners were unwilling to undertake with the restrictions imposed, even had there not been many legal difficulties in the way of their doing so; but they expressed their general approval of the object which the Society of Arts had in view in organizing the proposed Exhibition, and their readiness when the trust was accepted by the five gentlemen named, to afford assistance in advising the Trustees on certain important principles and financial points, and to elect as Commissioners those two of the five Trustees—Lord Chandos and Mr. Fairbairn—who were not already members of their body.

Meanwhile, the Trustees to the Commissioners, additional space being requisite, obtained the loan of an unoccupied portion of land lying between the western arcades of the Horticultural Gardens and Prince Albert's-road, as well as the south arcades of the Horticultural Gardens, to be fitted up as refreshment-rooms. A subsequent request for more space on the opposite side of the grounds to form another annexe was also complied with.

It may relieve the dryness of these details to quote from the *Quarterly Review* this more picturesque account of the new tenancy:—

"The Horticultural Society, which had since its foundation rusticated at Chiswick, came into prominence as the chief claimant for the Commissioners' favours. No one had a word to urge against its pretensions: it asked to come to town, and town was glad to receive the petitioner. In the creation of a metropolitan garden, there was a guarantee for a new lung of London. It was comparatively unimportant that the prospects of the horticulturists were somewhat problematic. They had not given up the useful old nursery at Chiswick, while it was well understood that the object of the new garden was to set up a 'moral Cremorne.' So the brave old trees which skirted the paddock of Gore House were felled, little ramps were raised, and little slopes sliced off, with a fiddling nicety of touch which would have delighted the imperial grandeur of the Summer Palace; and the tiny declivities thus manufactured were tortured into curvilinear patterns, where sea sand, chopped coal, and pounded bricks atoned for the absence of flower or shrub. The area had to be inclosed, for it was carefully stipulated that the lengthened frontages on the boundary roads should form no portion of the lease to the Horticultural Society. The result was Mr. Smirke's Renaissance arcades in brick at the upper portion, and the terra-cotta imitation of the Lateran cloister, produced by the Department round the southern half, neither of them, it may be, great works, but both of them graceful, and even refreshing architectural experiments by the side of their gigantic neighbour. To the south of this garden lay another plot of 1851 ground, predestined for the New Exhibition."

Thus, the site was determined on. In February, the Queen granted a charter to the Trustees. The Bank of England agreed to advance the necessary funds on the faith of the guarantors, and all was ready for deciding about the building, when the first step taken by the Commissioners was generally considered an unwise one. Without any appeal for suggestions to the country in general, or to the architectural profession in particular—without a hint to the guarantors to provide against loss, or even a single note of preparation, it was suddenly announced to the public that the design was agreed on, the plans were laid, the specifications written, and that tenders for the erection of the Building were sought for. Sir Joseph Paxton, as a guarantor, very justifiably objected to the looseness of the conditions, and to spending so large a sum of money as this Building should require, and this without allowing time for a fair estimate of the cost to be made; it being added, that the person who tenders for the erection of the Building, "must do so at great risk, *unless he has been so fortunate as to have had access to the plans before they were given to the public.*" However, these objections were overruled; and the design by Captain Fowke, of the Royal Engineers, was declared to be accepted. The circumstances under which the Commissioners arrived at this decision are thus described in a letter of Mr. F. R. Sandford, their Secretary, dated Feb. 20, 1861:—

"The most pressing point was the Building required for the Exhibition. In 1850, notwithstanding the possession of considerable funds, and the assistance of the most eminent architects and engineers, seven months elapsed before a design was adopted. The Commissioners therefore felt that if they postponed the consideration of this subject until they were a legally constituted body, the cost of the Building would be greatly increased, and a serious risk incurred of its non-completion by the appointed time.

"The arrangements made by the Society of Arts, when negotiating for a site on the estate of the Commissioners of 1851, and their arrangement that the Exhibition was to include Pictures, a branch of art not exhibited on the former occasion, rendered it necessary to contemplate the erection of a Building in some parts of a more substantial character than that of 1851.

"A plan was submitted to the Commissioners by Captain

Fowke, R.E., who had been employed by Her Majesty's Government in the British Department of the Paris Exhibition of 1855. This design was adapted to the proposed site, and was intended to meet the practical defects which experience had shown to exist both in the Buildings in Hyde Park and in the Champs Elysées. It appeared well adapted for the required purposes, and its principal features were of a striking character, and likely to form an attractive part of the Exhibition. The Commissioners submitted the design to the competition of ten eminent contractors, four of whom took out the quantities. Three tenders (one a joint one from two of the contractors invited) were sent in on the day named in the invitation, but all were greatly in excess of the amount which the Commissioners could prudently spend, with a due regard to the interests of the guarantors.

"The Commissioners have, therefore, had under their consideration modifications of the plan, which, without destroying its merits, would materially reduce its cost."

Its principal feature at first consisted in a great central hall, with arched roof and rounded ends, 500 feet long, 250 feet wide, and 210 feet high—"a veritable Hall of Eblis (says the *Practical Mechanics' Journal*), the designs of which we have seen, and which would certainly have been not only stupendous in size, but grand in point of style and duration; although we might ask here, *Cui bono?* However, this was a single central hall, a veritable central-point to the whole, however Brobdignaggian in height. The estimates for the original structure amounted, including this hall, to 590,000*l*. The Commissioners required such modifications to be made, as should reduce this amount within the manageable limits of their guarantee fund; and Captain Fowke appeals to the fact that he has had to preserve the main features of his design (exclusive of the great hall,) and yet so modify, or leave incomplete its details, as to bring the cost down to little more than half his original estimate, in explanation and justification of many incongruities and sins against form and taste, charged against him now by the public, but in reality chargeable to the conditions of the case as placed in his hands." The writer of this sound view of the matter in the *Practical Mechanics' Journal* had the advantage of access to the whole of the working drawings, general designs, and photographs of progress of the Great Building, placed in his hands by Captain Fowke: by which the journalist was enabled to describe for the first time to professional readers and the public its structural details from authentic sources; and access was given, as often as occasion required, to every portion of the structure required, for personal examination of its details.

The journalist's defence of Captain Fowke's Building is far more serviceable to him than all the fine flourishes of his non-professional friends.[*]

---

[*] This young and clever officer of Engineers attached to the Department of Science and Art, had previously engineered at the South Kensington Museum, the "Brompton Boilers," and the permanent Galleries for the Sheep-

The writer in the *Quarterly Review*, a journal long accustomed, as Byron sings, to "treat a dissenting author very martyrly,"— we consider, in this view, to be very fair to the engineer. "The authorities (he says,) had proclaimed so confidently that there was one building, and Fowke was its architect, that they left themselves no retreat. We do not blame Captain Fowke: he had been wafted into a false position, and it would be to set up a more than Roman standard to assert that he was in any way bound to refuse an offer so abnormally advantageous as that of becoming *per saltum* architect of the world's biggest building. How far those who placed him there were alive to the exceptional importance of their own act is a very different question, on which society has long formed its own verdict. The presence or absence of the central dome was, after all, an immaterial consideration in the value of the Building. If it had been carried out, it would have been a monument of purposeless cost and ineffective bulk. Its absence only creates a vast solecism, as purposeless, as ineffective, and as needlessly costly in proportion to its cubic contents."

Of the three tenders sent in, that furnished by Mr. Kelk and the Brothers Lucas being the lowest, was accepted; and these eminent firms became partners in the work. For the rent of the Building a sum of 200,000*l.* was absolutely guaranteed; if the receipts exceeded 400,000*l.*, the Contractors were to be paid 100,000*l.* more for rent; and they were bound, if required, to sell the whole for a further sum of 130,000*l.*, thus making the whole cost 430,000*l.* The Building was to be completed by the 12th of February, 1862.

Captain Philpotts informs us that the Commissioners for 1851 are to be the legal proprietors of the site; but to secure the greater portion of it for the intended 1872 Exhibition. they have agreed to reserve about 16 acres of it for that purpose on receiving 10,000*l* as a sort of ground-rent. It is already agreed that the Society of Arts, Adelphi, will be granted the lease of the central portion of the picture-gallery, one acre in extent, along the Cromwell-road, for 99 years, on payment of a ground-rent, and that it be given up unreservedly for the use of the 1872 Exhibition.

LAYING OUT OF THE WORKS.

The laying out of the works was commenced on 9th March,

shanks pictures. We have seen the former attributed to the late Sir William Cubitt. The galleries are a far superior work. Francis Fowke, Captain Royal Engineers, is distantly connected with the Leicestershire family of Lowesby Hall, in that county. Captain Fowke was born in the year 1824; and, having gone through the usual preliminary training at the Royal Academy at Woolwich, obtained a commission as Lieutenant in the Royal Engineers in 1842. In 1854 he attained to the rank of Captain; was selected for civil employment by the Government, and it was probably owing to his connexion with the Museum at South Kensington that he was appointed to design and carry into execution the above plan for the edifice intended for the Exhibition of 1862. Captain Fowke has received for his design the sum of 5000*l*.

1861, by three independent agencies—Mr. Marshall on the part of the contractors, while Mr. Wakeford and Sergeant Harkin, Royal Engineers, acted for the Commissioners.

Great care was taken with the measurements, for the slightest error would have thrown out the work considerably, and have occasioned great difficulty in fitting the girders. In the three separate measurements made, the mean variation was only three-eighths of an inch, a difference quite imperceptible in a piece of ground 1200 feet by 600 feet. A glance through any of the aisles will show how accurately the work has been conducted; and whether they be examined on the square or diagonally, the columns will be found to range in line as perfectly as they would show in a plan.

About two weeks were occupied in making the measurements, so that the Building may be said to have been actually commenced in the beginning of April, 1861, from which its progress became uninterrupted and rapid. It may be said to have been practically finished about the beginning of April, 1862, having been just about a year in progress.

The following statistics are given by Captain Philpotts as to the quantities of the chief materials used in its construction:—

"There were 7,000,000 bricks used; these were all supplied by Messrs. Smeed, of Sittingbourne. Nearly all the cast-iron work was supplied from the Stavely Iron-works, in Derbyshire; there are upwards of 4000 tons of this metal in the building; and to show what care had been taken with the castings, only four girders proved defective, by breaking in the proof.

"There are upwards of 820 columns, of 25 feet, equal in length to 4 miles; and if the 1266 girders used were placed end to end, they would reach a distance of 6 miles. The wrought-iron was chiefly supplied by the Thames Iron Company, Blackwall, London. This firm undertook the supply of all the iron for the domes, the groined ribs, the 50-feet roofs, and the iron trellis girders which support them; the total quantity of wrought-iron in connexion with these parts amounts to 12,000 tons.

"The timber-work was executed partly at the works of Messrs. Lucas, at Lowestoft, and partly at Mr. Kelk's works at Pimlico; the former prepared all the window sashes, &c., &c., by machinery; and the latter constructed the heavy ribs of the nave and transepts. Upwards of 1,000,000 super feet of floor has been laid.

"To cover the roofs 486,386 square feet of felt were used, equal to 11 acres; and to complete the whole of the glazing required 353,000 super feet of glass, which weigh 247 tons, and would cover 12¾ acres.

"The whole of the working drawings were prepared by Mr. Meesom, who had charge of the details of construction from the time that the building was put into the hands of the contractors."

PROGRESS OF THE BUILDING.

It may be interesting as well as instructive to reproduce a few of the many graphic accounts of the progress of the works, detailing the operations at various stages.

While the ground at South Kensington was only "marking out," the lines of tapering scaffold poles at its edges made it resemble on the outskirts a young plantation for colossal hops. Red sticks marked where the double columns of the nave were to be erected, and apertures were cutting in the ground for the great iron pillar from which the dome is to spring. In about a month the brick walls were more than thirty feet high; the floor of the picture-gallery was being laid, and the skeleton of the eastern end of the great structure was fast mapping out in piles of brown massive columns, with their interlacings of trellis and face girders, the number and extent of which visibly grew with every hour's labour. The rows of columns that lay about the ground diminished in their number every minute; and so admirable were the appliances for working, that they were whisked up into the air, placed on end, and bolted together, almost in as little time as it has taken us to tell it. The immensely increased rapidity with which iron structures of the most enduring kind can be run up as compared with those of brick or stone is shown by the way in which the metal portions of the building progressed over the picture-gallery. The latter part of the structure, though begun long before the rest, was only about thirty feet high, while in some parts the iron work was upwards of fifty. The works connected with the picture-gallery were, however, of no ordinary magnitude and substance, for all connected with this portion of the Building is most massive, and calculated for permanence. The story immediately beneath the picture-gallery is lighted on one side by a series of lofty windows fifteen feet high by fifteen wide, at intervals of fifteen feet apart. As above these the wall rises unbroken nearly fifteen feet higher, the arches over each are unusually strong, while in the wall itself, over the centre of every window, is what is called a pocket—a hollow flue made in the thickness of the brickwork to lighten as much as possible the superincumbent weight on the windows. The roof of this carriage department forms the floor of the picture-gallery. It is formed of thick flooring beams laid transversely over girders fourteen inches deep by ten inches wide. The ends of these girders rest on blocks of stone built into the walls, but as they have a span of fifty feet, each is further supported by thin iron columns down into the carriage department beneath.

This flooring was tested by being weighted with bricks laid equally over it on all parts five deep. This represented a weight of 140 lb. on the superficial foot, which, when we remember that three feet of the gallery on each side in front of the pictures is railed off, and portions of the centre floor occupied by seats, is a greater weight than by any possibility can ever come on it. As a matter of course the flooring stood this test with ease, and after a day or two more the weight was increased to 200 lb. the foot, in order that it may be seen if the floor is not only a strong one, but a "stiff" one. When this point had been satisfactorily established, the work of running up the remaining portion of the gallery walls was continued. This noble gallery is not one unbroken line of flat wall surface from end to end; there are two compartments of 325 feet long each, one of 150, two of 75, and four of 50. This subdivision, however, is only made by a lofty arch of brickwork, similar to the slight framings of the same description which had such a charming effect in breaking the long monotony of wall at Manchester. Of course, these partition walls are continued beneath the floor with cross-walls, which tie them in all together as one piece. Beneath the middle of the picture-gallery is one of the main entrances to the building, of enormous solidity: at this part there are four piers in the walls which are no less than seventeen feet wide by ten feet deep and sixty feet high, all of solid brickwork! Than the iron columns and girders, probably, cleaner and finer castings, or castings of a better description of iron, have never been seen. At both sides of nave and transepts, the columns are double—one square and one round, and each 12 inches diameter. The other columns for the side courts for exhibitors are 8 inches wide. Each column, in addition to what it has to support, is equal to about ten times the pressure that can ever possibly come upon it. In the Exhibition of 1851, the sub-divisions or bays, as they are called, were all 24 feet square or 48. In this structure they are all 25 or 50. The trellis-girders which support the floor of the galleries might, it is computed, under certain combinations of circumstances, which are scarcely possible, have to sustain a weight of from 28 to 30 tons. A number of them were accordingly tested and broken to ascertain that they were fully up to the strain. None broke under 72 tons, and some went as high as 76. With the jealous overcaution in all that relates to perfect strength which distinguishes both the Commissioners and contractors, it was, nevertheless, determined to increase the thickness of the girders, so as to make 80 tons the *minimum* breaking strain, thus rendering them equal to thrice the weight that can ever come upon them.

Engineers and contractors who visited the works were unanimous in the opinion that they were better "laid out" for facilitating the rapid progress of labour than any they had ever seen. Upwards of two miles of little tramways intersected the grounds in all directions, and along these a couple of men could move a truck with 4 or 5 tons of girders at a far greater speed than six or eight horses could move them in a waggon. With the same view, a small powerful steam-engine was placed in the centre of the works, and connected by a network of ropes passing through pulleys over all parts of the ground. By means of these, loads were drawn about the tramways, or columns and girders hoisted and bolted in their places, with amazing rapidity and ease. But the most astonishing and the most extensive of these labour-saving contrivances was a gigantic travelling scaffold, built on twelve wheels, to run on rails up and down the whole length of the centre nave. This huge structure was 60 feet square and 100 feet high, and weighed nearly 300 tons. Yet so equally was it balanced, and so smoothly did the wheels work, that four men with levers could move it very quicky to any part of the works. It was more than double the size, strength, and weight of any travelling scaffold ever yet erected. It was used in hoisting the upper columns, the huge circular wooden ribs of the roof, for painting, or, indeed, for any purpose connected with building where many men had to be employed at a great height. The annexe, or ingeniously planned shed for the exhibition of machinery in motion, progressed with marvellous rapidity. Of all the ingenious things that have been designed by Captain Fowke, he has done nothing in its way better than the plan for the framework for this strong, light, simple, and beautiful shed. It is the *ne plus ultra* of woodwork for covering in large spaces in the cheapest manner. Captain Fowke first sketched out the rough design to suit the South Kensington Volunteers, who wanted a drill-shed, but could not afford to spend much money on it. His plan combined such strength of frame with economy of material, that the Volunteers were actually able to build a shed 90 feet long by 50 broad for 82*l*. He again improved upon this design in the entrance to the Horticultural Gardens, and brought it to the perfection in which it now stands in the annexe to the Exhibition. The roof of it looks as if it would scarcely bear the weight of a man on it, yet the slight wooden arches of 50 feet span have actually been tested with a strain of three tons.

The vastness of the constructional labour is thus sketched, in a masterly manner, in the *Saturday Review:*—

"So complete are our mechanical contrivances for the utmost economy of expensive human strength, so admirable are the arrangements for concentrating as well as dividing labour, that we may pronounce the work, as work, a complete triumph of engineering. The travelling scaffold and the steam machinery by which girders and beams are hoisted into mid-air—the way in which mere labour seems to be lost in the absolute supremacy of force—the sense of power, apart from the multiplication of efforts of personal strength—is the striking thing in great modern works. When Thebes or the Coliseum was built we can quite understand what the aggregate of a thousand or two thousand pairs of arms pulling together at a single mass of stone could do. But here it is the fewness of the labourers and the might of screw, and lever, and steam which is remarkable.

"Indeed, we might go further, and say that this Building—and it is in various degrees true of all modern buildings—shows less of intellect than of the mechanical and abstract powers. All that is to be seen at Brompton is a vast and ingenious system of joinery. Scarcely anything is made on the spot. There is absolutely not one solitary fragment of work—wood, iron, or glass, which is not executed by machinery. It would be perhaps difficult to point out one single square inch of work which is due to skilled manual labour. The iron is all cast, the bricks are all machine-made, the wood is all machine-planed; the very capitals of the vast columns, the one and only feature in which ornament has been attempted, are all run in plaster moulds. The glass is all cast. All that man has to do is to screw and nail and tie and mortice and cement ready-made materials together. It is the tendency of modern work to destroy skilled labour which requires anything more than mechanical precision. It absorbs the man in the machine. The more the workman is brought down to the level of a piece of unerring and irresponsible machinery, incapable of praise or blame, the better he is fitted for our present great building works. No doubt this is the cause why this vast structure is probably the least satisfactory which has emanated from human skill. And its failure in one respect is exactly commensurate with its success in another. It is the very largest, the most complete and satisfying for one purpose; and because it fulfils this, we are disappointed, and even shocked, that it does not answer to other requirements. The ordinary critics repeat the stock phrases 'stupendous,' 'gigantic,' 'imposing,' 'vast,' 'impressive,' till they almost persuade themselves that the sublime consists in mere size. As to the magnitude of the buildings, they might have been ten or twenty or two hundred times as big without increasing their value as works of art. To the capacities of using up iron, bricks, roof, and flooring, there are absolutely no limits while iron and space exist; and it would have been just as easy to palisade all London with innumerable columns, and to cover it with a roof, and to circle it with a brick wall, as to erect this one building. It is merely the multiplication of the very rudest building which was ever constructed. There is a pleasure-dome and it may be stately; but when Kublai Khan enclosed with walls and towers twice five miles of fertile ground, he did only a work whose sole merit was its bigness, and Captain Fowke has, if the praise is worth anything, erected a very big work. This is the beginning and end of his achievement."

Among what may be termed *curiosities of construction* we find the following well-drawn picture in the *Builder*, Jan. 11, 1862:—

"The first effect on entering the building falls more upon the ear than upon the eye. There is a clanging vibratory roar as of a vast iron shipbuilding yard, a railway terminus, and a midland county manufactory, all in full career under one roof: then various distinct noises can be clearly made out,—the driving of nails into wood, with the preliminary tapping, followed by the full hammering that sends them home; the silvery ring of innumerable trowels; the chipping of bricks; the dull splash of plaster, with the gondolier-like chanting of the men who have close and comfortable quarters, such as generally fall to the plasterer's lot; the shrill screams and hissing steam from stationary engines; the clanking of iron; the rumbling of carts. Then the eye begins to take in impressions. These are, at first, almost droll. Pieces of iron of every size and shape are lying about in heaps, all lettered and numbered, ready to be fitted into their places. In the vastness of the building these appear of diminutive proportions; but on trying to lift some of them their colossal length and weight are evident. Many of these pieces of iron are of the oddest shapes, such as we might suppose young Vulcan had for playthings. Bolts, round-headed and wormed, like the staves of special constables; pieces into which the bolts go like great stair-rod eyes; others flanged and hooked, as though intended to draw teeth; rings of iron of all sizes, breadths, and thicknesses, some like the collars of ship-masts, others like great quoits, some plain, others bored with holes. Then there is an immense monkey, of gorilla proportions, for pile-driving, lying useless on the floor, its occupation gone; and iron nuts strung on wire rods like beads upon a string; piles of nut-plates; grind-stones; casks of oil; casks of tar; casks of putty; iron bracket pieces; ladders ninety rounds high; lengths of iron split at one end, tuning-fork fashion; others rounded, flanged and rebated, rebated and flanged, and double flanged; iron rods shaped like pincers at one end, with a nut and screw at the other; iron rods flanged and shaped like toddy ladles with long handles; great pieces of iron, arrow-headed and flanged, like so many battering-rams; boxes of glass, and piles of sash-bars are among the oddments lying about on all sides. An enormous travelling scaffold, on twelve wheels, occupying three sets of rails, each of 18 feet gauge, fills in the width and 80 feet of the height of the great central nave, and is moved backwards or forwards on the rails as it is wanted, so that all parts of the sides and roof of the nave can be easily reached. This is in form like the mediæval war-engine, called the cat, which was placed over moats to get at the parapets of castle walls, and was provided with flying bridges, or scaffold stages, capable of being adjusted to any height; and it also calls to mind the lofty permanent wooden scaffold on drum-wheels in St. Peter's, Rome, that is kept and used for the purpose of cleaning the ceilings. A little farther on, a monstrous Catherine-wheel-like framework, some 50 feet in diameter, calls the attention, and proves to be the complete framework of a gable end. More striking still are the great diagonal girders, forming, in heraldic phrase, a cross saltire, on which are being framed the double staircases to get at the galleries, and whose straddling form serves the two-fold purpose of a brace to the structure, as well as of a ground-work for the staircases. And so by degrees the eye takes in the specialities of the building.

"As we pass, the co-operative nature of the work is noticeable. The girders of roofs and floors and iron columns, when fixed, serve as scaffolds whence to fix more, and for slinging cages in which to move men up and down; and the floors of galleries and basements do double duty as drawing-boards. The grasp with which our modern appliances are brought to bear is also noteworthy—gas and water are laid on, railways and tramways laid down, and turn-tables, and every other mechanical contrivance for the saving of hard labour, thought of and used.

"The feeding of the building is going on all day. Large waggons, with the names of Kelk and Lucas painted upon them, drawn by handsome dray-horses, are bringing in supplies that appear inexhaustible. Foundries, factories, and workshops, in different parts of London, furnish various materials, and these are also continually flowing in. The supply of material, indeed, is one of the wonders of the work, and gives rise to the conclusion that, should there be any delay in the finishing of the Building, it cannot possibly be imputed to any failure in this department. As the respective trades are following up each other as closely as possible, —the carpenter coming quickly upon the bricklayer and smith,— the glazier keeping close up to him, and the painter pressing onwards close upon the heels of all,—the labour department on the spot would appear to be quite as removed from the liability of blame, should the ultimate want of punctuality incur any.

"To see 4000 men at work on one building is a sight worthy of contemplation. Among the skilled men in their allotted places at their allotted tasks, with no shirking anywhere and no driving taskmasters to be seen, there is an appearance of personal interest in the progress of the work that makes the spectacle even more telling. Shipwrights, sailors, ship-carpenters, bricklayers, plasterers, house-carpenters, joiners, coppersmiths, ironsmiths, steelworkers, painters, glaziers, labourers of all nations, are employed in honest labour for honest pay at a season of the year that is often characterized by compulsory idleness of many weeks' duration. By division of labour, and sub-division of contracts, each small set of men in the various trades and departments bring about a great result—all are for progress; and there is no coercion."

Probably there never has been raised a building where economy has been brought to bear so rigidly upon construction. There does not appear to be a superfluous ounce in the lofty iron pillars, nor in the great spanning girders, or the light-tied roofs; and the principals are placed at the greatest possible distance apart that is compatible with a likelihood that they will be able to perform the offices required of them. Yet, for the most part, all is considered to be satisfactorily solid.

Some idea of the magnitude of the undertaking so successfully completed by Messrs. Kelk and Lucas might be gathered from the immense mass of materials known as "builders' plant," used in the erection of the Building, including 12,000 scaffold poles, 18,000 cords, 10,000 boards, 6000 putlogs; 1000 loads of timber, used principally for the construction of the great domes; 5 steam-engines, 20 tons rope falls, blocks, chains, smith's tools, &c. &c. The whole of this plant was sold by auction shortly after the completion of the Building, and realized about ten thousand pounds.

The strength of the Building had now to be scientifically tested. The following is the Report addressed to the Commissioners of the Exhibition by Mr. W. Fairbairn and Mr. W. Baker, civil engineers, detailing the results of the proofs to which they themselves experimentally submitted the strength of the galleries and staircases. The strength of the domes, it will be seen, is but lightly touched upon :—

"*To the Commissioners of the International Exhibition.*

"My Lords and Gentlemen,—Feeling that it would be a source of satisfaction to the Commissioners, as well as to ourselves, as members of the Building Committee, and also a due precaution for the public safety, that the gallery and other floors of the International Exhibition Building at South Kensington should be thoroughly proved, we undertook a series of experiments on Monday last.

"We have to report that, in carrying out these experiments, the various floors and stairs were put to a more severe test than they would be subjected to with the largest number of people that could possibly be assembled upon them at any other time during the Exhibition. The results of these experiments fully bear out our calculations on the strength of the different parts of the structure, and we feel perfectly satisfied as to the stability of the Building for the purpose for which it was intended.

"The two large domes, in the strength of which we have taken great interest, were eased from their temporary support last week, and no observable settlement took place.

"The following are the particulars of the tests:—We first caused a large body of men, about 400 in number, to be closely packed upon a space 25 feet by 25 feet on one lay of flooring; we then moved them in step, and afterwards made them run over the different galleries, and down each staircase; at the same time we caused the deflections of the girders carrying these floors to be carefully noted at several places, and had the satisfaction of finding that, in each case the deflections were very nearly the same, thus exhibiting a remarkable uniformity in the construction. The cast-iron girders, with 25 feet bearings, deflected only one-eighth of an inch at the centre, and the timber-trussed beams of the same bearing placed between these girders deflected half an inch at the centre. In every instance the girders and trusses recovered their original position immediately on the removal of the load.

"We are, my Lords and Gentlemen, yours faithfully,

"WM. FAIRBAIRN,
"WILLIAM BAKER, } C.E.

"London, Feb. 13."

THE EXHIBITION BUILDING DESCRIBED.

The main Building occupies about sixteen acres of ground: it is nearly rectangular in shape, and measures about 1200 feet from east to west, by 560 feet from north to south. It lies south of the Horticultural Society's Gardens and the Kensington-road. The Cromwell-road forms the southern boundary; on the east it is shut in by the Exhibition-road; and on the west by Prince Albert's-road. The whole of this ground is covered by permanent buildings; and two long strips of ground, east and west of the gardens, were roofed in by the temporary sheds, or *annexes*, in which were shown machinery, and large and heavy objects. This additional area extends to seven acres.

The interior space is entirely covered in by roofs of various heights, and is divided into nave, transepts, aisles, and open courts: the latter are roofed with glass, as in 1851, but the other parts have opaque roofs, and are lighted by clerestory windows.

We shall now describe the respective fronts of the Building.

The *South Front*, in Cromwell-road, 1150 feet long and 55 feet high in the brickwork, has two projecting towers at each end, rising 16 feet above the general outline, and a larger tower in the centre, in which latter is the main entrance to the *Picture Galleries;* being about as long as the Gallery of the Louvre, in Paris. The exterior is chiefly brickwork, relieved with semi-circular-headed panels, separated by pilasters, and between the arches are circular niches; in the lower portion of each panel being a window, to admit light and air to the ground-floor, and to ventilate the Picture Gallery above. The panels are plastered in cement, and it is proposed to ornament them with English mosaics, dependent on the funds. This great frontage has almost unanimously been condemned as ugly and featureless; but Captain Fowke designs to incrust it with terra-cotta panels enriching the great pilasters and other parts of the face, the present blank window spaces being filled in from end to end with a grand series of designs in solid mosaics, rich in colour, emblematic of art and science, and other works.*
The Editor of the *Practical Mechanics' Journal* objects that the lower or glazed portion of the windows of this front, as now framed with timber lintels visible *en face*, and cast-iron perforated ventilators in them, can never be made to look well or to harmonize with any finished remainder. The windows must be solid carved stone or terra-cotta jambs and mullions, with arch or other headings of like material, and showing deep reveals, and perhaps projecting balconies, if ever this (at best awkward) appropriation of the whole arched height between the pilasters is to satisfy the eye of taste. Again, were all this done, it may be said, the site makes it useless; the opposite houses preclude our seeing the front of the Building except in small bits at a time. Quite true; but the architect did not make the site, it was dictated to him, and as we ourselves strongly surmise, with this in view, that should the Building become a national gallery, the houses at the south side of Cromwell-road should be purchased out, and a sufficient open space in front be thus ultimately obtained.

The *East and West Fronts*, though differing from the South, are not less imposing. They are, in all respects, similar to each other in their general aspect. Here the huge domes, rising to a height of 260 feet, show to most advantage, and the transept-roof, with its lofty clerestory windows, is in full view. To the observer below the form of each dome appears nearly that of a semicircle: this effect is obtained by making its height 11 feet

---

* Two of these mosaics are already executed.

more than its semi-diameter, which fully allows for the loss by perspective diminution.

From the crown of each dome rises the pinnacle to the height of 55 feet. Each dome is in the middle of each façade; its centre is the point formed by the intersection of the centre lines of the nave and transept, and the front of the Building is advanced from it 108 feet. Under each noble arched recess is the main entrance to the Industrial Courts, the effect of which forms one of the most pleasing exterior parts of the Building

Each of the porches contains a deep semicircular arched recess, 68 feet span and 80 feet high, in the tympan of which is the great rose-window, visible from end to end within. The window is one closing the vista as the spectator looks from a standing point beneath the other.

At the extreme north and south are two auxiliary picture-galleries, each 247 feet long. The main and auxiliary picture-galleries afford available wall-space covered by pictures, equal to 7600 square yards, or about one and a half acres.

The only portions of the Building which resemble the Crystal Palace of 1851 are the six courts north and south of the nave: they have glass roofs on the ridge-and-valley plan, supported by square iron columns and wrought-iron trellis-girders. As these courts are open from floor to the roof, they admit floods of light into the Building, with admirable effect.

The construction of the East and West Domes was a hardly contested labour: in fact, there was "a *battle of the domes*," and the victory was won by the eastern one.

The construction of the two Domes, and the whole of the roofing of the courts, was intrusted to the Thames Ironwork and Ship-building Company; the making and erection being placed under the superintendence of Mr. T. E. Hussey, an engineer of experience. He selected Mr. J. Mauldin (one of the sub-contractors for the erection of the transept and two towers of the Crystal Palace, under the inspection of Mr. Cochrane), to whom the erection of the two domes and the roofing of the courts were sublet. Mauldin hoisted the first column of the eastern dome on Monday, October the 21st, 1861; the first column of the western dome, Wednesday, November 13th, 1861; making three weeks and two days between the start of the two domes. Messrs. Kelk and Lucas then offered their assistance in erecting the western dome, which was accepted. From this time commenced the battle of the domes. The western staff showed great spirit in putting up large wooden ribs, of which the eastern staff could not see the utility. This staff still kept their steady and safe course, while the western tried all they could to overtake them by employing nearly one-third more men, and working till a late hour in the night, with the assistance of gas, the eastern men leaving work at the end of the day. The number of derricks rigged for hoisting and fixing the ground ribs for the eastern dome were nineteen. The whole of the main ribs of the eastern dome were hoisted and fixed by thirteen pairs of shear legs and thirteen derricks. The number of derricks rigged for hoisting the ground ribs in the western dome was twenty-eight. The number of shear-legs for hoisting the main-ribs was thirteen pairs, and twenty-six derricks: although this extra tackle and number of men were employed, yet they could not gain on the eastern dome. When the western found they could not gain the advantage they left off their nightly labour, and followed the eastern at a greater distance than when they started. The cost of labour for erecting the western dome was over 1000*l.* sterling more than the cost of the eastern. There still was an extra cost for tackling. The scaffold resembled forests of timber: they occupied nearly the whole interior space of the domes, and were cross-legged and cross-bolted, to enable them to bear the weight of the iron, 120 tons in each. The building of the scaffold occupied eight weeks, and every beam was hoisted by the steam-winch; very little of the timber was spoiled by cutting, and each scaffold contained 40,072 cubic feet of wood.

The plan of the groined roof-ribs of the domes, it must be allowed, is ingenious and novel. Each dome is at the intersection of the nave and transepts.

The dome-scaffolds were stated to have been upon a greater scale than anything of the kind ever executed. To this the Editor of the *Practical Mechanics' Journal* demurs as follows:—"To go no further, we imagine that the centering with which the tremendous concave of the central brick dome of the Baths of Caracalla at Rome must have been turned, probably involved more timber than the two dome scaffolds made into one. However, these scaffolds were most admirable examples of skilful combination, with great economy as to the injury done to the timber, nearly all of which was in whole or half bulk."

The two duodecagonal domes, 160 feet in diameter, and 250 feet high, are officially described as the largest of ancient and modern times.* The dome of the Pantheon is 142 feet in diameter and 70 feet high; the dome in the Baths of Caracalla was 111 feet; Brunelleschi's, at Florence, is 139 feet in diameter and 133 feet high; the dome of St. Peter's is 158 feet in diameter, and 263 feet high from the external plinth; the dome of St. Paul's Cathedral is 112 feet in diameter, and 215 feet high. The domes are of glass, with an outer and inner gallery; and it has been proposed to erect one of Messrs. Chance's dioptric lights at the top of one of them, and to illuminate it at night.

The *effect of the domes* is thus described in the official *Concise History*. "The Exhibition Charter provides that fifty thousand pounds shall be spent in the architectural completion of the central portion of the Building out of the contingent profits. The two great domes being each 300 feet from the south front, can never in any way enter into its effect. If the middle hall, with its great central dome, should ever be built, then the Cromwell-road front will not be without this ornament. Each dome keeps its place, as the centre of its own front, and its effect is utterly independent of its fellow, which is 1000 feet from it. The upper terrace of the Horticultural Gardens is the only point from which the two present domes appear simultaneously; and when thus viewed, so completely does the Building carry on the symmetrical lines of arcades and terraces, that the duality of the domes is at once accepted as the natural complement of the system which has governed the laying-out of the entire quadrangle."

* This is denied in the *Practical Mechanics' Journal*. The dome of the old Halle au Blé, at Paris, of timber, was 200 feet diameter; and after its destruction by fire was replaced by the wrought-iron and zinc dome, still in existence, of the same dimensions. There has been also this misconception as regards these domes. They have been compared with those of St Peter's and St. Paul's, which they exceed in size; but they do not rise to *so great a height* as either of the cathedral domes. The Exhibition domes rise 264 feet from the ground; St. Peter's, 434 feet; and St. Paul's, 340 feet.

In the best view to be obtained of the domes, they are striking, from mere magnitude. The Editor of the *Practical Mechanics' Journal* says:—" Seen from any point except one, directly in a line passing through the *centre* of one side of the polygon, or exactly through one of the angles, the outline appears gibbous and lop-sided. This is common to all polygonal domes; and although domes thus fashioned have the weighty authority of architectural names, such as those of Bramante and Brunelleschi, we venture heretically to say they are a radical mistake, and that every dome, whatever be its curve, should be a solid of revolution; and if *fully* discussed, we suspect the weight of past architectural authority would coincide with our view. But besides this, when pretty near, these glass domes are seen through and through, the glass, except at a few points where it reflects the light, seems to vanish almost from the eye, and we see the naked ribs and framing standing up as it were, and supporting nothing except the finials, the outlines, and indeed every part of which, appear to us graceful, and the lower portions extremely good. The only place whence these domes are really striking and grand objects is from a mile or two miles away. Seen in the clear light of morning from the high grounds of Wandsworth or Clapham, they look exceedingly beautiful, and still quite preserve their impressiveness as to size and altitude."

THE INTERIOR.

Entering east or west, the ascent is by two steps until the level of the daïs under each dome is reached. From either point the interior of the whole building may be seen in one view, at 6 feet above the rest of the floor. Thence three flights of steps, 80 feet wide, lead into the nave and transept on either side.

The supports on either side of the nave (800 feet long and 100 feet high) consist of square and round cast-iron columns, coupled together; the former carry the gallery floor, and the latter, advancing into the nave, receive the principals of the roof. From the capitals of the columns spring the roof frames, which consist of three thicknesses of plank, from 18 inches to 2 feet 6 inches deep, firmly nailed and bolted together, and so arranged that their ends break joint. The centre plank is 4 inches thick, and each of the outer ones is 3 inches; the lower edges are tangents to an imaginary semicircle, round which they form half of a nearly regular polygon. From the springing rise the posts of the clerestory windows, 25 feet high. The principal rafters of the roof-frames rise from the top of these posts, and are carried up, after passing a tangent, to the back of the arch, to meet at the ridge in a point 25 feet above the top of the clerestory. The angles over the haunches and crown of the arch are firmly braced together, so as to reduce the thrust as much as possible.

The rib is repeated thirty times in the length of the nave, and from its graceful curve and lightness it produces a fine effect. Between every roof-principal is a clerestory light 25 feet high, consisting of three arches springing from intermediate mullions. The roof is covered with felt and zinc on 1¼-inch planks. The transepts run from each end of the nave, at right-angles to it, and extend north and south 650 feet; they are the same width and height as the nave, and the ribs of its roof are of the same construction.

To these details, abridged from the *Official Description*, may be added the mode of fixing the principals in the nave-roof. This was done by the huge moveable scaffold already mentioned, which contained 4745 cubic feet of timber, and weighed 140 tons; notwithstanding, it was moved by four men, working crowbars under the wheels. One-half of a rib was first hoisted to its place; when in position, the other half was raised; and as soon as both were fixed true, they were joined together by completing the arch and bracing over its crown. As soon as one rib was up, the travelling scaffold was moved to the adjoining bay, and the next rib completed. The purlins and boarding were then fixed, after which the scaffold was again moved forward, and another bay covered in the same manner. When Mr. Crace's workmen came in to paint the roof, this scaffold was enlarged for their use until its weight reached 200 tons.

"The hoisting was all done by a most ingenious winch, or hoist, which has two grooved cast-iron barrels, made to revolve by means of a system of toothed wheels connected with a portable steam-engine. A rope is passed round the grooves. On the fall being manned and the barrels set in motion, the coils of the rope are gathered up, and a great hoisting power obtained. By means of snatch-blocks and pulleys ropes were led from this simple machine to all parts of the building, and the heaviest materials, such as girders, columns, scaffold-beams, &c., were hoisted to their position with the greatest ease and rapidity. As an instance, we need only mention that the heavy floor girders, weighing about one ton and a quarter, were raised in two minutes, each of the columns in about the same time, and the ponderous ribs of the nave, weighing six tons and a half, required only from ten to twenty minutes to raise them their full height." This Steam Hoist is the clever invention of Mr. Ashton, the engineer.

The ribs of the transept were differently fixed over a standing scaffold all through, which scaffold alone consumed 30,336 cubic feet of timber.

The construction of the galleries is very interesting. They form an abutment to the nave and transept roof, by a particular form of bracing, the ingenious suggestion of Mr. Ordish. As the roof thrusting outwards tends to throw the columns out of the perpendicular, this is counteracted by strong iron braces anchored to the foundation of the inner column, and carried up to the top of the opposite outer column. "Another bracing, anchored to the footing of the outer column, is carried up to the top of the inner column, to secure it from being acted on by the force of the wind. This vertical cross-bracing is repeated at every hundred feet, or every fourth bay, and by introducing horizontal diagonal bracing under the roof flats, they are turned as it were into a deep horizontal girder, supported at two ends by the columns vertically braced as just described. This horizontal girder therefore takes the thrust of the three intervening ribs. The way in which the bracing is introduced is very clever, and is an admirable example of the perfect control which the simplest mechanical means, properly applied, give us in dealing with enormous masses. The bracing is all adjusted by connecting screw-links on a plan very similar to the method of joining railway carriages; by this means it can be tightened at pleasure, and the position of the columns corrected to the minutest fraction of an inch."—*From the Official Description.*

The intersection of the lines of columns in the nave and transept aisles forms two octagons, which, though not mathematically regular, are regular in this one respect—their opposite sides are parallel and equal, the length of the sides being alternately 85 feet and 35 feet 5 inches. The columns at the angles of these octagons are the chief supports of the domes.

Though the chief points of support, however, are at the eight angles of the octagon, the dome is a dodecagon, the other four points being thus obtained:—The last bay of the nave and transept, instead of having a roof resting on wooden principals going straight across, has two iron diagonal ribs crossing it, forming as it were a groined arch, whose apex is a point in the centre of the bay and in a line with the roof ridge. By joining the apices of these groins and the points in the octagon already determined, we get a nearly regular dodecagon, having its opposite sides parallel and equal, and with eight sides in pairs, each equal to 43 feet 9 inches, and the four remaining sides coming between these pairs, each equal to 35 feet 5 inches. This dodecagon forms the base of the dome, which will thus have eight sides over the nave and transepts, and four sides over the corners of the aisles, equal respectively to the dimensions just given, and a diameter of 160 feet.

Each groined rib transmits the weight on it to two columns outside the octagon, so that the dome may be said to rest on sixteen points, its pressure on the angles of the octagon being nearly five times ($4\frac{9}{15}$) as much as it is on the adjacent columns of the nave and transepts. Thus, no additional columns of support but those actually coming in the sides of the nave and transepts are used, and thus an uninterrupted vista is obtained through both these channels.

The mode of lighting the interior is threefold: the nave, by means of clerestory windows on either side. The picture-galleries are lighted from the top with skylights and an inner roof of ground-glass, to modify the light, and make the interior more secure against the intrusion of wet; the courts and the *annexe* are also lighted from the top. The carriage-department and the refreshment-department are lighted from the sides.

Security from fire was, of course, a prime object in a Building to contain such treasures as the Exhibition consisted of. To have ample means at hand for the prompt extinction of fire, water under pressure was laid on to every part of the Building, and there were no less than eighty hydrants evenly distributed throughout. The water was supplied by the West Middlesex Water Company, and had a head varying from 100 to 200 feet. A 9-inch main traversed the Building from west to east, and from it 4-inch branch-pipes were led in all directions to supply the hydrants. This was sufficient to throw any amount of water on to the roof-flats, on the top of which there were portable fire-engines, to pump water on to the nave roof. As in 1851, there was a trained body of men always on the spot for working the hydrants, hoses, and engines. A new division of police, called the X Division, consisting of about four hundred men, four inspectors, forty sergeants, and one general superintendent, was specially appointed by Sir Richard Mayne to do duty in and about the Exhibition. The Contractors insured the building, in February last, for four hundred and fifty thousand pounds, in the Norwich Union Fire Office, at a premium, with the tax, of three thousand and thirty-eight pounds.

We may here recapitulate the main features of the Building:— The great nave, 800 feet in length—equal to the whole length of the Chester Railway Station—and 85 feet wide, and rising 100 feet in height to the ridge of the roof, which runs east and west parallel with the south front building; at either end of it are the great octagonal spaces between the two glass domes, each 135 feet diameter across the faces of the octagon, the domes themselves above being duodecagonal, and 160 feet across the angles. Passing through these and transverse to the nave, and therefore running north and south, are the two cross naves or *transepts*—as by a small abuse of language they are called—also 85 feet wide, and spreading each nearly 250 feet in length north and south of the domes, or nearly 600 feet in length right through. These rise to the same height as the nave, and the construction of nave and transepts is identical. The *ensemble* of these main portions form in Plan a letter H with short vertical legs. The space between the cross dash (nave) and the Horticultural Garden or refreshment rooms, and that at the opposite side of the cross dash (or nave) and main front building (picture galleries), are wholly roofed over with glass, and occupied by galleries ranging all round these spaces, and also crossing the last-named at two points to the right and left of the front central entrance. These galleries, floored with timber closely laid, are at 25 feet above the ground, and approached by several staircases of timber steps laid on cast-iron bearers. Running quite round the spaces that we have described, it will be seen that along with the transverse galleries they leave a central space north of the nave, divided into three open areas or courts; *i.e.*, open to the whole height of the glass roof from the ground level; and another central space south of the nave, likewise divided into three courts.

Such is a general idea of the distribution of space within the area. Along the east and west wings, at the extreme extensions, are numerous offices and adjuncts, lavatories, water-closets, &c.; and auxiliary or smaller picture-galleries along the wings.*

The whole structure may be separated into three classes of work —that which is meant to be permanent, viz., the front façade and the narrow strips of brick buildings at both wings running north and south; that which is *quasi* permanent, viz., the naves, transepts, domes, and covered courts and galleries; and that which is absolutely ephemeral in the annexes, and the refreshment-rooms over the arcades at the south end of the Horticultural Garden. Standing at the centre of the front in Cromwell-road, we have the front building of 1150 feet 9 inches extreme length stretching right and left, with a general width of 50 feet, and two stories in height. At the centre are the grand entrance-hall, vestibule, and within these, to the right and left, the grand staircases leading to the higher floor; returning southwards we enter a hall of 150 feet in length, for sculpture chiefly, and as a vestibule to the great ranges of picture-galleries to the east and west, and extending on into the wing tower buildings to a total length of about 500 feet each way.

The appropriation of the several portions of the Building is briefly thus :—the nave, transepts, galleries, and courts for the display of general industrial productions; the brick building on the north, inclosing the narrower courts, for refreshments; the grand picture-gallery extends along the south, and has auxiliary wings in front of the east and west transepts extending their whole length; these picture-galleries requiring to be lighted from the top, are placed above the entrances, which on the south side stretch to either hand for the display of carriages, &c.

DECORATION OF THE BUILDING.

This cannot be better described than by Mr. Crace,† who, in April, 1862, read before the Society of Arts a paper in which he

* Abridged from the excellent Scientific Record in *Practical Mechanics' Journal.*

† Mr. John Gregory Crace, under whose direction the decoration of the Building has been carried out, was born in 1809. His father and grandfather both practised the same art as himself—the latter having been extensively engaged for the Prince Regent at Carlton House; the former at Windsor Castle, the Pavilion at Brighton, &c.

Amongst the most important decorative works in which Mr. Crace has himself been engaged are those for the Duke of Devonshire at Chatsworth, Lismore, Chiswick, and Devonshire House; and for the Marquis of Breadalbane at Taymouth. He was specially selected by Sir Charles Barry to carry out the decorations of the Houses of Parliament; and to him was committed the decoration of the Art-Treasures Exhibition Building at Manchester.

Mr. Crace was engaged at the time of the lamented death of the Prince Consort in carrying out, under his Royal Highness' immediate direction, the decoration of the Waterloo Chamber at Windsor Castle; probably the last work of art in which his Royal Highness took a personal interest.

Mr. Crace has not confined himself solely to the practice, but has devoted much attention to the history and principles of his art, and has written several papers, read before architectural and other societies,—on colour, on art as applied to manufactures, on the Soulages collection, on fresco decorations, the history of furniture and of paper-hangings; he also wrote the Report of the jury of class 27 in the Exhibition of 1851.

informs us that it was the 23rd January last when he received his authority to proceed with the decoration, and it was to be all completed by March; that is to say—some twenty acres decoratively painted in about eight weeks. He proceeds:—

"After careful consideration I decided that the general tone of the roof must be light, and that the best colour would be a warm pale grey; that the arched principals must be made to stand out clear from the roof; that they must look well in a perspective of 800 feet; and that they must not look heavy or confused as they approached each other in the distance. No single colour would do, and after a pretty stiff bit of reflection of twenty-four hours, I confirmed myself in my opinion of what would be the most likely way of treating the principals.

"I have remarked that the form of these is polygonal, and in three thicknesses, the centres of the outer planks covering the joints of the inner ones.

"The form precluded the use of a continuous repeat ornament. I therefore decided on following the form of the construction, and adopted panellings of blue and red alternately, relieved by coloured lines, intersected at the joints by circles of black on which are gold stars, and from these spring ornaments in vellum colour with green in the filling, as shown in the coloured drawing.

"Following out this arrangement I had a pattern painted on paper of the full size of one of the principals, and it was fixed in its place within a week from the time of my appointment; part of that identical pattern is now in this room; it has never been altered, and thus exactly it has been carried out throughout the roofs of the nave and transepts.

"Until the principals were coloured, it seemed to me that the thicknesses were lost; I wished to make the construction evident, and I therefore coloured the two outer edges in chequers of black and vellum colour, and the centre edge full red. As to the bracings above the polygonal arches I coloured them the warm-wood colour, with red or blue coloured lines on the face, and the under thicknesses red.

"I have said that I decided on warm grey for the roof of nave. I did so because it gave space and lightness; and on its surface I introduced an upright scroll ornament in red, with gold, star-like rosettes, sparingly introduced. My object in this ornament was to raise the apparent pitch of the roof, and to relieve and warm the effect of the grey. The horizontal purlins, on the contrary, I kept purposely light, so as not to depress the rise of the roof, or interfere with or confuse the effect of the principals. The ridge piece of the roof, in itself comparatively small, I marked as strongly as possible, as the apex, in black and vellum white, *en chevronné;* on each side I coloured a margin of maroon red, and a little below that a bordering of very warm green, shaped to accord with the top scrolls of the red vertical ornament, the green being relieved with rosettes of gold colour. At the base of the slope of roof this green is again introduced in much the same way, and the band of maroon also. Below this are the clerestory windows.

"The next important features in the nave are the iron columns, supporting the principals as well as the galleries. These I have painted pale bronze colour, relieved with gold colour vertical lines. The capitals are gilt; the grounds of the ornaments being picked in rich red or blue alternately; the centre blocks of the columns are also coloured red, with bands of blue, or, *vice versâ*, the mouldings being gilt, and the same style of colour is continued to the bases. The top plate above the columns is painted bronze colour, relieved with light gold colour ornament on the upper part, and a Vitruvian scroll in gold colour, with a maroon red base on the lower part.

"The gallery railings are light bronze colour, the rose, shamrock, and thistle ornaments being partly gilt, and the whole backed with deep red cloth. The plate under the gallery is painted oak colour, relieved with deep brown interlaced ornaments.

"I have kept the part below the line of arches purposely quiet in colour, in order that the brilliancy and richness of the various articles exhibited may not be interfered with. The roof, on the contrary, is rather vivid in colour, to carry up, as it were, in some degree, the gaiety of the scene below; and this will be still further sustained by a series of banners of the various countries whose products are assembled in this International Exhibition.

"Much variety of opinion has been expressed at my introduction of the vivid colours in the arched principals of the nave; but I think that many who fancied it would look too powerful, will confess their surprise at its comparatively quiet effect now that it is completed. The colours being properly balanced, have neutralized each other. Most of you probably know that blue, red, and yellow, in the proportion of three, two, and one, when mixed with white, produce a grey, exactly the same as the grey produced by mixing black and white. I will show you. I take ultramarine blue three parts, vermilion two parts, and chrome yellow one part. I mix them together, add some white—you observe it is grey. I take some black and white, mix them, and identically the same grey is produced. If you paint on a disc radiated stripes of blue, red, and yellow, in proper proportions, and make the disc revolve rapidly, you find grey produced, the same as if they were stripes of black and white. The effect of the roof of the nave exemplifies this theory.

"I have heard it said by some that it would have been better to have employed panellings of one colour instead of two to each principal, and made the principals alternately blue and red; in my opinion they would have been utterly disappointed; the striped contrast would have by no means given the softness, richness, and glow of the present colouring. To convince myself, I, at one stage of the colouring, tried, by fixing blue paper over the red panellings in one principal, and red paper over the blue panellings of another, but the effect was not nearly as good, and I was confirmed that the principle I had adopted was the right one.

"This principle of counterchanging colours is adopted in most of the decorations of the early masters, which abound in Italy.

Those decorations, so beautiful, so interesting, rich, glowing in colour, full of fancy and taste in the ornament, the masses well arranged, show the most perfect harmony everywhere, and are dignified by often acting as the framework of the highest gems of art.

"In the roof of the Upper Church of Assisi, in the Chapel of St. Corporale, of Orvieto, in the choir of Santa Croce at Florence, and in the Palazzo Spinola, examples are to be found of counter-changing of colouring, and in the roof of the Cathedral of Lucca, of the chevroneze of black and gold.

"My principal difficulty in carrying out the decoration of the domes was, that I could see nothing of them. The scaffold formed a series of solid stages or floors, through which it was impossible to view anything; and I confess I never could mount the ladders above 100 feet; but even there the scaffolding was so thick that I could see nothing of the top, and very little of the cornice, facia, and walls.

"At last, Mr. Ashton, the engineer, contrived to get for me an open square box, into which I got, and I was drawn up by means of his beautiful little engine very pleasantly to the top; yet when I got there the ceiling almost touched my head, so that I had no opportunity of judging beforehand of the effect of distance and light upon my colouring, and I knew well that they were very formidable elements for consideration. The knowledge that the scaffold would be taken down before I could possibly judge of the effect, and that when once down I could never hope to touch my decoration again, caused me many an anxious thought.

"My drawing will best explain to you the colouring I adopted for the top of the domes. The main ribs are painted bright red, with spaced black and white at the edges, and a fine gold line up the centre spreads at intervals of about 4 feet into lozenges and circles containing gilt stars on a blue ground; where the main rings reach the ring plate I carry round the red, marking the points of intersection with black and white; thence the eight main ribs are painted deep blue, relieved with red, gold, and black, until they meet in the centre pipe or pendant, which is gilt bordered with red. The shaped covering, or umbrella, as I am accustomed to call it, is painted light blue; gold colour and gilt rays diverging from the centre and streaming a considerable way down the blue, the shaped outline of which is bordered with red and gold ornament.

"In decorating the walls of the domes, the solid parts between the arches, and the springing of the roof, it was necessary to consider the probable effect of the great mass of light above. On the one hand it was desirable to sustain it with sufficient strength of colour, on the other it would be dangerous to make it too heavy.

"The moulding of the cornice and facia are painted vellum colour, very slightly relieved by gilding; the trusses are gold colour; the facia between them is red, with a vellum patera; the soffit is green. The broad facia below is painted blue, and on it is inscribed in gold letters, three feet high, the exordium of David in the 29th chapter of the first Book of Chronicles, 'Thine, O Lord, is the greatness, and the glory, and the victory, and the majesty: for all that is in the heaven and the earth is thine;' and, 'O Lord, both riches and honour come of thee, and thou reignest over all; and in thine hand is power and might, and in thine hand it is to make great.'

"The large iron columns, which rise nearly 100 feet high, are painted dark maroon colour, their capitals being richly gilt. The panelling between the arches and the frieze is painted in shades of red, relieved by coloured lines; in the four broad compartments are inscribed, on dark green panels, Europe, Asia, Africa, and America; below, on a circle, are the initials of those so beloved by us all, Victoria and Albert. On the eight spandrils to the four main arches, are medallions, eight feet diameter, by Mr. Burchett, of the Kensington School of Art, emblematic of Manufactures, Commerce, and the various arts and sciences which lend their aid. These were executed in an exceedingly short time, and, like all the rest of the work, with no opportunity of judging how they would look in their elevated situation. I should add, that round the red panelling is a broad margin of sage green, on which are stencilled pateras. The moulding of the arches is painted vellum colour, the top fillet being gilt; and the face of them ornamented with Vitruvian scroll in dark colour.

"The walls at the gable end of the nave and transept are treated so as to recal the arched form of the principals. Under these a semicircular panel is formed of warm brown colour, bordered by a broad blue margin, on which are gold stars. Inside the panels are written the following sentences:—

"On the east end of nave—

"'The wise and their works are in the hands of God.'—Ecclesiastes ix. 1.

"On the east end of transept—

"'Alternately the Nations learn and teach.'—Cowper.

"On the south-east end of transept—

"'Each climate needs what other climes produce.'—Cowper.

"On the west end of the building the sentences are in Latin, being the part occupied by foreign exhibitors. At the end of nave is written:—

"'Gloria in excelsis Deo, et in terra pax.'

"At the north-west end of the transept—

"'Domini est terra, et plenitudo ejus.'

"At the south-west end of transept—

"'Deus in terram respexit, et implevit illam bonus suis.'

"Inside these semicircular panels are a series of radiating panels, painted maroon, and bearing the names of the various sciences and arts which have affinity with the objects exhibited. The coloured drawing will more directly explain what I have thus endeavoured to describe."

Altogether, the decorations beneath the domes are generally considered extremely grand, harmonious, and rich. As to the fitness of the Building, opinions of the merits, engineering or architectural as the case may be, have been very various.

Towards the close of the year, upon the reading of Captain Philpott's description of the Building to the Society of Arts, a critical discussion arose upon its architectural defects, especially upon the poising of the dome, almost upon the ridge of the roofs, and placing them so far back as to be invisible from the main façade. We have no inclination to enter further into the results of this discussion: it heaped coals of fire on the head of those who had "ignored the architectural profession," and undoubtedly tended rather to raise than allay the storm.

Yet the Building and its engineer have had their apologists. At a meeting of the Society of Arts, on the 29th of May, the chairman, Lord Granville, said:—" He had had the great honour of being intimately connected with the two great Exhibitions which had taken place in this country, and he might say that some of the happiest recollections of his life were associated with the Exhibition of 1851; and having now, under different circumstances, been connected with the management of that in 1862, he had felt the greatest interest, not wholly unmixed with annoyance and trouble, in the conduct of this Exhibition, though he did not look forward to having much connexion with another Exhibition, even if he were asked to do so. He (the chairman) had not forgotten the experience of 1851. He remembered that eminent men were called upon to give plans, the result of which was that none were considered satisfactory. He never should forget the feeling of pleasure with which he first saw the beautiful design of his excellent friend, Sir Joseph Paxton, which seemed to come so opportunely to relieve the difficulties of the moment; and whilst speaking on this matter, he might remark, that there was sometimes great advantage arising from vicissitudes. There was a strong feeling in the public mind that the two noble elm-trees in the park should not be cut down—the British public would not hear of such a thing; and hence that which was at first regarded as an obstacle, had, as Sir Charles Fox had stated, originated the idea of a transept which should enclose the trees. In comparing the present building with that of 1851, he believed nine people out of ten associated the latter with the beautiful erection now standing at Sydenham, but that was a very different structure, in a great many respects, to the Building of 1851. As it was, however, the Commissioners found a plan ready prepared. He might say that the late Prince Consort thought most decidedly that the present building was infinitely better adapted for exhibition purposes than that of 1851, and he (Lord Granville) thought it would have been folly on the part of the Commissioners to have rejected that plan.

He might add that the design was shown to Sir Joseph Paxton before it was finally settled upon, and he expressed his opinion that it was extremely handsome, and well adapted for the purpose. There had been some changes in the design, which had been adopted from motives of economy. That might be a misfortune, but it was a circumstance to which every one was more or less liable from a want of cash."

At the banquet given by the Lord Mayor, Earl Granville also said, "The Building would have presented a much more imposing appearance had the whole design been carried out."—"It was our poverty, and not our will, that made us build, like the ancient Romans, in brick." Upon this a Correspondent of the *Builder* observes:—"It is not the brick, however, but the purpose to which good bricks have been put, that is the grievance. Very fine buildings have been, and will again be, built of brick, or even with brick cased in cement; but if this structure had been built with Carrara marble, it would have been just as ugly as it is now. Does Lord Granville think that it is the material, and not the art that gives the value to the production? Did it not occur to him, before he made use of that argument, that there are small statues in mere baked clay that are priceless, and big ones in Carrara marble that are worthless?"

An apologist in the *Athenæum* maintains that Captain Fowke's "architectural work" has been unfairly found fault with: it having been blamed for not being everything that it ought not to have been, and that Her Majesty's Commissioners and the public never wanted it to be." The great merit of "the great shell," the *Athenæum* considers to be "the splendid possibility of exterior decoration which it admits of."

The great point of persistency in the arguments of the apologists for the Building is that it is *admirably adapted for its purpose;* but, on the other hand, it is asked, could not this advantage have been obtained with beauty of form, as well as with the unsightliness which the Building now presents?

The plea of the Royal Commissioners is, that their prime object was the suitableness of the Building for its purposes, and not architectural beauty. Now, Captain Fowke's Building is a vast engineering work, and nothing more: externally it resembles a huge railway station, relieved with pavilions, towers, and roofs, of the style to which Louis XV. lent his name, and Mansard his genius. They remind one, among other novelties, of the roof of the newly-erected Wellington College. The uselessness of the domes is not atoned for by their beauty; as in the case of the graceful glass dome of the royal stables of the Pavilion at Brighton —a costly freak of George the Fourth when Regent.

The critics who have been loudest in their condemnation of Captain Fowke's design, maintain that there was no reason why the Building should not partake of that excellence which was to characterize its contents, so as to show the advancement of Architecture *pari passu* with that of other arts: "An Exhibition

Building superior to that of 1851, would have just as much a note of progress as a superior building full of goods could be. Both one and the other would be alike symbolical of, and advantageous to, the art-industry movement. Clever minds had been naturally set thinking on the problem of architectural combinations of iron and glass." (*Quarterly Review*, p. 184).* It might also have been expected that the patronage of the Society of Arts, and the Department of Science and Art, would have guaranteed that the profession of architectural art would not have been overlooked.

Few persons will, we suspect, altogether assent to the following estimate of Captain Fowke's design :—

"As to the Building, it lacks the endless perspective of the glass shed in Hyde Park, and has not its unity of design. But for extent, for convenience, for elevation, for beauty of forms and lines, and for charm of colour, the present Building is far, far superior, to that in Hyde Park. Had any constant visitor of that Building, on the very day after its reluctant and regretful closing, while all were casting a longing, lingering look behind, stepped into the present Exhibition, he would have found all his admiration swallowed up in the new scene before him. He would have felt the Crystal Palace of the day before as much absorbed in the more beautiful fabric and collection before him as a bud is in the rose, or the fair girl in the woman. Besides being considerably higher and much wider, the new Building is something more than an arrangement of pillars and girders ; it is a simple and beautiful design. The graceful curve of the trusses that support the roof, and the nice choice of colours and tints, make a whole that will stand comparison with the finest edifices in the world. The domes are magnificent in form, in size, and in decoration. Springing as they do from four piers, after the Italian plan, they are vastly superior in point of construction to the dome, if dome it may be called, of St. Paul's, which springs from eight piers, like the 'lantern' at Ely Cathedral, a mere makeshift of construction. The only fault to be found with the domes is that which has already been found, and which might have been foreseen. Unless they are to be retained for gigantic tropical plants, in connexion with the adjoining gardens, they must be filled in with something else than glass. A tenth part of the light will answer every purpose." (This has been modified by *velaria*.)

It should, however, be recollected that in the journal wherein this opinion appears, the Hungerford Suspension Bridge was condemned as the ugliest of our metropolitan bridges ; and the

---

* In addition to the various exhibition buildings at Dublin, New York, Munich, Sydenham (so far as it differed from Hyde Park), Manchester, Mr. E. M. Barry's Conservatory in Covent Garden, and Mr. Owen Jones's sketch for "the Palace of the People," on Muswell-hill,—a Crystal Palace is in course of erection at Amsterdam ; and the Royal Academy Exhibition of 1862 contained the designs of a large iron and glass market for Preston, by Mr. Gilbert Scott ; and of an exhibition building at St. Petersburg, by Mr. E. M. Barry ;—both of them indicative of considerable study, and both as superior to Captain Fowke's structure as one thing can be to another.

Travellers' Club-house, in Pall Mall, rested equally low ; whereas, the Bridge was a most graceful engineering work ; and the Clubhouse is held to be one of Sir Charles Barry's masterpieces.

Probably, upon no point has there been greater difference of opinion than as to the merits of Mr. Crace's decoration. The writer of the following goes so far as to tax the artist with spoiling Captain Fowke's work by his capricious colouring :—

"The columns, with their pale bronze and stripes of *quasi*-gold, are well in themselves, but their caps of blue and red seem too violent for harmonious colouring ; and while the roof itself is delicately bright with pearly-grey and tastefully decorated, there is much unreposing character in the doubly counter-changed markings of its ribs. Thus coloured, the markings of the ribs, instead of aiding the long vista of the roof, fritter its effect into a sparkling glitter, where there should be rest for the eye, and prolonged bars leading it to the end. So strongly are these shortcomings felt, that every one acknowledges the unpainted machinery annexe to be the most beautiful and satisfactory part of the edifice, excepting of course the picture-galleries, which have been decorated on a wiser principle. The judiciously deep marone tint shown on the great iron shafts that support the domes manifests a feeling for decorative propriety which should have appeared throughout. As parts of the domes, the oblique ribs bearing the thrust outwards from where the gilt brackets are placed over the transepts and nave, should have had the characteristic ornamentation of the domes, and not that of the roofs. It is not fair, in estimating this building as a building and apart from the decorations, to compare it with the Crystal Palace. The mere fact of being open to the sunny day, and having the gorgeous sky-canopy for a roof, with all its islanded white clouds and sweeping masses of shadow to boot, gave charms which Captain Fowke cannot be blamed for not equalling. We believe, indeed, that the interior of his building is, for its purpose, admirable, but that the decoration has marred much that was worthy of high applause."—*Athenæum*, May 3, 1862.

The following we consider to be a fair estimate of the merits of the Decoration :—"Mr. Crace's transmuting performances are, undoubtedly, open to criticism, and, in particular, we think certain appositions of blue and red close to the clerestory windows might have been reconsidered. But, as a whole, when the railway speed at which he had to work, and when the impossibility under which he laboured of obtaining a fair sight of his own work, are considered, we must say that Mr. Crace has very honourably and very ably acquitted himself of a work which, in less willing hands, would have been both thankless and impossible. He deserves particular credit for having proposed all through to subordinate his own coloration to the advantage of the things exhibited." (*Quarterly Review*.) The latter is a paramount advantage.

The *Annexes* (a term borrowed from the French) are allowed to be engineering works of great merit.

The western Annexe is 975 feet long, and 200 feet and 150 feet wide. The east side is enclosed by the back wall of the west arcade of the Gardens, and the west side, which adjoins the road, has a plain lath-and-plaster front. It is covered by a ridge-and-valley roof, supported on light wooden ribs, similar in construction to those of the nave; that is, they are formed of planks nailed together. The circular portion springs at ten feet above the ground line. Its elevation is nearly half of a regular polygon, described about a semicircle whose diameter is 50 feet; it consists of three planks nailed together. The principal rafters, which are composed of two three-quarter inch planks, rise from a point 28 feet above the ground, and meet above the curved ribs, so as to make the ridge five feet above the crown of the arch. The upright, which has its foot mortised into a sleeper resting on piles, is formed of one and a quarter inch centre-plank, with a three-quarter inch plank on each side, having a strengthening piece four inches by three inches spiked to it on either side to prevent its bending. The principal rafter and upright are connected with the curved rib by radial pieces of one and a quarter inch plank, which are brought rather below the inner line of the curve, and finished off, for the sake of ornament, by a spear-head. The roof-frames are therefore merely planks nailed together, and so disposed that the weight comes on their edge. One half of the roof is covered with boards and felt; and the other half has a glazed skylight, with louvres for ventilation throughout the whole length.

The western Annexe, as before mentioned, is devoted to the exhibition of machinery in motion, for which purpose steam-pipes, water-pipes, and shafting are led through it. Its superficial extent is about four and a half acres. The entrance is through the north end of the west transept, from which point the ribs of the roof are seen from end to end in fine perspective.

Mr. Hollingshead awards the highest praise to this work, characterizing it as " of itself a perfect exhibition of its kind, and containing the most ingenious mechanical contrivances of the age." He instances its ingenuity, economy, and simplicity : "it required no bolting or framing, and any person of ordinary intelligence, able to drive a nail, could have constructed the ribs, which have nothing in them but nails and sawn planks. Each rib was made in a horizontal position, over a full-sized drawing, marked on a platform, and, when complete, it was hoisted vertically by means of a derrick. To prevent it from wabbling, which, from its extreme thinness, it was very liable to do, it was stiffened while being raised by having scaffold-poles tied across the angles, which themselves formed the scaffolding for finishing the roof. The frames are braced together at the top of the uprights, and the ribs are strutted from the wall-plate to prevent buckling."

The eastern Annexe is exactly similar to the western in its construction ; but it is 200 feet shorter.

The plea of cheapness in comparison with Sir Joseph Paxton's Building was confidently put forward by Captain Philpotts, stating, that no building in the world covering 24¾ acres has been erected at so low a rate, or at one enabling it to be bought in at 430,000*l.* Sir Charles Fox, however, has reminded the public that the cost of the Crystal Palace in Hyde Park, plus that of Sydenham, was only 396,540*l.*

"The comparison of cost naturally suggests some comparison as to structural stability. Omitting *early* or other structures of mere carpentry, and having no pretensions to permanence, we have had before us three principal Buildings, comprising as many distinct classes, as to the general idea of structure involved in each. We had the Building of 1851 purely of iron, timber, and glass, columnar only in support. The Building of 1855 (the Palais) of iron, timber (floors only), and glass, and an envelope of stone, columnar and mural in support. Lastly, the Building of 1862 of iron, timber, largely used (constructionally as well as in flooring), glass, slate, and a cancellated surrounding structure of timber, iron, and brick, columnar and mural in support; the brickwork not an envelope merely, but variously combined as an exterior with, and forming parts of a combined interior, to which it imparts support and stability laterally."—*Practical Mechanics' Journal.*

We have abridged the above details with the conviction that Capt. Fowke's very simple and economical mode of construction, in this instance, will be extensively followed in future sheds for exhibitions, or structures for temporary or brief purposes.

We may here observe that Mr. Hollingshead has written the *Concise History* with much care; but as his Book deals with facts, there is but rare opportunity for the embellishment of this ready and piquant writer: the pleasantries are, accordingly, but few and far between. His account of the Building is from Capt. Philpotts' paper, with many additions, corrections, and illustrations.

THE EXHIBITION ORGANIZED.

Upon the National and Local Committees devolved the labour of allotting the space and selecting the articles to be sent for exhibition. For the space, 9862 persons applied, the aggregate of whose demands was equal to more than seven times the whole available exhibiting area in the Building.

Among the applicants were the strange fantasies of amateur inventors, who may be described, generally, as a class of persons who betake themselves to eccentric employment of their brain as a change or relief to their own proper pursuits. In this they may be said to find recreation, just as a workshopful of men, at their dinner-hour, rush off to the very games of boyhood, as a relief to their daily toil.

The oddities of these applications were droll enough. Of course, there were perpetual motion seekers; and one ingenious gentleman proposed to exhibit a flying-machine in motion under one of the great domes: had his application been granted, and his success equalled his wishes, he might have shot upward through the costly glass cupola. When his offer was politely declined, he as politely thanked the Commissioners, feeling that their object in refusing him permission to exhibit was only to save him from making a very great personal sacrifice in preparing his machine.

The embalmed body of Julia Pastrana was offered to the Commissioners, to be shown at sixpence a head—but was declined; and the dead wonder became a Piccadilly show.

A penny loaf of the year 1801 was offered for exhibition as *the oldest piece of bread in the world;* it was purchased by the applicant's father sixty years ago, when wheat was selling at a guinea a bushel : it had been kept in a string net. What an illustration would this have been for the Anti-Corn-law League! It had been declined by the Exhibition of 1851, and the Commissioners for 1862 alike rejected it.*

A lively Frenchman proposed to put the whole Official Catalogue into flowing verse ; and to work up all the minutes, documents, and decisions of the Commissioners into an epic poem. Another thoughtful person sent a number of small physic powders, all the way from Baden-Baden, intended to recruit the exhausted frames of the overworked officials. Considerate philanthropists these : it is difficult to say which would have been the least welcome—the poetry or the physic, had it been accepted : the Commissioners would have neither. Another poet asked leave to exhibit an epic poem in the picture-gallery.

Among the prodigies offered were a giant and a wonderful child : a giant was offered as follows :—"I am the agent and interpreter of a grand subject ; he is a giant : his height is 8 feet, his weight 30 stone, his age is 25, of a pleasing exterior. I take the liberty to offer him to your lordships' notice. Dressed up in Henri Quatre style, he would make a very commanding usher for the International Exhibition," &c.

A clergyman asked permission to send breech-loaders and models of tremendously destructive shells : this application was not a whit more strange than Bishop Watson's improvement in gunpowder with which George III. ungratefully twitted the Bishop at a levee.

Here are a few instances in exemplification of what has just been said of persons flying off to these eccentricities for the sake of change :—

A "nurseryman and market-gardener" proposed improvements in surgical instruments ; a doctor "a new contrivance for forwarding the ripening of fruit on walls ;" a grocer in one of the busiest thoroughfares of the metropolis proposed—not specimens of souchong or twankay, but "a new axle applicable to carriages of all descriptions," "a new projectile for heavy ordnance," and "a novel method of propelling ships ;" a graduate of Cambridge

---

* This odd application reminds one of a short-weight loaf being suspended by a string from the statue of Charles I. at Charing Cross, on July 3, 1810. To the loaf was attached a ticket, stating that it was purchased from a baker, and was extremely deficient in weight, and one of a numerous batch. This exhibition attracted a great crowd of persons, until the whole of the loaf was washed away by rain.

offered "a model of an invulnerable floating battery," "a breech-loading gun and carriage," "a new cork poncho mattress," and "a life preserver;" an accountant in the City had prepared "a model of a self-acting water-closet," "an improved theodolite," and an "omnitonic flute;" a barrister wished to send "spring-heel boots and the drawing of a man equipped with ditto," "a type-composing machine," "illustrations of the wave line theory as applied to shipbuilding;" a bookbinder asked for space to exhibit his "plan of interminable suspension," as applicable to bridges and viaducts, and boldly proposed to do away with all such old-world absurdities as the present piers and abutments; a new paddle-wheel, self-acting railway signals and bolts, that would "prevent any gate being opened while a train was within a quarter of a mile, or any other convenient distance." From an insurance broker there came proposals to show improved floor-cloth, paper-hangings, and embroidery, machines for dressing stone, electric telegraph cable and conductors, junctions for iron pipes, and specimens of "wines acquired by a new process;" a gentleman described as a private secretary, proposed to exhibit some home-made gooseberry and rhubarb wines; another offered a photographic view of an organ-front, and also one of his own orchard; and for the picture-gallery a gentleman suggested a "model room for a working shoemaker, showing sanitary arrangements and economical furniture, cooking apparatus, and turn-up bedstead."—*M'Dermott's Popular Guide.*

Schemes were offered for showing widows' caps, peculiar wigs, and a patent moustache guard, with protection from soup while the wearer is dining!

We suspect the following to be a piece of chemical quizzing: an Exhibitor proposed to send "Evidences of one general metallic root," in these terms:—

"Hard labour and multiple experiments has proved to me the evidence of one general root metallique. Out of the fundamental principle, and by the developpement of the primitive formations often natural influences interferring, various mixtions are produced, but when the actives and passive agents are settled to a more or less neutral state and a homogene equilibrum of their parts of atomes is constituted, a homogene characteristic individualité is, or can be produced, and a so-called Simple Element is established, this Element, inseparable from his special Character and Indidual Unité, cannot be divided further by the ordinary Official Chemical Rule and Methode—from the Bar Metal to the Oxides from the Oxides to the fluid State and again (vice-versa) —but, when higher and most exalted Affinitys produced in a Philosophical Way might be known and applied, then, the homogene Equilibrum of the Individual Unités, affected by a higher affinité then its constituent Atoms posses itself, consequently chemical combinaison will follow on one side, reduction to a more primitive State on the other, and the parts of the so-called Unité of the pretended Simple Element returned to the primitive Root."

Mr. Hollingshead writes of another proposition, with some humour:—"A project was submitted to the Commissioners, for securing the money receipts of the exhibition by a system of astronomical checks based on the signs of the zodiac. The sun's radiations were to do a great deal in keeping the money and ticket-takers honest ; crowning honesty with a glory, and scorching dishonesty with the mark of the beast. The whole scheme was elaborate and confused ; and though put forward as a serious business proposition it read like one of those headstrong allegories written in imitation of John Bunyan."

The Commissioners had to *edit*, as it were—to pare down—the demands upon their space, according to their relative importance. The greatest number of applications was for iron and general hardware ; for steel and cutlery there were but 120 ; glass and pottery, few ; agricultural implements, 150 accepted. In the end, nearly 5500 British exhibitors were chosen.

The rejection of contributions kept up the semblance of the Commissioners' editorship. One said cynically : "If Diogenes were alive, he would find abundant use for his lantern in guiding the Commissioners in their search for truth." Another, more indignant, wrote to say :—"I am determined to exhibit, and shall petition all the Commissioners, even to the Prince of Wales himself, should this application be unsuccessful. If all means fail, I shall inquire through the press—the leading daily and literary journals—for an explanation of the system of preference which dictates refusal to one and the acceptance of another exhibitor."

A General Advice Committee for the arrangements of the Manufactures and Industrial Products was also formed of the Chairmen of all the Chambers of Commerce in England, Ireland, Scotland, and Wales ; the Presidents of the most important Societies ; and some noblemen and gentlemen whose names are familiar from the interest and prominent position they have taken in these matters. At a Meeting of the Society of Arts, a paper was read by Professor Ansted on the best method of exhibiting the mineral products, and it is but fair to say that the author's intention appeared to be that his paper should be suggestive. The scientific, or, as it may be more properly termed, the classified arrangement was met with unmistakeable disfavour. To take a manufacturer's package and distribute its contents in detail through every court in the building would be not only to destroy the most important features of national competition, emulation, and pride, but would reduce the whole collection to a gigantic museum of disarranged specimens—for who could arrange them ?—that would present the least attractive appearance to the thousands of visitors who are expected to be attracted by this display.

One of the chief pleasures we had in the Exhibition of 1851 was to go from court to court and view and compare not only the produce and manufactures of the various countries, but to observe also the differences of education, feelings, tastes, and social conditions of the peoples that were thus pourtrayed in these products of their culture or industry. The geographical is undoubtedly the best arrangement that could be adopted.

The Classification of the Exhibition was based upon that of 1851, but embraced thirty-six classes, besides those of the Fine Arts ; and when these were thrown into natural groups, but out of their consecutive *order*, they were as follows :—

THE CLASSIFICATION. 55

I.—RAW MATERIALS, AND MANUFACTURES DIRECTLY FROM THEM.
CHEMICALS, FOOD, &c.

Class 1. Mining, quarrying, metallurgy, and mineral products.
,, 2. Chemical substances and products, and pharmaceutical processes.
    Sub-Class a. Chemical products.
    ,, b. Medical and pharmaceutical processes.
,, 3. Substances used for food.
    Sub-class a. Agricultural produce.
    ,, b. Drysaltery, grocery, &c.
    ,, c. Wines, spirits, beer, and other drinks, and tobacco.
,, 4. Animal and vegetable substances used in manufactures.
    Sub-Class a. Oils, fats, and wax, and their products.
    , b. Other animal substances used in manufactures.
    ,, c. Vegetable substances used in manufactures, &c.
    ,, d. Perfumery.
,, 25. Skins, fur, feathers, and hair.
,, 27. Articles of clothing.
    Sub-class a. Hats and caps.
    ,, b. Bonnets and general millinery.
    ,, c. Hosiery, gloves, and clothing in general.
    ,, d. Boots and shoes.
,, 30. Furniture and upholstery, including paper-hangings and papier-maché.
    Sub-Class a. Furniture and upholstery.
    ,, b. Paper-hanging and general decoration.
,, 36. Manufactures not included in previous classes.
    Sub-Class a. Dressing-cases and toilet articles.
    ,, b. Trunks and travelling apparatus.

VIII.—PHILOSOPHICAL INSTRUMENTS, &c. ; PAPER, PRINTING, &c.
EDUCATION.

Class 13. Philosophical instruments, and processes depending upon their use.
,, 14. Photographic apparatus and photography.
,, 15. Horological instruments.
,, 16. Musical instruments.
,, 17. Surgical instruments and appliances.
,, 28. Paper, stationery, printing, and bookbinding.
    Sub-Class a. Paper, card, and millboard.
    ,, b. Stationery.
    ,, c. Plate, letterpress, and other modes of printing.
    ,, d. Bookbinding.
,, 29. Educational works and appliances.

Sub-Class a. Productions of publishers.
,, b. ,, apparatus makers.
,, c. ,, toy and games manufacturers.
,, d. Specimens and illustrations of natural history.

II.—MACHINERY, TOOLS, IMPLEMENTS.

Class 7. Manufacturing machines and tools.
Sub-Class a. Machinery employed in spinning and weaving.
,, b. Machines and tools employed in the manufacture of wood, metal, &c.
,, 8. Machinery in general.
,, 9. Agricultural and horticultural machines and implements.

III.—ENGINEERING, CIVIL AND MILITARY, NAVAL ARCHITECTURE, &c.

Class 5. Railway plant, including locomotive engines and carriages.
,, 6. Carriages not connected with rail or tram roads.
,, 10. Civil engineering, architectural, and building contrivances.
Sub-Class a. Civil engineering and building contrivances.
,, b. Sanitary improvements and constructions.
,, c. Objects shown for architectural beauty.
,, 11. Military engineering, armour and accoutrements, ordnance and small arms.
Sub-Class a. Clothing and accoutrements.
,, b. Tents and camp equipages.
,, c. Arms, ordnance, &c.
,, 12 Naval architecture—ships' tackle.
Sub-Class a. Ship-building for purposes of war and commerce.
,, b. Boat and barge building, and vessels for amusement, &c.
,, c. Ships' tackle and rigging.

IV.—IRON AND STEEL, METAL MANUFACTURES, AND PRECIOUS METALS.

Class 31. Iron and general hardware.
Sub-Class a. Iron manufactures.
,, b. Manufactures in brass and copper.
,, c. Manufactures in tin, lead, zinc, pewter, and general braziery.
,, 32. Steel cutlery and edge tools.
Sub-Class a. Steel manufactures.
,, b. Cutlery and edge tools.
,, 33. Works in precious metals, and their imitations.

V.—JEWELLERY, GLASS, FICTILE MANUFACTURES.

Class 33. Jewellery, imitation gems, &c.
,, 34. Glass.
        Sub-Class a. Stained glass, and glass used in buildings and decorations.
             ,, b. For household use and fancy purposes.
,, 35. Pottery, tiles—tesseræ; terra-cotta, &c.

VI.—TEXTILE MATERIALS AND MANUFACTURES, &c.

Class 18. Cotton.
,, 19. Flax and hemp.
,, 20. Silk and velvet.
,, 21. Woollen and worsted, including mixed fabrics generally.
,, 22. Carpets.
,, 23. Woven, spun, felted, and laid fabrics, when shown as specimens of printing or dyeing.
,, 24. Tapestry, lace, and embroidery.

VII.—GENERAL MANUFACTURES (HANDICRAFT).

Class 26. Leather, including saddlery and harness; manufactures generally made of leather.

THE PRIZE MEDAL.

To Mr. Maclise, R.A., was confided the designing of the Prize Medal given to the successful Exhibitors; and to Mr. L. C. Wyon was intrusted the execution of the same in bronze.

The obverse is of a more elaborate character than that of the Prize Medal of 1851. In the centre Britannia is depicted seated on a throne. In her right hand she holds a wreath, and in her left an olive branch. Emblematical figures, representing manufactures, raw produce, and machinery, are exhibiting to her their several productions. Behind Britannia, painting, sculpture, and architecture—who were to receive no reward beyond the tribute of admiration which their works induced—are seen, emblematically represented, and watching earnestly the decision of Britannia. Resting at the feet of the central figure, and occupying the whole foreground of the group, is "the British lion." The arrangement of the figures is admirable; and the whole design is worthy of the artists, and of the occasion.

The dimensions of the medal are identical with that given in 1851, as well as the material of which it is composed—namely, bronze. The emblematical figures tested the skill of the engraver to the fullest extent: for the elaboration and minute detail of their drapery and accessories are remarkable; indeed, elaboration, rather than striking effect, is the merit of the work. The reverse is a wreath surrounding the inscription.

THE EXHIBITION OPENED.

By a wonderful effort of labour, the executive staff of the International Exhibition were enabled to keep their promise to the public, and open the grand display, with all befitting ceremony, and even with more than hoped-for success, on Monday, May 1, 1862. It was altogether a more pretentious ceremonial than that at the opening of the Exhibition of 1851, which was a semi-state affair. There was, doubtless, a praiseworthy motive for investing the ceremonial of 1862 with more state than its predecessor. Well do we remember the glow of satisfaction approaching joy which mantled the countenances of Her Majesty and the Prince Consort as they entered the Exhibition Building in Hyde Park, on the morning of May 1, 1851. This interchange of delight as the royal pair advanced into the Building amidst the warm greetings of the assemblage was a touching testimony of heads and hearts working together for good.

There was no such incident of brightness—no such ray of splendour—in the ceremonial of May 1, 1862. In the words of the journalist next morning, "The day, indeed, had one dark shadow. Of the hundreds of thousands who lined the streets and thronged the building, few forgot the Prince by whom the great work of the day was encouraged and helped on—who sowed, but reaped not; and many were the kindly and regretful words spoken of the Royal lady who would have been so gladly welcomed, and who yesterday was so sorely missed. The absence of the Queen, and the cause of that absence, marred the state pageant, and produced a partial gloom which an impressive and imposing ceremonial could not wholly dispel."

In kindred spirit are written the following admirable remarks:*— "No doubt, as we have more than once said, and as the universal sympathy on Thursday so unmistakeably showed, the one marked deficiency and loss in this Exhibition, especially on the opening day, as contrasted with its memorable predecessor eleven years ago, is to be found in the absence of him, the great Friend of this country, to whom we owe so much, and whose presence and power on such an occasion we so much deplore. His memory was retained by the banner which was hung at the side of a throne which will never again be filled by a proud and happy wife. *Treu und Fest*, however, was written not only on perishable silk, but on an imperishable memory, but Cæsar as well as Cæsar's bust was sadly missing from the ceremony. The stately form which dignified a courtly procession, and the yet more royal mind which regulated and improved a great plan, were wanting; and the very shortcomings and mistakes of the day and of the Exhibition itself, neither few nor unimportant, only more and more attest our great national loss. It is a bootless task to recall the memory, too, of the Great Captain of these latter days, who in loyal attendance on the Sove-

* From the *Saturday Review*, May 3, 1862.

reign whom he had so long served, was a figure so conspicuous and popular in 1851. And why should we to-day recall, except for the sake of a mournful retrospect, the sight of our own good Queen surrounded by her fine family and in the very flush of happiness—surrounded, too, by emblems of universal peace, and anticipating for us all a future above which the little cloud had not yet begun to rise? All this is terribly changed. We live at quite another stage of history and life. A widowed Queen flies away to privacy, and almost solitude, from scenes which would only too forcibly recall a sad but memorable past; and though the Court assisted with all the regulation Court ceremonial at the Exhibition opening, it was not the Royal Court of which we have so long been proud."

In the out-door procession to the Building, this feeling of regret was painfully visible among the people. "Immediately following the Royal Commissioners was a *cortège*, the mournful aspect of which impressed the spectators more deeply by its contrast with all that had gone before. It was merely a file of carriages, driving at the same pace as all the rest; but the deep black liveries of the servants, and still more the associations connected with the event that was being celebrated, struck the minds of those who looked upon them as forcibly as ever did the slave's warning in the classic triumphs, or the *memento mori* of later times." (*Times*, May 2, 1862.)

We shall quote only the leading details of the State preparations in the Building. Here the company spread themselves over the area of the nave, transepts, and galleries; a portion of the nave being railed off for the passage of the procession. Entering by the south central door, and passing along through the nave, a privileged few were enabled to reach a raised daïs beneath the western dome. Here was erected a lofty throne, hung with crimson velvet and satin, and powdered with gilded roses and stars. On each side of a rich chair of state were placed large marble busts of her Majesty and the late Prince Consort; and in front of the platform on which the throne stood were ranged in a semicircle, gilt and crimson velvet chairs. Standing on this estrade, and looking down the nave, as one looked down towards the eastern dome, the army of singers and musicians, the ladies in their variegated dresses all grouped together, formed in the dim distance an exceedingly pretty boundary to the objects which the eye took in. It was on each side of this daïs under the western dome that the more distinguished visitors were admitted. A large number of the noblemen and gentlemen were in uniform and Court dresses, and the scarlet robes of the Doctors of Divinity, the dark robes of the clergy of lower rank, and the very various gowns of civic dignitaries, were all to be seen glaring along in rapid progress. On the right of the throne the diplomatic corps and foreigners of rank passed in. Remarkable amongst these were the Japanese Ambassadors, the President of the free American colony of Liberia, attended by two or three gentlemen of colour of the darkest hue,

The Royal Commissioners of the Exhibition, Her Majesty's Ministers, the Foreign Commissioners, and the other persons who had been appointed to form part of the procession, being joined by the Queen's Commissioners for opening the Exhibition, they started for the south centre of the nave, and proceeded by the south side of the nave to the western dome, where were mayors and corporate dignitaries, refulgent in many-coloured robes. There were Greeks, Turks, Albanians, Parsees, and Persians, all more or less embroidered and enriched, Hungarians and Highlanders, Swedes and Orientals—great men of almost every clime and creed and costume.

To the sound of martial music, the procession moved slowly along to the daïs. The Duke of Cambridge occupied the centre of the semicircle ranged in front of the throne; on his right were the Crown Prince of Prussia, the Archbishop of Canterbury, the Lord Chancellor, and the Earl of Derby; on his left stood Prince Oscar of Sweden, the Lord Chamberlain, Viscount Palmerston, and the Speaker of the House of Commons. The Royal Commissioners of the Exhibition were grouped a little to the left of his Royal Highness, at the bottom of the steps leading up to the daïs, and Earl Granville, stepping forward, spoke as follows:—

In the name of her Majesty's Commissioners who have charge of the International Exhibition of 1862, I have the honour of presenting to your Royal Highness and the other Commissioners for opening the Exhibition a most humble address. We especially offer to her Majesty our condolence for the loss irreparable which her Majesty and the nation have sustained, and we thank her Majesty for allowing herself to be represented by your Royal Highness and the other Commissioners on this occasion; and we beg to express our great gratitude to his Royal Highness the Crown Prince of Prussia and his Royal Highness Prince Oscar of Sweden for having honoured the Exhibition with their presence this day. We also offer our thanks to the Commissioners, British and foreign, who have assisted us in this work; and we venture to express our confidence that this work will be thought worthy of ranking amongst the international exhibitions which in the future may periodically occur.

Lord Granville then presented an address from the Exhibition Commissioners, which, however, was not read. The opening is as follows:—

"May it please your Royal Highness and my Lords Commissioners,—We, the Commissioners for the Exhibition of 1862, humbly beg leave to approach her Majesty through you, her illustrious representatives on this occasion, with the assurance of our devotion to her Majesty's throne and Royal person.

"And, first of all, it is our melancholy duty to convey to her Majesty the expression of our deep sympathy with her in the grievous affliction with which it has pleased the Almighty to visit her Majesty and the whole people of this realm in the death of her Royal consort. We cannot forget that this is the anniversary of the opening of the first great International Exhibition eleven years ago by her Majesty, when his Royal Highness, the President of the Commissioners of that exhibition, addressed her Majesty in words that will not be forgotten. After stating the proceedings of the Commission in the discharge of their duties, he concluded with a prayer that an undertaking 'which had for its end the promotion of all branches of human industry and the strengthening of the bonds of peace and friendship among all nations of the earth, might, by the blessing of Divine Providence, conduce to the welfare of her Majesty's people and be long remembered among the brightest circumstances of her Majesty's peaceful and happy reign.'

"When we commenced our duties, and until a recent period, we ventured to look forward to the time when it might be our great privilege to address her Majesty in person this day, and to show to her Majesty within these walls the evidence which this exhibition affords of the soundness of the opinion originally entertained by his Royal Highness—evidence furnished alike by the increased extent of the exhibition, by the eagerness with which all classes of the community have sought to take part in it, and by the large expenditure incurred by individual exhibitors for the better display of their produce and machinery. We can now only repeat the assurance of our sympathy with her Majesty in that bereavement which deprives this inaugural ceremony of her Royal presence; and, whilst bearing mournful testimony to the loss of that invaluable assistance which his Royal Highness was so ready at all times to extend to us, we have to offer to the Queen our dutiful thanks for the interest evinced by her Majesty in this undertaking by commanding your Royal Highness and your Lordships to represent her Majesty on this occasion."

The origin and organization of the Exhibition are then detailed, and are followed by this statement :—

"About 22,000 exhibitors are here represented, of whom about 17,000 are subjects of her Majesty, and 5000 of foreign States. The arrangement and design of the building is such that the exhibited articles have been generally arranged in three great divisions :—

"1. Fine Arts, in the galleries especially provided for that department.
"2. Raw materials, manufactures, and agricultural machinery, in the main building and the eastern annexe.
"3. Machinery requiring steam or water power for its effectual display, in the western annexe.

"Within these divisions the classification adopted is in most respects similar to that employed in 1851, the British and Colonial articles being kept separate from those sent by foreign countries, and each country having its own portion of the several departments allotted to it.

"The articles now exhibited will show that the period which has elapsed since 1851, although twice interrupted by European wars, has been marked by a progress previously unexampled in science, art, and manufacture.

"It is our earnest prayer that the International Exhibition of 1862, now about to be inaugurated, and which it is our privilege to conduct, may form no unworthy link in that chain of international exhibitions with which must ever be connected the honoured name of her Majesty's illustrious Consort."

The Duke of Cambridge returned the answer to the address, which was as follows :—

"We cannot perform the duty which the Queen has done us the honour to commit to us as her Majesty's representatives on this occasion without expressing our heartfelt regret that this inaugural ceremony is deprived of her Majesty's presence by the sad bereavement which has overwhelmed the nation with universal sorrow. We share most sincerely your feelings of deep sympathy with her Majesty in the grievous affliction with which the Almighty has seen fit to visit her Majesty and the whole people of 'this realm. It is impossible to contemplate the spectacle this day presented to our view without being painfully reminded how great a loss we have all sustained in the illustrious Prince with whose name the first great International Exhibition was so intimately connected, and whose enlarged views and enlightened judgment were conspicuous in his appreciation of the benefits which such undertakings are calculated to confer upon the country. We are commanded by the Queen to assure you of the warm interest which her Majesty cannot fail to take in this Exhibition, and of her Majesty's earnest wishes that its success may amply fulfil the intentions and expectations with which it was projected, and may richly reward the zeal and energy, aided by the cordial co-operation of distinguished men of various countries, by which it has been carried into execution. We heartily join in the prayer that the International Exhibition of 1862, beyond conducing to present enjoyment and instruction, will be hereafter recorded as an important link in the chain of international exhibitions, by which the nations of the world may be drawn together in the noblest rivalry, and from which they may mutually derive the greatest advantages."

Earl Granville then, on the part of the Commissioners of the Exhibition, presented to his Royal Highness the "key," technically so called, of the Exhibition. This is, in fact, a masterkey (manufactured by Messrs. Chubb), and which opens the entire number of the different suites of locks on all the doors of the buildings. It is beautifully wrought entirely by hand out of a solid piece of steel, and was inclosed in a crimson velvet bag.

This concluded that part of the ceremonial which took place under the western dome, and before the throne; and the procession, being re-formed, proceeded in the same order along the north side of the nave to a large platform under the eastern dome, immediately in front of the gigantic orchestra. Here had assembled a number of the visitors, British and foreign, distinguished for their rank and the high positions, official and diplomatic, which they hold. To this point the foreign Ambassadors had been conducted, and here her Royal Highness the Duchess of Cambridge, the Grand Duchess of Mecklenburgh-Strelitz, and the Princess Mary of Cambridge, had been allotted places. Seats, too, were provided for the personages taking part in the procession; and, as soon as they had been duly arranged, the music specially composed for this occasion was performed by an orchestra consisting of 2000 voices and 400 instrumentalists, conducted, with one exception, by Mr. Costa. It commenced with a grand overture by Meyerbeer, comprising a triumphal march, a sacred march, and a quick march, and an embodiment of "Rule Britannia;" then Dr. Sterndale Bennett's chorale, which had been composed for the words of the ode written by the Poet Laureate Tennyson, as follows:—

> Uplift a thousand voices full and sweet,
> In this wide hall with Earth's invention stored,
> And praise th' invisible universal Lord,
> Who lets once more in peace the nations meet,
> Where science, art, and labour have outpour'd
> Their myriad horns of plenty at our feet.
>
> O silent father of our Kings to be,
> Mourn'd in this golden hour of jubilee,
> For this, for all, we weep our thanks to thee!
>
> The world-compelling plan was thine,
> And lo! the long laborious miles
> Of Palace; lo! the giant aisles,
> Rich in model and design;

Harvest-tool and husbandry,
Loom and wheel and engin'ry,
Secrets of the sullen mine,
Steel and gold, corn and wine,
Fabric rough, or fairy fine,
Sunny tokens of the Line,
Polar marvels, and a feast
Of Wonder, out of West and East,
And shapes and hues of Art divine!
All of beauty, or of use,
That our planet can produce,
Brought from under every star,
Blown from over every main,
And mixed, as life is mixed with pain,
The works of peace with works of war;
War himself must make alliance,
With rough labour and fine science,
Else he would but strike in vain.—
Ah, the goal is far away,
How far is it? who can say,
Let us have our dream to-day.—

Oh ye, the wise who think, the wise who reign,
From growing commerce loose her latest chain,
And let the fair white-winged peacemaker fly
To happy havens under all the sky,
And mix the seasons and the golden hours,
Till each man find his own in all men's good,
And all men work in noble brotherhood,
Breaking their mailed fleets and armed towers,
And ruling by obeying Nature's powers,
And gathering all the fruits of peace and crown'd with
    all her flowers.

The performance of this Ode was a great success, and decidedly the most faultless and complete feature of the day. "Auber's Grand March" followed—spirited and melodious, and full of the best manner of the composer.

After the conclusion of the special music, the Bishop of London, with much fervency of manner, read an impressive prayer.

Handel's mighty choral hymns—the "Hallelujah" and "Amen" from the *Messiah*—which, coming directly after the prayer of the Bishop of London, formed a portion of the religious ceremony, towered above all in sublimity.

After the "Amen" the National Anthem was again sung, and with this the music to the religious part of the ceremony came to a conclusion.

The Duke of Cambridge then rose, and in a loud voice said, "By command of the Queen, I now declare the Exhibition open."

The trumpets of the Life Guards saluted the announcement with a prolonged *fanfare*, and the crowd echoed it back with a cheer, which was taken up and speedily spread from one end of the building to the other. This ended the official ceremonial.

Sweet, and yet sad, those thousand voices rung,
Winding and travelling through the long defiles
Of courts and galleries and far-reaching aisles:
And bright the banners from proud arches sprung;
But not the less their drooping folds among
Lurked a dim hoard of grief; for over all

> Chastening, not marring, our high festival,
> The shadow of an absent Greatness hung—
> Absent, but yet in absence present more
> For all we owe to him, and might have owed,
> For the rich gifts, which, missing, we deplore,
> Than if he were rejoicing at this hour—
> We with him—that the seed his wisdom sowed
> Had blossomed in this bright consummate flower.
>
> R. C. T.
> *Times*, May 2, 1862.

Among the illustrations of our great subject, which partake of a poetic character, may be ranked an Address read by Mr. Monckton Milnes, M.R., at the Royal Institution, on the day after the opening of the Exhibition, namely, on the 2nd of May. Mr. Milnes modestly introduced this paper to his audience as prefatory to a series of special discourses, to be delivered at the Institution, and as "a few considerations on the natural scope of this wonderful congregation of the industries and intelligences of the world."

It was the habit of this Society to deal rather with facts than speculations, and he would therefore direct their attention to the geographical and political conditions which alone rendered possible such an event as this. It had been written with sufficient accuracy for verse, that—

> " The total surface of this sphered earth
>   Is now surveyed by philosophic eyes:
> Nor East nor West conceals a secret worth—
>   In the wide ocean no Atlantic lies :
> Nations and men, that would be great and wise,
>   Thou knowest, can do no more than men have done;
> No wond'rous impulse, no divine surprise,
>   Can bring this planet nearer to the sun—
> Civilization's prize no royal road has won."

The accessibility of the ocean-waters of the globe was a first necessity to this end, and this had been now accomplished from the ice-bound fires of Mount Erebus to the grave of Franklin. We could not say quite as much of our knowledge of the land of the world, but we perfectly understood the limits of our ignorance, and could fairly assume that there was no position on the earth yet unsurveyed which could in any notable degree add to our physical science, or extend our observation of the habits and destinies of mankind.

Although great continents are represented in our Exhibition only by their fringes, we can hardly contemplate any such conversion of nature or man as should people the sandy spaces of Africa, the vast pastoral steppes of central Asia, or those huge fields of the unlimited liberty of animal and vegetable life which stretch in South America from the tropics to the polar snows, with the higher forms of industry, art, and civilization. It is enough that no longer can Tartar hordes swoop down on richer and fairer lands, and that the sage and saleratus prairies of North America cannot check the enterprising outgrowth of the Anglo-Saxon race.

And this brings us to another necessary condition of our Exhibition, the security of the seas and the general facility of our commercial intercourse. The exceptional piracy which obstructs the trade of the waters of Oceania, and which the energy of Sir James Brooke has done much to repress, was once the custom of the world, and carried with it no notions of cruelty or disgrace. This evil was partially remedied by placing commerce under the safeguard of religion. Where the modern state establishes a factory or a free port, the old state built a temple. Thus the Tyrian Hercules linked together the trade of Greece and Phoenicia in a common worship: thus the fame of Jupiter Ammon was the great resting-place and protection of the caravans of the desert: thus the lines of the chief Catholic pilgrimages were the paths not only of all travellers but of all merchants in the middle ages. The interchange of the gifts of God was sanctioned by Pagan and by Christian piety, and the notion of connecting trade with any inferiority of social station or intellectual power is a perverted remnant of the fendal system, where the jealousy between town and country tended to discredit labour and to idealize brute force.

The speaker proceeded to draw the distinction between ancient and modern trade. In the old Asiatic nations, where influence is still palpable among mankind on the score of authority and the bond of religion, the ideas of free trade and competition would have been incomprehensible. The exclusion of foreigners from the internal navigation of the several countries was universal, and none were permitted even to enter foreign ports, except with the *tessera hospitalis*, or some other symbol of a commercial treaty. Bars were thrown across the mouths of some rivers, as by the Persians across the Tigris after their conquest of Babylon; traces of which impediments to navigation still remain. And in modern Europe the growth of liberal commerce has been slow indeed, and it is one of the happiest privileges of our time, that as regards ourselves at least, we have come to see its consummation. In Sir Dudley North's *Discourse on Trade*, published in 1691, the principle is laid down "that the whole world as to trade is but as one nation of people, and therein nations are as persons." But the Hollanders and the Portuguese long remained the objects of a commercial animosity, which did not prevent the one from occupying our fisheries up to the very coast, and the other from sharing with us the dominion of India.

The social and political conditions represented by our Exhibition next occupied the attention of the speaker. The whole of this marvellous combination of energy and art is the result of free labour—of the spontaneous industry of mankind. It is not the mere application of local nature to local designs, but the collation and transmutation of most diverse and distinct elements to the use and benefit of our race: the juxtaposition of our coal and iron have suggested the manufactures of Sheffield, but it is the borax of Tuscany which assists the ingenious labourers of Colebrook Dale. It is the sign and symbol of the general education of the world, which renders it impossible that discoveries can be neglected or arts be lost. The ignorance and superstition which kept mankind in unnecessary physical pain after the invention of the "spongia somnifera" of the twelfth century, can no longer check the anæsthetic powers of a beneficial nature, nor would it require a Harvey to revive, however he might be required to develope, the knowledge that perished with the ashes of Servetus.

But besides the intercommunication of nations in space, the speaker remarked, our Exhibition surely owes much to what he would call the trade of time, the thoughts, the feelings, the interests, that pass from generation to generation; the arts of Greece, the laws of Rome, the religion of the Semitic peoples, the triple elements of modern civilization. The silent East gave the alphabetic character which has transmitted all the speeches and varied literature of the West; the Brahmin preserves the sacred language in which the linguistic science of modern times traces the mother-tongue of all the Indo-Germanic dialects that pass from mouth to mouth beneath these lofty domes.

The singularity of the circumstance that England should be the scene of the meeting of nations was next alluded to. It was an illustration of the advantage of our insular position, which being combined with sufficient territory, gave us at once the best political conditions of external power and domestic independence. Our greatest danger in history has been, not our own conquest, but the conquest of France, which must have absorbed us into the continental system. Now, the peril of our power lay in the rapid political and moral elevation of the other European nations; but we could well afford to sacrifice some individual superiority to the common gain of mankind.

Upon the probable effects of this great display, the speaker, in conclusion, observed:—" Large congregations of men had always visibly struck the imagination, and the Jubilee of Pope Boniface so occupied the mind of Dante, that he illustrates it by one of his supernatural pictures, and fixed it as the date of his spiritual journey. Such assemblies have always been looked on as harbingers of peace, and we know what were the expectations of 1851. But though that hope has proved delusive, we may yet feel thankful that, with the exception of the American calamity, all the disturbances of the world have since that time been the conflicts of a lower against a higher civilisation, in which the higher has had the mastery. The materials here brought together must impress on the spectators the mutual dependence of nations, and the interests of amity. One of the chief objects of interest would be, the various applications of art to industry; advantages, perhaps, somewhat balanced by the injury of the application of industry to art. As art becomes mechanical, it loves the spontaneous dignity which makes it most divine; and it seems impossible to diffuse and repeat it, without some diminution of its highest faculties. But this qualification does not extend to the relations between industry and science,—there the moral is as certain as the material profit : intelligent labour is substituted for the mere exertion of brute strength; the supply of comforts is extended from the luxurious classes even to the necessitous: the diseases consequent on physical hardships are diminished, and the average longevity of man increased. To the progress of scientific education not only the philosopher but the statesman looks for the diffusion of public happiness and the permanence of modern civilization. If the states that now rule the world are to escape the doom of Babylon and Rome, of Egypt and of Greece, it is in that they have not made their science the monopoly of a caste or a priesthood, but they have placed it more or less within the reach of the individual intelligence of the humblest citizen. Let the education that enables mankind to apprehend and value truth proceed commensurately with the discoveries of science, and the community will gradually but continuously absorb into itself that knowledge which makes decay impossible; and our country may boldly and confidently meet whatever destiny remains for it in the inscrutable designs of the Creator and Ruler of the universe."

PROGRESS OF ART-MANUFACTURES

EXEMPLIFIED IN THE EXHIBITION.

BEFORE we detail the most striking objects in the Exhibition, it will be interesting, as well as instructive, to glance at the Art-characteristics of the various countries, as represented in the Exhibition. These have been sketched by a master-hand in the paper in the *Quarterly Review*, to which such frequent reference has been made; and from this source we condense the following:—

"We need not linger long in lands where, for many generations, art has been feminine, not masculine, in its characteristics: among people who work by the heart and not by the head, by instinct not by reason; in those old Oriental regions where the appreciation of colour is instinctive; where the patient manipulation of detail knows no fatigue; where the goldsmith and jeweller are held in universal honour; where each nationality has its own limited series of forms, within which the artificer labours successfully, but beyond which he does not seem gifted to advance. India on the one side, and Turkey on the other, were the limits of this feminine phase of art, as exhibited at Brompton. Its educational value to us has not been sufficiently appreciated as our teacher in points in which the art of Europe—the art, that is, of the head, and not alone of the heart—is apt to be more deficient: such as the jubilant use of colour, the fearless employment of costly material, the delicate handling of minute detail. These, we say, are feminine attributes; and the masculine art of Europe—the art which is founded on the study of the human figure—must not despise their gracefulness if it aspires to tread the path of perfection. As it is, we were sorry to see, in some instances, a contrary influence at work, and the native instinct vitiated by a ridiculous aping of the vulgar forms of European trade production. In the Indian department, for instance, by the side of rich stuffs and elegant Bombay work, we beheld tables, sofas, and pianos, carved far away by native fingers, but modelled for the European market upon forms which are already happily looked upon at home as vulgar and ante-dated." The reviewer then passes on to countries living in or peopled by Christian Europe.

Russia, if not actually retrogressive, was stationary, and to be stationary with such an empire is next door to being retrogressive. Some silver and enamelled bookbindings and plate, chiefly for church purposes, exhibiting a style, combining modern feeling with reminiscences of Byzantine, of Renaissance, and even like its prototype, of the flamboyant, which we suspect to have passed from Poland into Muscovy, with some graceful ideas borrowed from the native art of Circassia, and a huge, vigorous mosaic of St. Nicholas, on a gold ground, flanked by two others of more recent type, sum up the novelties which this vast realm contributed. The large Imperial porcelain vases were merely good imitations on a Cæsarian scale of Sèvres. That noblest of veneering processes, the manipulation of malachite, of which Russia displayed such stupendous specimens in 1851, was wholly without a representative. We were in hopes that this time we might have seen equal excellence of handling, and equal grandeur of scale, married to purer forms. England is the last country which has a right to complain of Russia for the want of progress during the past decade, but the fact is significant. Perhaps, indeed, the character of the Russian exhibition may be referred to an altered policy and a better sense of the true interests of that empire, which lie in the development of raw materials, rather than in the production of manufactures, which, in a country destitute of coal, can only be regarded as exotics.

"The art-manufacture of Spain began and ended with M. Zuloaga's spirited revival of the Damascening process, which is so good as by its solitariness to be a reproach to a country which, with such a history and such resources, has not better profited by its opportunities. Judicious little Portugal rested comfortably content with the goodness of its material productions. The rival Courts of Italy and Rome, distinct nationalities for this term, testified, in the pictorial mosaics, and the cameos of the Papal city, in Salviati's successful copies of the Murano glass-works, and of the early mosaics of Venice, his elaborate table of glass marquetry; and his clever adaptation of the mosaicist's principle of gilding to the production of gold—enclosing glass mouldings and ornaments proof against all dirt and scratching; in the floral incrustations of Florence, and in Marquis Campana's artificial marbles, to that ingenious, toilful, and withal graceful industry, of which the modern Italian mind so well appreciates the value. The vigorous, though sometimes crudely-coloured porcelain, which Marquis Ginori, of Florence, has produced in copy of the old Capoda Monte ware; and Signor Castellani, of Rome's felicitous revival of the jewellery and goldsmith's work of Greek, Etruscan, Roman, and Mediæval days, stood in the first class of imitations." The reviewer then claims for England the Venus of Marriage, which Mr. Gibson has sent to the Italian Court in tinted marble.

Austria evinced, with all those characteristic differences which might be supposed to distinguish the Teuton from the Southerner, a ready-money yet artistic adaptability to present tastes. The various forms produced by the partnership of the glass-blower and the chemist may not be high art, but they were all ingenious, many of them decidedly pretty, all commendably cheap. Habenicht's stamped and coloured leather wall-hangings deserved more than a passing glance. The carefully revised maps and geographical models indicate the scientific bent of the graver minds of Austria. That conglomeration of the other German States the Zollverein, aimed at more and performed less. Prussia's costly porcelain and silver work were stiff, stately, and academic; and the crowded shop full of Dresden-China figurantes, showed how tamely this generation can go on copying a phase of art which lost all its value when it ceased to represent the feelings of the frivolous age which gave it birth. The Bavarian Athens proved at how moderate a price pictures can be copied and printed in oil-colours. Cheap art is good, but we wanted a little also of Munich's dear art. In Bavaria, and in Rhenish Prussia, and to a certain degree all over Germany, a school of revived Gothic art has sprung up within the last thirty years, having its centres at Cologne and at Munich, which claims to compete with the similar revivals of France and England; yet the German Gothicists only showed one small ivory shrine, besides a carved and painted retable, and a coloured statue. From Frankfort and Hamburg there was a lavish display of stags' horns twisted into articles of furniture.

Belgium, of course, revelled in laces. There were some coarsely-finished chimney-pieces and inferior Teniers tapestry. A tall gothic pulpit of wood, by Messrs. Goyers, of Louvain, was praiseworthy for its technical finish, but the whole design was spiritless. Belgium also boasted of a huge candle trophy; and so did Holland, which also displayed a wooden gothic pulpit, by Cuypers, of Ruremond. Sweden and Norway stood off from the art-contest, though the group of Wrestlers in the former country had a kind of rude energy; and so practically stood Switzerland, which has never found the way to improve the wood-carving and landscape-painting industries of Lucerne and Interlachen, into schools of art. Denmark was more promising. The Royal porcelain manufactory at Copenhagen is little more than a reflex of Sèvres, very creditable indeed for so small a nation, but in no way indicating original power. In the smaller contributions, however, of private manufactories, we observed a tendency to the reproduction of characteristic forms of ancient Scandinavian art, significant, we trust, of the rise of a national school. "When we state that against the pillars in the Danish portion of the nave stood statues by Thorwaldsen, and prominent among them the majestic Jason, we have said that in sculpture Denmark is foremost of the nations, although the world at large very justly claims some share in the man who worked at Rome, and whose genius was first fostered by one who, born in a foreign land, made himself a name in English literature."*

Greece showed its double nationality. In its rich embroideries —in Agathangelos's marvellous resuscitation of the old, though still living, school of minute wood-carving crystallised in Mount Athos, we see the genuine 'modern Greek' Christianized and Slavonized. In the busts of Codrus of Athens, and other mythological and typical worthies, we recognise the artificial Hellene of the Athenian schools. The 'Ionian' display belonged exclusively to the first class.

Some South American Republics were represented—that was all.

* The author of *Anastasius*, who was Thorwaldsen's earliest patron.—*Ed. Year-book*.

Brazil sent a tempting display of natural wealth and a little upholstery art. The United States, which in 1851, astonished us by its nuggets of gold, commemorated 1862 by a frame full of the innumerable notes of many banks, fancifully engraved with various emblems. Power, whose Greek Slave was one of the delights of the former display, again adventured a female figure; but in 1862, he only gave us a strapping stiff "California." However, that penchant for sculpture which has so curiously manifested itself in the American race, was represented by Miss Hosmer's Zenobia, shown in the Italian Court; and by Story's contributions to the Roman display, in his Cleopatra, and in his Libyan Sibyl.

"We have thus travelled round the world, and at last we find ourselves in the face of the two great rival exhibiting realms: the haughty, exulting, self-contained France, and the venturesome progressive British empire, with its growth of half a hundred colonies." The French display is described as a museum rather than an exhibition. The long iron screen, rich with hangings, and backed by the furniture of Fourdinois and Grobé, formed a sort of propylæum to the treasures within. Inside, streets of stalls, all artistically and uniformly designed, led to a splendid centre composed of the rich electro-gilt and electro-plated plateau which Christofle had executed for the city of Paris. The treasures around were innumerable. The jewels with their settings were of countless price, while the parures of artificial stones would even deceive the wary round the necks of the *demi-monde*. The state manufactory of Sèvres yielded porcelain which might almost atone in bulk for inferiority of execution compared with England or Italy. The looms of Beauvais and Gobelins had not been idle, and the full-sized copy from the latter place of Titian's Assumption required to be handled before the stranger could believe that he did not gaze on the veritable masterpiece of Venetian colour. In bronzes, Paris was always pre-eminent, and Barbedienne, in rivalry with Raillard, stood foremost in them; while he was great in every other school of metal-work, mediæval, renaissance, oriental, cast, chased, or relieved with enamel. In his hands the revival even of Limoges art has been attempted with very sufficient success. Bookbinding was very gay, as fitted the editions *de luxe*, which were prodigally displayed. Ecclesiastical metal-work of mediæval design was represented by several exhibitors, whose productions were all of them costly and elaborate, besides being artistic when due to M. Viollet Le Duc, and highly enamelled as Frenchmen can enamel; although, as a rule, deficient in fineness of chiselling, and overloaded with gilding. The huge hammered figures in copper and in zinc for the fleches of the Sainte Chapelle and of Nôtre Dame were bold and telling works, made to be viewed at a distance; while Christofle's female nudity, produced in dully shining electro-plate, stood as a beacon to avoid. The newly-discovered 'onyx' marble from Algeria, a species of alabaster of a light golden tint, semi-transparent, and easy to be worked, had its capacities displayed in various forms, notably as the dress of images, with hands, arms, and feet of bronze. "If the supply prove equal to the demand," adds the reviewer, "this substance is a gain to art, from the richness of its tone, and the ease with which it may be worked."

The writer then mentions the huge and sumptuous French iron fountain in the Horticultural Garden; and recurs to Christofle's great plateau for the Hotel de Ville, the merits of which, as a work of art, are thus estimated :—"Grace, no doubt, it possesses, but it is the grace of the Academy; it is dignified, but its dignity wants self-forgetfulness; its material is rich, but the richness is mostly on the surface; its technical execution is perfect, but in execution the spirit has evaporated. Considered as an allegory, it is one of ten thousand; it has about it no moral significance, hardly even mythology, but only some trite effigies of obvious material advantages."

The English display of industrial art was larger and more miscellaneous than that of France. There was vulgarity enough in the English department to send us home sorrowing, and there was progress enough to cheer us in our most desponding moments. The artist has clearly had to do with the producer during the last eleven years. His influence has often been thwarted, and his suggestions altered, but still he has been employed as he never used to be. * * * "For this development much credit is due to the schools of design which are at work in various places, but much also to the impulsion given by persons who have taught without a pencil in their hands, and whose lessons may be summed up in the one axiom, to seek utility of form and reality of material first, and then to ornament in accordance with that form and that material. In the present Exhibition the furniture, whether of the costly or the cheap description, paper-hangings and carpets, testified respectively to this upward tendency. Glass-painting alone was standing still, so far as we could judge by the Exhibition." The writer then refers to the substitution, in furniture, of spirited carvings, natural forms, and flowing lines, for the old upholstery patterns; a variety of woods was chosen for colour and grain, often artistically contrasted in delicately inlaid patterns; and the beauty of simple varnished deal, drowning its natural colour, was appreciated. The paper printers who work by machinery vied in the purity of their patterns with their dearer brethren who still employ the block process; gigantic bunches of lilac, roses, and peonies, shaded up in high relief, are no longer the *ne plus ultra* of taste in carpets; and as a whole, the looms are being daily more and more set to patterns combining geometrical forms with well-contrasted colours.

"In the porcelain of almost every European school—Faïence, Majolica, Palissy, and Neo-classical, not to talk of the revival of indigenous types—England, represented by its various Staffordshire and Worcestershire firms, stands supreme; and foremost among the exhibitors are Messrs. Minton, though well followed up by the Copelands, the Wedgwoods, and the Dukes.* As a

* To these we would add Messrs. Rose, of Colebrookdale.

contrast between life and death, we have only to turn from these displays to the cold Dresden exhibition. In tiles for mural decoration as contrast with porcelain, Messrs. Man have made valuable progress, and their large mosaic, designed by Mr. Digby Wyatt, in bold ceramic tessera, is a production not to be overlooked.

"The Ornamental Glassworks of England were not in proportion of so remarkable a quality as the porcelain; still they showed considerable aptitude in the imitations of several foreign schools; and one tazza of glass, delicately engraved, and shown by a St. James's-street firm, not unmeritedly won considerable praise.

"The performances in Brass-work and in Wrought or Cast Iron were of remarkable size, and very high merit. The praise of Skidmore's screen from Coventry was in every visitor's mouth. Messrs. Hardman's delicate wrought-iron grill, of Gothic pattern, from Birmingham, must not be overlooked; while another prominent work, Barnard's Norwich Gates, partly of cast and partly of wrought-iron, composed of spirited imitations of natural foliage, artistically grouped, deserves especial commendation. The cast and bronzed gates from Colebrookdale were as conspicuously bad.

"Mediæval Art in a surprising variety of forms was not only displayed by the artists we have named and by other workers in brass, such as Mr. Hart, but also in a court arranged by a Society, with the long name of Ecclesiological, out of which we should name some very meritorious embroidery and woollen work of rich colours, well contrasted, by Messrs. Jones and Willis, of Birmingham, under Mr. Street's instructions; and a specimen of the pavement of Lichfield Cathedral, by Messrs. Clayton and Bell, reviving the old art of incising stone, for designs to be executed in various cements—a process as applicable to walls as to floors.

"The Goldsmiths and Jewellers astonished with the monetary value of their cases. The price of these gems is not, of course, a question of art, and the settings were frequently nothing more than ingenious devices to show off the stones. But there was a prodigal display of glyptic work in the precious metals and their imitations. The nearly forgotten process of *repoussé* is now in vigorous operation. The French invention of oxydizing silver has been acclimatised here since 1851; and in the profusion of forms which racing and other 'cups,' memorial shields, and so on, assume, ideas are here and there struck out, which are capable of much further expansion. As a whole, this display, when its abundance is considered, may be esteemed as a hopeful indication of the homage which wealth now pays to art.

"In Tapestry England did not compete, and in Bronzes hardly at all; but Derbyshire very fairly imitated the pietra dura of Florence; while in a pavement by Mr. Slater, for Chichester Cathedral, we were glad to note the revival of marble mosaics of a constructural character."

In Architectural Drawings of modern buildings, Britain stood virtually alone. Very few arrived from foreign lands. The French catalogue has some names of architectural eminence, but affixed to restorations of ancient buildings. A few original designs came from Prussia and Austria, and one or two from Holland: the rest of Europe was a blank. The Commissioners, with characteristic indifference to architecture, reluctantly granted a range of galleries for architectural designs, and an adjacent court for portions of buildings. The Gothic drawings were ranged on one side, the Classical and Renaissance on the other, but peacefully commingled in the external galleries, which were partially devoted to the Scotchmen. In this large collection, England might point with honest pride to the cathedral-like church which Mr. Scott is building at Hamburg, even in an international competition; and to that other cathedral for Lille, where Mr. Clutton and Mr. Burges came off victorious over Europe, followed by Mr. Street, only to be defrauded of their work. Adjacent to the Architecture, a gallery was devoted to Art-designs by persons who have been living during the century. We have incidentally mentioned Scotch architecture. With this exception, neither Scotland nor Ireland took up any distinctive position in the industrial arts. Very little art, as might be supposed, came from the Colonies, but they contributed materials for future art-exploits of refreshing originality. Not to mention the marbles of New South Wales, and the malachite of South Australia, the prodigal array of woods of every grain, every hue, and every hardness, which came from Australia, South Africa, and New Zealand, from the West Indies and from Ceylon, and in a less degree from North America, were an alarum to the carver and the cabinet-maker and to the architect and the draughtsman to sharpen their pencils. We are glad to see that these colonies have, to a certain extent, contributed to the architectural appeal by the photographs which several of them had sent of their principal cities, such as Sydney, Melbourne, Geelong, Auckland, Montreal, Halifax, &c.

We have referred to M. Christofle's plateau as typical of French art; that of England may be considered to have attained its most characteristic expression in Minton's Majolica Fountain, designed by the late Mr. Thomas, and in Skidmore's Hereford Screen, carried out under Mr. Scott's directions. Both these works are emphatically monumental in their aim, and neither of them the fruit of artificial enterprise. Each is the largest work which has yet been produced from the manufactory which the late Mr. Minton in the one case, and Mr. Skidmore in the other, developed or set up, with the express intention of allying arts to industry. Each in its largeness transcends any previous exploit in the same materials produced elsewhere.

"Like Minton's Majolica Fountain, Skidmore's Hereford Screen is a debt which the present is paying to the past, no less than to the future. Its art is modern in its extent, but in its principles it is old, and its object is to enhance a large surviving monument of ancient art. Such also is the intention of many of the costly objects of Church silver-work in the cases of Bachelet, Trioullier, and Poussielgue Rusand; but while these productions, clogged with superfluous gilding, will in the end occupy some position where they must be inspected like cabinet pieces, the bolder Englishman commands the fabric itself, and raises metal-work to the level of architecture.

"We are not in despair," says the reviewer, in taking leave of this portion of his subject, "at the fact that so many of the contributions from all countries manifested absence of invention, along with great readiness and variety in adaptation; which critics have considered to be the sum of the lessons learned from the whole exhibition of applied art. It is by working at first from the models before them that the regeneration of art can at last attain that knowledge of the principles of art which can justify them in launching out in a bolder course at some later day."

In conclusion, this eloquent and well-informed art-critic glances at the causes which combine to make the English character of 1862, so old and yet so young, which is struggling for its artistic expression. "In the meanwhile, science is every day pouring its hard-won treasures into the lap of art: new processes, new minerals, new dyes, new easements of manual operation; the galvanic bath turning the artists' own clay into the everlasting statue; the sun slaving in the glass-house to paint man's pictures; the electric spark running along the wires to tell man's messages; the vapour of water doing that which no horses and no hands, no winds and no tides, could ever accomplish."

How much sagacity and finely-expressed thought are there in the author's closing reflections. "These agencies are Providence's instruments to work out results mightier than any Exhibition can make or mar. Yet Exhibitions have their value, as seats by the road-side, where the wayfarers may rest and compare their adventures. Much varied lore may there be gathered by those who will have the patience to sit at the feet of experience and industry, and many false impressions will be dispelled by the attrition of equal minds. Officials may have done their little best to spoil the good result, but, after every abatement has been made, great gratification to multitudes, tangible instruction to a smaller but numerous class, will be the gross result of the Exhibition of 1862, as it was of that in 1851. Whether there will ever be another in England, or whether there will not, these two will have left their mark on history. The names of the Commissioners and of the engineer will be forgotten, while the date of both will be remembered as occurring in the reign of Queen Victoria, and as having been among the many wise conceptions for the public good of that Prince who had so eminently the capacity of swaying events by his consciousness of quiet power."

OBJECTS AND ARTICLES EXHIBITED.

WE now proceed to select and describe the Objects and Articles which are entitled to special record by their novelty, or comparative rarity. The *classification* of these subjects which has been followed is that which is most likely to prove available by the largest number of readers, as most befitting the plan of a popular work—that is, a work for popular reading—like the present.

Raw Materials.

MINING, QUARRYING, AND METALLURGY.

We commence with a collection of Mineral Products from the Shropshire lead and copper mines, exhibited by the Rev. F. More. Besides felspar and china-stone ochres, oxide of manganese, and sulphate of barytes; the case containing Roman spades and pigs of lead. A case, devoted to Aluminium, showed the progress already made in the application of that valuable metal and of its alloys. The metal is obtained from the double chloride of aluminium and sodium by fusion with sodium. Amongst its advantages, besides non-liability to tarnishing, is the lightness. By its use, a sextant which in brass would weigh 3 lb. may be made to weigh 1 lb. 9 oz. It costs 40s. per lb. troy. The alloy of the metal with copper, called aluminium-bronze, contains five per cent. of aluminium, and costs 4s. 6d. per lb. avoirdupois. This alloy resembles gold in appearance; whilst it is stronger than iron. Keys are made of aluminium alloyed with two per cent. of nickel to increase hardness. Bell Brothers, of Newcastle-on-Tyne, were the exhibitors. As showing what our island contains, the collection belonging to Mr. T. A. Readwin, of Gold Ores from Merionethshire, was interesting. There were also shown ingots of Welsh gold, of 126 oz. 19 dwt., from 6 cwt. 21 lb. of quartz, the weekly yield. A large case contained specimens of Platinum, and various articles manufactured from it, as alembics and retorts used in the rectification or concentration of sulphuric acid. The usefulness of the metal in manufacturing chemistry is now greatly increased by the process discovered by Mr. St. Claire Deville, using the intense heat of combined gases, by which it can be made to assume complete fluidity,—the refractory nature of the metal constituting its value in the arts. Johnson, Matthey, and Company were the exhibitors. The value of the platinum in the case is 5180*l*.; one ingot, weighing 3200 ounces, being worth 3840*l*. Besides the platinum, and gold and silver, the case contained iridium, palladium, rhodium, uranium, cadmium, selenium, tellurium, osmium, and ruthenium, and the elements called non-metallic, silicon and boron, in various states and combinations. The platinum is recommended for the points of lightning conductors. An alloy of iridium and osmium is used for pen-points. Used in photography are the nitrate of silver, neutral chloride of gold (for imparting a delicate tone to the prints), the cadmium, and the nitrate of uranium. The oxides of uranium are used for colouring glass. In a corresponding position to that of the case last described, was one devoted to specimens and illustrations of the manufacture of German silver-plating, and the applications of nickel and cobalt. It was exhibited by Messrs. Evans and Askin, of Birmingham.—*From the Builder.*

The exhibitors of Iron Ores, iron in the rough state, and Cast and Wrought Iron in various forms for use, or to show the fibre and strength, were very numerous. There was probably no department of the Exhibition that evinced greater progress than this of late years. Mr. R. Smith's display of iron produced at the Round Oak Works, in the South Staffordshire district, from ores in the Earl of Dudley's estate, amounted to upwards of one hundred and twenty articles, besides the specimens of the coal and limestone. Nearly all, however, exhibited bars and rods doubled, or tied in knots, or fractured to show a fibre like that of wood, in ways quite opposed to the common ideas of the properties of iron. Amongst the specimens from the Earl of Dudley's Works was a bar of iron $1\frac{1}{8}$ inch square, which, tried at the Chatham Dockyard, stood a tensile strain of $64\frac{1}{4}$ tons without fracture, and broke two of the large cables of the testing-machine.

The articles, about fifty in number, from the Low Moor Iron Works, were sent by Hird, Dawson, and Hardy.

They included the Low Moor coal, hard and soft, and coke made therefrom, and used in blast or smelting furnaces and refineries; the Black Bed coal used for engine-boilers and house fires, and the coke for lime-kilns and other common purposes; the Black Bed stone lying immediately above the coal last mentioned, in six distinct strata, and containing about 28 per cent. of iron; the white ironstone; the calcined iron ore, prepared by roasting or burning in kilns, or in heaps on the ground, for the smelting furnaces, and the limestone from Skipton, used with the latter as a flux; furnace dross, or the earthy part of the ironstone combined with the limestone used for roads; pig-iron, of which the best quality is used for machine castings, the second for heavy machinery, and the third for forge purposes; refined iron, which is prepared from pig-iron by being exposed to a strong blast in the refinery; the cinder or impure matter separated from the metal in the refinery; puddled iron of two kinds—one adapted for boiler-plate, and the other for railway-wheel tires, the specimens showing fracture; chain iron, several specimens, bent cold in various ways to show toughness and strength, or fibre; boiler-plate, bent cold, with shorn edges; similar plate, doubled when hot so as to show pliability in working, and other specimens punched; knots tied cold; various specimens of bars, punched, doubled when cold, or broken to show grain of the iron; and other articles.

(Steel will be illustrated under the head of "Manufactures.")

Of Copper, in the Exhibition, there were specimens of ores from nearly every part of the world: Swedish, Norwegian, Russian,

Zollverein, Austrian, Italian, French, Spanish, Portuguese, Canadian, Nova Scotian, Newfoundland, British Columbian, Danish, from Greenland, United States, Brazilian, Costa Rica, Venezuela, Jamaica, Indian, Australasian, and New Zealand. Among the specimens of special interest, was, in the Zollverein, a series from the Prince Wilhelm mine, near Langenberg, illustrating the dressing of ores, consisting of copper pyrites, galena, and blende, the process at this mine being one of the most skilfully conducted in Germany. In the Italian department were the fine ores of Monte Catini, near Volterra, one of the most productive and profitable mines in the world. In the Portuguese department, among other ores, was the malachite from Western Africa. The Canadian copper ores, pyrites and variegated, were well represented. Sir W. Logan states that he has discovered a bed, not a lode, containing five per cent. of copper, and extending over a considerable area. In the United States department was shown native copper from Lake Superior, where it occurs in enormous masses—one weighing 500 tons. From Russia were several large pieces of native copper. Magnificent specimens, and large masses of copper ore from South Australia were exhibited: a mass from Wallaroo weighed 6 tons. From the Burra Burra Mines were specimens of variegated copper ore from the 60 fathom level, as well as green and blue carbonates: as was anticipated at a certain depth from the surface, the ores originally found are replaced by pyritic ores. The Connoree Company, Wicklow, Ireland, exhibited iron pyrites containing one per cent. of copper and other ores of copper. Mr. Bradley showed ores from Richmond, Yorkshire, a newly discovered locality, vitreous copper and blue and green carbonate. More than half the copper annually smelted at Swansea is obtained from Cornwall and Devon; which ores were not well represented in the Exhibition.

The Welsh system of Copper-smelting in reverberatory furnaces was well illustrated by the Swansea Local Committee; and there was an excellent display of the various kinds and forms of copper known in the English market. Mr. Hussey Vivian, M.P., was the only exhibitor from Swansea; Newton, Keates, and Co., of Liverpool, exhibited a fine collection of manufactured copper articles; and the Mona Mining Copper illustrated the smelting process; Mona copper is in high request for its great malleability. In the Swedish and Norwegian departments were excellent collections illustrative of copper-smelting in blast-furnaces. From the old Mansfeld works (Zollverein) were two large sugar-pans, each hammered out of one piece—one 1724 lb. (Prussian), the other 1833 lb.; and in the French department was a similar pan, weighing 1486 lb.

Next to Copper comes Spelter (ingots), in rolled sheets, Zinc. The Connoree Mining Company, Ireland, exhibited calamine, the ore of Zinc, from a new locality. Ores of zinc were also shown in the Belgian, Zollverein, Austrian, Swedish, Spanish, Portuguese, and United States departments. Mr. Vivian is the largest smelter, and exhibited spelter and zinc. In the Belgian department,

Muller and Co. exhibited spelter produced in a blast furnace; a process long attempted in vain. Some cast specimens of rolled zinc were shown in the Zollverein department.

Cadmium, generally found in zinc ores, was shown in the Polish and Zollverein departments, in foil and cylindrical sticks. Cadmium, combined with sulphur, forms a fine yellow, opaque, durable pigment much prized by artists. It is much in request for Wood's newly-discovered fusible alloy, which melts at a temperature far below boiling water.

Of Tin the Exhibition presented nothing remarkable or novel: the usual tin-stone, impure peroxide, was shown in the British department from Cornwall, in the Indian, the Portuguese, and that of Victoria.

Lead (galena) was shown in nearly all the departments, the Italian and Portuguese being specially interesting. The best illustrations in the British department were those shown by Mr. Sopwith, on the part of Mr. Beaumont; here, and in the Zollverein and Italian departments, the processes of dressing and smelting were well shown; there was, however, nothing in the Exhibition to indicate that progress has been made towards the solution of the great problem of condensing lead fume. In one year a large smelting establishment in the north of England obtained 800 tons of lead from the dust accumulated in their long flues.

Arsenic was sufficiently represented: Garland of Redruth, and Jennings and Co., of Swansea, and others, sent instructive collections illustrating the manufacture of white arsenic from the ore.

Nickel, recently become important in manufactures, when pure, is malleable and ductile, and is of much higher tenacity than wrought iron, but it is not yet employed in the state of pure metal. It is used in alloys for its whiteness; *German silver*, a name which our Teutonic brethren repudiate, is a simple alloy of copper, nickel, and zinc: it might be called white brass. It is now much used for electro-plated articles, and the nickel manufacture was first brought to its present perfection in Birmingham. Nickel is now employed in the coinage of Switzerland, Belgium, and the United States. Ores of nickel were exhibited by several manufacturers of German silver.

Cobalt, valuable for its forming blue colour, was found in the Zollverein department, and the United States. Oxide of cobalt is now largely employed by the potter and glass-maker in Birmingham: the fine "flowing blue" on our china was the result of the first application of this oxide.

True gray copper ore, containing a considerable amount of Mercury, occurs in Hungary: and although this ore had long been treated for copper and silver, yet it is only within the last few years that it was found to contain mercury, which has since been regularly extracted from it by a simple roasting process. No one would suspect the presence of mercury on looking at this ore, and it is probable that it may exist in other gray copper ores in which it has not hitherto been detected.

With regard to the illustrations of Silver, there is not much to be said. All galena contains it, though not always in sufficient proportion to allow of its profitable extraction. It is generally admitted that only lead, containing more than two ounces of silver to the ton, can be subjected to Pattinson's well-known process of desilverization with advantage. By this simple and important invention an enormous amount of silver has been saved to the world. The inventor most justly received one of the great medals at the last Exhibition—medals which were worth competing for. He now sleeps in his grave. He was a self-made, clear-headed, observant, upright man, whose name deserves to be recorded among the benefactors not only of his country, but of the world. Wherever lead is exhibited, specimens of silver will generally be found in concert. A curious story is told about the celebrated mine of Konsberg, in Norway. Not many years ago it might have been purchased by English adventurers for 50,000*l*., but was declined. In the following year it is reported to have yielded 80,000*l*. net profit. During the last twenty years or so, silver ores have been regularly imported into this country from South America; and they have been partly smelted by the lead smelters, and partly subjected to wet processes of extraction by Mr. Vivian and Dillwyn and Co., both firms of Swansea. It is to be regretted that the mineral resources of Peru and Bolivia were not represented in the Exhibition.

Antimony was well represented in the Exhibition. Its chief ore is sulphide, which has during many years been regularly and largely imported into this country from Borneo. Specimens of native sulphide of antimony were found in the Italian and Portuguese departments; in the French province of Constantine, Africa; in the Zollverein and Austrian; in the department of Victoria, whence considerable quantities have been imported into England.

Samples of metallic antimony were in most cases exhibited along with the ores. Mr. Hallett, the well-known antimony refiner in London, sent a good series of illustrations. We may here remark that the applications of antimony are not numerous. In the state of fine black sulphide oriental ladies have employed it from time immemorial to paint their eyebrows and the outer edges of their eyelids; and very palpable illustrations of this practice may now be witnessed on the stage as well as elsewhere in London. But the chief application of antimony is for type metal; and the title of Basil Valentine's famous treatise, *Currus triumphalis antimonii*, was prophetic of the mighty part it was destined to perform in the instruction of the world through the medium of the press.

The Exhibition contained several interesting and important illustrations of Mercury or Quicksilver. It chiefly occurs in nature in combination with sulphur, constituting the well-known mineral, Native Cinnabar. Magnificent specimens of this mineral from the Almaden mines were found in the Spanish department in the nave. Very fine specimens of cinnabar from the New Almaden mines in California were exhibited by Gibbs, Bright, and Co. Cinnabar and vermilion prepared from it were sent from Idria, in Carniola, in the Austrian department.

Rich sulphide of Silver has recently been discovered in Cornwall, but hitherto it has not been possible to procure even a specimen, as the adventurers are desirous of attracting the notice of the Crown as little as possible ; for a mine of which the ore is sulphide of silver would undoubtedly be a mine royal, and belong to the Crown. But would not the Crown do well to consider whether it is really expedient to retain this ancient privilege of claiming the so-called gold and silver mines ?

Gold was displayed in marvellous profusion in various departments. All native gold contains silver, which varies much in proportion, and tends to render the gold pale in colour. All lead contains gold in addition to silver, but in quantity generally so minute as to be valueless. But there it is, and it may invariably be extracted from lead, so as to be distinctly visible. The process of hand gold-washing was shown in the East Transept, near the Eastern Dome, and the Port Phillip Mining Company erected stamps of working size which had come all the way from Australia, and some of them were daily at work. The Australian departments, Tasmania, British Columbia, and Nova Scotia, presented a surfeit of gold.* The collection exhibited by the banks and mining companies of Victoria, was gorgeous, and, at the same time, highly instructive. It was very well arranged in an ornamental case. Specimens of gold were found in the departments of Canada, Costa Rica, Venezuela, &c. ; but the Ural did not appear to be represented. The large and beautiful water-colour drawings and the well-executed photographs of the "diggings" and the gold mining operations which adorned the department of Victoria possessed extraordinary interest. The "cradles" used in gold-washing might also be seen in this department. But there is gold in England—at least, in Wales. Auriferous ores from the Clogau mine, near Dolgelly, have been mentioned. This mine is, undoubtedly, a great success : a short time ago, with an expenditure of about 30*l.*, not less than 800*l.* worth of gold was obtained !

A series illustrative of the extraction of gold by chlorine water from the residue obtained at the arsenic works at Reichenstein, in Silesia, was exhibited in the Zollverein department. The application of chlorine for this purpose was first suggested at the British Association in 1848, and a paper was published on the subject in the *Philosophical Magazine* in 1850. It was first carried out practically by the late distinguished Professor Plattner. We know positively that this application of chlorine, whether employed as chlorine water or in the form of hypochlorites, has been notorious during many years, and that for some time it has been actually in operation at Swansea on a large scale. Yet we learn that a patent has just been granted for its use in England !— *Abridged from the Times.*

* The gilded pyramid facing the entrance under the Eastern Dome, is stated to have been an exact measure of the bulk of all the gold hitherto extracted in Australia; and though the conception was ingenious, its realization in the form of a pyramid was a failure.

Clays have been classified by Brogniart, into *fire-proof, fusible, calcareous,* and *ferruginous.* The samples comprised porcelain clays from the granite formations of Cornwall and Dartmoor; the Teignmouth pipe, or potter's, clay; the China-stone of St. Austell; the potter's clay of Poole and Wareham; the fire-clays, including the Stourbridge; and others. Clay and terra-cotta manufactures were represented chiefly by fire-bricks and retorts for various purposes. Mr. Walcott's retort-beds are believed to have an advantage of economy in the arrangement for returning the heat, absorbed by the mass of the brick-work, into the furnace to intensify combustion. The retorts are built three or four in a tier, with heat passages between; and are heated by one fire, the temperature being uniform.

There were specimens from the millstone grit in the form of millstones, and from the "Farewell Rock" of Dean Forest; Buhr stones, French, dexterously put together in England; sandstones, and flags; dolomites; oolites; and limestones, including the hydraulic, lias, and others.

The collection of different kinds of Stone exhibited by Mr. S. Tricket showed that a great variety of stone is brought to the London market. Oolite building-stone from the Little Casterton Quarry, near Stamford, was exhibited by Mr. O. N. Simpson. The Ancaster stone was shown in the form of a font, by Mr. John Wilson, of Grantham, who notes that the material has been in good preservation in buildings (of course not in London) four hundred years.

There was a good specimen of York Landing from Summerley's quarry at Idle, near Leeds. It would measure about 13 feet 4 inches by 7 feet, and 4 inches thick. Of Greaves's blue-lias lime from Stratford-on-Avon, favourable opinions were quoted from Mr. E. Smith, of Woolwich Dockyard; Mr. John Roe; Mr. J. Brown, of Birkenhead, who speaks of its value in setting masonry where exposed to a strong current; from Mr. T. Wicksteed, who used it at the East London Waterworks, in one part of the lime to eight of gravel; by the late Mr. Brunel and the resident engineers of the Great Western Railway, and others.

Grey Granites, in slab and column, well-worked and polished, were exhibited by W. and J. Freeman. The Cheesewring Granite Company also exhibited their material; and good specimens of grey granite were sent from the Craignair Quarries. Mr. A. Macdonald, of Aberdeen, also showed grey, red, blue, and pink granites: one column had the *frusta* of the shaft so well put together that the joints were hardly perceptible. Polished red Granite was also exhibited by the Ross of Mull Granite Company; there were also Granites from Ireland. A collection of rose-coloured granite, and of serpentine, were shown in the Swedish division. A fluted column, a candelabrum, a tripod, and other articles in blue-grey jasper, of good workmanship, were exhibited in the Russian department. M. Hermann, who lately erected the Brittany Granite fountain in the Champs Elysées, is said to work granite porphyry and jasper, by the aid of a newly-discovered black diamond. His vases of jasper of Savoy, with bronze ornaments, are noteworthy as works of art.

The Lizard Serpentine Company showed a chimney-piece, moulded and coped slab, and a font for Uppingham Church, of this beautiful material. Chimney-pieces, of Devonshire marbles, red and green, were shown by J. C. Stark, of Torquay. The grey fossil marble of Galway, and a marble from the Isle of Man, were also exhibited; as were the Connemara green and black marble. The Derbyshire marbles were poorly represented. Mr. Birley, of Ashford, exhibited a pillar table, inlaid, and elaborately ornamented with leaves, flowers and fruit, birds and butterflies—price 300 guineas.

Slate was shown in plain slabs, roofing forms, and decorated, that is, enamelled. The Llangollen Slab and Slate Company exhibited slabs of great size and good quality, 16 feet and 20 feet in length. The Rhiwbryfdir Slate Company showed that a block (18 inches by 10 inches) which is an inch and a half thick, may be split and dressed into 39 slates; and that out of a block (20 inches by 10 inches) half an inch thick, 8 slates can be sawn, the waste in such case being hardly perceptible. A model of a Slate-dressing machine, consisting of knife-edges, placed obliquely on a revolving drum, so as to work like the down-cut of a carpenter's saw, was exhibited by one of the Port-Madoc contributors, Mr. J. W. Greaves; and the Company there, above named, seem to have a machine that will dress 12,000 to 15,000 slates *per diem*, accurately and completely. The slate ridges and hips of Messrs. R. Williams and Co. also are shown.—*From the Builder.*

GRAPHITE FROM SIBERIA.

M. Alibert exhibited in the Russian portion of the nave blocks of Graphite or Plumbago, from an extensive bed recently discovered in Siberia. It takes so high a polish as to be mistaken for steel. The material, so highly prized for making lead pencils, is but rarely found in large quantities, and for many years the celebrated mine at Borrowdale was the chief source from which the best supplies were obtained. At one time the price paid for the plumbago from this mine was 2*l.* 5*s.* per lb., and as much as 100,000*l.* has been realized from it in one year; but for some time past—notwithstanding that it has been worked very sparingly—the supply has run short, and it is believed that the vein is practically all but exhausted.[*] In travelling through Eastern Siberia M. Alibert found some traces of this mineral in a remarkably pure state, and, knowing its value and importance, he set himself

---

[*] Messrs. Brockedon have replied to this statement in the *Times*, the journal wherein it originally appeared. They state that they have many tons of the finest Cumberland lead in store, from which the pencil-makers are supplied from time to time. This is the only plumbago, or pure graphite, that will rub out with india-rubber. The Siberian graphite, Messrs. Brockedon assure us, is as difficult to rub out as black chalk.

to work to search for the vein, which he felt satisfied must be in the neighbourhood. For fifteen years, at considerable expense, he persevered, and was at last rewarded by arriving at a bed of graphite. Geologists of all countries who have examined the samples shown speak highly of its quality—and it can be used in the construction of pencils without any of those elaborate processes to which inferior lead has to be subjected. The great drawback of the mine is its distance from those civilized portions of the world where lead pencils are much used, for it is situated not far from the Russian frontier of China, on the summit of the Mountain of Batougol, a spur of the chain of Saian. Even the most unscientific observer can form some idea of the quality of the graphite from the ease with which it is carved into all sorts of shapes. Besides several handsome blocks, which exhibit it pretty nearly in its raw state, M. Alibert showed some elegant busts, and half-a-dozen trophies of the material of various designs. These carvings—sculptures, we might almost call them—have all been executed by the Siberian peasants who work in the mines, and show no mean skill, while the clearness of the outlines and the smoothness of surface speak highly for the material with which they have worked. Other specimens of graphite, from a different part of Siberia, were also exhibited in the Russian Court, but the quality was very inferior; and in the gallery above were samples of graphite from Norway, Sicily, the East Indies, Malaga, Cumberland, and other places.

M. Alibert, among his Souvenirs of Siberia, exhibited a large mass of Nephrite, a mineral substance closely resembling malachite in appearance, but which has, in reality, a greater affinity to jade. In some respects it is superior to both, for it works up much more readily, and in small pieces has a transparent brilliancy which both those minerals lack. The mass which M. Alibert exhibited was 1280 lb. in weight, and he valued it at 1600*l*.

MINERAL WEALTH OF FRANCE.

The French Juries for the admission of specimens to the Exhibition, have indicated as amongst improvements in the course of the past ten years, in the extraction and fabrication of the products of this Class, the following : 1. The development given to the production of coal, and the persevering efforts made in different localities to discover and realize the value of new beds of combustible material; 2. The various *perfectionments* in the sinking of pits through the most difficult water-bearing strata, in the machinery of extraction and ventilation, and in the *exploitation* of thick beds of coal; and the processes for the agglomeration of small coal; 3. The development of the *exploitation* of pyrites of iron and copper for the fabrication of sulphuric acid; 4. Increase in the extraction of *kaolin*, and also in the manufacture of cements and hydraulic limes; 5. A notable augmentation in the quantity of wrought and cast iron produced; the use of hot-air become almost general in the high furnaces; utilization more and more frequent, of the gas and heat otherwise lost, in reverberatory and other forms of furnace; and the improvements, numerous and varied, in the rollers for the fabrication of special forms and dimensions of wrought iron; 6. The more active search for manganesic and spathose minerals for the fabrication of cast iron, using wood; and the tendency of this special fabrication to develope itself; 7. Increase in the fabrication of puddled, cast, and other steel, from cast iron, by new processes, with the aid of wood of the locality,—methods of which the use extends more and more every day; 8. A certain amount of progress in the treatment of the minerals of lead and copper, and in the elaboration of those metals; and 9. The creation in France of the production of aluminium, and the remarkable progress in the manufacture of a multitude of objects of this metal and its alloys; and the perfection of the treatment of the mineral of platinum, and in the fabrication of objects in which the metal is used.

The French Geological Maps of France were numerous and important. Among the more remarkable was an atlas of twelve sheets, forming a map of the ancient principality of Dombes in the department of the Ain, a curious district of about 100,000 hectares, of which area, more than one-sixth has been converted into fish-ponds, which are in number about 1600, and are emptied every two years to obtain the fish, and to be planted for cereals, and afterwards again filled with water and stocked with young fish. The insufficiency of the population and other causes, led to the method of cultivation. The method has, however, as might have been expected, been most injurious to health in the district. An instalment was shown of a great work, that of ascertaining the levels of principal spots over the whole of France continental, was suggested in 1857, by Mr Bourdaloue, who had already completed a similar work for the department of the Cher. The object is to render more easy and certain the operations having relation to new routes, water-courses, drainage, and irrigation. Great detail and exactness therefore were required, which would involve much expense. The first part of the undertaking, comprising the fixing the principal points, was commenced at the end of September, 1857, and will be finished before the end of the present year.

Those who would understand something relating to the climate and products of France, should examine the maps of the three regions, the wheat, wine of exportation, and silk producing, and the specimens of the principal types of animals and birds, useful or considered hurtful, belonging to those regions, and the botanical and geological collections, which are exhibited by Messrs. Éloffe, of Paris.—*Abridged from the Builder.*

MINERALS OF THE ZOLLVEREIN.

This collection, formed under the direction of Von Dechen, of Bonn, and arranged by Dr. Hermann Wedding, of Berlin, contains almost every known description of iron ore—namely, magnetic oxide, specular ore, red and brown hæmatite, spathose carbonate, and argillaceous ore, including black-band ; and even bog iron ore is not absent. The specimens, which are large and well-selected, are arranged in ascending geological order, and nearly every member of the series has its representative. Thus, ores are shown from igneous and metamorphic rocks, and the following formations :—The Devonian, the carboniferous, the new red sandstone, the magnesian limestone, the trias, the lias, the oolite, the wealden, the cretaceous, and the tertiaries. The gems are the magnificent spathose carbonates from Siegen. The upper Devonian beds of Westphalia and Nassau have been found very productive of red ores of good quality ; and a series of these forms an important part of the general collection. Complete information will be found in the special catalogue concerning the mode of occurrence, and the localities of all these ores. We would direct attention to the Nos. 620, 621, 622 of this catalogue, as illustrative of a process for converting the fine powder of a brown iron ore into compact masses suitable for smelting. The powder is separated by washing with water in the state of mud, which is left to consolidate sufficiently in shallow pits, and is then made into bricks ; these are dried and burnt, and so rendered fit for smelting.

CHEMICAL SUBSTANCES AND PHARMACEUTICAL PROCESSES.

The display of Chemicals in the Exhibition was the finest yet collected together. Not only were the exhibitors more numerous than in 1851, but there were more first-class names on the list, hardly one manufacturer of eminence being absent. In our leading branches of Chemical Manufactures the show was wonderfully good. The specimens of alkalies, alum, and the coal-tar dyes generally, constituted the great bulk of the Exhibition. Looking hastily through the range of cases, we met the familiar names of Allhusen and Co., Chance, brothers, the Jarrow Chemical Company, Hutchinson and Earl, Musspratt, the Walker Alkali Company, Gaskell, Deacon, and Co., and several others equally famous in the manufacture of alkali. The samples sent by these firms were fine in the extreme, some of the soda crystals being almost perfect in form. When all are so good it would be invidious to choose ; but the samples of mono and bicarbonate, contributed by Hutchinson and Earl, and Gaskell, Deacon and Co., appear to be as near perfection as they possibly can be. Mr. Peter Spence sent a splendid cone of alum, weighing nearly five tons. A hole has been cut in the side in order to render the interior visible. Another cone of equal size and excellence was contributed by the Metropolitan Alum Company. A very fine but small crystal of alum, sent by Bray and Thompson, attracted great notice. In Coal-tar Dyes, Messrs. Perkin were of course foremost. Their collection, illustrative of the manufacture of Mauve, was very complete. They were almost eclipsed in colour, although not in excellence, by Simpson, Maule, and Nicholson, who exhibited a magnificent crown of crystallised Acetate of Rosaniline, which presents the most dazzling appearance. In their wake followed Roberts, Dale, and Co. (who exhibited some fine samples of oxalic acid prepared from saw-dust), Rumney, Holliday, Dawson, Judson, Allen, and several others. Indigo and the lichen dyes were also well represented; the collections of Haworth and Brook, Pincoff, Wood and Bedford, Marshall and Sons, B. Smith and Son, and Haas, being especially good. The collections of specimens illustrating the improvements made in Dyeing and Calico-printing since 1851, formed by Mr. R. Rumney, afforded a wonderful proof of the activity displayed in this branch of Chemical manufactures during the last eleven years. It included the very fine collection of Madder products formed by Dr. Schunck, and exhibited by him before the British Association at Manchester last year. Other Chemical manufactures were well shown; some sulphate of copper in gigantic crystals, by Buck and Co., of Manchester; a sulphate of iron crown, by Buckley's trustees; excellent specimens of prussiates, by the Hurtley and Campric Alum Company; bichromate, by White and Co.; and prussiates by Bramwell and Co.,—were extremely fine. In fine and rare chemicals, Huskisson's iodides, Morson's lithia and nickel salts, Foot and Co's acids, the iodine products by Ward and Co., and a series of interesting products by Hopkin and Williams, were only a few of the fine displays in this branch. Dr. Stenhouse, Dr. Müller, and Mr. Church contributed interesting products, chiefly discovered by themselves, the specimens of orceine and nitrotheine in the collection of Dr. Stenhouse being wonderfully pure and perfect. Mr. Crookes exhibited the new element, Thallium, and several of its compounds. A series of Bile products, by Bullock and Reynolds, was likewise very fine. Chemical colours and pigments received adequate representation at the hands of Windsor and Newton, who sent over 1,000*l.* worth of real ultramarine ; J. W. Smith, whose Magenta lake is extremely beautiful, and a number of others. Bailey exhibited some very fine porcelain colours, and Emery and Co.'s case of specimens of these materials was a perfect gem in the taste shown in its arrangement. Wilkinson and Heyward, Mandor Brothers, Wallis Brothers, and Rea, send some fine samples of gums and varnishes. Lucifer matches were well represented by five or six of the first houses in the trade ; and the familiar names of Everett, Day and Martin, and several others, were here in all their sable glories. Laundry Starch was contributed by nine or ten well-known houses, amongst whom may be mentioned Orlando Jones and Co., J. and J. Colman, S. Berger and Co., Broomhall, Wotherspoon, Rickett, Stiff and Fry, and many more.

One of the great features in the class was the splendid collection of Drugs formed by the Pharmaceutical Society, which filled one of the finest cases in the whole Building. The series of

Cinchona products by Howard and Sons, could hardly have been produced by any other house. A magnificent mass of crystals of Codeine, measuring eighteen or twenty inches in diameter, and worth upwards of 200l., was exhibited by Macfarlane and Co., who also contributed some splendid specimens of anarcotine, morphia and its salts, sulphate of berberine, narceine, and other opium products. The trophy—which consists of a fine mass of alum crystals, surmounted and surrounded by crystals of prussiate, bichromate, sulphate of copper, and other chemicals, piled in artistic forms—was very effective.—*Chemical News.*

Superb crystals of Red and Yellow Prussiate of Potash, were shown by the Hurlet and Campsie Alum Company, and Bramwell and Company. Prussiate of Potash fills a very important place in our manufactures. It is made from such apparently worthless materials as rotten wool, rags, hoofs, horn waste, or any other azotized organic matters. These are mixed with the impure carbonate of potash and iron filings, and, whilst being stirred with an iron rod, submitted to a red heat in close iron vessels, the whole is afterwards treated with hot water, filtered and evaporated, when crystals are obtained of ferrocyanide of potassium. By passing chlorine gas through a solution of the ferrocyanide, the ferrid cyanide is formed, or by another process, too elaborate to describe here, cyanide of potassium is the resulting product so much used in electro-plating, gilding, and photography. Again, from ferrocyanide of potassium, or the yellow prussiate of potash and sulphuric acid, the deadly hydrocyanic or prussic acid is formed; and Prussian blue is an admixture of this same substance with a salt of iron.

A new product, for the first time, was exhibited—the Silicate of Alumina—a beautiful crystalline substance resembling glass. It is formed by mixing two alkaline solutions of silica and alumina; from the great affinity of the alumina for the silica, a union is formed between them of a most permanent character. The bases in the mixed solutions, however, showing a most energetic action in strong solutions, when diluted with water have that action so retarded that they remain in the form of a liquid for some hours, admitting of many useful applications, such as the preserving of stone by induration, and the manufacture of artificial stones, which processes were exemplified.

White Wine Vinegar is obtained, in the form of Acetic Acid, from the smaller branches of the oak and other hard woods, and it is now also obtained from—sawdust. This dust now finds itself entering the mouth of a long retort through a hopper, is coaxed forward by an endless screw occupying the whole diameter of the retort, and brought under a heat that implies *destructive* distillation, thus parting with its volatile products, and leaving the retort at the far end fairly exhausted, whilst assuming its sombre carbonaceous form, it becomes the parent of the acetates, whose names are legion, and are of so great a commercial value amongst dyers, as also in chemistry and pharmacy.

Cundy, of Battersea, exhibited the Permanganate of Potash, a most powerful and innocuous deodorizer and disinfectant : its oxidizing powers are beautifully shown by treating pure and impure water; with a small quantity of the fluid, each water may be perfectly pellucid or clear ; but if organic matter be in solution, it will instantaneously be oxidized and precipitated as a powder to the bottom, leaving the water colourless ; but if nothing of the kind exists in the water, it remains tinged with the pink colour of the fluid, which retains its normal condition.—*Mechanics' Magazine.*

Paraffine was well illustrated.—In the Great Exhibition of 1851 Mr. James Young exhibited specimens of Paraffine and Paraffine Oil, and one candle, the product of the distillation of coal. Soon after, he and his partners established a manufactory at Bathgate, near Edinburgh, which, we are informed, has grown to be among the largest chemical works in the world. Evidences of this appeared in the huge blocks and other specimens of paraffine now exhibited by Mr. Young. Paraffine was first obtained about 1830 by Reichenbach, by the destructive distillation of wood and peat. Mr. Young has been fortunate enough to make what Liebig some years ago said would be one of the greatest discoveries of the age—viz., the condensation of coal gas into a white, hard, dry, solid, colourless, odourless substance, portable, and capable of being placed upon a candlestick or burnt on a lamp. Mr. Young's paraffine oil will not take fire at common temperature, and is therefore much safer for household use than the numerous oils which bear that name now so largely sold.

Among the rare Chemicals shown by Mr. Church were Picric, Tuberic, and other acids, and their salts ; and Mr. Crisp's remarkable Bile products. Huskisson's specimens of Iodine and Iodides were there in beautiful crystalline forms : the iodide of arsenic was very elegant ; and some of the cubes of the iodide of potassium were nearly $1\frac{1}{4}$ inch in the side : the hollow truncated crystals of the iodide of ammonium, and a fine artificial crystal of sulphur, much interested students in crystallography. Foot and Co., of Battersea, exhibited a complete series of products illustrating the manufacture of Acetic Acid and its compounds, from the wood upwards : their specimen of glacial acetic acid was the only one which preserved its solidity despite the heat. An example of the exhaustive method of modern chemistry was given by Mr. J. Lewis, of Swansea, who, by the destructive distillation of various hard woods, not of the fir tribe, obtains tar, naphtha, charcoal, and acetate of soda, of which last he exhibited specimens.

Chemistry in its relation to Medicine was represented chiefly in the large cases of the Pharmaceutical Society, containing a systematic collection of the materials of the British Pharmacopœia. The Ethers (including the great anæsthetic, Chloroform) exhibited by Duncan, Flockart, and Co., of Edinburgh, were of especial interest ; as was the series of elegant crystals of various medicinal preparations set forth in the case of Bullock and Reynolds. The case of Messrs. Howard exhibited salts of the Alkaloids of great beauty, fine large crystals of Chlorate of Potash and Carbonate of

Soda, specimens of Calomel, &c., in its various conditions; then Hopkins and Williams showed fine specimens of pyrogallic acid, cyanide of potassium, caffeine, aconitine, &c., and also the rare salts of lithia; and Mr. Halle's salts of strychnine and quinine were clean and well crystallised. The specimens of narceine exhibited by Messrs. Morson were considered unique: and their Japanese purified peppermint and crystallised citrate of lithia were very remarkable.

In regard to Pigments we can only refer to the gorgeous collections of Windsor and Newton, Wilkinson and Heywood, and others too numerous to specify, as proving the high character maintained by British manufacturers. As a novelty we may notice that Gaskell and Deacon exhibited an artificial Ultramarine made by calcining together certain proportions of China clay, sulphate and carbonate of soda, sulphur and carbon, and specimens of vermilion of a very fine tone.

In connexion with Pigments we may here notice C. W. Vincent's specimens of Varnishes prepared by steam-heat, which secures uniformity of action on the part of the substances used as driers, and gives the power of regulating the consistency of the varnish itself with great certainty. These varnishes are said to possess great drying powers, and in special cases have permitted as many as twelve separate printings in as many hours. Samples of Printing Inks made from them, and several of the coloured supplements of the *Illustrated London News* in which they have been employed, were also exhibited.

Among the chemicals used in manufactures are the various forms of Borax and Boracic Acid. The obtaining them from the volcanic fumaroles in the lagoons of Tuscany has become a great source of wealth, through the enterprise of Count Larderel. Very interesting specimens of them were sent by Mr. E. Wood, of Stoke-on-Trent.

As an example of practical application of pure chemistry we must refer to Professor B. C. Brodie's specimens of Graphite or Plumbago, chemically disintegrated and purified by means of sulphuric acid and chlorate of potash, in an iron vessel. His researches in connexion with this substance, are well known to chemists. In relation to the now important manufacture of Lucifers, were the beautiful specimens of crystals of chlorate of potash, of amorphous phosphorus, &c., contributed by Albright and Wilson. By Schrötter's process, made known in 1851, common phosphorus is deprived of the properties which prove so injurious to lucifer makers, by causing frightful disease of the jaws and facial bones. We regret that this form of phosphorus has not yet come into universal application. Of the numerous specimens of Soaps, perhaps the most interesting was that exhibited by the firm of Gossage. It is a compound soap, the invention of Mr. Wm. Gossage, of Warrington, and made from ordinary fats, saponified by means of silicate of soda. It is stated that it can be supplied at the rate of 28*l.* per ton. The Gossages also exhibited some interesting specimens illustrating the manufacture of Soluble Glass.

Among the most extraordinary substances shown was a new material, called "Parksine," from the name of its discoverer—the product of a mixture of chloroform and castor oil, which produces a substance as hard as horn, but as flexible as leather—capable of being cast or stamped, painted, dyed, or carved, and which, above all, can be produced, in any quantity, at a lower price than gutta percha.

Here may be mentioned the principal improvements during the past ten years in France, in Chemicals and Pharmaceutical Products and Perfumery, including Colours. Such improvements are the use, already alluded to, of pyrites in place of sulphur, which has caused reduction in the price of sulphuric acid; the extension of the indigenous production of potash by the calcination of the residues of the distillation of beet-root juice; and the preparation of the *potasse du suint*; the development, in the process of extraction from the waters of salt-marshes, of the sulphate of soda and the salts of manganese which are contained in them; the improvements in the production of ammonia, and its salts, from the condensed fluid collected during distillation of coal; the development of the industries of the distillation of coal-tar, and the preparation of benzine and certain acids; the application, more and more frequent, of the silicates of soda and potash, to the conservation of monuments and sculpture; the new industry of the salts of alumina with a soda-base, and of pure alumina; the experiments for the industrial production of the prussiates and ammoniacal salts by ammonia and carbonate of barytes; increase of the production of pyroligneous acids and its compounds; development given to the fabrication of the vegetable alkaloids; extension in the manufacture of white lead, and artificial ultramarine; introduction of the yellow, red, violet, and blue colouring matters, resulting from the transformations of aniline; and the use of sulphuret of carbon for the extraction of fatty substances and perfumes.

COAL-TAR AND LICHEN DYES.

Strange and curious were the illustrations exhibited of the Coal Tar Dyes, and their wonderful effects already mentioned. Coal-tar is the basis of all the new colours we have lately got, such as Mauve and Magenta, and this field of chemical research seems boundless in extent. Thus, coal-tar is gradually refined upon and improved till the dirty mass becomes a liquid of glowing tints, the dye of which is shown by exquisite silks, feathers, and moiré antiques, tinted of the now so fashionable colours. Both these colours were discovered in England and by English chemists. Perkin, in endeavouring to make artificial quinine, found Mauve; and almost at the same time Mr. Nicholson, of the firm of Simpson and Maule, discovered Magenta. The way in which the colour is produced may be told in a few words. Coal-tar, when distilled, yields a colourless fluid called Benzole, much used for removing grease-stains from silk or cloth. This when mixed with nitric acid forms nitro-benzole, which when again distilled with acetic acid and iron filings forms those exquisite green crystallizations, called aniline. This when distilled again with different salts produces dyes of different colours, such as Mauve and Magenta ; and thus the coal-tar, which was of such little value that it almost puzzled gas factories to get rid of it, has become the basis of a most important manufacture. Aniline was but a few years ago so rare as to be known among chemists almost only by name. Now it is an article of commerce. A few grains of it suffice to dye many yards of fabric, and it is well that it has this power, for two gallons of coal-tar only yield ten grains of aniline. One circular block of aniline about twenty inches high by nine inches wide was shown which was the whole product of no less than 2000 tons of coal. This specimen is sufficient to dye 300 miles of silk fabric. Where two quantities are given it is easy to find a third. With the *data* which we have stated, therefore, as to two gallons of coal-tar yielding ten grains of aniline, and the product of 2000 tons of coal being capable of dyeing 300 miles of silk, any lady of a calculating turn of mind can reckon to a bushel the precise amount of coal consumed to colonr the mauve dress in which she is attired. A grain of the aniline dissolved in water tinges it at once of that reddish violet, the delicate colour of which can only be compared to the brightness of a flash of electricity.

Near these were shown the products of the Lichen Dyes, the beautiful blues and purples which are made from the common mosses and lichens. This was accidentally discovered, for the mosses have to undergo a particularly offensive course of treatment before they yield their tints. Where the specimens of the mosses used were shown, the fabrics dyed with their colours were displayed above them, so that, except in witnessing the actual process, the whole *modus operandi* was told to the visitor clearly enough. Near these were shown some specimens of indigo and indigo dyes, exhibited by Heyworth and Brooke ; while round about were displayed all the wonderful forms of crystallization, from masses of alum as big as grottos, and hollowed out inside with clusters of glittering prisms, down to groups of crystals of soda, of salt, and saltpetre. Some of the single block crystals of alum weighed from five to seven tons.—*Abridged from the Times.*

SUBSTANCES USED FOR FOOD.

The collection of these articles was numerous and considered very interesting. For the sugar-refiner there were Sugars of every kind, raw and manufactured, from all parts of the world, and almost from all substances known. In one case was a series of beautifully crystallized specimens of sugar from sugar-cane, beet, maple, liquorice, gelatine, milk, and fat ; also sugar from grapes, from starch, from ergot of rye, from manna, and "from flesh." Other curious sugars were likewise shown, including one of crystals made from sweet-pea.

Sugar, long considered a neutral substance without congeners, has, in consequence of chemical research, become the parent of a numerous and increasing family. Fourteen specimens were exhibited by Darby and Gosden, including not only beautiful forms of cane and grape-sugar, but also sugars derived from acorns, &c., muscular fibre, beets, and other animal and vegetable substances.

Mr. Hallett exhibited his wonderful examples of "Pedigree Wheat." He has applied to the growth of wheat the rules which every stockbreeder in the country knows—namely, that from the largest and best animals the largest and best progeny may be expected, and that, therefore, the agriculturist should proceed to develope the productive powers of wheat as if it were altogether a new species of cereal which he was trying to bring to perfection for the first time. Mr. Hallett, in 1857, planted only from ears 4½ inches long, containing 47 grains. In 1858 his finest ear was 6¼ inches long, containing 79 grains, and there were 10 ears from the finest plant. In 1860 the ears were imperfect, from the wet season, but they appear only to have reserved and husbanded their productiveness for a more auspicious occasion, as in 1861 the finest ear was no less than 8¾ inches long, containing 123 grains, and the number of ears in the finest single plant had risen from the starting number of 10 in 1857 to 52 in 1861. The various ears and their dates of sowing were shown.

Among the Articles of Food,—Port, sherry, claret, champagne, and brandy were openly exhibited as of British manufacture, with Havannah and other "foreign" cigars. The great Ale and Beer brewers alike exhibited. Bass, Guinness, Salt, &c., all were here, save Allsopp, who was wisely content with the practical exhibition of his manufacture at the refreshment counters in the Building, where it was consumed at the rate of some twenty barrels a-day. Huntly and Palmer erected a little temple case of Biscuits of every form and kind that were ever eaten; and not far from this were labelled specimens of cheap Confectionery.

Nor was the display confined to articles merely eatable or pleasing to the palate. There probably never was such a collection of Poisons brought together before under one roof, from the drug that kills instantaneously up to the British port that takes years to accomplish its deadly purpose. They were all here, and some in such attractive forms as crystals grouped like rare and costly gems, massive deposits of golden or ruby looking prisms, one grain of which would almost suffice to destroy life; piles of soft snowy crystals of caustic soda.

In Alum manufacture were some fine crystals, contributed by the Metropolitan Alum Company of Bow; very perfect specimens of the crystals of alum, magnesia, and copper, exhibited by Mr. F. Baker; and a great alum cone sent by Mr. Spence, of Manchester, who has devised a process whereby he is able to produce sixty-five tons of ammonia alum from fifty tons of coal shale; also alum specimens, including red and yellow prussiate, contributed by Messrs. Wilson, of the Hurlet Works, near Glasgow. A fine column of rock salt, by gradually dissolving, visibly manifested its remarkable power of absorbing moisture from the atmosphere: it was exhibited by the Salt Chamber of Northwich, Cheshire.

Mr. Vickars showed a case containing not only every kind of Isinglass as white as the purest snow, but the same material shown for the first time in what may be termed artistic castings, such as the leaves, tendrils and fruit of the vine as perfect as nature itself in everything but their wonderful clearness of colour. Fortnum and Mason exhibited a perfect collection of dried and preserved fruits.

Valuable improvements have been made in the Preservation of Meat and other articles of diet. Jones and Trevithick exhibited a raw leg of mutton and other meats, which appeared perfectly fresh after a long interval of time. In their process the meat is introduced into a tin vessel, the air is exhausted, and a small quantity of sulphurous acid gas is introduced, which is quickly absorbed by the juice of the meat. Nitrogen (or azote), which is incapable of exerting any putrefactive action on it, is then permitted to enter the vacuum, and the can is sealed. Should this process prove successful a great step will be gained. Mr. M'Call exhibited meats preserved in the old method—viz., expulsion of the air by boiling. The speciality of his process consists in a plan for the absorption of any oxygen remaining in the case. In the top of his can is a small capsule in which he places a button of fused hypo-sulphite of soda: this, when exposed, as the can is soldered, is supposed to take up any oxygen left in the vessel. The open case of beef appeared quite fresh.

The increasing demand for agricultural produce necessitates the application of Manure to restore to the ground the elements taken from it. Mr. Whitworth, of Bermondsey, has endeavoured to make still further use of Fish for this purpose, and exhibited specimens of his concentrated fish manure for cereal crops. Chemists of high reputation testify to the richness of this manure in soluble phosphates and nitrogenous substances.—*Abridged from the Times and Illustrated London News.*

INDIAN PRODUCTS.

Mr. M. C. Cooke, in the following paper, in *The Technologist*, characterizes the Indian collection as superior to that department in 1851; and interesting beyond the Exhibitions of either 1851 or 1855, from the closer association of India with the British Crown. We are taught by the recent Exhibition that India *can* supply us with cotton, tobacco, and tea, sufficient to compensate us for the deficiencies which events might occasion: what may be necessary to ensure such a supply does not fall within our province at this juncture to indicate. The fact that three hundred samples of tea were shown, and more than a hundred of cotton, with some tobacco, were features not to be forgotten in passing through the Indian collection. And of starchy products were two or three novelties. A kind of arrowroot from a plant growing wild in Cuttack is of very good quality. The manufacture has been but recently introduced into that province. This product, which is known in the bazaars under the name of *Palvoa*, is collected by the Sahars and made into cakes, or boiled with milk, and used as an article of food. The plant which produces it grows abundantly in the jungles. From Akyab, another kind of arrowroot was sent, which is known under the native name of *Rembowah*. It is said to be prepared from a root called Pemban Oo, which is obtainable in large quantities, and the cost of the article when manufactured would be about four rupees per maund.

From Chota Nagpore we had also a similar product, obtained from a wild jungle plant; and from Chittagong, "wild ginger starch." The wild ginger grows abundantly everywhere in Chittagong.

Behchandee is prepared by the Gonds, and is sold in the Bazaars of Jubbulpore. It is not an arrowroot, but bears some resemblance to it when pounded. The natives prepare it for food in a variety of ways, and use it on fast days. It is obtained from the stems of a jungle-plant, after being soaked in running water for several days.

The Elastic Gums contained some novelties. From Gorruckpore, four samples of caoutchouc were sent, stated to be obtained from sources new to commerce. From Chingleput, Dr. John Shortt contributed india-rubber, obtained from the Mudar plant (*Calotropis gigantea*), and also from the milk-hedge (*Euphorbia antiquorum*), and another species of Euphorbia (*E. tortilis*). Amongst the gutta-percha of the Malayan Peninsula was a substance greatly resembling it, called Gutta Terbole, and which is affirmed to be employed, not only as a substitute, but as an adulterant of the genuine article. What Gutta Gree Grip and Gutta Babee, from the same locality, may be, we have not yet had the opportunity of determining. Somewhat allied in its uses is the Buglar tree bark, from Chota Nagpore, where it is employed as a glue for joining wood.

Soluble gums and resins were similar to those exhibited on former occasions: Gum Kino, from Rangoon, probably the produce of *Pterocarpus Wallichii*, might be obtained in almost any quantity, the tree which yields it being one of the most abundant. Of Aleo-resin, the turpentine of *Pinus longifolio*, and wood-oils, are most important; of the latter, several kinds were exhibited. The Gurgun of Chittagong is obtained by cutting a hole in the tree, about three feet from the ground, and about four or five inches deep into the tree. The base is hollowed out to retain the oil. The hollow is cleared with fire, without which no oil exudes. After it is cleared the oil issues, and is removed as it accumulates. The oil is thus extracted year after year, and at times there are two or three holes in the same tree. The oil is allowed to settle when the clear part separates from the thicker portion. If a growing tree is cut down and cut in pieces, the oil exudes, and concretes on the stem and the ends of the pieces, very much like camphor, and with an aromatic odour. A tree yields from 250 to 400lbs yearly, and the same tree will yield for several years. This substance has been employed as a substitute for Balsam of Copaiba, and would be useful as a varnish. It can be had in any quantities, at ten rupees per maund.

In the Oil series, and amongst oil-seeds, were Nahor Oil, obtained from the seeds of *Mesua ferrea*, and the oils of *Aleurites triloba*, and *Rottlera tinctoria*. The curiosities in this section were the Oil of Cocoa-nut shells, and the veritable Oil of Macassar.

The Dye-stuffs attracted attention on account of the presence amongst them of the Roum dye of Assam, *Ruellia*-leaves; a series of illustrations of the green dye of Malda, with cloths dyed therewith; and a similar series illustrative of a new yellow dye, from the same locality, which can be obtained in any quantity. The flowers of *Trapa bispinosa* ; *Thitna* dye, from Akyab ; *Neepa* dye, of Burmah ; *Kamla Goondee*, of Cuttack ; *Jackwood*, of Akyab ; and *Mug* dye, of Chittagong ; were amongst the novelties in this section. A series of sixteen linches was contributed from Darjeeling, but these require testing before anything can be affirmed as to their tinctorial properties. Two or three new tanning substances were exhibited from Chittagong and elsewhere.

The stimulants, whether alcoholic or narcotic, were well represented: amongst the former were rice arrack, Mowha spirit, Mango whisky prepared from the Mango fruit, and cane-juice spirits. Amongst the latter, *Gunjah, Bang*, and varieties of *Churrus*, or hemp-resin. Full illustrations of the manufacture of opium, with specimens of the product, were shown; with *Bynee* seeds, used as a substitute for Betel-nuts ; Tobacco from a few localities, and other narcotics amongst the medicinal products.

The grains and pulses were more numerous than ever, and in connexion with these, Dr. Forbes Watson exhibited a series of the chief varieties, with the results of his analyses attached, showing the nutritive value of each.

Of woods there were from twelve to fifteen hundred specimens.

Amongst the curiosities of food, we had, in addition to the usual contribution of sharks' fins, birds' nests, trepang, agar-agar, &c., some potted fish gnapie, dried mushrooms from China, dried fungi, and other delicacies.

Here were also specimens of the principal soils of India—samples of iron ores, and various articles manufactured from them, and tin ores, gold washings, and all the principal minerals. The Government of India, the Madras Central Committee, and others contributed numerous samples of Cotton from different localities. Of the products of the Dacca looms there were many exquisite specimens, and the cases containing the magnificent shawls and gold-embroidered tissues were conspicuous from afar. The dazzling splendour of the gold and silver tissues of Kingcomb almost eclipsed at first sight the sober hues of the real cashmeres in a case hard by. From Bombay a native exhibitor, Bhimjee Byramjee sent some beautiful articles of carved furniture, including a grand pianoforte, which would bear comparison with the finest works of English manufacture. There were also other very remarkable specimens of carving in ivory, ebony, sandal, and other woods. Jung Bahadoor, the Rao of Kutch, the Maharajah of Ulwa, and other Indian princes contributed numerous articles of native jewellery and manufactures in gold and silver; and there was an entire case filled with the most elegant silver filagree-work.

The most suggestive, but least attractive, portion of the Indian display was at its entrance, where one of the great tests of a country's value was shown by a collection of its raw materials and natural products. Beyond these came its manufactures—native locks that would puzzle Hobbs to pick; cutlery from Salem that should astonish Sheffield. Beyond these were weapons damascened in gold, and then gold and silver work, and enamelled jewellery.

An Indian shawl is popularly supposed to be a mixture of gold and brilliant colours, while on to almost any and every scarf or shawl coming from the East has been tacked the name of "Cashmere." Those who wish to be learned in the matter of these exquisite fabrics, the manufacture of which it is to be feared is dying out, could, in the India Court, trace every step of the process; from the first rough groups of dirty hair and wool that are sheared from the shawl-goat, down to the cleaned wool and hair, the wool alone, the wool twisted, dyed, and woven at last into those wonderful patterns of sad colours which make the thick Cashmere shawl. Near these wonderful cases of textiles were shown a few specimens of a work, which, in its best examples, is almost peculiar to the natives of Goojerat. These were the steel objects inlaid with the arabesques in gold. Formerly it was almost entirely used for decorating armour, shields, and blades of weapons. Now none of these are made, and the natives confine the manufacture entirely to such things as paper-knives, caskets, jewel-boxes, &c. Some exquisite specimens of these were shown. In the same case with these was exhibited by Dr. Campbell a very curious collection of articles from Darjeeling and Thibet. Among others are the prayer cylinders—a common brass cylinder, filled with printed prayers, which the natives spin and turn round, and every revolution counts as so many prayers said. In some parts near Thibet, where the strictest Buddhism prevails, these prayer cylinders are made of great size, and turned by water power, so as to do the praying of the whole village in which it works without a moment's cessation. This easy method of invocation is so extensively practised by all the natives, that printing in Thibet is confined almost exclusively to the production of the innumerable prayers that are required by the people. The printing-blocks used for this purpose in Thibet and Darjeeling were shown in one of the cases. They are cut in coarse wooden blocks, and in workmanship are apparently on a par with what Caxton's first failures must have been.—*Abridged from the Times.*

Machinery.

RAILWAY PLANT.

LOCOMOTIVE ENGINES AND CARRIAGES.

Of Locomotive Engines there was a magnificent rank, eight or nine at least, with tenders attached, in complete working order,—brilliant with polished brass and iron and varnished paint. The London and North-Western, the Caledonian, and other railway companies, sent splendid specimens; as did the private builders, among which those by Sir W. Armstrong, and Sharp, Stewart, and Co., were the most conspicuous. Some of these engines were designed to attain the highest velocities with light loads; others had all the wheels small and coupled, and were intended to drag interminable trains of minerals at low speeds; and of those little handy engines now so common on the works of contractors and elsewhere there were numerous specimens. Mr. Ramsbottom exhibited an admirable invention for watering tenders of trains while at full speed. This was originally invented to facilitate still further the rapid progress of the Irish express train (better known as the Wild Irishman) between Holyhead and London. The plan simply consists of a sunk trough filled with water, laid at certain stations between the rails, and into which, as the engine approaches, a slanting, trumpet-shaped shoot is lowered, up which the velocity of the engine forces the water with such power as to fill the tender tanks in a single minute. Mr. Ramsbottom showed two engines and tenders, one full sized, as running on the North-Western Railway at present, and one a model, to run on a railway 80 feet long, with water trough between—to illustrate the invention. American engines were here with their hoarse whistles and balloon-shaped funnels; and here was Mr. Connell's Leviathan Express engine and tender, weighing 35 tons net weight, side by side with the Neath Abbey Ironworks locomotive, which only weighs 10 tons. The great facilities of the 5½-feet gauge in giving space to engineers to proportion locomotives properly were exemplified by the engines of Beyer, Peacock, and Co. for India; the engines of Sharp, Stewart, and Co. for Ireland; and the engines of the Armstrongs for the Spanish railways. Every possible variety of permanent way, with all the newest and most improved modes of fastening, was shown. The Great Northern (of France) Railway Company sent a monster Locomotive Engine, which has its boilers, cylinders, water-tank, and coal-bunk built up one above another to such a height that the wonder is how it can pass under an ordinary bridge. Its chimney, instead of standing straight upright, as is the manner with ordinary locomotives, has to be curled over its back like an elephant's trunk. It is intended for heavy traffic only, and its wheels are comparatively so small that probably no very great speed could be got out of it. Among other improvements it is fitted with a superheating apparatus. Opposite to it were two very handsome composite railway carriages. The saloon carriage shown in the Belgian department, which comprises a covered platform in which passengers may walk about and smoke at their ease, is no doubt a very pleasant innovation, though hardly calculated for travelling where, as on most of the Belgian lines, the dust is such a nuisance.

Mr. Ashbury, of Manchester, exhibited the raw materials, wood, pig-iron, copper, tin, lead, pigments, oils, &c., requisite to make one complete Railway Waggon, side by side with the finished waggon itself. This last waggon was constructed and completed from precise duplicates of the raw materials shown, in 12 hours.

Mr. Yarrow exhibited a simple but ingenious Steam-carriage for common roads, intended to carry 12 passengers, and the engines, which are connected with the driving axle, are about four-horse power, and are placed outside the framing. There are two propelling wheels, and the driver sits in the middle of the front seat, with the steering wheel before him and the reversing lever at his right, which give him control over the direction and speed of the carriage. The boiler is at the back of the tank under the seats. Under favourable circumstances a speed of from 18 to 20 miles an hour, it is said, has been obtained with the carriage, and no doubt it might be made particularly useful for working in conjunction with railways in carrying passengers between the stations and small towns in the neighbourhood of the line.—*Abridged from the Times.*

WHEEL CARRIAGES.

The Carriages not connected with rail or tram roads included every variety of vehicle, from a Bath chair to a velocipede, and from a four-in-hand to a perambulator or a self-propelling bathing-machine. There were barouches, landaus, single and double broughams, Eugenies, sociables, and phaetons, broughams under 7 cwt.; Stanhopes, phaetons, waggonettes, "diorophas," and one comprehensive vehicle which was "a barouche, sociable, coach, and landau" all in one. Among the novelties was a cart to form either a cart or sleigh; and the model of a plan for the prevention of all accidents to carters. Mr. Evans, of Liverpool, showed an improved Hansom cab, to accommodate two persons; and a very handsome Fitzroy phaeton came from Northampton, constructed with malleable steel and wheels of hickory. Mr. Mulliner, of Leamington, sent a four-wheel dog-cart, which folded open and formed a waggonette. Shillibeer exhibited an improved omnibus, described as a *vis-à-vis* omnibus, with separate seats inside, the outside seats on the roof and box being reached from the interior. Starey, of Nottingham, showed a landau with flat fall of head, elastic springs and noiseless wheels in chain tires. Vezey, of Long-acre, sent a carriage with noiseless springs in india-rubber bearings.

TRACTION ENGINES.

Bray's Traction Engine, considering its great capabilities, is a remarkably compact and simple piece of locomotive machinery. A specimen exhibited was built at the factory of the Company, by order of the Government, for Woolwich Dockyard. It combines many improvements upon the earlier contrivances for the purpose of transporting heavy weights by steam-power; but the feathering principle of the wheels, as originally introduced by Mr. Bray, is retained. This principle consists in the circumference of the wheel having a a number of small apertures through it. These apertures are the media which allow of the protrusion and withdrawal, by means of an eccentric, of a series of blades, or teeth. The teeth may be adjusted to the nature of the soil, or paving, over which the engine has for the time to travel: that is, they may be lengthened or shortened, so to speak, at the will of the attendant. In many cases the teeth are not required to be protruded at all, the friction of the periphery of the wheel being sufficient for the purposes of traction. In such cases the blades may be thrown out at the top, or on that part of the wheel not coming in contact with the road. On the contrary, in the event of the ground being soft and slippery, or of the engine having to ascend a steep incline, the powerful auxiliary aid of the teeth can be brought into action, and the requisite amount of biting ensured. Arrangements exist for altering the speed and the power, so as to suit the circumstances of the occasion upon which it is used. The engine exhibited was not intended solely for traction purposes; for it is fitted with a drum, which renders it available for driving any kind of fixed or portable machinery. It may thus be made available for an infinite variety of duties: is, in fact, an engine of all-work. Some other special features about this valuable steam appliance are:—the introduction of an improved mode of steering, and of outside bearings for the driving wheels, which also are mounted on springs on both inner and outer framings. A powerful engine of this kind was employed in the conveyance of ordinary locomotive engines, heavy castings, and machinery of various kinds, from the docks, railway stations and manufactories, to their destinations at South Kensington: it was thus a potent contributor to the magnificent display of machinery in the Western Annexe. The load conveyed, at one time, by this engine, occasionally amounted to 45 tons.

Taplin and Co. exhibited a Traction engine of a different form to those of other competitors. This has a singularly light appearance; but it has double cylinders, and is of 16-horse power. It has a peculiar apparatus for regulating the height of water when going up or down hill ; the mode of steering is simple and effective, and it will carry sufficient fuel and water for a journey of twelve miles.

MANUFACTURING MACHINES AND TOOLS, AND MACHINERY IN GENERAL.

A large portion of the Western Annexe was devoted to the display of Engineers' Tools, of every form and size, and for every description of work—either incision, excision, or circumcision; and nearly all under the head of lathes, planing-machines, slot-cutting, punching, shearing, and drilling, or boring machines. There were also engines for weighing, measuring, testing, shaping, bending, and drawing. Some of the machine-tools were of immense size, for turning railway-wheels; as were others for boring steam-cylinders and artillery.

Among the more striking collections exhibited, was that of Mr. Whitworth, comprising specimens of all the principal machines constructed at his works at Manchester: they were of the highest class of workmanship and design. The principal machine in the group was a large recently-introduced machine called a Self-acting Radial Drilling and Boring Machine; the radial arm carrying the drill-spindle is moveable through an arc of 200 degrees; it is attached to a vertical slide worked by a rack and pinion, with worm and wheel on the main frame; the drill-spindle works through a tube, and is adjustable horizontally by a screw and nut from one radius to another; it has a variable self-acting down motion, and retains its connection with the driving motion in every position. Fairbairn and Co., of Leeds, sent a large Planing-machine for armour-plates, with other important tools and machines. William Muir and Co., of Manchester, had a very large collection of tools, some of them are of immense size: they showed also a pair of grindstones arranged in a novel manner, one grindstone always rubbing up the face of the other. Beyer and Peacock exhibited many large specimens, several of them being constructed to prepare railway machinery: one lathe exhibited by this firm is for turning up large driving-wheels for locomotive engines.

Sharp, Stuart, and Co.'s display comprised a large Shaping Machine, driven by a crank, working in a slotted vibrating-arm (this is to give a quick return to the tool); a Marine Slotting-drill, bolt-cutting machines, and a Radial-drill, in which the drill-spindle may describe a circle twelve feet in diameter. Shanks and Co. exhibited two Drills of novel construction : the multiple-drill and the turnstile-drill. They had here also one of their large double slotting drills, with two tools working towards each other: it is capable of making a slot eighteen inches long.

Here were shown the File Cutting Machines of the Manchester File Making Company. It had been maintained obstinately for many years past, that the manufacture of files was beyond the machinists' art. Hand-labour alone could produce them, it was said, and in Sheffield it was stoutly declared that hand-labour alone could produce files. At length the problem seems to be solved; and from what we saw of the file-cutting machines in the Exhibition, and know of their performances in Manchester, we are bold to say that the days of hand file-cutting are numbered. The importance of this change can scarcely be over-estimated, as the price of files will be reduced enormously by it.

In the Foreign Department of Machinery, there was an extensive display of this class of machines, specimens being sent from France, Belgium, Prussia, Austria, Switzerland, and Sweden; but by far the finest collections were from the works of Herr Hartman and Herr Zimmermann, of Chemnitz, in Saxony. Here were specimens of nearly all the machine-tools in use in England, but not a single newly designed machine, nor an old one improved. The whole of them were of the approved Manchester pattern, and but for the name on them we should have thought they had been made there. The collection of Zimmermann showed what great progress the foreign machinists are making. The introduction of these tools is comparatively recent in England, yet we find ourselves competed with already by machinists in nearly all the countries of Europe. Zimmermann's tools are quite up to the English mark in quality.

STEAM-HAMMERS.

The name of Nasmyth is, of course, inseparably connected with this valuable implement for the forge; and Nasmyth and Co. were represented extensively in the Exhibition. Many modifications of the Steam Hammer have been made by different makers, with a view to overcoming some of the defects existing, or said to exist in its original construction. Of the modifications, Robert Morrison and Co., displayed their Double-Acting Steam Forge Hammer. The main point of improvement in this apparatus is comprised in the fact that the hammer-bar and the piston are forged solid together. In other cases, where a different mode of attachment is adopted, the piston and piston-rod have sometimes, from the violence of repeated strokes, parted company. In this instance such a catastrophe, we need not say, is next to impossible. The steam-cylinder is firmly bolted to the single frame which supports the whole. This frame also contains the steam-chest, steam-passages, and the steam and exhaust pipes. The hammer-bar is furnished at its lower end with a claw for holding in the different faces or dies required for various kinds of work. The piston is simple in its construction, and two small steel rings fitting into grooves on its circumference make it steam-tight. Above the piston the bar is planed flat on one side, a corresponding flat being left in the cylinder cover. This arrangement has the effect of keeping the bar and the hammer face constantly in the same relative position to the anvil. On the top of the hammer-bar there is a small roller which works in the slot of a lever. The lever, with the aid of a pair of links and a slide-rod, gives motion to an ordinary box-slide, which admits steam alternately above and below the piston. The Kirkstall Forge Company were also exhibitors of Steam Hammers, and rapidity of action is one of the principal qualifications for which they claim attention to their implements. No doubt in many cases this point is a momentous one, because the completion of a forging at one heat is very frequently a desideratum. The machines shown were massive and well constructed.—*Mechanics' Magazine.*

GWYNNE & CO.'S CENTRIFUGAL PUMPING MACHINERY.

This most attractive piece of machinery consists of a patent Centrifugal Pump, driven direct by two horizontal steam cylinders, and arranged so as to draw the water from a tank situated on the ground-floor of the building. After being raised to an elevation of 23 feet into an upper tank (the difference between the water-levels when the pump is at work, is 21 feet), supported on four columns, the water falls back into the lower one in the form of a cascade, 10 feet wide and 9½ inches deep; the water rising inside the upper tank to 12 inches above the highest level of the mouth-piece. The steam-cylinders working the pumps are 18 inches diameter; the pistons have a stroke of 14 inches, and are coupled direct to the pump shaft without any intermediate gearing. The revolving disc of the pump is 4 feet in diameter, the suction and delivery-pipes are 30 inches in diameter, and the pump, if worked with 25 lbs. steam-pressure in the cylinders throughout the stroke, discharges 110 to 120 tons of water per minute, or equal to three and a quarter times the contents of the lower tank. At a height of 6 feet (the same elevation as Messrs. Easton and Amos's Appold pump) it will discharge about 400 tons per minute, the engines having the same speed and power. For the discharge of the above quantity, the pump requires a speed of 210 revolutions per minute, which gives out a duty of about 80 per cent. on the power expended, a much higher result than has ever been attained by other centrifugal pumps. A centrifugal ball-governor suspended from an arch between the back columns regulates the speed of the whole machinery, which can also be adjusted, started, or altogether stopped, by means of a small hand-wheel. Surmounting the four corners of the lower tank, are four small pump-cases, connected by means of pipes with the large pump, and fitted with copper mouth-pieces. These last mentioned, on a valve inside the tank being opened, emit streams of water, which, although in comparison with the cascade they appear very diminutive, yet discharge a large quantity of water, and have a pleasing effect. A net-work of fine wire covers the under tank to break the fall of the water, and prevent sparkling and spray, as much as it is possible with such a large quantity of water falling.

This centrifugal pump is superior to every other form of pump for raising large or small quantities of water, and to any required elevation. We are informed that the following is a summary of its advantages:—

1st. It can be erected with ease and celerity, and works with an easy rotary motion, without any valves, eccentrics, or other contrivances, which consume power in friction.

2nd. It will discharge a quantity of water greater in proportion to the power applied than any other pumps, 70 per cent. being taken as the average; under favourable circumstances a higher duty has been attained.

3rd. It is economical in use, simple in construction, of great durability, and will discharge a continuous and steady stream without air vessels.

4th. Its cost, measured by the quantity of water discharged, is below that of all other pumps in use, and it is little affected by mud, sand, grit, or other foreign matter in the water which so rapidly destroys most other pumps.

5th. It will admit, in the large sizes, the passage of *solid bodies* six inches in diameter, and the smaller sizes in proportion, without injury, whilst it will pump with equal facility hot or cold liquids.

6th. It requires a very light and inexpensive foundation (having no vibration or oscillation in its working, as in reciprocating pumps).—*Mechanics' Magazine.*

THE UNIVERSAL JOINER,

The invention of Robert Henry Thompson, of H. M. Dockyard, Woolwich, is an ingenious apparatus, capable of being worked by hand or by steam-power, and applicable to a variety of purposes, as its name implies, connected with joinery. The copying principle is here employed, and thus diversity in the form of work to be produced is no barrier to its action. It may be used for any description of joiners' work, including gothic heads, elliptic and all other curves, mouldings of whatever form, the strings of stairs, with treads, risers, and handrails, together with plain or ornamental work for cabinet or coachwork. With some modifications, and, of course, with a change of cutting tools, the Universal Joiner may be converted into a general mason, for it does not object under such circumstances, to deal with stone. Mr. Thompson also exhibited a patent Tree-Feller, and a patent Sawing-machine, these being the natural feeders to the joiner. They perform the rough work, indeed, and the joiner the smooth.

FIRE-ENGINES.

A public trial of the merits of various Fire-engines, sent into the Exhibition by different manufacturers, was made on the banks of the Serpentine, near Kensington-gardens. The first experiment commenced with a trial of Shand and Mason's engine; Merryweather and Sons', of Long acre; and those built by Messrs. Rose, of Manchester. The number of gallons of water thrown was decided to be in favour of Shand and Mason, 1; Merryweather, 2; Rose, 3. Three other experiments were made with the same results, the engines throwing respectively, in thirty seconds, 78 gallons, 68, and 65 gallons. Many other experiments with different engines were afterwards made, the results of which, however important to the several manufacturers, do not call for special notice. During the trials the royal family passed over the bridge, apparently with a view to witness from their carriages the operations in progress. A great number of conductors of the engines were present to show how the machines could be most advantageously used in case of accident by fire. Another experimental contest took place between one of Merryweather's engines and another, Capt. Fowke's engine, and a third with Mr. Roberts' engine, the patentee, of Millwall. Roberts's engine, with a 57 stroke, threw 114 gallons, and with a 60 stroke, 117 gallons, twenty men only working at the engine. Capt. Fowke's engine, made by Shand and Mason, with twelve men, threw 109 gallons of water in two minutes. The decision of the judges may be stated as follows :—Shand and Mason, 1 ; Merryweather and Sons, 2 ; Hodges, 3.

SIEBE'S ICE-MAKING MACHINE.

This machine, exhibited by Siebe Brothers, of Lambeth, is the joint production of Messrs. Siebe and J. Harrison. The principle on which it is constructed is the removal of caloric by evaporating a volatile fluid in vacuo, and the condensation of the vapour by pressure. A strong solution of brine is employed as a carrying agent, which, after having been passed through the evaporating vessel, flows along the refrigerating trough, in which are placed vessels full of pure water, which becomes ice by the absorption of caloric. The great point in this machine is its perfect independence of all external, thermal, and atmospheric influences, which renders it equally effective in any climate ; its consequent value to the inhabitants of tropical countries cannot be too highly estimated. The refrigerator in use at the Exhibition was not only under the direct influence of the rays of the sun, but was surrounded by steam-machinery at work ; in fact, there were steam-pipes running underneath it, yet the blocks of ice were drawn forth with wonderful rapidity. For the salting of all kinds of provisions, or in the operations of brewing and preserving alimentary substances, these machines, by equalizing the temperature of different seasons, are commercially of the first importance.

LIFE-PRESERVING APPARATUS.

The ladders and uncovered baskets whereby men formerly passed into collieries are now being gradually replaced by safety-cages. The object of these apparatus is to protect life if the rope or chain raising or lowering the miners should fail, or any *débris* or gearing should fall into the shaft. The principle of nearly all safety-cages is the freeing of one or more levers which press against the guide-rods fixed to the side of shafts, when the hauling-tackle is not stretched by the chain. Mr. J. T. Calow exhibited an improvement in the levers or grips not being disengaged whenever the cage is supported, as by resting on the ground. This apparatus has been beneficially in use for some 'time at the West Staveley Colliery, the viewer of which, Mr. Moody, states in writing that it has preserved life on three occasions. In the open court there was erected in full size working order Aytoun's patent safety-cage. Mr. W. Heath Jordan likewise exhibited a model of a pit frame and safety-cages.

For the raising and lowering of goods through the different floors of warehouses, and at railway stations to and from the platform, as at Bristol, the miners' cage is used. The patent Hoist Company exhibited a safety-cage which is designed to obtain the same result by an arrangement brought into action by centrifugal force: Watt's governor regulates the velocity of the cage in transit. The advantage obtained by this mode is that when a chain breaks the cage gradually descends. Patent cages could easily be constructed to enable the inmates to lower themselves on a chain breaking. Mr. George Dodman showed also a patent safety hoist: the cage in this instance becomes stationary whether the chain breaks or is overwound.

The many contrivances invented for affording relief to the inmates of houses on fire have been well represented for some years past at the annual Exhibition of the Society of Arts. They principally consisted of chain-ladders for attaching to upper window-sills cages with incombustible curtains, lowered by cranes inserted into eye-bolts fixed in the wall. Some houses have still facilities permitting egress over the roof to the adjoining residence in cases of fire. These are all being superseded by the ladder fire-escapes; none like the two to be seen at the recent Exhibition was shown in 1851. Mr. Clarke's improved fire-escape reaches eighty feet high. The underneath part of the centre ladder of this fire-escape is encircled by canvas rendered incombustible by being saturated in alum and chloride. A wire-gauze further protects the canvas from the effects of flames. Into the wooden steps of the ladder are inlaid wire-rope, sufficiently strong to bear the weight of several men. The improvement in Clarke's fire-escape is in the lever-bars for raising the second ladder, which works on quadrants: this fire-escape is so light that one man can wheel it easily.

The mariner's daily risks appear to equal those of the miner. The sympathy for the former is displayed by the Royal National Life-boat Association, who possessed a prominent stand, containing models of rowing and sailing life-boats. Mr. Richardson showed a highly finished model of a patent tubular life-boat; another inventor, Mr. Coryton, his vertical wave line system and atmospheric guide propeller life-boat. The noted life-boat named the *Mary Anne*, belonging to the ports of Hartlepool and Sunderland, was represented by a beautiful model. This boat was subjected some years since to many tests in Ramsgate harbour, and fully showed its capability of being able to right itself immediately when purposely capsized, particularly in the instance when the boat was under sail. The crew of the *Mary Anne* have received, since 1857, the sum of 250*l.* from the Board of Trade, for saving life, besides salvage money for assisting vessels in distress.

Heinke's patent Diving Apparatus was employed for removing the old foundations at Westminster bridge, and is stated to have been in constant use for five years without any accident having occurred. Adjoining was shown A. Siebe's Diving-apparatus, used in the summer months from 1839 to 1844 inclusive, in clearing the anchorage at Spithead of the wrecks of the *Royal George*, of 104 guns, lost whilst engaged in partially careening the vessel in 1782; and the *Edgar*, of 70 guns, blown up and sunk in 1711. There was a very interesting copper pulley-wheel shown, recovered from the wreck of the *Mary Rose*, sunk in the reign of Henry VIII. The workmanship and skill used in order to combine strength and lightness in this pulley-wheel are remarkable; no improvement thereon could be effected at the present day.—*George Walcott, C.E.* ; *Mechanics' Magazine.*

SUGAR MACHINERY.

This class of machinery and apparatus was well represented: among the most stupendous instances was a mill constructed by Mirrlees and Tait, of Glasgow, which required 150 tons of iron for its construction ; its use being to express the juice from the cane. The mill is a three-roller mill, the rollers being 33 in. in diameter and 7 ft. in length. The bedplate, which forms a tank for the reception of the cane-juice which falls from the rollers, is of cast iron, and weighs five tons. On the opposite sides are fixed the great cheeks or head stocks which carry the bearings of the rollers; these have to receive the whole strain of the work, which is equal at this point to the maximum power of the engine, acting through a leverage of sixteen to one. The top roller is placed in a line with the shaft of the large gearing-wheel. The lower rollers are of the same size as the top one, but have on their outer edges a flange within which the upper one works : this is to prevent the canes escaping sideways over the ends of the rollers. The mill is driven by a six-columned, high-pressure, steam beam-engine, having a cylinder 22 in. in diameter, with a stroke of 4 ft. 6 in. The usual working pressure employed is 70lb. per square inch. The steam is admitted to the cylinder by the usual three-port slide-valve, cutting off at three-fourths of the stroke; while a further degree of expansion is provided for by a separate gridiron expansive-valve having a link-motion adjustable to any length of stroke when the machinery is in motion.

At the back of the great sugar-mill of Mirrlees and Tait was an extensive range of apparatus, consisting of three large copper vacuum-pans, with all the necessary fittings,—the whole of copper and brass, polished and burnished. The purpose for which they are employed is to evaporate the water of the cane-juice, and so extract the sugar. The operation is as follows. The cane-juice from the sugar-mill, after passing through the desiccators and bag and charcoal filters, is received into the centre pan, to be evaporated to a density of 15° to 17° Beaumé, after which it is discharged into one of the side pans to undergo a further evaporation to a density of 25° to 27° Beaumé. After leaving the second pan the concentrated syrup is passed through filters containing animal charcoal, and then enters the third pan, which is of larger diameter than the other two. In this it is finally concentrated to the proper degree of granulation : the skipping is then discharged into heaters, from which it is poured into moulds to be taken to the curing-house.

Manlove, Allnutt, and Co., exhibited some complete and ingenious machinery for completing the manufacture of sugar. The old plan was to place the sugar, on its leaving the boiling-pans, in conical-shaped moulds, in which it was allowed to remain for ten or twelve days. This machinery entirely does away with the use of the cones and the loss of time, and it actually produces the same result in as many minutes as the old system required days. The effect is produced by centrifugal force ; the pans containing the sugar being caused to revolve at the rate of 1000 revolutions per minute, by which means the treacle and molasses are perfectly separated.

PAPER-MAKING MACHINERY.

The display of Machinery for making Paper was very large, comprising several entire sets of machines exhibited by the principal manufacturers of England, and also by eminent machinists on the Continent. One of the most complete and beautifully-executed machines was constructed by Bryan, Donkin, and Co., of Bermondsey, and intended to manufacture an endless sheet of paper of any width under seven feet. The first machines ever used for making endless paper were erected by Messrs. Donkin, at Frogmore, in Berks, in the year 1803; and at Twowaters, in the county of Hertford, in 1804. The above machine is capable of making an endless sheet of paper twenty miles long in about twenty-four hours : the actual superficial area of this sheet of paper would be about seventeen acres. The combination of machinery exhibited by Donkin not only makes the paper complete from the pulp, but also gives to it the necessary water-mark, and cuts it into sheets of any desired size and form.

When the rags are properly prepared and in the state of pulp, they enter the machine which is to convert that pulp into paper. The first portion of the machine is the sand-catcher : this is a cast-iron tray or shallow tank coated with zinc ; the bottom of it is formed into lateral triangular channels, into which the sand or grit falls as the pulp passes through it. From the sand-catcher it passes to the knot-strainer, another shallow tank, beautifully made of gun metal ; the bottom of it is intersected with minute slots, the upper openings of which are exceedingly fine ; on the lower side they are much wider. The pulp, having entered, passes through the fine openings, leaving behind all the lumps or knots that may be in it; a rapid vibratory motion is communicated to the machine; and it has a parallel motion which secures an even action over the entire surface. The pulp, having been perfectly strained by the knotter, then passes to an endless wire table or apron, which is supported on small brass rollers. This travels forward, bearing a film of wet pulp upon its upper surface, and conveys it to the wove-rider, or dandy-role, which is made of perforated copper, the width of the sheet of paper being determined by an endless web placed on each side the wire-table. At this point most of the water is extracted from the pulp by pressure produced by vacuum and other means. The sheet of partially-dried pulp then passes through the couch-rollers, which are covered with thick blanket-felt; these press the pulp and further free it from water, so that it no longer requires to be supported by the wire-apron, having become sufficiently strong to carry itself. It then passes over, under, and around a series of iron rollers, the first covered with felt, the next are smooth surfaces of iron. These are of cast-iron hollow, heated with steam, and six in number. The pulp having now become dried has assumed the character of paper, but requires to pass through another series of rollers, to give it a proper surface. The paper is made to pass over, under, and around the surface-pressers in the same manner as it passes the drying-rollers; but the pressing-rollers are of smaller diameter, of great weight, and are still further made to press on the paper by having attached to them weights acting through compound levers. The pressing-rollers, like the drying-rollers, are heated by steam.

The cutting-machine completes the operation. It effects its object first by the action of circular steel-cutters (kept in their places by springs), which cut the sheet of paper longitudinally into strips, and afterwards by the action of a back cutter, which severs them the reverse way; a measuring apparatus secures uniformity of size; the cut pieces of paper fall upon a table, and are collected by attendant boys. Thus this beautiful machine effects the whole operation of Paper-making; the pulp being supplied in a liquid state at one end, it delivers it converted into sheets of paper, dried, faced, and cut, at the other.

Should it be necessary to give the paper a water-mark a copper roller, covered with wire-gauze, upon which a projecting wire is fixed, acts upon the paper after it leaves the travelling wire-table and before it is submitted to the action of the cast-iron rollers. This projecting wire is arranged in different forms, to indicate the name of the manufacturer, the character of the paper, or for mere ornament.—*Abridged from the Illustrated London News.*

BESLEY'S TYPE-CASTING MACHINE.

This interesting machine was exhibited by Messrs. Charles Reed and Benjamin Fox, successors to Mr. Alderman Besley, of the Fann-street Letter-foundry. The object of the founder has been to produce a type-metal which, uniting hardness of material with fineness of quality, should not be open to the serious objections which lie against a type so brittle as to fly off in its finer parts under extraordinary pressure. The desideratum has been provided by Messrs. Besley, who, in 1855, sealed a patent for their hard metal, having taken the first-class medal at the Paris Exhibition, and the result has been that every considerable type-founder has cast in hard metals all types expressly designed for the wear and tear of long numbers. Specimens of these types in various sizes have been exhibited, and have received the first-class award; Besley's machine has been engaged for two months in casting type used in the *Illustrated London News*.

The machine consists of a pan for holding the metal, with a well and piston, the latter with a side lever, connecting-rod, and cross-bar attached to the piston-rod and worked with a cam. To the pan is fixed a "jobber," used to prevent the return of the metal after it is pumped into the mould, which is fixed to the front of the machine, and held to the pan whilst the type is being cast. When the type is cast the mould is drawn back by means of a spiral spring, and the mould is opened by a bar and rod, which are also used for delivering the matrix. Other arms and plates are adapted for fixing and lowering the mould. The machine is driven by a lever and motion-crank.

YOUNG'S TYPE-COMPOSING MACHINE

Was shown at work in the Exhibition, and excited much interest. The inventor describes that this type machine is provided with separate compartments called "reservoirs," for all the letters of a fount; each reservoir being provided with a small lever, which, by means of a rod, is connected to a key like those used in a pianoforte. When a key is struck by the player, it pushes a type out of the reservoir by means of the lever mentioned above, and the type is thus caused to slide down an inclined plane, and thence into a receiver, where it is set up side by side with other types, by means of a beater. Thus, each type or letter can be set up by a player in the order required by a compositor's copy. This is now done with a speed of from 12,000 to 15,000 types set up in an hour's time.

The justifying apparatus is intended to replace the compositor's stick. The compositor places the galley filled with the long lines of type set up by the composing machine, slides one of them into the apparatus, divides it into the proper width of the page, and having justified it, moves a handle which depresses the completed line, and thus makes room for a succeeding one. It is found that a compositor can, by this means, justify at the rate of 4000 to 6000 types per hour.

The distributing machine separates all the different letters of a fount that may have been used for printing, into different channels ready for use in the composing machine. This is effected by one or more pairs of nippers, which takes every type singly from the reservoir in which all the types have been placed, and allows it to slide down an inclined plane, the upper part of which moves on a hinge. The thin or lower-case types slide down to the bottom of the fixed inclined plane, but the thicker, or upper-case letters, are retained on the moveable incline, which, on being raised, drops them into an appropriate receptacle, whence they are then taken and re-distributed by passing down a separate channel of the inclined plane. The thin, or lower-case letters, that have arrived at the bottom of the inclined plane, are pushed into the grooves of a revolving chain. This chain in moving passes underneath plates which are made of different widths in order to cover only certain nicks cut or cast on the edge of the types, and situated in different parts of their length, from 1-16th to 12-16ths of an inch from the tail of each type. When, therefore, a type passes underneath a plate, which allows its nick to be exposed, it is pushed from off the chain by means of a scraper which passes over the plate on to a tilting inclined plane. This plane in its descent allows the type to slide down, by means of an inclined channel, into a receiver, where it is set up by means of a beater, as in the composing machine. The distinguishing nicks are somewhat like those used by typefounders ; 71 per cent of the types require only one nick, 20 per cent. only two nicks, and the remainder have three nicks. One distributing machine, attended by two boys, will distribute and prepare for the composing machine from 14,000 to 18,000 types per hour. A saving of 50 per cent. in the cost of composition is said to be effected by the use of these machines.—*Mechanics' Magazine.*

BANK-NOTE PRINTING.

In the English gallery devoted to Printing was exhibited a case of carefully printed Bank of England Notes,—shown by the Governor of the Bank; containing samples of all notes, from 5*l.* to 1000*l.* In place of the usual signature is printed the one word "cancelled," but as, of course, in all other respects the notes are perfect, an attendant came every day from the Bank to keep an eye on the case ; for if any of the larger notes were stolen, it would be easy to erase the lightly-printed word "cancelled" and substitute a signature, when its payment at any foreign bank might follow as a matter of course. To have one stolen for presentation, however, is not what the Bank would fear ; but if some of the larger ones were stolen for imitation the affair would be serious. To the means of preventing or detecting forgery the Bank has its vigilance incessantly directed, more especially to the improvements in photographic art, from the progress in which, unless the tint of the present note-paper is changed, as has been done in America, the troubles of the Bank will surely come at last. The mere printing of the bank-notes offers no very great difficulties to forgers. Even Maclise's little vignette in the corner has been so copied in lithograph as to be scarcely capable of detection by the Bank inspectors; and the case of the servant girl who, with a pen and ink, copied her one 5l.-note on tissue paper with such perfect fidelity that she passed several, shows how easily the mere text can be reproduced. It is the paper and its watermark which are the forger's great difficulties; and though in 5l.-notes he can reproduce these so as to deceive the general public, he never succeeds in imposing upon the Bank. The paper for the Bank-notes is made by Mr. Portal, in Hampshire, and the manufacture is conducted under as careful supervision as the printing of the notes themselves; for if once the forgers could get a supply of the true paper, the rest would be easy enough. The watermark they imitate to perfection by a kind of embossing, so perfect as to deceive the most practised eye: in fact, there is only one method of detecting it, but that fortunately is simple, and infallible in its results. If the note is doubtful, a part at the back should be wetted with the tongue. If genuine, the watermark shows out brighter than ever; if a counterfeit, it instantly disappears. The paper for bank-notes is only made in small sheets, each sheet large enough to print two notes laid side by side. The paper where they join has what is technically called a "deckle edge," and in the manufacture certain slight flaws in the paper are caused by this edge or margin line being put into the substance of each note, so as to be barely perceptible and to look like an accident. These minute imperfections vary in their position according to the value of the note itself, and are, no doubt, subsequently reversed and varied by the Bank authorities according to the months in which they are printed. In like manner also are varied the little and scarcely noticeable spot above some one or other "O" in the figures of the large notes, and these private marks always correspond on the two notes, which are printed side by side on the small sheet as we have mentioned. Thus, a forger must always have two notes of following numbers to make a good counterfeit. In the case of 5l.-notes this is easily done; but in the instance of 1000l.-notes it is almost impossible. There are several printing presses for printing notes at the Bank, each of which can turn out 3000 notes an hour.

By the side of this case were specimens of the notes of the Government of India, which were looked upon with interest, as the design for them was drawn by the Queen herself. The amount of these notes is printed on them in the characters of four Oriental languages. Nearly all foreign Governments get the plates for their notes executed, and in many cases the notes themselves printed, in this country: a fine collection of these and of foreign postage-stamps was shown in Bradbury and Wilkinson's case.

Among them was exhibited an engraving of a new Bank of England note, designed by the late Henry Bradbury. This is exceedingly beautiful in the artistic merit of its design, and is printed in tints, pale pink and green, to avoid photographic forgeries. In this case was also shown some of those most exquisite specimens of Bradbury's Nature-printing. The process by which these flowers, ferns, and seaweeds are made, as it were, to print themselves is exceedingly simple; it is only the perfection to which Mr. Bradbury has brought the art which is surprising. It is by touch alone that the spectator can be convinced that wonderful groups of seaweed, spread on the sheet in all their rich variety of tints and minute structural organization, are not actually the pressed weeds themselves.
—*Abridged from the Times.*

FOLDING, PRESSING AND STITCHING MACHINE.

This compact little folding-machine, a Swiss invention, is constructed to make a perfect register, and to fold printed or white sheets of paper with far greater precision than the most experienced hands can do it, at the rate of 1400 to 1500 sheets of any size per hour; and it presses and stitches the sheets at the same time.

The machine works as follows :—The sheets are put singly by a boy under the points of the machine, in the same manner as with the printing-machine. A knife moving nearly vertically up and down takes hold of the sheet lengthwise in the centre, draws it through a slip in the table, and the first fold is made. The knife returns instantly, and the sheet is taken by a second vertical knife, moving from the left to the right, folding it at a right angle to the first fold. The double-folded sheet is now opposite a pair of ribbed rollers (cylinders). Before the third fold is made, the stitching commences as follows :—Two needles, provided with hooks, pass through the middle of the sheet, at about an inch distance from each other, drawing the cotton through, which is unwound from a bobbin, and cut to the required length by a peculiarly constructed pair of shears; the sheet is then folded a third time—viz. a knife in the shape of a T, acting horizontally, and consequently, at a right angle with the second knife, takes hold of the middle of the sheet, and pushes it between the above-mentioned ribbed rollers, whence it is passed directly to another pair of polished rollers, from which it comes glazed and pressed on to the table. The machine works very correctly, and folds the largest as well as the smallest sheets, and both the stitching and pressing apparatus, or each singly, may be detached by loosening a single screw. It can be worked either by steam or hand, a boy being sufficient for that purpose.

The same exhibitor showed a second folding-machine which feeds itself by an air or sucking apparatus that takes the sheets one by one from off a pile, under the horizontal folding-knife, thus enabling it to fold 3000 sheets per hour.

These machines, to fold sheets of any size, for two, three, or four breaks, are supplied at a comparatively low price, and are extensively used on the Continent.

SURFACE DECORATION BY BLOCK-PRINTING.

The British Wall-papers and Decorations produced by Block-printing are considered to have shown our advancement in this manufacture as marked and satisfactory.

The enriching a wall with raised ornament has hitherto been attended with great cost and labour; but through the recent improvement in our wall-paper manufacture, such treatment is attainable by a moderate cost and in a most perfect manner. Belgium exhibited a few papers in low relief (the relievo resulting from a process of embossing); they have, however, a metallic aspect which is curious. But the attaining a thoroughly satisfactory result in relief wall-papers has resulted from the energies of Scott, Cuthbertson, and Co., of Chelsea.

The mode in which relief is attained by this firm is by the repeated printing of flock upon flock either upon a gold or a plain ground: in the latter case the paper is hung with butt (not overlapping) edges, and, after being well sized, is reduced to one tint by an even coat of oil-paint. A simple lozenge pattern about three inches in height was exhibited, being in uncoloured flock on a gold ground, in relief, to the height of about a quarter of an inch; it is exceedingly pleasing, and demands special notice. But this is not the only form in which they presented patterns in relievo. Fronting the observer were exhibited three panels which, while differently treated, were yet all raised: these were repeatedly printed in flock, then painted, and finally subjected to a second printing for the sake of adding gold and other colours; and thus some of the best results were achieved which have ever been gained in the wall-paper manufacture. France and Austria exhibited patterns worthy of special consideration; but the display of M. Jules Desfossé exhibited one of the most marvellous specimens of block-printing which has ever been shown. This was of the beauties of many lands; plants from various countries and diversified seasons being pressed into the service of the artist. The delicacy of the tints, the harmony of the colours, the masterly power of the drawing, the feeling of light which prevailed throughout, and the skilful character of the grouping, constitute this a work of no ordinary kind. On the one side was a cedar in spring leafage; on the other a Virginian creeper in autumn foliage; and these combined with the bignonia, the strelitzia, and other plants.

AGRICULTURAL MACHINES AND IMPLEMENTS.

Cultivation by the Steam-engine was the paramount feature of this Department; one gallery and part of another being occupied by two rival systems of Steam-ploughing Mechanism. Fowler's Leeds factory contributed the steam-engines, with their wire-ropes, ploughs, and grubbers, of which about 150 sets are now at work in this and other countries. In Germany there are four, in Hungary two, in the West Indies three, at the foot of the Pyramids one has just been started; while several others have been manufactured in France, and an Algerian cotton company has taken another to facilitate its operations. Here, too, were the engine, windlass, grubbers, and new balance-ploughs of the Howards, of Bedford; their steam-cultivators, and new implements for the hay-harvest. Mr. Chandler, of Bow, exhibited models of his apparatus for steam-ploughing and cultivating. Mr. Steevens, of Hammersmith, showed a new balance-plough for steam-power; and Mr. Hayes, of Stony Stratford, his windlass, which won credit and honour at the Leeds steam-ploughing trials. Mr. Halkett's system of steam culture is as follows:—Permanent guideway rails are laid down over the fields, at intervals of 50 feet or more, upon which a locomotive cultivating machine traverses, performing a variety of tillage, weeding, and harvesting operations. The outlay of more than 20l. per acre is shown to promise reasonably a large return; but a modification of the system gives a traction engine and apparatus travelling upon strips of grass, instead of rails, at a cost of only 2l. 10s. per acre; and the inventor calculates that with an ordinary engine he can plough 60 acres a-day, or harvest, or strip off the ears (on the Australian plan) of no less than 400 acres of corn in that time.

The wonder of 1851 was the Reaping-machine. Now we have both a Reaper and (the corollary from it) a Grass-mower.

Burgess and Key exhibited their self-delivering screw-platform Reaping-machine (now improved and lightened, and made to shut up into a narrow compass for travelling, of which upwards of 3000 are employed in the United Kingdom. Their Grass-mower cuts any sort of grass or clover at the rate of about one acre per hour. The same machine, by the addition of a platform, becomes a Corn-reaper, with manual side-delivery.

The trustees of W. Croskill showed the original type of Reaper—Bell's machine, propelled by horses walking behind. Simplified and improved, and made to cut a width of 8¼ feet at once, with three horses, this machine will reap between 20 and 30 acres in a day, performing the work of 20 or 30 harvest-men.

Mr. Samuelson, of Banbury, showed his Revolving Rakes, to deliver the cut corn in bunches ready for binding. Mechanism causes an upright spindle to rotate, and as this supports four long arms, balanced, and carrying boards and rakes at their extremities, with a circular cam to regulate the elevation and depression of these rakes, they sweep over a quadrant-shaped platform as they revolve, delivering the corn in separate bunches with a smooth and steady motion. The alternate boards fulfil the office of the reel in ordinary machines, bending the standing crop to the cutters. Ransome and Sims, of Ipswich, produce the same idea in a rather different form.

America has produced a greater variety of reaping and mowing-machines than we English have done; most of our new notions in knife, or gearing, or delivery, having come a voyage across the Atlantic. In the United States Court we accordingly found several ingenuities of this order.

A striking object among these inventions was the Reaper of Mr. M'Cormick, which advertises itself as one of 40,000 made and sold in one shop. The platform is of a quadrant figure; the reel has but three, instead of four blades, the place of the fourth being occupied by a rake, which by a very peculiar but really simple and easy movement is made to sweep over the platform, delivering the cut corn at one side. Ashley and Co., of Stamford, exhibited that novelty of late years, the Circular Rotating Harrow, which does great execution upon tough furrow slices, matted weed, and obdurate clods. Mr. Aveling, of Rochester, showed his simply-contrived and practically-successful Locomotive for common roads, of which, it is said, forty are already in constant use. Barrett, Exall, and Andrewes, of Reading, were distinguished by their fixed Steam-engines; and especially the small Portable Thrashing-machine. On Mr. Bentall's stand we had that modern invention, the Root-pulper. Clayton and Shuttleworth showed what the Lincoln works can produce—mainly consisting of those portable Engines and Thrashing-machines which are famous all over the world: last year this firm sent out 566 engines. A. and E. Crosskill, of Beverley, exhibited their Clod-crusher; and Hornsby, of Grantham, showed his portable Engines and newly-improved Thrashing-machines. One of the most interesting sights in the Exhibition was that of busy Honey-bees at work in the transparent and humane hives of Neighbour, of Holborn; and Marriott, of Gracechurch-street. On the stand of Ransome and Sims, beside ploughs and other field implements, were to be seen portable and fixed Steam-engines, their newly-improved Thrashing-machine, revolving Corn-screen, Mills for crushing all sorts of grain, Root-slicers, Chaff-cutters, &c., sample machinery from their great and celebrated Orwell Works. Mr. Robey, of Lincoln, showed a Locomotive Engine for travelling along common highways. Ruston and Co., of the same city, exhibited a portable Engine and improved Thrashing-machine. On Messrs. Tuxford's stand we had their celebrated first-prize Steam-engines of all varieties; together with their new road Locomotive, which propels itself by means of a single roughened roller, avoiding the complication of driving by two wheels.

Professor Kaugh, of the Agricultural College of Hohenheim, Wurtemberg, illustrated the origin and history of Traction-tillage by 100 beautifully constructed models of ancient and modern implements, consisting of :—1. Ploughs, originated from the trowel-shaped hand-hoe. 2. Those from the spade, whence have descended the short, upright mouldboards that grub the American prairies, and the Continental model plough of Brabant. 3. Ploughs originating from the two-pronged hoe, the most modern form being seen in

Poland and East Prussia. 4. Turnwrest, side-hill, or one-way ploughs, such as that of Cincinnatus, and at this day used in India and China. It is impossible to enumerate here the successes of our great Plough-makers. "And as to comparing the best 'Champion,' 'Eclipse,' 'Criterion,' and other ploughs of nominal perfection, we should only be dwelling upon fine distinctions in the formation of the essential parts, and detailing *minutiæ* of the shapes and fastenings of coulters, the attachment of wheels, the adjustment of the position of shares, the regulation of the line of draught for varying depths and widths, and less important differences than those between trussed and solid beams, between having or not a draught-chain below the beam, or between constructing the body-frame in one piece with the beam or not."—*Times*.

The Foreign display of Implements was very numerous. In the French there was an obvious imitation of the English, but without the adaptation of parts, strength, perfection, and finish, which distinguish our implements. The French portable Steam-engines had some excellent points.

Belgium showed several specimens of the Plough, more or less made of iron, in place of the old-fashioned cumbrous wood; several thrashing-machines, chaff-cutters, drills, and churns.

Denmark contributed a novelty in the shape of long shallow Iron Pans for holding Milk in large dairies. A screw at the further end enables the pan to be slightly raised for emptying, and a broad blade of thin wood reaching across the pan and supported by rollers running along the edges of the pan, is drawn from end to end when the cream is to be skimmed off the milk.

Austria showed Ploughs, Hoes, and Drill-ploughs, not of a very advanced order. Prussia exhibited Horse-power for machines, and Broad-cast Sowing-machines. Italy had a fine show of ploughs, trench-ploughs, harrows, machines for thrashing maize, corn-thrashing machines, carts, the short-handled Tuscan plough, the plough of Parma on wheels, models of irrigation works, agriculturists' levels for operations in watering the fields, and apparatus for hatching silkworms' eggs.

Norway exhibited several Ploughs, constructed of wood and iron —one a very fair copy of the Scotch swing-plough in iron. The Norwegian Harrow, with its sets of rowels for effectually breaking the upper soil, was a great feature here; and so was the Broadcast Sowing machine. And there was the simplest contrivance in the world, in the shape of an iron clamp, by which hop poles, or garden sticks, can be thrust easily into the ground by the foot.

Sweden showed Iron Ploughs, with or without trussed beams, generally after the Scotch model. Among the Dairy Utensils was one churn, with warming vessel, cleverly made with a reciprocating rotatory motion, procured by a couple of straps wrapping round a spindle, and alternately unwound by the pressure of a lever.

Among the Russian implements was a peculiar grouping of three small Ploughs upon one frame, with regulating wheels.

Turkey had little better to offer than tools much like mattocks. Switzerland showed but few implements. Neither had the Netherlands sent many mechanical indications of their really great advance in tillage.

The United States we have already referred to as great in Reapers and Mowers. From our own colonies, of course, the few implements were of wondrously varied character,—from the extremely rude Indian ploughs and corn fan, to the ploughs, horse rakes, drills, and waggons of New Brunswick and Canada.

In the Australian Court was a Victorian Reaper from Melbourne, the original from which those of Ransome and Samuelson are taken and improved. But in South Australia the fine climate, ripening the wheat crops evenly and thoroughly, enables the farmer to thrash and reap all at once. A machine was exhibited resembling the ancient Roman Reaper. A box, upon a pair of wheels, is propelled by horses and a pole at the side; the forward end is armed with an iron comb, which does not, however, snap off the ears of the standing crop, but holds them, while the rapidly-revolving beaters of a drum, like that of a thrashing machine, strip out the kernels of ripe grain. The box receives the corn; sometimes a fan (driven like the drum, by wheels and a strap, by the rotation of the carriage wheels) winnows away the chaff, and the produce is thus collected ready for the market.

There is, unquestionably, great improvement in many foreign lands; but our implement trade has grown with such rapidity, that the annual production of our chief agricultural manufactories is estimated at 2,000,000$l.$; and that of the innumerable local makers may be much larger, while we have a great and rapidly increasing export of tools and farm-machinery to every country of the world.—*Condensed from the Times.*

CIVIL ENGINEERING, ARCHITECTURE, AND BUILDING CONTRIVANCES.

ENGINEERING MODELS.

The greater number of the contributions by engineers were Models of Iron Bridges and Viaducts, of which the principle of construction is remarkable for that subserviency of other considerations to one of rapid completion, which is generally of importance to shareholders. In most of these models, one of the forms of lattice-girder, or Captain Warren's diagonally-braced truss, as applied in many cases by Messrs. Kennard, is used, with piers likewise of iron construction. The Beelah Viaduct, Westmoreland, on the South Durham and Lancashire Union Railway, was illustrated in a model exhibited by Gilkes, Wilson, and Co., of Middlesbro'-on-Tees. It was designed by Mr. T. Bouch, of Edinburgh. It is 1000 feet long and 200 feet high in the deepest part of the valley, and was erected in four months. Three years, say the exhibitors, would have been required for the erection of a viaduct of brick or stone. Lieut.-Colonel J. P. Kennedy's "Elements Essential to Railway Success" was an exhibition of models and drawings of different Bridges on the Bombay and Baroda Railway, also of iron. Sir John Macneill's bridge over the Boyne has its three main openings spanned by lattice girders at a height of 90 feet from the water—the span of the centre opening being 264 feet. Each pair of girders, as in works of considerable dimensions, is cross-strutted over the line of railway, so that the perspective, looking from one of the approaches of the line, somewhat resembles that of a tubular bridge. Turner and Gibson, of Dublin, exhibited, besides Iron Roofs, balance Rolling-bridges for Railways over water and roads. Mr. Hawkshaw and Mr. W. H. Barlow exhibited a model of the Suspension-bridge proposed to be erected at Clifton, in which are to be introduced the chains from Hungerford Bridge.

The Chepstow and still more the Saltash Bridge, by the late Mr. Brunel, of which models were shown, are chief examples of this conjunction, in these latter days, of great constructive skill with the very worst art. The centre span of the Chepstow Bridge is 300 feet; and each span of the Saltash Bridge is 455 feet. The system of trussing is analogous in the two cases; the roadway being supported somewhat as in a suspension-bridge, whilst a great collar-beam, between points of suspension of the chains, forms abutment aloft in lieu of prolongation landward, and anchorage to the ground. In the Saltash Bridge the tubes resisting the tension of the suspension-chains are not straight, but they rise in a curve equal in height to the curve downwards of the chains: thus, say the printed particulars (which, considering the interest and importance of all points in the application of the suspension principle, it is well to quote), "the weight of the girders and roadway rests half on the tube, half on the chains, the girders being carried by vertical struts placed at intervals of forty feet, diagonally braced so as to give rigidity, and by intermediate attachments to the suspension-chains."

Not less important than the system of Trussing is the economy of recently perfected methods of Founding the piers of such bridges—for example, the compressed-air system of cylinder-sinking. Models both in the French and the Zollverein Divisions, showed that like improvements, and on a vast scale, have been made by foreign engineers; and, it is fair to add also, like offences against good taste. The French, to whose works we may return, are nearly as bad as ourselves when they are not dealing with the arch-form in iron; whilst they seem to be equally able to dispense with scaffolding.

A model of one opening of the Railway bridge across the Rhine at Mayence, was exhibited by Klett and Co., of Nuremburg. The Zollverein catalogue gives a view which shows that the whole bridge may compare with the Saltash for ugliness. The principle, called Pauli's System, seems to resemble that suggested in the course of the discussion at the Oxford meeting of the British Association, in the Mechanical section, after the reading of Mr. Barlow's paper on Bridges on the suspension and combined girder principle capable of affording requisite strength for passage of railway trains. In this Rhine bridge we see, in each complicated arrangement of bars forming the truss, a descending curve following much the same line as the chain of a suspension-bridge; but riveted to form one piece in itself, or, rather, as part of the whole truss; the combination of rigidity with the catenary; or the substitution of that form of resistance to the tensile part of cross-strain in a girder or truss, for the chain with links, apparently realizing the suggestion of the speaker at Oxford.

A model illustrative of another important Bridge of Iron construction—that across the Vistula at Dirschau, was exhibited by the Berlin Minister of Commerce and Public Works.

A contrivance was shown for Raising Vessels from one water-level to another without a succession of locks. The substitute is a carriage for the vessel, which is wound up an inclined-plane—an old idea, but one to which objections have been raised, such as that of injury to the framework of the vessel in the transport. The carriage of course is drawn on a line of rails. It descends into water at the foot of the incline, where the vessel steams or sails on to it; the sides of the vessel may be wedged tight, the traction-rope is brought into play, and when the load reaches the top, the carriage again descends an incline into water to set free the vessel. This arrangement is in use at Elbing, on the Oberländische Canal. It is necessary to add that the vessels are flat-bottomed. The rise of the incline is between 60 and 70 Prussian feet. The arrangement has been in action about four years.

Mr. Edwin Clark exhibited a model of his patent Hydraulic-lift Graving-docks, by which the vessel, cradled on a shallow pontoon, is raised bodily out of the water, by means of hydraulic rams, to the level of the repairing-yard, instead of being floated into a basin and then exposed by the displacement of the water; ready access being also afforded to the bottom of the vessel.

A large and interesting model, showing the course of the Tudela and Bilboa Railway across the chain of the Cantabrian mountains, in the Basque provinces of Spain, as designed by Mr. C. Vignoles, was exhibited. The manner in which the line, onwards, is carried along the faces of steep cliffs, deserves attentive examination; and the work will give ample scope for ability in direction and skill in construction.

Mr. J. Chalmers exhibited a large drawing of his proposed Channel Railway connecting England and France. One or other of the published designs for a passage of the Channel by a railway, is very likely, we think, to be attempted before many more years have passed; and there will be hardly more serious difficulties in sinking tubes, in ventilating them, and in preserving them by submarine embankment, than once might have been, or were, seen to a tunnel under the Thames or through the Alps, or to the construction of bridges without scaffolding from the ground.

Several Models and Photographs of Suspension-bridges, not all for the passage of railway-trains, were shown. The chief work was a Railway-bridge, that of the Niagara—still not sufficiently appreciated, we think, by British engineers, and having, be it admitted, the defects which are sought to be counteracted by the chains anchoring the under-side of the roadway to the rock.—*Abridged from the Builder.*

An admirable series of models contributed by the French Minister of Public Works, comprised representations of the Sea-walls of Cherbourg and the Harbour of Marseilles. The system of construction in both cases, if not identical, is closely analogous. In the greatest depths, where the disturbing action of the wave ceases, the smaller stones are placed, or, more properly speaking, sunk, being allowed to assume their natural inclination. Above these again the larger material comes, increasing in bulk in proportion to the action of the waters; the largest masses of natural stone being surmounted, and the outer surface faced by enormous blocks of concrete, of which also the superimposed masonry is principally formed. This artificial stone is composed of the débris from the quarries mixed with hydraulic lime. Some of our engineers have employed concrete in this way: for example, Brunel in the Chepstow bridge, Page in the bridges at Chelsea and Westminster, and Hawkshaw at Hungerford.

The principal Bridges of which models were exhibited in the French Department were that of St. Just, that over the Garonne of Bordeaux, and the swivel-bridge at Brest; but they present no features with which we are not familiar.

The models of Graving-docks in the French Court showed little or nothing beyond the mere form; though there was exhibited a beautiful and elaborate model of the dockgate and entrance of Havre which reveals the details of their mechanism.

The most remarkable objects remaining in this Court were examples of the different orders of the Catadioptric Light.

The displays of Diving apparatus by Samson Barnett and Mr. Heincke, exhibited considerable improvements over those shown in 1851,—more especially in these important respects—the supply of atmospheric air to the diver, and the increased facilities of communication with the surface.

A very interesting exposition of the Clay manufactures of the Shropshire Coal-field included every conceivable application of the material, from drain-pipes to mosaic floors and Ruskinesque chimney-pots.

The numerous examples of Portable Gas apparatus formed a striking feature in this part of the Exhibition. Foremost among these we have no hesitation in placing the simple, cleanly, and economic machine shown by Messrs. Edmundson, of Dublin.—*Condensed from the Illustrated London News.*

CEMENT, AND ARTIFICIAL STONE.

Knight, Bevan, and Sturge, of Northfleet, exhibited a block of Portland Cement, weighing five tons, besides two blocks, one of them of eight tons, composed of nine parts of shingle and two parts of cement, as adapted for the construction of breakwaters. Lee, Son, and Smith, exhibited Portland and Scott's Cement, and

Scott's Plaster. Mr. J. C. Part's Martin's Cement, which obtained a medal in 1851, is said to involve a saving of 45 per cent. in cost of the material, whilst it can be painted upon within twenty-four hours of its application. Mr. W. J. Taylor showed how Portland Cement may be coloured in the mixing, mouldings and panels being varied, as well as contrasted with a differently coloured ground; but the colours were not very brilliant in the model. Bellman and Ivey's Scagliola; the artificial stone from Farnham; that from the Company employing Ransome's process; and that from Messrs. F. and G. Rosher, we can merely name.

Besides Mr. Ransome's Indurated Stone, there were several specimens of materials to which preservative processes have been applied. The difficulty, obvious to any practical architect, which attends us in a notice of this kind, and which we know not how the jurors will grapple with, of course is not wanting in regarding these specimens. In the instance of the Creosoted Woods shown by Mr. J. Bethell, however, the evidence is clear and satisfactory. In the case of piles, fourteen inches square, used at Grimsby, half the substance is found to be eaten away by the sea-worms, in ten years or less, where the pile had not been creosoted; whilst the creosoted pile, after exposure for the same time, is shown to be in the original state. The collection of specimens included sections from railway-sleepers after twenty-one years' constant use; the wood being scarcely injured. Mr. Szerelmey applied his "Arabian Zopissa, and granitic preserving and indurating compositions," to a great variety of materials, claiming to be able to prevent decay of every kind.—*From the Builder.*

ARCHITECTURAL PRODUCTIONS.

Mr. George Maw, of Broseley, arranged a most interesting Court, with a "collective series of Architectural Productions, illustrating the clay manufactures of the Shropshire Coal Field," acting on behalf of his own firm and W. B. Simpson and Sons, J. and E. Burton, G. Davis and Co., R. Evans, W. Exley, G.W. Lewis and Doughty, Mrs. Thorn, and the Colebrookdale and Madeley Wood Companies. The productions of the Benthall Works, which were chiefly from the designs of Mr. M. Digby Wyatt, held the most prominent place. The divisions of the series comprised "Roofing Materials," which included tiles, common and ornamental; unglazed, glazed, and enamelled; plain-tiles and pan-tiles; roof-crestings, plain and flanged, and with fixed and loose ornaments; ventilating roof-crest tiles; hip and gutter tiles, and flanged hip crestings; "Paving Materials," including Illustrations of the Revival of Pictorial Mosaic, consisting of a pavement, the subject "Apollo and the Four Seasons;" a facsimile head from the pavement at Bignor, and various works in *tesserœ*, geometrical mosaic, and tiles, plain and encaustic, and their combinations: Moresque mosaics and majolica tiles for wall-linings, some of which may be fixed by ornamental brass-headed nails, without cement; "Draining Materials," "Fire-bricks, Furnace Materials, and Stove Fittings," "Bricks and Materials used in the Construction of Walls," "Accessories to the Decoration of Buildings," and other articles, including pillars and square shafts effectively treated in colour, and with ornamented capitals; and "Raw Materials" illustrated by a section of the Shropshire Coal Field, and specimens, some of which show the relative shrinkages of the clays. It should be recollected that there are other, and perhaps higher, aims in architecture, than demonstrating the serviceableness and scope of any one material; in other words, interests and feelings of manufacturers, and the tastes of architects, are not what should lead to the same conclusions; but the geometrical mosaic is doing excellent service in the decoration of houses; and some of the credit for the obvious future of popular taste will be due to manufacturers and to those whom they have called to their assistance.—*From the Builder.*

CLAY AND METAL PIPE-MAKING.

Clay-ware Pipes, by Zeller, of Ollwiller (Haut-Rhin), enamelled, and Bitumenized Paper pipes, by Jaloureau, of Paris, of good manufacture, for the conveyance of water and gas, were exhibited. The bitumenized pipes are favourably reported on in Paris, as regards durability, after four years' trial; and elasticity is one of their advantages. Tinned lead pipes were shown by Ch. Sebille, of Nantes. An English patent for a somewhat similar description of piping (Bennett's) was sealed in 1861. The French manufacture has been carried on five or six years; and the town of Nautes is served with these pipes. The English method is described as pressing and tinning the interior surface of lead pipe in one operation; and Dr. Letheby, reporting nine days' experiments with common water, rain-water, and distilled water, tried in straight and bent forms of tube, states there to have been complete protection from corrosive action, the most delicate tests failing to discover the presence of lead in the water; whilst common lead, with the same water (rain and distilled) quickly communicated to the water a metallic impregnation. Sebille's piping is, however, tinned on both sides. He exhibited another description of pipe, manufactured from pulverized slate-refuse, or cinders, and about one-fifth part coal-pitch. This compound slate-paste, having been heated and well mixed in an iron pan, can be moulded into pipes, bricks, or slabs, and becomes so hard, whilst free from cracks, that neither water heated to 180°, nor any cold, affects it: a 3-inch pipe of usual substance will stand internal pressure of ten atmospheres.

We condense these details from the *Builder*; in conclusion, the Editor pertinently asks: " Would it not be possible to collect all the specimens of pipes of different materials, for the conveyance of water, and subject them all, or duplicates, to similar experiments, chemical and mechanical; the latter including not only experiments to ascertain the resistance to bursting, but others on the resistance to collapse, as from a weight of superincumbent earth. The results being tabulated, with prices, a record would be left, the value of which after the Exhibition, in every question of supply of water to town or house would be immense."

Amongst the British exhibitors of Pipes, Mr. J. Chatterton, of Wharf-road, City-road, showed lead, composition, and pure block-tin pipes of the most perfect manufacture; also ordinary lead pipes of all sizes, from 1-32nd of an inch to 6 inches diameter; lead mouldings, polygonal, and multiple pipes, the latter being used for the purpose of conveying various liquids into spirit-vaults, are enclosed in the large pipe for neatness of appearance and facility of fixing on walls, down angles, &c. The three pipes combined are especially designed for domestic purposes, the object being to convey to the different parts of the house hard and soft water and gas. Lead pipes are coated internally with pure tin, for use in those localities where the water forms poisonous salts with the ordinary lead pipe. Lead pipes were shown, lined with gutta-percha, for similar purposes as last named. These were also, by their lightness and remarkable strength, particularly suitable for conveying water in mountainous countries, where they would have to sustain a great pressure; and, from the frost-resisting properties of the gutta-percha, they are invaluable in cold latitudes. The Composition tubes for gas showed a great superiority in material and manufacture, and placed by the side of tin tubes, not only rivalled them in brilliancy, but were found also to equal them in hardness and toughness. The pure block-tin tube specimens were unequalled. Mr. Chatterton also exhibited specimens of Cylindrical Projectiles for smooth-bore guns, intended to obviate the necessity of using a rifle-barrel, with its tendency to fouling; and at the same time to secure that force and accuracy, which under ordinary circumstances are only attainable by the use of the rifle. Instead of receiving a rotatory motion, as heretofore, from a grooved barrel, it derives it from the resistance of the atmosphere acting upon a suitable helical apparatus in the bullet itself. The projectile is in shape a hollow cylinder, open at both ends, and the internal screw is made of different patterns.

NAVAL AND MILITARY MODELS, WEAPONS, AND APPLIANCES.

NAVAL AND MILITARY MODELS.

In the Court devoted to these articles the visitor could study, almost in a glance, the progress of naval architecture for nearly three centuries past. All kinds of these models were here, from that of the *Great Harry* down to our last and greatest ship, the *Warrior*, with lines as fine as a Dover packet. Yet almost a finer model still than the *Warrior* was shown side by side with what used to be the crack sailing-ship of the Navy as it was in

1840—the old and much-praised *Queen*. By this now old line-of-battle ship was placed the model of the *Northumberland*, the newest and most improved of the iron frigates yet building; so that even the least initiated could, at all events, judge of the change which has taken place in shape and size since the introduction of 5-inch ironsides obliged us to build vessels large enough to float with such a casing. This model of the *Northumberland* is equal, in the minute perfection of its guns, rigging, and fittings, to that of the *Warrior*, shown by the Thames Iron Company, and higher praise than this it would be difficult to give it.

Close by these was shown a series of most wonderfully perfect Models of Lighthouses, made to scale; which includes all the chief of those great sea-lamps, from the South Stack and Smeaton's *chef-d'œuvre* on the little Eddystone rock, down to the still more ingenious red-legged tripods which mark sands where no base for a granite structure can be found. Not only were there models of such mechanism as the rough and ready bridges of the Royal Engineers, but models of almost everything which relates to the science of defence and attack, whether of or from land or sea. Models of saps, mines, and covered ways—principally illustrated from works carried out during that greatest of all sieges, Sebastopol—explain how the strongest places must yield to the gradual assaults of military engineering; close by this was another model giving a rough bird's-eye view over London, and showing how it is only necessary to turn the beautifully wooded hills of Surrey and Middlesex into bastions, re-entering angles, dry ditches, caponnières, &c., to make our quiet metropolis as strong a fortress as the lost mistress of the Euxine was before the attack of the Allies.

An important American invention was shown—a series of beautiful little working models of the various machines used in Thompson's patent for Making Boats by Steam, which do all, even to curving and bevelling the edges; so that a rough board passing in at one end of a machine comes out at the other, not only curved, but bevelled and planed. To make a large and strong boat 33 feet long requires at least from eight to ten days' work, and costs for labour alone, exclusive of material, from 12*l.* to 16*l.* By Mr. Thompson's machinery a similar boat can be completed from the rough timber in five hours and a half, and at a cost for labour and machinery of from 1*l.* 15*s.* to 2*l.*

THE ARMSTRONG AND WHITWORTH GUNS.

We now proceed to the Military Weapons. Here was shown the new Gun invented by Sir William Armstrong. It is a rifled breech-loading 70-pounder, but one in which the chamber ventpiece and screw are entirely dispensed with. There is no doubt whatever but that the ventpiece and the movement necessary to place and close it are the least perfect parts of Sir William's invention as applied to very heavy breech-loading ordnance. In this gun it is superseded by a mechanism so simple that it may almost be termed self-acting, and so massive that it cannot be injured by shot, and, above all, so evenly balanced and sliding on such true surfaces, that a child's strength would suffice to open and close the breech. The gun is built up of wrought-iron coils and rifled in the usual manner; but in the breech on both sides two narrow openings are cut, into which are fitted two wedge-shaped masses of iron with handles. These, when drawn aside, have openings in them corresponding to the bore of the gun, which can then be seen through from end to end, a hollow rifled tube. The shot and powder are then inserted in the ordinary way at the breech, and the foremost of the sliding iron wedges we have mentioned drawn across so as to close the tube. The second and most massive wedge is then drawn into its position so as to jamb both tight, and the gun is ready for firing. By a simple but more ingenious mechanical contrivance connected with the lock of the gun, which slides down a powerful steel bolt that keys the two wedges together, the piece cannot be fired till both wedges are in their place, nor can they be withdrawn until this again is lifted. Only five or six movements of the hand are required to load a 100 or 150 pounder. A gun of this construction has been severely tested, yet not the slightest escape of gas, or rather fire, has ever occurred; and while the breach is almost hermetically closed, a sufficient play is allowed for the wedges to permit of their expansion from the heat of rapid firing. This is, in our opinion, the finest Breech-loading piece of Ordnance that Sir William Armstrong has yet invented. It has all the advantages as to range and strength of material of his previous inventions. It is cheaper because simpler in its method of construction; and can be fired much more rapidly, as it dispenses with the hitherto awkward necessity of lifting in and out the breechpiece, which was, in fact, the only drawback on the use of his very heavy guns for sea service. The gun will, we think, before long supersede the first invention as applied to the heaviest artillery, though the value of what we may now almost call the old method remains as great as ever for light ordnance. The Armstrong trophy attracted a great amount of notice, though really not as much as it deserved, for the whole of that huge Building contained no finer specimens.* It was a tree of Armstrong ordnance, arranged in an exceedingly pretty shape as to outward form, and containing in its structure such specimens of forging and carefully finished workmanship as it is not too much to say had never been seen.

Near the Armstrong Gun were shown sections of Shells of all sizes, both time and percussion. The Time-shell is adjusted by distance—that is, the fuse is cut short to burst the charge so many seconds after it leaves the gun, every second representing a space of 400 yards traversed. Thus, after one or two shots for "range," the shell can be burst to a nicety of 50 feet. The Percussion shell, as its name implies, explodes instantaneously on touching any obstacles after it leaves the gun.

* This huge pile of arms was in the nave of the Building.

Sir William Armstrong's segment Percussion-shell is the most destructive missile that the science of modern war has yet brought to perfection. The visitor could judge at a glance of their tremendous power, for close by the shells was exhibited a kind of large iron bee-hive, in which one of the small shells was exploded. There is scarcely a superficial inch of this in which one or more pieces of iron and lead are not sticking.

Near to this were exhibited the Guns of Armstrong's great competitor—Mr. Whitworth, whose Gun is still that which has attained the longest range and greatest accuracy, and is still the only piece that has sent as light a shot as 70 lh. through 4½ inches of solid iron plate. The Blakeley Gun, also in this Court, is a very good piece of rifled muzzle-loading ordnance, very similar in principle to the "*canon rayé*" of the French. Even, however, as a rifled muzzle-loader it is inferior to Whitworth's, which has the advantage of being a breech-loader as well. A large Wrought-iron Gun was exhibited from the Mersey works, which, as a perfect triumph of forging, should have been shown side by side with the double-throw crank of the same firm. The Shells of the Monster Mortar —shells which, when loaded, weigh as much as 25 cwt., are another instance of extravagant invention of which this Court offers as many samples as any other in the Building. Every kind of breech-loading small arm was, of course, to be found here. And here, by comparison, might be seen the superiority of the American invention of Mr. Storm over others. In this piece there is nothing special in either the lock, or stock, or barrel; the only invention, in fact, being the Breech-loading Apparatus, which is applicable to any and every barrel, at a cost, it is stated, as low as some 16s. each. The breech, about an inch, or an inch and a half in length, is fitted to the barrel by an ordinary hinge, which is thrown up or open by a movement of the finger or thumb, the charge inserted, and the breech closed. A breech-loading rifle is the great military desideratum now; so much so that the Prussian army is entirely armed with weapons of this class—very inferior ones, it is true, but infinitely better than any muzzle-loader. Last year some wonderful shooting was made at the Wimbledon meeting with breech-loaders of Mr. Storm's patent adapted to the Enfield and Whitworth rifles. Since then it has been tried by some of the highest professional authorities on musketry, and has been pronounced perfect. Its great advantages may be summed up in the few words—that it requires no special ammunition, is adaptable at the low cost we have mentioned to any rifle, which can then be loaded at either breech or muzzle, it is so simple in its mechanism, that it can be fired easily from 12 to 15 times a-minute, and as rapidly in the dark as in the daylight.—*Abridged from the Times.*

From the Carriage Factory at Woolwich was shown a series of specimens of Gun-carriages and Ambulances, with which no carriages in the Building could compare for strength, and very few for finish. The utilization of the cask-hoops which lay in tons about the camp at Sebastopol to mabe gabions and sap shields, was fully shown by the models in this Court.

Mr. Lancaster exhibited his oval-bore Cannon, with shot and shell for its service ; and also examples of the rifle which proved so eminently successful in the recent official trials at Woolwich. The system of construction is briefly described thus :—"The inside of the barrel is cut by proper machinery in spiral form, the difference between major and minor axis being ·012 of an inch." While admitting the value of more recently-invented weapons, we should not overlook those of Mr. Lancaster, remembering the tried services both of his artillery and small arms in the Crimean war and in the Indian mutiny.

A very interesting collection of Guns and Projectiles was contributed by the Whitworth Ordnance Company. The guns ranged in size from the 1-pounder to the 70-pounder, and comprised examples of both breech and muzzle-loaders. In every case the bore is hexagonal in its cross-section, and in the rifling the pitch is equal to twenty times the diameter of the bore. Messrs. Whitworth state the range of their 12-pounder rifled cannon, with a 12 lb. shot, and 1¾ lb. of powder, as follows :—At point blank, 380 yards ; at 1° of elevation, 900 yards ; at 5°, 2600 yards ; at 10°, 4500 yards ; at 20°, 7000 yards ; at 35°, 10,000 yards, or about 5¾ English miles !

A very beautiful Gun of small calibre, and constructed of cast-steel, was forwarded from Russia. A label attached to it informed us that it has withstood a test equivalent to 4000 charges. This argues a degree of tenacity in the metal of which it is composed, second only—if second, indeed, it be—to that of which the Prussian cannon are made.

Prussia contributed an interesting collection of Gun-barrels of the famous steel of Messrs. Krupp, of Ensen. They were shown, together with various specimens of the metal, including one ingot of thirty tons weight, in the Western Annexe. "When we examine the illustrations here offered of the texture (so to speak) of this steel, we cease to be surprised that the guns made from it have borne with impunity the rigid test that has been applied to some of them. This consists of sealing securely the muzzle of the gun, after having previously filled the barrel with powder ; when, on application of the fuse, the whole charge burns away harmlessly through the touch-hole, leaving the barrel perfect and flawless."—*Illustrated London News.*

NEW CARTRIDGE.

A new seamless Skin Cartridge, the invention of Captain M. Hayes, and exhibited by H. Gladstone and Co., of London, excited much interest. The advantages which it possesses over ordinary cartridges are its waterproof qualities, greatly increased facilities of loading, cleanliness, and cheapness. In addition to the natural damp-resisting properties of the skin used in the manufacture, it is chemically prepared, so as to be impervious to wet. The ordinary paper cartridge cannot resist water, and naturally absorbs moisture. The facilities in loading gained by this invention are extraordinary. The cartridge requires neither biting, tearing, nor puncturing ; but by one action is passed entire, viz., powder and ball in one complete whole, into the muzzle of the arm used, and goes clean down to the point of ignition. The spark from the percussion-cap penetrates the skin, and the charge is exploded without the chance of hang or misfire. Three rounds may accordingly be fired in the time occupied by one when using paper or other cartridge: it is more cleanly, inasmuch as no loose powder is introduced into the barrel, no fouling takes place, the barrel remaining as polished and free from soil after 100 rounds, as before the first was fired. These advantages are multiplied under circumstances which render loading difficult: thus, the cavalry soldier, already engaged in the management of a restive horse, is occupied a long time in loading, and not unfrequently *loses* the greater part of his charge. The seamless skin cartridge thus renders a muzzle-loading arm almost equal to a breech-loader ; while for the latter it is adopted by inventors of guns on that principle. In boat service again, the injurious effects of surf and spray are avoided, which has induced Her Majesty's Government, after submitting this ammunition to the severest trials on our foreign stations, to adopt the skin cartridge exclusively for the Royal Navy. It has been successfully tried for lifeboat purposes, in connexion with a howitzer invented by Mr. Scott, of the Lutch Breech-loading Gun Company; by its means a line is projected over a ship in distress, either from boat or shore, with much greater power and precision than by any other plan yet devised.

MARINE ENGINES.

As might naturally be expected, the most important part of the exhibition of machinery was that where the object was Marine Propulsion. There were no less than seven pairs of Marine Engines fitted up complete for work, the aggregate power of which could not be less than 2000 horses. First was a magnificent pair of engines, by Maudslay, for H.M.S. *Valiant*, of 800-horse power ; by the side of them a pair of trunk engines by Penn, of Greenwich, of 300-horse power ; and near to these a pair of 400-horse power by Humphreys and Tennant. These engines were of the highest class of workmanship and design, and exhibited the extraordinary perfection now attained by the first-rate constructors of Steam Marine Engines.

Messrs. G. Rennie and Sons exhibited a pair of marine screw engines for H.M.S. *Reindeer*. These are of 200-horse power nominal. They may be nominated single trunk engines, and for compactness of arrangement rivalled any in the Exhibition. The projecting trunk, objected to by many, is absent in Rennie's engines, while they have the advantage of a long connecting-rod, which one misses in those of Humphreys and Tennant, just referred to. The cylinders are placed close to the condensers, and thus a good vacuum is likely to be ensured. The bottom bearing of the connecting-rod, too, is easy of access—a practical point, which those who are acquainted with the working of marine engines will know how to appreciate. The slide-valves are double ported, and the pressure of steam at the back is relieved by an arrangement first introduced into marine engines by Messrs. Rennie. These engines are simple in construction, and at the same time possess great strength; and are, therefore, apparently well calculated for the hard work contingent on constant steaming in long voyages. Messrs. Rennie were also represented by models of the following kinds:—One of the 14 double-screw gunboats, made by them for the Spanish Government for the suppression of piracy in the Pacific. A model of one of the 10 double screw-gunboats constructed for the East Indian Government, and used for river-service during the Mutiny. There were also models of the celebrated steel gunboats made by the Messrs. Rennie for the Russian Government, and used against the pirates of the Caspian Sea. These boats draw only 20 inches of water, and are thus enabled to pursue sea-robbers into the shallowest creeks and inlets of the Caspian.

Perhaps, however, the most interesting models of the Rennie group, were those of a portion of the Gigantic Floating Dock, constructed by the firm for the arsenals of Cartagena and Ferrol in Spain; and of an Armour-plated Frigate, in process of being docked. A very clear idea of the ingenious construction of the floating docks is conveyed by this model; a part of the outer skin or plating being removed, to show the pumps, sluices, and machinery employed in raising and lowering the dock.

There was also to be seen a model of an extension of the Rennie system of Docking as it is now being carried out at Cartagena. It consists of flat shallow slip-ways, so arranged that vessels may be hauled off the floating dock on the land, and thus the dock itself may be made available for docking many vessels in immediate succession. This operation has, indeed, been effected at the arsenal of Cartagena; and among the vessels so docked was the celebrated frigate *Novara*, which had just completed the circumnavigation of the globe on behalf of the Austrian Government.

Among the best marine steam-engines shown in the Exhibition were those manufactured by Humphrey and Tennant for the *North Star*, representing exactly the form and arrangement of all the screw-engines which Humphrey and Tennant have made for ships of war, amounting to about fifty pairs, within the last seven years, and fitted to vessels belonging to the British, Brazilian, Greek, Portuguese, Russian, and Turkish navies. They are technically known as "direct-acting short-stroke and short-connecting-rod engines." The short connecting-rod is found to give off more power to the crank than a long one, owing to the friction caused by the appliances necessarily introduced to enable a longer rod to be employed; and the short-stroke and short connecting-rod admits of a very simple and effective arrangement being introduced, as exhibited by the engines of the *North Star*. Practically there is no difference in the speed of a vessel of a given size with a given power, whether the stroke and rod be long or short; but the short stroke and short rod will drive a given ship a given speed at less cost than will a long stroke and long rod ; for although the short proportions cause a very slight increase in expenditure of fuel, the long proportions cause a considerable increase in the cost of lubricating material. Putting it in exact figures, a pair of engines of 400-horse power with a long connecting-rod will save 4s. 6d. per day in coal over a short one, but the short one will use 11s. per day less of lubricating material : indeed the effect is so nearly alike that both proportions may be considered equal ; hence the simplicity of the engines of Humphrey and Tennant. The engines of the *North Star* are nominally 400 horse; they have cylinders 64¼ inches diameter, and make a stroke of 2 feet 8 inches, going 70 revolutions per minute. A pair made from the same patterns, tried on board her Majesty's ship *Albion*, were worked up to 1865 horses.

Richardson and Sons, of Hartlepool, exhibited a working model of inverted Cylinder Marine Engines, as fitted on board of screw-steamers. The consumption of fuel in no case exceeds 112 lb. per hour for each 10 (nominal) horse power ; and the indicated horse power in each of the engines they have made is from three-and-a-half to four-and-a-half times the nominal power. The arrangement is very compact, and occupies little space in the ship. The cylinders are steam jacketed, and fitted with feed super-heating apparatus.

Every one of these engines was of the screw-engine type, for apparently paddle-engines are old fashioned now; though it is only eleven years since, at the last Exhibition, they were in the zenith of their fame, and screw-engines were almost in their infancy. —*Abridged from the Times.*

A pair of marine engines exhibited by John Penn and Son, were excellent exponents of workmanship : they are on the direct acting principle, and are intended for a screw steam-ship. The engines are of the collective power of 600 horses, and have been manufactured for the Spanish Government. The cylinders are 78 inches in diameter, and the length of the stroke is 3 feet 6 inches. The connecting-rods are 9 feet long. Several pairs of engines of a nearly similar character have been made for the respective navies, and they have been found to work with perfect smoothness and regularity. Each condenser is provided with a double-acting air-pump 23 inches in diameter, the length of stroke being the same as that of the piston.

PUMPING-ENGINES FOR WATER-WORKS.

Models of a Pumping-engine and Safety-balance valve, as erected and used at the Lea-bridge branch of the East London Waterworks, were exhibited by Harvey and Co., and Hayle, Cornwall. Having seen the originals of these we can vouch for the fidelity of the models. The Lea-bridge engine, which was erected by Messrs. Harvey some five or six years since, was at the time of its erection the largest in or near London. When working full power it pumps 9000 gallons of water per minute to a height usually of 140 feet. The water thus raised is conveyed into London by means of cast-iron pipes 36 inches in diameter.

In 1858 Harvey & Co. erected, for the Southwark and Vauxhall Water Company, at Battersea, a Pumping-engine, the cylinder of which is 112 inches in diameter, and weighs 36 tons. This engine, though the largest and most powerful ever built for such a purpose, is of the most simple construction. The steam-valves are all on the equilibrium principle, and the arrangement of parts is throughout such that this colossus of engines, so to speak, is as completely under the control of a pigmy, but intelligent engineman, as is the small engine in a factory. The quantity of water pumped up for the supply of London daily amounts to 115,000,000 gallons. Of this enormous quantity 79,000,000 of gallons are pumped by means of single-acting engines on Harvey's plan.—*Mechanics' Magazine.*

GAS ENGINEERING.

One of the best illustrations of the progress effected since 1851 was in the number of exhibitors of fire-clay Gas-Retorts at the Exhibition. This has been caused through iron gas retorts being superseded by earthenware retorts in almost every town exceeding 10,000 inhabitants.

Boucher and Keller, of Belgium, exhibited some very large pieces of Fire-clay goods, it is thought, larger than any ever made in England. Messrs. Cowen showed two Gas Retorts beautifully manufactured from the Newcastle fire-clay. John Hall and Co. showed a glass-house pot of superior make; and gas-retorts and crucibles, partly made from carbon incrustation.

The engineering department contained the beautiful Coal-gas Apparatus invented by Mr. George Bower, for lighting isolated country mansions and factories: it occupies only a few square feet of space, but will supply gas for twenty lights.

Bischoff and Co. exhibited Clegg's Gas-meter, an improvement on the wet meter; ensuring correct registrations, independent of a variation of the water-level, whether caused by evaporation or wilful abstraction. The principle consists in floating the drum by an air-vessel, which permits the revolving drum to rise or fall, according to the height of the water in the case, and to work free from friction on the bearings.

In Mr. Sugg's case were shown a photometer, eudiometer, exhauster-gauge, &c. Mr. G. Glover, of Pimlico, exhibited a meter, by which quantities of gas so minute as from $\frac{1}{100}$ to $\frac{1}{3000}$ part of a cubic foot can be measured with precision each second.

Mr. Warner advertised his patent anhydrous oxide of iron for purifying coal-gas; Mr. Cockey showed his patent Centre Valve which will perform the work of half a dozen single valves. The pressure and supply of gas to the Exhibition Building was governed by the regulating valves of C. Walker and Son's make.

A sample of the red tin canisters which uselessly disfigure the public lamps was shown at the Exhibition. Also Mr. Prossex's Oxyhydrogen Lime Lamp, the identical one used for three months at the South Foreland Lighthouse. The lime-light was fitted up two years since at Westminster Bridge; but the great cost of manufacturing oxygen gas, together with this mode requiring two lines of pipe, caused its discontinuance. Mr. Clarke showed his patent Gas Regulator, which, like those invented by Mr. Paddon and Mr. Hart, are useful for public lamps. There was also Mr. Hughes's safety whistling Gas Chandelier. In a similar manner whistles might be fixed a few inches above the lower curbs of gasholders, to make known when they are full. There were shown Bitumenized Pipes for gas and water purposes. Time alone will satisfy people whether such description of pipes will retain water under-pressure, or bear the chemical action of gas.

In 1851 the only Paraffine Candle exhibited was made from turf. The considerable display made by Mr. Young, and Messrs. Field, and many others, of blocks of Paraffin and Candles, proves the manufacture of this article to have arisen during the past ten years. In 1872, it is probable that the paraffine exhibited will be made from the lately introduced rock-oil.

Mr. Shepard's magneto-electric light was shown. This remarkable light has been two winters in use at the South Foreland Lighthouse, and is now fitted up by the Trinity Board at Dungeness. The light produced is intense—sufficient, it is stated, in a revolving lens giving off six rays, to enable any person with average sight to read at a distance of ten miles.—*Mechanics' Magazine.*

PHILOSOPHICAL INSTRUMENTS.

Amongst the general instruments exhibited were cloud-mirrors, sunshine recorders; and a galactoscope for measuring the transparency of milk. The Right Hon. Robert Lowe showed Spectacles which magnify without glass or any other refracting medium; and Dr. Lankester exhibited an Ozonometer for registering the hourly variations of ozone. The Stereotrope, or Stereoscopic Thaumatrope, the invention of Mr. W. T. Shaw, was shown: it applies the principle of the stereoscope to thaumatropes, phantascopes, plenakistoscopes, &c., which depend for their results on "persistence of vision," superadding the effects of solidity, so that the object is perceived as if in motion, and with an appearance of relief as in nature. The curious and beautiful effects of the plenakistoscope are wonderfully enhanced by the addition of solidity in this instrument.

The principal exhibitors of Microscopes were Smith, Beck, and

Beck, Ross, and Powell and Lealand. In the case of the first firm was shown the instrument from its rough casting to its finished state. We must not overlook a novelty in the display of these exhibitors. The late Prof. Hounslow suggested the desirability of a microscope which could be placed in a public museum and supplied with a stock of objects. Smith and Beck have carried out his suggestion, and the result is a Microscope containing five hundred different objects arranged so that they can be seen with three different powers, at choice; and placed on a revolving cylinder which, while it brings them successively under view, prevents their being injured.

The improvements effected by Mr. Wenham deserve mention: what Wheatstone did for the photograph, when he contrived the stereoscope, Mr. Wenham has done for microscopic objects. No longer a mere flat image is produced: the binocular microscope, by a contrivance for the use of both eyes, gives perfect stereoscopic relief, and at the same time saves much labour to the eyes of the spectator. We believe this to be the most important advance in the manufacture of the microscope since 1854.—*Condensed from the Illustrated London News.*

Mr. Norman showed a wonderful series of microscopic slides containing minute sections and preparations of almost every conceivable object, animal or vegetable: from sections of the tooth of a lion to the liver or skin of a man, from the lungs of a boa constrictor to the palate of a toad or the tongue of an alligator.

A machine was exhibited by Mr. Peters for Microscopic Writing, which is infinitely more wonderful than Mr. Whitworth's machine for measuring the millionth of an inch, which excited such astonishment in 1851. With this machine of Mr. Peters it is stated that the words "Matthew Marshall, Bank of England," can be written in the two and-a-half millionth of an inch in length. The words to be written microscopically are written in pencil, in ordinary characters, on a sheet of paper at the bottom of the instrument. But the pencil with which this is done communicates by a series of levers and gimbals with another minute pencil and tablet at the top, by means of which the ordinary writing of the pencil and the pencil for the microscopic writing both move in unison, though the motion of the latter is so graduated that a stroke of a quarter of an inch at the bottom is only a stroke of a quarter of a millionth of an inch at the top, the shape and character of both marks being nevertheless precisely alike in outline. As a matter of course, the microscopic writing at the top is only visible under powerful magnifiers; the object of the machine is chiefly to mark bank-notes with certain minute signatures for the prevention of forgery. Close by this curious instrument was Mr. Babbage's Calculating Machine, which will work quadrations and calculate logarithms up to seven places of figures.* It was the account of this invention written by the late Lady Lovelace, Lord Byron's daughter—that led the

* See a large Engraving of this Machine, never before published, in *Stories of Inventors and Discoverers*, by the Editor of the present volume. 1860.

Messrs. Scheutz, of Stockholm, to improve upon it to such an extent as not only enabled the machine to calculate its tables, but to print its results. This improvement was at once bought up by the English Government, but it is not now shown at the Exhibition. The small and by no means complicated machine of Mr. Babbage was in the gallery.

Negretti and Zambra showed instruments entirely new, and most of the important ones. Among these was a Thermometer so exquisitely sensitive as to rise at once upon the approach of the hand within two or three inches : this was made specially to test the temperature of the body and coils of the python during her attempted incubation at the Zoological Gardens.

Messrs. Elliott exhibited a number of Electrometers of the most delicate kind ; a large Electrifying Machine, with ebonite discs ; improved air-pumps on a large scale ; Drawing Instruments in aluminium, bronze, &c. ; Micrometer gauges for shot and shell ; improved Quadrant for levelling rifled cannon ; and a large and very beautiful sectional model of a Steam-engine, with all the latest improvements. Murray and Heath showed an improvement upon the Electric Lamp, by which the electrodes are kept at constant distances without the intervention of any clockwork motion. An improved instrument for observing the circular Polarization of Liquids, and an entirely new reflecting Stereoscopic Microscope, were also shown.

Frastré, Brunnier, and Dutron exhibited, in the French department, Meteorological Instruments of perfect manufacture. Naudet and Company, of Paris, showed some exquisitely sensitive Aneroid Barometers; and Colombi and Sons, from the same city, a collection which maintains their high character as optical instrument-makers. M. Kœnig showed a wonderful collection of instruments applied to the illustration of the theory of the conduction, undulation, and vibration of Sound. By a most ingenious but simple instrument— a common glass cylinder, coated with fine lampblack, and applied, turning, to a tuning-key when vibrating—M. Kœnig makes sound its own printer. From the impression left on this cylinder all the different vibrations and undulations of sound between A and G are here recorded from their outset to their latest tone, have been made to register themselves, and from the records thus left a most beautiful series of acoustic charts has been drawn out.

M. Bardou, of Paris, who is the manufacturer of three-fourths of the opera-glasses which come to this country, showed a beautiful series of Telescopes and Optical Instruments, though why he was not allowed to show opera-glasses as well it is difficult to say. The most important of French exhibitors was, of course, Duboscq, who, as in 1851 and 1855, sent a collection of the best made and the rarest philosophical instruments. Beyond all doubt, the finest constructed Solar Spectrum we have yet seen was shown in his collection. M. Deleuil, the inventor of the beautifully-adjusted Balance for the Imperial Mint, and from which our own, we think, is an adaptation, of course sent a number of wonderfully-adjusted scales, which the 1-1000th part of a grain or a sunbeam at either side would almost suffice to turn. He likewise showed what are apparently two powerful hooped Mortars, mounted upon high wheels, but which the chemist at once recognised as the receptacles used for the solidification of carbonic acid gas. M. Collot sent some Balances made of aluminium; and, as in 1851, Madame Gavard was in the French Gallery at her Pentograph— an instrument which, by a careful adjustment of gimbals and levers, follows the motion of a hand tracing drawings, to reproduce them by a pencil fixed in a rod at the furthermost extremity. Since 1851 an improvement has been made in this machine, which can now be applied to the purposes of the engraver, and made to produce on copper fac-simile copies simultaneously. In the Berlin Court of the Zollverein M. Wagner exhibited an Engraving Pentograph of a different kind, applied to the production of those curious bas-relief engravings with which the public have lately become familiar. M. Perreaux exhibited his straight line dividing instruments, such as are used at Kew and by all the leading philosophical instrument-makers. He also showed a novelty since 1851—a Spherometer, for measuring the curves of object-glasses. This instrument is of such extreme delicacy, that when adjusted to zero, even placing the hand on the ground-glass plane beneath, from which the slender index works, is sufficient to deflect it instantly. M. Bertrand showed some small Spheres of Iceland spar, and a good collection of Nicols Prisms for the polarization of light; and Hoffmann also contributed very fine specimens of the same kind. None in the Foreign Department showed good Photographic negatives of Microscopic objects but Roncoli, of Bergamo, in the Italian section. Some of these instantaneous photographs of the magnified blood and anatomy of the most minute insects were among the most wonderful *tours de force* that this chemical art showed in the Building. In the French Department was the Calculating Machine of M. Thomas—the Babbage of France. It is so small as to fit in a compass not greater than that of a good musical snuff-box. Yet, by simply winding a handle, 18 seconds suffice to multiply 8 figures by 8; to divide 16 figures by 8 figures only 24 seconds are required, and a square root of 16 figures is obtained within a minute! And all this is done by turning a handle rapidly, and the price of the whole apparatus is within the reach of most buyers.

In the Zollverein, M. Greiner showed such specimens of Glassblowing for the finer kinds of philosophical and chemical apparatus as are really almost indescribable for their wonderful skill.

The preceding details have been, in the main, selected and condensed from the excellent Report on the Philosophical Instruments, which appeared in the *Times* journal.

PHOTOGRAPHY AND PHOTOGRAPHIC APPARATUS.

Photography may be said to be an entirely new Class since 1851; indeed, the art itself can scarcely be said to have existed at that time, if we compare it with its now universal spread. It is true we had then the Daguerréotype and the Talbotype; the former the only process sufficiently rapid to take portraits, and the latter only suited to views and objects admitting of long exposure to the camera. We all remember the very beautiful specimens of both these processes exhibited in the Building in Hyde Park. They were, however, few in number, and exhibited as mere adjuncts of the philosophical instruments. Still they showed what was doing; for hitherto the workers had carried on their labours without knowing what others were employed upon; and this, combined with Archer's invention of the collodion process, gave a great impulse to the art; the extremest rapidity was obtained, the imperfection of the texture of the paper got rid of, and the power of multiplying copies to any extent at a cheap rate was achieved. Notwithstanding the very inadequate space which the Commissioners were able to allot for the display of the art, British photography need fear no comparison with its Continental rivals. The landscapes of Bedford Mudd, Robinson, the Earl of Caithness, Vernon Heath, Lady Jocelyn, Cundall and Downes, and a host of others, attested a supremacy in the art which, we venture to assert, very few, if any, Continental rivals will dispute. C. Thurston Thompson and Caldesi showed gigantic photographs of the cartoons of Raffaelle, wonderful as masterpieces of manipulation. In portraits, the well-known names of Williams, Claudet, Mayall, Lock and Whitfield, Mayer, Dolamore and Bullock, Maull and Polyblank, &c., were exhibitors: their coloured photographs are in reality miniatures, being so worked by hand as to leave no trace of the photograph.

Negretti and Zambra exhibited transparent Photographs on glass, similar to those well-known productions of Ferrier of Paris. Enlarged photographs were shown by Claudet and others, which were life-sized, and some of them coloured. Paul Pretsch, Pouncey, John Field, and F. Joubert contributed specimens of this class.

Mr. Warren De la Rue exhibited his most interesting series of Photographs, showing the progress of the late Total Eclipse of the Sun, as seen in Spain.

Colonel Sir Henry James, director of the Ordnance Survey, showed specimens of "Photo-Zincography," for the reduction, enlarging, and printing of maps and plans. Sir Henry showed adaptations of it to the production of fac-similes of ancient MS., and one of a page of Domesday Book. The photograph, by a simple and cheap process, is transferred to a zinc plate, whence any number of copies can be taken off by the ordinary plate printing process.

F. Joubert exhibited a series of very beautiful pictures burnt in on glass, a marvellous adaptation of the photographic art in an absolutely new direction. By a pure photographic process he produces on the glass, in ceramic colours, a picture, which, by exposure to heat in the furnace becomes burnt in like any other picture on glass or china. By a careful and artistic manipulation he has been able to produce effects in several colours. The process has been perfected, and a cheap and artistic ornamentation of our windows is brought within the means of the many.

Some of the best Photographs in the display were by English artists resident in France; some remarkably fine ones were sent by Mr. Maxwell Lyte, an amateur.

Mingled with the photographs were the instruments and appliances used in the art. In lenses, on which the artist is so greatly dependent, there has been great progress made since 1851. Ross and Dalmeyer showed some very fine specimens—marvellous proofs of a combination of mathematical theory with the skilful development of the practical optician. Horne and Thornethwaite, veterans in the field of photography, Murray and Heath, Bland and Co., attested what the English can do as makers of apparatus. One firm showed specimens of albumenized paper, in preparing which they use annually half a million of hens' eggs.

The Educational appliances in this department of the Exhibition likewise deserved an attentive visit.

The right of taking Photographs in the Building was purchased for nearly 2000 guineas, by the London Stereoscopic Company, whose Photographs for Stereoscopes are clear and sharp as instantaneous views; the tinted views especially bringing out every light and shade, and every tone of colour, in the Building.

In these pictures the statuary comes out with all the sharpness of high relief, and every column and rib of the nave may be counted. In some, such as the collection of glass in the English and Austrian Courts, the effect is more than stereoscopic—it is an optical delusion; less a picture of the places as we see them than the places themselves. The quaint, funny monstrosities of the Japanese Court were reproduced to the life; here we got the long vista of ponderous wheels and thrusting pistons of the Machinery Annexe; the veiled figures of Monti came out with beautiful distinctness; and the pale, earnest features of the Reading Girl were copied with all the force of the statue itself. This latter was apparently the popular picture, as nearly 200 gross of its copies were sold per week. On the whole, this pictorial record of the finest Exhibition that has yet been held was in every way worthy of the advance the chemical art has made since our last World's Fair in 1851.—*Abridged from the Times.*

CLOCKS AND WATCHES.

There were giants of Clocks in the days of the Exhibition o 1862, as well as in that of 1851, and although our great public clocks of late have hardly performed in proportion to their bulk, those in the Exhibition have, we believe, kept the promise to the ear.

The great Dial around the stained glass window at the eastern end of the Nave, measuring nearly 40 ft. in diameter, was the first lion of this class. It was worked by a clock made by Dent, maker of the great clock at Westminster Palace. In this clock the aim was to show that the hands for an immense dial can be worked by a comparatively small movement. In large clocks two-seconds pendulums, of about 15 ft. in length, are almost always used; the attempt was here made to show that one of 8 ft. long is sufficient for this great dial. The movement of this, with the exception of the escapement, is of iron. This firm had also in the eastern Transept a fine specimen of the Turret Clock striking the hours on a bell weighing between three and four tons, and the quarters on four smaller bells. The whole of the wheels are composed of gun-metal, and, though working four dials of only 7 ft. diameter in the Exhibition Building, the apparatus is capable of working the same number of 12 ft. diameter. There was also at work by the side of this clock a smaller one showing the time only, the construction of which demands special attention. The maintaining power which continues the performance of the clock while winding, has the advantage of exerting an equal force during the whole time of winding, as well as the capability of multiplying the winding-power at discretion. The rémontoire in this clock is driven by a weight hanging from a drum, thus equalizing the force and avoiding the effects of a varying temperature experienced in a spring rémontoire. The description of gravity escapement used in this clock is particularly safe, it being scarcely possible to make it trip.

Another gigantic work, termed *par excellence* "The Great Exhibition Clock," was placed in the central tower of the south side of the Exhibition Building. The maker is Mr. Benson, of Ludgate-hill. Its special peculiarity is a new double lever rémontoire, the application of which diminishes the friction or retarding force, and allows of great motive power, even to the extent of 20 tons, being used without disturbing the time-keeping qualities. In all cases where the works of a clock are at a great distance from the dial, as in this case, the outer dial being 300 ft. from the works, a great motive power is requisite. Mr. Benson's clock has a compensated two-seconds pendulum, 15 ft. long, and all the pivots will run in gun-metal bosses fitted in plummer-blocks. These plummer-blocks had never been applied to clockwork before: their advantages are, that they allow of any portion of the clockwork being removed without disturbing the whole. Every wheel of the clock is made of gun-metal, and the chimes are those of St. Mary's at Cambridge, remodelled, so that their intonation may denote first, second, or third quarters. The weights of the Clock are in the eastern corner of the Exhibition, some 200 ft. from the works; they were carried under the floor, and finally passed over a pulley, fixed 70 ft. above the foundations of the Building. The bells together weigh 50 cwt., and were cast by Mears, of Whitechapel. The foundations of the clock were erected by Kelk and Lucas, in solid brickwork, sunk 15 ft. below the floor of the Building. The ironwork is by Potter, of South Molton-street: it is richly decorated by Jackson, of Rathbone-place, and Mr. Crace.

The Commissioners are stated to have dwarfed its proportions by some 4 ft., and to have almost "spoilt the case." Besides the great Dial, 9 ft. in diameter, surmounting the entrance, four smaller ones were placed round the works at the four cardinal points.

Mr. Bennett, of Cheapside, also exhibited a large Clock, surmounted with a timeball and figure of Victory. This last work was in communication with Greenwich, so that the timeball was discharged at noon to the fraction of a second.

The great Watch and Clock Makers of Clerkenwell exhibited in full strength. After Clerkenwell, but at some distance, came the watches of Coventry; and last of all, the prettiest and cheapest, but much inferior, watches of Switzerland. In this class all the great watch and clock manufacturers of England showed their masterpieces of workmanship. There were reversible chronometers, steam clocks, marine chronometers, astronomical clocks, geographical clocks, silent clocks, skeleton clocks, Liliputian alarm clocks, electro-magnetic clocks, keyless watches, electric clocks, mercurial timepieces, clocks showing mean time and longitude at important places, and galvano-magnetic clocks; and gold and silver watches of every description.

Mr. Benson also exhibited a collection of horological curiosities, ranging from 100 to 250 years old, and intended in some degree to illustrate the gradual rise and progress of Watchmaking and Watch Ornamentation. One of the earliest was of the ordinary vertical construction, but has a gut instead of a winding-chain, and has no pendulum-spring. The case is covered with shagreen, ornamented with a regular pattern formed of small gold pins, which also serve to attach the shagreen cover to the body of the case. The dial is of enamel, the centre blue, surrounded by an edge of white, on which the hours are painted in black: the maker's name, "Goublons, Paris." There were also two curious old silver watches of an oval form, maker's name, "Grinkin, Fleet-street:" these also were without a hairspring, and a winding-gut instead of a chain. Of about the same date, and with the same peculiarities which mark the three preceding, was a watch with a case cut from a solid Brazilian topaz. Next was a small but beautifully-constructed verge-watch, remarkable for accuracy of construction: the case cut from an agate mounted in gold, set with diamonds: maker's name, "Archamb, London." The next was of the vertical construction, remarkable only for two very fine enamel paintings on the case—one of "The Adoration of the Shepherds," the other "The Flight into Egypt." The peculiarity of the next watch was, that it was wound up at the centre pinion by which the hands are set in modern watches, while to put the watch to the time it is necessary to move its one hand with the finger: maker's name, "Gaudron, à Paris." The next in the collection was of the same construction as that first described, but the watch demands particular attention from the very splendid enamels with which the case is ornamented. These enamels, one of which is outside and one inside the case (which is made of iron), are evidently portraits of some distinguished persons, thought to be Charles I., while the exaggerated hair and vivacious expression of countenance of its neighbour betokened a French original: maker's name, "Rigault, à Blois." The next is supposed to be a relic of the celebrated Parliamentarian, Pym. It is of the vertical construction, and repeats the hours on a bell, fixed within the case. The outer case is of brass, covered with tortoiseshell, ornamented in the same manner as the last described. On the inner part of the case is scratched "John Pyme, his watche, A.D. 1628." Maker's name, "Johannes Bayes, Londini." The last watch we have to notice is of the horizontal construction, and evidently modern make. Its great peculiarity is, that it shows the month, day of the month, day of the week, hour, minute, second; age, and first, second, or third quarter of the moon. This very curious watch has six hands, three of which are affixed to the centre, while the other three are opposite the figures 3, 6, and 9, respectively: maker's name, "Sarton, à Liège."—*Abridged from the Observer.*

Aubert and Linton exhibited an Astronomical and Geographical Clock, the work of M. Henry Grettillat, who devoted twenty-three years to its construction. It possesses a compensating pendulum, formed of nine branches, and carries at its lower extremity a dial, which by two hands indicates the variation to the eight-hundredth part of half an inch. It also gives thirty-five different demonstrations, and has twenty-six dials, which respectively indicate the revolutions of the sun; sunrise and sunset, with solstices and equinoxes; a perpetual calendar; the months, the date of the months, the days of the week; the equation of time; the changes of the moon; and the hour of the day in twenty-two towns.

A curious specimen from Nuremberg, the birthplace, so to speak, of pocket-watches, was a handsome and large Watch with an enamelled case enriched with pearls, the works in which play a variety of tunes. This, however, is a comparatively modern English specimen taken at the general "loot" of the Emperor's Summer Palace, at Yuen Min Yuen. There were also shown Chronograph Watches, which mark time to tenths of seconds. Many of these watches were in cases ornamented with designs for which prizes were offered at the various Government schools. Some of these designs were of great beauty, and attempt to compete with foreigners in decorative watches.

M. Oudin Charpentier exhibited several Watches of exquisite workmanship. One was a Chatelaine and Watch in rock crystal; the chatelaine itself the head of the lion surmounted by the British crown in gold. In its mouth is a ring of brilliants, from which is suspended a small repeater and self-winding watch, the dial of which is of crystal. Instead of the ordinary figures to denote the hours, there are twelve small scutcheons, which have the words "Dieu mon droit" traced in brilliants, these twelve letters representing the hours. The back of the watch is also of crystal, and is ornamented with a garter in brilliants; around are the three emblematic flowers of the United Kingdom. The same exhibitor showed some cruciform Watches, to be worn round the neck: one, in the antique style, and richly jewelled, was made for the Empress of the French; another, ornamented with brilliants, sapphires, and rubies, for the Queen of Spain; a third in jasper, with engraved ornaments, inlaid with gold, with the four Evangelists' emblems; and there was also one of these watch crosses made for the Pope, ornamented with a relievo carving on steel; and a watch made for the King of Spain, striking the hours and quarters of itself, and repeating the minutes at the will of the wearer. It has national escutcheons, and the Collar of the Order of the Golden Fleece and that of Charles III.; and these surround on one side the arms of the King, on the other the cipher of his Majesty; the backs are bordered with two circles, formed of chased fleurs-de-lis, more than two hundred in number. Both the dial and dome of the watch are of crystal, and the works are consequently exposed to view.

There were Watches with double running seconds hands, one stopping on pressing a knob; the other starts, and marks the number of seconds travelled, and when disengaged they both adjust themselves to the minute hand. Another showed the time of day in about fifty different parts of the world, by a dial, revolving within a circle, on which were marked the names of the cities or towns. The designs exhibited for ornamenting the cases of Geneva Watches were very beautiful, and showed exquisite effects of form and colour in their details. Those by Alphonse Dubois and Fritz Kimdert were amongst the most admired.

ELECTRIC TELEGRAPHS AND ELECTRICAL APPARATUS.

It has been aptly observed that the practical influence of electrical inventions met the visitor at the very threshold of the Exhibition Building, where the "Magnetic Tell-tale" of Prof. Wheatstone was attached to some of the turnstiles, and this, in a measure, controlled the financial department. This instrument was worked without battery-power of any kind. The electricity was generated by a peculiarly constructed magnetic-machine, so connected with the axis of the turnstile as to discharge a current of its force at each revolution of the stile. Thus, each visitor, on passing through it, unconsciously and telegraphically announced his or her arrival to the financial officers in whose rooms were fixed the instruments for receiving and recording the liberated current, which latter was conducted thither by a line of copper wire laid along the Building between those instruments and the turnstiles, and metallically connected to each. The registers thus obtained formed a complete check upon the money taken at the doors, and they were produced automatically, requiring only the current evoked by the revolving turnstile to set in motion the electrical apparatus whereby they were recorded.

The wires of the Electric and International Telegraph Company had their stations in the Building, whence messages could be sent to all the telegraphic stations of the world.*

In illustration, as well of the pure science of electricity, as of its telegraphic offshoot, there were in all sixty-eight exhibitors, whose nationalities may be summarized as follows :—Twenty-nine British subjects, fourteen French, five Austrian, five Dutch, five Belgian, four Italian; and two each from Switzerland, Prussia, and Denmark respectively. Their productions were more remarkable for careful manufacture than for novelty or originality.

First, the Gutta Percha Company exhibited two frames, wherein was pure gutta percha, rolled out to a tenuity little less than that of a soap-bubble, and stretched like a picture glass. The surface was perfectly even, and quite diaphanous, being infinitely less opaque than horn such as is used in lanterns. The same Company also exhibited good specimens of insulated conductors ranging from a thickness suitable for a 2000-mile cable, down to a size small enough for surrounding the coils of electro-magnets. One mile of this latter beautiful thread is contained in a ball about the size of an ordinary breakfast-cup. We had also numerous other specimens of "cores," or insulated centres of cables, of which the Company showed fifty-one specimens, being separate examples of each of the cores manufactured by them since 1850.

Glass, Elliott, and Co. similarly displayed specimens of thirty cables which they have completed from cores made by the Gutta Percha Company, and submerged by their own staff.

The great improvements and numerous inventions in Electric Telegraphy during the past ten years were strikingly shown by the various new instruments exhibited by the Universal Private Telegraph, the British and Irish, the Submarine, and other Telegraphic Companies. Prof. Wheatstone's ingenious and beautiful Domestic Telegraphs were shown in working order, and many inventions and contrivances to utilize this valuable discovery were

---

* One of the excluded companies (the Submarine) determined not to be beaten, having hired a piece of vacant ground in the Cromwell-road, nearly opposite the south-east tower, and erected thereon a gay little Kiosk-like building, supplied internally with all the requisites of a telegraph-office. Into this were brought the Company's wires, which, in connexion with their own cables and with the wires of the Magnetic Telegraph Company, were thus in communication with all the British and Continental stations. From this position, defiant with international bunting, they were enabled to wage vigorous competition with their privileged rivals, apparently not without success, for the large amount of telegraphic business evoked by the occasion.—*Mechanics' Magazine*.

to be seen in this Class. Mr. Tyer exhibited his patent Train Telegraph which has met with the strong approval of Captain Tyler and Colonel Yolland, of the Board of Trade. The apparatus for the use of the signalmen comprises a telegraphic-needle for each line of rails in each direction, and a bell and gong, having different sounds, the one for the up and the other for the down line of rails in each direction. The bell or gong is used to draw attention to the approach or passage of a train, and by the number of beats employed, to describe the train: while the needles are used solely to denote either "line blocked," or "line clear ;" and no signalman can alter his own instrument, it being the duty of each signalman to work the needles of the signalmen on each side of him.

The most interesting and advanced of these instruments were those which worked more or less automatically. The Automatic system of Mr. Allan is especially ingenious. It consists of three machines; the punching-machine is the first of these, and by this the ribbon paper to be passed through the sending machine is perforated with holes, representing dots and strokes of the Morse alphabet, at those points only where the current is required to mark on the unperforated ribbon at the receiving station; next is the sending-machine, into which the perforated paper is introduced. This machine winds up its own clockwork, whereby the paper is drawn forward, and stops of its own accord when the message is completed; and lastly, the receiving-instrument at the distant station, which is also so arranged as to start its own machinery on receiving the electric impulse, and stop it when the perforated paper at the other end has passed through the sending apparatus. Professor Wheatstone's Automatic Recorder was another very beautiful instrument of this class. M. Sortais exhibited a remarkable machine, whereby the ordinary Morse instrument can be made to start and stop itself by the electric current. Signor Bonelli showed in actual work, his ingenious Electro-chemical Recording Apparatus.

In Printing Telegraphs, the only instrument exhibited was that of Mr. Jacob Brett, which is memorable historically, as the instrument by which the first message was received through the first submarine cable.

The British and Irish Magnetic Telegraph Company exhibited an ingenious and novel system of controlling turret and other clocks, patented by Mr. L. Jones, of Chester, unlike any previously in use; the clocks being controlled only, and not moved either in whole or part, by electricity. The three clocks shown were in all respects, excepting the pendulum, of ordinary construction, and would go without the electric current, keeping their own time. The pendulum is a hollow electro-magnet, oscillating over or around permanent magnets. When a current is sent, second by second, from a controlling clock, the temporary attraction between the electro-magnet and the permanent magnet compels the controlled pendulum to copy the vibrations of the controller, even though there may be a discrepancy of several minutes in their daily independent rates. The above Company also sent the Acoustic Telegraph, a clever and extensively used instrument, invented by Sir Charles Bright and Mr. E. Bright. By its means a telegraph clerk, in taking off a message, writes it himself without being obliged to raise his eyes from the paper; the signals being produced by strokes on a pair of bells of different tones, one placed on either side of his writing-desk. There was also a Transmitting Relay, patented by the Messrs. Bright, for use in connexion with a needle telegraph, by means of which the taking off of a message at an intermediate station is rendered unnecessary, extra battery power being used instead. We also noticed a rarefied-air Lightning Protector, patented by these gentlemen.

Mr. C. F. Walker, the telegraph engineer, exhibited a pair of the bells, of which some hundreds are erected on the South-Eastern Railway, for signalling trains. There is no mechanism, and but one moveable piece, the hammer which strikes the bell. The battery employed is a one-fluid battery, the negative plate being platinized graphite. A counting index is attached to some bells to count if the signalman is absent or distracted. Two instruments record the signals. One of these drops black and white balls into a groove for the signals, and spotted and blue for the hours and quarters. The other imprints red and black marks on cotton thread for the signals, and the two combined for time marks. Mr. Walker also exhibited a Graphite Battery in work, remarkable for its simplicity of action, and the constancy of the power evoked; an audible system of Train Signals; an index for counting, and an apparatus for recording them.

The two Electrometers, portable apparatus for observing atmospheric electricity, and recently introduced by Dr. Thomson into the observatory at Kew, were shown: with Mr. C. F. Varley's Multiplying Electrometer for testing the electrical state of the atmosphere when its power is too weak for ordinary instruments. Messrs. C. and S. A. Varley exhibited a large ebonite Electrical Machine: the disc is three feet in diameter, and is excited by a soft amalgam composed of zinc, tin, mercury, and lead, to give out sparks from 16 to 20 inches in length. Some Voltaic Piles and other electrical objects were exhibited by the University of Pavia, as having once belonged to the immortal Volta.

SURGICAL INSTRUMENTS AND APPLIANCES.

The numerous and important display of Surgical Instruments in the Exhibition was subdivided into those used, first, for general surgical purposes; secondly, in ophthalmic surgery; thirdly, in orthopædic surgery; fourthly, in aural surgery; fifthly, in dental surgery; and, sixthly, in obstetric surgery.

In excellence of workmanship and perfection of manufacture,

the English makers still maintain their superiority; but Prussia, Russia, and France tread very closely on the steps of advance taken by some of our leading makers.

All the well-known manufacturers of Great Britain were represented in the Exhibition. Evans and Stevens, Weiss, Savigny, Coxeter, Ferguson, Matthews, Durroch, Bigg, Ernst, Ash and Co., and a host of others more than maintained their previous reputation. Evans and Stevens exhibited an ingenious Trephine, which possesses some advantages over that ordinarily in use; and a new instrument for Vaccination. Weiss and Son exhibited among the novelties a modification of the Ecraseur, an instrument by means of which the tissues of the body can be divided by a wire or chain saw, worked by a sort of windlass action. In that devised by Messrs. Weiss the power is obtained by an endless screw, and is so great that no part of the frame except the bones is capable of withstanding its almost resistless force. As it cuts in a slightly uneven manner, and the constriction is necessarily very great before incision commences, it follows that there is little chance of important hæmorrhage happening after its employment; it is therefore preferable to the knife for some operations, such as removal of part or the whole of the tongue, &c.

Messrs. Savigny showed the instrument suggested by Dr. Marcet for the Resuscitation of those rendered inanimate by Drowning, Suffocation, &c.: it is very ingenious, and likely to be very useful.

A very serviceable Stretcher, and also an hospital-bed appliance invented by Captain Russell, were shown.

Savory and Moore exhibited some Medicine-Chests and Cases which are models of successful arrangement; and also Panniers for field purposes, which contain plenty of surgical instruments, drugs, and other appliances, and which, by a very simple contrivance, can be converted into a firm substitute for an operating-table. Mr. Rein had a small glass room, in the centre of which was an ugly chair, intended to collect sound by means of the open mouths of two heads, which terminate its two arms and communicate with the interior, so that we imagine the patient sits on something like a drum, the vibrations of which increase his powers of hearing.

The Artificial Limbs shown by Masters were of exquisite workmanship. One of the artificial legs was of wonderfully small weight —viz., 2 lb. 7 oz., constructed of willow wood coated with leather, and furnished with strong though light articulations. Notwithstanding its lightness, it is capable of bearing the whole weight of an adult man.

In Orthopædic instruments Bigg and Ernst maintained their deserved reputation. Appliances of this kind, which are devised for the cure or relief of spinal or other deformity, are now constructed on really scientific principles, and the problem of combining strength with lightness seems to have been solved in a great degree.

Among the French exhibitors Charrière, Mathieu, and Luër fully maintained their claims to merit in invention and originality of construction. Charrière invented for M. Roger, the celebrated tenor of the Opéra Comique, an Arm. The novelty in its construction consists of an extra joint made in the centre of the forearm, to which a spring, with cords, is attached; and, the cords passing over the opposite shoulder, give the wearer the power of turning the hand and pointing the finger. The object is, however, attained by an awkward, ungraceful movement, required to be made by the opposite shoulder to procure the movements of the hand and finger. This invention is, however, disputed by M. Mathieu. Luër's instruments for Operations on the Eye are of a very superior kind. In the French gallery we also noticed the apparatus of Dr. Sales-Girons for the Pulverization of Liquids: by means of compressed air a small stream of mineral or medicated water is driven against a metal plate with such rapidity, that on striking it, it breaks into a finely-divided state, or, in other words, into a mist which the patient can easily inhale. An instrument invented by Dr. Marey, that not only shows the Pulsation of an Artery by the oscillation of a lever, but also draws on paper the curve defined by it at each beat of the heart, merits a word of mention.

Mr. Grossmith, of Fleet-street, exhibited an Artificial Leg (not of *cork*, as generally supposed), well-formed, of finished proportions, with knee, ankle, and toe articulations, performing all the movements of the natural limb, and sufficiently durable to give the wearer many years of active service,—weighing only $2\frac{1}{4}$ lb. This artist has introduced a new principle of joint articulation, a kind of spring-rod passing down the calf of the leg, and connecting the actions of the knee and ankle, which effectually causes flexion of the knee; and, at the same time, gives a feeling of safety to the wearer quite equal to that secured by a bolted stop, and without its awkward appearance. Mr. Grossmith also showed Artificial Eyes, which were fine specimens of glass-working, especially for beauty of colouring. The tint of the sclerotica, with the minute veins running through it; the colours of the iris, its radiance, and the transparency of the cornea; are all obtained with the greatest accuracy; so that, when inserted under the eyelids the deception is complete, and the artificial eye cannot be detected from the natural one.

Desjardins and Boisonneau, of Paris, also exhibited Artificial Eyes, with the latest modifications of form and thinness of material.

Leiter, of Vienna, had some instruments which were really original. His tubes used after the operation of Tracheotomy have a valve which allows the patient to speak, notwithstanding the opening in his windpipe. Dr. Hebra's Bath, in which he keeps patients for such a period as eight weeks, is a curiosity in its way. He was first led to adopt this in a case of extensive superficial burn; and conceived that immersion in tepid water, constantly changing, would be a good mode of treatment: it was quite successful. Drs. Czermak and Türck exhibited their modifications of the Laryngoscope, a mirror so arranged at the back of the mouth as to reflect a view of the state of the larynx. By this instrument it is quite possible to detect alterations in the state of the larynx and windpipe, and also to guide the operator in applying local treatment.

Among the Prussian exhibitors of surgical instruments we may notice two—namely, Lütter and Windler, of Berlin.

In a collection of instruments sent by the University of Pavia were several contrivances of very old date which have been either "invented" or resuscitated quite recently: indeed, it is believed that instruments have been disinterred at Pompeii, the originality of which has been claimed within the last few years.

America sent a "Sticking-Plaster" which is a distinct piracy of an invention of the late Mr. Liston. Mr. Bates, of Philadelphia, showed some small and ingenious instruments for the treatment of Stammering, the effect of which on an individual so afflicted is really remarkable.

Russia sent some beautifully-made instruments from the Crown factory at St. Petersburg, which are all constructed on well-known models; and when we have mentioned an ingenious though complicated apparatus sent by Mr. Nyrops, of Copenhagen, for operations on the Osseous System, we think we have mentioned all the surgical instruments and appliances which can be interesting to the general reader.—*Condensed from the Illustrated London News.*

SANITARY APPLIANCES.

Mr. J. W. Bazalgette exhibited the drawings and specifications for the Main Drainage of London which had been prepared up to this time: that is, inclusive of everything connected with the intercepting sewers, outfalls, reservoirs, and pumping-engines, to complete the system. J. Burton, Sons, and Waller's model showed different forms of pen-stocks, flushing-gates, and tidal-flaps, in position, and showed also Mr. Haywood's arrangement of charcoal-trays for disinfecting the escaping gases in the gullies. Mr. Lovegrove exhibited several drawings showing the defects which still exist even in improved sewer and drain construction, as in the matter of bell-traps. The trap which he proposes to substitute contains a valve, to act on the same principle as an ordinary tide-flap. Thus there is double protection; and the forms of trap, with water as interposing medium, are not trusted to. Objections to one of these forms, the common one for sinks, Tye and Andrews prevent by making the grate unremovable, and substituting the dip or elbow form of water-holder for the bell-trap. A screw boss on the elbow portion allows the opportunity of cleaning out, should that be necessary; or even of attaching a force-pump.

For the Water-Supply of London there were contrivances sufficient to show that there will be less difficulty with the mechanism of the service, than there is in the selection of sources. Immediately important are several different forms of Filtering Apparatus. Mr. Thomas Spencer exhibited one of them, the Magnetic Purifying Filter—as the only one known to science that effects a chemical purification. He says:—"Already, some of our greatest scientific authorities have pronounced that, 'with the magnetic filter, impure water is impossible.'" Even sewer water, "is instantaneously rendered by these filters pure, colourless, and tasteless." The discovery is, that magnetic oxide of iron, loadstone, is nature's chief agent of purification, and that any stratum containing iron also contains a small percentage of this oxide; and that where the oxide most abounds,—say, in the Malvern district,—water is purest. The oxide attracts oxygen; the molecules of that gas become polarized, or ozone: the latter attracts the carbon of moist organic matter; and carbonic acid results. The oxide is formed by Mr. Spencer by conversion of the ordinary ores.

The Silicated Carbon Filter Company exhibited their Filters of Dahlke's patent, formed of a combination of carbon with silica, as existing in the Torbane Hill mineral, which is represented as immensely more effective than mere carbon, both as an oxidizer and a promoter of chemical combination generally; carbon, indeed, acting mainly by absorption, or not chemically, being subject to saturation, and absorbing the carbonic acid. Instead of taking away the gas, the silicated carbon causes production of it, whilst nitrogenous products become changed. These filters have been adopted by the Metropolitan Free Drinking Fountains Association. They are represented as removing the poisonous salts of lead; and these Filters retain their properties undiminished.

Heating contrivances were exhibited by Mr. A. M. Perkins, Mr. S. E. Rosser, and others. Mr. Rosser's low-temperature air-warmer, high-temperature stove or desiccator, and radiating hot-water stove; were shown, with his flanged hot-water pipes and other apparatus; as well as drawings of the system of heating and ventilation at Guy's Hospital and St. Augustine's Prison, Canterbury; and of the details of drying-closets and desiccating-rooms at various buildings. Mr. Woodcock exhibited the Hot-water Battery for greenhouses, from the London Warming and Ventilating Company; the "Gurney Stove;" and a ventilating fresh-air grate which ejects the warmed air into the room by apertures concealed by ornament bordering the aperture.

Mr. McKinnel's Concentric Ventilator was exhibited, and explained by models. The working depends upon the self-action of an ingressing and an egressing current in concentric tubes fixed at one spot in the ceiling of a room. It is recommended by schoolmasters, by the Glasgow Professor of Civil Engineering, by Dr. Farr, and by the Commission on Barracks and Hospitals.

There were several inventions for Shutters and Window-fastenings; and for the exclusion of draught or the admission of fresh air. Mr. W. H. Elkin's arrangement which admits of the sashes being turned inside out, and of replacing sash-lines without removing the beads, deserves trial. Mr. P. E. Chappuis' Reflectors for use in dark places, as well as in artificial lighting, were applied with advantage in some parts of the Building. S. Hood and Son showed Iron Sashes and Casements; besides a cast-iron Staircase "which can be made of any radius without strings or plates." The staircase exhibited has no newel, but winds round a wellhole space, from floor to apron-piece, without intermediate support. Clark and Co. exhibited, besides their Shutters composed of laths rebated, a new kind which are in one sheet of corrugated steel, without chain, links, or rivets; they will coil in a small space, into which they can be pushed up, or from which they can be drawn down, without any other machinery than a long pole with hook. This improvement is applicable to openings of fire-places.

We abridge the above from the *Builder*, in which journal especial attention is paid to Sanitary subjects, the treatment of which is marked by intelligence and experience.

MUSICAL INSTRUMENTS.

Although the art of harpsichord-making was first introduced into this country from abroad by workmen from Germany, yet England has since become the country in which the Pianoforte has been brought to its greatest perfection: it is the centre from which most of the important improvements in the instrument have sprung. On examining the various Pianofortes exhibited in the Foreign Departments, we found adopted by the different Continental manufacturers the system of construction, mechanism, and forms of the instrument that were first introduced in England by our great improvers of the pianoforte—Broadwood, Collard, Erard, Kirkman, Wornum, &c.—all with more or less variation, but identical in principle.

England maintained its ground in the Exhibition, and holds its position as the first Pianoforte-manufacturing country of the world; and, although we have some remarkably fine instruments of different kinds from France, America, Germany, &c., still, as a whole, the display of pianofortes in the English Musical Court was of a quality and character that shows we keep the lead in this important branch of musical art-manufacture.

Any one examining the pianofortes in the English Musical Court, and remembering the Exhibition of 1851, could not fail to be struck with the great and general improvement in the instruments shown in the recent Exhibition in tone, touch, and construction, as well as in beauty of exterior. The stride made since 1851 is remarkable, and gives great encouragement for the future. The old and eminent houses of Broadwood, Collard, Kirkman, &c., still keep the first rank; but many others are pressing forward, and bid fair to attain the same degree of excellence. Messrs.

Broadwood added to the interest of their display by exhibiting a series of models and detached parts of instruments, illustrating the manufacture of their Grand Pianofortes. Messrs. Kirkman in one of their grand pianofortes had a new bridge to prevent the sinking of the sounding-board, which is applied in a very scientific and thoroughly mechanical manner, and for certain classes of pianofortes must be a valuable improvement.

Greiner and Sandilands exhibited Greiner's patent Apparatus for Tuning the whole note of either two or three unisons at one turn of the tuning-pin; this it professes to accomplish perfectly.

Mr. Knoll showed a handsomely inlaid Oblique Piano, with the peculiarity of the strings being at the back of the instrument, and the hammers also striking at the back. This is accomplished by an ingenious system of levers, something similar to that employed by organ-builders, where the keys are at a distance from the instrument. With this plan properly carried out, it would be quite possible for a performer to play in one room while the piano is in another.

Messrs. Chappell exhibited a Cottage Piano, with pedals useful for organ practice; and to the same instrument was attached a mechanism of ingenious construction to play octaves when single notes are struck, or to double the octaves when octaves are played. Mr. Glassborrow showed a newly-patented Cottage Piano, with a second sounding-board and another set of strings at the back of the instrument, by which contrivance he states he obtains a greater amount of tone from his instrument, in consequence of the strings at the back of the piano, which are tuned in unison with those in front of the instrument, sympathising with each other.

There were also specimens of Mr. Wornum's Grand and Cottage Pianos in walnut; and a new patent piano, which he names a "Folding Piano." It is, in fact, a small square or table piano, which, instead of being placed on legs, is hung on centres and suspended between two uprights. When played upon, it is put in a horizontal position; and when not used, can be swung back into a vertical position, in which it occupies very little room.—*Selected and condensed from the Illustrated London News.*

An American improvement merits special mention. Mr. Hulskamp exhibited a modification of the instrument, founded on the observation that tension was an important element in the vibratory action of bodies. Accordingly, applying, by the use of screws, a straining power to the sounding-board of a pianoforte, he is enabled to increase its vibration so materially, that a horizontal pianoforte exhibited by him, two feet shorter than the ordinary grand, has all the power of the larger instrument. The whole result thus produced, however, is not solely due to the tension applied to the sounding-board, but is in part referable to the oblique braces which transmit the vibrations from the frame on which the strings are stretched to the centre of the sounding-board. Mr. Hulskamp has applied the same principle of construction to the violin, increasing in a remarkable degree the volume of tone.

We necessarily confine our notices to novel appliances to the Pianoforte. Upon the instruments generally, we find the following notice by the able musical critic of the *Athenæum:*—"Our general feeling is, that less attention and cost have been devoted to outside decoration (especially in the case of pianofortes) than was observable in the great London show of 1851, or afterwards at Paris. Yet this Exhibition shows, in its ample display of woods hitherto unknown from every quarter of the globe, what exquisite varieties of colour and grain lie at the service of every cabinet-maker, though he be bent on no such fine fancies. Meanwhile, the general quality of instruments is improved:—this, we are assured by those who have gone scientifically into the matter, owing to improvements of structure. Speaking of pianos, the makers may be said to keep strictly to their own nationalities, so well known to the Liszts and Pleyels and Halles—whether the piano Viennese, or Parisian, or of London. The Americans, also, (M. Fétis assures us, in his Juror's Report, at present being contributed by him to the *Gazette Musicale,*) show signs of 'going ahead.' As for the *Orgues* Debain, &c., who would dare to venture into the contest among the conflicting makers, save to remark the obvious increase in popularity of this useful, but, we cannot help thinking, fatiguing instrument? It represents, however, the organ conveniently; and its cheapness and small size explain its acceptance. There are no foreign organs here. To the English ones our former remarks apply in the fullest force. Position is 'four points' of the law in such a case. In these instruments, again, while there remains much to be done (especially in the matter of that distinctness in the upper sounds which gives to the new French organs superiority—take, for example, those in the Parisian churches of St. Eustache and of the Madeleine), there have been great improvements both in point of combination and to facilitate the manual and pedal execution. M. Fétis, to whom power of minute examination as a juryman was, of course, accorded, complains of the materials used by us as being inferior; but as there is no subject on which Belgian critics and players are more touchy than that of English organs, it may be as well merely to state his objections. M. Sax had his usual case of carefully-made brass instruments. England, we fancy, carries off the palm in flutes. There seems nothing capable of being perfected in the article of violins : many old instruments, which must have not unpleasantly varied the 'consort,' having apparently died out of the family, not to be born into it anew."

THE PIPING BULLFINCH.

The Musical Boxes from Geneva attracted great attention in the Swiss Court; and Auber and Linton showed here a beautiful piece of mechanism which, though no novelty, drew a crowd of admirers. It was in the shape of a small musical box, just large enough for the waistcoat-pocket, out of which, when the lid was opened, popped up a pretty little Bullfinch, who piped a song, fluttering his wings in the most natural manner possible. The plumage, the action, and the peculiar note of the bird, were imitated with wonderful exactness. Automatic birds have had many admirers, but we question if any piece of mechanism ever obtained so enviable a celebrity as this Piping Bullfinch. It was a benevolent idea of the proprietors to make this mechanical wonder subserve "all mankind's concern," charity, by announcing that whenever the sum of five shillings was raised among the visitors, the bird should perform, and the fund so collected be appropriated to the benefit of the Distressed Cotton Districts. He seldom continued long without an audience, and sometimes realized from 10*l.* to 12*l.* a-day towards the Cotton Districts Fund. Through some misunderstanding, which it is not important to explain, the Bullfinch was moved from his sphere of charity, and the performances discontinued; but he was soon restored. In the meantime, another warbling automaton appeared, scarcely larger than a common bee; yet it skipped out of its little box, and trilled and fluttered about with the vehemence and fulness of note of a grown skylark.

MISCELLANEOUS MACHINERY.

COTTON-SPINNING MACHINERY.

This important branch of machinery was largely represented; and Dobson and Barlow, of Bolton, contributed a fair quota of the whole. They exhibited, in fact, a series of machines for opening and cleansing, preparing and spinning Cotton. The whole of these were replete with the most recent improvements of detail, and they may be briefly mentioned in the order in which the operations named follow each other in ordinary working. The first is named a Cotton Spinner, and it is adapted for spinning and cleaning long or short shaped cotton. The feeding parts and the inside gratings, are of a novel construction, the object in view being to open out and clean the cotton without injuring the staple. The second is called the Single Scutcher, and it is supplied with feeding rolls, which have been patented by the firm in question: the merit of the rolls consists in their holding the cotton sufficiently firm without breaking the seeds or shells. Then follows the Breaker Carding-engine, which is a combined patent machine; Wallmann, of the United States of America, and Dobson and Barlow, each having a share in it. Its chief merits are that the cotton is well opened and cleaned by the working rollers, before the upper rollers will allow it to pass the self-stripping top-flats: these flats can be taken out at pleasure by the attendant, and readjusted without the use of a screw-key. A Finisher Carding-engine stands next, and it works automatically—an improvement on the plan of stripping flats by hand, as is usually done. Ashworth's patent Lap-machine is used for making laps for the finisher carding-engine, and combing-machine; and a grinding-apparatus is so contrived as to grind two rollers and a flat at the same time.

Then follow five frames, known respectively as the drawing-frames, with forty-four spindles, each ten inches by five inches; the intermediate-frame with fifty-four spindles, each eight inches by four inches; the roving-frame of seventy spindles, each seven inches by three and a half; and the jack-frame of eighty-eight spindles, five inches by two and a half.

The Patent Self-acting Mule, of Dobson and Barlow, made the total of the cotton-spinning arrangements at the Exhibition contributed by that firm.

Platt, Brothers, and Co., of Oldham, figured extensively in the same branch of manufacturing industry, the space devoted to their machines and contrivances being very large. As the *Illustrated Catalogue*, Part III., however, does elaborate justice to their Cotton-working Machinery, we need not further refer to it than to say it reflects the highest credit upon the firm, who must have gone to very great expense in forwarding the whole to London, and keeping a large staff of workmen and girls to attend to it.

The Cotton-machinery of Hetherington, of Vulcan Works, Manchester, was not inferior in many parts to that we have already referred to.—*Abridged from the Mechanics' Magazine.*

CARPET-LOOMS.

There was an extensive collection of Carpet-weaving Machinery exhibited by Jackson and Graham, of London; Henderson, of Durham; and an American loom for weaving Axminster carpets. The Power-loom by Tuer and Hall, of Bury, near Manchester, for the weaving of pile, velvet, patent tapestry, or ordinary Brussels carpet, any width required, either with or without jacquard, was shown in operation. All the working motions are outside the loom, except the crank from which it is driven: by this means free access to the working parts is obtained, and an hitherto much-complained-of inconvenience removed. It will admit larger yarn beams in the same space than any other loom we know of. The wire-motion inserts forty-five wires per minute, at two picks per wire; it recommends itself by the facility with which it inserts the wires on which the loops or pile is raised, and by its simple arrangement for holding the wires when inserted, withdrawing and transferring the point of the wire for reinsertion. The whole of the motion is governed in its action by one cam. It produces six yards of carpet per hour, much more than ordinary looms, and requires less space than most of them with the same width in the reed; six such machines may be driven by one horse's power. This loom is also applicable to the weaving of Utrecht velvet, for the lining of carriages, omnibuses, &c.

WASHING MACHINES.

Of these Machines some were exhibited which professed to wash by knocking the clothes about in water, in which wooden balls floated; others beat, and thrashed, and winnowed the clothes until the dirt was effectually removed. Another machine, shown by Mr. Williamson, imitated, as nearly as it is possible, the various motions of rubbing, and squeezing, and turning over and over, which the washerwoman uses at the wash-tub. The squeezing of the clothes after sluicing in the water, was performed by an elastic or yielding pressure, which was so applied as to change repeatedly the position of the articles to be washed. Each movement of the spring washboard and the press caused the roll of clothes to make a partial revolution, and thus expose a constantly changing and new surface to the washing action of the machine. It can be applied with equal success and safety to the washing of the most delicate fabric, or the heaviest and coarsest blankets and counterpanes. After undergoing a very severe trial, the machine was placed on board the *Warrior* and the *Black Prince*. The larger machines are worked by steam-power, and one of them, as a moderate day's work, has washed 3000 blankets.

[Before we close this Division it may be as well to insert here the two following groups of Machinery—the one selected from the leading countries of Europe, and the other forming great portion of the Contributions from North America.]

FOREIGN MACHINERY.

The progress made by Foreign Machinists during the last dozen years is most extraordinary: here we are still the leaders, but French, Dutch, Belgians, and Germans, judging by the specimens in the Exhibition, will not be long in the rear.

The value of the machinery exported from Great Britain last year was never exceeded in any previous twelve months, steam-engines having figured for 1,243,467*l*., and other kinds of mechanical apparatus for 2,976,221*l*., while in 1860 the totals were 1,238,333*l*. and 2,599,488*l*. respectively. In 1850 the value of the steam-engines exported was only 423,977*l*., and of the general machinery 618,189*l*., so that during the last ten or eleven years a vast development has taken place in the demand for British machinery in foreign countries and in the colonies.—*Parliamentary Returns*.

The collection of engines and machines in the Foreign department comprised almost every description now in use—marine, fixed, and portable steam-engines, locomotives, mills, machine-tools; apparatus for brewing, distilling, dyeing, making ice, and hundreds of other purposes.

Of Marine Engines the most important were a pair of engines of 400-horse power, of French manufacture, having been constructed by "La Compagnie des Forges et Chantiers de la Mediterraneanée." These engines are horizontal, with double piston-rods; the eccentrics are not, as in ordinary cases, fixed on the main shaft, but are on a separate shaft worked by gearing. The screw is fixed on a short piece of shafting, and the whole machinery was shown in motion.

Escher, Wyass, and Co., of Zurich, exhibited a pair of small Paddle-wheel engines, with a portion of the section of the vessel through the engine-room. The paddle-wheels, with feathering floats, were placed on the shaft. The engines were oscillating, and of the ordinary pattern in general use for small river-steamers. The workshops of foreign nations must be rapidly improving when such a remote place as Zurich can turn out such work as was here exhibited.

Of Locomotive Engines there was a strong array, besides a number of Portable and Agricultural Engines. With one exception these were exact copies of such as are usually constructed in England; they were exceedingly well built, and doubtless, good, serviceable engines, mostly of the class used for drawing heavy loads at low velocities. The specimen exhibited in the Austrian department was an immense engine; but in weight and heaviness of appearance was entirely eclipsed by a colossal one built in Paris, the design of which is entirely novel.

Of fixed engines there were numerous examples, varying in power from one to a hundred horses. A preference seems to be generally given to the horizontal principle of construction. There were some large specimens of this class from France, Germany, and Belgium, well designed, and thoroughly well made, quite equal in every respect to the best produced in this country. Machine-tools were exhibited by numerous persons, but by far the finest was the collection of J. Zimmerman, of Chemnitz, Saxony: it comprised specimens of all the machine-tools in ordinary use for boring, cutting, turning, planing, punching, shearing, and other operations. Nearly the whole of these tools were copied from English patterns: the workmanship was excellent.

Blowing-engines were shown by Perard, of Liège: these machines were for the purpose of creating the blast for ironworks: they were large, powerful, and well built. Two powerful horizontal steam-engines act direct upon the piston-rods of two air-cylinders, at each end of which is a revolving disc. As the piston travels backwards and forwards in the air-cylinders the ports of the disc are opened and shut, and the air either admitted or forced into the air-receiver. The action is simple and convenient, and, we think, preferable to the ordinary system of upright cylinders, beams, and very expensive framework.

A large and elaborate system of Bolting Apparatus for making fine flour was exhibited by S. J. Marie, of Belgium. A portable Saw-mill, by Frey and Son, of Paris, was a well arranged and constructed machine, and would be invaluable in the colonies, as saw-mill and engine are complete in one frame and carriage. One of the largest contributions in the Foreign Department was the entire Apparatus of a Distillery: it occupied an immense space. A Sawing-machine in the Belgian department attracted much attention: it is capable of sawing out the most complicated shapes, giving at the same time every description of cant or bevil to the piece of wood that may be required: the saw is an endless narrow band of steel running over two pulleys. An improved kind of Railway-carriage was exhibited in the same department. The carriage is divided into three divisions, the middle portion being roofed over, but open at the sides, an open iron railway only inclosing it; the entrance to the two end compartments is from the open middle space. Ladies may thus travel in elegant comfort, while the gentlemen sit outside and smoke. A Railway Tank-truck was a large and important contribution from Paris. It will contain ten tons of liquid, and is provided with apparatus for filling and discharging the contents. A Refrigerating Apparatus excited a good deal of attention, blocks of ice being made by it with rapidity.

Machines for the manufacture of Textile Fabrics were exhibited in large quantities, comprising looms, spinning-machines, carding and dressing-machinery, and a great variety of other machines for similar purposes.

From Switzerland two Looms were both exhibited at work, in weaving broad ribbon. In one the pattern was a portrait of her Majesty (black lines on a white ground); the other produced the Royal arms in beautiful colours, also on a white ground. This latter machine weaves several ribbons at one time. It is a beautiful piece of workmanship, but so elaborate and apparently complicated that it is perfectly bewildering to a stranger to endeavour to trace out the meaning of its parts—such piles of perforated cards, such masses of threads in the gears, and such innumerable little bobbins and shuttles. It is in machines of this kind that we see the real genius of the French or Swiss mechanic develop itself. In such machines they surpass all the rest of the world, as we do in our large and ponderous though equally beautifully constructed and contrived marine engines and locomotives.—*Abridged from the Illustrated London News.*

AMERICAN MACHINERY.

From causes on which there is no necessity to dwell, our kinsmen across the Atlantic were very imperfectly represented at the International Congress. Private energy and enterprise to some extent supplied the deficiency, and the south-eastern corner of the Building contained a numerous and exceedingly interesting collection of various contrivances for simplifying and facilitating the operations of ordinary trades.

Among the machines was Conroy's Cork-cutter: the man in charge simply puts down a square of cork on a small ledge, and as the machine works, two fingers are pushed out, which grasp it, and fix it on a rapidly rotating pin, where it is applied to the edge of a circular knife, revolving horizontally : in a couple of seconds the square assumes the desired shape and size, and immediately drops into a reservoir beneath to make room for another. A man and a couple of boys can cut 150 gross of corks with this machine in a day. The Rope-making machine, which stood next, compresses a rope-walk of some 800 or 900 yards into about 8 feet, and it spins a 12-strand rope quite as stout and in much less time than it could be done by hand. Close by the rope-spinner was a Machine for Shifting and Securing Machinery-belts, by which, no doubt, many accidents may be prevented. By pulling a cord the belt is moved either on or off the drums ; and as the guides move they are secured in their place by a self-acting lock, so that the belt cannot slip either one way or the other. Eckell, of New York, sent one of his new Presses, by which 1000 lb. of cotton may be pressed into 18 cubic feet, or 800 lb. of hay into a truss of 5 feet by 2 feet, with a height of 32 inches, in a space of four minutes, and with a less expenditure of labour than by any other press yet invented. They are capable of exerting from 100 to 1000 tons pressure, and one man working alone can bring 100 tons to bear. The machinery is very simple, and may be applied with equal advantage to presses for extracting oils. Hansbrow's California Pump was chiefly distinguished for the ingenious adaptation of the leverage, by which immense power is saved and gained, so that a child might work it. The stream rises on the slightest movement of the handle, and when full power is put on it will throw a stream from a depth of 30 feet to a height of 85 feet through 50 feet of hose.

A Cotton Planter's Machine was exhibited close by, which was just coming into use in the Southern plantations when the War broke out. This machine, which promises to be a great success, with two men and a horse will do the day's work of eight able-bodied "chattels." There was also a Corn and Bean Planter, which, it is said, will plant 20 acres of corn per day, either on even or uneven ground, and will do the work of 30 men per day. It requires but one man to work it, and is designed to plant two rows of corn or three rows of beans, the rows being made at any distance apart. It marks the furrows, drops any desired number of seeds, covers them, and presses the soil over them at any required pressure or depth.

Among the most important machinery was a Power-loom for Weaving Tufted Carpets. In a practical point of view it was perhaps one of the valuable novelties in the Department. By a single throw of the shuttle, it will insert, weave in, cut off, and complete one whole range of figuring tufts across the width of the fabric in less time than is required for the making of a single tuft by the hand-loom. Any medallion design can be woven in parts, which may easily be united so as to have the appearance of being woven in one piece, as the selvage produced is such that when sewed the seams are not visible. The strain on the material is so slight that common worsted or woollen yarns of any quality may be used, so that the cheapest kinds of carpets may be produced in it. The Americans are very confident of this loom; and Earl Granville has publicly stated that it is destined to achieve greater results than any other machine in the Building.

Besides these there were various other contrivances of minor importance, but all displaying wonderful ingenuity. Mr. Bates's mechanical Apparatus for curing Stammering, deserves notice, though it is impossible to give any verbal description which would afford an adequate idea of its operation. Mr. Ward exhibited a complete series of his Signal Lanterns, which form perhaps the simplest and most intelligible system of ocean telegraphs yet invented. We must not omit to mention the Sewing-Machines, of which half-a-dozen might be seen hard at work at all hours of the day. There were a few specimens of Cereals, and the mineral wealth of the States was represented by a few cabinet specimens, the chief of which are from the Washoe silver-mines. In this case were shown two or three samples of quartz said to be worth 2000*l.* per ton. The Arts of the States were represented by Kentze's fine statue of "America," and a few pictures, all worthy of a position where they would attract more attention.

The Pianofortes were highly praised by experts; the most remarkable novelty among them was a piano exhibited by Mr. Hulskamp, in which, by applying an extraordinary tension to the sounding-board, and by an arrangement of oblique braces transmitting the vibration, he obtains an unusual volume of sound in a very small space. This improvement has already been described at page 150.

Mr. L. A. Bigelow, Boston, Massachusetts, exhibited several machines connected with Boot-making. First was a machine for splitting the leather, or rather, as we would describe it, for paring the leather intended for soles to a uniform or required thickness. This is effected by passing the leather between two rollers, one grooved and the other smooth, behind which is a knife that may be adjusted in relation to the frame according to the thickness of the leather required. The cutting is accomplished rapidly, and with more precision than can be done by the hand and knife. Then we had a machine for cutting up the leather into soles, which it does at the rate of twenty pair a minute, all fitted exactly to the last, without the use of a hand-knife, and the edges sufficiently smooth to finish. Further, there was a "heel trimmer," that is, a machine which, carrying the boot or shoe on a pivot, subjects it under a circular motion to the action of a cutter, which in a minute pares the rough edges to the form of heel, whatever the thickness may be. At last came the sole-sewing machine, much on the same principle as the sewing-machines for lighter material, with which the public are now familiar. Of course it is more ponderous and powerful, having a force to penetrate the thickest leather, or even a board half an inch thick. It uses a heavy waxed thread, drawing the thread more tightly than can be done by hand, and making the work both strong and solid. This machine will sew on the soles of one hundred and fifty pairs of boots or shoes per day.

Another very simple contrivance of great use was a Machine for Addressing Newspapers, exhibited by Mr. Sweet, of New York. A wooden disc, from the edge of which project all the letters of the alphabet, is made to revolve by a treddle; a small wooden block is pressed against the letter required, till the address is cut out on the face of the block. It is then placed along with hundreds of others similarly cut upon an endless band, and having been inked, the band carries them round; and as one by one they descend on a small table, the newspaper, or whatever is to be addressed, is pressed against them by a pressure of the foot, and a thousand addresses are copied in a few minutes. This apparatus is in use in most of the newspaper offices in New York, and must greatly facilitate the despatch of journals which are supplied directly from the office, and not through the intervention of newsvendors.

Scholl's Life-boat was constructed on a novel principle. It looks like a great green porpoise, with a lid opening into his back. Look into the interior, however, through the lid, and you discover the arrangements for the accommodation of a crew and passengers —for the saved and the rescuers, as the case may be. The object of the boat is to pass through a heavy surf with safety. The internal fittings of the boat are below the centre of gravity and of flotation. They are hung in the manner of a binnacle compass, that is, be the motion of the external shell or hull of the boat what it may, the persons within are always maintained in a horizontal position. Indeed, let the boat turn round and round like a spindle, which is hardly possible, its passengers are nevertheless unmoved. The steering apparatus is within, and so are all the arrangements for a screw propeller. This boat has no outer deck; indeed, as we have said, in form it resembles a porpoise in the model, and on a large scale it must be something "very like a whale."

Some ingenious small Hand-Labour Saving Machines were the most looked after. One of the most curious of these was the Machine for Milking the four teats of a cow at the same time, and in a manner precisely similar to the action of the calf's mouth upon the teat. In point of time, labour, and cleanliness, the operation of the machine is said far to surpass milking by hand. In this court also was a very ingenious Machine for Making Paper Bags, which turns them out folded, packed, dried, and finished, at the rate of 46 a minute.

A Wringing-Machine, of great efficiency and economy, was shown. Its principle consists simply of two rollers of india-rubber, kept at a tight pressure by means of screws, and on turning a handle the articles of clothing, when washed, are drawn between the rollers and pressed dry without the slightest injury to the fabric. So equal is the pressure, that the same machine will press dry a thick woollen carpet, lifted direct from a tub of water, or a thin sheet of writing-paper that has been immersed for hours.

A Caloric Engine, by Wilcox, was shown. It is an engine of low power, quick in its revolutions, not liable to derangement or explosion, and of which the consumption of coal is as low as 100lb. per day of 10 hours. Some good folding and revolving Drying-Machines were shown in the American department, the prices of which were as low as 30s., of which 10s. is sent to the Lancashire Relief Fund. They had a good sale, and the 10s. charitable deodand was regularly acknowledged by the Relief Committee.

SEWING MACHINES.

In the *Mechanics' Magazine*, a journal which has paid considerable attention to the invention and progress of the Sewing Machine, it is stated to be "now clearly established, that, whatever a needle can accomplish, the Machine can do, from the finest and most delicate fabric for female adornment to the heaviest and coarsest habiliments of the sturdy labourer, either at home or at the antipodes."

There were about thirty different Sewing Machines in the Exhibition, each having, or professing to have, some distinctive peculiarity : in the American Court, the Processes Court, and in the French Court.

Howe's Sewing Machine is entitled to priority of mention among those exhibited in the American Court. This is the basis of all successful machines : its essential characteristics are thus enumerated :—

1st. A mechanism for making stitches, or interlocking of thread, combined with an apparatus for making tension on the thread, and drawing up and securing each stitch when formed.

2nd. An apparatus consisting of two surfaces, between which the material to be sewed is contained, and which support it against the thrust and retraction of the needle, and in such a position as to permit the stitches to be drawn tight.

3rd. An automatic, intermittently-acting feeding apparatus, which causes the material to pass with a regular movement between the holding surfaces in the intervals between the punctures of the needle with an unerring precision and uniformity of effect, impossible to obtain by hand.

But Howe has improved marvellously and effectively, even upon these properties, by the invention of a Cylinder Machine, by the introduction of an entirely new principle in sewing by machinery. All shuttle sewing-machines make their stitch by the needle entering the material, and remaining there until the shuttle passes and takes up the loop. By the cylinder machine, the needle pierces the material to be sewn, carrying its loop with it in its downward course, and leaves it within the material ; then returns, when the shuttle starts forward, takes the loop and tightens the upper thread ;

the needle-arm is then lifted considerably, and the shuttle-thread by that means tightened. It will be seen that the stitch is thus made when the needle is *out* of the material; and, as a consequence, very close sewing, closer even than by hand, can be made. The award of a Prize Medal to Howe's Sewing-machine will, we think, be acquiesced in by all its competitors.

Wheeler and Wilson's Machine is very remarkable on account of the novelty of its construction. Here we have still the double stitch; but the "lock" is accomplished by means of a rotating hook instead of a shuttle. The underfeeding bobbin differs also from those used in other machines. This bobbin is about the diameter and thickness of a florin; but between the two surfaces there is a deep groove, containing the requisite supply of thread. The bobbin is placed within the rotating hook, and winds off according to the demands of the machine. The rotating hook itself, larger in diameter than the bobbin, is the segment of a circle—a complete circle almost, but interrupted in its periphery by a kind of gash. The effective segment of the gash has a pointed end, which catches into the loop made by the needle, drags it round about three-quarters of its circuit, when the thread is released and pulled tight through touching a rest. The hooked wheel revolves again to catch a loop, and again to make a close stitch.

These exhibitors gave a curious table of the time required to stitch a number of articles of clothing by the machine as compared with the hand. We find that a man's shirt may be made by machine in 1h. 16min., which by hand would occupy 14h. 26min.; a coat may be made in 2h. 38min. by machine, and by hand in 16h. 35min.; a silk waistcoat in 1h. 14min. as against 7h. 19min.

The Sewing-machine of Wilcox and Gibbs is a single thread chain-stitch, against which some persons have a prejudice, from its liability to ravel, or "run out. It is certainly possible, by undoing the finishing loop, to draw the whole out, but ordinary wear will not do this; and its beauty of stitch and great rapidity of operation render it useful for many kinds of domestic work. The striking peculiarity in the mechanism is a "spur looper," which catches the slack down-loop, retains it, and by its peculiar conformation holds the next down-loop distended so as to be caught again at the next revolution of the spur. By this arrangement, there is no chance of a stitch being dropped, and the seam is as even and tight as can be desired.

These machines have become the family instruments for sewing in a great many households in England as well as in America, and their great simplicity and ease of operation are strong evidence in their favour.

The Machine of Mr. J. M. Singer has little in it to be described beyond the ordinary shuttle-machine. This firm has manufactured, from first to last, about 60,000 machines, 8000 of which have been sold in England: their manufactory in New York gives employment to 800 persons.

For details of other Sewing Machines, see the *Mechanics' Magazine*, July 18 and Aug. 8.

Manufactures.

COTTON FABRICS.

A contributor to the *Illustrated London News*, who furnished that journal with the Report of the Cotton Manufactures at the Great Exhibition of 1851, thus speaks of its comparison with the recent display. "It is greatly to be regretted that the illustration of the Cotton Manufactures of Great Britain is not more complete. In 1851 it was very indifferent. On this occasion, if not worse in itself, the defect in the exposition is aggravated by a much smaller display in a dependent industry—that of Calico-printing. Happily the Manchester manufacturers made up for their shortcomings in 1851 by a more practical and efficient display at the Universal Exposition at Paris in 1855; and while we feel the contrast so much the greater on this occasion, still the loss in an industrial aspect is less than it would have been had the admirable series of illustrations of the cotton trade not appeared in 1855.

"Looking back over the eleven years which have elapsed since 1851, whilst many and varied improvements have arisen in the details of manufacture, the industry, as a whole, may be said to be practically the same.

"We decidedly keep our position, positively if not relatively, as regards our Continental competitors, for the goods shown are excellent in quality and finish. It must, however, be carefully borne in mind that Great Britain no longer has the exclusive use of that superior machinery which at one time placed us so far ahead of other nations, and that the last decade has fairly inaugurated a gradual extension of those more refined mechanical contrivances which for a period appeared to give to the British cotton spinner and manufacturer a monopoly of the markets of the world. Much of this has been gradually changed, and the fact is fairly illustrated on the foreign side of the Exhibition Building.

"In Fine Yarns, for instance, there is a much nearer equality existing between the spinning of French and English yarns than in 1851. This may be attributed to two causes: one being that above named, the extensive use of machinery formerly used only in England; and the other the application of a French invention of great importance, the combing-machine, which greatly facilitates the production of the fine numbers—in fact, renders that comparatively easy which formerly appeared almost impossible, and indeed was so, except in the hands of the special few. English spinners are, however, still pre-eminent ; and with that pride in superiority, great experience, and thorough intelligence which characterizes our Houldsworths, and Bazleys, and Murrays, we are not likely to lose our ground, for a period at all events."

The most extensive series of exhibit in the Cotton Class was that comprised under the head of Sewing Threads, in this respect contrasting favourably, in quantity at least, with 1851. The two most noticeable exhibits were those of J. Brook and Son, Miltham Mills, Huddersfield, and Edmund Ashworth and Sons, Egerton, near Bolton. The former sustained their old and well-earned reputation for the production of their goods ; and the exhibits comprised a complete illustration of their manufacture in Sewing, Embroidery, and Crochet Cotton. Walter Evans and Co., Derby, had a very practical display of Sewing, Knitting, and Crochet Threads of admirable make and finish, together with a valuable record of the strength of the thread according to a fixed system of tests.

The Paisley display of Threads was a very remarkable one, well and ingeniously arranged by each exhibitor, yet coming together admirably as a whole. The dyed threads of Clark and Co. were very excellent, and the same may be said of Messrs. Kerr and Clarke's. The finish of the threads of J. Carlisle and Co. was perfect. These three firms, together with J. and P. Coats, whose threads were of excellent quality and prettily arranged, all received an award of a Prize Medal; so that Paisley threads achieved a triumph on this occasion. The exhibit of Coots, Neilson, and Co. was a very interesting one, inasmuch as they illustrated the process for No. 90 in a very pretty manner, giving examples of carded and combed cotton ; then the same, after passing through the drawing-frame, with bobbins, and finishing with cops from mule.

In the Great Exhibition of 1851 the Turkish Bath Towel made its first appearance, and in a short time, owing partly to its quick adoption in the Royal nursery, the article got into great favour. W. M. Christy and Son, of Fairfield, near Manchester, had an excellent exhibit of these useful adjuncts to the bath. The make is perfect, and the Blankets specially noticeable as supplying a great want. The Counterpanes exhibited by this firm were of good design and excellent manufacture. The Jury recognised the merits of the whole with a Prize Medal.

Barlow, Goody, and Jones, of Manchester, displayed some goods which showed what may be done in the way of producing Cotton Damasks in colours, both sides being alike. With good and carefully considered designs—that is, designs properly adapted to the fabric and mode of manufacture—very beautiful results might be obtained. The designs exhibited seemed to be based, strangely enough, upon a type of pattern used for "one-colour" prints, instead of the more legitimate style of woven damasks. It should be borne in mind in producing such things, that prints originally aimed at imitating the effects of the loom in a cheap

M 2

form, and that the details of the design had to be adapted to the method of printing. For the loom to be lowered to the imitation of printing processes, whether block or cylinder, is a degradation and a waste of means.

There were a few important exceptional exhibits in this Class which deserve special attention. The Imitation Silk Velvets and Cotton Velvets manufactured and exhibited by Kesselmeyer and Mellodew, Manchester, were of admirable character. The dyes were very rich and the finish perfect. In fact, these goods are in their way quite a triumph of manufacturing skill aided by science in dyeing. The Jury awarded, and most deservedly, a Prize Medal. A kindred exhibit, though different in individual character, was that of Mr. J. Moore, of Manchester. This consisted of Ribbons and Trimmings of a very pretty and useful kind, manufactured in the manner of cotton velvet by patent machinery: the goods were excellent.

There were some Skirting Welts and Sateens, the latter made from "Surats," exhibited by W. J. Smith and Co., Manchester. These are of excellent quality and finish, showing of what East India cotton properly selected is capable. In fact, there were abundant proofs in the Exhibition that the way to get cotton will be found when there is a will to do it.

The contributions from Glasgow consisted almost entirely of Harness and other Muslins, and exhibited a great general advance alike in taste and perfection of manufacture. In Cottons, Glasgow keeps as high a place as Paisley does in shawls. Some of the printed Cottons shown by Orr and Co., Monteith and Co., and Stirling and Sons were beautiful specimens of printing. The hardness of effect of cotton prints is overcome, or at least diminished, by a very skilful combination of colours, which blend with each other with as much ease and softness of outline as woven fabrics. Some representative specimens of that huge class of exports which find a ready market in all parts of India, Africa, and South America were gorgeous pieces of colour.

R. Owtram and Co., of Watling-street, made an admirable display, especially of Figured Muslins of a very high quality, both as regards weaving, design, and finish. Manufacture can scarcely go further. The imitation French Cambric and the Jaconots and Nainsooks were also excellent. The Quilts exhibited by this firm were also of a very high class. A Prize Medal was awarded for the exhibit.

France exhibited largely in this Class, and did justice to the power of production, alike in tasteful design, beauty of mechanical result, and brilliancy of colour. The finest Yarns, and in its way the most complete exhibit, were certainly those of Mallet Brothers, Lille. The display made by this eminent firm illustrated the application of the yarns produced by them in several distinct phases.

The Sewing-threads exhibited were of first-class quality and finish, and the specimens of Muslin and Lace showed the yarns in their application to these fabrics to great advantage. The Ribbons in which the fine yarns are used as warp were superior goods of their class, and proved to what an extent fine cotton may be employed in fabrics not usually associated with the use of this material. Mallet Brothers received a Prize Medal for their exhibit.

There were several exhibitors of lower numbers of Yarns from 20s to 40s, and these were chiefly produced in the neighbourhood of Rouen. There appeared no essential difference between these and English Yarns of the same kind, and within the two numbers quoted above, they showed an advance during the past eleven years in the production of the chief essential of the cotton trade.

The best display of Cotton Threads was that of M. Cartier-Bresson, Paris. The Sewing and Crochet Threads were of superior quality, dye, and finish: our sewing-thread manufacturers must look to their reputation.

The Quilts and Quiltings exhibited by French manufacturers were generally of a very superior make, and in no instance was there attempt at eccentricity in deesign.

The application of Quilts to ladies' collars and cuffs was well illustrated by this firm. These are very ingenious and useful articles, and the effect of those embroidered after the sewed-muslin fashion is especially noticeable.

The Figured Muslins especially for curtains, exhibited by M. Hugues-Cauvin, St. Quentin, were especially deserving of notice for the admirable character of the designs employed, which tend to show rather than to conceal the true character of the fabric, and thus both ornamentation and tissue gain immensely thereby. A Prize Medal was awarded to this exhibit, and also to that of M. Boucly, marchand, St. Quentin, for some most ingenious and elegantly woven Shirt-fronts. Some are very beautiful, and were embroidered in the loom.

The city of Roanne, Loire, was well represented by a capital display of coloured cotton goods for dresses, mostly Ginghams, and heavier fabrics of that character.

M. Thivel-Michon, Tarare, brought together specimens of Muslins manufactured from yarns spun by the leading spinners both of the Continent and England. The finest were by the latter, and fabrics were shown made of 220s and 300s spun by Murray and Co.; of 250s by M'Connel and Co.; and of 300s and 440s by T. Houldsworth and Co., all of Manchester. The specimens of muslins made from cotton grown in Algeria were very suggestive, but none seemed to go beyond 180s.

The dyed examples shown in M. Thivel-Michon's case were very beautiful. The colour seemed little more than suggested, yet the effect was very rich, and displayed great skill and taste. To this exhibit was awarded a Prize Medal.

In the French Court was a most elegant exposition of Tamboured Work in net and muslin. M. V. Dubois, Paris, showed some admirably-tamboured muslin curtains. The work is done with great ability. The foliation in one example was based on tropical plants, and the effect of some portions was very superb

Fèrouelle and Rolland, St. Quentin, made a first-class display of tamboured muslin curtains and the harness curtain.

The contributions of Cotton Goods from Switzerland consisted chiefly of goods said to be manufactured for exportation. This Swiss cotton exhibit says much for the ability and enterprise of the people, and has been liberally recognised by the Jury: the total of awards was eleven Medals and three Honourable Mentions to twenty exhibitors: a very remarkable proportion.

The Belgian contributions in this class were of a very practical character. There were two considerable exhibits of goods manufactured in the apprentice schools of East and West Flanders.

Probably the most remarkable exhibit of Cotton goods in the Austrian Department was that of C. Burckhart, Vienna, and, with that of M. A. Spitzer, also of Vienna, illustrating the most novel use to which cotton has been recently applied. The articles consisted of shawls and other articles of ladies' dress, with neck overties for gentlemen, made of chenille in cotton.

The Cotton goods of the Zollverein were cheap and strong clothing for working men, such as already noted in Belgium and Austria. An admirable example of this class of goods, which seem to be confined to the locality of Gladbach, in Rhenish-Prussia, was found in the display of Wolff, Schlaffhorst, Bruel, and Co. Some of these goods were made with a plushlike face, soft and downy, and, whilst the patterns and dyes are well selected and in excellent taste, the finish is equal to woollens of the same character.

Klemme and Grube, Crefeld, exhibited excellent Cotton Velvet Ribbons and Trimmings similar to those manufactured by Moore, of Manchester. The make of these goods was excellent, and the designs and finish very good. The Jury awarded a Prize Medal to G. Klemme, of the firm.

Saxony had some useful exhibits of Cotton: the contribution of Wæntig and Co., Zittau, consisted of cotton and mixed linen Tickings: excellent goods, and suggestive of a useful class of fabrics for vestings for working men.

The Milan Chamber of Commerce exhibited a series of useful fabrics in Cotton, and E. Lualdi showed good yarns. There was also a curious, but we fear not a very practical illustration of the produce of Italy in Raw Cotton.

The only exhibitors of Cotton goods from the United States were Gardner, Brewer, and Co., of Boston, Massachusetts. The goods shown were a very superior quality of fine shirtings, which were certainly not produced a few years ago in any part of the States.

Here we may record that three Prize Medals were awarded to exhibitors of Raw Cotton grown in New South Wales, and the same number to the exhibitors of the same material grown in Queensland. This is a distinct proof that the British Colonies of the Southern Hemisphere can produce raw cotton which will satisfy an International Jury of cotton factors.

FLAX AND HEMP.

This important section of textile industry presented few novelties. Here the Sailcloths of Arbroath and Dundee, together with the Jute fabrics of the latter place, were arranged. The Damasks of Dunfermline, the Yarns and Linen cloths of Leeds, the Diapers and Huckabacks of Barnsley, occupied one side of an erection in the centre of the gallery; Ropes, Matting, Twine, and kindred products being placed in the other. The chief display, however, in this class was from the north of Ireland, in which the Belfast manufacturers and merchants were fairly represented in everything except high-class damask table linen, and in this direction, two or three of the principal houses were absent. Belfast also contributed a trophy of the Irish Linen-trade, which was placed on the north side of the central nave, near the centre of the Building.

On the whole, the Flax and Hemp manufacture proper may be said to have been stationary since 1851. The manufacture of Jute has, however, progressed enormously, and it is stated that 40,000 tons of this material are now worked up annually in Scotland. Its success may be chiefly attributed to its analogy to cotton, the ease with which it can be mixed with other fibrous substances; and, as illustrated on this occasion, its ready affinity for certain dyes, although their permanence in this material is rather doubtful.

The Foreign productions in Flax and Hemp were pretty much on a par with those of 1851; for, whilst the cotton and silk manufacture has increased in most countries, the linen trade seems to have been stationary.

Among the Flax-machines exhibited was an improved Power-loom, by Harrison and Sons, Blackburn. It is supplied with a self-acting positive letting-off motion, which delivers the warp as required by the taking-up motion for the cloth, which motion is also positive. These two motions work in concert, and with such precision that the warp is delivered from the yarn beam with the same regularity when the beam is almost empty as when it is full. The taking-up roller of the loom is covered with a patented surfacing material instead of that in ordinary use, made of emery. It is also supplied with the weft-stopping motion, and other important appliances. A loom of this description is capable of weaving upwards of 180 yards of linen per week. Messrs. Harrison exhibited a series of other machines for weaving cotton, and for all the processes necessary for converting the yarn into cloth.

Flax-machines were also exhibited by Lawson, of Leeds, Fairbairn, of Leeds, and others, for carding, heckling, and spinning.

SILK AND VELVET.

The English Silks made a great show in themselves, and there has been nothing yet displayed by foreigners which equals our best specimens of loom manufacture. Spitalfields was as great as ever in the massive richness of its fabrics and softness of colour. Ballance and Co., and Kemp and Stone, of Spital-square, had exquisite specimens of this kind, both in Silks and Velvets; the latter especially were good and rich, equal to anything ever produced by Lyons or Genoa. Grant and Gask sent some gorgeous specimens of English-made Silk Curtains, where the brocade fabric is interwoven with designs in spun glass, as fine as silk. These *tissues-de-verre* are of a similar manufacture to the hangings that are now in the Throne-room at St. James's, and which have been some thirty years in use, though still as bright as ever. These massive fabrics were decidedly the richest and most beautiful of the kind shown; and, as exemplifying a not very costly and most desirable combination of silk and glass, attracted especial notice. Campbell, Harrison, and Lloyd showed the finest collection of Figured and Watered Silks and Moire-antiques. In the figured silks, harmony of colour and beauty of design were carried to their utmost in these specimens; while the watered silks had a most brilliant lustre. Seamer sent various samples of Silks and Velvets, second only to those of Campbell and Co. But the most beautiful and most varied collections of fabrics of these classes were found among the Irish Poplins. Fry and Co., and Pim Brothers, exhibited every kind of Poplin, either watered, embroidered, or figured. One of the best examples was a copy in white silk of the various forms of snow crystals worked on a blue ground, by which, of course, an almost endless diversity of beautiful little stars is obtained. The Manchester Silks, it is feared, attracted but little notice amid this fine display; for, generally, their colours were not well chosen, and nearly all had a dull aspect. One very good collection was, however, shown by J. Chadwick, all the samples in which were woven by the power-loom. Those who remember the same classes in 1851, could judge of the improvement which has since been made. Both in an artistic and manufacturing point of view the whole collection far exceeded even the highest anticipations.—*Abridged from the Times.*

The show of Ribands sent by Coventry was magnificent. There were ribands here of all kinds,—from fine delicately embossed webs to broad flowered silk textures, wide and massive enough for curtains. Newsome and Co. showed a collection of every possible variety of fineness, texture, and pattern; and those sent by Franklin and Co. were almost equally good. There are apparently very few ribands made anywhere in England but at Coventry—certainly none which can compare with them, either for fabric or design.

WOOLLEN AND WORSTED, AND MIXED FABRICS.

In these great and important industries, the chief exhibits were the collective ones from Huddersfield, Bradford, and Leeds, as representing the great Yorkshire district, Halifax and Dewsbury falling in as part of the arrangement. The display was a highly suggestive and satisfactory one, and the ground taken so successfully in 1851 was well maintained, a most decided improvement being manifested in the general taste of the goods and perfection of dye and finish.

The West of England and the London houses followed with their exhibits, and the Cloths of the West are up to their usual standard.

The Mixed Fabrics and Poplin of Dublin and Norwich, with the shawls, tartans, &c., of Glasgow and Paisley, came next. Norwich took the post of honour; and the richly coloured Shawls arranged in the central compartment of the great mediæval case erected by the three or four manufacturers who sustain the honour of that city of textiles, was an effective feature of the Building at this point, apart from the fact that these articles would have been considered an impossibility in 1851.

Then followed a miscellaneous collection of Woollens and mixed goods, in which the manufacturers of Hawick, Kendal, Chipping Norton, and Darlington, took the lead.

On the Foreign side, France, Belgium, Austria, Prussia, and Saxony (the two latter as States of the Zollverein) exhibited largely and effectively alike in Woollens and Mixed Fabrics; and marked improvements have taken place in certain directions which show that the lessons of 1851 and 1855 were not thrown away. France has probably made the most decided improvement in the greater substantiality of her Woollen Cloths; in shawls and the more ornate mixed fabrics, her pre-eminence in certain points remained much the same. In Merinoes she has found, however, a serious if not a triumphant competitor in the Bradford exhibits on the British side.

CARPET MANUFACTURE.

The artistic principles upon which the selection of designs for Carpets is sought to be established is, we suspect, too often overruled by the taste of the public to be capable of satisfactory development. However, the object of the art reformers is legitimate: and with the view of aiding its progress, our notices of the specimens of Carpets exhibited will be framed, as far as practicable, with a view to this object.

Whytock and Co., of Edinburgh, showed a work, in every respect of a commendable character. "It is founded on a geometrical basis, is simple in the arrangement of its parts, soft and low in tone of colour — the ground being green and the ornament in maroon enlivened with red—and the whole is margined by a border of great simplicity and beauty. As a work it fulfils all requirements. Besides being of the radiate type, and having its parts subjected to a geometrical disposition, the welcome quality of flatness pervades its parts, which of itself is a feature worthy of the highest commendation in the case of a floor enrichment. Nothing can be more erroneous than the idea that, because rugged paths are picturesque, lakes beautiful, and blackberries sweet to the taste, they are hence agreeable things to walk upon. A flat surface is that which is welcome as a floor, and holes, bushes, and trees are alike avoided whenever we wander abroad. While flatness of the floor is essential to comfort, and the very appearance of unevenness is unpleasant, the hispid nap of the carpet is very grateful to the sense of touch, and the soft floor covering is pleasant to walk upon, just as the turf is, which is the velvet-pile of nature."—*Illustrated London News.*

Whytock and Co.'s Wilton or Scoto-Axminster is produced by an ingenious process, which combines numerous and vivid colours with much that is pleasing and harmonious in effect.

In this process each thread of the warp carries its share of the rose or thistle, the leaf or the briar of which it is intended to form a part; thus the entire warp presents a mottled appearance and variegated aspect that would have its exact counterpart in a printed cotton dress that should be carefully separated into its constituent threads, and these threads spread out upon a plain surface. The appearance presented by a printed cotton so dismembered may easily be conceived. Each thread would be covered by innumerable patches of colour, and the restoration of these to their original position in the once beautiful design of which they constituted a necessary part may appear a hopeless task; but this is precisely what is accomplished by Mr. Whytock's ingenious patent. His warp is bespattered with colour, apparently confused and variegated without a purpose, but it is in reality mottled with design, and parti-coloured with a method that ensures each tint and hue being gathered up by the weaver to take its place in the development of some graceful form or some beautiful flower. The principal Carpet is in design a very good example of the Byzantine style of ornament, with much careful drawing and well harmonised heavy colouring.

Woodward Brothers and Co., of Kidderminster, exhibited several Carpets of a commendable character.

Palmer Brothers showed two Rugs which have many excellences and features worthy of careful consideration. "They are flat, low in tone, simple in treatment, founded upon a geometric basis, and the little star-like or floral forms are of a circular character. Not only is every plant, as seen from above, of a radiate nature, but the head of flowers and the individual flower have also the same structure, while flowers which are seen laterally are frequently bi-symmetrical. It will, however, be said that the flower of the candytuft is of a bi-lateral character, and that it enjoys a horizontal position. This is the case; yet occurrences of this nature are rare; but even here the manner in which the flowers are grouped together brings about the production of a circular ornament, for the small portion of every flower is directed to the centre, and the larger portion to the circumference; hence the radiate structure is perfectly restored. In the mats under consideration we have added to the other merits the welcome full view of the flowerlike forms, which is ever pleasing in the case of decorations for horizontal surfaces.

Watson, Bontor, and Co., exhibited some fabrics to which considerable interest attaches, as they are the produce of their India Carpet establishment, commenced in the Madras Presidency in the year 1848. This manufactory is left entirely to native superintendence, and is carried on by local talent and energy, no personal communication having at any time taken place between employed and the employers; but it is a significant illustration of the mixed character of most manufactured articles, where great attention is paid to quality, that in this particular instance the material for the groundwork, or "back" of the carpet, is spun in England, and sent to India to supplant the less enduring native fabric that would otherwise be employed as the basis of the manufacture. These carpets have the lower part or "back" of the carpet formed of twisted cords of hemp, and the entire upper surface of chenille, which, by an ingenious process, is woven into the various forms that constitute the pattern.

Watson and Co. showed their Patent Axminster Carpet, the filling of which is very judicious and beautiful, and consists of quatrefoils, with low-toned blue grounds, the interspaces being filled with red. It consists of a subdued geometrical form, a simple ornamental arrangement (repeated as a diaper, and stars which tell out somewhat strongly from the low-toned reds in which the other portions are wrought. The border is simple, but the white here introduced is rather strong; yet, when considered as a whole, this work has great beauty, and is of a highly meritorious character.

Templeton and Co., of Glasgow and London, exhibited some patterns which have superior merits: a Border Carpet with a blue hue, is founded on a geometrical basis, and consists of quatrefoils with low-toned blue grounds, leaving between them spaces filled in with red. The filling consists of conventionally-treated flowers and foliage of great simplicity. About this carpet there is a justness and suitability to the purpose intended which few possess: it is rich yet low in tone, well varied, and not obtrusive; the pattern is equally distributed over the surface, and the border is pleasing, consisting of pointed quatrefoils, simply arranged. This carpet appears to suggest its true office, that of a background. Such is the opinion of the writer above quoted; yet this design hardly comes to the flatness just insisted on.

Templeton and Co. also showed two Hearth-rugs, in which the ornamental treatment of the flowers was beautifully symmetrical —an example of the true treatment of flowers for floral patterns. The carpets of Harvey, Nichols, and Co., were defective in flatness, but had many good qualities, marred by the festoons of flowers in the borders, than which nothing can be more inconsistent.

Another carpet by the same manufacturers has the filling very rich, and consists of small star-like floral forms in two reds, falling softly and pleasantly on a maroon ground. The border is in good Italian ornament, harmoniously coloured, yet it is rather strong, the ground here being white. Altogether this is a very excellent work.

The Velvet-pile Carpets of Messrs. Jackson and Graham are made in the Jacquard loom, worked by steam-power, and the designs might be seen in process of weaving in a loom which the firm had at work in the Western Annexe. The rhododendron design, the bay-leaf pattern, and the jasmine trellis, were very successful. Two Persian designs were remarkable for their richness and harmony of colouring, and close imitation of the beautiful Oriental originals.

Jackson and Graham also showed a large square carpet, which, while very florid and strong in its contrasts of colour, has yet delicacy and beauty and a certain amount of repose; the colouring, also, is harmonious, and the masses are well disposed.

Lapworth Brothers, Old Bond-street, showed a very large carpet, the greatest merit of which was its flatness: blue prevailed, and the pattern was good. Lapworths' carpets were admirable examples of woollen fabrics: they are the production of the hand and not of the loom, and they still maintain an enviable superiority over all the varieties of textile carpets. These carpets are the produce of their establishment at Wilton, which enjoys a special celebrity in carpet-making: it was here that the Flemish weavers found refuge from religious persecution, in the reign of James I., and set up their looms to manufacture Brussels carpets, under the patronage of William, Earl of Pembroke, then chamberlain of the royal household.

Crossley and Son were among the largest manufacturers in the country of Velvet Pile and Brussels carpet, to the production of which power-looms have now been applied in the place of the hand-looms which were in use at the time of the Exhibition of 1851. Of their designs it has been said that they will not please the Professors of the Kensington School of Science and Art. Kidderminster carpet calls for few observations; its texture remains the same, and the mode of production the same as at the Exhibition of 1851.

A noteworthy specimen of Axminster carpet, designed for and intended as a wall-decoration, after the style of the Gobelin tapestries, was manufactured and exhibited by Tapling and Co., of Gresham-street. The design is by Mr. W. A. Parris. It contains figures, considerably larger than life, of Louis Napoleon presenting the treaty to Queen Victoria, and is designed to commemorate the Treaty of Commerce between France and England. The figures are surrounded with an elaborate framework of laurel and oak-leaves in gold colours. The panels are of a rich maroon, having an interlaced ornament alternately of the rose and bee, emblematical of the two countries. The French emblem is introduced on a shield at the top of the design, surmounted with branches of the palm, depending from which are large swags of fruit, symbolical of Peace and Plenty. At the base are the English and French flags, supporting the Rose, Thistle, and Shamrock, with a blue ribbon containing the motto, "La reciprocité est la base vraie et durable de la Paix." In a work of this character, so novel in design and treatment, there were many difficulties to contend with, but they have for the most part been successfully overcome. The work is woven in one piece, twenty-two feet by eighteen feet.

Messrs. Filmer, of Berners-street, exhibited Velvet Pile and Brussels Carpets, from designs by the Government School of Art. The latter present a conventional treatment of flowers, without shading, and presenting the appearance of a uniform flat surface, following in this respect the patterns of the carpets of the East. In the velvet pile carpets six strongly contrasted colours are so well and evenly balanced, and are mixed in such small quantities, that no one colour offends the eye; and the whole blends into a soft, warm, greyish tint, forming a very appropriate ground for the furniture and decorations. Sewell and Co., of Compton House, were exhibitors of a fine Axminster carpet, the pattern of which is an adaptation of an original design by Mr. Digby Wyatt. It is deserving of notice on account of its fineness of pile and texture, the beauty of its colours, and the symmetrical arrangement of all the parts of the design.

FOREIGN CARPETS.

It may be convenient to notice here, for the sake of readier comparison, the Foreign Carpets in a group, rather than under their respective countries. The paper in the *Illustrated London News* will best supply the staple, inasmuch as its writer shows very considerable knowledge of the general subject, and a judicious amount of artistic taste.

The Carpets both from India and Turkey are, in some respects, widely different from each other; yet they have features in common, and both may be said to be founded upon equally correct principles. Thus, both are rigidly flat in treatment: that is, no attempt at light and shade is made, nor is the evenness of the surface (which is a very desirable quality in a floor) in any way disturbed. The decorative shapes employed, and the arrangement adopted, are such as does not give to the patterns a right and wrong way upwards, but emphasizes them equally in all directions, which is the only treatment consistent as a floor enrichment. Yet in how many cases does this requirement remain unfulfilled in the carpets which we see in the shop-windows, and even on the floors of the opulent; yet no arrangement in which the pattern runs in one particular direction can be satisfactory, as it must of necessity be wrong way upwards to the greater portion of the occupants of the room, and thus impart pleasure only to the few.* A low neutral aspect also marks these carpets, which is due,

---

* Prayer-carpets have a pattern running in one direction; when in use the pattern points to Mecca.

primarily, to the nature of the colouring, but also, in part, to the judiciously vague distribution of the shapes used for the purpose of enrichment. We are thus led to see that the Indian and Turkish designers are possessed of most valuable knowledge, which has led them to endow all their carpets with this neutral aspect. But the artists of the two countries achieve their results in different ways; for we find in the Turkish carpets large masses of negative colour employed as general and partial grounds, such as low-toned or tertiary red, which is their favourite colour; and forms of a semi-geometrical character filled in with ornament of various hues, in which blue and green predominate; they, however, depend for their effect chiefly upon the exact tone of the colour which is to prevail in the work as the ground-tint, and throughout the colours are used in such masses as to affect the eye separately. The Indian carpets, on the contrary, owe their negative aspect to the precise balance of colour which is introduced into the works, whereby a neutral colour-bloom is produced: thus, they impart a glowing effect by letting orange slightly prevail. Yet, while we say that the Indians adopt this mode of producing their neutral effect, and that the Turks use masses of colour which are in themselves low in tone, we only mean that such modes are the more general with these people: yet in some cases the Turkish works exhibit a very full admixture of colours, and the Indian rugs have grounds of a single tint.

Excellent examples of the more characteristic Carpets and Rugs of the Turks were exhibited by Watson, Bontor, and Co.; Tapling and Co.; and Lapworth Brothers; and of the Indian Carpets and Rugs by Major M'Andrew, who exhibited a carpet made at Lahore by the Thugs; Watson and Co. showed one from Masulipatam, a carpet made by the prisoners in the gaol at Meerut (which closely resembles that shown by Major M'Andrew), and a series of rugs. These, together with a carpet made by the native Thugs at the Government School of Industry at Jubbulpore, were the most important works, and their excellences can scarcely be overrated.

The Carpets furnished by the natives of Hindostan are unrivalled in every respect, but unfortunately their production requires a considerable length of time, the Thugs being ignorant of the modern process of carpet manufacture. To remedy this evil, an attempt has been made to introduce the Kidderminster process amongst the natives, but with this result: the beautiful patterns of the natives having been thrown aside, and some of the worst of a worn-out English school substituted. Thus we had one of the hideous specimens of Kidderminster exhibited side by side with the beautiful productions of the native loom which had fortunately escaped the debasing influence. In the carpets of the natives due regard is paid to the relation of the carpet to the furniture of the room. The Kidderminster carpet exhibited, on the contrary, by its coarse vulgarity, immediately calls the chief attention to itself. Though this importation of bad taste into India was pointed out and strongly-deprecated eleven years since, it is still continued. In the first Great Exhibition some specimens of this Anglo-Indian daubing were displayed, and were condemned in the following words in the " Supplement to the Report of the Jury on Class XXX. :"—" Having spoken thus highly of the decoration of such goods (carpets) in India, it is painful to observe the attempts ignorantly made to vitiate the sound taste of the native artists." Let us hope that the next decade of years may be productive of better results.

Two works, of a character new to us, brought from the Summer Palace of China, were exhibited: they rather surprised than pleased upon first viewing them, yet meritorious qualities quickly appeared, for there is an amount of vigour displayed in their ornamentation and a revelation of power to deal with most difficult matters of art, such as cannot fail to make an impression upon the observer who attentively considers them.

The more important Carpet, of large dimensions, is in form a parallelogram, has a set border, and a blue-black velvet ground. The enrichment of the field consists of the conventional forms so well known as the symbolic clouds of the Chinese, coloured blue, green, and two shades of vermilion, and outlined with gold, together with a number of grotesque creatures flying and running in every direction, and animated by excessive life. These are fine examples of the grotesque, and combine with the clouds to fill a wonderful sky, which undoubtedly represents the Elysian plains of the Chinaman, their much-coveted hunting-ground; and, while it may seem remarkable that the "world in the sky" should be portrayed on the floor, the producers of the work probably deem it nothing but right that the chief of a celestial empire should be seated upon the clouds, and some such notion has probably possessed the mind of its originator. The border consists of a simple alternate arrangement of a conventional cloud, and the Chinese ornament corresponds with the Anthemion of the Greeks.

The smaller carpet is of a less interesting character, and has a yellow ground, on which are spread butterflies sporting with the flowers; yet in this the manner in which some of the flowers are treated must be commended.

TAPESTRIES OF GOBELINS AND BEAUVAIS.

The Tapestries of the Imperial manufactory of Gobelins and of the sister institution of Beauvais at this very day are as highly prized as when the Royal works were first established two centuries since. Their exhibit consisted of four tapestries and two carpets—the large central tapestry containing a full-length portrait figure, and the two carpets are from the parent institution (Gobelins), and the fruit pieces to the right and left from Beauvais. The central work, of great magnificence, is after the celebrated picture

Venice—"The Assumption of the Virgin," by Titian. Here we have needlework entering into competition with the pigments of the artist, which can be spread as transparent films, heaped in effective masses, modified by mediums so as to be fitted for producing the most varied effects; having tackiness in the one case, which renders them fit for "dragging;" and fluidity, which renders them adapted for "glazing" in another; and, with all this, being susceptible of diversified modes of hanging.

The "Assumption of the Virgin" realizes all the charms and delicacies of the original work—expression, energy, delicacy, and tone of colour being rendered with the utmost truth, the rich harmony and glow of refulgent light being also fully embodied in the work. The toil and labour necessary to the production of such a work it is difficult to conceive: not a thread can be placed without the most careful consideration, and not a colour used without the sanction of a most experienced eye, as colours when juxtaposed acquire abnormal hues: yet this tapestry in which the figures are lifesize, finds its commercial equivalents in 6000l. To the right of this central and most important work was the portrait tapestry of Louis XIV. of France, in which the flesh is rendered with a faithfulness seldom witnessed.

The Tapestries from Beauvais were in no way inferior to those of Gobelins: yet they differ so widely in character that a mere glance will suffice for the distinguishing between the works of the two manufactories. Those from Beauvais are of still-life and fruit, while those from Gobelins are of an historical character.

FLOOR-CLOTHS.

To Floor-cloths the Exhibition were less indebted for any general ornamental effect than to carpets. Smith and Baber exhibited two large cloths of considerable merit: the one, a simple design of marbles, with a border that is elegant in effect; and the other a geometrical pattern, having sprays and flowers in imitation of a mosaic inlay on a marble ground. Downing and Co. exhibited several very good specimens; one of 10 yards or 30 feet wide had a combination of the squares of a chess-board and samples of encaustic tiles. James Rolls and Son showed an example of a tile pattern cloth, admirable for its fidelity to the simple forms that make up the detail of the design, and for its excellence in colour. Hawksworth, of Doncaster, exhibited some remarkable specimens of Mosaic Floorcloths. Nairn and Co., of Kirkaldy, exhibited a number of "carpet patterns" where the attempts to produce roses and leaves were very creditable under the circumstances. Their specimens of marquetrie and parquetrie were also commendable.

Kamptulicon was exhibited by Taylor and Co., and is a Floor-cloth made of cork and India-rubber. It is admirably adapted for all situations where the floor is damp, being exceedingly durable. The quantity manufactured of this most useful material has hitherto been exceedingly limited, and the probability is that the demand will never be great at any time, as it cannot be produced for the price of ordinary floorcloth, and does not, therefore, enter into competition with it.

PRINTED AND DYED FABRICS.

Probably in no Department of the whole Exhibition has there been so thorough a change since 1851 as in that of Printed Fabrics: mousselines-de-laine, barèges, and other printed fabrics of kindred make having been superseded by alpacas, mohairs, and various light and elegant mixed fabrics. Nevertheless, the leading printers, both of Manchester and Glasgow, contributed little to the display. In the matter of design the great body of English and Scotch Calico-printers are pretty much where they were fifteen years ago; except that in the English Division, simple effects were worked out in one or two colours, instead of elaborations in form and colour, which are generally costly and failures.

There can be no doubt that in mechanical modes of production, as well as in the chemistry of the art of Printing and Dyeing, considerable progress has been made during the last ten years; and that by these means the British producer is enabled to meet the wants of the various markets of the world with much the same, if not greater advantage than heretofore.

The French printers made a great effort to completely illustrate everything they were doing, especially in the way of improvements in Printed Fabrics: the result was, they made a valuable display, and deservedly carried off the largest proportion of the honours.

At the suggestion of Dr. Lyon Playfair, a systematic illustration of the various improvements in the Chemistry of Calico-Printing and Dyeing since 1851 was given by Mr. Rumney, of the Ardwick Chemical Works, Manchester. All the new dyes and chemicals of any importance introduced into the trade during the last eleven years were here shown, as illustrating "the latest chapter in the history of Calico-printing." The various dyes and chemicals were exhibited in bottles; and the examples in cotton, silk, wool, and mixed fabrics were also shown. Amongst them was the application of Mr. Perkin's discovery of Coal-tar and its remarkable product Ailine as a colouring agent. Aniline colours were shown in their varied forms of dyeing and printing as applied to cottons, cotton-velvets, silk, and woollen, in shades of purple, reds, and blues, known as mauve, magenta, &c. The colours in silk were especially brilliant. There were also illustrations of murexide colours on cotton and woollens. Murexide, generally called Roman purple, was in great vogue amongst printers and dyers about 1856. This is a guano colour, as the uric, and is found in sufficient quantities in that substance, which is first treated with hydrochloric acid and subsequently with nitric acid. The final result was seen in the specimens exhibited. To these were added pigment colours fixed with glue and mercury, under

Lightfoot's patent; also aniline and pigment colours. Pigment colours fixed by albumen and substitutes for albumen, such as lacterine, gluten, &c., were shown; and coal-tar colours in combination at one operation with dyeing and printing. Specimens of emeraldine, a new green, and azurine, a new blue, were contributed by Mr. Crace Calvert, F.R.S., of Manchester. Emeraldine is produced by preparing cotton with chlorate of potash; then printing with an acid chloride of aniline, in a given period a bright green appears; next the green is subjected to the action of a solution of bichromate of potash, and the tint is changed to a deep blue, which has been called azurine. Altogether, Mr. Rumney's exhibit proved how actively science has been working for the industrial arts.

The practical application of these Dyes would far exceed our limits. Probably the most remarkable display was that of Butterworth and Brooks, Manchester, to whom was awarded a Prize Medal; the award stating that the firm was the first to fix aniline colours in cotton by a new method—a most important improvement, as in the various illustrations given of the result. These were madder and aline colours printed in one process; dyed mauve colour, giving very clearly printed and elegant effects; aniline, a subdued purple, and opaline, a subdued blue of very pleasing tone, both in mixed fabrics.

Littlewood, Wilson, and Co. were distinguished by excellence in Madder Styles; besides their new method of fixing, with tartar-emetic, aniline in cotton fabrics; and for machine-printed furnitures with the gum-roller.

Muir, Brown, and Co. sent a wonderful case of very fine Muslins, some of which were printed with a delicacy equal to the French; and others with a thread of gold or silver tissue running through them. The latter had a beautiful effect.

Joseph Lockett, Sons, and Leake, Manchester, illustrated their eculiar methods of Engraving the Cylinders employed in Machine-printing, or rather the results of these methods as shown in the fabrics printed. These showed the character of the grounds produced by machinery, such as "eccentrics," imitations of watered effects, &c. The smaller geometric patterns, sea-weed, and striated effects are produced by "millwork." Handwork is still employed in the introduction of the larger effects, but such is the present demand for cylinders for calico-printing that no available amount of handwork could possibly keep pace with it. Among their numerous mechanical contrivances, this firm showed an adaptation of the principle of the pantagraph to engraving copper rollers. The pantagraph arrangement and the pattern being placed horizontally instead of vertically, and the "nippers," which in the embroidery machine are armed with double-pointed needles working through the vertical fabric, are in this engraving-machine fitted with points which, when in action, scratch the pattern in repeats upon the copper cylinder, which is covered with an etching-ground. Of course this pattern is bitten into the copper surface by immersion in a corrosive acid. The advantage of the machine is, that a variety of sizes of the same pattern can be engraved; whilst the work, being reduced from an accurately drawn and enlarged original, comes out so much the more perfect in the reduction, and there seems no limit to the amount of elaboration to which any pattern can be carried. Messrs. Lockett were awarded a Prize Medal both for their patterns and the machine.

Glasgow made a much more limited display than Manchester. The only printers of Linens who exhibited were Girdwood and Co., Belfast, whose specimens were good.

Furniture Chintz-printing, represented by two exhibitors, stood where it did in 1851; the Printed Table-covers were as stationary. Of Printed Felts there were better specimens.

In Dyeing, pure and simple, a great triumph has been achieved by English dyers on this occasion. The French almost acknowledged themselves beaten; for purity of colour and excellence of finish, commend us to the British goods, especially silks and woollens.

The most perfect display was that of Mr. Samuel Smith, Bradford,—a series of admirable illustrations of Dyes, as applied to wool, shawls, alpacas, and other lustres; Coburgs, Orleans, corded figured reps, &c., all of excellent tint and finish.

The English Silk Dyes were superb. Coventry stood first—in the aniline colours shown by Mr. B. S. Richardson, and the brilliant dyes by Hands: the new crimson from aniline, and a dark mauve, were great successes. The blacks and whites amongst these Coventry dyes were also very pure.

Adshead and Co., of Macclesfield, showed greens, yellows, and crimsons in perfection. Picric acid, obtained from carbonic acid by the action of nitric acid, is used for the yellows, which, with coal-tar blues, produce greens.

Altogether, English dyers and printers made a decided stand against traditional French Dyes on this occasion.

France exhibited largely, and did justice to the power of production alike in tasteful design, beauty of mechanical result, and brilliancy of colour. Austria made a great advance; but the most remarkable progress was that of Russia, for, notwithstanding the disastrous war and political distractions since 1851, Russia produced in this Exhibition most remarkable specimens, probably the best of the kind shown considering that eleven years ago the industry may be said not to have existed.—*Abridged from the Illustrated London News.*

A beautiful combination of science and mechanics as applied to the art of Engraving was shown in the Electrograph Engraving Machine of Mr. Henry Garside, of Manchester. This is intended for the engraving of copper cylinders used in calico-printing, and may be described here. The distinctive feature of this apparatus, apart from its mechanical arrangement, consists in the application of voltaic electricity in communicating movement to important and delicate portions of the machine. The cylinder to be engraved is first coated with a thin film of varnish sufficiently resistent to the continuous action of the strongest acids. The required number of copies of the original design are then traced on the cylinder by means of a series of diamond points arranged on the machine, in a line parallel to the cylinder. The metallic surface of the latter thus becomes exposed at the parts required to be engraved. A bath of nitric or some other potent acid is afterwards used to deepen the exposed portions to the extent required, and thus the operation is completed. The diamond points are all in connexion with as many small magnets, and these are so arranged that intermittent voltaic currents are established in unison with the original design. The results are that the diamonds are withdrawn or advanced at the proper moment, and the tracery forms an exact counterpart of the copy. There are, also, adjustments, which enable the operator to enlarge or diminish at will the size of the patterns to be engraved.—*Mechanics' Magazine.*

LACE-MAKING.

The respective positions of the countries which may be said to compete in the Lace Manufacture have, we think, continued unchanged since the last Exhibition. England has made a wonderful advance. France well supports its ancient reputation; but, undeniably, Belgium has contributed the most exquisite specimens. In them is displayed the marvellously patient study of detail characteristic of the country, combined with a delicacy and grace of design in which some branches of its art have hitherto been found wanting.

In the Belgian Department M. Hoorickx exhibited a beautiful novelty—a handkerchief which presents every variety of point stitch, and several styles of design. At the extreme edge of the lace border is a wreath of convolvulus leaves and flowers; within that is a kind of arabesque pattern enriched with *plumetis* or satin-stich, which is quite a new feature of the Belgian laces; and then comes the triumph of art in a border of exquisite little bouquets; the miniature flowers are all in relief, the rose showing its circling petals, and other blossoms their natural forms. The small centre of cambric is enclosed within a mechanical design of heavier substance. The price is about 200*l*. A section of flounce, half a yard wide, with flowers in the same style of relief, was also dislayed: the value of the set of two, 800*l*.; that of a tunic with berthe and handkerchief, about the same. Van Rossum showed point sets of handkerchief, lappet, collar, and sleeves: each set is worth 240*l*., and occupied four years in making.

The French have much improved the "Guipure," called by them "Maltese." Among various shawls and flounces of Chantilly was M. Seguin's half-shawl, valued at 140*l*., pattern, a Chinese garden. The Compagne des Indes showed a point d'Alençon flounce, priced at 1000*l*.

The exhibition of British Lace was admirable, not only for its beauty and richness, but for the variety of object in which Honiton, Ireland, and Nottingham compete for supremacy. Among the Nottingham manufacturers, Barnett and Maltby, Vickers, Robinson, Adams, Northcote, Marlowe and Co. were foremost, both for exquisite fineness of texture and beauty of design. Howell and James sent a kind of Trophy Piece of Lace Needlework; with a dress of the most elaborate kind, on which it is stated that upwards of 200 persons were employed: it was certainly one of the most wonderful pieces of handwork in the Building. The Industrial Society of Ireland exhibited a small, but very fine collection of Irish Laces: the Countess of Erne sent some Irish Valenciennes; and Messrs Forrest, of Dublin, showed Limerick and other Laces, which, with the various Irish imitations, gave the sister-island a decided pre-eminence in this class. There was one large case of mixed Honiton and Irish Laces, unsurpassed. The larger kinds of lace-work, as curtains, &c., came almost entirely from Nottingham: the honours were carried off by the exquisite designs of Copestake and Moore. The Nottingham imitations included Spanish shawls and mantillas, and black Chantilly, remarkably improved. In fact, in design the machine-made lace of Nottingham has turned the tables upon our French competitors in 1851. Reckless and Hickling, of Nottingham, exhibited laces, flounces, tunics, mantles, shawls, coiffures, and barbes in one piece, all made by the pusher machine, with the application of the jacquard; all the fabric pattern being made by the machine, and the outline being entirely needlework. These goods nearly rival the hand-made laces of Cambray, Chantilly, and Bayeux.

A case of Spanish blondes contained articles richly embroidered in colours and gold thread; the real gem of the collection, however, was a white Mantilla—the pattern, wreaths of flowers supported by flying cupids, of solid texture; the ground light guipure. Saxony is remarkable rather for the low price than the quality of its laces; but Berlin added to the attractions of the Exhibition a very creditable suite of Brussels point on real ground.

FURS, FEATHERS, AND HAIR.

The finest specimens of this Class were grouped or displayed in trophies. Messrs. George Smith and Son, Watling-street, displayed, in this form, various descriptions of Sable, and eight varieties of Fox; and beneath these, magnificent paletots, with smaller articles intermixed. The most striking feature of the group was a mantle of pure white ermine, without the usual intermixture of tails, but trimmed with a broad border of delicately-marked chincilla. Messrs. Smith also displayed two other paletots of ermine—one adorned in the usual style, the other minivered in a scalloped pattern round the edge, together with specimens of sables and other furs. The handsome trophy of Mr. Nicholay, the Court furrier, formed one of the most attractive ornaments of the Nave. Here the Russian sable was to be seen in perfection : a complete set of it, including trimmed velvet mantle, is valued at 500*l*. Next were a cloak of the fur of the Siberian squirrel; skins of the Astracan lamb; paletots of seal skin, trimmed with other furs, including the beaver, and made into a bonnet edged with miniver and decorated with a plume of white feathers. Among the treasures of the collection was a sea-otter skin, worth 50*l*. Messrs. Poland showed a splendid rug of the white Arctic fox, and large cloaks of sable and ermine; and Mr. Jeff a swan-muff and tippet from Holland, and a curious mantle formed from the crest and neck of the king eider-duck, a kind of green and black pattern on a white ground.

Russia contributed little : the most noteworthy specimens were a manufactured Fur Carpet ; an elegant mantle of Down; and eight species of stuffed Sables, exhibited by M. Alibert.

In the next section of this Class, De Costa, Andrade, and Co. displayed an Ostrich-feather trophy, in which as many as ten different colours of tints were presented in one single feather. The white plumes were examples of purity of colour and excellence of finish ; they were selected from 5000. A Veil of Marabout Feathers was also an ingenious novelty. Here also was a Pelerine and Muff of white marabout feathers ; and white, grey, and black Ostrich Feathers, in their rough state, as sent from the Barbary States and the Cape of Good Hope.

The third division of the Class included Artificial Hair, suited to every requirement and demand. Flowing white locks for majestic old age ; or a light sprinkling of grey hair to assist the expiring efforts of Nature ; and wigs adapted to middle life, and more or less advanced.

Among other Curiosities exhibited was a case containing specimens of Human Hair of great length, shorn from the heads of English, German, French, and Italian ladies-hair of every hue, from pale auburn to jet black, and of every degree of fineness and silky gloss. The honours in this Class, however, were carried off by some fair unknown of our own country, from whose head had been severed a lock of jet-black hair, no less than 74 inches in length!

INDIA-RUBBER MANUFACTURES.

There were upwards of 20 exhibitors of various manufactures in this material, besides those of Gutta-Percha, and other analogous substances.

Prominent amongst these were the original patentees in England, C. Mackintosh and Co., of Manchester, who exhibited beautiful specimens of the raw material, showing the process of manufacture, from the masticated lump to the finished sheet.

They had also tubing for the Lighting of Railway-carriages by Gas, which has been found practicable; and an inflated India-rubber Globe, three yards in circumference, for the use of schools. Silver and Co. showed their Ebonite Tubes, which are not affected by acid, for vinegar and dye works; bottles and funnels, photographic baths and dishes; coated harness-irons; bracelets and chains in place of jet, &c. In soft vulcanized India-rubber was shown a Door-mat, produced by making incisions with a sharp knife at regular intervals, which being kept open, during vulcanization, a mat is produced, firm to the foot. They also exhibited washers, valves, steam-packing hose, &c.; insulated telegraph wire, and ebonite pole insulators.

Warne and Co. showed their novel Junction Rubber for piston-rings and pump-buckets, made of soft and hard rubber combined; and their Screw-shaft Water-stop for ocean-steamers, which prevents the necessity of stoppage for repacking when at sea. This is effected by the inflation of two rings so arranged as to answer the end required, whilst the stuffing-box is being repacked. They also showed an elastic Bath-towel, having a rubber warp alternate with cotton; "mineralized rubber;" "ferruginous cement packing;" a very ingenious flesh-brush, and their "aromatic bands;" also an "Archimedean screw Rifle-cleaner." Warne and Co. were the first to introduce the use of India-rubber for door-mats, formed of cross-sections of tubes cemented together.

The North British Company, of Edinburgh, excelled particularly in their over-shoes, which is a branch of the trade hitherto only carried on in France and America. The shoes exhibited here, however, very far exceeded in beauty of make and finish those of either of the other makers; as did also their valves, hose, and beltings. They showed, let into the floor, the largest valve which has ever been made; being 6 feet 4 inches in diameter, and 1½ inches thick, made of pure rubber, in the manufacture of which no solvent had been used.

Cow and Co., of Cheapside, showed their Water-proof Cloths; a knapsack and haversack combined, and a lady's yachting-jacket. Mr. J. L. Hancock exhibited a portable air Bedchair for invalids. Hooper, and Hall and Wells showed their India-rubber coated Telegraph-wires for submarine and aerial purposes. Spill and Co. exhibited their Vegetable Leather made up in various forms; and there were several exhibitors of Kamptulicon (India-rubber and cork) floorcloth.

Walton and Co., of Chiswick, showed samples of their "Campticon, or India-rubber substitute," made from oxidized oil, freed of unctuous matter, and formed into semi-elastic resin, which, for steam-packing, driving-bands, and hose, answers as well as India-rubber, and at a considerably less cost.

The Gutta-Percha Company displayed a good collection of their manufactures; and Mr. C. Hancock showed some beautiful Mouldings in Gutta-percha, on a sideboard. There were several French exhibitors of Tubing and Vulcanized India-rubber goods;

and three or four from Hanover. There were also exhibitors from Berlin; and the Russian Company of St. Petersburg displayed superior Overshoes, Hose, and Belting; and Boots specially adapted to Russian wants.—*Abridged from the Mechanics' Magazine.*

Cohen and Co., of Hamburg, make the most extensive display of any one in the Building, consisting of India-rubber goods generally—overshoes, clothing, tubing, toys, and a very elegant and useful mat or carpet for doors, stairs, railway carriages, &c. They resemble more than anything a grey carpet with a raised honeycomb pattern.

As a *curiosity*, we may here mention a statue of Vulcanized India-rubber, contributed by Herr H. C. Meyer, of Hamburg, who also exhibited a large trophy of articles of the same material. The statue was modelled by Herr Engèlard, the Hanoverian sculptor, and is intended to represent Hermann (the Arminius of the Roman historians), the son of Sigmier, the chief of Cherusci, one of the tribes of North Germany, after the victory gained over the Roman legions under Quintilius Varus, in, as is supposed, the Teutoburg Forest. The head is surrounded with the victor's wreath, the foot rests on a Roman eagle, and the sword is being sheathed triumphantly. The figure has considerable artistic merit; but the material is ill adapted for the purpose.

PERREAUX'S PATENT PUMP-VALVES.

This method of constructing Pump-Valves (says the *Illustrated London News*) is extremely ingenious, simple, and efficient: it is copied from the valves contained in the human heart. Perreaux's valves are made of India-rubber vulcanized for the purpose; they are of the form of a tube flattened at one extremity, similar to the mouthpiece of a hautboy. The thickness of the sides of the upper part diminishes gradually to the top, where the two sides meet and form two lips, which when the valve is in a state of rest are in close contact, and prevent the downward passage of the fluid. With any upward pressure, the lips freely separate, and allow of the upward passage of the fluid; the gradual diminution in the thickness or tapering of the sides forming the lips of the passage enables the valve to open and close with the slightest variation of pressure. The passage for the fluid through these valves is larger than in any others of the same dimensions; they also possess the advantage of having a "clearway," there being nothing whatever to retard the flow of water; and, owing to the self-acting principle imparted by the elasticity of the material, they close perfectly and instantaneously the moment the pressure from below ceases. The lips of the valves being flexible and elastic, any foreign substance which may enter the suction-pipe, such as sand, gravel, coal-dust, cinders, grain, cotton, tow, rags, chips of wood, &c., passes freely through without in the least interfering with or deranging the action of the valve; semi-fluid material, as tar, passes freely through. Should a pump of this description remain dry for any length of time it requires no priming by pouring water into it, as other pumps do, but is always ready for immediate use. In practice these valves answer exceedingly well: they are extensively used in soap and alkali factories and by paper-makers, tanners, bleachers, and dyers, in pumping paper-stuff, chemicals, tan-liquor, &c. The pumps exhibited had glass cylinders or barrels, so that the action of the valves might be seen. It is found advantageous to use glass barrels, as they are free from corrosion and lubricate themselves with the material which is pumped through them.

LEATHER, INCLUDING SADDLERY AND HARNESS.

Additional warranty was given to the old fable of "Nothing like Leather" by the contents of a small Court of British specimens, remarkable both for material and manufacture.

From the head-quarters, Bermondsey, Hepburn and Son sent an enormous Butt-hide of Black Enamelled Leather, 11 feet long by 10 feet 3; and a large number of tanned English sole butts, the average weight being 43 lbs.; the thickness and texture being very remarkable. Samples of all the Tanning Materials used in England were shown in front of these butt-hides:—English oak bark, valonia, gambier, shumac, mimosa, hemlock oak-bark, and others. Bevington and Sons had a large black enamelled coach hide. Harness Leather was shown by Brown and Sons and Santley and Co.; capital hides and skins, coach and harness leather, by Wilson, Walker, and Co.; coloured moroccos, and leather for bookbinding, as fine and delicate in tone and colour as the best fabrics of Manchester, by Fitch and Co., of Leeds. Coloured moroccos were also shown by Bevington and Sons, and coloured seal-skins by Matthews, all remarkable for the excellence of their colour. Leather for boot-tops, thin and light in texture as a lady's glove for jockey-boots, contrasted strongly with the enormous thickness of the leather made from the walrus-hide. There was also buff leather for soldiers' accoutrements. In Saddlery and Harness, Mr. Cuff showed a magnificently embroidered military State Saddle, the property of the Duke of Buccleuch: it is covered with blue velvet, richly worked in silver and gold, and is a gorgeous piece of work, rivalling some of the state trappings of India. Saddles for officers of the 13th Hussars and the Enniskillen Dragoons, by Mr. Gibson, of Coventry-street, were also exhibited by Davis, Strand; with an embroidered Side-saddle, from designs by Delamotte. Merry, of St. James's-street, sent a beautiful Saddle and suite of Harness, made to the order of the Prince of Wales. The Whips, by Swaine and Adeney, formed a brilliant and tasteful display, a case of theirs being valued at more than a thousand pounds. Horses fully harnessed were shown by Blackwell; and the Saddlery Ironmongery of Walsall was largely represented. Among other applications of leather, were specimens of that once fashionable accomplishment for ladies, Potichomanie; Snuff-boxes; and Embossed Leather for walls, screens, and covering furniture—a tasteful item in these times of decorative revivalism.

In the Nave there was a Leather trophy by Bevington and Sons, which was grouped with considerable effect: it was nearly forty feet in height, the summit being occupied by a fallow-deer, standing on a miniature rock. The cornice was diversified by a display of the heads of wild boars, bullocks, elks, African goats, rams, seals, and red deer. Between these was a glass-case, divided into compartments, in which was exhibited every description of leather, from the most delicate texture which covers the lady's hand down to that in which the greatest strength and durability are required. In the lower compartments were photographic representations from the works of the exhibitors, showing the process of the manufacture and preparation of leather through its different stages.

The supremacy of British Leathers and Saddlery was thus fully maintained. There was also a large show of Cape leathers (the so-called dogskin gloves being all made from the skin of Cape sheep); and, among the furs, Lillicrap exhibited a collection of all kinds of Sealskins from the Falkland Islands, to procure which the greatest exertions had been made.

ARTICLES OF CLOTHING.

This display was an epitome of the wants of man, woman, and child, as the title-pages of histories say, "from the earliest period to the present time," and strongly illustrated how "the world is still deceived by ornament."

The Class was divided into, 1. Hats and Caps. 2. Bonnets and general Millinery. 3. Hosiery, Gloves, and Clothing in general. 4. Boots and Shoes.

In this *wide-awake* age it is not easy to describe the varieties of head-gear. Gaimes and Saunders exhibited their light ventilating Hats; Lincoln and Bennett, some Black Hats, of exquisite finish; and Ellwood and Sons, a series of Military Hats and Caps for the army in India; so made as to admit of the cool air ascending round the forehead, to drive the hot air out at the top of the cap, the sound principle of ventilation, whether applied to the House of Commons or the head of one of its Hotspurs. Westland and Laidlaw, of Glasgow, showed a patented Hat, that is ventilated, and so expanding as to fit every kind of head easily and fully. Mr. Stollady showed Hats 3¼ oz. in weight. How much has been done to improve the manufacture of our hats since the days of the miscalled "beaver hats;" yet, next to nothing has been done to alter the shape of the hat, except it be to make the wearer more ludicrous: we have read newspaper leaders written upon "hat reform!" A really droll article is the "reversible bonnet," exhibited in this quarter: on one side it is a hat, while, worn on the other, it is a bonnet. Umbrellas were shown in this section—doubtless, as coverings for the head. The Bonnet was shown in its *ad libitum* variety; the Artificial Flowers were of gold and silver; and one exhibitor showed a May-tree made of muslin and cambric, reminding one of the good old days when a wagon was a head-ornament for a lady of fashion.

Among the Hosiery novelties was a patent Dress fastening without sewing; Leglets for ladies, to keep the wet and dirt from their shoes; and "a Corset made in fifty parts, to insure elasticity in conformity with the various motions of the body .... There was a Crinoline that expanded and contracted at the will of the wearer, and was so adjusted that when touched by a spring it would contract, and enable the wearer to pass on without inconvenience."—(*M'Dermott's Popular Guide*.) There may be some truth in fairy tales, after all! Chivalry had its knights in steel; we have our ladies in the same defensative metal.

A large display of Academical, Ecclesiastical, and Civil Robes almost made us imagine ourselves in the High-street of Oxford, instead of the south-east angle of the Kensington Building. Of graver import was the show of the Robes of the Scotch Church, sent by Middlemas, of Edinburgh.

There were Gloves from the ancient city of Worcester; from the still 'town of Woodstock; from Chipping Norton, Milbourne Port, and Yeovil. But more remarkable was a specimen of Gloves made from Australian cotton, soft as silk.

The show of Nottingham Hosiery was good in quality and pattern. The Scotch Hosiery included Belts and Braces from Wilson and Mathewson, of Glasgow, who also showed an Umbrella embroidered in scarlet and gold, and made to keep off the burning sun of Africa.

Among the novelties (or oddities), was a pair of "Reversible Trousers, for civil and military wear," sent by M. Mendelson, late of the Garrison, Gibraltar. There were, also, a Seamless Coat and Trousers, by Mr. Halliday, of Dundee, who is stated to have occupied four years in making them: they are felted, soft, and cloth-like in texture.

Boots and Shoes, which really have so much to do with human temper and comfort, were well represented, and must have been specially interesting to all who have undergone the martyrology of tight feet-coverings. To the adage, "many men, many minds," may be added "many feet," and the model is the only certainty to insure ease. Still, here was a legion of contrivances—boots and shoes with adjustable heels, and detached heels and fastenings; self-adjusting and ventilating boots; boots "to prevent splashing;"

"chameleon shoes, changing colour," &c. A case of Boots exhibited by Mr. Gullick, of Pall Mall, presented the more rational qualities of elegance of design and workmanship: they included a lady's Hungarian mauve morocco Riding-boot, which has a spring-spur that will not injure the habit, while it spurs the horse. Next was "the Napoleon Boot," elaborately embroidered with the French eagle, and fitted with a richly-gilt spur, of antique design. This was succeeded by a handsome Austrian long Riding-boot; then, a new style of Top-boot, "the Equestrian," with a spur in the form of a bird, elegantly chased. A military dress Carlton Boot was shown, with, inserted in the heel, a patent Eclipse Spur-box, which raises the spur to the top of the heel; and to illustrate this improvement, the fellow boot had the Spur-box fitted in the old manner. The Two-decker Shooting-boot was of novel make, extremely thick, yet very light. There remain to be noticed some wrinkled Hessian Boots, with steel ornaments, and elaborately chased silver spurs; a pair of such boots was supplied by the maker to one of the Foreign Commissioners, who wore the same at the opening ceremony of the Exhibition: these boots cost the wearer 27 guineas. To Mr. Gullick, for the excellence of the entire collection, was awarded a Prize Medal.

PAPER-MAKING, AND STATIONERY.

The French paper-makers made a far more satisfactory appearance than the British; and any one, after a stroll through their Court, could form a very fair judgment concerning the peculiarities and excellences of French Paper. In France linen rags appear to take the place of cotton in England, and the average quality of the papers is therefore higher. In the commoner kinds of Printing-papers, such as are used for our newspapers, France cannot compete with England. Very cheap French papers seem to be produced by a free admixture of clay, and they drop apart under tension, like tinder. These Printing-papers are generally unsized, one advantage of which is, that the paper takes the impress of the type with greater perfection. In their Writing-papers they mix their size with the pulp, whilst we commonly spread it on the surface, and often by this skilful glaze a poor paper is passed off for a good. In fancy writing-papers we know nothing in England to compare with the French delicacy of tint and finish; and there were coloured note-papers with a variety of ornamental water-marks. French writing-paper if sufficiently known would, like French gloves, have many purchasers. It is easily written on, is light, and finely finished. For foreign letters there is nothing to compare with the thin French paper. We noticed some foolscap light as tissue-paper, weighing only 6 lbs. to the ream, and which can be written on both sides.

Paper made from the roughest material was shown; and strangely enough the coarsest descriptions of old cordage produce the finest qualities of paper used in the potteries for fixing the patterns on porcelain. There was also some paper made from the hop-bine, by Barling, amidst the hop-grounds of Kent; and some board made of paper of which the exhibitor, Mr. Towle, more than twenty years ago built himself a house, which has once at least successfully resisted a fire, that burned to the ground the adjoining substantially brick-built residence. The application of silicate of Zopissa, a description of Arabian gum, to paper by Mr. F. Szerelemy has been found to give it so much strength that the material may be used for rocket-tubes, planking for ships' sides, water-pipes; and, it is even said, for heavy artillery. There were specimens of paper made from straw, from the Spanish Esparto; and some charming flowers made from coloured papers by Mrs. Stodhart, Mrs. Weatherfield, and Mrs. Higgins. Mr. Leighton, who had the superintendence of this Class, obtaining a very perfect representation of these important and curious branches of manufacture.

[The exhibition of Bank of England Note Paper, and its manufacture, has already been described at pp. 110-112.]

Mr. Barclay, Bucklersbury, showed his Paper for Cheques to prevent Forgery: and a new paper for press-copies of letters, containing some ingredient which produces a sharper impression than hitherto.

Mr. T. H. Saunders, of Queenhithe, had perhaps the most generally interesting, and, on the whole, unquestionably the best show, of Papers; with specimens of rags from all parts of the world; also other materials for paper. His hand and machine made papers were very good; but his water-marks were surpassingly excellent. One large sheet which he showed contained in its water-mark a very complex border encircling a bust, over which is a wonderfully exact copy of Raffaele's "Madonna and Child"—a perfect marvel of manufacture. Burgess and Ward, of Mendip Paper Mills, near Wells, showed excellent specimens of Straw Paper, with samples illustrating the various processes of its manufacture and application. These makers claim for their paper superiority over that made of common rags, and to prove its capabilities, showed its adaptability for newspapers, railway time-tables, placards, &c. They also exhibited book-work, music, fine engravings, and lithographs, printed on their papers; also paper-hangings, enamelled papers in various hues, fancy box papers, in gold colours; and a delicate polychromic printing, executed on their paper by Day and Son. All these specimens showed good surface and texture; proving that the richest work tells upon straw-paper as well as on the finest rags; and Ward's paper has less of the objectionable brittleness than any other straw-paper. Greer and Co., of Cork, showed very good writing-papers; and Mr. Routledge, of Eynsham Mills, Oxford, exhibited very creditable paper made from foreign fibre, with which much more is to be done than our paper-makers have yet attempted. Hook, Townsend, and Co., of Snodland, near Rochester, had a very creditable show of Writing and Envelope Papers; and Messrs. Turnbull, of

Shoreditch, exhibited excellent Drawing-paper and fine Cardboard, in the latter of which, however, they were surpassed by Woolley and Co., of Holborn. The best Writing-paper in the Class was found in the case of Marcus Ward and Co., of Belfast, who, collecting from the bleach greens the cuttings and trimmings of unworn linen, send them over to a mill near Maidstone, where they are turned into hand and machine made paper, which in texture and finish was beyond anything of the kind shown in the Exhibition.

In purely Commercial Stationery were some very good account-books of Jones and Causton, of Eastcheap, which deservedly got a Medal, but which were not equal to the books of Ward, of Belfast, medalled by the Jury as "superior." Than these ledgers we cannot conceive anything better. The paper of which they are made is manufactured from pure linen; the binding is of vellum, banded, not with Russia leather as is the custom, but with morocco, which is much more lasting and more elegant; and the sewing is double, and secured both at top and bottom, the leaves being sewed with linen thread on stout linen belting in addition to the usual vellum slips. It is, therefore, impossible that the leaves can come out or even protrude without actual violence. All these books open perfectly flat, and the edges, instead of being marbled in the ordinary way, are highly polished, to exclude dust.

Messrs. Goodhall and Dinsdale, of Pancras-lane, City, had a well-earned Medal for account-books, as all they showed were of excellent quality. Hyde and Co., of Fleet-street, who had a Medal for Sealing-wax, of which they showed the best in the Building, also exhibited a clamp Copying-book, which is exceedingly simple and good. As far as the wetting, &c., is concerned, this book is the same as the other Copying-books, but the pressure is effected by a clamp which is slipped on, and which effectually secures an impression. The great advantage of the clamp is that it is portable, and is especially suited for commercial travellers who may require to copy letters, and yet cannot carry with them a press for the purpose. Messrs. Hyde also exhibited Inks in various colours; and their famous Gold Pens; and excellent Sealing-wax. Straker and Sons, of Leadenhall-street, showed an account-book with a patent index, the "stops" of which coming through the binding indicate the letter whether the book is open or closed: for heavy books this index would be very valuable. Letts and Co. showed their world-famed Diaries, with the merits of which every one is acquainted; and which are in their various forms adapted for the merchant, whatever be his line of business, and the professional man, be he clergyman, lawyer, or medicus. A Copying-machine shown by this eminent firm was perhaps the best in the Exhibition.

In the sub-class of Stationery were shown the Pencils of Brookman and Langdon, and Mordan's Pencils and Appliances; and some beautiful specimens of the seal-engraver's art, from the masterpiece of Wyon down to simple letter punches. Here, among them, was the Great Seal of England—if not the finest, beyond all doubt the most important, of all Wyon's works. Mr. Mansell showed a collection of Decorative Stationery which is curious as exemplifying the uses to which paper has been turned by modern manufacturers: there were ornamental lace-edged paper handkerchiefs, paper flower-pot cases, and cut dish-papers, perspective valentines, &c. Mr. M'Clashan showed the stiff gilt and silver papers which are used for theatrical armour, shields, helmets, &c. ; and Messrs. Corfield a collection of marbled papers, in which the English excel.

There were also shown samples of a very successful English imitation of a French manufacture,—the highly decorated Plum, Bonbon, Cake, and Glove Boxes: their tinsellings and coloured velvets, in good hands, might be made effective enough. Mr. Bennet showed a case of these boxes, of various kinds, which in their quiet good taste had no superior in the Building. Mr. John's display was also very good; in fact, both these and the cases shown by Mr. Bauerrichter contained such perfect imitations of similar French articles, that the Jury on their visit required proof that they had all been manufactured in England. This branch of industry has entirely arisen within the last two or three years, and it promises eventually to give employment to thousands of men and women.

We should mention the new manufacture of Paper Collars for ladies and gentlemen; and a Machine for manufacturing them, in the Exhibition, shown by Newbery and Co., President-street West: these collars possess the peculiarity of having *cloth faces*.

PRINTING.

Plate, Lithograph, and other modes of Printing were well illustrated; but it has been aptly observed:—" Printing in all its various branches was shown, except in that most important one of all which ministers so much to the instruction and amusement of all England—that process, by which the thought and eloquence of the kingdom are embodied in a few hours and sent forth in the form of a daily newspaper by hundreds and thousands before daylight. It would require a very large court indeed—more, in fact, than ten times the whole space that is given to this class, to show the various processes which even a paper of small circulation has to pass through before its sheets are submitted to the public."— *Times.* *

In this Class were exhibited specimens of Printing Types from all the chief type-founders, Caslon, Figgins, Besley, Miller and Richard, &c. For good clear-cast and very durable type no country has a higher reputation than England; but, on the other hand, all relating to the decorative parts of the art ranks almost

* There was nothing of its Class to match the *Illustrated London News* Vertical Printing-machine, shown in the Great Exhibition of 1851, at the cost to the Proprietors of 1000*l.* or 1200*l.*

as low in the cultivated judgment of our Continental neighbours. None of our printers' ornaments will stand comparison with those put forth in the exquisite pattern-books of Paris or Vienna.

There were shown two samples of what may be called the extremes of printing—one the New Testament printed on a single sheet of paper, exhibited by Collins, of Glasgow. The print is, of course, exceedingly small, but wonderfully clear. Unless, however, a reduction in the price of the book is to follow the reduction in the size of the type, we can scarcely see its use. Mackenzie, of Glasgow, on the other hand, showed a magnificent illustrated Bible of the largest size. This work has been set up entirely by a Type-composing machine; the paper and print are both beautiful, and the illustrations are furnished by Frith's admirable photographs of the Holy Land.

Miss Emily Faithfull, of the Victoria Press, Coram-street, showed "a specimen of Printing by Women;" the work is neat and tasteful.

Clay, Son, and Taylor, of Bread-street-hill, exhibited specimens of their admirable printing of Wood-engravings; and to them was most deservedly awarded a Prize Medal. They were likewise the printers of a considerable portion of the *Illustrated Official Catalogue.*

Probably the most curious feature of this Department was the collection of Trübner and Co., of Paternoster-row, consisting of their Russian publications. From information supplied, it appears that the Russian press, the first ever introduced into that country, was established in 1853; and so signal seems to have been its success, that it boasts now of more than fifty original works, which have exercised an enormous influence on the development of Russian affairs. The works hitherto produced are of a political, historical, literary, and theological character. We remark among them the first volume of a Russian Bible containing the complete Pentateuch. It should be remembered that the Russian Church never allowed the Bible to be translated into the vernacular, and all honour is, therefore, due to Mr. Trübner for having been the first to do what one would have thought to be the peculiar province of the British and Foreign Bible Society. The books are all very creditably got up, paper and printing being very excellent—indeed, it is reported that the London Russian type has become the model from which modern native Russian founts are being cast.

Mr. Austin, of Hertford, exhibited some well-printed specimens of Oriental books: when the East India College was near Hertford, Mr. Austin was constantly employed to print Sanscript works.

There were some good specimens of Whittingham's Printing among the Books exhibited by Bell and Daldy; but the best printed book in the Exhibition was in the Austrian Department.

Among the Writing Inks was Blackwood's Jesoline, the colour of which, being held in solution, never deposits, and the ink therefore does not get thick. Messrs. Hyde showed excellent Black Ink, and Marking-Ink; remarkably good Sealing-wax; and a Clamp Copying Apparatus, of novel construction.

Black-Lead and Coloured Pencils were exhibited. Brookman and Langdon still maintain their position in the first rank, and they have reduced the price from 6*d*. to 3*d*. each. Mr. B. S. Cohen showed a Pencil-making Machine at work in the Exhibition, and his Drawing Pencils show as many as twelve varieties of hardness or colour. Banks and Co., Keswick, who use the celebrated Borrowdale lead in its native state, also exhibited a great variety of pencils of every description. Melville's Solid Red Ink deserves notice, so also Messrs. Wolff's Coloured Crayons in Cedar; and in the Foreign Courts was to be seen how far the pencil manufacture can be carried, and at what prices the pencils may be obtained. Grossberger and Kurz, of Nuremberg, manufacture pencils the full length, which they sell at the very low rate of 1*s*. 1*d*. the gross.

In Steel Pens English manufacturers reigned supreme. We had not only the well-known names of Gillott, Mitchell, and Perry, but the comparatively unknown firms of Hinks and Co., Myers, Schelhorn, Turner, and Sommerville; all of whom exhibited pens and holders of a much larger variety than most persons who use a pen could believe possible. Here, for instance, is the description of those exhibited by Sommerville and Co., Birmingham, who alone have 708 different kinds, scarcely one of which is known in this country; yet they are not only equal to the general average, but some are of a very superior make, besides possessing more than average elegance. Here is the characteristic description they give of their several kinds of Pens :—

Our pattern card shows 708 different kinds of pens, all of current sale in the Continental countries of Europe, where our business lies. In the counter case we exhibit our series of Carbonized Pens, most of which have been registered, and the Gilt-pointed Pens, of which we are the inventors and sole makers. These pens are of the very highest finish, and are not surpassed by any made in England and France for material and general workmanship. Amongst these pens we mention especially: the Patent Regulator Pen—a pen which can be made hard or soft at will, by moving the slide up or down the pen, the Fountain Spear-pointed Pen, known as the Alfred Pen, the Classical Pen, the original St. George, the Humboldt Pens, and the Constantinople Pens. All the above have been invented by us, as well as the celebrated Fleury and Emanuel Pen, represented in our series by Nos. 2120 and 2330.

All the above pens are put in very nice special boxes; and we have also brought out of late the Garibaldi, Victor Emmanuel, the Pope's, the Russian Emancipation Pens; the boxes of which have a steel engraving of these historical persons on. Still the gross of these last pens to the wholesale trade is 1*s*. net only. Our pens are as well known on the Continent as Gillott's in England, but hitherto we have not tried for a home trade. We also show in the Exhibition a Pen Machine, viz., a large pen model, showing the action of our Regulator Pen by clock-work.

Playing Cards were exhibited by Goodall and Sons, Camden Town; and by Reynolds and Sons, Vere-street, who have contrived some cards for the use of the blind; the pips being cut out and mounted on ordinary cards, so as to stand out in relief. They have also some other varieties said to be much liked by players. Mr. Owen Jones sent some beautifully-ornamented backs, which he designed for Delarue.

To the assemblage of choice examples of Colour-printing Leighton Brothers, of Milford-house, Strand, contributed a collection of their Chromatic Prints, such as are occasionally given away with the numbers of the *Illustrated London News*. Of some of these prints as many as 230,000 copies have been printed. Nearly all of them contain from twelve to fifteen colours, and have to be passed through the machine once for each colour they contain, so that the machine is used nearly 5,000,000 times to get the required number. The two large prints issued with the above journal, August 30th, 1862, representing the Opening of the Exhibition, and Minton's Majolica Fountain, are beautifully executed.

The Leightons, of Buckingham-street, also showed Wood-engravings and Processes connected with Printing Surfaces.

In Printing Surfaces the Electro-block Company showed their most ingenious process of enlarging and reducing blocks. This, with Mr. W. J. Linton's Kerographic Process and Mr. Wallis's new art of Auto-typography, illustrated one among the very many attempts to effect that long-sought desideratum—an effective metallic relief produced without engraving.* The makers of the bank-note paper and printers of the bank-notes for the Bank of England showed some valuable and interesting specimens of Note-paper, Bank-notes, Stamps, &c. Bradbury and Wilkinson exhibited minute engravings for the prevention of forgeries in notes; and the exquisite specimens of the Nature-printed Books produced by the late Henry Bradbury were also shown—an honour to any country.

The specimens of Lithographs and Chromo-lithographs, shown by Day and Sons, Rowney, Vincent, and Hanhart, were among the finest that have ever been displayed. It is difficult even for the most practised eye to detect the difference between some of the best specimens of these and carefully finished water-colours. Rowney showed a very fine one of the cave beneath the Holy Rock at Jerusalem, copied from Carl Haag's picture, taken for the Queen.

* *Kerography* is a new process, invented by Mr. W. J. Linton, to take the place of Engraving on Wood. It has the advantages of wood-engraving without its disadvantages; can be worked at hand-press or machine, with type or without; costs less than wood-engraving in production, as little as wood-engraving in printing, and is even more durable. Wood-engravings are, at best, only translations—and generally very imperfect translations—of the artist's drawing on the block. By the new process, which is a secret, an engraving is necessarily a facsimile, even to the minutest touch, of the draughtsman's work. Where an artist's manner is of any value, the new process is superior; capable, also, of giving greater delicacy, and very much more minuteness and elaboration. As Mr. Linton is the most artistic engraver of his day, the above statement by him may be received with confidence. It is accompanied by specimens of the New Process, applied to a variety of subjects: they are of great beauty, delicacy, and characteristic expression.

On a screen was hung a wonderfully vigorous picture representing Her Majesty's ship *Agamemnon*, with the Atlantic cable on board, in the hurricane on the night of the 21st of June, 1857. The artist, Mr. E. Concanen, has selected the moment when, with her coals and boats adrift, her cable shifting, and screw-guard broken, the noble ship was in the crisis of her distress. The tremendous nature of her difficulties, the rush of wind and sea, are given in Mr. Concanen's picture with such a force and truth to nature as we have never yet seen in any mere drawing of a storm at sea. The process by which the waves are rendered with such clear and terrible distinctness is a secret of the artist: this picture was shown to the Prince Consort just before his fatal illness commenced, and his approval of the artist's merits was expressed in high terms of admiration.

BOOKBINDING.

One of the finest cases of Bookbindings in the Building was shown by J. and J. Leighton. This contained some magnificent specimens of tooled books in the modern mediæval and antique style. There is a richness, solidity, and good work about these books to which nothing in the art bore comparison except the costly volumes from Vienna. They had a large show of extra leather bindings, &c.; of processes connected with the restoration of many portions of books—as copper and wood-cut illustrations; also letterpress, produced by them in MS., fac-simile; plates (reduced from folio to 8vo. size) produced by the photo-zincographic process; likewise samples of paper-splitting, which is often very useful in bookbinding. They also showed choice book-plates produced for various literary collectors.

The extra bookbinders showed a very fine collection, especially in the most elaborate kinds of hand-tooled works. In publishers' works in the neat cloth binding which is so peculiarly our own that it is known abroad under the title of *toile Anglaise*, we stand unrivalled. Both for design and rapid execution of this work, Leighton and Hodge, Bone, and Westleys held their own against all comers. Leighton, Son, and Hodge's work displayed most artistic skill combined with some special excellences: amongst the items most noteworthy, were "The Sermon on the Mount," the largest block ever engraved or worked in gold in one piece. The arming-press by which the impression was made, is the most powerful in the world: it weighs upwards of ten tons. This firm was the first to introduce for the ornamentation and lettering of books, aluminium. The designs of Owen Jones, Luke Limner, and others have within a few short years worked a complete revolution in this branch of art-manufacture. The Annuals, it will be recollected, were beautiful specimens of binding in silk; but it was reserved for their successors, the Illustrated Gift-books, principally of standard literature, to bring out the tasteful talent of our binders in cloth and other ornamental processes and designs. A case of these illustrated and illuminated gift-books, of great merit, was shown by Griffith and Farran.

Of Foreign Bookbinding we have space to say but little. M. Schavy exhibited some books, mostly from the Royal Belgian Library, and representing the highest state of the bookbinder's art in that country: some are good reproductions of old styles, but the morocco-bound books were not superior to English.

In matters of taste and delicacy of manipulation, the French are in advance of us; as exemplified in M. Engelmann's large volume bound in red morocco, inlaid with dark green; and a square volume in green morocco, inlaid with small dice of orange and yellow. In clasping, the French likewise excel. MM. Maine and Son, of Tours, showed a copy of *La Touraine*, unique, and one of the most beautiful vellum books in the world: the plates are like sheets of ivory: binding, morocco, inlaid.—*See the Bookseller*, for its really useful Reports upon this branch.

EDUCATIONAL WORKS AND APPLIANCES.

It was judiciously intended by the Committee to whom the Educational Department of the Exhibition was intrusted that the contributions to it sent by the various countries should be in juxtaposition; to insure their being seen and compared with greater facility. But the Foreign Commissioners determined upon keeping each educational collection separate: nevertheless, we shall describe the more noteworthy objects of the several collections in one group.

The British Educational Collection was not very extensive; but this was not the fault of the contributors, since *fifteen* times as much space was demanded by them as could be granted. The books exhibited were numerous and well chosen; some eminent publishers sent their most approved Educational Works. The various well-known educational institutions showed what they have done in providing books and requisites of a useful and convenient description. There were books for the blind, and untearable books for children; excellent Maps, and a Projection of the two Hemispheres, representing the globular form of the earth in such a way as to prevent or remove the usual crude ideas of young persons on the point. Of the many good Globes which were exhibited that of Macintosh, made of India-rubber, seemed to be the most convenient; when not inflated it occupies very little space.

Mr. John Curwen, of Plaistow, exhibited books and diagrams on the Tonic Sol-fa method. About the year 1812 Miss Glover, the daughter of a clergyman of the Church of England, commenced teaching children to sing by means of a "Musical Ladder" and a simple notation of letters taken from that ladder. At the close of

1840, Mr. Curwen taught himself to read simple music by the help of this book, and became convinced himself, by experiment and study, of its educational and scientific truth. On this system he founded, with Miss Glover's consent, the Tonic Sol-fa method. He has endeavoured to adapt this method to the various wants of the school, the home, and the church, by publications; and he has recently obtained census returns from a thousand teachers who are now giving lessons to 47,000 children, and about the same number of adults.

Mair and Co. exhibited a "School List," comprising the names and addresses of 20,000 school proprietors, particulars of 900 endowed schools, and information respecting Continental and Colonial establishments. This work is the first attempt at compiling a school directory.

The National School Society showed excellent models of School Furniture, and among them Telescope-desks, which are very simple, and can be made to occupy very little room. The Home and Colonial School Society exhibited admirable specimens of School Fittings, and models of Gymnastic requisites. A model showed the benefits derived from Reformatory and Ragged Schools: the rescue of the young from vice and crime, and their career of training until they join some useful trade or calling, were very effectively represented. Among the Toys and Games exhibited, there were numerous small collections of a very useful kind: thus the Home and Colonial School Society showed a number of common objects, with many of which children are familiar only by name; also objects illustrating the manufactures of Great Britain. There were chemical apparatus and chemicals for the simpler kinds of elementary instruction; collections of minerals, some of them having particular reference to the teaching of geology; fossils and shells; zoological series and anatomical specimens; mechanical and other diagrams; models illustrative of the elements of physical science: in a word, between private exhibitors and public bodies, nearly everything was shown that is required for a sound and practical elementary education.

The Home and Colonial School Society also displayed an interesting series of articles used in the "Kinder Garten" system, which has been so successfully adopted by that society in its infant schools.

The Globes of Messrs. Newton, Stanford, and Wyld; the Orrery of the Rev. J. Latouche, and the Collection of Messrs. Griffin;— were shown; with a Scientific collection of Mr. S. Highley; a curious case of Small Birds by Mr. Ashmead; and large cases of Stuffed Birds by Ward and Bartlett—remarkable evidences of the perfection which the art of taxidermy has reached in England.

Mr. Cremer sent a capital collection of Toys; Mr. Novra his Conjuring Apparatus; Mr. Loysel an ingenious Drawing-room Game; and Mr. Dark and Mr. Page all kinds of Cricketing implements. M. Montanari, M. Pierotti, and others, fitted up cases full of Dolls, that were admired by old and young; and amongst the most popular models (which by many visitors were mistaken for dolls) were Dr. Roth's series of Gymnastic Figures. These models are in high relief, and they show an infinite variety of gymnastic positions and movements for educational, sanitary, and military purposes, as well as for the physical development of the blind, deaf, and dumb.

Education has its Fine Art branch, and under this head Mr. Brucciani showed some excellent Casts of Fruit and Foliage from nature, prepared as Art-studies for Schools. The list comprised apples, blackberries, hops, sunflowers, and lilies. The colour-makers were well represented by a very attractive display, in which most of the new chemical Colours had a place; and Mr. Green, Messrs. Rowney, and others, sent some very useful Rustic Drawing Models.

The specimens of Embossed or Raised Type, of Writing and Ciphering frames, of Musical Notation, and of Maps in relief used in the Blind Schools, were very interesting. Mr. Moon (of Brighton), F.R.G.S., exhibited Reading in several languages, Maps, Diagrams, &c., of this character.

Missionaries are continually carrying books from the establishment at Brighton to every corner of the globe. Twenty-seven societies are established in various parts of our country for teaching the blind at their own homes, and lending them books from free libraries; and for several years past Mr. Moon has from time to time visited the Continent for the purpose of benefiting the blind by the spread of this system, and both he and his system have met with a very cordial reception in Holland, Germany, and France. His publications comprise the whole of the Bible in English, and portions in fifty other languages, a good variety of other books in English, such as the "Pilgrim's Progress," "Biblical Dictionary," "English Grammar," "Geography," "History of England," &c.

A beautiful embossed Globe, used in the School for the Indigent Blind, was shown in this Section: and specimens of the work done in various blind asylums was displayed on the walls and screens.

The Austrian Educational Collection was attractive; the Government priding itself on having directed education, in a special manner, to practical purposes, the country being well provided with schools of every kind and for every class. Among the requisites for teaching shown by Austria was means of instruction in Shorthand, a branch not often considered as belonging to ordinary education. We found Maps printed, not on paper, but on woven fabrics, and hence more convenient and durable than the ordinary kind; also aids in the way of rendering formal lessons unnecessary; Pictures and other objects for the instructive occupation of youth; Models of Schools, &c. A variety of Mechanical and other Toys was shown.* The models and apparatus connected

* The trade in toys in Austria is very great. The Gröden Valley, in the Tyrol, exports annually three hundred tons of wooden toys, that reach every quarter of the globe.

with *Realistic* Schools, or those affording, in addition to ordinary instruction, facilities for acquiring special branches of knowledge relating to manufacturing and trading pursuits, were very interesting. Philosophical apparatus used in the higher grades of instruction was also shown ; and illustrations to anatomy and comparative anatomy.

Belgium had objects devoted to the School of Industry, besides ordinary apparatus, such as books, models of school-desks, &c. ; a collection of substances used for domestic purposes ; historical and mechanical diagrams ; designs for shawls, &c., some of them extremely beautiful ; and specimens of the work done by the pupils. In a Belgian school museum were diagrams and other illustrations of natural history ; collections of minerals and philosophical instruments ; specimens of the works of the blind, and of deaf mutes, &c.

France had arranged her Educational contributions in a very pleasing and convenient way, in two compartments : the first devoted to the means and appliances for instruction ; the second, to the results obtained from them in the shape of works executed by the pupils. In the former, besides an excellent collection of books connected with pedagogy, globes, maps, &c., was an Orrery, placed within a sphere of glass, having the fixed stars depicted upon it. There were also models of solids and curves, photographic copies from antique busts, anatomical and mechanical diagrams, natural history and botanical collections, &c. In the compartment which contained the works of the pupils, was a painting on porcelain, by a young workman only eighteen years old ; and some beautiful specimens of flower-painting, sent by the School of Design of the City of Paris. The works executed by the blind, and by deaf Mutes, was very striking.

The Educational collection of Italy included some good diagrams; models of crystals and solids ; a collection of chemical substances ; a small museum of economic Botany, containing the various agricultural products of the country, mineralogical and natural history specimens, &c.

Prussia, long distinguished for her exertions in the cause of education, among her educational apparatus exhibited some good Maps and Globes, both plain and in relief ; apparatus for teaching the rudiments of Geometry by superposition of the surfaces, or parts of surfaces, which are to be proved equal ; some very excellent elementary collections of Minerals, &c.

The Educational contributions of Russia included models of animals and fruits, and representations of the different varieties of the human race. Switzerland had done little to show the progress which she has really made in education. Her contribution was nearly confined to a few neat mechanical diagrams, collections of common substances, objects relating to Natural History, and herbaria.

Among the countries which exhibited nothing connected with the subject were Spain, Portugal, and Rome : how suggestive are these shortcomings !

The Bible Society, instead of taking their place among booksellers and publishers, entered their collection among Educational Works and Appliances. At a high elevation in the Central Tower, in a place out of the thoroughfare, difficult to find, and seldom visited by any except inquisitive and long-winded climbers, their case, containing copies of the Scriptures in 191 languages, was set in the corner of the gallery. An influential petition was made to the Commissioners to have the case removed to a more conspicuous position; but, on second thoughts, the Society took the matter into their own hands, and opened a handsome booth in the Cromwell-road, which the eye of no visitor could miss. In the Exhibition Building S. Bagster and Sons displayed a tasteful selection of their exquisitely-printed editions of the Scriptures, bound in morocco, vellum, ivory, and oak. Eyre and Spottiswoode made a grand show of Bibles and Prayer-Books, in all sizes. Some large Family Bibles, with heavy gilt brass clasps and rims, found many admirers.—*Abridged from the English Churchman.*

FURNITURE AND UPHOLSTERY.

There was a large show of excellent Furniture, which not only impressed one with its sumptuousness and magnificence, but also with its bold and elaborate beauty of design, its art-workmanship and high finish. And in no class of the Exhibition were there better proofs of the advancement of the national taste since 1851 than in the Furniture display. Some of the fine forms reminded one of the furniture artists of last century, when the cabinet-maker was an artist as well as an artisan. Our success in this branch assures us that we need no longer ransack old mansions, or curiosity-shops, for furniture of beautiful design as well as craft, when it is so readily produced by the workers of our own day.

All our great firms competed here, and the result of their combined efforts was an exhibition which defied comparison with that put forward by any other country. The Sideboard Bookcase, inlaid with Wedgwood plaques, and the Robinson Crusoe Sideboard—the former for exquisite and most harmonious decoration, and the latter for its spirited carved work, which brings Defoe's romance before the mind's eye like a picture—were among the most successful specimens in this Court. The inlaid bookcase appealed only to those of the most refined and highly cultivated tastes; but there was a life and vividness in the Robinson Crusoe sideboard which told its own tale to gentle and simple. It needs no explanation whatever. From the first coming of the storm—the landing of the goods at the wreck—the footprint in the sand—the man Friday—goats, seeds, garden, cave, and wooden almanack, all were here portrayed in solid wood, with the ease, humour, and freedom of a drawing by Leech.

Among the more economical novelties was a set of Bed-room Furniture in varnished deal, showing how even the commonest woods may be made to answer decorative purposes.

Here, too, were Wall and Ceiling Decorations in carton-pierre, by Jackson and Sons; the earliest application of which, upon an extensive scale, is, we believe, in the Renaissance re-decoration of Ironmongers' Hall.

A Cabinet made from New Zealand woods, by Levien, was remarkable for its beautiful markings and rich tone of colour.

Messrs. Filmer, Berners-street, showed some novelties in Furniture, entitled to special mention. First, was a Circular Dining-table, capable of enlargement, not in the usual way by adding leaves in the centre, but by increasing the circumference by the addition of circular segments, keeping the centre entire. The frame-work on which these segments rest is extended by an ingenious combination of racks, moved by a central pinion. One rack is moved by a screw turned by a handle, and communicates the motion to the other three through the pinion. The action is excessively easy and simple, and not likely to get out of order. The table itself is of old pollard oak, and the scroll supports, festooned with fruit, are well designed and executed. The making of the additional pieces fit accurately the external moulding round the edge of the table involves a difficult piece of workmanship, but is well achieved; and the grain of the wood being continued by a careful adjustment and adaptation of the veneers from the central piece to the outer additions, the expanded table looks as like one piece as can possibly be contrived. Another novelty exhibited by the same firm is a Central Ottoman, which, if required, dissolves into two small settees and two arm-chairs. Messrs. Filmer showed some specimens of Chintzes, the result of a prize offered by the firm to the pupils of the Government School of Art at South Kensington, and to the Female School of Art, Queen-square: of these a convolvulus pattern, designed by Miss Charlotte James, is very graceful. Considering the difficulties required to be overcome in these designs, which are limited to two colours, and have to be applied to two distinct fabrics very different in their mode of production, they reflect great credit on the schools from which they have emanated.—*Abridged from the Times.*

In the English Furniture Court was an extraordinary Singing Bullfinch, the property of Mr. Wertheimer, which is stated to have equalled the philantropic bird in the Swiss Court, whose merits have been so highly extolled.

A Cabinet of Oak, by Taylor and Son, Edinburgh, was a marvel of elaborate carving: opposite were some groups of Dead Game, exquisitely carved by Kendal, of Warwick. Next were Wardrobes in rich walnut, birchwood, and rosewood; and Sideboards, Cabinets, and Buffets, of admirable work: the subjects of the carvings were well chosen from the vintage, bacchanals and nymphs, and fish and fowl, in oak, walnut, sycamore, &c.

Decorations for portions of rooms were exhibited with excellent effect. Jackson and Graham showed a specimen in the style of Louis XVI.—crimson, white, and gold; and a chimney-piece of Algerian onyx.

A Sideboard, made by Morant, for the late Earl of Ellesmere, is in fine Italian style : gold-winged chimera supporting a slab of enamelled white; the back purple velvet, with the crest on a gilt scroll; and festoons of fruit, scroll-work, frieze, and mouldings, of great richness. The Gillows exhibited a Renaissance Sideboard of English walnut, except the slab, unpolished. The same exhibitors showed a Cabinet of elegant Italian design, for the display of gems and china. Pool and Macgillivray exhibited a central Cabinet for showing articles of vertu: it is of novel form and material, circular, upon four finely carved supports; inclosed with bent glass, with three interior shelves, also of glass, resting around a central column, so that the articles displayed upon them are seen to the greatest advantage.

Mr. Wertheimer, of Bond-street, exhibited an exquisitely carved console Table and Cabinet, in the style of Louis XVI. Of the table, the ground is of steel in silver, and the ornaments upon it mat-gold, or bosses in mat-gold. Swags of flowers, laurel, and ivy leaves, also in dead gold, hang gracefully from the front and sides, and in the centre is the head of a bacchante wreathed with flowers. The carving of these decorations has scarcely been surpassed in cabinet-work. Every leaf is wrought out with the utmost care, and even the fibres are shown in delicate relief. The mounts are in the style of Goutière. Another Cabinet, after the celebrated Reisner, is of simple but elegant outline: the doors of choice marqueterie.

A magnificent Buffet, or Sideboard, by Jackson and Graham, was shown among the trophies in the nave of the Building. It is ten feet in length, of pollard oak, enriched by carvings in brown English oak. On the doors of the pedestals are carved boys gathering grapes, and reaping: the friezes are ornamented with the hop-plant springing from shields. The frieze of the centre division has a richly-carved shield with fruit enrichments, with barley as supporters. Above the slabs, and over the pedestals, are plinths, with characteristic carved panels,—the one representing a wine-cup entwined by the vine; and the other a tankard, amidst the hop-plant. Two female caryatides support the cornice and pediment, which has a boldly carved central shield in the centre, and festoons of fruit, pendent and partly resting upon the cornice. The caryatid figures are flanked with pilasters richly carved, one of game, surmounted by the head of a retriever; the other, river and sea fish, surmounted by the head of an otter. The centre and side panels are filled with looking-glass.

The same makers exhibited a large Wardrobe, of walnut-wood, planned in three divisions. The plinth, cornice, and end-panels are inlaid with lines; and finished with ornamental corners of amboyna, purple wood, and holly. The central door is panelled with looking-glass, and the side-doors have small oval mirrors in rich floral marqueterie; the pilasters are inlaid with various woods: the caps and bases supporting the cornice and pediment are finely carved; and a hollow worked upon the angles of the wardrobe receives inlaid and carved columns completing the support of the cornice.

Litchfield and Radclyffe, Hanway-street and Green-street, exhibited a group of Ebony and Ivory Furniture, of great merit for design and execution. The group consisted of a carved Ivory and Ebony upright Cabinet, on stand, the doors inlaid with cornelian, marble columns, plinths, &c.; the inside lined with silvered glass, and decorated with groups and fine specimens of Sèvres, Dresden, Berlin, and Viennese porcelain. There were also three Ebony Library Tables, of Italian design, with inlaid ivory, and richly carved mouldings and panels in ebony; therm legs, relieved with discs of ivory; and the tops bordered with inlaid and engraved ivory marqueterie. Next was a fine old Venetian engraved Looking-glass, adapted as a cheval-glass by a stand of richly-carved ebony, inlaid with ivory, manufactured to the order of the Earl of Craven. For these beautiful Works, Litchfield and Radclyffe deservedly received a Prize Medal.

The adaptability of the French Renaissance for drawing-room decoration by means of light, elegant panels, rendering it capable of great pictorial effect, and the introduction of classic medallions, pictures, jewels, brackets, vases, &c., was well exemplified here.

Wright and Mansfield, of Great Portland-street, exhibited a Cabinet, carved and gilt in the English style of the last century, with plaques of Wedgwood-ware in the panels and frieze; a fine Louis the Sixteenth marqueterie Cabinet with ormolu mounts; a Chimney-piece and Glass frame in the English style of the eighteenth century, of gean-wood, or wild-cherry of the Scotch Highlands, with medallions of black Wedgwood-ware in the frieze; also, a noble specimen of Room Decoration and a Bookcase, both in the style of last century: the bookcase of the wild-cherry wood, with Wedgwood medallion—the design and the medallions of the frieze and door-panels after Flaxman.

Another superb object was a Pianoforte, by Erard, in a case o fine Amboyna wood, richly inlaid with trophies of musical instruments, and flowers of fine marqueterie; the front, above the fall, of perforated purple wood, forming three finely-painted plaques of porcelain; that in the centre representing a group of children playing upon musical instruments; on the left is a medallion of a boy playing the Pandean pipes; and on the right, a corresponding medallion of a boy playing cymbals.

The *Paper-hangings* in this division were mostly well designed and beautifully printed. Green and King, Baker-street, showed some effectively painted washable Wall-decorations; Lea, of Lutterworth, Wall-decorations for churches; Muslin and Co., Foley-street, imitations of British and Foreign Marbles and Serpentines, on paper; Stather sent from Hull washable photographic oak Paper-hangings, and a granite Column imitated with machine-printed paper; M'Lachlan, St. James's-street, artistic

Decorations for dining and drawing-rooms; and Williams and Cooper, West Smithfield. Wall-decorations in Italian and other styles. Tasteful Paper-hangings were shown by Woolams, Scott, and Jeffrey; clever imitations of figured Silk, by Kershaw; and Glass Mosaics, by Stevens. The Pyrography, or woodwork, ornamented by the agency of heat, and exhibited by Mr. G. J. Smith, of Wenlock-street, was very effective.

The *Papier-maché* (English manufacture, with a French name), of Bielefield and Bettridge, was shown in tasteful decorations and suites of furniture, and ornamental articles.

Among the *Carvings in Wood*, those of Wallis, of Louth, from nature; and Flowers in walnut, by Winfield, were excellent.

Mr. Rogers exhibited several Works of rare beauty of design and execution: including a Glass Frame, richly carved in light wood, in the style of Grinling Gibbons, and mounted on Amboyna wood; an oak Clock-bracket, in the style of Holbein; four highly-finished plaques, charming studies of Flowers in Box-wood—cranesbill, buttercup, ivy, and passion-flower; a very elaborate Roundel, carved in Boxwood, bordered with Italian foliage—the centre, two Genii holding a cartouche; a carved Vase of Fruits and Flowers, executed for Boodle's Club; a foliated Cross carved in Ebony, with silver mountings; a magnificently carved Salt-cellar, highly enriched with Italian ornamentation; and several Boxwood Frames and Brackets in rich and elaborate taste: and a set of Chess-men carved in Ivory—the Holy War—the Turks under Saladin, and Christians under Richard Cœur-de-Lion—the costumes from ancient authorities. These several Works are, in treatment, full of artistic thought and poetic fancy; and in execution, rich and elaborate.

Cox and Co. exhibited a large Lectern, surmounted by an eagle standing on a rock, with spreading wings: carved from the solid, in oak. The work is octagonal in plan, tapering upwards; the base is of moulded work, above embellished with crockets all different in design, worked from natural foliage and flowers of English growth. The capital of this lectern represents the foliage and flowers of the horse-chestnut.

Kirk and Parry, of Sleaford, showed a fine Carved Font, of Ancaster stone, surmounted by a beautifully-carved cover in English Oak, by Mr. David Sharp, who also exhibited a carved Bracket in the classical style, which is tasteful and skilful. Mr. Sharp is entirely a self-taught artist.

There were shown here some clever illustrations of *how far* machinery can be employed instead of hand-work in carving: in this subdivision of labour, the mechanical stage is likely to be carried so far as to reduce to the minimum the life, feeling, and finish of hand-labour.

MEDIÆVAL ART.

The very interesting collection of Works exhibited by the Ecclesiological Society,* well illustrated the great advance made in their particular epoch of art, since the formation of the Mediæval Court, in the Exhibition of 1851.

The arrangement of the similar Court in the recent Exhibition was carried out by Mr. Burges and Mr. Slater, the eminent architects. They showed amongst other things, a Reredos by Mr. Street, executed by Mr. Earp; and a portion of that for Waltham Abbey, with the cartoon of the rest. There was likewise a cast of the Sculpture by Mr. Farmer, in the Bedminster Reredos, which excited so much controversy a few years since. Mr. Redfern contributed casts of his sculptures of the Ascension, for the Digby Mortuary Chapel at Sherborne; and for the Westroop monument in Limerick Cathedral, the latter being arranged in connexion with a portion of the actual carved work of the monument.

A cast of Dr. Mill's Monument (designed by Mr. Scott) and Effigy at Ely was exhibited. Mr. Nichol sent another Effigy arranged on a high tomb in connexion with some subjects in relief; as also, the late Lord Cawdor's High Tomb; and one of the circular panels, with a cut subject, for the Lichfield Pavement. In woodwork there were the Stalls of Chichester Cathedral; a rich Bureau, which was shown about two years ago at the Architectural Exhibition; and a Decorated Organ.

Fonts in alabaster and marble, by Mr. Norton; and a cast of the Renaissance Font at Witley, by Mr. Forsyth; were also shown.

In Metal-work, one exhibitor sent a rich Iron Font-cover; the Ecclesiological Society exhibited the Frontal which it is about to present to St. Paul's Cathedral, designed according to the Cologne method; and the Dean of Peterborough kindly lent the new Frontal for his cathedral, executed by the Ladies' Ecclesiastical Embroidery Society.

An appreciative *précis* of the contents of the Mediæval Court appeared in the *Builder*, to which the reader is referred.

IRON MANUFACTURES.

Previously to describing the more striking Articles, we shall quote the following *précis* of the recent larger operations and results of the Iron Manufacture, abridged from the *Times*.

Yield of Cast-iron.—Great progress has of late been made in this respect. In the Great Exhibition of 1851 there was a Model of a Blast Furnace from the Cwm Celyn Works, Monmouthshire, which yielded a weekly average of 209 tons of white pig iron during twelve consecutive months. This was regarded as a very large amount. The gradual increase in yield in different districts is certainly one of the most interesting points connected with the

---

* See "Progress of Art-Manufactures," p. 72 of the present volume.

development of the iron trade in modern times. Not many years ago, a weekly return of 70 tons was considered good, but now a single furnace has yielded the enormous amount of 600 tons in a single week. Some of the Aberdare furnaces are reported to have done excellent work, and to have yielded a weekly average of 400 tons. This has been effected by what is called "driving hard"—*i.e.*, sending a large quantity of blast through the furnace in a given time. An instructive Model, to scale, of one of these Furnaces, together with numerous Illustrative Specimens, was exhibited by the Aberdare Iron Company. Great yields have recently been obtained at the Barrow-in-Furness works, Cumberland. These works are quite of recent construction, and were represented by a costly mahogany Model, occupying a very large superficial area. There was also a single Model, made to open, of one of the furnaces. The average yield in one of these furnaces per day during the fortnight ending the 16th of April, 1862, was 91 tons 7 cwt. 3 qrs., or the enormous amount of about 640 tons (short weight) in a week of seven days. In one week this furnace yielded not less than 684 tons (short weight)! The qualities of the pig iron were 3-5 between Nos. 1 and 4, and 2-5 between Nos. 5 and 6, inclusive of 35 tons of mottled pig. It is exclusively rich red ore that is smelted at these furnaces, and the fuel is Durham coke. The waste gases are economized in raising steam, and their propulsion to a distance is aided by the exhaustion of a fan. The pipes conveying the gases are provided with expansion joints. Great advantage is attributed to the manner in which the gases are taken off from the furnace, and to the mode of fitting.

In the Austrian Department Charcoal Pig-iron was shown, which, it is stated on the best authority, is produced with a consumption of less charcoal than is known in any other locality. The ore is brown decomposed spathose ore, containing, when roasted, 52 per cent. of iron, and the products are gray iron and spiegeleisen. Only 60 parts by weight of charcoal are required to produce 100 of pig-iron. Models of Furnaces for smelting Iron and Copper were found in the Russian Department. They are long and rectangular in horizontal section, and are provided with numerous twyers. One of these furnaces is reported to have been in operation for smelting iron during a year and a half. A large yield and reduction in the amount of fuel are stated to be the advantages of this kind of furnace.

Forged Iron.—Some of these specimens were interesting as illustrations of remarkable malleability, others as displaying skilful workmanship, and others on account of their large dimensions. A deep round vessel, with everted rim, at the top of the Lowmoor collection, furnished an example of malleability, as it was fashioned out of a flat piece under the hammer. Some of the crank shafts were admirable specimens of forging—such as the locomotive straight and double-crank axles from the Monkbridge Works. The straight axles contrasted very favourably with some in the Belgian Department, which showed a want of finish which would not be tolerated in this country. The Monkbridge Company exhibited Locomotive and Agricultural Fire-box Plates, flanged both ways inside and out, which demonstrate excellence in the iron and soundness—qualities essential in such objects, which otherwise would soon become blistered. In the collection of the Kirkstall Forge Company were excellent specimens of forging, &c., which fully maintained the character of this long-established firm. With regard to forgings remarkable on account of their large dimension, the two objects which stood out pre-eminently were the enormous Crank Shaft and the large Armour-plate manufactured by the Mersey Steel and Iron Company. The monster shaft weighs about 25 tons, and is destined for one of Her Majesty's ships. During the process of forging, this heavy mass was moved by powerful and skilful mechanical appliances, with ease and rapidity, just as a blacksmith handles his iron. The plate bears the following inscription:—"This armour-plate, 21 ft. 3 in. long, 6 ft. 3 in. wide, 5¼ in. thick, having a superficial area of 133 feet, weighing upwards of 13 tons, was forged at the Mersey Steel and Iron Works, Liverpool, and has been neither smithed nor tooled since it left the steam-hammer. This plate would have been made 15 ft. to 20 ft. longer if space could have been obtained." It is an admirable specimen of forging. The great Horsfall Gun, of which every one has heard, is another testimony to Mr. Clay's (the manager of the Company) skill in forging large masses of iron. This gun was made several years ago: it is 10 in. in the bore, and has stood charges of 80 lb. of powder.

Welding.—The Exhibition contained many very interesting illustrations of Welding under difficult conditions. The Butterley Company's large girders, of which one was in the form of a double T, 12 in. across each end and 3 ft. deep, was welded longitudinally. In the English Department was shown a stamped, solid, wrought-iron Wheel, made by an ingenious process invented by M. Arbel, a Frenchman: it was forged under the steam-hammer, and combines strength and cheapness. In illustration of the successful welding of steel and iron in railway tire bars, we may refer to the specimens in the Monkbridge Company's collection. The iron tire being heated to whiteness, and dusted over with borax powder, the melted steel is cast round it: the union seems to be perfect, and we have examined specimens which have been hammered out into thin plate without presenting any sign of separation. This process is also the invention of a Frenchman, and promises well.

The French appear to have made great progress in the manufacture of Iron, and we are indebted to them for many ingenious mechanical contrivances. Two instances in the case of railway wheels have just been mentioned, and to these might be added a third—the process of Pétin, Gaudet, and Co., of making "weldless tires," of which the Blaenavon Company exhibited specimens manufactured by themselves.

Rolled Iron.—Specimens of boiler-plate were shown, doubled hot and doubled cold, and punched under various trying conditions. The Butterley Company exhibited a Rolled Boiler-plate, 12 ft. 9 in. long, 7 ft. 6 in. wide, and 1¼ in. thick. This company had a truly magnificent collection of rolled iron, which does honour to the country. It was stowed away under a miserable shed adjoining the Eastern Annexe, and though undoubtedly one of the most important in the whole Exhibition, may, we fear, from the obscurity of its position, have escaped general attention. The Shelton Bar Iron Company exhibited a boiler-plate of considerable length (No. 322), which was placed vertically. It was not easy to roll so large a plate, as, owing to its thinness, the iron cools very rapidly. In the Butterley Company's collection the solid-rolled engine-beam slab well deserved attention : it is 31 ft. 6 in. long, 7 ft. wide in the middle, 2⅜ in. thick, has a superficial area of 163 square feet, and weighs 7 tons.

Sheet-Iron.—Of Sheet-iron there were numerous fine illustrations. The Belgian sheets were, of their kind, unrivalled, and were specially characterized by their smooth and dark bluish-grey glossy surface. The colour is obviously due to a thin and firmly adherent skin of oxide of iron, which has been detached here and there near the edges of several of the sheets, clearly revealing the colour of the subjacent iron. Russia still continues without a competitor in the production of a peculiar description of sheet iron, which has long been highly esteemed in commerce. The quality of the iron, which is both smelted and worked with charcoal throughout, is excellent, and the dark polish on the surface is remarkable. The process of manufacture is not known: mythical stories are current as to the precautions taken with a view to secrecy, and the lamentable fate of those who have gained unlawful access to the works, in order to possess themselves of the mystery. In tin-plate works we have frequently seen portions of "black plates," which reminded us strongly of the Russian sheets, in respect both of tint and lustre. The manufacture of this description of sheet-iron in England is a desideratum. The Russians are said to anneal their sheet with charcoal dust interposed, and finally to hammer them in packets. They are not all obtained equally good, and a selection is accordingly made. Austria exhibited excellent sheet-iron, and so did the Zollverein, except the specimens of the so-called transparent iron, which are a sham. This iron is not transparent at all, but is perforated with innumerable small holes through which light passes, thus showing how inferior in malleability iron is to gold.

Bars, Rails, and Girders.—This display was magnificent ; and in no branch of the metallurgy of iron has greater progress been made since the first Exhibition of 1851. The mill-power required to produce some of these articles is enormous, but we are probably far from having reached the *maximum* limit. There were gigantic rails exceeding 100 ft. in length, but these were to be regarded as curiosities, interesting as exhibitions of power and effective mechanical appliances, showing what might be done if required. In general they were admirable specimens of rolling. The Butterley Company sent a Rail 117 ft. long and 5¼ in. deep, and a tension bar for Girders, 83 ft. long, 1 ft. wide, and 1 in. thick. The Dowlais Company exhibited two rails of the following dimensions:—one 53 ft. 6 in. long, 4¾ in. across the head, and 10 in. deep, the other 31 ft. 6 in. long, 5½ in. across the head, and 15 in. deep. In the Zollverein was a section of rolled rail 5⅞ in. across the head, and 18⅜ in. deep. Belgium made a very creditable show of rails and rail sections; and it is declared that in certain foreign markets she has beaten the English producer of rails, both with respect to quality and price. The Austrian Society of State Railways exhibited specimens of rails—some with the head of granular and the foot of fibrous iron, and others of puddled steel. This is a great manufacturing company, established in 1855, with the view of producing everything required for the use of railways. They not only smelt and manufacture iron, but meddle with copper, lead, gold, silver, paraffine, &c. The catalogue which the Society has printed in elucidation of their display in the Exhibition contains much valuable information, scientific as well as commercial, and is well illustrated. It more especially concerns railway engineers.

Dupont and Dreyfus (France) exhibited a fine and extensive collection of objects of interest, especially with reference to Building constructions. There were flat bars and girders in great variety and profusion, indicating excellent workmanship. In France iron is more extensively used for building purposes than in England, and is, we believe, applied with much science. Why should our architects and builders lag behind the French in this matter? Captain Fowke has set them an example of the use of iron in the new permanent buildings at South Kensington; but something better will be done than this: surely iron is capable of being applied so as to produce a building less resembling a modern workshop in structure.

The Bridge-links for Suspension Bridges manufactured by Howard, Ravenhill, and Co., Rotherhithe, were interesting as having been made by rolling. One of the links exhibited weighed 6¼ cwt. We have witnessed the process, and observed that from the time the slab left the furnace to the complete formation of a large link about four minutes elapsed.

We must not omit to mention as deserving of notice the Rolled Iron Wire exhibited by the French, and which, though thick as compared with drawn wire, is yet fine, considering the mode of production.

Armour-plates.—There were no metallurgical illustrations in the Exhibition of more interest than the rolled Armour-plates for ships.* Of these two were sent by John Brown and Co., Atlas

* No false economy must be tolerated with regard to the iron intended for Her Majesty's ships. We have reason to know that the authorities, both military and naval, are now fully impressed with the absolute necessity of em-

Works, Sheffield. The immediate dimensions are as follows:—
(No. 1) length 21 ft. 8 in., width 4 ft. 2 in., thickness $6\frac{1}{2}$ in., weight 10 tons 12 cwt.; (No. 2) length 24 ft., width 3 ft. 8 in., thickness 5 in., weight 7 tons 17 cwt. A few years ago the rolling of such enormous masses of iron would have seemed incredible. In the Exhibition of 1851, Bagnall, of South Staffordshire, presented a rolled round Bar, which was considered extraordinary on account of its size, but it weighed only $1\frac{1}{4}$ ton. In the Paris Exhibition in 1855, we believe there was a much larger bar, but still nothing to compare in weight with the gigantic plates above-mentioned. Brown and Co. also exhibited large, but much thinner plates outside the Building in Exhibition-road; one was intended for gunboats, and is 22 ft. long, 7 ft. 2 in. wide, and 2 in. thick; and the other for engine beams. These two plates were thus manufactured. The metal consisted of "best new scrap," obtained from a mixture of Swedish, Shropshire, and Derbyshire refined iron. It was balled under a 4-ton steam hammer, piled under a 6-ton helve, and rolled into bar, re-rolled into slabs, all crossed, then rolled into "moulds," and lastly, rolled into the finished plates. There are 360 layers in the $6\frac{1}{2}$-inch plate.

The Butterley Company sent two Armour-plates, each 14 ft. long, 5 ft. wide, and $4\frac{1}{2}$ in. thick, and weighing when finished six tons. Experience teaches that it is quite impossible to form a satisfactory judgment as to the resisting powers of armour-plates from their outward appearance. Plates which externally have presented every sign of excellent workmanship, and which have been made of high-class iron, have been shattered like glass by heavy shot at high velocities; whereas others which in all respects would have been considered unsuitable, have stood comparatively well under fire. The expense of manipulating such enormous masses of iron as these armour-plates is necessarily very great; and the present cost of them to the nation ranges between 35l. and 45l. per ton! We are informed that all the experimental results hitherto obtained lead to the conclusion that they should be made of the softest possible iron.

Canadian Iron.—Enormous deposits of Magnetic Iron Ore—which, when pure, is the richest of all the ores of iron—have been discovered by Sir William Logan in the Laurentian rocks, which present no traces of organic remains, and are the oldest sedimen-

---

ploying, irrespective of cost, only those qualities of iron which have been found by experience best adapted to the various purposes of war. The experimental investigation on Iron Armour for Ships has now extended over eighteen months, and is still in progress. Information has been collected on the subject from every source; the opinions of the proprietors or managers of many of the leading iron-making firms in different parts of the country have been procured and recorded; plates of iron of various kinds, and manufactured in different ways, have been tested under conditions calculated to afford decisive comparative results; the maker of each plate has been invited to witness the effects of its trial; and a spirit of laudable rivalry has thus been excited, which cannot fail to secure the best results for the nation.

tary series in the world. The ore occurs interstratified with the rocks containing it. The accumulation of this ore in some localities is so great as to appear incredible. Thus, one bed is not less than 500 feet thick ! On the Rideau Canal there is another bed 200 feet thick, which is now worked at Newborough, and from which the ore is conveyed to Kingston on Lake Ontario. From this place it is put on board vessels at a cost of $2\frac{1}{4}$ dollars per ton, and taken to Cleveland, on Lake Erie, Ohio, whence it is sent to Pittsburgh, Pennsylvania, to be smelted. The best quality of ore is met with in a bed 25 feet thick in the township of Madoc. Canada also possesses extensive tracts of Bog-iron Ore on the north side of the St. Lawrence, and this is the only ore which is at present smelted in the country, charcoal being the fuel. The smelting is conducted at the Radnor Works, which include a forge for the manufacture of iron. At these works a large number of railway wheels are made of cast-iron derived exclusively from bog-iron ore. Cast-iron from ordinary bog-iron ore is about the last kind of metal many founders would dream of employing for such a purpose; yet in the Canadian Department was exhibited a pair of Railway Wheels which have travelled, without showing much evidence of wear, not less than 150,000 miles, or about six times round the earth. And it should be remembered that in Canada there are great alternations of temperature, the heat of summer being intense, and the cold of winter extremely bitter. The bog-ores must be exceptionally free from phosphoric acid; otherwise they would yield a tender, and not a strong iron like that of which the wheels above mentioned are stated to consist.

Iron in India.—There was an interesting series of specimens shown in the Indian Department. Iron ores, chiefly earthy-brown hæmatite and magnetic ironsand, occur abundantly in several parts of India, and have been smelted, from time immemorial, by the natives, in small furnaces. The East Indian Iron Company sent an instructive collection of Iron Ores and the various products which they yield. There are several Blast-furnaces in India on the European model, using charcoal as fuel. It is a remarkable fact, that in one locality in the Nerbudda Valley, good Bar-iron, but only in small pieces, can be made and sold by the native smelters under 5*l.* per ton. But the selling price of native iron in most parts of India is generally about double this sum. In the native process the iron is obtained direct from the ore in the malleable state, and pig-iron is not formed. All iron was formerly produced by this direct method; and to this day it is still practised in the Pyrenees, Finland, and some of the northern parts of the United States.

Swedish Boat-plates.—Sweden's chief ore is Magnetic Oxide, of which fine and characteristic specimens from various localities were exhibited. An instructive series of the far-famed Dannemora ores and the associated rocks specially deserved attention. The ores from this locality are among the finest in the world; and the iron which they yield always commands a high price, on account of its producing good steel. The Swedish iron ores differ much in quality, even when in appearance they closely resemble each other. One cause of the excellence of such as are considered the best is, without doubt, the absence of phosphorus, which is constantly present in sensible proportions in nearly all British iron ores, except the red hæmatites.

One of the remarkable objects shown was the fore-part of an iron paddle steamer, 200 feet long and of 120-horse power, which, during a fog in September, 1860, and while going at the rate of eight or nine knots an hour, struck on a rock. The iron was "crumpled up like a piece of brown paper," and yet the vessel got off and proceeded without difficulty to Stockholm, about 100 miles distant. The plates were made and the vessel was built at the Motala Iron Works. No object in the entire Exhibition appeared less attractive to the eye than this; yet, when its story is told, not one should excite greater interest, at least in the minds of Englishmen. Here we have ocular demonstration of the rough treatment which a ship made of really good iron has received with comparative impunity. Plates to be used in the building of iron ships ought, like boiler-plates, to be made of the most tenacious iron; whereas it is well known that in the manufacture of the so-called "boat-plates" the worst iron has often been employed. We know not how many lives have been sacrificed to cheap "boat-plates."—*Abridged from the Times.*

GALVANIZED METALS.

Amongst the exhibitors of Galvanized Metals were Morewood and Co., who say that their materials are more durable than zinc. They may be applied in the form of tiles, which are 3 feet by 2 feet, and are curled at the edges to finish as rolls, and are stiffened by transverse grooves. They are also made in sheets of 500 feet and upwards in length: thus they can be laid with great expedition by any labourer who can use a hammer; whilst considering that boarding is not required, the cost, say the patentees, is less than asphalted felt. Amongst the other productions of the same manufacturers, were welded-iron water and gas tubes. Tupper and Co. also exhibited "Galvanized Iron Manufactures connected with buildings and architecture." H. Vavasseur and Co., also exhibitors, used the Galvanized Corrugated Iron (No. 16 gauge, with a 10-inch flute) in covering the Amsterdam station on the Dutch-Rhenish Railway, and (No. 20, with 5-inch flute) in the construction of the Palace of Industry, Amsterdam. Mr. John Walker displayed articles belonging to the same branch of manufacture. S. C. Hemming and Co. showed what they have done in Iron-building and Roofing. F. Morton and Co., of Liverpool, exhibited a variety of articles, including Galvanized Corrugated Iron roofs, and patented improvements in Railway Fences and Telegraph-poles. Their wire-cable fences, with tapered oval iron posts, are fitted with winding straining pillars, by which 400 to 500 yards of fence may be kept perfectly tight and rigid; indeed, the pillars are called "self-acting." With galvanized corrugated iron Morton and Co. can cover an area of 100 feet square (plates and uprights only, furnished them) in five spans, for 370*l*. They can provide and erect an iron cottage with five rooms and entrance-porch for 120*l*.

For Zinc Roofing, the Vieille Montagne Company, and their manufacturing agents, F. Braby and Co., were exhibitors. The "Italian-formed Corrugated Zinc" which is simply a formation of the sheets with rolls at close distances, is used for the verandah of the Horticultural Society's conservatory, and on the refreshment-rooms of the Exhibition. We may observe that zinc is now constantly employed in Paris, for buildings much larger in scale, and more substantial in construction, than the London houses.—*Abridged from the Builder*.

Tylor's Zinc Work illustrated improvements in the Manufacturing and Laying of Zinc, as applied to building purposes, whereby the metal is made to last much longer than it does when improperly laid. There were models, showing the method adopted to lay the sheets, 8 feet long by 3 feet wide, to allow of free contraction and expansion, without confining the sheets of zinc with nails or solder; the whole being secured with clips, so that each sheet of zinc can be removed without breakage or injury. The falls of the boarding and gutters are arranged to have a drip at every eight feet or sixteen feet; and the falls are so arranged that no water or sediment can remain on the roof, and will clear away with every storm.

MALLEABLE CAST-IRON.

The James Foundry Company sent to the Walsall Division a collection of Iron-foundry Goods, showing to how great an extent Malleable Cast-iron is used, and the perfection to which it is brought. All kinds of builders' odd work was represented: Buckles, Slides, and other lighter articles made of cast-iron were shown, with fine specimens of bronzing, and samples of polished cast-iron goods.

IRON PAINTS.

Here may be mentioned Wolston's Torbay Iron Paints for coating materials which are to be under water, or in a position to be affected by damp. They are manufactured at Brixham, Devonport, and are successfully used in dockyards and public works. A caisson in Woolwich Dockyard, painted nine years since, is said to be in a perfectly sound condition, both under water and between wind and water. It is also said that the Torbay paints have been found to stop corrosion that has set in; so that in Pembroke Dockyard, where in 1859 two iron-roofs had been found so corroded as in the opinion of the authorities to need entire renewal, but where two coats of the paint were applied, the result has been such that the expense of renewal is no longer necessary. The experience in the case of corrugated iron-roofing at the Aberdare Iron Works is even more satisfactory. Two coats were there applied in 1853, and one coat since. The specimens exhibited were taken from roofs in the dockyards and arsenals: the greater number of them bear out the preceding statements.

BIRMINGHAM WARES.—WIRE-WORKING.

All the leading branches of the industry of Birmingham were fully represented in the Court appropriated to the Exhibitors. Here were raw materials of every kind for the use of brass-founders; a fine display of metallic bedsteads and gas-fittings, and stamped and general brass foundry. To these were added, tin-plate and japan wares; stoves, grates, and fire-irons; iron safes; hollow wares in copper and iron, tinned and enamelled; tubing of all kinds; scales and weighing machines; medals and dies; hooks and eyes; pins; steel pens; locks and general hardware; knife-cleaning-machines; steel toys; metal mountings for the use of bookbinders; fire-guards; coffin furniture; saddlers' ironmongery; ornamental panels, screws, nails, hinges, &c. Guns and swords, and Japan-ware were also shown in great number and variety.

Webster and Horsfall exhibited a case of Iron Wires, including music, needle, and flat spring wires, the latter manufactured from the patent steel wire, which was also shown; with samples of submarine telegraph cables, coal-pit ropes, and ropes for ships' rigging. There were shown two coils of Steel Wire without a weld, of the extraordinary weight of 1 cwt., said to be the heaviest coil ever manufactured. The whole power of a 100-horse engine was required to roll it, and Webster and Horsfall's mill is the only mill in the country at which it could be made. This wire is to be used for pit-guides, in lieu of the ordinary iron guides, liable to frequent breakage at the welds.

Smith and Co. sent from Halifax a bloom, or piece of the best Swedish Iron, and specimens of all the stages of manufacture from it down to the smallest sizes of wire. The first stages down to the rod gauging No. 2 or 4, are manufactured while the iron is hot; after that the iron is drawn cold through steel plates similar to the small model exhibited, with some sizes of wire in it; and as the process of drawing hardens the wire, it has to be annealed or softened at various stages, and then drawn again. The above piece of bloom, measuring only $8\frac{1}{4}$ inches long and 3 inches square, and weighing 20 lbs., would, if drawn as small as the finest wire exhibited in the same case, measure 110 miles in length. They will give you 1000 feet of wire out of a brass farthing; 70,000 feet of wire, or a sheet of brass, 12 feet square, that will not exceed one pound in weight.

By similar processes the same firm makes all kinds of wire for wire ropes for collieries, ships' rigging, &c., also for carding cotton, wool, silk, and tow, weaving into wire blinds, &c. ; bottling wires, and wire covered with cotton for ladies' bonnets, artificial flowers, &c., specimens of which were shown.

THE HEREFORD SCREEN.

We must describe in detail this truly artistic work—the Rood Screen, made by the Skidmore Art Company, at Coventry, for Hereford Cathedral, and probably the finest piece of modern metal-work in existence. It has been executed from Mr. Scott's designs since January, 1862 ; it is much larger in its dimensions than its companion at Lichfield, and, indeed, is the largest piece of architectural metal-work ever executed. Iron is of course the principal material used, though in the decorative details copper and brass are largely introduced. In these combinations the fine examples which the early metal-workers have transmitted to our time are studied with conscientious care, so as to adhere to the lessons of the past in a work that in itself is perfectly original. Thus, in the Hereford Screen we find the iron wrought both into true grilles, and also elaborated after the manner of the early chasers into the richest iron filagree. The brass and copper work has been dealt with in the same spirit, and the capitals supporting the Screen are most happily adjusted to the requirements of architectural conventionalism. The copper flowers by which these are enriched have the softness and beauty of nature, though all, after the old style, are worked out with the point of the hammer from sheets of copper. The copper is throughout left of its own natural colour, but the brass work is intermixed with broad masses of vitreous mosaic. Where paint is used upon the iron, all the colours employed, with the exception only of the green, have been obtained from oxides of the metal itself ; though the colouring and gilding have been applied only with a view to the effect of the whole piece when shown in the subdued light of a cathedral nave. In the Exhibition Building, it was seen to great disadvantage.

The whole composition consists of a double arcade of five primary and ten secondary arches, blended in a single group, though each retains its own individuality. The centre arch, forming the passage, is very lofty, and is enriched with the most exquisite scrolls of flower and foliage. The shafts for the arches are of mixed brass and iron ; and, as at Lichfield, the whole is adorned with examples of architectural sculpture, figures of angels, &c. These figures are perfect studies in themselves. Every one can understand them at a glance, and from the centre statue of Our Saviour to those of the Praying Angels, the fulness of their meaning may be felt without the aid of any inscriptions beneath their feet to set forth who or what they are. Above the Screen was hung the gas corona as it will hang at Hereford. Close by the Hereford Screen were the side Courts fitted up, one by Hardman, and the other by Hart and Sons, with mediæval ecclesiastical ornaments in brass, stone, and wood.—*Abridged from the Times.*

THE NORWICH GATES.

The Wrought-iron Park Gates, by Barnard and Bishop, also merit detail. The work consists of four massive piers, a pair of central and two side gates. The piers are connected by girders, or horizontal members of a somewhat massive character. The large portions of these gates are in cast-iron, and the smaller parts are wrought; the cast members being enriched with ornament, which is judiciously in low relief, while the enrichment wrought by forging is of a very different class.

In the designs, the quatrefoil is very pleasing. The foliaceous filling of the entire work consists chiefly of the vine, hawthorn, oak, ivy, rose, convolvulus, bryony, and periwinkle.

The two central or chief piers are crowned by capitals enriched with wrought-iron foliage. The shafts of the piers are panelled, and are filled in with leafage and flowers.

Over the central gates is a terminal enrichment, formed of the oak and holly, surrounding a shield bearing the arms of Norwich; and over each of the side gates is a similar arrangement of hawthorn-branches which lean towards the central mass of the gates, and are of a bright, bracket-like character. Each pier is also surmounted by a griffin supporting a shield.

Here may be mentioned a pair of magnificent Gates, executed by Messrs. Kennard, for the pleasure-villa of the Duke of Salamanca, near Madrid. They are of elegant design; the style of colouring, applied by Mr. Owen Jones, is Alhambresque.

MEDIÆVAL METAL-WORK.

The Court characteristically fitted up by Hart and Son (the ceiling designed by Crace) for the exhibition of Mediæval Works in Metal, showed on the sides some fine Monumental Brasses, and from the ceiling hung Chandeliers of Gothic design. The body of the Court was filled with furniture, every article being in harmony with the general character of the Gothic decorations. The fenders, fire-irons, candelabra, moderator-lamps, candlesticks for ecclesiastical purposes, even the tables and chairs, were Gothic in their style. There were candlesticks with gold and silver plate, for ecclesiastical purposes. Hart and Son also exhibited Stoves, Mantelpieces, Clocks; specimens of Ornamental Wrought-iron; a pretty Wrought-iron Gate, put together in small pieces, and ornamented with birds and foliage.

Mr. Hardman also fitted up a Court, presenting many fine examples of the mediæval style. Mr. Benham, of Wimpole-street, showed Stoves, Wrought-iron Scroll-work, and Fenders; Bailey, of Gracechurch-street, also contributed Stoves ; and Feetham, of Oxford-street, Stoves, Fenders, and other useful and ornamental work.

WOLVERHAMPTON GOODS.

Clark and Co. sent a fine collection of Hollow Manufactures ; among which was prominent a set of Stable Fittings in Enamelled Iron, consisting of manger, rack, water-troughs, stall, posts, &c. : these fittings being readily taken to pieces for removal instead of requiring to be finally adjusted before leaving the manufactory. All descriptions of tin, and enamelled hollow Iron-ware, adapted to culinary and sanitary purposes, were also shown.

Mr. T. Smith sent all kinds of Locks, Bolts, Carriage-springs, Axles and Blocks, Cart-axles, Blocks for the heavy bullock-waggons used at the Cape, Iron Safes ; heavy Edge-tools, Table Cutlery, Plated Spurs, Stirrups, &c. Also, Mills, from Corns's Snow-hill Manufactory, elaborately ornamented and of beautiful design. A large and highly finished Padlock, of very singular construction, intended for the foreign market, was also shown here ; besides Iron Pipes and Castings, Kettles, Saucepans, Frying-pans, &c.

BEDSTEADS.

Winfield and Son, Peyton, and Whitfield and Sons contributed Iron and Brass Bedsteads, which, in their light and elegant forms, contrasted strangely with the lumbering wood bedsteads of our forefathers. Among Whitfields' specimens were two handsome instances: the first an Iron Tube Bedstead, to which is applied a recent patent in using iron stampings of various patterns, instead of the plain tube : the second is of similar character. One is coloured in imitation of malachite, picked out with gold ; the other light blue and gold.

COOKING APPARATUS, RANGES, AND STOVES.

In the Hardware Court were several descriptions of Cooking Apparatus, of which one showed great novelty of arrangement, namely, the patent Duplex Range, by Edward Deane and Co. It has two fires of different sizes, separated and backed by a T boiler. Each fire has a separate oven of proportionate size, flue, and hot-plate. In combination with the patent Revolving Roasting Apparatus—also the invention of Mr. Edward Deane, and with which as many as nine joints can be roasted at one fire—120 pounds of meat may be roasted ; the same quantity baked in the ovens ; and the same quantity again stewed on the top of the stove ; while the steam boiler at the back will boil 3 cwt. of potatoes, and the circulating boilers will keep 60 gallons of water constantly hot, the whole cost of the fuel per day being one shilling. The roasting apparatus consists of a cylindrical meat-screen, within which three sets of joints, one above the other, revolve first round a general centre, and secondly round their own axis, each joint having a separate dripping-pan.

Brown and Green, of Bishopsgate-street Within, obtained the Prize Medal for a large Kitchen Range, fourteen feet in length, containing four roasters, or ovens, and three boilers. It is stated that this range is capable of doing all the plain cooking for more than 2000 persons with a consumption of less than one ounce of coal per head per day, this being one of the results of a practical trial of this range before it was placed in the Exhibition : these results are certified by the inspector of cookery for the army, who conducted the trial by command of the War Office. This large Kitchener also provided for the certain cure of smoky chimneys ; the ventilation of the kitchen through the upper part of the range, whereby are prevented oppressive heat in the kitchen, and close smell of cooking ; and the facility for roasting meat in front of the fire at the same time that the whole of the apparatus is kept going.

Gigantic Ranges were shown by Thomas and Sons, and Radclyffe, of Leamington, a place famous for its Range and Cooking Apparatus. These are fitted with ovens and boilers, and supplied with valves and appliances that will do any amount of roasting, boiling, frying, toasting, or heating. One consumes its own smoke, and also all the odour which arises from cooking. There was one apparatus adapted for French cookery, to burn only wood, and another immense one suitable for large ships. There were Stoves and Ranges exhibited by Benham, suitable for all establishments, from the cottage to the club-house ; for the ocean-going steamer or small pleasure-yacht.

An admirable notice of the Heating, Ventilating, and Cooking Apparatus, shown in the Exhibition, will be found in the *Builder*, No. 1022.

Prominent among the Stoves was a Gothic Dining-room or Hall Grate, in electro-bronze, with brass ornamentation and polished bars. Wright and Co. showed a Register Stove, bi-valved, to regulate the draught : also Gill-stoves, upon the principle of the gills of a fish, so as to give a large radiating surface.

CHANDELIERS, GASELIERS, AND LAMPS.

Messenger sent from Birmingham some Gothic Chandeliers, suspended on a frame, of extraordinary beauty. In the centre is an octagon, the lower portion saw-pierced with minute ornamentation. Some of these tasteful works were designed by Mr. Digby Wyatt, and range in price from 50s. to 100 guineas. Mr. Philip, also of Birmingham, exhibited a large collection of Lamps in bronze and gold, and Grecian designs, with snake burners ; besides Chandeliers in Italian and Renaissance styles. Hinks and Son sent a case of new patent Lamps for the complete combustion of the commonest oils, without glass chimneys: some were glass elaborately gilt, and others of opal and bronze.

Harrow and Son, Portland-place, exhibited an Eight-light Gaselier, cast in brass, from models designed and carved by Mr. Rogers. It is constructed in form of an ancient grillier, or fire-pot, the upper bar consisting of eight inverted friezes, richly wrought and divided by heads of dragons, from whose mouths issue fire, and lightly-poised gas-jets. At the bottom is a very bold boss, composed of two large salamanders, intertwined in fierce struggle, their feet grasping the lower ring or bar of the suspended fire-pot, and thus forming its base. This composition is a welcome relief to the bare conventional forms of brass chandeliers.

THE BRASS TOY TRADE.

Mr. Nettlefold exhibited a tasteful display of Nails and Screws in Iron and Brass, pictorially arranged. The famous Birmingham Buttons, of gold and steel, and fanciful descriptions, were also tastefully shown. So perfect is the machinery for making buttons, that the manufacture is completely effected by the single revolution of a wheel.

Brass Tubing, some of it 9 inches in diameter, was shown here; a case of Bookbinding, in metallic covers; Brass Hinges, Door-knobs, and Handles, in endless array. The Cornice Poles and Brackets, by which small houses are most economically fitted, were exhibited here, made by the stamping process of Mr. Hill: the metal is struck by die after die, each gradually increasing in convexity, until the highest relief or most minute outlines are brought out.

LOCKS AND SAFES.

Mr. Harley, of Wolverhampton, contributed a case of Locks, remarkable for their mechanism and elaborate and artistic finish. It contained all kinds of chest, trunk, drawer, wardrobe, carpet-bag, portfolio, ledger, till, and padlocks. Two specimens of Detector Locks, with outer dials, which require to be set to a given time before the locks can be opened, comprise no fewer than three thousand changes, and defy all attempts at opening by those who do not know the time at which the dials were set. Another description of Detector Lock contains a small gong, which rings out when the key is turned, like a lock in the Turkish collection. Some of the padlocks were as small as the stone of a ring, and others as large as a cheese-plate; and some of the Folio Locks are also so minute that a dozen of them might be sent by post for two stamps.

Messrs. Bramah maintained their old reputation by exhibiting models and specimens of their well-known Locks, as manufactured in their ordinary business. Hamilton and Co., Royal Exchange, showed a Lock to be locked without a key, by merely turning a brass knob, but which is opened by a very small key. Tucker and Reeves, Fleet-street, showed a collection of Lever-locks, some with novel tumblers, scarcely to be picked, or destroyed by gunpowder. Mr. Tann showed a Lock, with the novelty of a self-acting lever, which takes the pressure from the bolt, and places a very simple but efficient obstacle in the way of the lock being picked.

Hobbs and Co. showed every part of a Lock and Key in course of manufacture by their machinery : they also exhibited a series of twenty-six Locks, varying in size from that suited to the smallest cabinet to a large cupboard, so constructed as to be opened with one and the same key. One of their larger Locks, the "Protector," by a peculiar arrangement of certain parts behind the bolt and levers, is stated to be unreachable by any lock-picking instrument whatever. When any tampering is attempted on the lock by pressure on the bolt through the key-hole, to discover the opening position of each lever, the bolt-protector comes into action, preventing the pressure affecting the levers in any way. Specimens were shown of an "Indicator Lock," which tells by an index on the outer side whether it is "open," "shut," or "locked."

Mr. George Price, Cleveland Safe and Lock Works, Wolverhampton, exhibited his Drill-proof Safes, and unpickable and gunpowder-proof Locks ; which were remarkable for their excellence in manufacture.

Chubb and Son showed a splendid and unique collection of Locks and Keys, manufactured by them at Wolverhampton, where they had been exhibited to thousands of visitors. Here it may be observed that no Locks or Safes of inferior quality are made by Chubb and Son, their aim being excellence of workmanship rather than excessively low price. There were about 300 Locks exhibited, varying between a gigantic rim lock weighing more than 2 cwt., and as finely finished as a lady's watch ; and an elegant little gold lock, with four tumblers, set in a finger ring, and weighing 16 grains ! Some fifty keys were shown with elaborate bows, three so much so, that, although small, they are valued at upwards of a hundred guineas ; the bow of each being composed of minute particles of steel, all separately riveted, and resembling so many brilliants.

Among the specially ornamental examples were—

1. A large Door Lock, encased in polished steel, the surface overlaid with an elaborate mediæval design in ormolu, and the key wrought in corresponding style.

2. Another Door Lock in a walnut-wood casing, the front covered with a rich Gothic foliated design cut from a single plate of steel, hardened and polished.

As examples of security for special purposes, there were—

1. A Wheel Lock for Bank Strong-rooms and Safes, throwing out with the greatest ease any requisite number of bolts on every side of the door, the whole being secured in their positions by four of Chubb's Patent Gunpowder-proof Locks. Each of these has its own distinct key, so that, if desired, access can only be obtained to the Safe when the holders of the different keys are present.

2. An Index Lock, in which the action of unlocking for every time moves the index-wheel one number onward, thus registering the exact number of visits paid to any depository on which the lock may be placed, and thereby giving notice of the improper use of its true key, should that be surreptitiously obtained by any unauthorized person.

3. The Banker's Lock, containing eighteen Tumblers, and many features of novelty and additional security. By the application of sliding pieces of metal with a triple-curtained barrel, all access to the tumblers and bolts is entirely cut off and closed while the keyhole is open, and it is not until the key has been inserted and turned, thereby causing the steel curtains to cover the whole of the keyhole, that these obstructions are removed. By another contrivance, any pressure applied to the bolt effectually fastens down the tumblers which secure it, and only when all pressure has been removed from the bolt can the tumblers be lifted at all.

4. A set of twelve Patent Detector Mortise Locks, each having a different Suite Key opening that lock only; also eleven Sub-master-Keys, and one Master-Key, to open all twelve Locks, and to double-lock, and thereby shut out any and all of the Suite or Sub-Master-Keys.

Among the Wrought-iron Safes were two ornamental Safes of different designs, as Jewel-cases, the designs being executed in mixtures of dead and burnished steel, inlaid gilt scrolls, gilt raised ornaments and mouldings, and the interior spaces are fitted up in fancy woodwork. The doors are secured by Wheel Locks throwing bolts all round, as in the larger Safes, and have very small keys.

A massive Banker's Safe, weighing about four tons, was also shown. It has drawers, and two distinct closets, or inner safes, each having its own different key, besides a master-key to pass the whole. The outer doors of the safe are constructed of wrought-iron plates, and hardened steel combined, and fitted with Chubb's Gunpowder-proof Wheel Locks, throwing thirty-one bolts all round, the main keyholes being further secured with case-hardened iron scutcheon locks opened by a key so small as to be set in an ordinary gold finger-ring.

There were also a Banker's Door and Frame for a Strong Room, and a smaller Bank Safe, of similar construction to the foregoing.

Messrs. Chubb, it will be recollected, made all the Locks for the Exhibition Building. The Master-Key to the whole is a very handsome implement. Within the bow are the Royal cipher, V.R., elegantly combined, and the date of the year, 1862, in Gothic figures, surmounted by a crown: the whole of the filing and chiselling was done by hand. The key was used by his Royal Highness the Duke of Cambridge, as First Commissioner, at the formal opening of the Building.

STEEL MANUFACTURES.

"The manufacture of Steel and Steel Articles, on anything like a large scale, (says the writer of a practical paper in the *Daily News*), is confined to very few countries: we exceed all others in this branch of industry. In 1851 it was ascertained that while we produced annually about forty-five thousand tons of Steel, Austria, which came next to us, produced only thirteen thousand, and all the states of the Zollverein taken together, but eight thousand. From the recent Exhibition, though there was an abundant display of Steel and Steel Articles, it was manifest that the production of Steel in any considerable quantity is still a very limited industry. A large amount of it, obtained directly from Pig Iron, was shown at the Exhibition of 1851; but Bessemer's process had not then been discovered; nor was the art of making Steel in very large quantities by other methods so well known as it is at present. Perhaps nothing indicates the progress which has been made during the past few years, so clearly as a comparison between the Steel found at the Exhibitions of 1851 and 1862.

"The so-called homogeneous metal, which has excited much attention of late, is extremely malleable and tough, and may be placed midway between wrought Iron and ordinary Steel; it may be regarded as Steel containing a low per-centage of carbon. This is the metal of which Mr. Whitworth has formed so high an opinion. Examples of it were exhibited by Shortridge, Howell, and Co. Pieces of Tubing formed of this metal were shown flattened down vertically, which might readily be mistaken for caoutchouc. It is stated to have been produced by melting pieces of Swedish Iron and carbonaceous matter."*

In the French Department, Jackson, Son, and Co. exhibited Steel objects made by the Bessemer process. The Swedes sent both Iron and Steel made by this process. Bessemer Steel was sent from Kloster Works, Dalecarlia: at these works are the largest charcoal blast furnaces in Sweden, each producing about 100 tons of pig-iron weekly. The process has not yet made its way into Austria: the Prussians have tried it, but failed.

The process of Uchatius excited some attention a few years ago, especially in London. Samples were exhibited in the Swedish Department. This steel, strange to state, finds a ready sale at prices ranging from 50*l*. to 60*l*. per ton, which are higher than can be obtained for Bessemer steel in Sweden. It is said to be especially good for sword-blades. It is made by melting Bispberg

---

* In the specification of a patent, No. 2369, A.D. 1856, it is stated that scale, which falls off from steel or iron during the process of hammering or rolling, is employed in addition to the ingredients in common use for cast steel. In Mushet's *Papers on Iron and Steel* (1840, p. 525) is the description of a metal which exactly applies to the so-called homogeneous metal. The process of manufacture appears to be essentially the same, and was patented by Mushet in 1800 (No. 2447), who is reported to have sold the patent to a house in Sheffield for the sum of 3000*l*.

iron ore, mixed with charcoal, in Belgian crucibles. This ore is remarkable for its purity.

Cast steel, made by melting together wrought iron and charcoal pig-iron, was shown in the Swedish Department, by Rettig, Geffe. Cast steel, made by melting together wrought iron and *refined* pig-iron, was exhibited by Dr. Price, in the British Department. It is maintained that coke pig-iron may be sufficiently freed from silicon and certain other impurities by the refining process as to admit of being employed with advantage in the manufacture of this kind of steel. There may be more in this method than is now supposed.

In the Austrian collection were specimens of the so-called Wolfram Steel, made by melting together cast steel and the mineral wolfram. The quality of the metal, it was believed, would be much improved by this addition. It breaks with a very fine grain, and is hard and tough. We have learnt on excellent authority that this alloy has not been found successful.

In the Austrian Department were drawings of Mayr's Furnaces for Casting Steel on Siemens's principle by his "regenerative furnaces." Lignite is the fuel used, of which three parts by weight are required to melt one of cast steel. In six days between five and six tons are melted in one of these furnaces.

A handsome Fitzroy Phaeton was sent from Northampton, constructed with malleable Steel, and Wheels of Hickory, and was shown with other carriages.

An interesting Machine, constructed by Greenwood and Bailey, for testing Steel, by crushing, pulling, and rolling, was a prominent attraction.

In 1851 the flourishing state of this manufacture in Great Britain, was evinced by the fact that 45 per cent. of the exhibitors of articles produced by it, and far more than the proportion of the articles themselves, were from the British Islands. Austria, which was the next to Great Britain in this respect, furnished only about 27 per cent., the Zollverein only 8 per cent., and France only 3 per cent. The proportions were somewhat different. Thus, while the British Exhibitors amounted to 126, those of Austria were 58, those of France 47, those of Prussia 18, those of Russia 15, those of Turkey 14, those of Sweden 9, those of Switzerland 2, and the United States sends but 1.

Cutlery and Edge Tools.—Sheffield produced every article of this class: other places confined themselves more or less to particular branches; and this is especially true of those countries where the manufacture has been more recently introduced, the artisans of which direct their attention in a greater degree to special productions. Thus, the Cutlery of Canada consisted chiefly of forest tools; that of the States of the Zollverein, of common articles and the more simple implements; that of the Austrian Department, of agricultural requisites. In the Belgian Department, were Spiral Cutters, which are required for finishing their woollen fabrics; and in the Swiss, Files and other necessaries for the manufacture of Horological Machines, which they carry on so extensively. The Cutlery of the various parts of France varied with the industries of the localities where it is produced.

Moseley and Sons well sustained the reputation of the London Cutlery, and showed some specimens of that old Salisbury style of work which is so different from that of Sheffield. Milward and Son, of Redditch, showed Needles, Fish-hooks, and Fishing-tackle. The firm was established in 1730. Six millions of needles are produced by them weekly, each needle passing through thirty distinct processes before it assumes its finished shape. By the machinery adopted in this manufactory, one man can point twelve thousand needles in an hour.

KRUPP'S CAST-STEEL.

We now arrive at one of the most extraordinary and most important collections in the Exhibition, the truly magnificent display of Krupp's Cast Steel: its wonderful soundness and the enormous size of the castings. Krupp affects considerable mystery in his processes. His works in Essen are reported to occupy 180 acres of ground. It is stated that he employs puddled steel, which is broken up, assorted, and re-melted in crucibles. This variety of steel does not appear to be adapted for cutlery. He consumes all the spiegeleisen produced by Müsener and Co. It is affirmed that there is a great consumption of plumbago and leather parings at the Essen Works. Each crucible is said to contain 70 lbs. of steel, and the furnaces in which they are heated vary much in dimensions, the smallest holding two and the larger twenty-four crucibles. When a large casting is required, the organization has been carried to such a remarkable degree of perfection that at a given signal all the crucibles needed are ready to be taken out of the furnace at the same time. Their contents are poured with the utmost rapidity into a large reservoir, and from this the metal is cast. By this means, as in bronze-founding on the large scale, homogeneity is attained. The apparatus for working the steel is the most gigantic yet constructed. There is a steam-hammer weighing 50 tons. The anvil face weighs 185 tons, and cupola furnaces were built expressly to melt this large quantity of metal. The largest casting in the world is the great bell at Moscow, reported to weigh 192 tons; but it cracked in cooling, and was never removed from its birthplace. Krupp's anvil rests on eight blocks of cast-iron, weighing from 125 to 135 tons each, and making a total weight of 1250 tons of cast-iron! This solid structure of iron is supported on a wooden foundation, 40 feet square. The largest Casting exhibited by Krupp in 1851 weighed $2\frac{1}{4}$ tons, and the largest in the recent Exhibition weighed 21 tons. It is in the form of a solid cylinder, about 9 ft. high and 3 ft 8 in. in diameter. It has been broken across to show fracture. The largest casting Krupp ever made weighed 25 tons. Now, when we reflect that this enormous mass of metal is melted in comparatively small crucibles, we get an idea of the perfect organization requisite to have every crucible ready and the pouring effected at almost the same moment of time ; and it is in this organization that we are disposed to think one great merit of Krupp consists. Krupp exhibited Shafts, Rolls, Railway Tires and Wheels, Locomotive Axles, and Guns. There was a good Catalogue in German, also a Price List of the Cast-steel Guns. A Finished Gun of eight inches calibre, turned, bored, and rifled, without breech-closing apparatus, is advertised at 975*l.* Krupp has supplied locomotive axles to some of our largest railway companies, and crank-axles of marine engines to some of our most celebrated marine engine-makers. The large steel bell was cast at Bochum's Works, it is said, by the same process as Krupp's foundry, hard bye. Steel cannot be compared with bell-metal for quality of sound, but is a cheaper material.—*Abridged from the Times.*

BESSEMER'S STEEL.

Bessemer made an admirable display both of. Iron and Steel produced by his process ; with specimens illustrative of the quality of the metal, as shown by hammering, punching, bending, twisting, stamping, rolling, drawing into tube and fine wire, turning, polishing, &c. A Rail was shown 84lb. to the yard, which may be supplied at 13*l.* per ton.

Mr. Bessemer had a resplendent "Trophy Court," in which were shown some of the most important of the various applications of the Bessemer Steel. There were a Crank-shaft of a 50-horse engine in one piece ; piston-rods for Engines of from 50 to 250 horse-power ; the powerful Screw of a Fly-press used in the Mint ; and a Circular Saw made from one disc of steel over 7ft. in diameter, with teeth of 10in. in length. There was, however, a larger saw than this shown in another part of the Building, made from steel by the old process ; and either of them, turning at the rate of 500 revolutions a-minute, would cut through the thickest timber as fast as a man could walk. With these massive examples were shown smaller ones, such as plates used in Boilers, Ships, and Bridges, rising in regular gradations from 1-50th of an inch to nearly 4¼ inches thick. Specimens of Steel were also shown, from a thickness too great for a strong man to bend down to the 250th part of an inch in diameter.

Among the applications of Steel Wire were exhibited several

---

* The great success of Krupp's productions in cast-steel led to an erroneous impression that Sheffield had been beaten by her Continental rivals, during the last eleven years. But the Jury have awarded to Sheffield a greater portion of Medals than to any of her rivals. Certainly, Krupp was the first to develop the manufacture of large castings of steel, which was practically unknown in Sheffield a few years ago, and his excellence is the great size of his castings. This is no proof that Sheffield has lost her supremacy in the older branches of manufacture, for excellence in which she has so long been famous —that is, for the quality of steel, tools, cutlery, and the productions of her other staple trade.

specimens of Cotton Cards, used in the best carding-engines, with steel in round, flat, and square bars of every size. Two important examples of Steel Ordnance were shown—one illustrating a mode of Mounting Guns without Trunnions, the elevation being effected by a screw, and the axles of the wheels admitting of adjustment; the other a 24-Pounder, with Trunnions forged on it out of one solid ingot of Steel. Mr. Bessemer also showed samples of Railway Bars made of his steel, some few hundred tons of which have already been laid on various lines for trial. He claims for these metals that they will last between four and five times as long as ordinary rails, and that they are not liable to snap in frosty weather, in proof of which was shown a Bar bent double during a hard frost by an eminent railway engineer. Naylor and Vickers also showed hereabout a fine Trophy of large Castings in Steel, and a peal of beautifully sounding Steel Bells. Another peal of Bells, by Warner and Son, were of the ordinary bell-metal, but were so arranged that one man could ring a peal on the whole of them.

WORKS IN THE PRECIOUS METALS.

The workers in Gold and Silver have, unquestionably, made great progress in their cunning art since the Exhibition of 1851. In this age of gold, and nobler enterprise than that of gold-seeking, and nobler successes than those of gold-finding, it was natural to expect a large increase in costly works of art, and luxurious ministrations to the vanity which are too often showered upon individual success. But the advancement of art has not gone, *pari passu*, with this increment of the precious metals, and this liberal employment of those who fashion them. Art has been beaten, in common phrase, "by the weight of metal;" and though the *quantity* has been superabundantly increased, the *quality* of the workmanship has suffered in this plethora of the earth's wealth. These shortcomings of art, must not, however, be set down to the artists themselves, but to the want of taste in their patrons, who estimate by the hand and not by the head—by the weight of the material, and not by the art displayed in working it.*

Messrs. Garrard, as Crown-jewellers, exhibited, by permission of Her Majesty, the following Articles:—

The Koh-i-noor, shown as a specimen of diamond-cutting. The history of this celebrated gem has been so often told, that we shall not repeat it. Since its recutting (at which the Duke of Wellington, it will be remembered, was present) it has been, with greater propriety, called "the mountain of light," although mineralogists

---

* See "Progress of Art Manufactures," page 72 of the present volume. Such of the visitors to the recent Exhibition as paid a visit to the Works of of Art on loan in the South Kensington Museum, must have been forcibly convinced of the vast superiority of the workers in metal centuries since, in comparison with those of the present day.

are still divided in opinion as to its purity. When shown at the Exhibition of 1851, it was an unshapely dim-looking gem: since its recutting in 1852, it has so much improved its shape, though it has diminished its size by about one-third, its brilliancy is greatly increased. Visitors could judge at once of its recent improvement, for by its side was placed a perfect model in crystal glass of its form, cutting, and colour when first exhibited: and although, as a great portion has been split off at the cleavage-plane, the cutting could only be effected by a great sacrifice of weight, yet there an immense brilliancy has been acquired, and even an apparent increase in size.

Three large and fine ancient Rubies, from the Treasury at Lahore: they are set with three very brilliant drops in the Indian style, as a necklace for Her Majesty. Persian inscriptions on these stones prove them to be of great historic interest. They bear the dates of A.D. 1070, 1125, 1153, and 1168 respectively.

An Ornament for the centre of the table, designed in Alhambresque style, and executed in silver, silver gilt, and enamel. This will be remembered among the Royal table-plate: it was shown at the Society of Arts several years since. Around the base is a group of horses (portraits of favourite animals the property of the Queen), and on the lower portion of the base, which is designed to represent a ruin, are introduced the flamingo and the vulture, and various plants. The whole appearance of this piece is, however, gaudy and rococo, and the eye is very far from satisfied with it.

A Jewelled and Enamelled Cup, in silver gilt, the gift of Her Majesty and the Prince Consort to their grandchild and godson, the Prince Frederic of Prussia, on the occasion of his christening, is in better taste. The figures are typical of baptism; on the stem are the arms of England and Prussia, and on the base a group of St. George and the Dragon.

A Tazza-form Cup, presented by Her Majesty the Queen to the Hereditary Duke of Baden, on his christening. It has wreaths of wheat and the vine, symbolical of the sacrament, surmounted with a group typical of baptism; and on the body the arms of England and of Baden are introduced.

A richly-chased Christening Bowl, in Renaissance style, presented by H.R.H. the Princess of Prussia to the daughter of His Excellency Count Bernsdorff on her christening. It has winged figures supporting coronals and wreaths of flowers, and on the edge of the bowl is an emblematic figure pouring out water.

The work of these three cups is minute, sound, and satisfactory in every respect.

Hunt and Roskell exhibited two other articles, by permission of the Queen: 1. A Vase, by Vechte, in oxydized silver, damascened: subject, the Centaurs and Lapidæ. 2. A Vase and Pedestal, by Vechte, in oxydized silver: subject, Thetis giving to Achilles the armour forged by Vulcan.

Messrs. Garrard also exhibited the Collars, and Badge, and

Stars of the Orders of the Garter; the Bath, the Thistle; and the very tasteful decoration of the new Order of the Star of India; the ornament of the latter consists of a miniature enamelled portrait of Her Majesty, surrounded with brilliants.

An Equestrian Statuette of Cœur-de-Lion, a model of Artillerymen with Fieldpiece, and two Sideboard Dishes, in the centre of which are the cancelled Great Seal of England—were interesting. The dishes were presented by the Queen to Lords Campbell and Chelmsford, and the cancelled seal set within them forms a graceful and appropriate memento to the Chancellor's office which those noblemen held.

More ambitious but less successful works were a large Table Ornament and a pair of Candelabra, made for his Highness Dhuleep Singh, which have been carried out, we are told, "in a style purely Hindoo, without any admixture of Mohammedan or otherwise."

A beautiful Silver *Repoussé* Table was exhibited by Messrs. Elkington, designed and executed for them by Morel Ladeuil. The work, which it took three years to execute, preserves all its delicacy, and entirely avoids the broken lights and reflection which polished silver must ever give. The subject is the poetical influence of sleep: the artist, to simplify his idea, has limited himself to three principal figures—Agriculture, Music, and War: and under these three exhibits some of the doings of Queen Mab as described by Shakspeare. Round the border is a fantastic creation in the German manner, not unworthy of Wagner, formed of reptiles and monsters, and intended to represent the nightmare dreams of the sleepers. This silver table was removed to Windsor to be shown to Her Majesty and replaced next day. In the same description of work, and not inferior to the latter in merit, were a silver Dish and Ewer, and a most elaborately magnificent Desert Service in silver and enamel, value 2000 guineas.

Messrs. Elkington also exhibited several examples of their Silver and Gold work, which had been specially lent by Her Majesty, for whom they were manufactured. Among these was a present made by the Queen to the Prince Consort on his last birthday—a statute of Lady Godiva in silver on a pedestal of mixed silver and gold; also, a pair of Candelabra for Balmoral, of mixed silver and gold, the designs for which were drawn by the late Prince himself.

Smith and Nicholson showed several fine examples of Presentation Plate; including the Hayter, Montefiore, and Mechi Testimonials; and Mr. Thomas exhibited the Plate given to Lord Stamford, as the result of a penny subscription among the people of Leicester, for his Lordship's liberality in throwing open to the public his park at Bradgate.

Mr. Emanuel showed a model, by Marshall Wood, of his Royal Highness the Prince of Wales as Colonel of the 100th Regiment, acknowledging a salute: the likeness of the Prince is accurate, and the horse is spirited and free. A Silver Ewer in *repoussé* throughout, 27in. high, and covered with chasing illustrative of

La Motte Fouqué's "Undine," was very praiseworthy and delicate. In the same case were some novelties in silverwork combined with wood ; a Service made of English oak, polished, ornamented with silver mountings ; and a complete Service, the design of which is taken from old hanaps in the Louvre, parcel-gilt, with figures in oxydized silver.

Hunt and Roskell exhibited a large assemblage of Works in Silver, mostly English Race Prizes, from the year of the Exhibition 1851, with many other works. Almost all these works are in cast silver, from models ; but not only have the models been carefully executed by the artists themselves, but they have been thoroughly well finished and chased afterwards.

Mr. H. H. Armstead was the designer and chaser of the Outram and Pakington Shields, the Kean and Manchester Fine-arts Testimonials, and other pieces of work, chiefly in oxydised silver. The Pakington shield illustrates the career of Sir John Pakington, and is full of really fine work ; the figures are well conceived and drawn, the faces have character and life, the draperies are excellent. The Outram shield is marked by the same painstaking accuracy and artistic taste, in the groups of Bhils in their conquest and civilization, the death of Meer Mahommed Khan, the charge of the Bombay Cavalry on the Persian square, and the other incidents which fill the circle. The centre contains a group of mounted officers, portraying Sir James Outram receiving the command of the force from Sir Henry Havelock, to whom he had so chivalrously intrsusted it : his work is conventional, but bold and spirited.

Mr. Armstead has been less successful in the Kean Testimonial, consisting of a tall Vase for a Centrepiece, two Candelabra, Groups, and Dessert-stands : bearing scenes and groups from those plays of Shakspeare in which Mr. Kean has achieved his greatest successes : the character portraits of Mr. and Mrs. Charles Kean and Miss Chapman, are admirable likenesses. An equestrian Statuette in bronze of the Duke of Wellington is a good and graceful work, very much better than half of our public statues ; and the Manchester Fine Arts Testimonial, formed of a single Pillar, around the mid base of which are three figures of Painting, Sculpture, and Industrial Art, and surmounting which is a figure of Genius struggling with an Eagle, is both graceful and excellent in execution.

To those who prefer the Frosted Silver to the Oxydised, the productions of Mr. Thomas Brown and Mr. A. T. Barrett afforded a pleasing contrast. The works of the former artist are very solid and thorough, full of painstaking endeavour and finish. Such is the Masterman Testimonial, and those presented to Sir R. M. Stephenson, Canon Dale, and others. More ambitious are his efforts in the Scarlett and Seymour Testimonials, in which much good modelling and artistic merit are to be found.

A Rose-water Fountain in Silver, partly Gilt, presented by the Queen to his Highness the Maharaja Runbeer Sing, is a favourable specimen of the power of Mr. Barrett—the figures of a Shiek soldier, an officer, and an English General and soldier, all correct and spirited.

Mr. Hancock made a remarkably fine display of *Repoussé* Work, the most original being a series of Vases illustrative of the Poetry of England. The centre one is dedicated to Shakspeare, and on each are Cups and Tazze to the honour of Milton, Byron, Moore, and Burns;—each of them being ornamented with scenes from the principal Dramas and Poems of those whom they are intended to honour.

Other works in Plate shown by Mr. Hancock included a large copy of an old Majolica Vase, made of Silver and Gold, with all the details and ornaments given with marvellous truthfulness. There was a most artistic group representing Gurth and Wamba, from *Ivanhoe:* the modelling of the figures was very fine, and the entire conception highly artistic. Near this was a Tazza in Silver, crowned by a figure of an archangel; it was designed and made for the Prince of Hohenzollern: it is a fine specimen of chasing, and remarkable for its extreme finish and pleasing outline. A Cup made for Her Majesty has a Zephyr standing on a Globe, and represented as borne through the air by the wind on her fairy-like sails: the foot of the vase is ornamented with allegorical figures of Commerce and the Sea. The Battle of the Standard is a stirring group of plate presented by the Earl of Sefton to his Regiment of the Guards upon his giving up the command. The body of the work is a clock-case of ebony. Two Figures in frosted silver are above the clock-face, and at each of the four corners of the base is a soldier of the Guards, portraits of men who had most distinguished themselves in the ranks. Another characteristic group in silver is one belonging to Lord Forester: it represents several of the members of the Belvoir Hunt. The figures—men, horses, and dogs—are all portraits. We are assured that throughout Mr. Hancock's splendid collection, the Plate is the work of English artists and workmen.

Mr. Keith exhibited Chalices for Sacramental uses, which were much admired. In one, the hexagonal stem was ornamented with diamonds and carbuncles; the figures on the foot personifying the Crucifixion, the Lord's Supper, and the Evangelists. Another chalice had the base set with rubies, carbuncles, and pearls—on the knop, turquoises and carbuncles. A third Chalice was jewelled with large diamonds, amethysts, and pearls, coral, and a cameo of the Madonna; the knop enamelled, and set with turquoises and pearls.

With few exceptions, the English Works in Silver gave a flat denial to some discreditable reports circulated by the French press, viz.—that our metal is heavy, tasteless, and cumbrous, that our artists are untaught and ignorant, and that when we do succeed our chief artists are Frenchmen. These calumnies are merely noticed to be denied.

Messrs. Emanuel exhibited a superb Cup, cut from a single

Topaz, mounted on enamelled gold work, in general form of design and outline resembling the celebrated Nautilus cup belonging to the Queen; but representing the story of Perseus and Andromeda, instead of St. George and the Dragon. It is treated entirely in the Cellini style. This cup, which cost 2000*l*. to manufacture, has been purchased by Mr. Marjoribanks.

A Toilet-glass and Stereoscope, executed by Mr. Emanuel, for the late Sultan for one of the ladies of his harem, by its costly splendour, gave rise to uncomfortable recollections of the national balance-sheet at the commencement of the present reign. The frame and stand of the toilet-mirror (of crystal), are of fine gold, richly chased, and thickly studded with large diamonds, emeralds, pearls, and rubies. The Stereoscope stand is an ordinary-shaped box of ivory, on a pillar and stand of the same materials, set all over thickly with diamonds, emeralds, and rubies. The value of these two little presents is about 15,000*l*.

Of Imitations of the Precious Metals, the specimens exhibited were very numerous, including Argentine and Electro-plate; Sheffield and other plate; plated Gold Jewellery; Medals; Enamelled Gold and Silver Jewels, in antique style; Electro-gilding, &c. Elkington and Co. exhibited a fine assemblage of Manufactures in Silver, Electro-plate, Bronze, and Enamelled Metal, including a Silver Dressing-table and Mirror, in Alhambresque style; and a large centre-piece and other portions of a Dinner-service for 100 persons in Electro-plate, made for the Duke of Brabant.

ALUMINIUM ARTICLES.

Aluminium, first obtained in England in the spring of 1855, alloys well with copper, forming what is now called Aluminium Bronze. When an alloy of this kind, containing from three to five per cent. of Aluminium, is "dipped" in aquafortis, it acquires a tint so like that of gold that it is impossible to distinguish one from the other, even when seen side by side. It is susceptible of a fine polish, and may be cast, rolled, hammered, and drawn out into fine wire. The Bronze usually made contains 10 per cent of Aluminium. It possesses great tenacity, but tarnishes by exposure to the air. According to Sir William Armstrong it has properties of much value in the arts.

M. Morin and Deville, in the French Department of the Exhibition, had an admirable display of Aluminium, exemplifying every important quality of the metal. There were statuettes and various cast objects, including latch-keys, which combine lightness with strength; there was the metal rolled into large sheets beaten into leaves, drawn into fine wire and woven into lace, coined into medals, plated upon copper; and Aluminium Bronze was shown in profusion, wrought as well as unwrought. The eagles on the standards of the French army are of Aluminium; and examples of these were exhibited. Aluminium Medals were shown; there was also an Aluminium Helmet; and what metal can be so suitable for this purpose, on account of its extreme lightness.

In the same department, P. Mourey presented beautiful specimens of Cups, &c., partially electro-gilt. There were also shown soldered Aluminium Tubes. The soldering of this metal has been attended with much difficulty. We understand that it is now effected with zinc in an atmosphere of hydrogen. Mourey's collection has been secured by the Conservatoire des Arts et Métiers, in Paris, and this is ample testimony to its value.

In the English Department, Bell Brothers, of Newcastle-on-Tyne, showed among other Aluminium objects, a large Bowl fashioned under the hammer; ornamental groups of Horses, Timepiece, Candlesticks, Telescopes, &c.; and the figure of an Owl in Aluminium, cast, and subsequently chased. They had also a series showing the materials employed in the manufacture of Aluminium and Sodium. Leaf Aluminium has lately been used for lettering, in bookbinding. Among the *Curiosities* of this new metal should be mentioned a small Aluminium Casket, made for Miss Burdett Coutts, at the cost of about 150*l*.

JEWELLERY.

The large Diamond, "The Star of the South," was shown in the Foreign Nave, as a contribution from Amsterdam, by M. E. Coster; this Diamond is of immense size, weighing no less than 125 carats. It is set in the centre of a magnificent star of brilliants. Its colour, however, is by no means so good as that of the Koh-i-noor. Around the stand on which "the Star of the South" was shown was a most interesting collection of Diamonds from various mines, in every stage of progress, from the rough stone to the finished brilliant; and a brief printed description at the foot of each made the whole method of cutting and polishing as clear as if the process took place before the eyes of the visitor.

A large Brilliant Drop, the property of Mr. Dresden, and the largest now for sale in Europe, was also exhibited: it weighs 76¼ carats, or 306 grains: price 50,000*l*. Messrs. Garrard also showed a magnificent Necklace of four rows of Pearl, with a Sapphire and Diamond snap; a superb Brilliant Necklace of thirty large and very fine Brilliants, with Earrings and Bracelets to match. There was also a magnificent collection of tiaras, necklaces, bracelets, and brooches of every variety of precious stone; pink Pearls and black Diamonds, Rubies of every tint, Amethysts, Emeralds, and Brilliants.

Mr. Hancock exhibited, in his well-appointed display, a Diamond Necklace, the price of which was 85,000 guineas. Amongst his noticeable gems were an Emerald and Diamond suit of good colour and lustre; a Diamond and Sapphire suit. Diamonds have greatly increased in value of late years, having been much in demand, through the frequency of the rapid attainment of wealth, of which the diamond is regarded as the paramount representative.

In Mr. Hancock's case was also exhibited the Devonshire Emerald (the largest in the world), and the Devonshire Jewels, one of the rarest and most artistic collections of antique gems in existence. These were shown amid a perfect galaxy of Pearls, Opals, Rubies, Brilliants, and Topazes : in this case were exhibited jewels to the value of 300,000*l.* Altogether, the Diamond bouquets, bracelets, pendants, and other ornaments of our chief firms were unrivalled ; and the many customers amongst the chief nobility of the Continent, and the passion which both Russian and French gentlemen have for English jewellery, will confirm us in the assertion that in this class our nation has borne away the palm.

London and Ryder exhibited a wonderful specimen of Diamond-setting, with a miniature Portrait of the Queen, composed of distinct Brilliants almost as fine as diamond-dust, and of which more than 2000 were required to complete the portrait.

Hunt and Roskell exhibited the Nassuck and Arcot Diamonds, the property of the Marquis of Westminster. The Arcot consists of three gems, a round one, 125 grains, and two drops, 223½ grains : of the very finest quality and water. The Nassuck weighs 340 grains : it was bought by the late Marquis of Westminster for 7000*l.*, and was once worn by his lordship on the hilt of his Court sword. Hunt and Roskell also showed a string of 32 remarkably fine Pearls, each 39 grains, and the whole valued at 8000*l.* They contributed likewise a parure of diamonds intermingled with very large turquoises of perfect colour ; another, very delicate, of brilliants and pale coral-tinted pearls ; a bouquet of diamonds, consisting of full-blown rose, carnations, fuchsias, and other flowers, tied with a ribbon, and mounted on springs to form a stomacher ; various tiaras of excellent arabesque, star, and scroll patterns ; and a dazzling bracelet, with emerald set diamondwise in the centre. Among the minor objects were a brooch and earrings of small diamonds, each representing a leaf with pink coral berry adhering to it ; and a moss-rose-bud with leaves, also imitated in diamonds, the flower pink topaz. They likewise exhibited a very large and fine Ruby, the property of Mr. R. S. Holford. Two other stones of great purity, colour, and brilliance, were a Sapphire, 680 grains ; and a Ruby spinelle, 323 grains ; both surrounded with large brilliants : the ruby has been cut from a stone possessed by various Kings of Delhi. There was also shown a Necklace of the choicest Hungarian opals, set round with dim imitative emeralds ; likewise fine black Pearls, Pearls in the shell, Emeralds in the matrix, Opals, Rubies, and Sapphires. Widowson and Veale exhibited two strings of fine Pearls, with two pendants, valued at 2800*l.*

Mr. Emanuel, in an ebony and bronze trophy in the Nave, exhibited some costly articles ; as an Emerald brooch, mounted in Diamonds, valued at 10,000*l.* ; a very fine suite of Opals and

Diamonds; and an effective diamond and pearl Bracelet, with butterfly clasp—the centre, pearl with diamond and emerald wings.

Mr. Phillips, of Cockspur-street, exhibited som every beautiful Ornaments made of pink and fancy coral: some almost white, other specimens variegated, others of a kind of flesh-colour: the price which fine pink coral has now attained is enormous. Never, probably, has such a varied display of the rarest corals been brought together before—of every shape and tint, from pure white to pink, deep red, and amost black. Some of the coral tiaras shown must have excited the astonishment even of the Italian exhibitors, who themselves showed some wonderful specimens. Mr. Phillips's reproductions of the Etruscan, Greek, and Egyptian jewellery rivalled even the famous specimens of M. Castellani, especially in the Etruscan work, which is equivalent in fineness to the rarest examples of Indian and Maltese filigree gold. Howell and James, among their Jewels, showed a suite in Turquoises, Pearls, and Diamonds, designed in Etruscan style; a Holbein suite, in variegated enamels, with Carbuncles, Emeralds, and Diamonds, as neck pendants.

Mr. Lambert's greatest novelty was some Crystal Intaglios engraved by Mr. Charles Cook, and afterwards coloured to the life; pretty objects of jewellery, either as lockets, brooches, or solitaires. Thus the semblance of some brilliant bird, or characteristic head of dog, horse, or stag is rendered with the colours and roundness of nature; this effect being gained by cutting into the reverse of the crystal an intaglio of the form and depth required, which is afterwards coloured.

Thomson and Profage showed an Opal of a very large size—probably, they state, the largest yet found—set as a brooch with brilliants; and a fanciful piece of jewellery called the "dolphin suite"—a necklace composed of diamonds and pearls, with dolphins of green enamel, from the mouths of which hang escallop-shell pendants of pink enamel, each holding a pearl.

Messrs. Emanuel, of Portsmouth, exhibited some very rich jewels extremely well set, and equalling the general run of jewels exhibited by London firms. Messrs. Loenstark, of the Strand, had a display of Masonic Jewels and "Paraphernalia," and Filigree-work. Messrs. Marshall, of Edinburgh, showed some Gold and Silver Jewellery in the antique style, enamelled and worked in that way which has been prevalent in Scotland for some centuries; and Rettie, Middleton, and Sons, of Aberdeen, a whole series of Scotch Jewellery. Professor Tennant, of the Strand, exhibited a series of the principal stones used in jewellery, which gave the visitors an insight into the difficulties as well as the material of the jeweller's art, and showed them how much practical skill and knowledge is wanted to give effect and beauty of form to the stones with which the lapidary furnishes the jeweller. Mr. Tennant's house has long been celebrated in connexion with Diamonds; he having succeeded John Mawe, who many years since, travelled into the diamond countries of Brazil, and wrote practically upon the history of the gem.

Amidst a blaze of modern jewellery, the visitor was brought face to face with the most ancient: In the case of M. Castellani, of Rome, already mentioned, we found goldwork imitated from jewellery taken from the cemeteries of Etruria and Greece. Coral Necklaces, Earrings, and Brooches were exhibited by Ambrosini, of Naples ; Red Coral and Lava work by G. Fusco; and Filigrane or Filigree Work in Silver by Emilio Forte, of Genoa. The gondola, vase, casket, steamer, entourages for the hair, pins, and books in this ingenious but trifling work, were very good. Peluffo, of Cagliari, showed some peasants' jewellery. From the peasants Castellani gained the chief of his hints towards the resuscitation of his art; and in the recesses of the Apennines, far from the centre of civilization, he found existing a special school of traditional jewellery similar in method and workmanship to the antique.

France and other countries also showed very beautiful Jewels and specimens of workmanship in gold and silver ; but the united value of all the foreign collections would not amount to half of that shown by the London jewellers alone.

M. L. Rouvenant, of Paris, exhibited a Diadem (style of Henry II.) in diamonds ; *une grande broche dragon*, formed by diamonds, rubies, emeralds, and pearls set in gold and silver, and ornamented with exotic foliage. In jewelled work M. Rouvenant showed a Pompeiian Bracelet in gold, decorated with enamelled ornaments, and bearing an emerald of a light colour cut as a cameo and surrounded with diamonds.

M. E. Granger, of Paris, showed an interesting collection of " Bijoux historiques pour costumes de Théâtres ; " and imitation Jewellery, taken from pictures, statues, and other known examples. M. Payen exhibited some Jewels of matted filigree ; M. Casalta some Sculptured Coral and Cameos of rare beauty ; and M. Dontin some delicate Enamel-work ; a Head-ornament of wheat-ears and diamonds, and a ring in which are ingeniously set diamonds of every colour. MM. Marret and Beaugrand exhibited six strings of very fine Pearls said to be worth 18,000*l.* ; colour very good, their tint orient, and form nearly perfect. M. Petiteau produced a very fine Brooch of diamonds with drop-shaped emerald pendants ; a Diadem of diamonds ; a Brooch of antique cameo, mounted in a pure Grecian style ; and a complete Parure, formed of cabochon emeralds and diamonds, in the Oriental style.

M. Phillippi showed a very fine Necklace of diamonds and pearls ; and another of brilliants, with emeralds cut as cameos. This cameo-cutting upon hard stones, rubies, emeralds, sapphires, and amethysts is carried on to an apparently large extent in France and Italy.

M. Bonnebakker, of Amsterdam, and Messrs. Toon, showed Netherlanders' Gold and Silver head-dresses, very curious ; and in the Norway Court was a collection of Norwegian peasants' bridal ornaments in silver.

Austria exhibited some excellent Jewellery. M. Peppe, of Vienna, had a Bracelet of Gold, so constructed that the wearer may not lose is.

In Imitative Jewellery, Mr. Emanuel exhibited some ornaments made in ivory and gold inlaid with various gems—a process which he has patented—which certainly produce a good effect; combining cheapness, softness, and a certain adaptability of colour to almost any complexion or dress. In the same case was shown a suite of Stones cut upon a new method (Mitford's), by which the facets are rendered mathematically correct, and the face of each facet is a perfect level, which, under the old system, was the case with neither. By this means, more actual reflexion of light is given from the stone; and this was shown in the specimens, but more especially in the large white topaz and a nine-sided brilliant of common brown quartz.

Howell and James exhibited a small suite of white Sidmouth Pebbles with antique setting brightened with small beads of Purple Enamel; also, some Intaglios belonging to the Marquis of Breadalbane. The novelties in Mr. Attenborough's collection were Gold Ornaments of a large buttercup pattern, the open petals forming a shallow basin with central tuft in jewels.

Among Scotch Jewellery, Messrs. Muirhead, of Glasgow, displayed Native Minerals in very attractive dress. A Cairngorm Brooch, in which the stone is supported by diminutive stags' heads and antlers in Silver, is very well designed; also, a suite of the same stones mounted in Gold inlaid with Pebbles, imitative of the popular cinque-cento.

In the French Court were shown some Imitations made by M. Savary, including a tiara of Mock Diamonds and some Rings and other Ornaments set with paste, rubies, and emeralds, exceedingly close imitations of the real, which might be worn at a party without any risk of detection.*

M. Vales showed some real and imitation Pearls strung alternately on the same string; and so well made are the false that unless a jeweller had them in his hand and tested them by the weight and size of the bore, he would be unable to distinguish the imitation from the real. M. Topart had also four strings of Pearls, two of them real and two false, which the uninitiated could not distinguish; yet one may be set down as costing about 8f., and the other about 800*l.*

A fine specimen of Cameo-cutting was exhibited,—a head of the Emperor of the French—an admirable portrait—set in Diamonds, which was bespoken by the Empress, at the price of 250*l.*

---

* The writer (in the *Illustrated London News*) relates:—"We have indeed heard of a certain Dowager Duchess who, taking advantage of her rank and position, wears imitation jewellery almost exclusively, and yet gets the credit of airing the old family jewels without the risk of exposure or the danger of losing gems of great value. We have reason to know that this lady is not a solitary instance, even without quoting the celebrated Hoggarty diamond, the history of which was once written so pleasantly by Mr. Thackeray."

GLASS, FOR DECORATIVE AND HOUSEHOLD PURPOSES.

STAINED GLASS.

The display of Painted Windows in the Exhibition was a very large one, and the first of the kind that has been seen in this country. It was, however, fuller of promise than performance,—in the original treatment of subjects, in place of copying epochal styles and methods of execution. Some years have elapsed since Mr. Ballantine published his treatise exposing the absurdity of continuing to copy bad drawing and other antique grotesqueness; and it has, doubtless, contributed to the improved taste evident in this branch of art. In the *Builder*, No. 1019, is an excellent review of this progress; and from this source we borrow the substance of our notes.

Among French exhibitors, M. Gloner, of Nancy, showed a Window, 12th century, good as imitative art: but in a Window of the 16th century ("Christ crowned with Thorns"), the artist has made the leaded joinings as inconspicuous as possible.* M. Bougens, of Rheims, showed an example, in which no brilliant colours are made use of, but all the effects are produced through subdued tones of comparatively pale colour. M. Lusson had some powerful imitations of old glass. Some of the cleverest Foreign Glass was exhibited by Maréchal and Co., of Metz; but, it is remarked, in the *Builder*, "their works are rather *pictures on glass* than glass-painting." Signor Bertini, of Milan, exhibited a "Virgin and Child," to which a Medal was justly awarded "for colour, design, and execution."

Hardman and Co. showed their fine series of Windows for All Souls', Oxford; each wholly filled with figures rising one above the other. This series and the artists' Window for the Norwich crypt gained their Medal. Their immense Window for Doncaster Church was the largest work of painted glass in the Exhibition: it consists of eight lofty lights, each containing three pictures from the life of Christ: the ornament is better than the figure-subject. It is admirably engraved in the *Illustrated London News*, No. 1166.

Chance Brothers showed a small three-light Window, "The Adoration," 16th century, of high finish. But their chief work was their Robin Hood Window, designed in the Albert Durer feeling, or still later German style; the canopy-work is florid flamboyant.

Ballantine and Son, Edinburgh, exhibited three Windows, Italian, late Cinque-cento, executed for the Glasgow Commercial Bank: the figures, Commerce, Agriculture, Mechanics, &c., are

---

* This concealment of the frame-work was well carried out in the large Painted Window of the Tournament of the Field of Cloth of Gold, executed by Wilmshurst, and exhibited in Oxford-street, in 1830: in this window, which occupied the entire end of a room, all the frames were concealed in the dark shadows of the composition, which resembled a vast sheet of painted glass: it was, unfortunately, burnt in an accidental fire, which entirely destroyed the premises. The size of the window was 18 by 24 feet.

good. The artists had also a large "Crucifixion" Window, for Prestonlee Church, in which the compositions are so managed that no leadwork joinings are visible.

Lavers and Barraud gained a Medal for their Window of "The Last Judgment," with a myriad of figures, marvellously minute—the most intricate stained glass in the Exhibition—in fact, a transparent mosaic.

Messrs. Cox showed in a Window some brilliant effects, by the irregular thickness of the glass—sparkling with "palpitation of light." Heaton and Co. received a Medal for their Window for St. Alban's Abbey. Baillie and Co. showed a portion of an "Adoration" Window for Morton Church, Lincolnshire, rich, yet sober in colour, and cleverly shaded. Clayton and Bell showed a 13th century Window, with excellent qualities; the subjects commencing with "The Temptation," and ending with "The Death of Abel." Messrs. Warrington exhibited examples of the gradations of this class of art during the whole of the Pointed Period: the subjects large, and the work sound: the heraldic work of this firm was specially commendable. Messrs. Powell received a Medal for their very skilful reproductions of Mediæval examples: an elaborate specimen of Grisaille was very fine. Altogether, our artists distanced Foreign competition, in the Exhibition.

The Embossed Glass of different colours is well spoken of for its rich, jewel-like effect.

HOUSEHOLD AND FANCY GLASS.

The manufactures of works of art in Glass proved as attractive as any class of the Exhibition; and British superiority over foreign competition was marked, and frankly and cordially acknowledged. France made very little attempt at rivalry; the Austrian glass was good in colour, and in their chandeliers was most effectively and artistically arranged; the Bohemian and Hungarian glass are special manufactures which were also admirably represented in the Building; but the pure cut crystal glass, for exquisite forms, whether cut, blown, or moulded, and, above all, for the very highest effects of the engraver's art, the visitor found in the English Court. The display was really wonderful. Here Dobson and Pearce, Pellatt, Phillips, Defries, Copeland, Green, Hodgetts, Naylor, Powell, and, in short, all the great glass-manufacturers and glass-dealers in England, sent their finest wares. Here were such triumphs of the engraver's art as Venice never knew: even wine-glasses fetched 6l. and 7l. a-piece. There were lustres and chandeliers, too, of all descriptions and almost every grade of excellence—from the simple classic design of Dobson and Pearce, worth 12l., up to the gorgeous crystal temple of Defries, which cost over 3000l. to manufacture.

First, for fine art work, both in form and marvellous perfection of engraving, was the collection shown by Dobson and Pearce. One of the great gems in this collection—an engraved Glass Tazza,

12 inches high, was purchased almost the first day it was shown for 250 guineas, incomparably the largest sum ever paid for a single and very small piece of modern glass-work. The panels in the cup, with their fine cut designs, are as delicately marked as steel engravings and as deep as intaglios, all cut with the wheel, even to the minutest chasing of its flower scroll-work. A very small Engraved Cup, not much larger than an ordinary tumbler, exquisitely engraved, was bought for 50 guineas the first hour it was seen. No piece of Venetian glass of the same size ever fetched so high a price.

A Claret Jug sold for 50 guineas, one side of which is deeply cut with a grotesque Raffaelesque design, of surpassing excellence; the foliage scroll-work—apes, dragons, and other monsters—being a perfect chapter on the weird combinations of Raffaelesque ornament. The birds in this piece seem to have an actual plumage, so exquisitely is every feather worked out in the cutting. In a somewhat similar work, the centre ornament is a group of water-lilies floating in a lake, produced with an effect almost equal to an optical delusion. So also with fountains on another class of works—they are not so much engraved as they seem to flow and ripple from the very body of the vase. Above Messrs. Dobson's collection was hung a wonderful Venetian Chandelier, of their modern manufacture, which in design and drooping of festoons was equal to the rarest old Venice types, only much more brilliant in its metal. In this Collection were also shown the cheapest, simplest, and most beautiful designs of Mr. Marsh, of the Lord Chamberlain's office, for table decoration, which took the first prize at the Horticultural Society's fête last year. Messrs. Phillips exhibited in the form of a Crystal Table, the most brilliant piece of cut glass in the Building. Behind it was placed a kind of épergne, or centre-piece for fruit and flowers, representing a pool with weeds and bulrushes in glass, and surrounded with nautilus-shells at the base, which altogether made up the most original and effective piece of this class in the display. Both these were manufactured by Messrs. Webb, of Stourbridge. Messrs. Pellatt's Engraved Glass also attracted such admiration that the firm received orders to make large Dessert Services of the same kind for the Prince of Wales and the Viceroy of Egypt: each service is to be so elaborate in design that many months will be required to complete them. The same firm showed cups, tumblers, and jugs of the most beautiful forms, covered with a perfect embroidery of exquisitely engraved designs: their copies of the Koh-i-noor in Crystal Glass, cut in the form in which this great diamond was first exhibited in 1851, were infinitely more brilliant than the renowned gem on its first *début*.

Alderman Copeland exhibited a few but most exquisite specimens of Engraved Glass, which, both for shapes, colour of metal, and minute elaboration, of engraved design, were inferior only to the gems of the same kind shown by Dobson, though the interval is wide between the comparative excellences of the two competitors. But in the general average of his exhibition of Cut Glass, Alderman Copeland had no superior. The jewelled Dessert Service of the brightest crystal, was a signal triumph of manufacturing skill: each piece has a lustre of its own that is brilliant beyond description. It is but just to add that this magnificent service was made from Mr. Copeland's designs by the firm of Webb, of Stourbridge.

Mr. Green, of the Thames Cut Glass Works, had a beautiful display of Cut Engraved Glass of every kind.

One of the newest and most effective objects in Decorative Glass was shown by Powell and Co. These were Vases of double glass, the outer one of pure flint, the inner coloured to resemble dark serpentine marble. Between the two are placed lightly printed photographs of statues, designs, flowers, &c., which show out as if finely engraved upon the marble; and these artistic effects are produced at the lowest possible cost. Messrs. Powell also showed some glass Chandeliers of a mixed twisted crystal and blue glass, which have an exceedingly pretty effect as branch lustres for a wall.

Naylor exhibited some exquisite chalice-shaped Cups, on which were engraved copies of the celebrated picture of the "Last Supper," equal to anything shown in the whole Class.

Among the more immediate novelties exhibited were Lloyd and Summerfield's Glass Window-bars; Moore's Ventilators and self-shadowed Glass; Mott's "Vessels for vivifying draught beer;" Rust's Soluble Glass, &c.

Osler, of Birmirmingham, the artist of the Great Crystal Fountain in the Exhibition of 1851, had in the recent display a pair of magnificent Glass Candelabra. But the most gorgeous attraction was one of the eight Prismatic Mirrors, which Messrs. Defries made for the late Sultan's new palace on the Bosphorus. This mirror is 15 feet high and 8 feet broad, and contains 1000 prisms. All the prisms join each other at the sides, so as to form one piece, and at the ends are dovelocked together and held into their place by a peculiar arrangement of copper rods. The weight of pure crystal is one ton, and the metal back one ton more. By the side of this Messrs. Defries showed their examples of Cut and Engraved Glass, decidedly the best for their very low price in the Building. Messrs. Defries also exhibited a vast Chandelier, with a base 14 feet in diameter, and 22 feet high.

> The body consists of three dishes beneath each other, formed of richly-cut prisms, each 3 feet 6 inches in length; a size which has, we believe, never before been attained. From these spring 112 lights. Then we have columns, and diamond-cut pillars; the upper tier of 56 lights being a prismatic vase, again supporting eight pillars. The dome, surmounted by a coronet and plume, is formed of a single piece of elaborately-cut glass resting on pillars and prisms, the interspaces filled by diamond-cut glass and spangles.

The Bohemian Fancy Glass exhibited was very beautiful, especially in its combinations of glass-enamel colours and painting.

POTTERY.

In the highest efforts of Ceramic art the English exhibitors were as successful as in their superiority in Glass.

The largest Work of this class in the Building was the Majolica Fountain, placed under the eastern dome. In its variety of form and colour it harmonizes with the internal arrangement and decoration of the Building: it was designed and modelled by Mr. John Thomas, the sculptor, and executed under his superintendence for the display of Minton's modern Majolica. The design, while very elegant and symmetrical as a whole, has that bold distribution of parts which is essential in a fountain to be in keeping with the wild play of water, especially in the open air. The mass of the fountain is in stone; the figures and ornaments, which are for the most part emblematical, being added in majolica. This is the finest work of the kind ever executed in this country, and proves that majolica may be made a most important department of industrial and decorative art. The following are the details of the design:—

The central portion is circular in form; having four niches, enriched with diaper pattern in blue and gold. Between these niches are caryatides, emblematical of Victory, bearing between their outstretched arms a wreath of laurel. Each figure is crowned with a coronet of laurel, coloured after nature. The faces and arms are also of natural tints. The wings, which meet in the lower extremities, are white, slightly relieved with grey. The frieze above carries the motto "St. George for Merrie England and Victory." Above these figures is a cornice, capped with ornaments, the red and white rose, twenty in number. Surmounting the centre stands the figure of St. George, about 7 feet in height, destroying the Dragon. Against the lower part of the pedestal stands a vase, opposite each niche, supported on a tripod formed of winged griffins. Between these, but rather lower, is a lion seated, holding a shield with the cross of St. George emblazoned upon it. These lions are placed at the angles of the main base, which is square on plan, with a truss projecting from the angle. At the end of each of these trusses stands one of the bird fountains, with nymphs and shell-basins, which adorn the Royal Dairy at Windsor. Between the trusses are basins, semicircular in form; the upper one being devoted to plants, and the lower to the receiving of water flowing from above. On the enclosure of the large basin which surrounds the whole are eight tazze, upon pedestals. The outer edge of this basin is decorated with the laurel, of its natural colour, banded, and the rose in full bloom, upon a chocolate ground. The entire height of the fountain is about 30 feet. The diameter of the outer basin is 40 feet. Seven thousand gallons of water per hour are required to supply it. The water was frequently perfumed by the process of Messrs. Rimmell and Co.

Minton's display comprised Earthenware, China, Parian; and specimens of Majolica, Palissy, and Limoges; imitations of the Crackle china of the East; and examples of the Henri II. Oriental style of Pottery. Two large candelabra of Palissy were of beautiful form and fine colour. Here were also reproductions of the famous old Sèvres *Bleu de roi*, *Rose de Barry*, turquoise, and others: some magnificent Jardinieres are painted from the famous Boucher pictures in the Louvre; and others with the Muses, from Lesneur. Minton's specimens of Majolica included five large dishes painted with the Triumphs of Julius Cæsar, from the tapestries of Mantegna, at Hampton-court Palace. Porphyry and Malachite were imitated in vases, with gold enrichments.

There were busts in parian of the Queen and the late Prince Consort, by Marochetti; and statuettes of the Royal children. A parian Venus, cast from the antique, and Summer and Autumn in the Renaissance style, were also shown. The floor of the Court was a pavement of 150,000 pieces; and on the walls were glazed tiles, in enamel colours, from designs by the best architects and artists.

The Wedgwood Collection, exhibited by the descendants of Josiah Wedgwood, nobly represented his famous ware in Etruscan vases, Nevers blue vases, and classic forms, painted with pastoral and other subjects.

The next display was from the Hill Pottery of Sir James Duke and Nephews, and comprised a superb Dessert-service of Parian figures and groups, and Vases from the antique, with amethystine Baskets, classic and other paintings, with gold enrichments; and the plates painted with flowers, and poetical figure-subjects. Their Parian Statuary included a bust of the young Augustus from the antique. Some Jet-ware, upon dead-black bisque grounds, was very effective.

A costly dessert-service, manufactured for Her Majesty at the Royal Porcelain Works, Worcester, by W. H. Kerr and Co., is unique in its application of colour to enamels, enamel decoration to a service, and the general treatment of the design: its cost and difficulty of production being immensely increased by no device being repeated; while each plate contains five subjects, and for the plates alone upwards of four hundred designs were made.

All the enamels of past ages have been wrought upon dark grounds, which is inapplicable to a dessert-service—hence the older colour had to be abandoned, and it has been judiciously replaced by a beautiful Oriental turquoise, which not only forms a novelty in enamel-work, but contrasts pleasingly with the chased and burnished gold.

The whole of this service was produced under the immediate approval of the late Prince Consort, and the design for each article was submitted before being modelled. His late Royal Highness took the deepest interest in encouraging this manufacture.

The Worcester cases also contained a number of beautifully executed objects, of unique design: as the Oyster-shell and Puck salt-cellars, wonderfully grotesque and original; and the coloured statuettes from the Shakespeare service presented to the Dublin Society. The Worcester Enamels were very fine; and the decorative articles of peculiar elegance.

Alderman Copeland exhibited a collection of articles remarkable for their extreme beauty and artistic excellence. Here was a Parian dessert-service, the centre piece being groups of nymphs supporting golden baskets for fruit and flowers, the draperies being delicate blue, and the ornaments gold: the plates are pierced and chased, and hand-painted with flowers. Here likewise was shown one of the largest vases ever made in England, 5 feet high: on the neck and foot are Cupids wreathing flowers, in raised and chased gold, upon pale-green, relieved by panels of

French white. There were likewise some admirable works in the new Ceramic Marble invented by Mr. T. Battam, including a set of classic urns, and statuettes from Monti's designs of Night and Morning, in which the difficulties of the massive drapery and the veils over their faces are surmounted in a manner that makes these specimens a perfect mystery to foreign manufacturers. A dejenner-service, the largest piece painted after Turner, the English Claude, by Lucas, a Staffordshire artist, was much admired. Here likewise were an ewer and flower-vases, excellently imitated from the old Limoges ware.

The Works exhibited by Rose and Co.,* of Coalport, included vases of every period of Sèvres, most successfully reproduced; two of these examples were awarded Prize Medals. There were also some large pieces of original design, which entitle the artist and modeller to special commendation. The nucleus of this fine display was the "Paul Potter Tray," which has been secured for a ducal collection. The material, form, and painting of this beautiful work, have been rewarded by a Prize Medal. To Messrs. Rose's delicate and brilliant turquoise and *Rose de Barry*, they have now added the Mauve and Magenta tints, in various articles of tasteful design: a dessert-service in turquoise also showed great advancement in porcelain-painting. We need scarcely say anything of the high repute of the Coalport Works: their productions are remarkable for purity of colour as well as form: their excellent white we are glad to see employed in goods for ordinary use; and we must not forget that English artists and artisans have produced the whole of these works. We should not omit to mention some perfect specimens of the famous Egg-shell China, which the Chinese themselves have lost the art of making, but which by Messrs. Rose can now be equalled, if not surpassed, in one of our English factories.

It will be most convenient to notice the Foreign Porcelain under the respective countries.

THE PROCESS COURT.

Few places in the Building proved more attractive than this new Court. Here Day and Son, the great lithographers, showed the whole process of Chromo-lithography and Steel-plate Printing. The art of printing in colours has been brought by this firm to such perfection, that pictures, whether in oil or water, are reproduced with almost the force of drawing and delicacy of sentiment of the originals themselves. The copies from Landseer's and Haghe's works, shown by the same firm in the gallery, are masterpieces of this kind of printing. The mode of printing in colours was shown by working off impressions of the tinted lithograph views of the Building from the Horticultural Society's Gardens. This was produced in three printings. The first impression is that taken

* With whom are associated, in the *Official Catalogue*, Messrs. Daniell and Co., London.

from the drawing-stone, where only the black lines are produced; the next gives the warm tint or brown shading of the foreground; and the last fills in the blue fleecy sky. Thus, by printing from a mere stain upon a stone and relying upon the antagonism that exists between grease and water, the most variously coloured pictures can be produced at almost nominal cost.

In this Court was also shown the process of the Colour-printing of the large pictorial Work illustrative of the *Masterpieces of Art* in the Exhibition, about to be produced under the superintendence of Mr. J. B. Waring, who will be recollected for his able services to the Exhibition of 1851. In the above process there was to be seen much that was curious in the mode in which the colours are laid on, the paper having to pass through the press every time a new colour is added. The projectors have had, we understand, great difficulty in inducing the foreign exhibitors to permit their beautiful designs to be copied, but all the gems of the British side will be adequately preserved.

Miss Lavinia Jones, of Bradford-on-Avon, Wilts, exhibited her miniature Albion Printing-press, which she aims at introducing not merely as a source of amusement in parlours and libraries, but as a means of inducing women to learn the art of printing, for their subsistence in cases of necessity: some of Miss Jones's specimens were very elegant.

Here was also exhibited Steel-plate Printing, from the fine line engraving landscape of Church's celebrated picture of the Heart of the Andes. Unlike the more rapid movements of lithography, the printer has to be almost an artist himself to repeat on each impression the aerial effect and tone of colour that it has taken the engraver years to sketch upon the steel. This, like most other artistic labours, is of course a slow process, so that not more than seven good impressions are taken in a day.

Mr. M'Queen also showed the process of Steel and Lithographic Printing. Close at hand Mr. Reynolds exhibited the simple but most skilful process by which the common Clay Pipes are made: a roll as soft as putty is bored through its stem, moulded, and turned out a complete pipe before the visitor has time to observe what is being done. In another portion of the Court the Milwards showed the method of Needle-making, partly by a series of pretty models, where the manufacture went into branches that could not be attempted in the Building, such as the furnace-work, &c., and partly by the manufacturing process itself. Mr. Pinches exhibited his great Coinage-press for striking commemorative medals of the Building, in bronze and German silver, and which the demands of visitors kept in active operation all day long. Cohen's exceedingly simple, but most efficacious process of making the best Lead Pencils was shown in all its branches, from turning the rough sticks of cedar to pointing the finished pencil itself; and Mr. Kennan showed a very ingenious machine like a copying lathe, by which the most intricate forms of sculpture can be copied with the fidelity of the original model. The powers of this machine and the delicate work which it is capable of turning out were exemplified by a series of models in ivory, all produced by the apparatus in the hands of an amateur.

Here likewise were exhibited some experiments made for introducing mosaic wall-pictures into England, as at Rome, Ravenna, and, indeed, most parts of Italy. A committee, consisting of the Marquis of Salisbury, Mr. Layard, and Mr. Henry Cole, was formed for the purpose of making these experiments, and the result was shown in the Building by a Staffordshire workman making the mosaics out of dry powder by means of a hand-press. With this the powdered earth used in making them is compressed to about one-fifth of its bulk into a hard mass that can scarcely be broken, and in baking it again shrinks still smaller. These mosaics are made of various geometric forms, and by a very simple machine, which was also shown, can be cut to any shape required. The committee look forward, therefore, not merely to the introduction of a comparatively new and cheap decorative art in England, but one which will give large employment to women. The placing the mosaic of their manufacture is a very simple operation; any one with a knowledge of drawing and copying can as easily perform it as any kind of Berlin woolwork. The simplicity of this process will enable the mosaic pictures to be produced in a tithe of the time and at a fifth of the cost of Italian mosaics of the same kind. These latter are not cut geometrically at the commencement, but the piece is ground and cut expressly; and instead of being backed with cement, is copied from the front of the picture and stuck into it. Two of the panels of the Picture Gallery facing the Cromwell-road have two large mosaic pictures, executed after this English method; and a subscription is open for filling the several panels with similar pictures.

To the uninitiated each Sewing-machine seems twin brother to its neighbour. In this Court was shown almost every variety of sewing-machine working by hand-labour, and literally turning out yards of well-sewn cloth in the space of two or three minutes. Several of the Sewing-machines are described at pp. 160, 161.

Robinson and Co., of Milk-street, Cheapside, had at work a Silk-Velvet Loom capable of producing half a yard per day of fine velvet. It seems strange that, with all the advance in mechanical science, there has never yet been produced a silk-velvet loom capable of throwing its own shuttle, and cutting the pile of the web.—*Abridged from the Times.*

Among the new art-processes in this Department of the Exhibition to which a prominent place was assigned may be mentioned a cast of colossal size, of the Moses of Michael Angelo, illustrating a peculiar process of preparing plaster moulds by backing them with canvas, invented and patented by Owen Jones. The present figure is, however, to be regarded rather as *tour de force* in the application of the process than an illustration of the usage for which it is chiefly intended, which is the production of mouldings and every kind of sculptural decorations for the walls and ceilings of apartments. By the process in question, these can be produced, of the most elaborate design, at a much smaller cost than with plaster, papier-maché, or any other composition in use; and when injured they can be repaired more easily, and, of course, far more cheaply.

Another less ornamental, but perhaps more useful, article exhibited in the same quarter was the silicious preparation patented by M. Leoni, and which has obtained a Prize Medal: it is intended for the purpose of superseding the use of metal in machine bearings, gas-burners, and wine and beer taps. M. Leoni asserts for his invention that in the first two articles it will not heat, and will therefore remove a great source of danger; and in the latter will not permit the wine and beer to become sour.

SALVIATI'S MOSAICS.

These exquisite productions, by Salviati, are, probably, the most successful imitations of the ancient Byzantine mosaics which modern art has produced. In Venice, naturally, from its connexion with Constantinople, the traditions of the art were long preserved; and Signor Salviati, who was originally a doctor of laws, has devoted many years' labour to an investigation of the methods of the ancient workers in mosaics, in practical endeavours to reproduce all their characteristic effects. With what success he has worked might be seen in his exhibition; but a still stronger proof is that a year or two ago the Administration of the Church of St. Mark, at Venice, after a long and careful examination of various manufacturers of modern mosaics, entered into a contract with him, by which, for the next fifteen years, he is to keep in repair the magnificent ancient mosaics which adorn the church, and to supply any new ones which may be required. In addition to the mosaics there were also exhibited imitations of ancient chalcedony, which were perfectly unique. The materials with which Signor Salviati works are gold and silver enamels, coloured enamels, and chalcedony, which, perhaps, may be described as enamels of precious stones. The common base of all the three is glass, subjected to such varied treatment that it is difficult to recognise it in all the forms which it is made to assume. The characteristics of the coloured *smalti*, or plates, are that they may be produced in an infinite variety of shades; that they are pretty nearly indestructible, and can be cut readily into the most minute sections. In them the colour is diffused universally throughout every particle of the plate; but the gold and silver *smalti* are produced, apparently, by laying a thin sheet of metal on discs of glass, with the thinnest possible coat of glass over it, so that the original brightness of the gilding can never be tarnished or damaged by any external influence. Signor Salviati can produce any effect of which mosaics are capable, and with this additional advantage, that no polish is needed to give brilliancy to the colours, nor any layer of cement needed to fill up the interstices between the ill-fitting pieces. Of its adaptability to all kinds of works we had here numerous examples, from large church mosaics and pavements, to the most exquisite enamelled brooches, rings, and bracelets. These ornaments are made still more attractive by being mounted, in the peculiar Venetian style, in thick settings of dead gold with delicate tracery in relief, or wreaths of gold-filigree.—*Abridged from the Times.*

One of Salviati's specimens is of an early Byzantine character, being the figure of a saint on a gold ground, of course accurately reproduced from one of a series in the ancient Church of Monreale, near Palermo. The second is a copy of a fine head of St. Nicholas, the original of which forms part of the magnificent mosaic decorations that clothe a large portion of the interior of St. Sophia, at Constantinople. It is a very interesting specimen of late Greek art, and has, like many of the Byzantine illuminations in the manuscripts of the period, the name of the saint in Greek characters of a late style at the side of the head. It reads ΝΙΚΟΛΑΟΣ. The third specimen is a half figure of Christ from St. Mark's, at Venice, which is superior both in design and workmanship to either of the other specimens. It is in a style which would blend far better with our modern Gothic than the works of more Oriental character.

There were also in Salviati's display some tasteful vases, formed of a modern imitation of that kind of old Venetian glass-ware which, by an admixture of glasses of different colours, produced a marbled effect that is very pleasing. The reviver of this old style of glass-ware, Mr. Lorenzi Radi, has termed it "Agate chalcedony," which is a very pretty name. These glass vases are very gracefully mounted in silver filigree, and light gold or gilt work, of very delicate device; the form of the vases and the elegance of the mounting showing how the hand of taste may elevate into novelty and elegance the most ordinary materials. Mr. Beresford Hope is the purchaser of one of these elegant trifles.

In the Roman Court also were several fine specimens of mosaic; among which was a fine view of St. Peter's and a clever general view of Rome. There were some small specimens, composed of branches of flowering plants, produced by a mosaic inlay, which is encrusted in plain black marble. They are very superior to the Florentine specimens of coloured marble inlay, the flowers in these specimens being represented by the mosaic process with all the accuracy and beauty of painting. The flowers executed by this process in the actual specimens are forget-me-not and jasmine, both being treated with great taste and delicacy. The display of mosaic work in the Roman Court was rendered all the more interesting by the exhibition of a large case containing a selection of the tesseræ of which mosaic work is composed: the gradations of shade, of every decided tone, being very numerous, and produced with unvarying accuracy. The tesseræ of the ancient mosaics are said to have been formed of stones naturally of the colour required; but on the modern revival of the art, coloured glass or earthenware was substituted, the gold tesseræ being gilt, and then protected with an additional glaze.—*Abridged from the Builder.*

SUBSTANCES USED IN MANUFACTURES.

This Class included not only raw materials, or substances, but the manufactures themselves. It was very miscellaneous, and presented comparatively few striking novelties. It is scarcely possible to arrange them, except in large and comprehensive groups.

The first group—Oils, Fats, Wax, and their Products, included Candles and Soap. Langton, Bicknell, and Sons, of Newington Butts, showed samples of Sperm-oil and of Spermaceti in large crystalline masses of great beauty. Ogleby and Co., of Lambeth, exhibited specimens of refined Spermaceti in crystalline masses, which assume the form of large coral branches of Paraffin and of Stearic Acid; together with candles manufactured from those substances, all, but especially those of Paraffin, remarkable for the beauty of their appearance. Neighbour and Sons arranged a collection of Oil-seeds and Nuts, together with samples of the Oils for manufacturing and machine purposes procured from them. Brecknell and Turner made a fine display of Coloured Candles of various materials. A collection of large and elaborately-ornamented Tapers for church use in the mediæval style was shown by Tucker and Co. The stand of the Price's Patent Candle Company was composed of gilt palm-trees with their branches arching over the upper part of the case: within were arranged, in decorative as well as instructive order, specimens of Palm Oil and Glycerine, of Candles and Soap in the composition of which they enter; and of other products connected with their manufacture.

In Soap the Eastern Annexe was particularly rich; not a few of the exhibitors having sent large blocks of several cubic feet as samples of their manufacture. The most conspicuous of these colossal cakes of soap were those sent by Cowan and Sons, of Barnes, and by Cook and Co., of Bow. In the case of the latter, which contained every variety of household soap, the white curd, the pale yellow, the mottled, and the old-fashioned yellow, there was an obelisk of marine soap, such as may be used in sea-water. In the same Sub-class, Field, of Wigmore-street, had a remarkable collection of Paraffin Candles, of brilliantly clear and transparent appearance; and the West of England Soap Company contributed the various descriptions of Soaps used in silk-throwing, spinning, and dyeing woollen manufactures, &c. Lastly, we had "Soap from Grease recovered from Soap-suds."

In advance of the grease of other days, the "Anti-attrition," Alderman Rose sent railway train and other Greases and Lubricating Compounds, which may have more to do with our progress than Wax Flowers. Of the latter, though in ill-assorted company of Oils and Fats, there was a very interesting display, by several exhibitors, besides ornamental Leather Flowers: the most noteworthy of the former was a Kentish bunch of flowers in July, modelled in Wax, contributed by E. R. Lambert, from Tunbridge.

Other Animal Substances used in Manufactures included Wools and Hairs. The Royal Agricultural Society of England sent a collection of Wools, and some of the processes of cleaning and dressing were shown. Samples of Cotton grown in every part of the world, with specimens exhibiting the length of the staple, were exhibited by the Cotton Supply Association. British Silk and Flax were also shown here. Ivory, and turnings and carvings in it were shown in great variety: the collection by Jaques and Son included many beautiful articles. Tortoiseshell and other Combs, the Pearl-oyster and other shells, Brushes, Size, Glue, and Gelatine were of this miscellaneous class.

The Aberdeen Comb Works sent a large collection of their Combs, the manufacture of which is very extensive. We are told:

Nine millions of combs are produced every year; and if the combs so made were laid together lengthwise, they would extend over 700 miles. The annual consumption is 730,000 horns and 4,000,000 of the hoofs of horses and oxen. Nothing need be wasted in this manufacture. The chippings and parings of these hoofs, amounting to 350 tons in the year, are used in the manufacture of prussiate of potash; and from the waste in this process is obtained the delicate pine-apple flavouring used by the confectioners. Ladies' side-combs, which are now sold retail at a penny per pair, go through eleven operations in the process of manufacture. Twenty years ago, the same article was sold to the trade at 3s. 6d. per dozen; the price now is 2s. 6d. per gross, a reduction of about 1600 per cent.

Vegetable Substances used in Manufactures included the fibres of the Aloe and Cocoa-nut, as substitutes for horse-hair. Articles in Cork were shown here; with foreign Hard Woods and Veneers; and Canes, used for fishing-tackle; Vegetable Ivory, &c. India-rubber and Gutta-percha applications were shown here, with the novel substance of Parksine, already noticed.

Perfumery completed this Class, to which the leading manufacturers of perfumes contributed specimens. Bayley and Co., Delcroix, Gosnell, Rimmel, Piesse and Lubin, and Atkinson, Breidenbach, Cleaver, and some twenty others, exhibited. The chemistry of perfumes was well illustrated in the Exhibition of 1851, and the lecture then given upon the subject. It was until lately popularly believed that the perfumes of flowers are obtained by distillation. This was incorrect; for we learn from Mr. R. Hunt's excellent *Hand-book* for the recent Exhibition, that "The odours of tuberose, jasmine, acacia, orange-blossom, violet, jonquil, &c., are only to be obtained in their natural fragrance by the process of *enfleurage* and maceration. This process is based on the fact that pure grease, fat, butter, oil has the power to absorb the odour of flowers, and to become perfumed when in contact with fragrant blossoms." In proof of this we have only to turn to the receipts in books of the last century for making jasmine butter by close contact with butter. "Grease absorbs odour," Mr. Hunt continues, "as salt absorbs water from the atmosphere; then, if such odorated grease be put into rectified spirit, the odour leaves the grease and enters the spirit. Nice, Cannes, and Grasse, in the South of France, are the present chief seats of this process, where are annually scented about 200,000 pounds of grease and oil." Messrs. Piesse and Lubin exhibited samples of this scented fat; also oils of the flowers. Mr. Perks sent excellent specimens of his Essential Oil of Lavender, from his lavender farm at Hitchin; Messrs. Condy sent Oils and Extracts, and Fruit Essences; and Ede's Perfumery was represented. Then we had Stolen Kisses; likewise Frangipani, for this family gives name to a handkerchief perfume as well as a tart. Pastiles and Incense were shown here; also perfumed soaps and powders, and sweet-scented waters; smelling-salts, and toilet-vinegar; sachet powders; hair-dyes, oils, washes, bandolines and bear's grease; milk of almonds, &c. There were also fountains of perfumed waters, Rimmel's perfume-vapourizer, &c. Here was the "Prince of Wales Perfume," so expensive that the smallest bottle costs 20s. Piesse and Lubin showed an ingenious little Fountain Ring: you wear it on the finger; touch a small spring, and forthwith there issues from it a jet of perfume. In fine, chemistry is, in these days, the Lady Bountiful of perfumery, and the laboratory her still-room. Nor is this a trifling matter, seeing that Perfumery, in this country, involves a trade of more than a million sterling per annum.

In the North Gallery was a group of costly Manufactures, of which Dressing-cases and Travelling-bags formed the principal portion. Some of the dressing-cases for ladies and gentlemen were marvels of silver and silver-gilt mountings. The price of some was nearly 1000*l.* In the trophy, under the eastern dome, was a dressing-case set with 900 carbuncles and pearls: the outside was mounted with turquoises, and the interior ornamented with coral.

Since the commencement of railway-travelling, and the carpet-bag of other days, what an amount of ingenuity has been expended upon the improvement of Travelling-bags, so as to pack the greatest number of articles in the smallest possible amount of space; until we have reached the capaciousness of the wonderful ark of a bag which Morier has so cleverly described in *Haji Baba*. Mechi and Bazin, Leuchars, West, and Mappin were paramount exhibitors of dressing-cases and travelling-bags.

Oils for Machinery.—Among the American novelties were exhibited the machine Oils in glass cylinders of various altitudes. We had coal-oil for lubrication; oil from tar for machinery; also signal-oil, that is, oil which may be used on locomotives, on the foremast of a ship, or on a railway signal; we had oil so limpid that it adapts itself excellently to the rapid motions of the sewing machinery, as it never gets gummy. There was a sample of oil from compressed lard of amazing transparency. The latter goes by the name of winter oil, as at 3° under freezing point it never coagulates, and is admirably adapted for the lamp in cold climates on that account. The engine and machinery oil is equal to sperm, and much cheaper: it stands a greater degree of heat and a greater degree of cold than sperm oil, and does not consume so fast. Mr. Pease had samples of petroleum in the crude and refined state, which cannot be exhibited in the Building on account of the fire insurance policy. There was, further, an oil shown called "armour oil," intended especially for gun-locks.

FIRE-ENGINES.

To the notice of the Fire-Engine trials at p. 103 we are desirous to add some account of the patent Steam Fire-Engine, by Merryweather and Son, for which they received a Prize Medal. In the fire-engine, as in all other constructions for aid in emergencies, simplicity is most important for instantaneous service. Merryweather's engine is so constructed that steam may be raised whilst travelling, and so rapidly is it generated that a pressure of steam 40 lb. per square inch can be obtained, and the engine set to work from nine to ten minutes from lighting the fire, cold water being used. The boiler is of steel, with copper tubes; and, by a system of perfect circulation, no priming—that is, carrying water with the steam—occurs to interfere with the working of the engine. It is fed by a Gifford's injector, and fitted with bunkers and tank for carrying fuel and water.

The engine part consists of one steam cylinder, 9 in. diameter, with 15 in. stroke, working direct, without any intermediate gearing, one of Merryweather and Son's patent double-acting Fire-pumps of 6¼ in. diameter and 15 in. stroke. Steam-cylinder and pump are tied together with strong guide-rods. The slide-valves are ingeniously arranged, so that a fly-wheel is dispensed with, and there are very few moving parts: the equal motion imparted by this arrangement is very advantageous for steam fire-engines, as an unusually steady jet of water is produced. The pump is in one solid casting of gun-metal, with large valves, all placed beneath the cylinder, thus preventing any grit from injuring the pump-cylinder, and the arrangement is such that immediately the engine stops working all water must leave the pump, thus avoiding accidents by frost. The pump, although double-acting, is provided with a simple means of lubrication. The valves are extremely easy of access, a capacious copper air-vessel surmounts the pump, and there are two delivery-ways, with stop-valves for attaching one or two hoses. To start the engine nothing more is required than to open the steam-valve, when it will run at any required speed (according to the distance the valve is opened) from one, or any intermediate number of, to 160 double strokes per minute, as there are no dead points. The engine discharges, when working at full speed, fully 500 gallons per minute.

No wood is used in the construction of the engine, except the wheels, which are high, for rapid travelling: the front wheels lock completely round, and in the box for carrying the hose, tools, &c., which forms a seat for six men, the suction-pipes are carried at the sides. When loaded with six men, hose, &c., it has frequently been drawn by two horses at a rapid rate; provision is made for three or four horses if required.

The handsome Fire-engine also built by Merryweather, and presented to Mr. F. Hodges, by the inhabitants of Lambeth, was also shown in the Exhibition. It is of the kind used by the London Fire Brigade, and the case is superbly decorated from designs by Sig. Casentini. The various improvements consist in arranging the valves and passages in as direct a line as possible, so that the water is delivered free and uncrippled; also in constructing the passages so that no water can possibly remain in any portion of the works when at rest, so as to prevent accidents or stoppages from freezing. The jet of water from this engine may be projected 130 feet in height. It discharges 140 gallons per minute, thirty men being employed at the pumps.—*Illustrated London News.*

COAL IN VARIOUS COUNTRIES OF THE WORLD.

In the British Department all the typical varieties of Coal in Great Britain were represented with one exception, and that is the lignites of Bovey Tracey, Devonshire.[*] We include the lignite, or brown coals of the Germans, under the term "coal." Newcastle and South Wales sent their rival steam coals. There were several collections illustrative of the measures of particular districts. We would observe—and this we do with the conviction derived from long experience—that it is impossible in many cases to form even an approximately satisfactory judgment of a coal from looking at a specimen, however carefully selected. An analysis may tell us much; but nothing short of actual trial on a sufficiently large scale will lead to perfectly reliable conclusions.

One of the purest coals for the smelting of iron is that known as the "better bed," which occurs in part of the Yorkshire coalfield. It is to the use of this coal that is so frequently ascribed the superiority of the Lowmoor iron; but we are inclined to think that this is far from being the only cause. It may be estimated that a seam of coal will yield about 1000 tons for every foot in thickness; but if the Lowmoor iron had been produced exclusively with coal from the "better bed," an enormous area would have been quite insufficient to supply the demand of this great establishment. A section of the measures, with illustrated speci-

[*] It deserves to be more publicly known than it is, that Miss Coutts has, with her accustomed munificence, recently defrayed the expenses of an elaborate scientific investigation of the fossil plants occurring in this remarkable deposit. The exploration was intrusted to the able hands of Mr. Pengelly, of Torquay, and the botanical part to Professor Heer, of Zurich, one of the first authorities in this branch of science.

mens, was exhibited. There is undoubtedly no better coal in the world for the smelting of iron than is raised in some parts of South Wales.

The specimens of Cannel Coal in the British Department received special attention. This coal derives its name from its property of burning with a luminous flame like that of a candle, of which "cannel" is stated to be a corruption. A single bit of coal may be readily ignited, and will continue to burn, which is not the case with common kinds of coal. Cannel coal is invaluable for gas-making, and accordingly fetches a very high price compared with other coals. G. H. Ramsay and Sons exhibited a fine specimen of cannel coal from Northumberland, in which district it is rare. A large and characteristic sample of the fine cannel from the Earl of Balcarres' property at Wigan was shown. The seam is stated to be 37 inches thick. We have had the opportunity, at one time or other, of examining the coal raised in every part of the United Kingdom, and in most parts of the world besides; and we have never seen a finer cannel, properly so-called, than that exhibited by the Leeswood-green Colliery Company, near Mold, in Flintshire. There are two varieties of this cannel occurring together, the "smooth" and the "curly;" but the latter is decidedly the best. Its composition per cent. is as follows :—Carbon, 77·81; hydrogen, 8·47; oxygen and nitrogen, 6·32; sulphur, 0·71; ash (chocolate in colour), 6·01; water, 0·68. Exclusive of ash, &c., the proportion of which is very small as compared with the famous Boghead cannel, or "Torbanehill mineral," the percentage of hydrogen is 9·15. Gas-makers and paraffine oil manufacturers will know how to estimate the value of this statement.*

In Belgium it is estimated that there are as many as 140 workable beds of coal, of which the total thickness amounts to 90 metres, or about 296 feet! In 1860 the quantity of coal raised was 9,610,895 tonnes (nearly the same as our tons), of the estimated value of 107,127,282f., or about 4,285,080*l*. There were a few small specimens of Belgian coal in the Exhibition, but no collection illustrative of the important coal-field of Belgium.

* The extraction of coal in this country is proceeding at a prodigious and continually accelerated rate. Last year it may be computed that we raised about 80,000,000 tons! A year or two ago, the probable exhaustion of our coal was much discussed in the House of Commons with reference to Mr. Cobden's Anglo-Gallic commercial treaty, and exception might have been taken to much that was advanced on that occasion. Our *data* are in many respects vague and unsatisfactory. Geologists present us with maps in which large areas are marked black to indicate coal measures. This is all very proper and very useful, but it should ever be borne in mind that the occurrence of the so-called "coal measures" by no means necessarily implies the existence of *workable coal seams*, at least in the present circumstances of the country. The coal may have thinned out, faults may have greatly disturbed the district, or the coal may be of bad quality, and where numerous faults exist, as is the case in the South Staffordshire basin, the coal in the *same pit* is subject to extraordinary variation in quality. Then, again, many of the seams are so thin that for all practical purposes they are utterly valueless, and in some localities, as in one part of the South Wales basin, the coal lies at such an *enormous depth* as to render it very doubtful whether, under existing geological conditions, it will ever become accessible to man.

The collieries of France, in 1859, produced 74,825,718 metrical quintals of coal, or in round numbers nearly 7½ millions of tons, of the estimated value of 94,979,163f. The committee of coal proprietors of the department of the Loire and Mining Company of Montcel, St. Etienne, sent a very fine series of their Coal, Coke, and other products, together with illustrative maps and sections. The "Compagnie des Mines de la Grand' Combe" also sent a good series of their Coal, Coke, and patent Fuel. Fine Lignite was shown.

Numerous specimens of Coal were found in the Spanish Department. Portugal exhibited a fine block of Anthracite, and several specimens of Lignite.

Lignite occurs extensively in the States of the Zollverein: in the lowlands of North Germany, between the rivers Elbe and Vistula, its development is greatest and most important. Lignite is largely used in Germany, especially in the lowlands of North Germany, both as fuel for domestic purposes and in manufactories, especially under steam-boilers. In Prussian Saxony it is extensively applied to the manufactures of coal oils and paraffine.

In the Zollverein catalogue not fewer than 12 distinct coalfields of the carboniferous epoch are enumerated. The most important are in the Rhenish provinces of Prussia, and the other two in Prussian Silesia. It is an interesting fact that in the Ruhr district, where the cretaceous rocks lie unconformably immediately over the greater part of the coal measures, an additional number of shafts is annually sunk through the former, extending northeast, and continually increasing in depth. The deepest is now sunk to about 400 yards. The total area of this field as yet explored is not less than 500 square miles, and there is reason to believe that it will be found to extend much further. The five minor coalfields are those of Ibbenbüren, Black Forest, Thuringia, the Harz, near the river Saale, and the Erzgebirge. Every variety of coal occurs in these districts, and was represented in the Exhibition. In 1860 the total production of coal in Prussia was 10,656,725 tons, besides 3,153,544 tons of lignite or brown coal.

Prussia sent to the Exhibition an ingeniously coloured map, showing the production, consumption, and circulation of mineral fuel in the kingdom in 1860.

Austria sent an extensive and highly instructive collection illustrative of her mineral fuel, formed by "the Imperial and Royal Geological Institute of the Austrian Empire," and accompanied with a special explanatory catalogue in English. "There are 239 boxes with specimens of peat, lignite, brown coal, black coal (our common bituminous coals), and anthracite from different geological positions, from the modern deposits through the miocene and eocene strata, chalk and lias, down to the genuine coal measures, from localities in Bohemia, Moravia, Silesia, Galicia, Hungary, Transylvania, the Military Border, Croatia, and Esclavonia, and along the Alps from the Tyrol and Vorarlberg, Salzburg, Upper and Lower Austria, Styria, Carinthia, Carniola, and Dalmatia." The whole number of tons of coal raised in 1860 in the different provinces represented in the catalogue was 2,059,080; but according to Haidinger (by whom the catalogue is signed) the total amount raised in the Austrian empire is 3,500,000 tons. A very large proportion of the fuel here included in the general term coal consists of lignite or brown coal. The production of coal of all kinds in the Austrian empire has increased twelvefold within 30 years.

Coal of the carboniferous epoch occurs in Nova Scotia, and is worked in the counties of Pictou and Sydney and elsewhere. It is stated that the most important coal measures yet explored are those of the Albion mines, in the first-mentioned county. "In one section at this locality the vertical thickness of the two large seams of coal, the main and deep seams, is 37½ feet and 22½ feet respectively." An attenuated pyramid of coal, representing the entire thickness of the first of these seams, was exhibited.*

In the New Brunswick Department were exhibited specimens of the beautiful coal from which Albertine is obtained. (*See page* 267).

New South Wales contains valuable beds of carboniferous coal, one of which, at Port Stephens, is stated to be 30 feet thick. Cannel coal has been found and worked. Some of the colleries have been named after districts in the north of England. Thus we have the Newcastle Coal and Copper Company and the Wall's-end Company. Practical details of value will be found in the New South Wales catalogue, which is worth possessing on many accounts. Smelting operations will, no doubt, greatly increase in this colony as the coal becomes more extensively worked. Mr. Keene, the Government examiner of coalfields, sent an admirable and instructive collection, illustrative of the coal measures and fossil flora of this important colony. A large block of fine bright-looking so-called steam coal from the Bellambi Mine, near Sydney, was shown. Apparently good coal from the "Bore-hole seam," Newcastle, was exhibited by the Australian Agricultural Company.

* The thickest seam in England is the well-known 10-yard coal of South Staffordshire, which has contributed so largely to the wealth of the Earl of Dudley. A gigantic column of the entire thickness of this seam was sent to the Exhibition of 1851 by Messrs. Bagnall. Not much remains of this magnificent seam, of which an inconceivable quantity has been wasted in the getting, especially in former times. Where nature has been most lavish of her resources man has generally been most wasteful. This coal has chiefly been gotten by the "pillar" and "stall" method, gigantic pillars from ten to twelve yards square being left to support the roof. These have been subsequently extracted. The coal, unfortunately, is extremely liable to spontaneous combustion, and great losses have frequently been sustained in consequence by those who have worked it. Of all mining in the world, perhaps none is attended with greater risk than that of the 10-yard coal on the usual system. The danger arises from the fall of coal or rock from the roof. A lump of a few pounds falling from a height of thirty feet more than suffices to kill an unhappy collier; and serious maimings and actual deaths from this cause are of *very frequent* occurrence. An explosion sending fifty victims to their account at a time produces a great impression on the public mind, while the destruction of a collier or two every week excites no notice. If any one would take the trouble to ascertain and publish the total number of deaths during the last few years from falls of the roof in the 10-yard collieries, the effect, we are convinced, would be extremely startling.

The colony of Victoria sent coal from Griffith's Port Bay.

Tasmania possesses coal both bituminous and anthracite. One seam, about four feet thick, at Tasman's peninsula, has supplied Hobart Town with coal during the last twenty-five years. Mr Charles Gould, son of the well-known ornithologist, of London, is now engaged in the exploration of the mineral resources of this interesting country, and will, no doubt, soon present new and important information as to the probable extent of its coalfield. He sent over specimens exhibited in the Tasmanian Department.

Coal has been discovered in New Zealand, and specimens which we have examined at different times wo have found to be of good quality. In the New Zealand Department, blocks from the Opaheke mines were exhibited by the Waihoihoi Coal Company; including Gas Coal from the Great Pakawau Mine, Nelson.—*Abridged from a valuable Paper in the Times.*

There were likewise in the Exhibition several contrivances for the economizing and utilization of coal : as the "step-grate" of the Germans, for burning coal-slack : also Siemens's regenerative furnaces, about to be applied to iron puddling : the principle is precisely that on which a handkerchief is tied round the mouth, or a "respirator" applied to it on a frosty day. The word "accumulative" would, probably, be more expressive than "regenerative :" there is no regeneration, but simply retention and accumulation.

Several very fine examples of Coke were shown; but no improved models of coke-ovens. Of patent fuel there were numerous illustrations in the British and French Departments; and in the Belgian Department were clever mechanical drawings of machinery for the manufacture of this fuel, which is said to work successfully.

Various kinds of Safety Lamps were exhibited, but with no decided improvement upon those in actual operation. The ventilation of collieries was also illustrated by instructive models of apparatus. The successful search for coal under enormous difficulties at the Shireoak Colliery, Worksop, was shown by the shaft tubbed with cast-iron tubbing, to keep out the water, which at the lower part was under the pressure of 200 lb. to the square inch. There were many models, some on a working scale, of Safety Cages, and the underground carriage of coal to the shaft by steam-power was represented. The subject of "boring," of great importance with reference to Artesian wells, and the exploration of coal, was exemplified by the implements used; and the French Government sent the beautiful model of the Artesian well-boring at Passy, near Paris.

A block of coal was shown, in which a living frog was stated to have been found imbedded : the hole was in the coal, and the frog was shown for a few days, when it died; but it appeared from evidence, that the frog was not found *in the coal*, but in a stratum of shale, technically called "pricking."

THE BRITISH COLONIES.

We have already adverted to the great superiority of the display of the exhibitors from our Colonies to that in the Exhibition of 1851. Then the Colonies were, as a whole, almost unrepresented. The East India Company, however, made a noble display.

Our Colonial Empire is more than twice as large as the whole of Europe. The space which the colonies occupied in the Building was not a very large one—about 16,000 feet; and they were nearly all arranged in the north end of the east transept. First on the right-hand side down the steps from the eastern dome, were the West India Colonies.

JAMAICA.

There was an abundant display of specimens of the products of this colony, such as Sugar, Rum, Indigo, Cotton, Indian Corn, Rice, Bread-fruit, and Bananas; besides some rude specimens of the manufactures of the white and coloured population.

First were not less than 144 specimens of Rum of the highest proof, in bottles; of all shades, from the pale pine-apple colour to the dark purple of port wine. Near the rums was a fine collection of the Liqueurs and choice Wines of the island, most exquisite in flavor, such as the pimento, the orange, the jamboline—a delicious liqueur, closely resembling Maraschino; and there was the delicious Santa wine, with flavour like that of shrub.

The Vegetable Oils of the country were represented by forty-eight specimens, some of which are of great value in the arts and manufactures, and useful as medicine. There was the wonderful Croton oil, and the sand-box oil, still more potent in operation: and an oil called the "French Physic-nut," which is not so well known as its merits deserve; for a dozen drops will be as efficacious as an ounce of castor-oil, and its effects may be neutralized by a glass of white wine. In a glass-case was shown a dry branch of a shrub, something like that of a palm-tree, which is called the "Burwood," and is a specific against cholera: when some years since, the cholera had almost decimated the population of Jamaica, it was found that a decoction of this burwood would arrest the disease. There were some pods shown, from which the famous "Oil of Bur," used in watch-making, is obtained.

Fine specimens of the native Woods were displayed, polished, to show their markings: they included the scarlet cordia, remarkable for the richness of its colour; the lignum-vitæ, hard as iron; the yacca, of whose lace-like bark the ladies of Jamaica make dresses, and use for other ornamental work. Here, too, was the venerable trunk of a coffee-tree; and by its side a thick Bamboo, the inside of which was hollowed out to some distance, in which state it forms a vessel, in which the coloured people carry water. Sugars were shown in various shades of colour; and near them a collection of the starches for which Jamaica is famous, such as arrow-root, tapioca, *tous-les-mois*, &c. The thunburgia, made from the root of a gorgeously flowering plant, and the bitter cassava, were also shown; the latter is ground into powder, and used for bread; and in the casserope, made from its liquor, meat is stewed; this is the famous "Demerara pepper-pot."

TRINIDAD.

The produce sent from this island consisted of specimens of its minerals; asphalte, from the famous "Pitch Lake;" glance, tertiary coal, and lignite; the latter, it is said, will bear comparison with the best lignites from any other part of the world.* The food substances included rice, ground nuts, seramum, cocoas, coffee, nutmegs, Brazil nuts, flower of bread fruit, plantains, yams, tania, sweet potatoes, curl-curl, bitter and sweet Canada arrow-roots, cloves, and black pepper. There were also vegetable oils and ivory, skins of sharks, sponges, seeds, &c.; textile materials, wild and cultivated cottons; cork, and fibres of wild cane; native woods, plain and ornamental calabashes, fancy baskets, Indian wickerwork, &c. Here were also shown some good Photographs from Port of Spain.

The Mineral wealth of the island was represented by fine specimens of copper, manganese, zinc, cobalt, ironstones, barytes, arragonite, iron pyrites, sands, clays, and other matters, which had been very carefully prepared, by order of the colonial government, by Mr. Barret, geologist to the colony; and on the wall was a large map showing the geological features of the island. Turtle was shown here in its native delicacy, unadulterated by bad cookery.

The productions of British Dominica, Demerara, and of British Guiana, had much in common with those shown from Jamaica.

NATAL.

Owing to some unfortunate disputes between contending sectaries in the Cape Colony, our South African possessions were represented in the Exhibition almost solely by the contributions from Natal. The natural products of this rising colony were very fully illustrated. Sugar, in particular, within the last ten years has become one of the staple products of the country. Twelve years ago a sample manufactured from Natal canes was handed about the colony as a curiosity; but within the last two years 2000 tons, exceeding 50,000*l.* in value, have been exported. The specimens shown here were pronounced to be of excellent quality. The rapid development of this capability of the climate and soil for sugar-culture has led to a rise in the price of land in the colony almost unprecedented. Of Arrow-root, for which the colony has

---

* An account of these Lignites will be found in a monograph on the Geology and Mineral resources of Trinidad, by Messrs. Wall and Sawkins, published by Her Majesty's Government.

also a speciality, there were some fine specimens shown, as well as of Coffee, Wheat, Barley, and Maize. Within the last few years the Assam Tea-plant has been introduced into the colony, and is said to thrive with great rapidity: some samples of it were exhibited side by side with a small quantity of the Bushman's tea. The colonial Cayenne pepper is said to command excellent prices. Natal is trying her hand at producing Cotton, and some specimens were shown of fair quality. The plant grows readily here, but the chief difficulty is in finding labour. The Colonial Government is making great efforts to induce the Caffres to take to the growing of it: the cotton shown was both grown and ginned by the natives. There was also shown a sample of Wool produced from a wild plant indigenous to the country.

The walls of the Natal Court were ornamented with magnificent skins of antelopes, leopards, and other animals shot in the neighbourhood of the colony; among them was the skin of a boa, eighteen feet long. Elephants' Tusks are a considerable article of export, and one was shown here weighing 126 lb. A very interesting portion of the Exhibition was the collection illustrating the habits and modes of life of the Caffre. His great luxury seems to be snuff, and here was every variety of snuff-boxes and snuff-spoons, generally carried in his back hair, along with his nose-scraper and other useful articles, some of them showing considerable skill in carving. A few of them smoke; and by sticking a reed with a bowl made of soapstone at the end of it into a cow-horn, which they fill with water, they manage to extemporize a very rude kind of hookah. Their greatest ingenuity, however, is shown in their Musical Instruments. The Caffre lyre is a bent bow strung with twisted hair, which beaten with a stick will give out some four or five distinct tones; while the Macabere piano, which is a series of strips of wood, each backed by a sounding chamber formed of the rind of some dried and hardened fruit, has one or two notes very nearly approaching to the music of a cracked bell. The extraordinary top-knots which are most characteristic of the Caffre costume were illustrated by a specimen which was torn off the head of a native in a scuffle at D'Urban some little time ago. Two or three articles of red Pottery-ware, which belonged to the famous Moshes, were excellent in quality. I Timbers the colony appears to be rich, for there was a great variety shown, some of the specimens possessing durability, while others are useful only for ornamental purposes. One of them—the "Sneezewood," is of extraordinarily tenacious fibre, and stands exposure to the weather admirably, is named from the pungent qualities of its saw-wood; and the "Stinkwood" is a furniture-wood somewhat resembling dark walnut, which, while green gives out a most disagreeable odour.

St. Helena, and one or two other African settlements, sent small contributions.—*Abridged from the Times.*

THE BAHAMAS,

The next compartment to that of Natal, offered Cotton, the Pine-apple Fibre, the Palmetto, the Banana, and other plants containing fibres useful for the manufacturer. Sponges and Liquorice berries, and shell-work, of various kinds, were arranged in the cases; and Jumbie Beans exhibited specimens of his handiwork in the production of ladies' bags and reticules.

CEYLON.

From this large and beautiful island was sent a fine collection of produce, natural and artificial. There were bows and arrows, and peacock's-feather fans; rude ploughs and yokes; carved cocoa-nut shells; native lace and gold embroidery, and musical instruments. In the centre of the Court was a spacious tent, formed of the leaves of the talipot palm. In furniture there was a pair of lyre-tables; a fine ebony foot-stool; and a jewel case. Also, a Dalada shrine, some fine specimens of kitool fibres, billhooks, and walking-sticks; and more especially interesting was a Davenport carved in ebony, in the English style, by a pupil in one of the industrial schools recently established in the island by the local government. Paddy and rice, coffee, and cinnamon and other spices, were shown; and there was a very fine collection of native gems, among which the pearl, the emerald, the ruby, were superbly represented. The native woods and serviceable fibres were also shown. A very large proportion of the articles exhibited were collected by a Committee appointed by the Government for that purpose.

Mauritius sent some fine specimens of sugar, fruits, and vegetable substances.

HONG-KONG

showed a small but interesting collection of Chinese produce and manufactures; and took under her wing a number of British merchants, officers, and some exhibitors, who showed some choice examples of Chinese industry, in silk, rich velvets, silk and gold embroidered carpets; china and enamels; and articles of raw produce.

MALTA, AND THE IONIAN ISLANDS.

The show made both by Malta and the Ionian Islands will probably surprise those whose attention has not been attracted to these countries. Malta came out very strong in her three great specialities—Lace, Silver Filigree, and Stonework. The beautiful black lace is made principally by the women in the small island of Gozo,—and an industrious worker by keeping at it assiduously may earn from a shilling to eighteenpence a day. In the patterns there is scarcely any departure from ancient ideas—though the schools of design which have been established in Malta are beginning to tell both on this and other branches of manufactures—but the workmanship is so excellent that for wear the lace is unsurpassable. One of its distinguishing and most valuable characteristics is that it is impossible to crease it. The rarest piece in the case—the shawl arranged over the yellow dress—will form part of a royal trousseau. The black lace is all of silk, obtained from Naples. There were also some very beautiful specimens of white thread lace, mostly made in the charitable institutions of the island. In the silver filigree work, wherein Malta takes a high stand, the delicate tracery is executed with quite as fine a finish as the best samples of the Genoese ware; and there is in addition an appearance of solidity and durability about it which the other lacks. The stonework exhibited was equally good. The forms all showed taste, and the carving of the ornaments, flowers, figures, and the like, is wonderful, when we remember that it is the work of men entirely destitute of artistic education; drawing, in general, their own designs, and working with half a dozen of the simplest tools. Here were large stone garden vases marked at half-a-crown.

From the samples of indigenous Cotton exhibited here, the whole of the last cotton-crop of the island were bought up for Manchester consumption at an average price of from 9d. to 10d. per lb.,—and the next crop, in all probability, will be secured by the same buyers. Among the cotton manufactures exhibited were very comfortable-looking Counterpanes, marked at 6s. each. The straw-work, particularly the Straw Hats, of remarkable lightness, made from rushes obtained in the Sicilian marshes, are another feature of the Exhibition which ought not to be passed. Neither should we omit to mention the imitations of the Italian *pietra dura* manufactories sent by Mr. Darmanin, which show great taste. There was an ample collection of agricultural products and seeds; and soup-pastes—such as Vermicelli and Macaroni made from semola—are to be bought at Malta for 2½d. and 3d. per lb. Among the seeds the most remarkable was that of the *Ceratonia siliqua*, the "locust bean" of the Scriptures, which grows abundantly in the island.

The chief articles which the Ionian Islands offered to commercial enterprise were their Wines. In sweet wines there were qualities which could hardly be distinguished from Muscat and Alicante, though the selling price in Cephalonia is only 1s. 6d. a bottle; and amongst the dry Wines the Vostillidi and a Wine of Argostoli resembled closely the Rhine vintages. The common country Wines of Corfu and Cephalonia sell at 3½d. and 4½d. a bottle, and the Wine made from the Zante Currants has a flavour of peculiar delicacy. Very excellent Liqueurs too, similar to Maraschino or Curaçoa, are made on the island, and of which samples were shown. The features of the show which attracted most attention were the life-size figures of the peasants of Corfu, Paxo, and Cerigo in their holyday dresses. The embroidery is richly and tastefully worked, and some of the ornaments worn by the young ladies are very curious. In the same case were some beautiful specimens of Lace-work manufactured in the islands, the most remarkable of which was a handsome *burnouse* made from the fibres of the American aloe. There were several fine pieces of inlaid and decorative Furniture : such as tables, escritoires, &c., of inlaid cypress, olive and walnut woods, which bore comparison with any furniture of the kind in the Building, both for design, elaborate finish of workmanship, and, above all, for reasonableness of price. The Ionian Court had some exquisite specimens of Gold Embroidery in velvet, the wonderful Albanian caps and jackets, which are seen nowhere in such perfection as in the Ionian Islands, and only there on festa days. Of specimens of the gold embroidery of Zante, there was a large display in the shape of girdles, caps, pouches, cigar-cases, book-covers, &c. Among the Girdles was the *facsimile* of one made for the Empress of Austria—it measures exactly 16 inches. The islands produce Cotton in considerable quantities ; but the specimens of their cotton fabrics were not of the same excellent quality as their Silks. The crotchet-work and the embroidery from Ithaca and Santa Maura were much admired. Samples of the famous Zante Currants, of the Wheat and Maize, and other agricultural products of the Islands, formed part of the Exhibition ; as well as building Stones and Marbles. Lastly, there was a large quantity of the indigenous Papyrus, which might be made of use in the manufacture of paper. The collection was very carefully selected and arranged by Mr. Drummond Woolff.—*Abridged from the Times.*

INDIA.

The management of this large and important portion of the Exhibition was confided to Dr. J. Forbes Watson, the reporter of Indian products, who has devoted so much attention to the due development of the staples of India.

The collection, one of the best arranged in the Building, was more varied and extensive than the former one in 1851 : the articles for which space could not be given, were removed to the Indian Museum, Fife House, Whitehall-yard, and there constituted a supplementary collection.

The Indian Museum itself contributed from its varied resources a collection of very considerable interest ; and several firms in this country, in their capacity as importers, as well as a few private individuals, exhibited valuable specimens. Some samples, showing the aptitude of cloth made of Indian cotton, for taking dyes, received special attention.

The collection from Bengal, the North-western Provinces, Oude, the Punjab, Burmah, the States of Ulwar, and the Tenasserim and Martaban Provinces, including the Straits Settlements, amounted to nearly six thousand specimens ; of these we can only mention a few recommended by their novelty.

The products of the soil were oil-seeds, oils, gums, resins, medicinal substances, fibres, and timbers. Tea occupied a prominent position; the tea-districts of Assam, Cachar, Sythet, Darjeeling, Dehra, Dhoon, Gurhwal, Kumaon, and Hangra, being all represented.

Among the articles contributed were several which showed the great improvement that has undoubtedly taken place in a variety of manufactures, and even of works of art. Among the latter, were the paintings on ivory from Delhi, several faithful copies of photographs taken at Lucknow.

A small but important display was some samples of the first Silk attempted to be raised in Oude, under the auspices of the Indian Government. The silk thus produced is not only greater in quantity, but infinitely finer in quality than any raised in Bengal: in fact, it is in every respect equal to the best China Silk. Eggs of the Cashmere variety of the worm were sent to the Mahomdee district of Oude, were they were hatched, and the insects continued remarkably healthy, yielding at last upwards of 2000 cocoons. Those first formed are considered to be remarkably fine, and the worst—namely, those that spun during the great heats—are only described as being no better than the Bengal cocoons. Beds of mulberry-cuttings have been planted out in this district of Oude with a view to the continuance of the experiment on a much larger scale next year. The floss silk embroideries on Cashmere cloth and net from Delhi were fine; greatly superior to what had been sent on former occasions; also of improved patterns and extraordinary cheapness. Of Cashmere shawls the collection was very large. Some sent from Sirinuggur, the capital of Cashmere, and from Umritsur, were considered very superior. Carpets showed a considerable advance in workmanship, and the blending of colours was remarkably fine.

The collection contained a variety of articles under the name of Papier-mâché, those made at Cashmere being deserving of notice. The specimens sent showed considerable improvement in comparison with those contributed in 1851 and 1855.

The assortment of Silk cloths from various parts of India was very large. Some from the Punjab and other parts were excellent, and of brilliant dye. The Embroidered Silks and Brocades from Benares stand unrivalled. The workmanship is of the highest finish, whilst the interweaving of the gold and silver threads with the silk shows exquisite taste. The kinkobs or brocades were also very rich.

The greater portion of the collection under the head of Manufactures in Cotton and Hemp consisted of specimens of Cloth, &c., made by prisoners in the various jails. The specimens of Paper formed a large variety. There was the famous paper made of the daphne plant at Nepal, illustrated by the fibre of the fresh shrub and specimens of all stages of its preparation. Of Sculpture there was a large variety of specimens in stone, ivory, marble, and various kinds of woods,—all of them much superior to any hitherto forwarded.

The collection from Bombay was interesting and important.

Cotton, its preparation and manufacture, was well represented: the Rao of Kutch contributed samples of raw and manufactured cotton from Bhooj, Kutch, and Mandanee; and the Cloth as made largely at the last-named place for exportation to Muscat and the Arabian coast. There were also specimens from Soebee, Jacobabad, and Shikarpoor, of the raw material; and from Khyrpoor, Meer Ali Morad sent cotton cloth and chintz clothing.

Rich samples of raw, manufactured, and dyed Silks, were forwarded; while most of the contributing places furnished specimens of mixed Silks and Cotton fabrics.

The Embroideries generally, on velvet, silk, leather, and cloth, were of a high degree of excellence, both in design and execution.

In works of art or skill, were the elaborate Carvings in black-wood, sandal-wood, and ivory; and in a material termed "Ratanglee," from Malabar. Inlaid ivory, and Enamelling in the precious metals was well represented by arms and armour contributed by Meer Ali Morad of Khyrpoor, and the Rao of Kutch. The last-named also presented costly specimens of skill in Gold and Silversmiths' Art: including a shield from Mandanee.

The models were mostly copies of Agricultural Implements, showing the local mode of preparing the land for the culture of cotton, grain, pulses, &c. There were samples of Cutlery, Jewellery, Lac-ware, &c., from Bombay and Scinde; and of Mineral products and works in Stone, &c.; Alum, Saltpetre, Subcarbonate of Soda, from Scinde; Indigo from Jacobabad; Sulphur, Lead, Copper ores, and Galena, from Beloochistan; Agates and Carnelians from the Ruttinpoor mines in Rewa Kanta.

The collection from Madras under the head of Raw Products, included timbers, oils, seeds, gums, dyes, &c. Of the important article of Cotton, were Oopum and Bourbon cotton from Salem in small quantities, and raw and manufactured specimens from other localities.

The rich Feather Ornaments from Kurnool and Vizagapatam, the large Straw Mattings from Pulghaut and North Arcot, the Writing-paper from Madras and Salem, and the Carvings and Constructions in ivory, sandal-wood, buffalo-horn, and porcupine-quills—were attractive.

Hydrabad and Burmah contributed specimens of Lac-ware.

The models of useful appliances included a portable Kitchen and compendious Sandwich-box from the Andaman Islands; and the works of art and skill, an exquisite Temple from Burmah, a curious Model in pith from Tanjore, and some copper Figures from North Arcot. Of Arms, Cutlery, &c., Salem, Malabar, and Burmah supplied the best specimens.

The Fine Arts in Madras were represented by a collection of engravings, photographs, and drawings. Some miniatures on ivory especially illustrated the delicacy of finish, minute detail, and brilliancy of colour, ever remarkable in native drawings.

The Pottery from the School of Industrial Arts in Madras, and from Bangalore and North Arcot, as well as most of the examples of native manufacturing and artistic skill, afforded abundant evidence of the existing will and ability to adapt the wealthy resources and produce of India to the requirements of advanced civilization.

From Burmah, a large collection comprised a series of grains, woods, medicinal roots, seeds, spices, pulses, and cotton; and specimens of metal, ivory, and precious stones, and gold-dust from Ava. The samples of Burmese Manufactures, &c., included musical instruments, jewellery, models of boats, implements, &c., and some curious Burmese pictures.

The mineral classes were represented by coal from Borneo and Malacca, iron from Saigoor (Cochin China), earths and clays from Singapore, Malacca, and Penang. The tin ore of Kassang and Malacca affords from 40 to 60 per cent. of metal after a rude process of washing and smelting.

There was a choice collection of woods and fibres from Malacca, Penang, &c.; vegetable tallow from Cochin China, Siam, and Borneo; gutta percha from the Malay Peninsula and the Eastern Archipelago; and tobacco from Bally and Penang.

Another important feature in this consignment was the collection of medicinal substances and processes, oils and gums, from Malacca, Siam, Sumatra, Java, and Cochin China.

Of Cotton, the principal specimens were from Singapore, Malacca, and Penang; the manufactures consisted principally of arms from Tringanu and Malacca. There were also Embroideries and Silks from Singapore and Penang, and Lace from Malacca.

The works in metals, &c. (including Implements), came from Malacca, Penang, and Singapore; while the Lac-ware of Tringanu and Singapore was very curious.

There was also a collection of Photographic Portraits of natives.

A splendid collection of fibres, assembled from almost every part of our Indian empire, was sent by Mr. Dowleans, Secretary to the Bengal Committee. The recent premature announcement that jute might be so prepared as to be operated upon by cotton machinery has led to many inquiries being made for specimens of that and various other vegetable fibres, which it was thought might be turned to useful account; but which Dr. Watson considers unprofitable. The Cotton Supply Association of Manchester illustrated the value of cotton grown in India for printing purposes, and showed some excellent specimens of prints executed on fabrics produced solely from East India cotton. Of course, with the prejudices existing against this kind of cotton, and the fact that, in all human probability, the quality of East India cotton has deteriorated since the importation of the first cotton goods from India gave them the name of calicoes, as derived from "calicuts," it is now necessary to prove that good and useful fabrics can really be made from the vegetable fibre grown in the country which first developed a cotton trade at all, and whence cotton goods were brought to Europe when the Southern States of America were under the rule of the red Indian.

THE NORTH AMERICAN COLONIES.

CANADA.

The large and prosperous colony of Canada was nobly represented in the Exhibition : not in her special riches, but in her vast natural resources, the raw material of boundless wealth—the produce of the field, the mine, and the forest.

The most remarkable portion of the Canadian display was that of her Timber, of which there was a gigantic trophy in the north transept. It was three stories or stages in height. Some of the logs of which this trophy was formed were of enormous dimensions. On one side was a log of black walnut five yards in circumference : it was cut from a tree 120 feet high, the first limb being 70 feet from the ground, and 350 years old. On the opposite side was a large block of white oak, more than four yards in girth, and 380 years old.

The collection of Woods of Lower Canada comprised the linden, the maples of various kinds, but especially the bird's-eye maple ; the moose-wood, and the curled maple ; the dogwood, the willow, and the birch. In commercial value the most notable were the thirteen varieties of *coniferæ*, including pine, spruce, and cedar, the oaks and beeches, the hickory and the maples. These woods were, however, surpassed by those of Upper Canada, the most remarkable being the white oak, a plank of which is four feet wide ; the black walnut, a beautiful wood for cabinet furniture ; the sugar and soft maples, from three to four feet in width ; and the pine, one plank of which is, we are told, "12 feet long (it could have been cut 50 feet long) and 50 inches wide, without a knot, sawn from a tree 22 feet in circumference, and 120 feet to the first limb."

The white oak is the most valuable : of the twenty varieties of oaks in North America it is the best. For shipbuilding it is the only reliable substitute for old English oak, and is well known in our building-yards.

In the collection were specimens of branches and leaves, which Dr. Tache and Dr. Hurbert had arranged for the gratification of botanical students.

Canada was most worthily represented, thanks to the Director of the Canadian Geological Survey, Sir William Logan. Since 1842, he has resided in Canada : in that year he commenced a geological survey, *pari passu* with a geographical one. In this great work, he is often compelled to penetrate the trackless primeval forest, to force his way across the tangled cedar-swamp, and brave the dangers of Canadian rapids in a frail canoe. Thus, Sir William has striven during many years to develope the vast mineral resources of Canada, comprising about 300,000 square miles, of which about 100,000 have already been surveyed by the Director and his small staff of assistants.

The lumps of bog and other iron ores attested in the Exhibition the wealth of the country : a pair of carriage-wheels, made from bog-iron, was shown; they have run 150,000 miles, yet their surfaces show scarcely any signs of wear. Iron ore occurs in the colony in beds from 5 to 200 feet thick; and the produce varies from 60 to 70 per cent. Copper ores exist on the Lakes Huron and Superior, for more than forty miles: a lump was shown, weighing 9 cwt., cut from a block several tons in weight; the discoverer of this mine has realized by it a large fortune.

There were also shown earths and ores for paints; stones adapted for lithographers; mineral manures, as gypsum, phosphate of lime, shell marl, &c.; trap-rock for grindstones; talcose slate for whetstones, flagstones, and marbles. A large proportion of the contents of the Court was made up of wheat, barley, Indian corn, and buckwheat.

Among the Agricultural Implements was one which does the work of plough, drill, and harrow at one operation.

There was a stand of New South Wales hermitage, Madeira, amontillado, claret, and other wines grown in the colony.

NEW BRUNSWICK.

The most attractive portion of this display was a trophy formed of native Indian moccasins and dresses, including a complete suit made up under the direction of Mrs. Manners Sutton, wife of the Governor of the Province: these dresses were profusely decorated with beadwork. There was a cap and coat formed of the skin of the beaver, now becoming very scarce. There were also the furs of the lynx, the bear, and other animals of the province. Two travelling sleighs were shown. There were likewise models of the suspension-bridge over the St. John; of carriages, engines, and snow ploughs, such as are used on American railways; and models of saw-mills, and circular saws, that are used for cutting timber. Specimens of the native woods were shown in their rough and in their polished state: some bound in the form of a book, for the purpose of being more easily examined. Among the minerals were specimens of the Albert-coal, black and glittering as jet, which will burn like a candle; and from which Albertine oil is distilled in large quantities. The mine is worked extensively by a company in New Brunswick, who have sunk one shaft to the depth of 750 feet, and are now sinking another, which it is expected will be continued to the enormous depth of 1500 feet. One ton produces from 16,000 to 18,000 cubic feet of gas, or about eighty gallons of Albertine or paraffin oil. Some specimens of shale found a short distance from these works yield about sixty gallons of oil to the ton.

Models of improved steering apparatus and windlasses; a horizontal windmill, which will work by the wind no matter in what direction it may be blowing; hay-making machines; and a model of a suspension-bridge over the Falls of St. John, were among the most interesting mechanical products. Among the industrial work was a mantelpiece of enamelled iron, brightly coloured and decorated.

VANCOUVER ISLAND.

This island, more than twice as large as Wales, was represented by some stuffed specimens of the native deer; models of native canoes; and bottles of preserved fruits of the country. The country is rich in metals and minerals: not only gold, but silver, copper, lead, iron, coal, zinc, and quicksilver have been discovered, besides coal, limestone, slate, and granite. Specimens were also shown of the red bricks, made near Victoria, the capital of the island. Vancouver, in 1858, drew from San Francisco 40,000 gold-seekers, when thousands perished in the adventure; and experience shows gold-finding here to be less profitable than agriculture in Canada, or shepherding in Australia.

A spar of Douglas fir, of which specimens were exhibited, was brought from the island: it is 220 feet long, and now reared as a flagstaff in the Horticultural Society's Garden.*

PRINCE EDWARD'S ISLAND.

From this smallest of the group of North American colonies were sent a mowing-machine; a variety of agricultural implements; and an ingenious running block, promised to create a revolution in ships' rigging. There were canoes and native spear-handles, carved by the Indians; also samples of hemp, of enormous lengths and fibre equal to the best of that imported from Russia; samples of wheat, barley, and Indian corn. Here was also shown the pork for which the island is famous; together with preserved lobster, salmon, and other fish; and a large skin of a black bear indicated one of the native animals of the settlement.

NOVA SCOTIA.

The Zoological specimens of this colony were prominent in the collection: a large stuffed moose deer stood in the centre. On one side was a case of grouse and partridges, and on the other ducks and waterfowl. Here were specimens of the fish, obtained in such large quantities in the neighbouring waters: mackerel, in three sizes, as sorted for the markets of the United States and the West Indies: salmon, pollock, haddock, hake, and cod. There were also specimens of the alewife and the Digby chicken fish—esteemed of considerable delicacy amongst the Nova Scotians—preserved in spirits; behind them were others, salted and dried.

The grain and meal of the colony were shown under glass-cases, and upon the wall hung a picture, formed of the natural wild flowers of the country. Then came samples of ales, wines, and

* This is stated to be the largest and longest spar that has ever been seen in this or any other country. That at Kew Gardens, 190 feet high, was thought to be the largest single stick that was ever seen, but this gigantic pole from Vancouver Island completely dwarfs it, being no less than 220 feet from end to end. Placed straight on end by the side of the Monument it would overtop even that lofty column by 19 feet.

ciders; honey from the bees lately introduced into Nova Scotia; preserved and potted fruits, meats, and fish; perfumes, and sugar from the maple-tree; apples, pears, cherries, gooseberries, currants, and other fruits similar to the old country, were shown, preserved in spirits, so that their form and colour might be seen. Here also were skins of the lynx, the silver-grey fox, and the bear.

Pearls, and the fresh-water mussel in which they are found, were shown here; and grains and small nuggets of gold evidenced the fortunes of the gold-seeker of Nova Scotia.

Of the bird's-eye maple furniture there were some well-made specimens; and here was a chair, made of the wood grown at Prince's Lodge, the residence of the Duke of Kent, the father of our beloved Queen, when Governor of the colony; the chair was sent as a souvenir to Her Majesty.

Among the mineral products was shown a column of Coal, 36 eet in height. There were also displayed large lumps of brown hæmatite and specular iron ore, which supply the furnaces of the Acadian Ironworks. Pig and bar iron from these works were also exhibited. In the useful descriptive catalogue of the articles sent by this province it is stated that 1200 tons of iron are annually made there, of the value of 16*l*. per ton.

THE AUSTRALIAN COLONIES

Of the almost unlimited natural wealth of the colonies of Great Britain, displayed in the Exhibition, Australia attracted most attention; as well from the unprecedented rapidity with which her resources have been developed, as from the fine quality of some of the objects displayed. At the Exhibition of 1851 this great continent was represented by a few ores and cereals, a block of timber here and there, and a case or two of wools; but now were shown in rich profusion samples of all the gifts with which nature can endow a land to make it great and flourishing, such as can hardly be surpassed by the most prosperous countries in the Old World. Geologists examined with the greatest interest the specimens of gold and of copper; agriculturists never tired of handling the wheat and maize; and wools and cottons were highly praised by the best judges. The endless variety of woods, useful and ornamental, also came in for a large share of admiration, and gave some idea of the vastness of the primæval forests, which, no doubt, will form an important element in the prosperity of the colonies.*

NEW SOUTH WALES,

the parent colony of the Australian group, takes the lead in pastoral industry. The colony owes its prominence in the production of wools to the enterprise of Captain Macarthur, of Camden, who, noting the effect of the natural grasses on the fleeces of ordinary sheep, imported at his own expense three rams and five ewes of

* These abstracts of the contributions from the Australian colonies are principally abridged and condensed from the excellent Reports in the *Times*.

pure Spanish breed, with which he crossed all the coarse-woolled sheep. The result of this patriotic enterprise was that in 1860 the export of wool from Sydney was 12,809,362 lb., and its estimated value 1,123,699*l*.

The samples of Wools, fleece and scoured, were of admirable quality; and there were two or three fine Merino fleeces, one of which, the produce of an imported French merino lamb, weighed 7¼ lb. Mr. Ledger exhibited a beautiful sample of Wool from the Alpacas, which he introduced into the colony from Peru with great success; the natural grasses suit them admirably, and Mr. Ledger is said to be confident that they will attain to maturity at an earlier age than in South America, with a larger form and a heavier fleece. In 50 years it is calculated that the flock introduced by him will have increased to 9,760,000, producing a clip of 68,320,000 lb.; and the rapid increase of the flocks of merino sheep within the past sixty years appears to be some justification for this apparently extravagant estimate. In a large case were shown seven stuffed specimens—a pure lama, a pure alpaca, and five crosses between them. The lama is the largest animal, but has short coarse wool, with bare head, belly, and legs; while the pure alpaca has finer, heavier, and longer wool, with head, face, and neck covered. The changes produced by cross-breeding were very curiously shown in the other specimens. The alpaca fat is said to be at least two degrees better for ordinary purposes than mutton fat, and in Peru it is in great request for pomade: a specimen bottle of alpaca pomade was exhibited. The Woollen goods shown were made from the Australian wools by English manufacturers. The merinos and mousseline-de-laines, contributed by Messrs. Pease, almost rivalled the Cashmere fabrics in exquisite fineness of texture; but the most generally admired pieces were two splendid lengths of blue and black beaver cloth. In the French department, Seydoux, Sieber, and Co., of Paris, exhibited a shawl manufactured from Australian wool, which is of remarkable beauty.

The finest Cotton exhibited in the Building was to be found in the New South Wales Court, and some of the samples have been priced as high as 4s. per lb.: a sample which attracted much attention was grown 50 miles from the sea-coast, in south latitude 33°.

In Cereals, too, the colony took a high rank. The best sample was grown at Bathurst, and the three samples of white wheat, which run from 64 lb. to 68 lb. per bushel, grown at Camden-park, were much admired. As a flour-making wheat it is said to be of first-rate quality. Maize seems to be a crop with which the soil and climate of New South Wales agree capitally, and some splendid cobs, both for size and close packing, of the grain were shown here. A sample of a most productive kind yields as much as 100 bushels to the acre; the large pure yellow sorts weigh 65 lb. to the bushel, and the smaller yellow 66 lb. There were numerous specimens of the products of the Vines of New South

Wales, including all the varieties grown there—Hungarian light wines, Tokay—to which the Muscat has a great affinity—Hermitage, Madeira, Bordeaux, and Burgundy. Since the Paris Exhibition, when the jurors reported strongly in their favour, the market for Australian wines has very much increased. Among the other products exhibited were Cayenne pepper, preserved fruits, tobacco, sponges; and sugar-canes, for which some parts o the colony are said to be admirably fitted.

The portions of the show, however, both here and in the Victoria Court, which were looked at with the deepest interest by most people, were the specimens from the goldfields, which, by the enormous tide of immigration they attracted, are the true cause of the rapid rise of our Australian colonies. A glass-case in front of the Nave, contributed by Lady Cooper, contained a large nugget, weighing 80 oz.; also some very curious specimens, showing the fantastic way in which the gold deposits itself. The contributions from the Sydney Mint, however, were the most interesting and complete of the collection. The first contained samples of all the principal goldfields of the colony, and some of them are of remarkable purity. From Moruza, for instance, there were two samples, worth 4l. 3s. 6d. and 4l. 3s. 7d. per oz. respectively. Another cabinet was very ingeniously arranged so as to show at a glance almost all the various strata the miners had to pass in the different fields, with their character and depth. Both cabinets were prepared with great care by the deputy-master of the Sydney Mint, Captain Ward. The yield of the New South Wales goldfields, though inferior to that of Victoria, is steadily on the increase, and in 1860 amounted to nearly 2,000,000l. in value. Two characteristics were represented by two figures in gold, the Emeu and the Kangaroo, sent by Sir John Young, the governor of the colony.

The colony has a great advantage over its neighbour in the possession of one of the most extensive Coalfields in the world. The upper seams alone are being worked at present, and the pits in operation at Newcastle, on the Hunter, are capable of yielding 1,000,000 tons annually, at prices ranging from 13s. 6d. to 15s. per ton. Samples of the principal pits have been sent over and have recently been tried at Woolwich. Of four sorts the report is most favourable, the percentage of clinker and ash being considerably less than in the Welsh coal. There were also specimens of the silver, lead, copper, and iron ores of the colony; of porcelain-clay, pumice-stone, alum, plaster of Paris, pipe-clay, meerschaum, sulphate of antimony, and sulphate of magnesia, all of which are said to exist in great quantities in various parts.

QUEENSLAND,

the latest-born of our Australian Colonies, made an excellent display, notwithstanding the settlement is only in its third year. First, of Cotton there were numerous samples. The quality of the Sea Island cotton is remarkably fine, and has been priced by such authorities as Mr. Bazley and Mr. Ashworth at 3s. 3d. and 3s. 6d. per pound. One sample, grown 200 miles from the sea-board, rivalled in quality that grown on the sea-coast. The principal export of the colony at present is wool, of which upwards of 5,000,000 bales, the produce of 3,500,000 sheep, are annually exported. A dress-length was exhibited here by Mr. Bazley as an illustration of the Queensland cotton and wool. It is manufactured from No. 250-lace thread, spun from pure cotton grown in Queensland; the wool having been spun from the finest sheep's wool, also produced in the colony. There were also a few samples of Silk of excellent quality, and the climate is said to be well adapted to the growth of the mulberry-tree. The specimens shown, both of wheat and flour, were very fine. The most generally cultivated crop is Maize. There were some splendid cobs shown here, and one sample is said to have been grown 1600 feet above the level of the sea. Samples of arrow-root, coffee, tobacco, sugar-canes, tamarinds, manna, wine, and honey furnished additional illustrations of the capabilities of the colony; and we must not omit to mention the fibres of the banana, the phormium tenax, and a malvaceous plant said to grow with great luxuriance near Brisbane, which are all of remarkable strength. Another of the most remarkable natural products is the dugong oil, procured from the blubber of the dugong—a fish which is found in large herds at the mouth of the Brisbane. The flesh was exhibited as a substitute for cod-liver oil : it contains no iodine, but, on the other hand, it is sweet and palatable, and does not produce nausea. There was also a collection of medicinal barks of some value, and a specimen of coal from the Red Bank Pits. The collection of woods was one of the finest in the Building. The Moreton Bay pine, the iron bark, the blue gum, the box, which are of the highest value for all building purposes, grow to an immense size in the Queensland forests; while in the violet-wood, tulip, acacia, and cypress, the colony possesses furniture woods of unrivalled beauty. Mr. Justice Lutwyche sent a very elegant set of chessmen and a table of myall and cypress wood mixed. One of the handsomest pieces of colonial furniture was a table inlaid with various woods, at the entrance to the New Zealand Court. Lady Cooper contributed a case of Queensland jewellery, the chief objects in which were a pearl of considerable size, mounted in gold, and a brooch of white topazes. There were also several cases of interesting Queensland birds.

SOUTH AUSTRALIA.

Although this colony is not, like New South Wales and Victoria, a gold-producing country, in return, she is unusually rich in copper, and the Burra-Burra, Kapunda, and the Wallaroo mines —from all of which, and other mines, there were ample specimens in the Exhibition—are reckoned among the most productive in the world. The Burra-Burra has been at work since September, 1845, and the annual yield for many years past has averaged from 10,000 to 13,000 tons of from 22 to 23 per cent. of copper. The specimens exhibited from the mine included sulphuret of copper in matrix of limestone; red oxide in silicious matrix; green carbonate with manganese; sulphuret associated with iron, from the lowest depth of the workings, yielding 50 per cent. of copper; and a number of beautiful pieces of the green carbonate or malachite. These specimens of Burra-Burra malachite completely eclipsed the famous Russian doors which attracted so much attention at the Exhibition of 1851. The ores exhibited from the Kapunda comprised almost every variety—as yellow ore or pyrites, blue and green carbonates, muriates, grey and black sulphurets, peacock ores, and malleable copper; the percentage varying much, from 66 per cent. downwards. The Wallaroo ores average from 15 to 25 per cent. of richness, and they possess the great advantage of easy access to the seaboard. The specimens included green carbonate, irony copper ore, vitreous copper ore, silver grey ore, black ore, copper pyrites, and horseflesh ore. There are also other copper mines which are rapidly rising to importance in Yorke's Peninsula, such as the Moonta and the New Cornwall: from the latter was sent a large block of ore composed of rich grey oxide and gossan, weighing 6 tons. In the district north of Port Augusta, which is also of rich promise, the chief mine open is the Great Northern, from which we had here a large block of rich red oxide of copper. In addition to these were specimens from the Karkulto, the Durea, the Cumberland, the Worthing, and other copper mines; and from the Wheal Ella, and from the Aclare silver-lead mines. The English and Australian Copper Company and the Kapunda Smelting Works sent some fine ingots of copper, and there was also a case showing the various stages of Rodda's patent process for smelting copper ores.

There are in South Australia about 400,000 acres of land under cultivation; the colony not only produces enough to feed itself, but is the chief granary of its neighbours, Victoria and New South Wales. The samples of Corn exhibited were of first-rate quality, superior to anything shown from the Old World, and only missing by an ounce or two the honour of being the heaviest in the Building. About 3500 acres are under cultivation as Vineyard, and their produce amounts to 300,000 gallons of Wine, besides 1000 tons of table grapes, which are exported by steamer to Melbourne. Among the samples exhibited were a red Burgundy and a pure Riesling, grown at Pewsey-vale; a Shiraz and Donzelinho, a superior claret; an excellent Verdeilho from the Auldana vineyard; and a wine of a peculiarly delicate fragrance, something between a Hock and a Sauterne, from the Clarendon vineyard. Owing its discovery and its foundation almost to the development of the pastoral industry of New South Wales, and the success of Mr. M'Arthur's experiments for the improvement of the breed of Sheep, South Australia takes a high

T

rank among the wool-producing countries of the world. The samples of wool exhibited were of excellent quality; with specimens of alpaca wool, and emu-eggs, richly mounted.

The representative of the Colonial Commission exhibited, as a specimen of the progress of Printing in South Australia, a complete set of the Colonial Statutes and of the South Australian *Hansard*. A Reaping-machine, invented by Mr. Ridley, was shown, which the colonists have so highly appreciated that they presented him a handsome silver candelabrum, to be seen here. In woods there were some pretty specimens of native turnery, and a pair of steam-made wheels composed of blue gum and other South Australian woods. Two large slabs of slate, six feet square, were sent from the Mintaro slate quarries. Mr. Dutton also exhibited a collection of colonial minerals, and a small quantity was shown of gold from the Victoria mine, eight miles from Adelaide.

WESTERN AUSTRALIA.

Passing to the West Australian Court, the chief resources at present developed appeared to be timber and minerals. The colony in the Jarrah possesses a wood which, for strength, endurance, and adaptability to a variety of purposes, is hardly to be surpassed. Of this and the Tooart—another wood of remarkably close grain, and almost as hard as iron, also specially useful for ship-building —Admiral Stirling told a committee of the House of Commons some years ago, that there was enough in the West Australian colonies to build a score of British navies. A pile of this wood was shown, which had been under water since 1832, and yet showed no symptoms of decay: it has equally resisted the ravages of the teredo and the white ant. There was also a mahogany post which has been seventeen years in water, with about three feet of its length in mud, without any damage. The Royal Engineers' department sent a cabinet which showed the various woods of the colony very effectively—sandal-wood, Banksia, cypress, peppermint-tree, and raspberry-jam-tree: this last, which is of the Eucalyptus species, is so called by the colonists from the similarity of its scent to raspberry-jam. The fragrant sandal-wood of the colony, of which there was a log here weighing 454 lb., is largely exported to Singapore and China: a cabinet was shown here, the work of convicts, and Messrs. Robson and Redpath had each a hand in it. Among the barks shown was the bark of the Tea-tree, so easily reducible to a pulp that it probably might be made available for papermaking. Mr. Ranford also exhibited samples of Wattle Barks, very valuable for tanning purposes; and a collection of colonial Leathers, including sole leather, calf, kangaroo, and sheep skins. The mineral wealth of the colony is at present little known: it consists of large quantities of copper and lead, with silver, iron, plumbago, and antimony in smaller quantity. Seams of coal have also been found, and occasionally in the beds of streams minute specks of gold. From the leading mine, the Wheal Fortune, we had numerous specimens both of lead and copper ore; and from the Geraldine Mine a fine sample of lead ore, part of a mass which weighed a ton. The Royal Engineers' department sent a bar of iron reduced from magnetic iron ore, which has been proved in conjunction with a bar of the iron of commerce and one of Swedish iron, the result being a deflection of about five to eight in favour of the colonial iron. There were also specimens of porcelain clay found in the colony, and of the Wilgi, an ochreish clay, with which the aborigines anoint themselves when they wish to appear particularly well dressed. Mr. Drummond, who also exhibited gums of extraordinary tenacity from the Boro Blackboy, sent a curious formation of rock in which asbestos forms a principal ingredient—so soft that it may be cut into any shape by an axe. The Vine grows most luxuriantly and produces magnificent grapes, but the wine, from want of skilled manufacturers, is not particularly good. The samples exhibited chiefly resembled Frontignac, Fontainebleau, and Madeira. The Central Committee and other exhibitors contributed wools of beautiful texture; and there were samples of West Australian Wheat, one of which is reported to weigh nearly 70 lb. to the bushel. Among other substances used for food were cases of preserved meat, including kangaroo tail—said to be of delicious flavour; also, 50 ounces of jelly seaweed, prepared from 63 lb. of the living weed, and capable of producing 100 quarts of jelly or blancmange. The gorgeous birds of the colony were entirely unrepresented, except by two or three beautiful feather screens and ladies' muffs of cockatoo and parrot feathers, and a magnificent carriage rug of the skin of an emu. Of opossum and other skins there were some handsome samples; and there was a numerous collection of native weapons.

VICTORIA.

The colonists had evidently taken great pains in this collection to illustrate the unexampled prosperity and almost boundless resources of their favoured country. In 1851, the colonies of Victoria, Queensland, British Columbia, and Tasmania had no existence. In the short ten years that have intervened since then, they have grown into what may be termed distinct States, and one of them at least—Victoria—contains such elements of wealth, such boundless mineral and agricultural resources within itself, as must in a few years make her the foremost and most powerful of the great cluster of our young Southern empires. The rise and suddenly acquired and vast material prosperity of this colony transcend all that has yet been told of colonial enterprise. When the Exhibition of 1851 was opened, the only habitation on the site of the present town of Ballarat was a shepherd's hut, built of slabs of wood, and roofed with bark. In a circle, having Ballarat as a centre, with a radius of 40 miles, the population then did not exceed 500 persons. The population of the same area in 1861 was 105,996 persons, the town of Ballarat 22,111.

From such a colony, the youngest and most favoured and vigorous of all our offshoots, a great collection for the Exhibition was to be expected; and such a collection arrived, rich not only in its gold and silver and tin, but in its almost superabundance of wools, corn, tallow, and hides. At the east end of the Building, in a beautifully carved wood case, was 50,000*l.* worth of Gold in every form in which it has been known or supposed to exist. There was a suggestive model illustration of this vast amount of Victoria gold.

The tall pyramid under the eastern dome 44 feet 9½ inches in height and 10 feet square at the base, represented the bulk of the Gold exported from Victoria from the 1st of October, 1851, to the 1st of October, 1861—the period from the close of the Exhibition of 1851 to the date when it was necessary to send the goods from Victoria to the recent Exhibition. The quantity of gold which it represents is 20,162,432 ounces troy; 1,793,995 lbs. avoirdupois; or 800 tons, 17 cwt., 3 qrs., 7 lbs. It is equal in solid measurement to 1402½ cubic feet; while the value of the gold thus represented, all of which has been exported to England, is 104,649,728*l.*, or more than one-eighth of our national debt. On the surface of the pyramid were represented models of some of the larger nuggets which have been found, with reference to the names of their fortunate discoverers. On other portions of the surface there were representations of the ingots into which the gold was formed previous to exportation.

Here was gold in nuggets worth 10,000*l.*; gold in bars and massive ingots; gold almost black, red, yellow, and brown; rough masses crystallized into the most beautiful forms; gold mixed with crystals of iron spotted over the milk-white quartz-like rare gems, or cased in bottles in an impalpable powder got from the blankets of the crushing-machines, and so fine that it floats in water like a metallic lustre. The labels attached to these specimens stated how they were got, and at what depths. To judge from the amount of labour required to bring them to the surface, gold must be almost as hard to win in Victoria as in England. The Maryburgh Mariner's reef is 550 ft. deep, and the shaft had to be driven through a bed of granite 250 ft. thick! The Cosmopolitan Gold Mining Company has had to take its shaft first through 4 ft. of surface soil, and then through 112 ft. of solid rock, then 16 ft. of hard clay, then 27 ft. more of rock, then 7 ft. of red clay, and finally 200 ft. of quartz rock, when at last a "seasoning" of gold was reached, but, as the label states, by "no means too much of it." The average depth of most reefs in Victoria is 300 ft.; the average depth of the common "wash dirt" surface diggings, 12 ft. The richer kinds of Quartz yield from 5 to 15 ounces to the ton.

The Victoria Commissioners, Sir Redmond Barry and Mr. C. E. Bright, were most anxious to carry out the wishes of the colonists and show the English public how the gold was washed, and how the quartz was crushed, and the most minute grains of the metal extracted from it. For this purpose the colonists went to the expense of sending over a ship laden with gold quartz, with a crushing-machine and some tons of "wash-dirt," to show the common mode of washing in the surface diggings. The crushing-machine was not allowed to be shown in the Building nor in the Machinery Annexe, but was exiled to the open Court off the Eastern Annexe. Water-power was the only power allowed, and though this had been laid on at much expense, it only yielded sufficient force to turn six out of the twenty-four stampers, and these so feebly and slowly, that the working of the machine was virtually discontinued. The process of washing the gold from the dirt was shown in the south-east transept. Before leaving the gold we may mention a Gold Inkstand, presented to Mr. J. V. Bruce by the workmen employed on the Melbourne and Murray Railway. Near the great collection of gold was also shown a very fine Bracelet made entirely of nuggets; and close by this was a small piece of Quartz studded over with small knobs of gold about as large as a pea. This little piece is as suggestive in its way as the great pyramid of which it is the parent: it was the first piece of gold found in Victoria by a shepherd near Ballarat—*the* piece which led to subsequent examination and the discovery of all the gold regions which have since wrought such wonderful results both for this country and Australia. Close by the gold was shown the firstfruits of another great source of colonial wealth—namely, the first sackful of Coals ever raised in the colony, from a mine near Cape Paterson. With gold, coal, iron, tin, copper, and silver in abundance, what prosperity may not Victoria look to in the future!

Specimens (weighing nearly 1 cwt.) of what may almost be termed native Iron, so pure is the ore, were exhibited, containing between 80 and 90 per cent. of metal: they are found strewed over the surface of the earth in some parts of the colony like boulders.

Among other curious objects shown in this collection was a Meteorite found near Ballarat, and weighing 30 cwt. A section of it shows graphite and magnetic pyrite in nests or patches through the mass, with chloride of iron exuding from the interstices. This most wonderful specimen of meteoric iron is, however, only a quarter the size of one found in the same colony. Among the natural produce exhibited were some samples of very fine Tobacco, the cultivation of which, in a few years more, promises to be as lucrative as the trade in gold, wool, or tallow. The kind chiefly grown is the Virginia leaf, but said to be of a far finer flavour than that raised in America. With the tobacco Victoria also sent Pipes, mounted with solid gold. The Vine comes to full and most luxuriant bearing three years after the slip is planted: already the South Australian wines are forcing their way into the market; at this Exhibition they have taken many Medals. A remarkable collection of samples of Wool was shown, representing the "clips" of more than a million sheep of various breeds! This was probably the finest colonial exhibition of the kind ever shown, both for the length of the wool, its general condition and combing properties, and to this part of the show most deservedly several Prize Medals were awarded. The great bulk of the wool shown was merino.

Some exquisite French shawls and merino fabrics were shown, made entirely from Victoria wools; the former the most perfect specimens of the kind in the Building, and the latter equal to any of the best real Spanish merino manufactured in France. In Cereals, the success of Victoria was even greater than with the wools. No other colony or country represented in the Building showed such a collection. Some specimens of Wheat weighed as much as 68 lb. 8 oz. per bushel. Another fine collection, which weighed 67 lb. 14 oz. a bushel, was stated to be the produce of the *sixth* crop reared in succession on the same land. As with the wheat, so was it also with the rye and barley, the Victorian produce carrying off the palm from all competitors. The indigenous and acclimatized Fruits were shown in a fine collection of wax models, cast from originals in Victoria for the purpose of being sent to this Exhibition. Some of them, especially the pears, were wonderfully fine, the pears attaining sometimes to a weight of 3 lb. There was also exhibited a fine and numerous display of highly-scented essential Oils from various native trees and plants. True Kaolin, or the best porcelain clay, which enters largely into the production of soap wherever it is cheap enough, is found in abundance in Victoria. The manufacturers are utilizing the tallow by the production of candles, called "sperm," though made from stearic acid: some remarkably good specimens of these candles were displayed. There was shown dried meat called "charqui," which is almost peculiar to Victoria: it keeps fresh in the hottest climates during almost any length of time.

A Victoria street-cab was shown of immense superiority over any vehicle of the kind we English possess, both as regards form, size, and comfort. It is a kind of very broad dog-cart, with high wheels like those of a Hansom; well balanced on its axle; it has three front and three back seats, sheltered by a large hood. A very good collection was shown of the principal fishes of Victoria, dried and stuffed, including, among others, a specimen of the celebrated Murray cod: it is probably the largest fresh-water fish known, 150 lb. being a not very unusual weight for it.

Altogether, for variety and importance, no collection in the Exhibition equalled that of Victoria. It showed a most complete and interesting collection of the chief buildings and objects of interest in the colony, and its fine oil and water-colour paintings were the only colonial works of the kind to which Prize Medals were adjudged.

Lastly, Victoria occupied nearly 6000 ft. of the Exhibition, and received more Prize Medals and Honourable Mentions than any other dependency of this country, save India.

TASMANIA.

This colony (formerly Van Diemen's Land, and one of our penal settlements,) made a good display of its products, of which useful and ornamental timber was most prominent. The Australian woods were perhaps seen to most perfection here; and in the octagonal trophy, in the north-eastern transept, were splendid specimens of all the principal trees of Tasmania : there were planks and spars of the blue gum and of the stringy bark, showing at once the immense thickness to which these trees attain. There were also samples of the white gum, silver wattle, blackwood—all timbers of great value for ship-building purposes; and in the Horticultural Gardens might be seen planks of 80 and 90 feet long, for which room could not be found here, and a spar of 230 feet long. From Port Arthur there were some magnificent ships' knees, which before the days of iron ships would have been almost invaluable.

Among the ornamental woods was the myrtle tree, remarkable for the beauty of its veins; and Huon pine, dog-wood, pinkwood, and musk-wood, for cabinet work. The Southern whale fishery was illustrated by two handsome whale-boats, fitted with their gear, and by the jaws of two full-sized sperm whales, one of which produced 1150*l.* worth of oil. There were also specimens of the oil of the black whale, sperm whale, and porpoise. The beautiful furs, mostly of black and gray opossum, were also shown. The Tasmania building-stone, of which many of the public buildings in Melbourne are constructed, was exhibited : and there were fine specimens of black and gray marble. Of coal, too, the island possesses several seams, both of anthracite and bituminous, of which there were samples; as well as a combustible mineral called dysodile—from which the colonists manufacture petroleum. A small portion of Tasmanian gold was shown; and in the same case were some brilliant topazes from Flinder's Island, mounted with great taste. The fruits of Tasmania were represented in admirably-executed wax models. Of wheat there were fine samples; and, lastly, there was a showy collection of the birds of the colony of every variety of hue.

NEW ZEALAND.

Adjoining the New South Wales Court, having a bay fronting the nave, was represented New Zealand, "the Britain of the South." Each of its provinces sent chiefly its natural produce. Nelson contributed its specimens of gold; and the Dun Mountain Mining Company showed the commercial products obtained from chromate of iron, found in their mines, as well as specimens of copper. From the North Island were specimens of the magnificent woods of its forests : some has been tested and found superior to English elm, and nearly equal to the British oak. Of the kauri there were many planks and logs : it has been used to a large extent in our navy for ships' masts, and sticks from 70 to 100 feet in length, tapering from 40 inches square at the bottom to 18 inches at the head, are often to be met with in these vast forests. There was also shown the *phormium tenax*, a fibre available for many of the purposes to which flax and hemp are applicable. Coal was sent from Nelson and Canterbury. There were samples of wool, for the growth of which the island is well adapted; corn, and vegetables, and fruits of the same description as are produced at home. Photographs of the rapidly growing towns of this fine colony were interspersed with drawings of the natural scenery and portraits of the native chiefs.

THE SANDWICH ISLANDS.

From this remote group in the Pacific, Lady Franklin, who had been making a visit to the islands, brought with her to England a small collection of objects of interest from Honolulu, made without any reference to the Exhibition. The only two products of mercantile value shown were pulu, a silky fibre surrounding the base of the rachis of a large fern, and which is extensively used both in the islands and in America as a substitute for wool and feathers in stuffing mattresses and pillows; and the root of the awa plant (*piper mephysticum*), from which an intoxicating drink, having also medicinal properties, is prepared. There were also a feather tippet, a feather wand of office, grass hats; and cloth made from the paper-mulberry bark, with the implements of manipulation and colour. More interesting were the literary specimens exhibited: the New Testament, translated by the American missionaries in the islands, and printed in Hawaiian and English in parallel columns; the entire Bible; books of mental arithmetic for children, and an advanced book for adults, a child's primer, and an atlas, all in the Hawaiian language. Beyond these were a volume of the statute laws of the Hawaiian kingdom in English; two or three newspapers, both native and English, published at Honolulu; and copies of the King's speech at the opening of the Legislature, &c. There were portraits also of King Kamehameha IV. and Queen Emma.

FRANCE, AND HER COLONIES.

This very important display was a most interesting collection of works of art and industry, contributed by no less than 5495 exhibitors, from France, Algeria, and her colonies. It was the best-arranged Court in the Building. The entrance portico was a noble work, of cast iron, manufactured by M. Barbezat. It formed a corridor extending the entire length of the Court: the portico had three divisions: the east and west were entrances to the Exhibition; the centre division was backed by a noble sheet of spotless plate-glass, perfectly transparent, manufactured at St. Gobain—its dimensions were ten feet and a half broad by sixteen feet and a half high. At the foot of the glass was a richly-ornamented couch or divan—the sides protected by lions of cast-iron, the size of life, placed on pedestals of granite: the central division was surmounted by the imperial arms, and flags; the side-entrances had bronze gilt chandeliers, six feet in diameter, inlaid with crystals. In the centre of the Court was found the gold and silver work; in the diagonals were set out various textures for dress or household purposes; on two sides was deposited in various stages of preparation, a vast assortment of edibles. The real worth of the collection was very great. In tapestry it was unique; in bronzes it bore the palm; in porcelain it was of extraordinary value; some of its glass was perfect; we may say the same of its gold, its silver, and its jewellery; the printing of the Imperial press has never been surpassed; French furniture sustained its old fame amid much rivalry; France is the queen of silk; we have a hard fight to keep up with her in certain musical instruments; and though we could show many great engineering works of the last ten years that may hold their own beside the best in the world, yet, as we have not chosen to do so, except in a very few instances, the French, as represented in their models of public works, stood forth in a very enviable light in this Exhibition. Such was the estimate given in the *Times*, a few weeks after the opening of the Exhibition.

The most conspicuous object in the Court—a great banner hung aloft, and attracting every eye—was the Gobelins tapestry—a glorious picture by Titian of the Assumption of the Virgin reproduced in wool. Beside it was a portrait of Louis XIV. in his robes. On either side were two wonderful fruit-pieces, the manufacture of Beauvais. These magnificent works have already been described at pp. 175-176.

In glass-cases on the floor were other specimens of Beauvais work—chairs and sofas, the seats and backs of which were covered with the most marvellously-wrought groups of flowers. Scarcely less marvellous in result was the splendid tapestry of Aubusson: its woven pictures and its flowered seats were triumphs of skill.

Here we may mention the elaborately tinted specimens of French Paper-hanging: some of the paper pictures are copies from old masters, and when shown as in the French Court, framed and hung a short distance from the ground, are such good imitations as to deceive all but practised eyes. In the production of some of these paper-pictures as many as 250 blocks are used, yet the price of the best of them (without their frames) is only 40£.

CERAMIC WARE.

At the head of the Ceramic collection stood the magnificent manufactures of Sèvres. Here it was at once shown that the character of Sèvres is changed. It produces little of the old sort. Its royal blue is nearly as good as of yore; but its turquoise blue is dull, its *Rose de Barry* is very far from the mark, and its gilding wants lustre. Instead of these, however, we were presented with other hues—with many other hues. Here were vases and cups of every form, and of many tints. Perhaps the most interesting part of the collection was a small case containing three or four dozen cups; every cup almost was different—not merely in pattern, but in more essential qualities. There was not one which had not called forth the highest skill of the French artist, and would not fetch a fabulous price. The production of a sort of seagreen ware—they call it *"céladon,"* and a variety of it *"céladon changeant"*—which first appeared in the Paris Exhibition in 1855, may be regarded as the leading feature of the Sèvres display.

The colour is characteristic of modern Sèvres in this respect, that it is of a low tone. The primary colours are for the most part eschewed; so also the secondary ones; and those which are sought are the tertiary and still more complex combinations. What is here called *céladon* is most feebly translated in the epithet seagreen. It is a gray, dull seagreen of many shades, more or less allied to some old oriental ware, which it is more easy to recognise than to describe. This *céladon* is a body-colour, it pervades the paste, and on it the French artists have succeeded in pencilling with a similar but white paste various designs, chiefly leaves and flowers, which stand out in gentle relief upon the vase or cup, white upon the *céladon* ground. The effect is very beautiful, especially in a variety of the *céladon* which is called *changeant*, because of the singular ease with which it reflects local colour. By gas-light this *céladon* looks pink.

Some of the little tea-services were very beautiful, but perhaps the finest specimens were two great pitchers (if we may call them by so common a name) which were mounted with gilt bronze, and divided in the middle by painted friezes, beautifully drawn by an artist named Froment, and represented peace and war. They were done in a peculiar red tint, which contrasted well with the gray seagreen of the pitcher. It must be remembered that the most valuable sort of *céladon* is the changing kind. The unchanging was very fairly imitated by a private maker, Pillivuyt, in the same court; the changing is as yet inimitable.

The Sèvres manufactory has been attempting something of everything, among others majolicas, here enamels on iron, there enamels on copper. What is their chief strength, what is, indeed, the strength of all French ceramics, is their skill in the higher kinds of figure-painting. The old Sèvres produced in its perfection was shown on the stand of a private manufacturer—M. Bettignies. Some of his pieces were wonderfully like the original, and but for the want of the original mark, the place of manufacture, they might by many persons be mistaken for the reality. It is well known that for years past the market has been rather loaded with modern imitations of old Sèvres, bearing, too, the old marks. The imitation is so well done that if the articles were found in the collection of any well-known fancier they would at once pass for real.

Another manufacturer had outdone the old Palissy ware. A small case bearing the name of Avisseau, of Tours, contained two pieces in imitation of Palissy ware—one a dish with a pike and other fish on it, the other a plateau, on which a heron is contending with a snake. It was extraordinary work. The glancing light on the skin of the pike and the eel in the one case, and of the snake in the other, was quite marvellous. In drawing, in action, in colour, everything was perfect. In the whole Exhibition it was the very best of its kind. The other pieces were intended for reproductions of the ware of Henri Deux. They were very fair; but no one who has seen the modelling on the real ware can have a doubt as to the backwardness of the imitation. Next to M. Avisseau's case was M. Chablin's clever species of ware, in which gold or silver is burnt into the enamel in considerable quantities, with very rich result. Next was the ware of M. Pinart, who paints his designs on unfired enamels. He puts the enamel paste on his ware, paints on that, and then fires the whole once for all. His drawings are very free and skilful, and the plates fetched prices which are almost incredible—15*l*. or 16*l*., while there were larger ones for which the prices asked range from 50*l*. to 80*l*. They have rather the appearance of majolicas, and the figures are supposed to show a softer outline in consequence of being drawn on the raw enamel. Next to M. Pinart were M. Macé and M. Pillivuyt, rivals in the production of a remarkable ware, printed from chromo-lithographs, even to the gold; the work is good: and sets of china executed in this process can be sold very cheaply.

The pure white china of Limoges was next shown: the material is beautiful. It is of great strength, so that, although the articles are very thin and semi-transparent, they do not break more readily than common earthenware. M. Pouyat was the maker, and the price told to a juror was 10s. 6d. a dozen. The beautiful transparent porcelain of M. Pouyat is worth remembering. So is the metallic lustre on that of MM. Gillet and Brianchon, some of the biscuit china of M. Gille, and almost every piece in the splendid displays both of M. Lahoche and of M. Rousseau.

To sum up the novelties of Ceramic ware in the French Court,—the most important of all was, of course, the *céladon* and the changing *céladon* of Sèvres. M. Pillivuyt's imitation of this will be distinguished by the most inexperienced, if he will merely look inside the vase, and note whether it is white or of the same tint as the outside. M. Avisseau's Palissy ware was next in importance. M. Pinart, with his paintings on unfired enamel, probably deserves the third place. M. Daniel has invented a process of engine-turning for working upon cups and other vessels various patterns which are really very pretty. The printing process of Pillivuyt and of Macé was excellent; the pure white porcelain of M. Pouyat it is not necessary to dwell upon; and we have only further to mention the singularly beautiful lustre produced by Gillet and Brianchon. Of the biscuit china of Gille one scarcely knows how to speak: the drawing of the figures was unsatisfactory.

SILK MANUFACTURE, ECT.

Of Silk, the most important manufacture of France, the finest specimens were from Lyons; but their adaptability for the present taste is another matter. It has been suggested that while the elaborately figured silks were in fashion, France was unrivalled in the manufacture. There was proof of this to be found even in the recent Exhibition. MM. Schulz set out two pieces of white silk—the one embroidered with orchids, and the other with birds of paradise. The work was a perfect marvel; it was the most astonishing piece of silk in the whole Exhibition; and along with it were shown 300 reels of thread of various tints, which had been required for the production of the figures. Now, although such a dress would not be worn in the present day, still the fabric itself is a miracle of ingenuity, and was worth exhibiting as a specimen of what France can do when she pleases.

The most beautiful silk fabric which the French now make, and which is in common use, goes by the name of Chiné. They excel all the world in this. The peculiarity of it is, that the pattern, which may display any amount of colouring, is printed on the warp and on the warp alone, and that as a consequence it appears, after the weaving has been completed, with a vague and misty outline; to produce a good pattern by such means requires the nicest care.

In Satins, Velvets, and ordinary Silks, France is still the great mistress of the art, though her manufacturers are of very unequal merit. In satin produced by first-rate houses, instead of the beautiful glossy surface in which all appearance of texture is lost, are seen threadiness and tendency to stripe longitudinally, which are characteristic of a poor material. This is attributed to the failure of the rich Lyons silk, and using instead, the China silk, which is irregular in size, knotty in composition, not yet understood. In the manufacture of the beautiful Moire Antique which France brought into fashion a dozen years ago, she has been surpassed. It is the richest sort of watered silk that has yet been produced; but the fabric was seen in the highest perfection in the specimens sent from the looms of Spitalfields. Nothing can be more lovely than the surface which was presented on these latest triumphs of our looms, which threw into the shade the quality of moire antique which the Lyons manufacturer was content to show, and which, till lately, was considered very good work indeed. In the manufacture of the black silk of a peculiar lustre, known as glacé silk, the French hold first rank, and showed some beautiful examples. For a short time the French supplied the entire demand; by and by Spitalfields and Manchester successfully competed for a second and third place in the race; while Switzerland beat all the world in the production of this kind of goods at a low price. At last the German entered into the field, and his goods now rank with those of Manchester.

In no respect was the superiority of France as regards its silk manufactures more evident in 1851 than its Ribands. The ribands of Coventry were formerly much inferior to those of St. Etienne. They are not so now. Tested by the excellence of design, of colour, and of texture, the ribands produced in Coventry are in no point inferior to those exhibited by the French manufacturer, while they greatly surpass the fabrics shown by the Basle houses—their only other competitors. The colours are so brilliant and so exquisitely arranged, that it is clear the art of dyeing has kept pace with the art of design. This change of position may have arisen from the indifference of France to rivalry with Coventry; or from some great effort of the Coventry manufacturers, to gather up their strength, and recover by one effort a portion of their lost prestige. The recent display, therefore, may not truly represent the faculty either of Coventry or of St. Etienne. The French may be under-represented and the English over-represented if tested by the daily productions of the looms. But judging by the samples in the Exhibition, the fact is indisputable that, while France in her ribands showed no marked advance in any respect, the progress of the English had been in every way such as to astonish the foreign manufacturer. These remarks apply not only to the rich figured goods produced more for the display of manufacturing ingenuity than for the direct purposes of trade, but also to the plainest fabrics and simplest designs which are more in harmony with existing fashion.

Of other French fabrics we need not say much. It will be admitted that no one can dye like the Frenchman; in referring to which we may mention as a curious fact, that the dyer of cotton fails in the dyeing of silk, and that the silk dyer does not know how to dye other materials. In this respect the French superiority is undoubted, and the same may be said of certain well-known productions—as a French shawl. There were many French shawls in the Exhibition, though not many of them very remarkable. The best was one displayed by M. Duché; it was a miracle of delicate workmanship and beautifully blended colour; finer than Indian work, though not so durable, and whereas this cost but 60*l.*, an Indian shawl to be compared with it would cost 500*l.* As no country in Europe can match the French in their shawls, we may say the same of much of their Lace. Some of the Venice point, Alençon point, and Brussels lace which they exhibited was superlatively beautiful, and not to be surpassed all the world over. In meaner fabrics we have little to say of them, except that they displayed great heaps of woollens; but we may pass all by, with the exception of the merinos, in which no country can touch France. Under the head of woollens, indeed, carpets ought to be mentioned, and tapestries; but upon the best of these we have already remarked.

GLASS MANUFACTURE.

The display of Glass was certainly meagre, two of the greatest houses having declined to contribute to it. The principal stand was furnished by Maës: here were designs of every kind in cut-glass, in engraved glass, and in glass adorned with colours. Here was glass of the richest ruby tint, there clearest crystal eked out with glass emeralds; here again vessels glorious in gold of vermicelli pattern, and there again some capital imitations of old Venetian work. In one or two curious specimens the glass was wrought in a most ingenious manner. In all the little lozenges formed by a very regular system of cross lines distributed over a glass tazza or other vessel, air-bells were introduced, with a certain glittering effect. In Stained Glass for windows not much of the work could be called good. Among the best was Maréchal's bright picture of the Glorification of St. Catherine, intended for the Cathedral of Metz, and a striking portrait sent from the museum of the town of Metz.

Altogether, the French display of glass was very poor. We have made immense strides since 1851, and now more than match our competitors. Our metal (or glass) is unsurpassable for clearness and lustro; our forms are purer than those of the French; and what our glass engraving is now, the branch of the art in which ten years ago we were most backward, the visitor to the Exhibition could at once see by turning into the British Court to look at the wine-glasses that fetched 5*l*. a-piece, and the little glass tazza which has been sold for 250*l*.

ONYX MARBLE.—BRONZES.

We have occasionally mentioned Algerian or Onyx Marble, which is a new and beautiful material. There was shown the sea-green variety; and the coppery tinted kind, which is less pleasing. Combined artistically with other materials, the result is often wonderful, as was shown in two lamps exhibited by Larolle. Two bronze slaves are holding on their shoulders two lamps: they are draped in onyx marble; their faces, hands, and feet come out in dark bronze, while the dress flows down in marked contrast, provided by the pale-green marble. The transparency of the material and the naturalness of the folds make the dress look like gauze, an effect which is heightened by thin lines, like threads of gold, forming stripes upon the drapery. Barbedienne showed a combination of enamel and the onyx marble: the vase or cup is banded with copper, which is illuminated with colours of brilliant enamel. The sale of the chief objects exhibited by the Onyx Marble Company was very good: some of the larger pieces fetched very high prices: its first introduction at the Exhibition proved a very profitable venture for the exhibitors.

The bronzes of Barbedienne were mostly reduced copies of well-known works, as the Venus of Milo; the Night and Day of Michael Angelo; and the restored group of the Fates, from the pediment of the Parthenon, now in the British Museum. The minute finish and singularly light appearance of the bronzes is their merit. In two cabinets displayed in the same stall was shown the application of bronze to woodwork. The one, an ebony cabinet, was profusely adorned with silvered bronze in arabesques, flowers, and figures: the effect was brilliant. The other was a cabinet in which bronzes were introduced as bosses, finials, and other ornaments, of corresponding tint with the brown wood. M. Barbedienne also showed some *repoussé* work in silver, well finished: two vases which are adorned with *cloisonné* enamel have been bought for the South Kensington Museum. M. Paillard was much more original in his bronzes: one of his best pieces was a mirror in the style of Louis XVI.: it was mounted in gilt-bronze; set off with small figures of children, one playing the flute, another painting, and so on; while it was further adorned with soft porcelain from the manufactory of Bettignies. In other examples children were holding candelabra, a child was catching a carrier pigeon, &c.: the modelling was clever, and the grouping good. M. Paillard, now the most celebrated French artist in bronze, it may be interesting to add, raised himself from the grade of a workman by his genius and by his wonderful aptitude for every branch of the art to the head of his profession.

With these bronzes we may mention the iron castings of Barbezat, Ducel, and others, which were of fair merit.

The most imposing piece of bronzework in the Exhibition, however, was a gilt and silvered centrepiece, intended for the great banquets at the Hôtel de Ville, by Christofle. The principal object is a ship, symbolical of the arms of the city of Paris: it floats in a sea of glass, and on its deck is a group of four nymphs, who support on their shoulders a lady, the emblem of the city of Paris. The details of the work are ably treated, and the modelling is singularly good. Some other of Christofle's bronzework is remarkable for its applicability to the adorning of woodwork as a substitute for ormolu. The finest dies are procured, and bronze cast in them by an electrotype process that gives every detail clean and sharp, without any necessity for chasing. The inside of this bronze casting is filled up with some brass material, to make it stronger and at the same time less brittle; the outer surface is then gilt, and an ornament is produced which far excels the usual ormolu such as is seen upon ordinary cabinet-work.

PLATE AND JEWELLERY.

M. Christofle's work in gold and silver was very fine, as shown in part of a silver-gilt service, and a *surtout de table*, both ordered by the French Emperor. The former has the French eagle for a handle to the dish-covers, and is coppery in tint. A silver tea-service, gilt and enamelled, was also good. Christofle also displayed some aluminium articles, which were only novel.

Though the art was not of very high character, the church plate shown by Poussielque and Rusaud was very superb; and a reliquary-box, which they have manufactured for Nôtre Dame, profusely adorned with precious stones, presented for the purpose by the ladies of Paris, was a commendable work. Rudolph sent some most beautiful specimens of his oxidized silver, and the enamels of Dotin were of the highest class.

The best French Jewellery was found in the case of Mellerio: among it was a wonderful sapphire, supposed to be the finest in the world: it was exhibited in 1851 by Hunt and Roskell. Here was shown a beautiful diamond head-ornament, in which the Greek key prevails, and another head-ornament bearing the Egyptian symbol of divinity. In the latter a large emerald, with a small ruby over it, formed the centre, and the Egyptian wings spread out on either side in countless rows of diamonds. A little vessel for holy water, with the Madonna and Child inlaid in enamel and gold on a topaz, displayed abundant fancy and excellent taste. In the setting of their diamonds MM. Mellerio approached more nearly than any of their Parisian competitors to the fineness of the English mode of setting: their usual mistake in France is showing too much silver.

Marret and Baugrand exhibited a very curious breast-ornament formed of pearls of every colour; also, a necklace of diamonds in the form of a fringe, with a diamond drop at the end of each thread of the fringe. Bonvenant showed a fantastic ornament for the bosom, of a dragon and a bird in diamonds; and another representing corn and corn flowers.

Of imitation jewels, there was a fine display; the French greatly excelling in this branch of art. Greiger showed several highly descriptive stage crowns, badges, collars, and stars of various orders, all cleverly designed. M. Valès imitated pearls so exactly, that it was almost impossible by merely looking at them to tell the false from the genuine; he claims for his work the merit of not being affected as imitation pearls usually are, by perspiration, by water, or by any other effect of wear. In connexion with these imitative jewels may be taken the process of setting invented and exhibited by Bouret and Ferre. Bezels, and clawsettings, and the frame-work of rings and earrings are struck out of dies in every form and size. This is an elaborate and very successful mode of getting up cheap jewellery for the American and other markets.

FURNITURE, CARRIAGES, ETC.

In the highest class of furniture the French metal-work is seen to advantage. An ebony cabinet of Fourdinois showed carving of every degree, in low relief, in high relief, in the round, and inlaying of ivory, all beautifully done. But here the bits of lapis-lazuli inserted on the doors of the cabinet, like the ivory in some English work is inharmonious in effect. Comparing 1851 with 1862, the advance on our side is enormous, while the French have not advanced much. Their most striking example was Christofle's electro-bronze as an ornament instead of ormolu: the metal-work used upon their cabinets appears to be clearer and sharper than that which we use. Another point of French excellence is, in setting glass in a cabinet, or in the back of a sideboard; we simply lay it in the framework, whereas the French bevel the edge all round (as in Vauxhall and other old glass), which gives the glass a more brilliant appearance, and denotes that the mirror has been specially prepared for its place. In addition to his ebony cabinet, Fourdinois exhibited a very elaborately carved chimney-piece, with delicate bronze bas-reliefs on darkveined marble, the effect of which is very questionable. M. Marchand contributed an extraordinary chimney-piece of black marble, relieved with green bronzes, and surmounted with a gilt statue of Minerva; the artist was M. Piat, who had shown great originality in the treatment of the style.

Behind the French Court was a very large display of French carriages of handsome design and tasteful execution; and a Bois de Boulogne omnibus, exhibited by the Company which rules the streets of Paris. There were also in this Department French Sewing-machines in full work, such as are used in making the clothes and shoes for the French army. There were likewise a great number of "things not generally known," from the most intricate-looking machines to the simplest and yet very useful contrivances. Amongst others were Brown's cloth padded strips for stopping superfluous chinks in doors and windows, protecting books in book-cases from dust, and applicable to any case, door, or window by any ordinary carpenter. Clergymen, students, merchants, and lawyers have testified to the value of the padded strips, and the inventor has patented his discovery. Then, in the Music Court there were one or two novelties. One manufacturer exhibited a piano in which, it is stated, a note and its octave may be obtained from the same key—an improvement which will be appreciated by those whose small hands render "stretching an octave" difficult and fatiguing. Another improvement of somewhat similar intention was exhibited as applied to the double bass ; professing to do away with the necessity of the player apparently flinging his whole body up and down the fingerboard of his huge instrument.

WINE AND FOOD.

The whole display was remarkable for the number of collective exhibitions, especially in the Wine and Food Class, more than forty of these being sent from various Departments of the country. Amongst the special groups were the forest products of the Landes ; a collection of French mammalia and birds, both useful and mischievous ; an exhibition of oak wood for ships ; a geological collection ; and paintings of animals and plants for forage.

M. Vimorin-Andrieux, the great seedsman of Paris, exhibited in a very interesting little Court, a bird's-eye view of the whole flora of France, from the mightiest monarch of the forest to the humblest pot-herb which grows in a cottage garden. There were first all the seeds which the French soil is capable of bringing to maturity ; then the plant as it grows, and the uses it is put to. In the case of trees we had small slabs of the timber, samples of the bark, the charcoal made from it, and even the sabots. The cereals were shown in the ear, the flour they produce, the hemp and the cordage made from it, beautiful collars, the ultimate end of the fibres of flax, vegetable dyes—in fact, every possible object which arboriculture, or agriculture, or horticulture can be imagined to produce. Close by was a curious case illustrative of a subject which has been much discussed of late—the destruction of small birds. It consisted of a collection of preparations of the stomachs of birds of various kinds, the contents of which had been analyzed so as to show the nature of their food,—a portion of the results of inquiries extending over twenty-five years, made at the Museum of Natural History at Paris.

The Acclimatization Society of the country made an exhibition of all the animals which they have succeeded in introducing into France. Among them are the alpaca, the llama, the ostrich, and a large number of birds, game, and water-fowl. The Vines of Bordeaux, Burgundy, and Champagne, and the wines and brandies of Montauban, were represented by artificial plants and fruit, showing the mode in which they are trained in the different vine-producing districts, samples of the earth in which they are grown, and the wines which they produce, were near them. There was a magnificent display of Tobacco, and Cigars, and Snuff, made by the Imperial Government establishments. The wheat, oats, barley, flax, and other cereals and farinaceous grain of the country, were tastefully arranged, so as to form an arched entrance to the Court from the Zollverein side. Prince Napoleon was President of the French Commission, and M. le Play vice-president. The admirable mode in which the Court was arranged attested the excellent manner in which they discharged their important duties.

In the items of gain in the last ten years, in industries, the French Juries of admission set down the progress in the fabrication of manure derived from towns and farms, and the elevation of the proportion of azote in such manure. There was exhibited by M. Chodzko, a model of a timber-framed building, which is described as for the complete disinfection of towns by the instantaneous transformation of the human *excreta*, solid and liquid, into perfect manure, and called the atmospheric system, and which seems to consist in the absorption of the liquids by faggots, shavings, or bones, on which the *excreta* have been placed.

MACHINERY AND MANUFACTURES IN METAL.

The French Machinery, which was distinguished for its mechanical finish, included all known types of machines. It had much beauty of form, and showed a judicious distribution of parts in relation to the strain to be supported. As regards vessels, the great marine engines used in the Mediterranean ships were also remarkable for the above qualities, and they included a direct application of the screw. The Railway Department presented some remarkable models of locomotives—the inventions of engineers, whose object has been to utilize the adherence of the wheels on the curves, to increase the power of the steam, and to introduce largely the employment of coal as a combustible.

Several improvements in Boilers were exhibited, showing how these machines may be made so as to be easily taken to pieces and cleaned. The means were also shown of purifying water from matters likely to form incrustations. The Giffard feeder, as a piece of ingenious mechanism, is, perhaps, the most striking invention of all. The hydraulic machines showed great progress since 1851.

In Mechanics and Metallurgy there were some new improvements both in form and in construction; and some important machines are exhibited for making sugar from cane or beet-root on a large or small scale. Every practical metallurgist must have been delighted to observe the magnificent unsoldered copper tubes of Estivant Frères, in this Department: they are produced entirely by hammering.

An excellent paper upon the Mineral Wealth of France will be found at pp. 83-84.

The Jury reported very favourably upon the following cast and wrought-iron work. M. Durenne exhibited a cast-iron monumental Fountain, remarkable for the execution of the details and delicacy of the moulding. And with this may be favourably classed the productions of Monduit and Bechet, and Grados and Michelet, of Paris, who have executed many fine ornaments and statues on the Sainte Chapelle, and other Mediæval buildings of Paris, in embossed lead or zinc. These materials are less apt to be affected by the atmosphere than iron, and some are of colossal size, evincing great boldness and finish, and refined artistic treatment at the same time. In order to counteract the action of water on iron, which threatened to destroy some of the finest monumental works of art in Paris,—as the fountains in the Place Louvois, by the late M. Visconti, and the fountains in the Place de la Concorde, and the Champs Elysées, by M. Hittorff,—executed in that metal, M. Oudry, having made various experiments, discovered a process of coating in bronze, which has been applied, with great success, to those noble productions, and to more than 1000 elegantly designed lamp-posts. M. Christofle, the eminent silversmith, has also of late years applied his galvanoplastic system to architectural details, such as stair-rails, balconies, elaborately enriched mouldings, capitals, and other portions of columns; so that architects may find in this system the possibility of carrying out their ideas even of the most elaborate ornament, at relatively moderate cost.

ALGERIA.

The French Government had evidently been at particular pains to present to the world an adequate idea of the resources and natural capabilities of its great colony; Algeria, in fact, occupying as much space as all the rest of the French colonies put together. The soil of Algeria still retains that wonderful fertility which made it in ancient times one of the granaries of Rome; and by far the most important part of the show was the long array of Cereals, Provender of various kinds, and Vegetables. Natives as well as colonists exhibited here, and some of the finest specimens of barley were grown by indigenous cultivators. Of wheats there was an immense variety, but the hard brown wheat which is indigenous to the country seems to suit the soil better than the *blé tendre* which has been introduced by the French. The best sample shown was by M. Declonfié, of Constantine. Maize, too, white and yellow, is extensively grown both in the Oasis of the Sahara and the Tell: occasionally as many as from 700 to 800 grains have been counted on one cob. The exhibitors of barley, oats (a crop of European introduction), and rye were numerous; and at the entrance there was a sheaf of each crop of the year's reaping. The Acclimatization Society exhibited a collection, in which there were not less than 58 varieties. Potatoes, however, cabbages, and such vegetables as were classed under the head of *tubercules*, flourish in great abundance, and there is a large export not only to France, but occasionally to this country. Algeria is rich in fruits, and besides a very ample exhibition of *conserves*, there was a beautiful stand of fresh fruits of this year's growth.

The results of the Cotton cultivation in Algeria were very interesting. Cotton has been cultivated more or less in Algeria from time immemorial, but it is only within the last few years that it has attained to any extent. Specimens of Algerian cotton were shown in the Exhibition of 1851 and received prizes: since that time the French Government has taken up the matter warmly, and by offering considerable prizes for the cultivation, has brought cotton into favour with the planters.

The Cotton-tree was shown in leaf and nut, with here and there the beautiful white cotton bursting from the pod. In the cases was an immense number of specimens of raw cotton, disposed in glass vases. Sixty planters were here represented. The finest samples were decidedly the long staples, grown exclusively in the province of Oran ; the two other provinces growing the short staple only. Mr. Hardy exhibited samples produced from seeds from all parts of the world which are in process of naturalization in the Jardin d'Acclimatation at Algiers, of which he is the director. Samples of the tissues woven from Algerian cotton were shown by the firm of Dolfus Mieg and Co., of Mulhouse, and other eminent French manufacturers. There were what we call calicoes, twists, and threads (filature), in every description and variety, from Lille ; some exquisite fabrics (muslin) to which a Prize Medal has been awarded ; some specimens of lace, known as "Nuns' Lace ;" and some handkerchiefs of such beauty and quality that they won for their exhibitor a Prize Medal.

The production of Silk in Algeria may be said almost to be one of the results of the French occupation of the country ; for when they arrived in 1830, though the mulberry-tree flourishes readily in all parts of the country under almost all circumstances, the last traces of the art were rapidly disappearing. Silk culture was pursued with great success until the year 1854, when the disease which had been so fatal to the silkworms of France extended to Algiers. The production has fallen off every year since. The Algerian silk is highly valued for certain branches of manufacture, and cocoons were exhibited from all the provinces. The most remarkable were shown by M. Hardy as the results of an attempt to substitute the *ricin* of Japan for the mulberry—apparently not a very successful one.

There was a considerable display of Wines, both red and white : one special wine called vermouth, from Oran, has been described as an imitation of the famous Hungarian vermuth. The specimens of spirits and liqueurs included the renowned and familiar "absinthe," and the more recondite and almost unattainable "chartreuse ;" both the result of French industry and manufacture in the colony. A considerable space was allotted to

Tobacco grown in Algeria, in its raw state and manufactured, in the shape of cigars and snuffs: its appearance was good. Here may be mentioned a very curious plant, like our common thistle, and from the pod of which is extracted a beautiful and delicate material which is woven into as beautiful and delicate silk, which is, besides, stout in substance, and the artificial colours of which are at once tasteful and rich. To this article a Prize Medal has been awarded.

Various specimens of Algerian Wool were shown: some coarse in quality, and dark, not to say dingy-dirty, in colour, but others apparently good; fine fabrics have been manufactured from this produce, and thick, dark-coloured, blankety fabrics are made from the rougher raw material. Here were examples of paper, writing and common, manufactured from grass-fibre; the former of which, though apparently flimsy in substance, is yet white, clear, and smooth, and is probably as well adapted for writing as the ordinary run of French paper: also, specimens of rope and cord woven from grass-fibre, and a lady's bonnet, manufactured from the fibre of the aloe.

Of the thuya, the olive, and the other beautiful Algerian woods which are in such request among Parisian cabinet-makers for *meubles de luxe*, there were numerous specimens. M. Lambert in particular, an Inspector of Forests in the province of Constantine, sent a large collection which gave a very complete idea of the forests of Algeria. The mineral riches of the country, too, were well represented, and the fine marbles, such as the onyx, which we have already described, and others. In that part of the collection which illustrated the native industries the most remarkable objects were the arms of the Kabyles; the woollen carpets, made principally in the provinces of Oran and Constantine; and the case of embroidery from the *ouvroir Musulman* at Algiers, an institution in which Arab orphan girls are received and educated. The burnouses exhibited by native manufacturers were of great beauty; and for all works in leather they seem to have a special proficiency. The *bijouterie* and *orfèvrerie*, too, which are principally the work of the Jews of Algiers and Constantine, showed very patient finish. We must not omit to mention the Arab pottery, which was very curious. M. Limbery, who contributed many pieces, also exhibited some fine specimens of Arabic printing, illuminated by himself.

Amongst the specially characteristic features of the Algerian Court were the skins of African wild beasts. There was a magnificent tawny-haired hide of a lion, and examples of skins of leopards, hyenas, and other native animals.

OTHER FRENCH COLONIES.

The French Colonies were admirably represented. Commencing with Martinique, we find that for some time past the efforts of the colonists have been turned almost exclusively to the extension and improvement of the cultivation of Sugar. Some of the samples shown were of very fine quality; and it is stated that, with the introduction of new machinery, there is a continued improvement in the quality. The Martinique rum, too, is rapidly rising in the market. A few samples of Coffee were exhibited, of excellent character, and M. Belanger sent a packet of dried husks of the coffee-cherry, from which an agreeable stimulating beverage is made, not unlike tea. The medical flora has always been exceedingly rich, and we had here a long row of healing herbs found in the colony. Here were, too, numerous specimens of the colonial woods, some of them of great value for building purposes. Martinique grows pretty good tobacco: there were shown the curious *bouts de négre* cigars, about a foot long; and samples of the once famous Macouba snuff. The other productions exhibited were textile plants, cotton, tanning and dyeing matters, gums and oils, and a curious manure produced by the bats. Of the riches of Guadaloupe there was a very ample collection. The samples of cotton, some of which were of first-rate quality, and the yarns and goods manufactured from it, attracted a great deal of attention, and went far to prove that this colony, which claims to be the mother country of the famous "Sea Island," is capable still, under good treatment, of rivalling, in quality at least, the best productions of Georgia and South Carolina. Of textile fibres, woods, dyeing substances, spices and medical plants, there were here specimens. The samples shown of Sugar were fine. Of liqueurs there was a great variety, among which *la crême de magnolia* was distinguished for its delicate flavour and rich aroma. The magnificent woods were the chief objects which attracted admiration of the contributions from French Guiana. Cotton, sugar, coffee, and cocoa—though not in great quantities, of excellent qualities—were among the products of the colony; and among the medical plants may be mentioned the Ayapana—a species of tea—which by the natives is esteemed a sort of universal specific. Fine skins, and a few groups of feather-flowers, made by the natives were shown. A native Indian in full costume was one of the greatest attractions of the Court. Samples of gold from the colony were shown. The chief contributions from Réunion were the sugars, of which there were numerous samples, some of them among the finest in the Exhibition. Of medical plants there was an immense variety; also specimens of the useful woods and vegetable fibres. From Senegal we had cotton, gums and oils, coffee and grains, and a few specimens of gold. Marabout and Ostrich feathers were well represented here; and close by were various articles manufactured from the skin of the hippopotamus. The collection of native arms and utensils, some of which showed great skill in manufacture, was very interesting. From Madagascar Mayotte, and Nossibe, other African colonies, we had nothing calling for special mention; nor was there anything of interest to be seen from the French Indies, beyond woods, dyes, gums, grains, and cotton.

From the fishing settlement of St. Pierre and Miguelon, were sent jars of dried cods' tongues, said to be a great delicacy. From these islands we had samples of a peculiar kind of tea, said to rival the Chinese in delicacy of flavour. The new settlement of Cochin China sent edible birds'-nests, *bêche de mer*, fishes' stomachs, deers' sinews, and dried fish.

Sandal and aloes woods of great beauty were shown, with gums, oils, and dyeing substances. The wool sent from New Caledonia was of beautifully fine quality. Of wild cotton there were several varieties. The contributions from Tahiti were chiefly woods, fibres, and oils. Both from New Caledonia and Tahiti we had turtle and pearl-bearing oysters, &c.—*Abridged from the Times.*

BELGIUM.

Belgium was well represented by a large collection spread through all the thirty-six industrial classes. The Ministry of Public Works of Brussels showed the Mineral products of the country; but her Iron industry could hardly be considered as fairly illustrated. The Belgian coalfield, like that of Northumberland, is deficient in workable measures of clay iron ore. There were some fine specimens of a somewhat peculiar variety of red hæmatite, which is stated to occur at or below the base of the carboniferous limestone at Vezin, near Liège. Ore extremely similar to this in all respects has recently been discovered in South Wales, in a similar geological position.

In the Department might be seen daily in operation a Blast-engine of novel construction, the invention of M. E. Fossey.

The section of Manufactures was well filled by more than five hundred exhibitors. About seventy-six apprentice-schools sent examples of cotton and linen manufactures. The Belgian Government also exhibited silk and velvet goods, and woollen and mixed fabrics; the flax and hemp classes were especially well filled. The show of Brussels lace was remarkably fine: here was a silk lace shawl, of such fineness as seemed to have been made in a fairy loom, rather than by the poor lace-workers in the back streets of Brussels: its price was 250 guineas. Near it were the pillows and the bobbins by which these exquisite productions had been fashioned: there were collars, and cuffs, and handkerchiefs of the most costly description. There was a brilliant display of flint and other Glass, pure in colour, and much of it elegant in form. Gorgeous church services and missals, and a noble book of the engravings of the Musée at Antwerp; leather, stamped and embroidered in all colours and all designs, came next. Then leather, tanned and dressed in the ordinary manner: among them some large black enamelled carriage hides; harness, cumbrous in its character, such as one is accustomed to see the Flemish horses in the country labouring under. There were bands of leather for machinery, and leather for military accoutrements. The Food products, and the Animal and Vegetable Substances, were very numerous: there was a huge candle-trophy, to match a similar absurdity from Holland.

Manufacturing machines and tools, and machinery in general, were well represented. There were some admirable specimens of wood-carving, by Goetz and others: the Goyers, of Louvain, sent a tall Gothic pulpit of wood: "its technical finish is praiseworthy, but the whole design is spiritless; and the carved panels cannot be acquitted of the sensuous sentimentalism which haunts the religious art of the modern Roman Catholic Church, both in its Italian and its Gothic shape."—*Quarterly Review.*

Belgium exhibited very little in textile fabric printing; the best exhibit being some clouded woollen yarns, contributed by M. R. Rave, senior, Curreghen, in Brussels. These were very beautiful for the neat and accurate manner in which the juncture of the colours was managed, and the Jury rewarded the exhibitor with a Prize Medal.

AUSTRIA.

This Department was one of the grandest, most interesting, and best arranged, in the entire Exhibition. The Mineral productions, as might be expected from the great range of the empire and the mountainous character of many of its provinces, were exceedingly diversified; they included fossil fuel, the useful and ornamental metals and minerals, and rock salt in immense quantity.

A singular mixture for stalled cattle was shown, consisting of rock-salt mixed with 2 per cent. of oxide of iron and 1½ per cent. of powdered charcoal. The Geological Institute exhibited a very complete collection of Austrian coal, valuable as indicating the amount of fossil fuel raised in the kingdom.

The same Institute showed a series of Crystals of soluble chemical bodies, 360 in number; they have been artificially prepared by M. Von Hauer, and certainly have never been excelled for the extraordinary correctness of their form. This unrivalled collection has been purchased for one of our museums.

The products connected with the manufacture of iron, exhibited by the Prague Association, were very complete. This body employs upwards of 5000 workmen, and smelts annually one million and a half hundredweights of iron ore.

The chemical products of Austria are of great importance. Sulphuric acid is now produced in large quantity from pyrites, until recently a waste mineral; during the last year 300,000 cwt. were obtained in this manner, and 50,000 cwt. of the celebrated concentrated acid of Nordhausen, which is obtained by heating green vitriol, from whence the acid derives its common name of oil of vitriol.

The Persian insect-destroying powder was shown in its various stages by Zacherl: it consists of the central florets of a daisy-like flower, growing wild in the Caucasus; its botanical name is *pyrethrum roseum Caucasicum*, and except in colour, it is not unlike the common feverfew of our hedgerows.

Samples exemplifying Kuhn's process for obtaining tin from the worthless scraps of tinned iron-plate were shown; the most important being pure tin in bars, Prussian blue, and weldable iron.

Wheat, flour, rye,' barley, beetroot-sugar, tobacco, were contributed in great abundance, and there were numerous exhibitors of flour of the first class. Hops of very superior fragrance were shown by Schöffe, of Saaz, in Bohemia, by Prince Schwarzenberg, and others.

The Wines of Austria were fully represented in the Exhibition, there being nearly one hundred exhibitors from different parts of the empire. Schwartzer's list included twenty-five different sorts, the titles of which seldom penetrate so far west as England; yet many of them are of the highest excellence, and admirably adapted to the English palate.

Nearly a million quarters of oil-seeds are annually produced; and the yearly growth of 700,000 cwts. of wool proves that the animal no less than the vegetable kingdom adds to the wealth of this huge empire. Prince John Schwarzenberg exhibited merino and negretti wools; and Dr. Robert Czilchert showed his merino fleeces, bred from carefully selected stock.

Flax from Pesth was exhibited by J. Birnbaum. There were several exhibitors of stearic acid Candles, and the quality of the articles was apparently of nearly uniform excellence. Those exhibited were chiefly formed of stearic acid, obtained from animal fat: their opaque whiteness, lustrous surface, and extreme hardness were remarkable; they are said to be free from the smallest trace of greasiness, and to burn with a large, pure white flame, without tendency to gutter when carried. Samples of the solid stearic acid were formed into vases and cast in large medallions, offering the appearance of the whitest statuary marble.

The Imperial Manufactory at Vienna exhibited no less than 964 pieces of porcelain, illustrating the manifold application of the manufacture. The establishment employs 200 workmen and artists, and there is a chemical laboratory for the preparation of the colours and gold for painting, and the glazes.

In Machinery, there was a Locomotive exhibited, to be used only on mountains: it had four cylinders, with a rate of speed equal to 90 English miles an hour. This was shown by the Staats Eisenbahn Geschellschaft. To the iron industrial Department, was sent a collection of knives, tools, and general cutlery.

The Austrians manufacture a legion of articles out of leather; and in the Exhibition the stalls or shops of Klein, Enders, Breul and Rosenberg, all from Vienna, presented a front which might suggest the idea of a great leathern Regent-street. Leathern cardcases, and leathern cardplates, picture and mirror frames, scentbottles and ladies' reticules, travelling-bags, portfolios, writing and dressing-cases, were made out of leather. We had china cunningly inlaid in leather, flat plates, convex and concave plates with wood and leathern borders. Some few of the leather wonders exhibited by these Viennese, however, belonged to the very highest branch of ornamental art. Breul and Rosenberg laid out an Oxford quarto Bible edition of 1851, bound at their establishment—and one of the most beautiful and costly specimens of bookbinding in the whole Exhibition; the binding is in leather, overlaid with ornaments in garnet and malachite, the whole cased with gilt-bronze chased, ornamented with rich devices.

Breul and Rosenberg also showed an album of Goethe's *Heroines*, lithographic copies of Kaulbach's *Cartoons*, executed for the King of Bavaria; the album is done up in leather, ebony, and gilt-bronze, bordered with iron-coloured bronze. There was another huge album, by Rollinger, dedicated to the city of London, with the arms of the corporation in a sort of leathern mosaic.

The educational establishment showed the Austrians have made great steps in most branches of the typographic, lithographic, and photographic arts, but they are unrivalled especially in anything connected with geographical studies. There were a map of Bohemia and raised plans of Vienna and its environs; the Austrian Government claiming the merit of having been "the first to present to the scientific world an accurate picture of the configuration of Italy." A trophy of arms, and other implements of war and the chase, from the Alpine districts of the Tyrol, were exhibited; and there were some mountain works of horn, wood, &c. There was a goodly display of furniture, Gothic clock-cases, papier-maché tables, &c. Besides the immense produce of the field and the mine, which constituted one of the chief attractions to the Austrian Court and galleries, there were linen, cotton, and woollen fabrics from Bohemia, Moravia, and Silesia.

Next to France, Austria made the most systematic display of Dyed and Printed Fabrics, remarkable for design, and brilliance of colour. Leitenberger's calico-prints, from Bohemia, were works of superior character; as were also Liebieg and Reichenberg's de-laines and shawls, and Bossi's wool and silk fabrics. In other Austrian prints and dyes, the garnucine style was shown to great advantage, and the mechanical adjustment of the patterns good. Liebieg's woollen table-covers were remarkable for their style of execution, and admirably drawn patterns, and bright colours. Among the dyes, the Turkey-red yarns were excellent.

There was a fine collection of Musical Instruments, including a glass Harmonica, consisting of a number of glass belts, or globes, of gradually progressing sizes, affixed horizontally to an iron spindle, which was set in a case, and which a very simple machinery turned by the motion of the foot. The sound was produced by the fingers moistened with water, and impressed with more or less force upon the glasses as they revolve, and the tone was exquisitely soft and beautiful.

The Bohemians in their show maintained their ancient renown for coloured and jewelled glass; their varieties were as follow:

There were greenish, canary-tinted sets, richly coloured and inlaid, at the stall of Mayer and Nephews; two large white glass vases, jewelled, exhibited by Count Harrach, were not easily to be matched either in design or workmanship; Lobmeyer, of Vienna, had a great display of lustres and chandeliers, and other glass articles; while the granulated glass produced by Hoffmann, also of Vienna, the surface of which resembles that of the leaf of the ice-plant, baffled anything that has been attempted in this country in emulation of it. Some of the hanging glass lamps by the same Hoffmann, especially those in the Chinese style, evinced uncommon taste.

A very interesting collection of the products made from the leaves of the maize-plant was shown: they included a nutritive bread-stuff; a fibrous material to be spun or woven like flax; and a pulp from which a most beautiful paper can be made. The latter process, as carried on in the Imperial Paper Manufactory at Schloegelmuehle, Lower Austria, gives a produce of 100 lb. of paper from 300 lb. to 350 lb. of head-leaves, irrespective of the other materials. And, what is important in this new material, it is very abundant; for, according to official accounts, the maize planted in Austria yields, annually, head-leaves estimated at 2,750,000 cwt., which, worked up into paper, would exceed 1,500,000 lb. So strong and durable is *maize-paper*, that if ground short it can be used as an excellent substitute for glass, so great is its natural transparency and firmness.

The collection of Meerschaum pipes from the great workshop, Vienna, was very curious, and may be thus described:

M. Freidrich's case of Pipes was full of admirably carved specimens, with chariots and horses, and an almost endless variety of figures, artistically produced upon the stems and bowls. M. Hoschek excelled in the plain pipes, and his name is well known to the dealers in this country. M. Beislgel had also some finely-carved specimens; and M. Hartmann showed, in addition to his finished specimens, an unusually large block of the meerschaum, as it was found in Spain, also a piece of fine amber of very extraordinary dimensions. Some pipes of M. Jaburek were shown in the different stages of colouring, and the more advanced ones had a peculiar rich dark brown colour. The imitation meerschaum pipes of M. Franklin obtained a Prize Medal. They are formed, we believe, of the waste materials made in carving the finer specimens, the chippings being ground into powder, and compressed by powerful machinery. Many of these highly-finished pipes were of great price, some as high as 500*l*. or 600*l*., while others ranged as low as one and two florins.

There were also shown wonderful little figures, Vases and Statuettes, which had been petrified in the mineral springs of Carlsbad; the water of which converts into a red-coloured stone anything immersed in it for a week or so. The above examples, originally formed of soft clay, had been sent to the springs by M. Behr.

M. Theyer showed some ornamental wood-work, which, though of a higher character, was almost as new in its kind as the Carlsbad petrifactions: it consisted of desks, cabinets, jewel-cases, portefeuilles, &c., of various woods, carved after old patterns, and inlaid with malachite and coloured marbles, chosen with admirable effect as to taste and colour.

Here also were shown large pictures and coats of arms formed of the heads of the round parti-coloured lucifer-matches used throughout the Continent: they appeared like mosaics, or pieces of Berlin wool-work.

We must say a few words of the Austrian Clocks. Here were eight-day clocks, in very handsome cases of dark wood, for 1*l*. 8s.; clocks which will go for a month at 4*l*. and 5*l*.; and three months and even 12 months' clocks—at proportionally low rates. Here, too, were sets of chairs and tables—with joints so flexible that they all pack up easily in a common sized wardrobe; also a suitable christening gift, a "growing child's bedstead:" the mechanism is so arranged that the sides will pull out to any length; in fact, it will grow with the child's growth.

It has been well observed, with regard to some of the ornamental articles of Austria—"The various forms produced by the partnership of the glass-blower and the chemist may not be high art; but they are all ingenious, many of them decidedly pretty, and taken all round commendably cheap. Habenicht's stamped and coloured leather wall-hangings deserve more than a passing glance."—*Quarterly Review*.

In this Department were two or three objects which an ordinary observer would regard with indifference. Nevertheless, they represented a process of manufacturing oxide of uranium of considerable interest by Patera, one of our best and most ingenious metallurgical chemists. Vanadiate of soda is separated in this process, and a specimen of it was shown. We found no representation of titanium, a metal which is abundantly diffused in nature, and which will one day find important application in the arts: the acid of titanium is employed to produce the peculiar tint of artificial teeth, and it has also been used to communicate a fine straw colour to porcelain.

To these contributions from Austria may be added the drawings of a hydraulic Forge-hammer, which is said to answer remarkably well: it is the recent invention of Mr. Haswell, who has long been resident in Austria, and was formerly a pupil of Mr. Fairbairn.—*Abridged chiefly from the Times*.

THE ZOLLVEREIN.

Rather than travel through the legion of articles contributed by the Zollverein and Hanse Towns, which occupy some 50 pages of the *Official Catalogue*, we shall particularize some of the more prominent objects.

The Saxon china works of the Meissen Royal Factory, near Dresden, keep up their old-established renown. There were shown several small bedroom tea-services, of the finest colours, and a few tables of the richest workmanship; while the paintings on the wall and the miniatures exhibited real artistic talent, and a high degree of finish.

The Royal Prussian ware, at Berlin, however, very nearly reached the Dresden in the form and colour of the ornaments, but not in the general shape of the articles: there was a superb "china trophy" of these articles exhibited by the King of Prussia.

Among the decorative porcelain produced by the Royal Prussian manufactory, several things deserve mention on account of their fitness for blending with rich architectural effect, both in galleries and private living-rooms. For instance, as chimney ornament, there were sculpturesque groups, in biscuit-ware and gold: the side-pieces were compositions of considerable size, formed by swans and Cupids supporting flower vases, extremely elegant—the details of a very high class of decorative art. The price of these handsome compositions was only eighteen guineas each; while the magnificent centre-piece, composed of a group of nymphs supporting a large and magnificently modelled sea-shell, was valued at no more than 67*l.* 10*s.* The colossal vases, which were the masterpieces of the Prussian porcelain works, were priced at 345*l.* each; the paintings of Nereids, &c., were highly wrought, and the gilding of the finely-moulded handles equals the finest ormolu. There was also a pair of low, basin-shaped vases, at only 52*l.* each. In their enrichments, the general effect of majolica had been aimed at, with more blending of tone and depth of colour, and a general velvety richness far beyond that usually obtained in any examples of ancient majolica. There was no porcelain painting of precisely similar style in the whole Exhibition.—*Abridged from the Builder.*

Besides the Prussian and Saxon china manufactories, those of Gotha and Bavaria also sent a few good specimens; and the latter State endeavoured, not without success, to rival the glass works of Bohemia.

The solid silver Vase, Table, and Candelabra, presented to the Prince and Princess of Prussia by the city of Berlin, as a wedding gift, were exhibited. The designer and modeller is Prof. A. Fischer; the table is of tripod form, and has three sitting figures of Faith, Love, and Hope. On the table-top are a ground-plan of Berlin, and armorial enamels. The vase is nearly 4 feet high, and round its body is a bas-relief of the entry of the Prince and Princess into Berlin. The candelabra are in corresponding style, but somewhat exuberant in scroll-work. Near it was the silver shield, presented by the Rhenish nobility. Here, too, was shown the Coronation Sword presented to the Prussian King by Luneschow, of Solingen, a very fine work. Here were a charming statue of Venus, by Froüken; a large architectural model of the Bourse, at Berlin; and some bronze statues. A state-coach and harness, with heavy silver mountings, was also shown here, from Berlin.

Of stag-horn and ivory carvings, a kind of ingenuity in which the city of Hamburgh appears to take the lead, there was an assemblage from all parts of Germany. Of deer-horn is made everything: from chairs, tables, and chandeliers, down to brooches and bracelets. We confess we like but few of them. Rampendahl, of Hamburgh, however, had something new to show, both in matter of ebony carving and also in amber-work, a branch of trade in which he may well claim the first honours. The Hanseatic department made a good show of furniture, among which were some excellent articles in oak and an inlaid table, by Werner and Pighlein. In cane summer-house furniture, Saxony, the Hanse Towns, and other parts of the Confederacy vie with each other. Here, too, was the vulcanite statue of Arminius, already described at page 184.

From Berlin were coloured glass chandeliers, with imitations of grapes and vine-leaves, of striking beauty. In the Bavarian collection Steigerwald's show of cut crystal and coloured glass was very fine: and there was among it a service of gilded glass, almost equal to Bohemian. Of iron-work and cutlery, brass ornaments and lamps, there was also a fine display. Germany did not fail at this juncture to set out a vast mass of cheap toys for "the juveniles of all nations." The Germans supply the rising generation with the best or at least cheapest playthings, and by producing the best-contrived, or at least most widely-spread, educational works and methods. In point of toys you would say that the whole of Germany is little more than a nation of overgrown children. For cheapness of production the Zollverein exhibitors stood almost unequalled. For instance, in the Würtemburg Court there were some pretty little inlaid tables, priced at 9s. 8d., of which the exhibitors sold many dozens. Here, too, were shown some flexible ornamental table-mats of wood, which are sold at 8s. the dozen. But the marvels of cheapness were certainly the oil-coloured prints from Munich, for effect hardly inferior to oil-paintings, yet the price for a good-sized print was only 18s. Some of the best photographs in the Exhibition were to be found here: the full-length portraits were very warmly praised by the best judges; but the specimens of the art which probably attracted most attention were the photographs from Kaulbach's famous *Beauties of Goethe*.

From Pforzheim was sent a large display of gold and jewellery, remarkable for its cheapness and lightness of design; and here was a great show of clocks from the Black Forest.

Bavaria sent some of its celebrated hops; but more noticeable was a case of impressions of seals and coats of arms, engraved by Kirubeck, of Munich: the beauty and sharpness of the engraving were much admired.

Bremen contributed some chased and embossed silver-work in the genuine old German style; but the chief display was Forguignon's show of lace, so arranged as to form a room. Next came wicker-work furniture from Hamburg; and then from the Duchies of Mecklenburg and Strelitz, some furniture, a carriage, and a pair of oak folding-doors.

The Mining Products* from the several States were arranged in systematic order: amongst them was a pillar of rock-salt, remarkable for its purity, from Stapfurth, near Magdeburg. The machinery and iron and steel manufactures included some remarkable castings from Krupp's foundry in Westphalia; a cannon

---

* See also "Minerals from the Zollverein," p. 84.

of cast-steel; and a locomotive engine from Berlin. The iron foundries from Berlin and Hanover sent some large ornamental works in bronze, and the latter two colossal couchant lions. There were also shown pantographs used for executing guilloche works on printing rollers and copper-plates. A collection of models of ploughs of every century, from the Academy at Hohenheim, was very interesting. Amongst the musical instruments were an orchestrion belonging to the Grand Duke of Baden; pianofortes from Leipsic and Berlin; and a large display of harmoniums from Stuttgart.

HUNGARY.

In spite of the sore discouragement of political influence, we had in the Exhibition, a "collective exhibition, systematically arranged, of raw produce of the kingdom of Hungary, with statistical notices, and illustrated with photographic representations of the places most in renown for wine culture, of national costume, races of cattle, and agricultural implements of Hungary," by Vincent Jauko.

This collection formed the nucleus of the Hungarian exhibition. First were photographs of the national costumes of the different districts, each of which keeps up its own traditional dress, which becomes, as it were, a visible sign of the municipal spirit which forms the very essence of Hungarian national life.

But more than the costumes, the type of those who wear them claims interest, for few indeed are the countries where the lower classes can be compared in independent bearing and manly expression to the specimens of the people which we have there before our eyes.

Only a few hundred square feet were allowed, in which to set forth the riches of a country, boasting above all its bulky national productions: grain, wine, minerals, wool, hemp, flax, silk, tobacco, &c. Yet this was done, by a crowd of samples. Handfuls of wheat, barley, rye, oats, &c., stood there for a yearly production of 20,000,000 quarters of grain, more than one-third of which is available for exportation. A few leaves of tobacco represented 2,000,000 cwt. of tobacco, which are grown in good years. Two little glass barrels of wine were the samples of 300,000,000 gallons of wine a year. Little bits of wood, a few inches long, represented 4000 English square miles of forests, from which well-nigh 20,000,000 cubic feet of timber are exported yearly. Little pieces of bacon and lard stood there as the representatives of 8,000,000 hogs, the few specimens of flax and hemp for 1,500,000 cwt. of yearly production, the few handfuls of rape and hempseed for about 500,000 quarters yearly, more than one-half of which is exported, the few fleeces for above 15,000,000 sheep, and so on.

But in no case is it more difficult to carry away an adequate idea of the production from the few samples which the limited space admitted than in the specimens of ore, coal, and metal which were shown as illustrating the mining wealth of a country which includes almost all metals known—above all, gold, silver, copper, iron, antimony, sulphur, coal, and saltpetre.

The productions of the porcelain manufactory at Herénd, were a successful imitation of Japanese and Chinese porcelain, especially in small fancy articles, such as *tête-à-tête* tea and coffee services.

Such were the principal articles shown in the Hungarian Court: but there were several others scattered and mixed up with productions of the same kind exhibited by the other countries of the Austrian empire; the native wine-merchants contriving to group themselves near each other.

RUSSIA.

The Russian Court presented an exceedingly fine display, complete and interesting of its kind. Its front was decorated with some noble works, in green jasper, and violet porphyry. One of these was a magnificent Vase five feet in diameter, with the handles richly ornamented with delicately sculptured faces; another was a Candelabrum 17 feet high. The materials for these fine works were found in Siberia, where they were wrought to perfection entirely by hand-labour; the toil of years. The porphyry vase, for instance, had a Russian inscription upon it, stating that it was commenced in 1856, and only finished at the close of 1860, though this, in comparison with other works of the same kind, was speedily accomplished; for in the Hermitage, at St. Petersburg, is one magnificent vase of jasper which it took no less than 25 years of uninterrupted hand-labour to carve and polish. Another candelabrum was carved out of blocks of lapis-lazuli, which has lately been found in comparatively large quantities in Eastern Siberia. There were also large blocks of graphite and other mineral products of that little-known region. We missed those grand ornaments in malachite which formed so great an attraction in 1851 : there were only a few large lumps of the material, in its natural state, but polished on the surface and sides.

The choice specimens of pietra-dura mosaic, which were not to be surpassed by any in the Building, were the productions of Russian artists who were sent to Italy by the Emperor Nicholas in 1845 to study the art; and the exquisite taste and delicate workmanship displayed in these works proved that the pupils were already worthy competitors of their masters. The masterpieces were a cabinet and a jewel casket, contributed by the Empress, and nothing could exceed the skill with which the natural colours of the stones—ruby, carnelian, nephrite, malachite, chalcedon, agate, and jasper—were blended together in the lovely groups of flowers with which they were ornamented. The nephrite vase is the largest object which has yet been manufactured from this new substance. The mosaics in the Byzantine style were of equal excellence.

The Imperial Glassworks exhibited some beautiful specimens of ornamental glass, among which was a superb turquoise blue and white vase, ornamented with ruby beads in the Moresque style. The Imperial china manufactory exhibited three large porcelain vases : one painted after Greuze, the other two with likenesses of John Locke and Inigo Jones. The *déjeuner* services also deserve notice : one was ornamented with portraits of various persons belonging to the Romanoff family, and another with quaint paintings in the old Russian style. Among the chief attractions of the department were the elaborately-finished bronzes of Lieberih and Baron Clodt.

One of the most curious and characteristic portions of the Exhibition was the collection of church Plate, such as Communion cups, crosses, and jewelled bindings for the New Testament. Most of these articles belong to the Grand Duke Nicholas, and the precious stones with which they are adorned were the property of the late Empress Dowager. Goobkin, of St. Petersburg, showed plate in quite a different style, and among them was a binding in silver *repoussé* work which deserves high commendation.

Turning to the industrial arts, we had samples of the clothing of almost every rank of society, and all the various nationalities of the Russian empire. The wild Bashkirs and Caucasian mountaineers showed their home-made cloth of camel and goats' hair ; and the Cossack women exhibited shawls of the fine goats' hair as light as a cobweb. The manufacturers made a very full display of cloth, alpaca, and worsted goods. The Moscow manufacturers sent a very interesting collection of goods manufactured for the Chinese markets. The worsted manufacture was represented by Armand, Goochkof, and Schepeler, who showed alpaca, merino, &c., of very beautiful colours. Russia proved herself to have made a remarkable progress in Calico-printing since 1851 : the Turkey-red, produced from the madder *marena*, was admirable. Prokorof showed cotton prints intended for the markets of Central Asia ; and Madame Baranova exhibited the red stuffs and chintzes so highly prized by the Russian peasants. The splendid gold and silver brocades and the rich furniture silks sent by Sapojnikof were great attractions. In leather, Russia maintained her ancient prominence : there were specimens here of pretty nearly every article which can be manufactured of leather,—boots and shoes of every pattern, portmanteaus, bags, &c. One of the chief novelties of this Department were the boots exhibited by M. Hübner, of small strips of plaited leather, which make a light elastic material, very agreeable for summer wear. In the display of magnificent furs also and skins of all sorts, Russia was conspicuous : there were two splendid sea-otter skins which were worthy to be compared with any in the Building. A complete collection of the vegetable produce of all the provinces of Russia, including cotton grown in the Caucasus, was contributed by the agricultural department.

There was scarcely one department in the Exhibition which was more successful in a commercial point of view than the Russian. Very few of the articles shown here returned to Russia, for most of them were bought at good prices; and, in addition to that, Russian exhibitors have made openings in the English market which may be expected to be most profitable to them hereafter.—*Abridged from the Times.*

ITALY.

The Kingdom of Italy contributed an extensive collection of Minerals, highly interesting, especially in reference to ores of copper and lead. It contained beautiful and characteristic examples of specular ore from Tuscany, of brown ore and spathose carbonate from various districts. The vicinity of Bergamo will be remembered as classic ground in the history of iron-smelting.

The Italians, with their true artistic instincts, in their exhibition of articles made rare excellence their rule of selection. Thus, from Castellani's magnificent establishment at Rome were sent some five dozen specimens of his reproduction of the gold trinkets of the ancients—from models of the Greek, Etruscan, Roman, early Christian, Byzantine, Mediæval, and Cinque-cento styles. Of these articles none was more attractive than the beautiful crown or diadem from Cuma, a Grecian piece of workmanship made on purpose for this Exhibition, the original of which is in the Campana collection—a minute tissue of gold and coloured gems. There was also a variety of wreaths, necklaces, earrings, bracelets, and other ornaments, Greek, Etruscan, and Roman; and a jewel-casket in the latter-named style, bearing the name of *Mundus Muliebris*, and containing all the trinkets belonging to a fine lady's toilet in the best period of Roman art—wreath, bracelets and comb, hair-pins, rings for every day in the week, winter and summer rings, earrings: and a mysterious tiny pot in lapis-lazuli, supposed to contain a secret spell for ensuring the imperishable freshness of the lady's complexion. Still more interesting than these ancient specimens were the early Christian and Byzantine brooches, mosaic crosses, and other devices. Besides the classic jewellery, Castellani contributed the very tasteful sword of honour presented by the Romans to King Victor Emmanuel. This sword formed the most beautiful ornament in a trophy of other fine weapons, surmounted by a bust of the King of Italy, and by a wreath of enamelled oak-leaves, subscribed for by the ladies of Italy in commemoration of General Cialdini's achievements at the siege of Gaëta. Next to these specimens of goldsmiths' and jewellers' work, the filigree silver-work of Genoa deserves honourable mention.

Some rich and varied samples of porcelain manufacture were sent by the Marquis Ginori from his factory at Doccia, in the district of Sesto, six miles from Florence. This manufactory dates from the year 1735, and rose at the same time as the Royal establishment at Sèvres, about a quarter of a century after the first introduction of this branch of industry at Meissen, near Dresden. The Doccia manufactory has been from the outset a purely private speculation, undertaken by a wealthy and benevolent nobleman, with a view to give employment to the poor peasantry on his estate. The Ginori family, from father to son, for four generations, have bestowed the utmost care on their favourite pastime, and their fabric has attained high excellence: most of the specimens at the Exhibition were sold. The paramount merit of the Ginori porcelain artists is their high and bas reliefs; their majolica, their imitations of Luca della Robbia's works, may be considered less as art manufacture than as pure art.

The great beauty of the Mosaic Tables of Florence and Rome presented the closest point of contact between art and industry. Some of the finest specimens were sent by the Papal, or Royal Manufactories, working under Sovereign patronage. The artists of these beautiful Roman and Florentine tables must make but a poor living by their work. Monachesi, for instance, must have spent half his life in the accomplishment of his marble table which formed one of the greatest objects of attraction in the Roman Court. Five hundred pounds, the price asked for Betti's table in Florentine mosaics, would hardly repay the care which must have been bestowed upon it for so many summers and winters. Two tables in pietra-dura by the Florentine artists, Torini and Vecchi, were much admired for their singleness, elegance, and lightness of design. The one design consisted of a Grecian border in lapis-lazuli, with a bouquet in the centre; the other had also flowers in the centre, with a border of pearls and birds. Somewhat in the same style was one of Montelatici, an arabesque border with birds and flowers, and flowers in the middle.

Of the Roman tables, the masterpiece was that by Barberi, which combined the two styles: it had a mosaic Roman border of flowers and medals, and in the centre a view of the Piazza of St. Peter's of Rome, also in mosaic; but between the border and the centre a large space was filled with specimens of marble of chance shapes, the simplest sort of pietra-dura work, so arranged that the natural colours made up a kind of perspective intended as a set-off to the central view: the effect was beautiful and novel.

The table presented by the Pope to Her Majesty, with its marginal border ornamented with views of Rome, had rare merit. So also had another fine mosaic replica of Raphael's great picture of the Holy Family—sent by the Papal manufactory; the smoothness of texture and fineness of colouring of this was equal in effect to the best oil-paintings of the old masters.

This art of inlaying tables has lately been introduced in Derbyshire, and in Russia at Peterkof, and in some Siberian districts. With the Derbyshire marbles, artistic excellence is by no means the workman's aim; but the Russian specimens in pietra-dura presented rare costliness of the precious stones employed in them (the ground of one is lapis-lazuli), and very careful and highly polished execution of the work itself, and the exquisite loveliness of design. These are the first-fruits of the work of the Russian apprentices, maintained in the mosaic factories of Rome at the charge of the Emperor of Russia.

The Roman Court, enclosed from the rest of the Italian Collection, was one of the most frequented portions of the Exhibition. Much was expected from the famous Pontifical manufactory of mosaics, and from the Roman engravers of cameos and gems, as well as something from the native painters and sculptors of Rome, the great art-capital of the world. But the result fell short of this high expectation. The foreign artists contributed the best works; but the Roman works scarcely equalled those from other parts of Italy: the painting was not superior; the sculpture was not better. The two statues by Story, the American sculptor, a Pietà, by Jacometti, the cameos, and a few mosaics, were the objects chiefly of artistic excellence. Story's African Sibyl and Cleopatra were two noble works;* Ruth the Gleaner; the group of Love Captive, by Engell; Zephyr and Flora, by Benzoni; Pandora, by Ives; and the Fortune-teller, by Guglielmo, were also fine examples of modern sculpture.—*Abridged chiefly from the Times.*

SWITZERLAND.

The industries displayed in this Court were mostly the results of the labours of the French Swiss and the German Swiss; the Italian Swiss contributing scarcely a single article.

The French Cantons—Geneva, Lausanne, and Neufchâtel—attempt to monopolize the watch-trade of the world; and in the Exhibition they achieved great success. Of Watches, intended for use no less than ornament, we had here a most charming display. There were ten or twelve houses from Geneva,—Lang and Padoux, Baume and Lerard, Moulinié et Lagrandroy, &c., not only claiming the merit of timepieces of the greatest precision, but also rivalling each other in the production of those trinket watches, watches to be enclosed in a bracelet, in a brooch, in a crown-piece, in a ring almost. Masterpieces in the same style, of equal merit, were sent by Audemars, Aubert, and others in Canton Vaud; and by Courvoisier, Grossclaude, &c., from Chaux-de-Fonds and other localities in Neufchâtel. Several of these master-workmen exhibited the whole of their workshops, with the various pieces, wheels, hands, cases, and other parts that go to the composition of a watch. Artists of very high pretensions give the design for the endless variety of cases and faces; there were gold-engravings by Alphonse Dubois, and by Fritz Kundert, both of Chaux-de-Fonds, some of whose specimens had been made for the Exhibition. Here were exhibited hour, quarter, and minute repeaters; some exquisite ladies' watches, enamelled with diamonds; and close by a case of silver watches of wonderful

* These statues have been purchased by Mr. Morrison for the sum of 3000 guineas.

cheapness. Messrs. Aubert added to their show several fine specimens of the roseate amethyst—the new stone not long since discovered.

From most of the eastern German cantons, especially Zurich, St. Gall, Appenzell, Glarus, &c., were industries of a very different kind—Woollen and Cotton factories; and of machine Embroidery, Tambourwork, and other frame and hand embroidery we had capital specimens, especially by Rudolph Ranch and Stäheli, both of St. Gall; Steiger-Schoch and Eberhard, and Tanner and Koller, both houses of Herisau, in Appenzell.

There was a great variety of Silk, Riband, and other manufactures, chiefly from the cantons Zurich and Basle. In Swiss manufactures in general, much of the work connected with them is carried on by the workman in his own home. As you cross some of the happiest, though naturally poorest, districts of Appenzell, Glarus, &c., you are agreeably struck with the multitude of women and children busy at their looms, at their frame, or with their spindle, at the door of the cottage.

Berne, Geneva, Vaud, and other cantons sent specimens of their *stutzen*, or rifles, plain and solid, somewhat ponderous weapons.

The Swiss showed their good sense this time in sparing us all that farrago of carved beechwood, all those chamois, chalets, and other knick-knacks without number, of which every hotel, every cabin, by lake, glacier, or waterfall, is a shop in the Bernese Oberland, as well as every nook and corner of the forest cantons.

In the Official Catalogue of this Department is mentioned metallic manganese; but the superintendent stated it to have been stolen. This metal, in the metallic state, is of great interest, and will assuredly, at no distant day, be extensively employed in the arts as a constituent of alloys.

HOLLAND.

The collection from Holland, as far as manufactures and raw produce were concerned, was very complete. There were some handsome specimens of Lacquer-ware from Rotterdam, much more elegant and pleasing than those which were found in the Japanese Court; but scarcely equal to them in solidity of workmanship. The Furniture, too, was of a high class: the woods chiefly employed were amboyna wood, rosewood, and palisander, and great ingenuity was shown in the way of secret drawers and other elaborate contrivances. For instance, there was one piece of furniture which could be turned from a console-table into a sideboard, and *vice versâ*; and a tall bureau, on a spring being touched, unbosomed itself of a flight of steps by which the higher shelves are reached. Perhaps the finest works of art in the Court were a very beautifully carved oak pulpit and a shrine intended for a church in Brabant. There were also some exquisite Photographs from rare etchings by Rembrandt and Ostade, and so clearly were even the finest strokes brought out that it was almost impossible to distinguish them from originals. The curious cinctures of brass and wire with which the Dutch peasant-women bind their brows were amply illustrated. There were two or three very fine specimens of Dutch Carpet Manufactures. A machine for teaching schoolchildren their notes was shown here, and was a very ingenious and entirely new invention : it was no larger than a good-sized musical-box ; on the face was printed the gamut, and on turning a handle the barrel inside ran up and down the scale, while a moveable finger in the front indicated each note as the appropriate sound was given out. Among other pieces of educational machinery may be noticed a very simple contrivance for explaining the principles and action of the thermometer. A very important part of the Dutch display was the Preserved Meats and Vegetables, some of which had made a voyage to Batavia and back before being sent here, and seemed none the worse. In the application of the arts to the manufacture of sweetmeats the Department seemed to be unrivalled. A hatter of Amsterdam showed a case of cork Hats weighing only 2 oz. each. Among the textile fabrics the Blankets attracted most notice: some of them were of extraordinary thickness, and the patterns were of the gaudiest hues. The Linen fabrics were not very largely represented, but there was a case of beautiful hand-made Lace from the South of Holland which was almost equal to anything displayed from the neighbouring country of Belgium. Among the Agricultural Implements a model of a rick-thatching machine, which can be moved up and down to any height by the simplest machinery, appeared to be a novelty here, though it is said to be in common use by the Dutch agriculturists. Of the Carriages shown, all very handsomely decorated, the majority of them were early sold. When we have mentioned a very elaborate Saddle for army-surgeons, which affords accommodation in a very small compass and within arm's reach for the principal medicines and instruments needed on active service, we have pointed out all that was of general interest in this Court.

DENMARK.

There was no country represented at the Exhibition which, all things considered, made a more creditable figure in art-manufactures than Denmark. Copenhagen is the Paris of the North, and some of the articles exhibited in this Department were scarcely inferior, either in design or workmanship, to the productions of the most famous makers of Paris or London. The Danish artists, instead of servilely following French models, preserve a specialty of their own, which is much more effective than the finest copies. Almost all the copies noticed here were from classical models. There were two stands of porcelain works of a high order. Nothing can be more beautiful than the paintings on the vases and cups exhibited by Bing and Grindhallse ; the combinations of biscuit and porcelain were executed with great skill ; one in the style of Christian IX., and another lent by the present King, challenged admiration by the quaintness of their forms and the richness of their decoration ; but perhaps the gem of the collection was a breakfast-service, ornamented with copies of Thorwaldsen's bas-reliefs. Another service of a similar kind illustrated the heraldic devices of the Danish monarchs. The works of the Royal Factory at Copenhagen excelled also in exquisite ornamentation, and the services in the old Danish style were very interesting. There were also some excellent specimens of biscuit statuettes, chiefly copies of Thorwaldsen's works. The Copenhagen Art Society also exhibited various specimens of porcelain ware, and some very clever works in silver and bronze. There was a piece of *repoussé* work, intended for the top of a lady's worktable, of considerable merit. A case of brooches, bracelets, and other ornaments in gold, after Etruscan and Roman patterns, spoke highly for the taste and skill of the Copenhagen goldsmiths. Among the jewellery was shown a very beautiful suite of Diamonds, the setting of which is little inferior to the work of the best London or Paris jewellers.

One of the chief attractions we can hardly call it—but certainly curiosities—of the Danish Court was the "Osteotome," an ingenious mechanical contrivance, invented by Professor Nyrop, of Copenhagen, for performing difficult operations on bony substances. Another interesting feature of the Department was the very ample collection of Greenland furs and Esquimaux dresses.

SWEDEN AND NORWAY.

The mineral wealth of Sweden has already been illustrated (*see* page 212). The manufactures were chain cables and anchors ; and kitchen utensils in tinned ware, including some new articles. Its collection of woods was also fine ; and a trophy of carpenter's work showed what machinery has already enabled the Swedes to accomplish. Flax and yarn, and linen goods, curiously printed, were displayed among the manufactures of the country. There was a roughly-made carriage and harness ; and a few agricultural implements were shown.

Some Swedish views, carved in cork and birch, possessed artistic merit ; as did a bronze group, representing two men strapped together, after the old Runic fashion of duelling, and fighting to the death with knives. The story of this fatal affair, from its first outbreak to the widow weeping before the Runic stone at the grave of her husband and lover, was told in a series of bas-reliefs beneath the group,—some of them copied from the old Runic originals.

The Norwegian natural products, manufactures, and arts were well represented. There was a collection of the rich silver ores of Konigsberg ; the iron was also excellent in quality, some of the specimens contained more than 60 per cent. of iron: there were shown an admirably-made anchor of 70 cwt., and some excellent chain and rope cables. The cereals proved that even in the high latitudes wheat may be produced of first-rate quality; and an Agricultural Association at Tromsø sent samples grown in the 70 deg. of north latitude, or 20 degrees north of London. The Norwegian lines and fish-hooks were shown in proximity to cod-liver oil; and there was an aboriginal display of peasants' bowls, tankards, and beakers in wood, well-carved. Among other subjects was a peasant girl with a goat by her side: it was the work of a poor peasant, who was sent by the Norwegian Government to Italy to study the works of greater masters. The provincial costumes were shown in an interesting collection of photographs.

The carioles and sledges exhibited were numerous: there was a luxurious sledge fitted with bearskin; a rude reindeer sledge used by the Laplanders; and samples of the peasants' snow-shoes and skates. There were some admirable specimens of furs, and clothing made from them. The Christiania Industrial Union for Indigent Women sent a collection of hats, boots and shoes, and baskets of wicker-work, and a variety of domestic utensils made by its inmates. Among the mechanical contrivances were an ingenious moveable jet-piece for fire-engines, a self-acting harpoon for catching seals and otters, a sounding apparatus, with arrangements for bringing up samples of the bed of the sea, and a very useful sail-cloth hose for conducting steam to extinguish fire on board ship. The Government Department, and the Board of Ordnance of the country sent a good collection of ordnance breech-loading rifles, pistols, and revolvers, in use in the Norwegian army. The Admiralty contributed a very useful steam pumping-machine; and agricultural science was represented by a number of ploughs, some cultivators, and a number of other implements.

SPAIN.

Spain exhibited a trophy of inlaid furniture and pianos; near which was a curious rifle-gun for mountain-service; a case of military models; a display of swords, from the manufactory at Toledo; and other military equipments, and rifled fire-arms. There were also carvings in wood and cork; and a few enriched daggers. The tobacco and snuff manufactures were well represented; and the show of wines, cheese, and grain was good: nearly half its exhibitors showed food and wines. There were specimens of embroidered silk goods and cotton fabrics; lace for the mantilla; curious straw-work and wax-flowers.

A collection of elegant figures, almost a specialty of Malaga, placed in the Spanish portion of the nave, was attractive. They represented the various stages of the bull-fight, from the first attack of the picador, the tantalizing diversions of the chulillos and bandilleros, the *coup-de-grace* of the matador, and the final exit of the victim at the heels of the mules who drag him ignominiously from the arena. Some of these incidents were represented with great spirit; but as a whole the groups did not show the same artistic finish as the figures exhibited by Cubero, of Seville.

The more important mineral wealth of Spain, which of late years has been rapidly developed, was but poorly represented; although more than 100 cases of minerals were lying in the docks for want of sufficient space in the Exhibition. This is to be deplored, as both Spain and Great Britain would have been mutually benefited by a display of their contents.

PORTUGAL

Shone chiefly in woollen and mixed fabrics, silks, and lace: a piece of embroidery in silk of the monument to Don Pedro at Lisbon closely resembled a fine engraving. Its poncho-blanketing was exhibited; and near it, a satin towel, embroidered with gold. There were likewise shown snuffs and cigars, grains, pottery, and soaps. The collection of raw materials was respectable; save that there was nothing relating to iron. The exhibits of wines were, as might be expected, numerous.

TURKEY.

The Turkish collection gained high honour in the list of awards, and substantial recompence in the sale of goods. The gold-embroidered muslins and embroidered Broussa silks shown here were the finest of their kind in the Building. The exquisite fineness of texture and effective though rather gorgeous admixture of colour in these silks were almost exclusively confined to the fabrics which are sent to the bazaars of Constantinople. The specimens of Turkey carpets were very fine. A Turkey carpet, like a Cashmere shawl, can never be successfully imitated or reproduced beyond the limits of the land from which each fabric takes its name: there is a quiet richness in their patterns, a subdued tone in their colours, and above all a solidity of manufacture which we find nowhere else. It is said that the climate and soil of Turkey in some parts of Asia Minor are most admirably adapted for the cultivation of Cotton, and the samples shown on this occasion would seem to establish the fact. Most of the specimens exhibited were from Adana, on the borders of Syria, where cotton has hitherto been raised in quantities sufficient to supply all the wants of the Turkish Empire, where all the population are more or less clothed in cotton stuffs from head to foot. The fibre is long, clean, and very strong, and shows to good advantage, in spite of the fact that the ginning-machines used in Turkey are of the very worst description. This year cotton has been planted over a very large extent of country, and a crop of nearly three times the usual amount is expected; while next year the supply will be, it is said, double this again. The great bulk of this is being raised to meet the sudden requirements of the English market. Silk is another product which Turkey exhibited largely, and the production of which in Syria and Broussa has lately received the most practical form of encouragement from the French manufacturers. The Italian method of winding off the silk has been introduced into Asia Minor by the French, and this improvement alone has increased the value of the Turkish silk in the market nearly two-fold. The silks woven by the native weaver after his own Oriental tastes and fashions are as inimitable as the Turkey carpets. Specimens of all kinds were shown from Broussa, Bagdad, Aleppo, Damascus, and Monastir in Albania, each and all very rich and beautiful, and distinctly characteristic of the localities. Some of the silks were perfectly stiff with the gold interwoven in their patterns; while others were as light and fleecy as the transparent yashmaks of the Turkish belles of rank. Some of the gold-woven meshlahs or cloaks of the Arab chieftains, which are made at Lebanon and in parts of Kurdistan, had no equals of their kind in the whole Exhibition for strange beauty and richness of design and colour. The Sultan exhibited, through his Imperial manufactory close to Constantinople, a series of embroidered silks of the purely English type; also, gold-embroidered Kurdish tunics, fit only for Sultanas. Nothing of the kind shown in the Greek or Indian Courts equalled the richness and beauty of these dresses, which though amply large, were priced as low as 20l. and 25l. The embroidered felt prayer-carpets were also shown: they had the strength of oil-cloth, twice the thickness of ordinary carpets, and were as soft as Cashmere wool. Perhaps the richest piece of embroidery shown was a Turkish saddle-cloth, stiff with bullion; yet the price of this most Oriental housing was only 45l., to outward seeming scarcely the value of the gold-thread consumed in its manufacture. There was a very perfect collection of Turkish musical instruments: including, of course, the peculiar harp, the form of which has apparently undergone no alteration from the days when it was cut on the obelisks of Egypt; and the inevitable cymbals, without the musical assistance of which even a corporal's guard is not relieved in Turkey.

In the Department devoted to the exhibition of the luxuries of the chibouk and narghilla, there were pipes—embroidered, embossed, carved, inlaid, and jewelled—of almost every length and price, from the stick of three feet to the tube of thirty, from 1l. up to 500l.; and near them was a beautiful collection of beads of clouded amber.

Of Turkish agricultural produce there was a small but good show: the wheat, peas, beans, and maize were fine and heavy of their kind. One the great staples of Turkish commerce, the fig

trade of Smyrna and the Levant, was well represented. The
great secret is to pack the figs so as to preserve the fruit almost
any length of time: this is only done at Smyrna, whence P.
Giudici exhibited figs of last year's growth which had the bloom
of the fruit upon them still: to these, as the best of the best Smyrna
kind, a Prize Medal was given. From Samos some splendid
raisins were sent. Mr. S. G. Nacouss exhibited a fine collection
of native dyes, galls, madder roots, saffrons, yellow berries, &c.
Of Tobacco there was of course every known Turkish variety: the
collection shown by Mr. Theodoridi contained the finest samples.
A few specimens of the Pottery manufactures of the Turks were
exhibited; and though of the coarsest and ugliest kind, every
piece was sold at enormous prices: common Dardanelles jars,
worth two or three piasters (6d.), fetching almost as many pounds.
Some fine coffee cups and sweetmeat stands of gold and silver,
with lanterns and mother-of-pearl chests, found a ready market.
There was a small collection of Turkish arms, but scarcely one
single specimen of the most curious inlaid antique weapons which
abound in every town and village of Turkey.

The collection included food, fruits, woods, wool, silver articles
and filigree-work from Thessaly; textile fabrics, silk-worms' eggs,
exported in large quantities to France and Italy; an alarm-clock,
which rings a bell when it is opened; and a copy of the Turkish
national jest-book. This very characteristic assemblage of Turkish
produce and ingenuity was gathered by the indefatigable Mr. Hyde
Clark, at the request of the Ministry of Commerce; and by the
Governor-General of Turkey.—*Abridged from the Times.*

GREECE.

The products of Greece were exemplified in each of the thirty-
six classes of the Exhibition. The native marbles and variegated
stones were shown; the Home Department of Athens contributing
seventeen specimens of marbles from the Peloponnesus. There
were two or three samples of "wild tea." The Agricultural
School of Tirynth sent samples of wheat, barley, maize, rye, and
honeycomb; wines of 1851 and 1861; aniseed, colza, tobacco,
&c. Haricot-beans were sent by general exhibitors; and champagne, the hippocras of our days, by the Wine Company of
Patras. Dye-woods and roots, cotton-wool, and sponges, were
among the natural produce; a calico-printing machine was sent
from Athens, and a small steam-engine from Syra. There was a
group of carvings in wood and marble, Pentelic and verd-antique:
some of the wood-carving in its details almost rivalling the work
of the patient Hindoo. A few cotton-silk fabrics were shown;
and several Greek costumes, including some finely embroidered
goods. An exhibitor sent from Tripolis a strange item—"a
butcher's knife." Little was shown associated with the old classic
fame of the country; but of its regeneration there were a few

memorials in sculpture. Statues told some affecting episodes in the struggle for Greek independence. There were some busts also of famous chieftains and warriors who assisted in this great work. Among the sculpture was one figure, Kodros, of whom the oracle said the war could not succeed until he was killed : forthwith he went into the thickest of the fight, received a mortal wound, and as his life was ebbing away, drew aside the cloak which concealed his features, and showed himself the chief who had thus sacrificed himself for his country. Another chief, after having slain a crowd of enemies, had his sword broken in his hand, was surrounded by Turks, and killed. There were some promising specimens of Greek sculpture by young artists of Athens.

PERU, COSTA RICA, AND URUGUAY.

The South American States contributed various articles of produce and manufacture. Peru sent silver, silver and plated articles, and mercury ; wools, including alpacas ; and cotton and wine. There were also shown some silver works of the time of the Incas ; and some coverlets of great antiquity made from cotton recently found in the ruins of an Indian city. Costa-Rica contributed mining and chemical substances ; skins and furs, and a small quantity of gold and silver filigree-work. Uruguay sent specimens of wool, roots, and skins ; timber and wheat ; lead, iron, copper, and coals ; some wine and food ; and a few coloured marbles.

BRAZIL.

Few foreign countries made a more complete and instructive display than the empire of Brazil, in which the Emperor took a personal interest. The national products were for the most part of a semi-tropical character. Of tea twenty-four varieties were shown, including "Matti," which is largely consumed by the natives : it is somewhat pungent in flavour, having a fragrance very closely resembling tea, but is ground to a fine powder for use. Coffee and Sugar were both well represented ; as were also wheat of good quality, and very heavy ; tapioca, starch, arrowroot, and flour from various descriptions of grain. Some splendid specimens of Cotton indicated fresh sources of supply of this much-needed fibre to meet the American famine.*

The specimens of Tobacco shown were finely grown, but deficient

---

* It is surprising how many countries exhibited native Cotton in the Exhibition. There was cotton from Egypt, Turkey, Algiers, Cochin China, Natal, Queensland, Malta, British Guiana, Jamaica, Trinidad, Demerara, Mauritius, the Gaboon district, an immense number of varieties from India, and some specimens from other countries. There is scarcely one of these countries which would not produce almost sufficient to supply our manufacturers with the raw material if sufficient encouragement were given to its cultivation.

in flavour compared with that produced in the Havanna. The Minerals shown included some remarkably fine iron ores, so pure that one might suppose they had been smelted: specular iron of great richness; gold, lead, and other metals. There were specimens of the gold as crushed out from the quartz, a small button not larger than a fourpenny-piece being about the quantity usually obtained from a ton of the quartz rock. Some gold in the dust, and nuggets found in the alluvial washings, were also shown. Near them were diamonds in the rough state, magnificent amethysts, emeralds, and other precious stones.

We now come to a miscellaneous list of Brazilian manufactures shown: oils, including oil from the alligator, a black, thick, pitchy looking material; stearine candles; furs and skins tanned and dressed, the skin of an immense boa constrictor; boots and shoes of excellent shape and finish; cloths of various kinds; and felt hats of extraordinary lightness and fineness of texture. There were specimens of excellent rum and native wines; and with those of beeswax and honey was shown a case containing twenty-four kinds of bees. There were creditable specimens of iron-casting, paper-hangings, wood-carving, and decorations of various kinds. The manufacture and cutting of glass was exemplified in some good specimens of design and engraving. Self-feeding pistols, a variety of fire-arms and weapons, native spun cotton and woollen dresses, and artificial wild flowers, as they may be seen in the Brazilian forests, were also exhibited; and among the less important articles was shown the celebrated patchouli scent.

Photographs were exhibited of the Emperor and Empress of Brazil and the imperial family; also of Brazilian scenery. And a candelabrum in silver, presented by the Emperor to an English captain in recognition of his services to a Brazilian vessel in distress, was an excellent specimen of art-work.

THE UNITED STATES.

But for the Civil War in North America, the space allotted to the States would have been very insufficient for the articles that would, in all probability, have been sent. Still, there was a good display of the latest inventions and industrial resources of the country. The Machinery has been already described at pp. 156-160. A very complete museum of the Minerals of the country was sent by Dr. Feuchtwanger, of New York. There were also specimens of the petroleum, or earth-oil, from the wells of Pennsylvania. This extraordinary oil flows to the surface from the wells in immense quantities. The surface of the Delaware is covered with the oil that has run to waste: such is the yield that the supply of barrels and hogsheads cannot keep pace with it, nor store the treasures which the earth pours forth in such lavish profusion; even when secured, it baffles all the powers of the

Atlantic and Great Western, and Erie railways to convey it to the ports.

There were a few specimens from the Washoe silver mines. In this case were shown two or three samples of quartz said to be worth 2000*l*. per ton. Mr. Hulskamp's pianoforte improvement has already been noticed.

JAPAN.

Although no collection of articles was sent to the Exhibition by the Japanese themselves, there was shown a series of cabinets containing specimens of the industrial and art manufactures of the country collected by the very few individuals who have seen it, the chief exhibitor being Mr. Rutherford Alcock, Her Majesty's Envoy to the Tycoon.

Among the works was a collection of little metal Buckles for fastening the dress; the designs of these buckles were irresistibly grotesque—not mere sketches, but solid little pieces of metal-work, the background being of bronze and the raised figures in relief being either gold, silver, steel, or platinum, or of all four metals intermixed. It is evident from the platinum being so freely used here that this metal must be much more common with the Japanese than with us, and that the secret of melting it, to which our chemical knowledge has only of late attained, has long been known to them. In the adaptation of bronze to ordinary domestic purposes, such as inkstands, tobacco jars, candlesticks, and the like, there was wonderful ingenuity shown; there was a Bronzed Tripod Candlestick so ingeniously hinged that it folded up into the size of a small envelope, and not much thicker. By the side of this case was shown an object which was one of the most curious of all in the whole Building: it was a small Window-blind made apparently of rods of twisted glass strung together; the rods were as hard, as clear, and as sharp as glass; yet it was made of *rice*, or, as Mr. Alcock asserts, from a gelatine of rice. We found also in a collection of Ivory Carvings, fresh proofs of the art, skill, and genius of the people—a comic scene was distinctly represented—yet they were so small that they might be worn as brooches. Opposite was a collection of Porcelain, in which was a large plate representing two Japanese ladies wearing French bonnets and shawls, with deeply-flounced silk dresses spread out by such an amplitude of crinoline as even our belles seldom venture on. One had a telescope with which she was pointing to the sea with an air of fashionable nonchalance, while the other figure, to still further exemplify European habits, had her gloved hand filled with green apples. In the background were two other Japanese ladies dressed in the costume of the county, and who were shrinking with horror and astonishment from their strangely-attired sisters. This ceramic caricature told its own tale: the attitude of the Europeanized Japanese lady pointing to the sea whence the barbarians are to come, the fidelity with which our dress and very walk is copied, all showed it to be meant as a warning satire of what will result to Japanese costumes and customs if once the Europeans are admitted within the pale of their strange community. It is a curious illustration of manufacturing skill that a passing joke like this should be represented in such a costly medium as this beautifully-finished porcelain.

The specimens of eggshell porcelain shown in this collection were, if anything, almost thinner than eggshell.

The show of Arms and Armour was not great. Among the weapons was a formidable short double-edged sword, taken from one of the party of assassins who attacked the house of the English Embassy at Jeddo by night last year. The best Japanese swordmakers, it is said, get as much as 100*l*. for a single blade.

The Coinage was completely illustrated. The silver coins are thick and square; those of gold are large, but thin, and have the corners rounded off. The largest coin of the latter kind is about 3 in. long by 2 in. broad, yet its value is only equal to 30s. of our currency: it is certainly thin, but there must, nevertheless, be at least 3*l*. worth of gold in it. Yet amply as they seem to be supplied with gold and silver, the Japanese have found their way to a paper currency, and their notes for various amounts, all of which are oblong, like the coins, were shown near the money.

In Paper, the manufacturers of Japan have undoubtedly attained an excellence and skill of which we in Europe know little. Here were paper Waterproof Coats, paper Leathers, paper Parasols, and paper Pocket-handkerchiefs. Some of the paper leathers were as strong apparently as any hides that ever left a tanyard. There was a large collection of the different kinds of paper used for paper-hangings, for writing, printing, and for wrapping up parcels. The different specimens of Printing were also shown: there was a Japanese Court Guide—a Directory which gave the names, ranks, and abodes of all the notabilities of the empire; there were a set of Japanese playbills—for the theatre is even a more fashionable place of resort in Jeddo than in London—a Japanese encyclopædia, and some children's story-books, which the comic genius of the people enables them to illustrate with the most racy humour. At the eastern end of the Court was a most valuable collection of Japanese Drugs and Surgical Instruments. Of the value of this pharmacopœia we can, of course, give no opinion, beyond saying that all their medicines seem derived from herbs. Their surgical instruments, however, were numerous and formidable. One thing is evident of their surgery, which is, that the terrible practice of resorting to actual cautery is still maintained, and the irons used in this dreadful operation were shown with the other instruments.

Of the Lacquer Ware, with which the name of Japan is most intimately connected, there were numerous specimens, some of them of great beauty and of unrivalled workmanship. A large Cabinet in hard wood, elaborately carved and lacquered, with cameos of finely-chiselled ivory and embossed metal handles, was said to be very old, and perfectly unique of its kind. Two cabinets, contributed by Mr. C. Copeland, were also very handsome; but the finest, perhaps, in this class was a gold-lacquered waiter, which bore the crest of the Minister for Foreign Affairs. In many instances European patterns have been copied with great success, and some of the most beautiful articles, not only in lacquer, but in bronze, were of Pompeian and Etruscan form. The lacquer and enamel on ivory, tortoiseshell, and mother-of-pearl showed great delicacy and minuteness of finish; and there were fine samples of the inlaid and carved woodwork executed principally by the mountaineers, who pass the winter months in the production of such articles. Of Straw-work many samples might be seen here in the shape of ornamental boxes, baskets, cigar-cases, &c.—*Abridged from the Times.*

CHINA.

The Chinese exhibition, from the similarity of the peoples, much resembled that of the Japanese in its lacquered ware, its porcelain, its carvings, and its metal-work in bronze. Among other things from China was the autograph of the "Heavenly Chief," the redoubted leader of the Taeping rebels, who writes himself "Yeh-ngam-fung-t'ien-ta-tor," which being translated means, "By the Grace of the Lord appointed Heavenly King and Great Chief." There was also a fine collection of medical drugs from China; with complete sets of Chinese types, rare ornaments in jade, and an exquisite wood carving, which formed the back of the Emperor's throne in his Palace of Yuen-Min-Yuen. Another of the spoils exhibited was a skull set in gold in the form of a drinking-cup, which is popularly reported to be the head of Confucius, but which is more likely to be the skull of a rebel chief who succumbed to the arms of the Pekin Government when it was a little stronger than it is now. It was looted from the Summer Palace by one of our private soldiers, and sold for a very small price, though the value of the setting is over 1000*l*. Lady Michael sent a pair of beautiful lacquered vases of considerable size and evidently of great age, from the same place; and two ivory hexagon vases in their way were unsurpassed by anything in the Exhibition.

AFRICA, CENTRAL AND WESTERN.

In these two Collections, there would be little to notice, even had they been more favourably located than "under Staircase." The articles consisted mostly of tobes and native wrappers; grass-cloths and mats; cotton cloths and sundry native manufactures. The Commercial Association of Abeokuta sent fourteen specimens of Cotton, in various states.

Throughout the Yoruba country cotton is grown extensively, especially to the east and north. Great quantities of cotton cloths, of a strong texture, are annually made, and find their way to the Brazils, and into the far interior. To obtain a largely increased supply of cotton, it is only necessary to open roads, and bring money into the market. There would also be abundance of jute for exportation, if in demand. Very nice leather is done. The art of dyeing Morocco leather has been introduced from the interior. The metal is good, and the natives manufacture all their own implements.

MADAGASCAR.

This important island, which has just been thrown open to European commerce, sent to the Exhibition ores, cloths, and other native manufactures: the scarfs in silk were very showy. Specimens of the minerals were likewise shown.

Radama, King of Madagascar, hoisted the national flag over the products of his country. There was a portrait of his Majesty, dressed in the uniform of an English admiral, and inscribed "Malagassa" ("God preserve the King"). There were shown also, specimens of working in gold and silver: a sword-scabbard, finely chased in gold; a "unicorn's horn," mounted in gold, for a walking-stick; silver chains; and a chair of thin bar-iron, to show the quality of the native metal; this was sent a present from King Radama to the Exhibition Commissioners.

HAYTI

Was represented by some Iron ores, Saddlery and Harness, and a few rude specimens of Pottery. Adjoining Hayti was a case in which were exhibited Walking-sticks, Whip-handles, Picture-frames, and Veneers made from the "sea-serpent," or rather from a gigantic specimen of algæ, or sea-weed, growing sometimes to the length of 1000 feet, and, when floating in the water, stated to have been easily mistaken by a seaman for this monstrous creature. M. Gheslin has turned this substance to useful account, and depriving it of its hygrometric qualities, makes it available for many purposes for which, heretofore, gutta-percha and other substances were available.

THE EGYPTIAN COLLECTION.

This collection consisted of the products of modern Egypt, of the Soudan, and the relics of ancient Egypt. The looms of Cairo contributed the largest proportion of the first division—and the silks were remarkable for the strength of their texture. In the patterns there was hardly any departure from the traditional stripes, but the lustre of the colours, even in the ordinary fabrics used by the fellahs for their fête dresses, was unusually splendid. The woollen and the cotton goods, too, were well represented; and what made the Exhibition more valuable and really interesting was that we saw,

Y

not what the select Egyptian looms can turn out on special order, but the ordinary fabrics produced for general use and export. The Viceroy was the sole exhibitor in the Department. In many cases the articles shown here had been bought in the bazaars, and there were hardly any which had been manufactured for this Exhibition. Almost the only articles *de luxe* which appeared were specimens of tent-cloths, manufactured for his Highness, which are certainly very magnificent, being a mixture of silk and gold tissue. The scarves for the officers of the army of scarlet and gold, the slippers, the stems of the chibouks (which had an extraordinary amount of gold-wire lavished on them), and the saddlery, were also very creditable samples of what the Cairo workmen can do. There was a beautiful case of saddlery, of which the most important was a dromedary saddle, of green velvet and silver embroidery, on which the Viceroy made his pilgrimage to Mecca. A saddle of purple and gold by the side of it was the ordinary harness of the Cairo donkey. In the ladies' dresses, which occupied another portion of the same cases, were shown specimens of a new industry in Cairo—an imitation of the thick massive gold embroidery of the West, as distinguished from some single thread, which is the leading characteristic of Egyptian embroidery. From Soudan were exhibited some marvellous specimens of gold filigree work, executed by the negroes, which in beauty of finish equal anything shown in silver from Genoa and Malta, without making any allowance for the rough tools they use. The gold was from the province of Fazogolo. There were numerous specimens of the manufactures of the Southern provinces of Egypt.

The Arms, the ordinary Domestic Utensils, the Musical Instruments, and the Ornaments of these remote peoples were shown; and there was also a complete display of the Pottery of Assouan, which for lightness and beauty of form is perhaps one of the most remarkable productions of an uncivilized people. To the manufactures of the South they contribute ivory, which we see worked up in several elaborate sets of chessmen; ostrich feathers, which appear in the shape of exquisite fans; and other articles of minor importance. From the arsenals of Cairo there was exhibited a stand of admirably finished Rifles, Bayonets, and other arms, all used by the Egyptian army, and all produced by Arab workmen, under the direction of M. Minié, who has been for some years in the service of his Highness. The fertile soil of Egypt was but imperfectly represented here, though there were a few specimens of Wheat, Oats, Cummin, and other products. There was a small sample of the Cotton which is produced in large quantities along the coast. Of the ordinary Leather-work of the country there were numerous samples, the most important of which was the camel harness in ordinary use among the Bedouins.

But the most interesting portion of the Exhibition was the contributions from the Cairo Museum, which the Viceroy is now forming, his Highness being the first Mussulman sovereign who has formed a museum. In one of the cases here was exhibited a collection of ancient Egyptian Jewellery of extraordinary rarity, all the results of researches carried on by M. Mariette at Thebes, and with one or two exceptions all forming part of the funeral ornaments of Queen Aah-Hoteh, the mother of Amosis, the first king of the 18th dynasty: her Majesty lived about 1900 B.C., or 500 years before the time of Moses, about the time of Joseph. Among the principal objects was a Poniard, the blade elaborately chased with figures representing the fight of a lion and a bull; and close by the hilt was the cartouche, or private seal of King Amosis. Behind was a diadem of massive gold, in the front of which was a box, with the cartouche graven on it, supported by two exquisitely carved sphinxes. The posterior portion was set with coloured stones, lapis-lazuli, cornelian and turquois, and it had a peculiar tongue rising above the head, which served to divide the hair of the wearer. A hatchet—the symbol of divinity —had on the blade a curious representation of Amosis sacrificing a barbarian captive, and on the handle a complete genealogy of his Majesty. Next was a massive Gold Chain, nearly a yard long, suspended to a scarabæus of marvellous workmanship; and near it was a collar of equal beauty, with three large golden bees suspended from it. The most curious article was a Golden Boat mounted on four wheels, with twelve oarsmen in silver, and a figure in gold seated in the midst, probably an effigy of the dead queen. This is supposed to symbolize the voyage of the soul after death, and may be regarded as another proof of the belief of the Egyptians in the immortality of the soul. The most elaborate of all the ornaments was a *Pectoral*, or brooch, which represents King Amosis between two divinities, who were pouring over him the water of purification. Both sides of this ornament were beautifully finished—one side in gold, the other in coloured stones. There were a profusion of other Ornaments—Bracelets, Rings, Necklaces—in gold of excellent quality, all of which were found on her Majesty's person; and all of them, it is conjectured, made specially for her adornment in the coffin. Two great Earrings were of a later date, and bear the cartouche of Rameses, of the 20th dynasty.

A case contained a complete Pantheon of the Egyptian deities, among which a beautiful figure of Isis was, perhaps, the rarest and most beautiful. The most curious object in the case was a sort of model mummy case: by the side of the body sits the soul, and on the side of the coffin are inscribed prayers supposed to be addressed to the body by the soul, beseeching it to remain undisturbed until the day of resurrection, when the two will be found together again. A small figure of another deity in blue enamel—the *bleu d'Egypte*, which the moderns cannot reproduce—destroy the theory that the Egyptians had no knowledge of the art of enamelling.—*Abridged from the Times.*

Fine Art Department.

WE have now completed our notices of the Industrial portion of the Exhibition. There remains the division of Modern Fine Arts, comprising Paintings, Drawings, Sculpture, and Engravings—British and Foreign. These were fully described in special catalogues; and to each subdivision in the Official Catalogue was prefixed a Descriptive Introduction, the writer of which has amply exemplified the notion, "nothing if not critical." It does not fall within the plan of this volume to do more than very briefly note these Collections. With the history and details of the majority of the Works here exhibited the public are familiar, or they are to be found in catalogues and lists of very easy access.

The Picture Galleries, a noble suite of saloons, if not fully entitled to the extravagant encomiums which they have received, are certainly the best portion of Captain Fowke's Building. In space, proportions, and lighting, they are admirably adapted for the exhibition of the finest collection of Works of Art ever assembled—from public and private galleries, and liberally lent by many art-patrons. The space was divided into two equal parts; the south-western angle being appropriated to foreign artists, and the south-eastern portion devoted to the exhibition of works by masters of the British School.

PAINTINGS IN OIL: ENGLISH SCHOOL.

This collection was much finer than that at Manchester in 1857; and what was of greater importance, more comprehensive and truly representative. Not only were there specimens of the leading painters, but when, as in the case of Turner, Wilkie, Mulready, Poole, Hook, Maclise, Dyce, and Philip, the painters have different manners, there were generally examples of each; which result is due to the care and judgment of Mr. Redgrave, R.A. The period of art represented was that between 1762 and 1862; the contribution commencing with the works of Hogarth, who died in 1764, and extending, by regular gradation, through all the links of our best art, down to the works of the most celebrated painters of our own day. Such a collection of Hogarths was never got together: embracing the whole series of the Marriage à la Mode; the only two of the Harlot's Progress not destroyed at Fonthill fire; the Election pictures, Rake's Progress, from the Soane Museum, &c.; the early-painted Mall, the March of the Guards, Captain Coram, Mrs. Hogarth, two Conversation pictures, and some half-dozen more.

There were some 40 works by Sir Joshua Reynolds, including the Age of Innocence, Penelope Boothby, the Infant Samuel, Mrs. Siddons as the Tragic Muse, the Princess Sophia, the Duchess of Devonshire, the Angels, Miss Boothby, Iphigenia, &c. Of Gainsborough's works there was an equally perfect collection, including the famous Blue Boy, Mr. and Mrs. Hallett, Dr. Fischer, Girl feeding Pigs, Georgiana, Duchess of Devonshire, Girl with Pitcher, Mrs. Sheridan, and Mrs. Tickell, &c. Of Richard Wilson's works there were his famed View on the Dee. Wright was represented by his Ulleswater; George Morland by his Gipsies, Sea-shore, Wild-fowl Shooting, and Sheep; Patrick Nasmyth by his Pond with Burdocks, and Ringwood. Of the portrait-painters towards the close of the last century, there were Opie, Jackson, Raeburn, Ramsay, and Copley. Sir Thomas Lawrence was admirably represented by the Calmady Children, portraits of Pius VII., Lord Eldon, and Lord Liverpool. Northcote, Harlowe, Stothard, Callcott, Hilton, Fuseli, Haydon, and Shee, with Briggs, Crome, Bonington, and J. F. Chalon, were here, with Martin and Danby.

Wilkie might be studied in some early pictures and some later Spanish works. Turner stands supreme master of poetical landscape, but was inadequately illustrated here. Etty's claims to be esteemed as a most consummate colorist were supported far better here than at Manchester. There were good specimens of other recently-deceased artists—besides Constable, Müller, and Danby; J. Ward—the large bull painted in emulation of Paul Potter's; Leslie's well-known pictures from Don Quixote, and the Merry Wives of Windsor scene; and a scene by Frank Stone.

Haydon was represented by his Judgment of Solomon, his most equal work, and approaching very near the standard of large academical or historical painting. His other picture here was the Mock Election in the King's Bench Prison, in 1827, which George IV. purchased of the painter for 500 guineas; but the picture is worth little without the descriptive story which Haydon has told better than he painted it.

At the head of the living painters was Mr. Mulready, with pictures in his earlier manner, as the Firing a Cannon; and his later, as The Bathers. There were excellent examples of the principal living artists—Stanfield and Roberts; Maclise's Caxton Exhibiting a Proof-sheet to Edward IV., and perhaps his finest oil picture, The Banquet Scene, Macbeth; Sir Charles Eastlake (his finest picture of sacred art) Christ Weeping over Jerusalem; Hurlstone at his prime; F. R. Pickersgill, J. and W. Linnell; Frith, Ramsgate Sands; Paton, the admirable Scotch painter of Home—The Return from the Crimea; Sir Edwin Landseer, several of his largest and most impressive Highland pictures; Leighton, his great picture of The Procession of Cimabue; Hook; O'Neil, the Eastward Ho!; Solomon, Lance, John Faed, J. Clark, Horsley, Frost, Cope, Egg, T. S. Cooper, F. Goodall, Dobson, Phillip, Poole—Ward, Charlotte Corday Going to Execution,

The Fall of Clarendon, and The Antechamber at Whitehall; J. F. Lewis, Cooke; Dyce—Titian's First Essay in Colouring, and Pegwell Bay; Creswick, Webster, Ansdell, Lee, Herbert; and Elmore, The Tuileries in 1792. The Pre-Raffaelites were represented by Millais; and by Holman Hunt's picture, The Light of the World; by Mr. Watts there were portraits of Mrs. Russell and the Poet Laureate.

The first effect of the Collection upon the visitor entering the English Gallery was well described as in the eye being at once sensible of the mellow splendour diffused over the right-hand wall, where were gathered examples of our earliest, and as yet greatest, masters in incident painting, portraiture, and landscape. Or, "be it the mellowing hand of Time or the magic of their art which gives its subdued but intense glow to this section of our English gallery, none but must be sensible of the contrast between even the most powerful colour of our living, or recently living painters, and that which steeps the first half of the walls devoted to our great dead."—*Times*.

"The English Gallery," says another able critic, "affords an admirable opportunity of gaining an acquaintance with most of what is worth knowing and studying in the history of Painting in England. The limits of time assigned to the exhibition of English pictures include all that there has been of painting in the country, while almost all, if not quite all, of those painters who ought to have a place in such a gallery are represented here. It is a collection as instructive as it is interesting. It is a condensation of all that we most wish to know, and most love to see in English art.

"In the first place, there are the pictures of Sir Joshua and of Gainsborough. Secondly, there are the pictures which represent the peculiarly English art of landscape-painting. Thirdly, there are the pictures of the incident school. And lastly, there are those pictures marked by the brilliancy of colour and minuteness of detail which we generally associate with the name of Pre-Raffaelitism. There are many other things to be studied in this gallery. There are other kinds of pictures. There are general notions of the historical sequence or intrinsic excellence of the gallery as a whole. But any one who determines that he will understand and recollect these four groups, and examine minutely a few chosen pictures in each, so that each may be represented by distinct types in his mind, will have made a use of the gallery that he will be glad of, and will have protected himself from that general feeling of indolent business of thought that is so often the only result of passing through a series of things which we may, perhaps, have most sincerely admired."

All who have studied the collection in this manner will have profited by an opportunity not likely to be again afforded them:

"Turner is only feebly represented here. All the pictures in this gallery are in his earlier manner, before he attempted to conquer those great difficulties in painting sky and land which have been the means of exciting in the breasts of his admirers such rapture of adoration. In the pictures to be seen in this gallery Turner is quiet, masterly, but not superhuman. Still, his Schaffhausen was there, to show how great he really was.—Turner may have done greater things than this, but very few men have done anything like it. But the merit of the gallery as an exposition of English landscape-painting lies in this—not that Turner or any one man is to be seen, but that the whole series of masters who have given their lives and thoughts to this branch of art comes before us here. We can see the variety of modes in which nature has appeared to her worshippers, and the fidelity with which each in his peculiar walk has tried to render her."

After a judicious reference to the ready appreciation of the old pictures in this collection, and the learning required to appreciate the modern school, the critic concludes—

"At the same time, it ought fully to be admitted that there are in this gallery pictures characteristic of the modern school in its highest degree of success, which show that study of a picture at first sight hard to understand may be amply repaid. 'The Light of the World' is an instance that must occur to every one. There are also pictures here that show how minute detail and brilliant colouring can be used so as to make a painting intelligible and pleasant to every one, while yet it is really masterly in design and execution. If any spectator wishes to take away the memory of such a picture as his last impression of the English Gallery, let him examine Martineau's 'Last Day in the Old House,' and he will find himself repaid and satisfied; and, if he is an Englishman, he will pass on to the Foreign Galleries with a proper pride in the paintings of his own country."—*Saturday Review*, June 28.

ENGLISH WATER-COLOURS.

Our truly national school, founded by Girtin, and above all, by Turner, the greatest landscape-painter that ever lived, was admirably represented. Turner's Works illustrated both the commencement and the full perfection of the art; those who laboured to extend its scope—as Edridge, Robson, Dewint, Copley, Fielding, Prout, and Varley, were not overlooked; while the works of Barrett, Blake, Stothard, and Cox, led up to the living representatives of this charming art. And there were Herbert and Lewis, Cole and Branwhite, Dodgson and Duncan, L. Haghe and Nash, Fripp and Warren, William Hunt, Birket Foster, Corbould and Wehnert, Fripp and Topham, Haag, Redgrave, Goodall, and Vacher, Roberts and Landseer. Turner shone forth in his long trail of artistic light—from his earliest work to his latest style; thus atoning for his feeble representation in the gallery of oil-paintings. "But that the drawings by Turner in the Water-colour Gallery in some measure make up for this poverty of oil-pictures by this great master, foreigners who wish to understand the estimation of Turner in this country ought to be specially warned to study him in Trafalgar-square, in the pictures bequeathed by him to the nation. As seen in his oil-pictures at the International Exhibition, Turner is the sober controller of great powers, both as a draughtsman and a colorist. The enormous range of his works, and the peculiar magic of his rendering of the vastness and mystery, as well as the beauty and terror, of Nature, are in some measure indicated, but only indicated, by his drawings."—*Times*.

ARCHITECTURE.—DESIGNS AND MODELS.*

This class of contributions reminded one of the "Architectural Room" at our Royal Academy Exhibition, with this advantage— that its groups of designs were selected from more years than one. They included drawings of edifices already built, and of many, in all probability, never to be built, but still useful as architectural

* See also pp. 72-73.

examples and studies. We had new hotels, government offices, halls and picture-galleries, churches, schools, railway buildings, and drinking fountains, with their pretty architectonic sentimentalism—altogether, exclusive of Models, some 600 in number. By the late Mr. Thomas we had the Royal Park Dairy, and the Queen's Boudoir, at Windsor; and two views of the New Lodge in Windsor Forest, by Mr. Talbot Bury; all pleasing and picturesque. Mr. Gilbert Scott's thirteen contributions included his Restoration of the Westminster Chapter-house, the noble church which he is building at Hamburg, and his prize design for the Hotel de Ville in that city. Mr. Digby Wyatt contributed some thirty Drawings, and Mr. Owen Jones one-third of that number —the latter including the projected People's Palace at Muswell-hill, the ceiling of Hancock's show-rooms, Bond-street, the artistic skill and taste of which are admirable. Ordish and Le Feuvre sent their Crystal Palace, now being erected at Amsterdam, in contrast with the Fowkeian edifice, not to our advantage. The executors of the late Sir Charles Barry contributed eight Drawings, including Bridgewater House, and reminding us how death removed the architect and two noble owners, leaving the mansion uncompleted. The Models, some twenty-five in number, comprised Mr. Tite's noble portico of the Royal Exchange; St. Paul's Cathedral, by J. Slie; and a few of our provincial Cathedrals.

ART-DESIGNS FOR MANUFACTURES.

The Art-Designs for Manufactures, in a subdivision of the same class as the Architecture, were divided as works of *deceased* and *living* artists. The whole number of the designs did not much exceed three hundred, scarcely one-third of them being the productions of the deceased artists—about twenty names in all of the latter. Each section contained some designs which either were of great merit, or had a certain interest historically. The names of deceased artists included those of Robert Adam, Cipriani, J. Bacon, Brettingham, Catton, Sir Wm. Chambers, Sir F. Chantrey, Chippendale, Cotterill, Flaxman, Joseph Gandy, Sir John Soane, Kent, Kilburn, Matthias Lock, Nollekens, Pitts, A. W. Pugin, Stothard, Vardy, James Wyatt, and W. Wyon. Out of the whole number of productions to which these names are attached, about half were by Stothard. Here were shown the detailed drawings of the Wellington Shield, by Stothard, in which he excels in his successful composition of battle-subjects, and his conscientious study of costume. His designs for silver-work, also shown here, were graceful and elegant; and his Frieze for Buckingham Palace is one of the few redeeming art-glories of that much-abused palatial pile.

Among the Architects' designs most noteworthy were the following: a Chimney-piece by Adam and Cipriani, showing the use of inlaid ornament; Chambers's designs, including one "for Guilloche and Capital," "for Ceiling," "for Chimney-piece," "for an Ewer," and "for Decoration of Vase and Frieze," each illustrating how that architect gave attention to architectural detail and some branches of ornamental and decorative art. Besides the drawings, a model was exhibited by Messrs. Vezey and Co., of Her Majesty's State-coach, which was designed by Chambers: the panels of the coach were painted by Cipriani, who also painted the original sketches on the model. Six sheets of designs by Kent included the same number of designs for fireplaces, the best of them having looking-glass frames over. Of this arrangement there are eighteenth century examples remaining in many houses in London; and there is a disposition to return to it among our artists in furniture. There were in the gallery three frames of designs, by Chippendale, and four by Matthias Locke, which well sustained their reputation. A design for a Candelabrum, with an unicorn at its base, by Catton, was also shown. Some of Kent's fireplaces, chimney-pieces, and ceilings, shown here, were classically elegant. By Brettingham and Vardy there were specimens of interior decoration. By Pugin, an artist of earnest excellence, there were designs for a portrait-frame, and for metal-work, comprising crosiers. Here, too, were drawings of race-cups, by Cotterill, shown by Garrard; and Hunt and Roskell exhibited the Shield of Æneas, designed by Pitts. There were some designs for silver-work, by Flaxman, contributed by the South Kensington Museum, scarcely worthy of our greatest sculptor.

Amongst the productions of living artists, Mr. Armstead's designs, illustrating the history of the Shirley Family, deserve high praise. The Department of Art, the Female School of Art, and the provincial schools, contributed designs for watch-cases, breakfast services, drinking-fountains, black flounces, chintzes, paper-hangings, majolica dishes, silver prize-cups, carpets, chandeliers, glass, book-covers, and many other articles, the majority deserving the attention of manufacturers. Mr. Jackson's designs for metal-work; Mr. Cable's for paper-hangings; Mr. Barrett's and Mr. N. Roskell's for Goodwood and other cups; Mr. Owen Jones's designs for covers and pages of illuminated books; Mr. J. Leasels' designs for book-stamps, frontispieces, and embossed glass; Mr. Maclise's series of beautiful designs for ceramic ware—the Seven Ages of Man, contributed by the Art-Union of London, and his designs for a bracelet, and for a cup; and Mr. W. H. Rogers's several designs for wood-carving—all deserved particular notice. Mr. Godfrey Sykes's design for bronze doors of a school of art was good. Mr. M. Digby Wyatt displayed a large number of designs, and for a great variety of objects—including railway carriages; and some of the late Mr. Thomas's designs were found here. Designs for stained glass were exhibited by Messrs. O'Connor and Mr. S. Powell; also a design, probably not recent, by Mr. Dyce, for a stained glass window for Alnwick Church, Northumberland: the mullions cut through the figures—the lights not designed separately. In a design for mural decorations by encaustic chalk drawing, exhibited by Mr. B. E Duppa, the drawings were in part by Sir Edwin Landseer. Mr. Alfred Stevens's designs, contributed by Minton, Campbell, and Co., especially one for a vase in Nevers ware, and Mr. F. Smallfield's designs for metal-work, including a loving-cup and a jewel-cup—were excellent. There were also some elegant designs for Honiton Lace, and for etched glass.—*Condensed from the Builder.*

SCULPTURE.

The collection of Sculpture, Medals, and Intaglios, under the management of Mr. E. Oldfield, was an important addition to the Fine Art section. For the first time, perhaps, in the history of such exhibitions, Sculpture held a prominent and recognised position side by side with painting. Here the works of our great sculptors were carefully arranged about the Building, to add to the general effect of the display, and add to its life, with the exception of one room devoted to the productions of deceased sculptors. This room contained fine examples of Banks, Nollekens, Bacon, Flaxman, Chantrey, R. J. Wyatt, Westmacott, and Campbell. Here were Banks's Falling Titan, and a plastic bas-relief of his Thetis and Achilles; Nollekens's poetic statues, and his noble busts; Flaxman was admirably demonstrated by his large marble group, the Fury of Athamas, his Cephalus and Aurora, and here was this great sculptor's Shield of Achilles, from the description of Homer. R. Wyatt's figures were next after Flaxman's; his Girl Bathing is a charming work. Bacon, prolific as he was, was represented by one work only—a statue of Mars; Westmacott, by his marble Nymph and Cupid, and a Nymph. Here were Campbell's clever bust of the late Earl Grey; Rossi's bust of Lord Thurlow; and striking busts of Sir W. Ross and A. H. Layard, by Patrick Park.

The majority of our modern sculptors exhibited, and the result was, a fine collection of about 120 statues, 40 or 50 busts, and 20 or 30 bas-reliefs. Among the good specimens of later art were Baily's Eve, Marshall's Ophelia, Westmacott's Peri, pleasing figures by the Thorneycrofts, Cupid by Behnes, and Love by Woolner. A critic in the *Saturday Review*, says of the latter sculptor:—"There are no busts of the present day which can, we think, be compared to the busts of Mr. Woolner. They stand by themselves for the mode in which they give the human face, when the face is that of a man of high intellect or of forcible character. The two busts of Mr. Maurice and Mr. Tennyson are as speaking likenesses, as plainly marked with the thought and the genius of the originals, as marble can be expected to produce. The Poet Laureate is perhaps slightly idealized. It is the man as he may be seen, not as he is sure to be seen. But the bust of Mr. Maurice strikes us as being quite as much like Mr. Maurice as he is himself. It is the man in stone."

Foley well sustained his reputation as the most imaginative of our living sculptors, by his group of Juno and Bacchus, his statues of Caractacus and Egeria, and his matchless equestrian statue of the late Viscount Hardinge. The works of Noble, Adams, and Munro, also had many admirers. Mr. Gibson contributed seven works, at the head of which was his celebrated tinted Venus. It is erroneously supposed that Mr. Gibson tints his statues to represent life, whereas he only endeavours, by colour, to soften the general effect, and to give the appearance of ivory, a material much used by the ancients. Apart from the colour, this is one of the finest works of modern sculpture : his Venus is the Goddess of Marriage, a dignified and beautiful matron, with a tortoise at her feet; this work had never before been exhibited.

A small collection of Intaglios, Cameos, and Medals—the latter containing many fine works of the Wyons, father and son—completed the general feature of this important Department.

Here may be noticed the colossal monument in plaster of Shakspeare, modelled by the late Mr. Thomas, both as a portrait-statue and a national monument. The bard is seated on the wings of a pair of swans, and is wrapt in thought. The face and head differ both from the Chandos portrait, and the bust at Stratford : the pedestal is very massive, and relieved by colossal seated figures and bas-reliefs. The figure of the bard is placed on too great a height to be seen to advantage : the accessory figures have greater merit, those of Comedy and Tragedy being very finely modelled, and the groups in the relief scenes from Shakspeare's plays are well chosen, and artistically executed. "A melancholy interest (says the *Illustrated London News*) attaches to this monument, for it is said indirectly to have hastened the sculptor's death. It is stated, on good authority, that the Royal Commissioners for the International Exhibition, or their agents, had refused him space for it, after considerable discussion with him not of the most conciliatory nature ; that he had been indisposed for two or three weeks previously from excessive labour and anxiety, and that he went home after his last interview with the authorities at Kensington, took to his bed, and died in a few days." Strange to add, this stupendous monument, although 20 feet in height, was overlooked by the Fine Art Catalogue maker.

ETCHINGS AND ENGRAVINGS.

If this Class was less attractive than others of the same Department, the cause was evident—prints being, from their multiplicity, in nearly all cases, better known than pictures. Our School of Engraving dates from about the middle of the last century ; and the Committee divided the specimens which the liberality of collectors had principally enabled them to exhibit, into five principal classes—etching, line-engraving, mezzotint, stipple, and wood-engraving ; and these were subdivided into works of deceased and works of living engravers.

The earliest etchings exhibited were those by Mortimer, who studied under Hudson and next under Sir Joshua Reynolds : they were clever but coarse. Next were two classic scenes by Barry ;

but more interesting was Schiavanetti's etching of the Canterbury Pilgrimage, from Stothard's celebrated picture. Next we had etchings of some of Wilkie's early works; Boys Fishing, by W. Collins; and some most expressive outlines by J. M. W. Turner.

The line-engravings commenced with a selection of Hogarth's prints, from the well-known collection of Mr. Felix Slade, and included the Harlot's Progress, and the Rake's Progress; and Morning, Noon, Evening, and Night, which, we do not use the phrase in a disparaging sense, were the art-furniture of the last century.* Vivares, Woollett, and Browne succeeded, with their landscape-engravings; and then Sir Robert Strange's masterly productions, as his Cleopatra, after Guido; and Charles I., after Vandyke. Bartolozzi's specimens included the diploma of the Royal Academy, after Cipriani; and a few benefit tickets. To these succeed a dozen of Woollett's conscientious works, including the Death of Wolfe, and the Battle of La Hogue, after West; and then we had a group of William Sharp's fine engravings of great pictures, comprising Sir Joshua's portrait of John Hunter. Then followed Heath and Bromley's clever book-illustrations. Rainbach's prints of Wilkie's pictures came next; and next, G. and W. B. Cooke's charming prints of Turner's coast-views; and the fine works of Charles Heath and W. Findoe brought us near the close of the *line* engravers, who were not altogether well

---

* Art-critics will never tire of lamenting the want of a biography of Hogarth which shall give a fair estimate of what they regard as his life-struggle for his art. By his prints, however, Hogarth succeeded—for a reason which does not appear to have been generally recognised by those who have written about the painter and his works. Elsewhere we have remarked:—

"How much of the moral effect of Hogarth's works is due to their being engraved, and the prints sold at prices *available by all classes*, must he evident to every one who has bestowed any thought upon the subject. If we refer to the list of "Prints published by Mr. Hogarth; Genuine Impressions of which are to be had at Mr. Hogarth's House in Leicester Fields, 1781," we shall find the price as low as One Shilling, and rarely to exceed One Guinea. For example, the Harlot's Progress, 6 prints, cost but 20s.; the Rake's Progress, 8 prints, but 42s.; and the Industry and Idleness, 12 prints, 12s." (*Anecdote Biography* of Hogarth, pp. 93, 94).

Mr. Leslie, the painter, has thus admirably illustrated the same view: "To the art of Engraving it is scarcely too much to say that we owe the very existence of Hogarth. His patrons were the million. The great people were told by Walpole that he was no painter; and Walpole being one of themselves, they believed him. But for engraving, therefore, Hogarth must have confined himself to portraits, on which he might have starved, for he was never popular as a portrait-painter. But when the prints of the *Harlot's Progress* appeared, 1200 copies were immediately subscribed for. This was the beginning of the patronage produced for painting by engraving."—*Autobiography*, p. 214.

The genius of Hogarth has unquestionably been advocated with great ability, eloquence, and ingenuity. If Walpole traduced him, and Reynolds slighted him, and Ireland and Nichols undervalued him, and Fuseli estimated him falsely, Charles Lamb has manfully vindicated him; Leslie has fully appreciated him, and J. T. Smith has circumstantially defended him; while, in another view, his genius has been picturesquely illustrated by Thackeray, one of the best art-critics of his day; by Sala, in his own clever manner; by Hannay, in his able essay; and in a hundred pages of the Anecdote Biography already referred to.

illustrated. The mezzotints were better represented by MacArdell, the two Watsons, Green and Earlom, the two Woods, Bromley and Clint, Say, Reynolds, J. M. W. Turner, and a few of his pictures engraved by C. Turner; Martin's Belshazzar and Nineveh brought the series near its close. The stipple specimens commenced with Bartolozzi's plate of Copley's great work, misnamed "The Death of Lord Chatham;" followed by those of Howard, Caroline Watson, and C. Scriven.

The living Engravers' specimens included George Cruikshank's etchings, works by the Etching Club, and Sir E. Landseer's Animals. The *line*, Allen, Burnet, E. W. Cooke, Doo, Goodall, Greatbach, Pye, Robinson, Rolls, Wallis, and Wilmore; *mezzotint*, Bromley, Cousins, T. Landseer, T. Lupton, and G. R. Ward; *stipple*, F. and W. Holl, and W. Walker.

The deceased Engravers on Wood represented were Bewick, Branston, Clennell, Nesbit, S. Williams, and E. Landells.

The Engravings on Wood included William Harvey's matchless Dentatus, after Haydon; and a few truly artistic works by W. J. Linton, J. Thompson, and J. L. Williams; there was little of the rapid engraving of the present day.

Of Lithography there were a few fine specimens by Boys, Harding, Lane, Lynch, and Maguire.

FOREIGN PAINTING AND SCULPTURE.

The foreign display of Paintings, Drawings, Engravings, Sculpture, and Intaglios, was numerically as strong as the British exhibition.

France led off with about 200 oil-paintings—specimens of the great French School; nearly 40 water-colour pictures; 50 groups of sculpture; and about 130 engravings, lithographs, and architectural drawings. The pictures selected by the Imperial Commission were those painted by living artists since 1850, or those painted since 1840 by deceased masters born after 1790. The greatest novelties represented were the recent school of natural landscape, and domestic subjects. We can only enumerate a few of the more striking works. There were six specimens of Paul Delaroche, namely: a portrait of M. Péreire; a Martyr in the reign of Diocletian, founded on an ancient Christian legend, that a nimbus floated over the head of a drowned female martyr; Marie Antoinette; the Virgin in contemplation before the Crown of Thorns; Good Friday celebrated by early Christians; and the Return from Calvary.

The high level of feeling and of art reached in these three little scenes from the history of the Virgin at the time of the Crucifixion is thus characterized in the *Saturday Review*:—"They are pictures to study, inch by inch. Everything is so simple and so true. The Virgin is so thoroughly a plain Jewess, and yet a woman torn by an agony of deep grief, and exalted by her meditations and her trials. This is the religious art which we feel sure will, little by little, drive into oblivion the dreams and the fancies of modern Continental mediævalism."

There were also the very intellectual portrait of Mdlle. Rosa Bonheur, by Dubufe fils; the Dying S. Francesco d'Assisi, by Benouville; St. Augustine and St. Monica, his mother, the only work by Ary Scheffer; the Spring, a female figure nude, the only example of the great master Ingres; the Landing of the French Army in the Crimea, and an Incident at the Battle of the Alma, two colossal pictures by the young painter, Pils. By Yvon there were small copies of the great pictures at Versailles, painted for the Emperor—the Battle of Solferino, Curtain of the Malakoff, Gorge of the Malakoff, and the Attack on the Malakoff—all well known by engravings; the Landing of the French Army in the Crimea, by Barrias—another colossal picture from Versailles; Flandrin's over-finished portrait of the Prince Napoleon; Winterhalter's large portrait of the Empress; a portrait of the Emperor, by Flandrin; Vipier's full-length portrait of Abd-el-Kader; Gerôme's well-known picture of Roman Gladiators saluting Tiberius in the Roman amphitheatre; Embarkation of Ruyter and De Wytt, by Isabey; and the Arrival of Queen Victoria at Cherbourg, by Gudin. There were two portraits by Horace Vernet, of Marshals Bosquet and MacMahon; there were three of the minute pictures of Meissonier; and charming examples of Trayer, Lambinet, Ziem, Marilhat, and Edouard Frère. Horace Vernet's only war-picture here was his Battle of the Alma.

Among the drawings was a large and elaborate composition by Decamps, of Joshua commanding the Sun to stand still.

Among the French sculpture we can only enumerate a few specimens: as a bust of a Negro and Negress, in bronze and marble, by Cordier; a noble marble bust of President Boileau, by Iselin; Mené's Death of the Fox; Pradier had but one subject—Sappho; Guillaume's bronze Tomb of the Gracchi; and Barge's Theseus subduing the Centaur; Vechte's chased Silver Vase; Cavelier's bust of Ary Scheffer; Fauns, by Gumery and Lequesne. Canova's colossal marble bust of Napoleon I. was in the French Gallery: it has not gained in estimation by the lapse of years.

THE GREAT GERMAN SCHOOL OF PAINTING was well represented by the Zollverein, and other German States. Prussia sent nearly 200 works of art, in architectural designs, oil-paintings, sculpture, and engravings. Berlin and Dusseldorf each sent a fine collection of paintings; and the engravings from the former city were choice and numerous. Among the sculpture from Berlin was a case of medals by Carl Fischer. Only one specimen was sent of Peter von Cornelius, and two of Oswald Achenbach. The oil-paintings from Dusseldorf included a series of 11 pictures by H. Mücke, representing the Life of St. Meinrad.

In sculpture, Cauer and Eichler contributed the greatest number of groups; and most of the works of art from Prussia generally were exhibited by these artists. Bavaria sent about 40 works of art, chiefly oil-paintings, amongst which were seven pictures by

Carl Wilhelm Müller. One of the grandest pictures was Nero after the Burning of Rome, by Piloty, of Munich, full of skilful drawing and expression; and "a conspicuous instance of the power of rendering human emotion and expressing human action on a large and free scale." Saxony was represented in 30 paintings, drawings, and groups of sculpture: the Grand Duchy of Baden sent a small fine-art collection. The Duchy of Brunswick, Frankfort-on-the-Maine, the Electorate of Hesse, the Duchy of Saxe-Coburg and Gotha, and Wurtemburg were represented by about 40 works of art. North Germany and the Hanse Towns also sent a small collection, Hamburg having contributed about 20 works. Among these were three pictures by F. Heimerdinger, one a scene of fairy life from a tale by L. Tieck, and three pictures by B. Mohrhagen. A cartoon by Peter von Cornelius, of the Four Horsemen of the Apocalypse was the only work in the Exhibition that represented by its chief master one of the highest forms of modern German art. There was a cartoon of Charlemagne meeting Duke Thessilio at the monastery, by C. Adamo; and one of the Deluge, by Herr August Hovemayer; there were also 17 Cartoons from the Odyssey, by Friedrich Preller; and a very German and conventional study of King Lear with his Fool, by Hermann Wislicenus. Somewhat allied to the cartoon-painting were the illustrations, in long perpendicular strips, to Goethe's Faust, Prometheus, &c., by Herr B. von Neher; and the spirit of the cartoon-drawer and fresco-painter was expressed in miniature by three frames of small sketches painted in oil, by the Baron Hugo von Blomberg, 27 in number, to illustrate Dante's Divina Commedia. We searched in vain for any of the grand historical works of Overbeck, Iteinle, Deger, Schnorr, or Kaulbeck, or for the clever incident pictures of Bendemann, Köhler, Hildebrandt, Schadow, or Sohn; or for the pleasing landscapes of Lessing or Koch. "In the religious art which represents the scenes of Gospel history as incidents of human life, but appeals most forcibly to our sympathy and veneration, this collection was very strong; of which art Richter's Raising of Lazarus was a most conspicuous and striking example." (*Saturday Review*.)

THE AUSTRIAN SCHOOL was represented by about 80 oil-paintings, 16 water-colour pictures, 19 pieces of sculpture, and a few engravings and architectural sketches. Here was a remarkably pleasing portrait of the Empress of Austria, by Schrotzberg. There was likewise Eugert's portrait of the Emperor of Austria, in which a solid mass of red velvet is cleverly kept by the artist subordinate to the main effect of the picture.

HOLLAND exhibited about 120 oil-paintings, and two engravings. Amongst the pictures were 7 by D. Blas, mostly good, and 8 by P. Van Schendel. There were a few flower and fruit pieces, and views with dykes, canals, and water-courses; the finest coast picture was the Shipwrecked, by J. Israels.

SWEDEN was represented by about 40 works in oil-painting and sculpture. The rustic scenes of J. F. Heckert and Miss A. Lindegrön were the most numerous amongst the pictures. Among the sculpture, a group, and bas-reliefs, in bronzed zinc, illustrating a story of jealousy, by Molin, were very interesting.

NORWAY was represented by some 50 oil-paintings, including nine specimens of Boe—pictures of flowers, fruit, birds, and jewellery—six landscapes by Gude—landscapes by Dahl and figure-pieces by Tidemand. Several portraits in ivory were in the small collection of sculpture. Altogether, the Swedish and Norwegian pictures astonished by unlooked-for excellence.

DENMARK sent about 110 works, including six groups of sculpture by Thorwaldsen, and five by J. A. Jerichau. Among the oil-paintings, E. Jerichau was the artist most largely represented. The Danish portraits have been described as "the very feeblest efforts of the art ever seen out of the parlour of a country inn." Among the sculpture were a colossal portrait-statue of Oersted, by Bissen; six of Thorwaldsen's masterpieces, including Mercury and Jason; and a Dancing Faun and Bacchante, by Peters.

RUSSIA sent more than 100 works of art; 80 oil-paintings, five groups of sculpture and medals, three architectural sketches, and seventeen engravings. Amongst them was a collection of medals exhibited by the Academy of Fine Arts of St. Petersburg, and a monument representing the Empress Catherine II., by Felix Chopin. The earliest picture exhibited was one by Anthony Losenko, who died in 1773; and there were seven specimens of Axenfeldt, and five portraits by Demetrius Levitsky. The other pictures were remarkable for the insight they afforded into the Russian manners and ways of life, its humour and character.

BELGIUM contributed the most complete display: about 113 oil-paintings, about 26 groups of sculpture, and two engravings. The great features were nine pictures, historical figures of the full life size, by L. Gallait: his Last Moments of Count Egmont is full of poetry, and is highly finished.—The Joan of Arc of Van Lerius is described as "bright with an intensity of colour which makes us think of Hunt and Millais; and it would not be difficult to find an English parallel to the picture of Leys—so painstaking, so full of sentiment, and so carefully conceived after the manner of an antiquated school." (*Saturday Review.*)—That Belgian art is much more like English than the art of any other country was shown by two sketches of heath scenery, with no marked differences from English landscape. Alfred Stevens's single-figure studies, the Nosegay, At Home, and the Widow, were wonderfully perfect. Very attractive, but painfully impressive, was Slingenmeyer's large picture, a Martyr in the reign of Diocletian,—a Christian youth asleep in a cell of the Roman amphitheatre, the door of which is held open and gives a glimpse of the arena in which he is to be thrust to be devoured by wild beasts, one of which is just about to spring upon the victim. Of the Belgian sculpture the finest example was the Venus Aphrodite of Fraikin.

SWITZERLAND sent more than 100 oil-pictures, amongst which were fifteen specimens of Jules Hébert; some quiet and truthfully expressive little works of Van Muyden; with a few pieces of sculpture and engravings. Of the pictures, the landscapes were most remarkable, and excelled the German works in quality.

SPAIN was represented by 30 works, in oil-painting, sculpture, and engraving, one of the former was Gisbert's fine historical work, the Execution of Padilla. Velasquez and Murillo were only illustrated by prints. There were remarkable for colour two fruit pieces, oranges and pomegranates in growth.

PORTUGAL sent only two oil-paintings (by Annunciação, and Da Silva), five photographs, and a few woodcuts.

ITALY was characteristically represented by about 40 architectural designs and 80 oil-paintings and drawings; about 70 groups of statuary and busts—some of them by English artists formed the sculpture-class; and the engravings reached 50. Francesco Harjez and Luigi Marchesi were represented by the most numerous specimens amongst the paintings; and the engravings included 7 plates by Luigi Calamatta of Rome; and some works by Giuseppe Longhi, Raffaelle Morghen, and Paolo Toschi. The most noteworthy figure-picture was Jephtha's Daughter musing in the Wilderness, by Ignazio Affanni.

ROME sent about 57 pieces of sculpture, including eight specimens of G. M. Benzoni; valuable cameos; a few fine drawings; many engravings; a collection of medals; and a large assemblage of mosaics, including a contribution from the Vatican. Its oil-paintings were chiefly modern; the best was G. Muller's Head of a Ciocciara, charmingly painted. The sculpture has been already noticed at page 308, describing the Roman Court, where Monti's Sleep of Sorrow and the Dream of Joy, and Magni's Reading Girl, were the paramount attractions.

TURKEY, for the first time in the history of all Exhibitions, filled a place as an exhibitor of pictures. Five portraits and still-life sketches were sent by M. Paul Musurus Bey.

GREECE sent two oil-paintings, five groups of sculpture, and engravings; the sculpture being chiefly marble statues and busts by L. and G. Phytalæ; and a few wood-carvings.

BRAZIL contributed a few paintings, and a pen-and-ink portrait of the Empress; two carvings in wood; and medals and coins.

UNITED STATES.—The American fine-art numbered only about a dozen pictures and engravings, the chief of which was Mr. Cropsey's Autumn on the Hudson: but several Transatlantic sculptors exhibited elsewhere in the Building.

DECLARATION OF THE AWARDS BY THE JURORS.

On Friday, July 11, the Grand State Ceremonial of the Declaration of the Prizes took place. The Duke of Cambridge acted as the representative of Her Majesty on the occasion; the various Foreign countries appointed what were termed "International Representatives" to receive the awards for their respective countries, and gentlemen were similarly appointed to act in the same capacity for the Colonies. The arrangements were of a simple and practical character, and everything which, in the regretted absence of the Queen, could be provided to give *éclat* to the ceremony, was adopted. The Ministers of State, the *corps diplomatique*, the representatives of foreign countries, wore their official costume; officers of the army and navy, and volunteers were in uniform; and not a few of the company appeared in academic robes. The dresses of the ladies imparted a pleasing and elegant appearance to the Gardens of the Horticultural Society, and there was music in abundance. On the upper terrace of the gardens a dais was erected, similar in its general appearance to that of the throne at the opening of the Exhibition. Here the special International Representatives were received by the Commissioners; and here the Jurors, arranged in their respective classes, and preceded by silken banners, presented their awards to the Duke of Cambridge. Her Majesty's ministers, and the *corps diplomatique*, and distinguished foreigners assembled in the conservatory. Among those who were present in addition to the Ministers of the Crown, were Mr. Disraeli; the Commissioners for 1851, and the Secretary, Mr. Bowring; the Building Committee; Lord Frederick Cavendish, secretary of the finance committee; members of the Council of the Society of Arts; the Council of the Horticultural Society; and the Commissioners of the Exhibition.

The proceedings of the day were commenced by Earl Granville, who, addressing the special International Representatives, said: "I have the pleasure of welcoming, on the part of Her Majesty's Commissioners for the International Exhibition, the distinguished representatives of foreign nations who honour us by taking part in the proceedings of this day. The readiness with which the Governments of foreign countries have responded to the invitation of the English Government is highly appreciated by the people of this country. I have now to request that the special representatives will receive the Report of the Council of Chairmen of juries. The awards will then be delivered to Her Majesty's Commissioners. We invite the assistance of the special representatives to make the awards known in the Building, as it will be agreeable to the exhibitors of the several countries to learn from a distinguished representative of their own nation the appreciation by the juries of their successful labours. In passing through the Building the special representatives will not fail to observe that the industry of all nations has shown a remarkable development since the last International Exhibition—a development which, justifying the anticipation of an illustrious Prince, now, alas! no more, owes much to the facilities given by such exhibitions by comparing the state of industry in each country, and affords a starting point for further progress."

Lord Taunton, the Chairman of the Council of Chairmen, then presented the following Report :—

"The work of the several juries having been brought to a termination, it becomes the duty of the Council of Chairmen to explain the manner in which the juries were constituted, and the result of their labours. The juries consisted of English and foreign members in varying proportions. The English jurors were in the first place nominated by exhibitors, and these nominations having been considered, Her Majesty's Commissioners invariably appointed such persons as appeared to be named by the general agreement of a trade or district. In cases where the nominations were not made on a common understanding, the Royal Commissioners were guided in their choice by the number of votes given to particular individuals, and in some instances by the desire expressed by exhibitors that the Commissioners should themselves select persons possessing the necessary qualifications. The British Colonies were represented by jurors recommended by the several Colonial Commissioners. Foreign nations taking part in the Exhibition had a right to nominate one juror for every class in which they were represented by twenty exhibitors, and for every section of a class in which they had fifteen exhibitors. As an alternative, each nation had a certain number of jurors allotted to it, in proportion to the space which it occupied in the Building, and several countries accepted this alternative. Her Majesty's Commissioners, without fixing any arbitrary proportion between foreign and English jurors, appointed as many of the latter to each jury as the experience of past exhibitions showed to be necessary for its efficiency. The juries were sixty-five in number, grouped so as to form thirty-six classes, or head juries, corresponding to the thirty-six industrial classes under which the objects are arranged in the Exhibition. Each of these head juries, when subdivided into sections, acted as a united body for the confirmation of awards. Before, however, the awards were considered final, they were brought before and received the sanction of a council consisting of the chairmen of the thirty-six head juries. The chairmen forming the council which regulated the affairs of the juries, were nominated by Her Majesty's Commissioners from the jurors of different nations, a number being allotted to each country relatively to the space assigned to it in the Building. The Council was presided over by a chairman appointed by Her Majesty's Commissioners. Her Majesty's Commissioners decided that only one description of medal should be awarded by the juries. This decision considerably facilitated their labours, as it became necessary only to reward excellence wherever it was found, without reference to competition between exhibitors. As the work of the juries advanced, it was ascertained that many articles possessed excellence of a kind which deserved a special mention, without, however, entitling them to a medal; and, although it involved some departure from the principle that had been originally laid down, yet the Council of Chairmen acceded to the wish of the juries, and permitted such cases to be classed and published under the title of "honourable mentions." The jurors and their associates engaged in examining the objects of the Exhibition amounted to 613 persons, of whom 287 were foreigners, and 325 English. They are men of high social, scientific, and industrial position, drawn from nearly every civilized country in the world. Their labours have occupied two months, and have been of the most arduous description, as they had to examine the objects displayed by at least 25,000 exhibitors. It can scarcely be expected that none of the articles exhibited have escaped their attention. In a few instances the delay of arrival or of arrangement has rendered it impossible for the juries to examine every article now within the building; while in other cases, errors in classification have rendered it doubtful to which of the juries the duty of examining some particular object should fall. Every effort, however, has been made to conquer these obstacles, and the omissions, if any, must be very few in number, and are not owing to the want of attention of the juries, or of the officers engaged in facilitating their work.

"The number of medals voted by the juries amount to nearly 7000, and the honourable mentions to about 5300. The proportion of awards to exhibitors is greater than in the International Exhibition of 1851, but less than in that of 1855. Notwithstanding the varied nationalities represented in the juries, it is gratifying to record that the utmost harmony has prevailed during the whole time that the jurors have been associated in their labours. The mutual dependence and intimate alliance between the industries of the world have been illustrated by the zealous and impartial efforts of the jurors of different nations to recognise and reward the merit displayed in the exhibition of their industrial competitors. We are glad to observe that the state of industry, as shown in the International Exhibition, gives evidence of a singularly active and healthy progress throughout the civilized world; for while we find every nation searching for new raw materials or utilizing products hitherto considered as waste, we are struck especially with the vast improvement in the machinery employed to adapt them to industrial purposes, as well as with the applications of science, and with the great and successful attention which is now given to all the arts necessary to gratify our taste and sense of beauty. We cannot conclude this report without expressing our obligation to Dr. Lyon Playfair, the Special Commissioner for Juries, for the constant and intelligent assistance which he has rendered to us throughout our labours, as well as to the Deputy Commissioners and Secretary, who have acted under his direction, and have afforded efficient aid to the several juries during their inquiries."

The Duke of Cambridge, in reply, said: "In performing the duty entrusted to me by Her Majesty on this occasion, I have great pleasure, on behalf of the representatives of the various nations which have taken part in this Exhibition, in receiving from your lordship an account of the labours of the juries. All countries owe a debt of gratitude to the large number of jurors who, at a great sacrifice of time and personal convenience, have gratuitously undertaken a work of such an arduous description. The efforts made by so many distinguished men of different nations to recognise and reward the exhibitors from all parts of the civilized world cannot be too highly appreciated. I have every confidence that the decisions of the jurors will meet with general approbation, and that the knowledge acquired by them in the discharge of the duties which they have so well performed will be the means of giving a new impulse to industrial progress in the countries which selected such eminent representatives of their scientific and manufacturing skill."

At the close of these addresses, a procession was formed, headed by State trumpeters, and composed of Her Majesty's Ministers and the distinguished personages and public bodies already mentioned, who proceeded by way of the eastern annexe, along the nave of the Building, and the western or machinery annexe; the Duke of Cambridge delivering on his way, and at appointed stations, the list of the awards for each class, colony, and foreign country. These stations were decorated with flags and banners, and occasionally with some of the choicest or most characteristic of the products exhibited. Bands of music were also stationed along the line of the procession, the foreign bands including the Zouaves, and the Gendarmerie de la Garde, the Guides from Belgium, a small band of blue-jackets from one of the Danish ships of war, and the band of the Pasha of Egypt; the latter performance was remarkable only for its oddity: the admixture of the "international" music is best described as a *charivari*. Having completed the distribution of the awards, the procession returned to the daïs in the Gardens; as many of the bands as could be brought together in time assembled near it, the National Anthem was performed by the united bands, and the ceremonial was brought to a close. In the Building and in the Gardens, 44,278 persons were present; a number far short of that which had been anticipated.

CLOSE OF THE EXHIBITION.

SATURDAY, November 1st, 1862, was the last day of the International Exhibition. It had been proposed to commemorate the close by a performance of music, as at the opening. This design has, however, been deferred until the Presentation of the Medals, appointed to take place early in January, 1863.

Nevertheless, the closing scene, on the 1st of November, was marked by a simple ceremonial—the singing of our National Anthem—that impressive tribute of national affection which, in fervour and sincerity, has no parallel in any other country of the world.

The day was gloomy—but some 40,000 persons were present. Before the hour of closing, it was interesting to remark how eagerly were paid the visits of anxious groups to their favourite Courts and Classes for the last time. Their Imperial Highnesses the Prince and Princess Napoleon were there, with the Prince and Princess Edward of Saxe Weimar, the Duke of Cambridge, the Princess Amalie of Schleswig-Holstein-Augustenbourg, the Dowager Duchess of Sutherland, the Duke and Duchess of Buckingham, Lord and Lady Ashburnham, Viscount Sidney, Viscount Torrington, Viscount Chelsea, &c.

Towards 4 o'clock, the members of the Sacred Harmonic Society were partly in the west gallery, by the side of Walker and Hedgeland's organ; and partly, also, around the daïs, under the west dome, used at the opening on the 1st of May. The Duke of Buckingham, Sir Wentworth Dilke, Mr. Fairbairn, Mr. Sandford, and Mr. Lindon, with a number of ladies and gentlemen, were also near the daïs, around and about which the visitors were collected. The succeeding incidents are thus graphically narrated in the *Times* report:—

"As the clock struck four the well-known words of our National Anthem were begun, at first with diffidence, but gradually swelling out into a sound which, if it did not fill the Building, at least sent its clear solemn tones up the nave, bringing together the scattered groups from all parts, hurrying down on tiptoe and bareheaded, to assist by their presence at what to all Englishmen is almost a religious ceremony. It was curious to watch the great mass of quiet, upturned faces, as they listened with that peculiar mingling of pride and reverence to every note of the strain—listened with an earnestness of feeling and attention not common even in this country. For a few moments after its close there was a pause, and then, as at a signal a loud cheer broke forth, with clapping of hands and waving of handkerchiefs, which was renewed again and again, and 'one cheer more' led to another and a louder, till there was no method of restoring silence but by singing 'Partant pour la Syrie.' To this compliment to our foreign visitors the same respectful attention was paid, and the same cheering greeted its termination, when again and again came the heavy rolling cheer and calls for an encore, which made the Building, large as it is, echo again. To this fresh demand the members of the Society kindly lent an indulgent ear, and sang 'Rule Britannia,' and, to do them justice, the audience spared no efforts to make them sing it half a dozen times more, so loud and long-sustained was their applause. But there was no response to this emphatic and vigorous encore. Some concession was, however, made to popular opinion by playing 'Auld Lang Syne,' but even the plaintive strains of this fine old melody were soon overwhelmed and buried under the tremendous clamour with which every bell in the Building commenced 'ringing out.' They seemed at once to open at full cry from every nook and gallery—high overhead, in side courts and main avenues, and down in secluded bays where no one dreamt that bells lay lurking—all gave tongue at once, filling the air with such a hideous jangle of varied sounds as ought at once to have emptied the Building, though it did not. Visitors sat and promenaded though dusk was fully on, and the great vista down the nave was almost dark, and would have been quite so but for the little jets of gas which flared out here and there. It was quite 6 o'clock before the place was clear, and for the last time, as an Exhibition, given over to the custody of the police, who from the commencement have guarded its contents so well, and who, when marshalled in the centre transept and their last daily reports given in, openly rejoiced that their long monotony of duties at the Building was at length over."

At the moment we write, the financial results of the Exhibition cannot be exactly stated from official information. The proximate results are a deficit on receipts as compared with expenditure, of about 20,000*l*., which, however, will not fall upon the guarantors; but, it is believed, will be mainly made good by Messrs. Kelk and Lucas—that is to say, that in addition to whatever may be the shortcoming on the third 100,000*l*. they were to receive under their agreement, they will submit to a still further reduction to cover the liability of the guarantors. The daily returns of money taken at the doors show a total received of nearly 315,000*l*., excluding, of course, the admissions by shilling day tickets. The season tickets, it is said, realized nearly 80,000*l*. and the shilling tickets also a considerable sum. Altogether, the receipts from every source, including refreshment and photographic contracts, waiting-rooms, umbrella stands, sales of catalogues, &c., were, up to November 1, within a very small amount of 500,000*l*. sterling, and are not unlikely to be 510,000*l*., or even 520,000*l*. before the nnal closing of accounts after the distribution of prizes by the Prince of Wales.

The cost of constructing the Building was originally estimated at 200,000*l.* ; but the extra expenses of the annexes, gilding, foundations for machinery, &c., bring the total cost to nearly 20,000*l.* more. A large sum was disbursed by the office and staff expenses, though very low ; by road-making ; hire of police ; receipt and re-delivery of goods, &c. The following results, as compared with those of other Exhibitions, are from the *Times* returns :—

"As compared, then, with former Exhibitions, that of 1862 will be found to be the greatest, both in the number of its visitors and even in the amount of its gross receipts. That of 1851 was open during five and a half months, and was attended by 6,039,135 visitors, *including staff and exhibitors' attendants*, as estimated daily by the police. The total amount paid at the doors was 356,800*l.* The produce of the sale of season tickets amounted to 67,800*l.*, and the gross total received from all sources was 505,107*l.* 6*s.* 7*d.*, *including* the 67,400*l.* which was subscribed before the undertaking commenced, and which was afterwards carried to the capital account and made to swell the gross total. The actual money taken from all sources, *less* this subscription, was therefore only 438,000*l.*

"The Paris Exhibition of 1855 was attended in six months by 3,626,934 visitors to the industrial department, and by 906,530 visitors to the fine arts department—in all 4,533,464, who paid for admission to each department the sum of 117,866*l.* This display left a deficit larger than our surplus, and which had to be made good by a grant from the Imperial Government.

"The present Exhibition has also been open six months, or 17 days longer than that of '51. The total number of visitors, *excluding* the staff and exhibitors' attendants, has been 6,117,450, or 87,000 over the gross numbers on the first occasion. The comparison between the two English displays, however, to be perfectly fair should include on this occasion the staff and exhibitors' attendants, which were used to swell the total of '51. This would give the Exhibition that has just closed a majority of quite a million over its predecessor, while its gross receipts will, we believe, be between 80,000*l.* and 90,000*l.* greater than on the first occasion, if we exclude from the total of 1851 the 67,400*l.* subscribed throughout the country at the first conception of the scheme, and which it is quite needless to say was never returned to the subscribers."

Such were the results to November 1. The Exhibition was reopened November 3, for the sale of goods exhibited ; and was finally closed November 15. The total number admitted during this last fortnight was less than had been anticipated, a whole week recording no more than a bad shilling day : on the last day, November 15, the attendance was unusually large,—13,000 in all. In round numbers, the visitors each week were 45,000, bringing the gross total of all admitted since the commencement up to 6,207,450, or 177,000 more than the numbers of 1851.

Throughout the present volume we have, at the proper points, quoted the opinions of leading contemporaries as to the organization and administration of the Exhibition ; and to these opinions of others we have added, from an impartial review, our own appreciation of the results, special and general. To recapitulate these matters, in this place, would be extraneous and tedious ; but it may be interesting as well as useful to summarize a few of the leading points.

The Commissioners have, to our thinking, achieved a success, if we rightly consider the obstacles with which they had to contend. When this second Exhibition was projected, its want of novelty was predicted against its fortune. The successful experiment of 1851 had been repeated in most of the leading capitals of the civilized world, with by no means uniform success, and it was thought the world had had enough of these displays. Even our own results in 1851 were a hard-earned success: we all remember how the Government of the time gave the design "the cold shoulder;" how certain of the titled classes, unconnected with the Court, stirred idly in the matter; how conspicuous were Her Majesty and the Prince Consort throughout the Exhibition; and how largely their repeated visits contributed to its popularity, from the first commencement of the Crystal Palace to its close. Already, our second Exhibition had been postponed, and there were grave doubts as to its realization, which, indeed, may be said to have been hastened by the courtesy shown by our Parisian neighbours, in postponing their Exhibition to give place to ours, which it was, at length, determined to hold in 1862. The design for the Building was decided on early in 1861, and had, substantially, advanced, when, in the last month of the year, the death of the Prince Consort struck with dismay all who were engaged in carrying out this great work. This "was a loss it was impossible to replace. For two reasons, the Exhibition of 1851 was mainly indebted to him for its triumphant results. In the first place, he was a far abler man than any of the subordinates who served under him. But even if he had been less able, his assistance would still have been the main element in its success. His value was that he was indisputably the first. He gave a unity to the operations of the Commission which no other man was in a condition to impart to them." When the country had partially recovered from the first shock of the death of the excellent Prince, the first question asked was—" What will become of the International Exhibition?"—an inquiry which better conveys his paramount value in the scheme than the most laboured eulogy can impart. To defer the Exhibition was found impracticable: it was now within four months of the opening day; arrangements had been completed nearly all over the world, and many contributions were ready, if not on their way to England. It was, moreover, understood to be the wish of the bereaved Sovereign that the desire of her lamented Consort should be realized; and the country responded to this wish—" as a fitting memorial of respect to the Prince who made the scheme of international exhibitions his own."

The reader need not be reminded how this "heavy blow and sore discouragement," by the death of the Princely originator, led by natural sequence, to the absence of the Sovereign, and the comparative seclusion of the Court. To these calamities must be added those of a "dreadful civil war, involving thirty millions of our own race and language; and the entire stoppage of the chief staple of our own country, reducing half a million of people into objects of private charity or public relief."

Notwithstanding these drawbacks,* the Exhibition has proved numerically and practically a success; and but for these depressing influences, would have been a great triumph. As it was based upon the broad international principle, we must be content with our relative share in the credit of the great display. Nor have we reason to be dissatisfied with our position in this respect; since the manufactures of the United Kingdom showed not merely a gratifying advance upon those of 1851, but a still greater improvement as compared with those of other countries. Commercially, the exhibitors have largely benefited by the sales of works of industrial and fine art, home and foreign; a result which, it is to be hoped, will contribute to the artistic advancement as well as the trade and commerce of the respective countries.

In conclusion, we may observe that the success of the Exhibition was, from the first, an object of national concern; and in this anxiety arose differences of opinion as to the standards of merit by which the value of the display was to be appreciated. In our endeavour to chronicle the results we have maintained strict impartiality; and hope, by this means, to have succeeded in realizing, as far as circumstances will allow, a true record of this great international event.

---

* The unfortunate adoption of the design for the Building at South Kensington has been adverted to in the early portion of the present volume; but it will be important to add, in this place, the opinion of one of the leading architects of the day, which, we are persuaded, must be the general sense of the profession. At the meeting of the Institute of British Architects, on Nov. 3, Mr. Tite, M.P., in his introductory address, as President of the Institute, referred to the International Exhibition, stating that, although as to the Building itself it would be most becoming for architects to observe silence on the subject of its artistic qualities, yet they certainly might record their protest against its being in anywise considered as a representative of the architectural taste of our age. It was unfortunate, he said, that a gentleman whose studies and pursuits had not been of a nature to develope the artistic faculties required for the successful cultivation of their profession should have been selected to design and execute a structure necessarily intended to illustrate before the assembled nations the actual state of art among Englishmen. The very merits of the construction were of a nature to indicate that its author had solely directed his attention to the scientific and technical details of the problem submitted to him, without being able to grasp its æsthetical or moral signification. The goods were exhibited in a shed, tolerably lighted; the pictures and sculpture were also placed in rooms where they could be seen, speaking generally, in a very advantageous manner; but there was an absence of artistic treatment in the plan of the Building, while the general elevation and the ornamental details of the exterior particularly were very objectionable. No architect could have designed a work so unsatisfactory had he but studied the rudiments of his profession, and yet British architects were unhappily represented to assembled Europe by this eminently unarchitectural building.

INDEX.

AWARDS, DECLARATION OF, BY THE JURORS, 339—341.

BRITISH POSSESSIONS.

AUSTRALIA:—
 NEW SOUTH WALES:—Cereals and Cotton, Coal-fields and Gold-fields, Sheep, Wool and Woollen Goods, and Wines, 270, 271.
 NEW ZEALAND:—Coal, Copper, Corn, Fruits, Gold, Photographs, Timber, 279, 280.
 QUEENSLAND:—Cotton, Dugong oil, Flax, Grain, Maize, Silk, Timber, Wool, 272.
 SOUTH AUSTRALIA:—Copper, Corn, Malachite, Printing, Wines, Woods, and Wool, 273, 274.
 SANDWICH ISLANDS:—Awa-plant; Paper-mulberry, portraits, Printing, Pulu, 280.
 TASMANIA:—Coal, Fruits, Fur, Gold, Timber, Wheat, and Whales, 279.
 VICTORIA:—Corn and Fruits, Gold, Iron, Hides, Meteorite, Minerals, Tallow, Wools, 277, 278.
 WESTERN AUSTRALIA:—Birds, Kangaroo meat, Minerals, and Timber, 274, 275.

NORTH AMERICAN COLONIES:—
 CANADA:—Agricultural Implements, Copper, and Iron, Geological specimens, Stones, Timber, Wheat, Wines, 266, 267.
 NEW BRUNSWICK:— Coal, Dresses and Furs, Models, and Woods, 267.
 NOVA SCOTIA:—Fruits, Gold, Grain, Honey, Iron, and Meal, Pearls, Woods, Zoological specimens, 269.
 PRINCE EDWARD'S ISLAND:—Agricultural Implements, Canoes, Fish, Hemp, Ships' block, 268.

VANCOUVER'S ISLAND:—Bricks, Douglas fir spar, Metals and Minerals, 268.
BAHAMAS:—Cotton, Fibre, Jumbie Beans, Sponges, 260.
CEYLON:—Furniture, Gems, Talipot tent, Woods, &c., 260.
HONG-KONG:—Chinese produce, 260.
INDIA:— Agricultural Implements, 264; Art-works, improved, 263; Burmese produce, 265; Carpets, 263; Carvings, 264; Cashmere Shawls, 263; Cotton and Hemp manufactures, 263, 265; Cutlery, Jewellery, and Lac-ware, 264; Fibres, 265; Fine Arts, 264; Manufactures, improved, 263, 264; Medicinal substances, 265; Minerals, 265; Metals, 265; Paper and Papier-Maché, 263; Photographs, 265; Pottery, 264; Sculpture, 263; Silk raised in Onde, 263; Silks, various, 263; Woods and Fibres, 265.
JAMAICA:— Liqueurs, Rums, Sugars, Vegetable Oils, and Woods, 257.
MALTA AND THE IONIAN ISLANDS:— Agricultural produce, Cotton, Lace, Silver filigree, and stone-work, costumes, Wines, and Liqueurs, 260, 261, 262.
NATAL:—Arrowroot, Assam Tea, Caffre-life Coffee, Cayenne Pepper, Cotton, Ivory, Timber, Wheat, 258, 259.
TRINIDAD:—Asphalte, Coal, and Lignite, Minerals, Food substances, Vegetable Oils, 258.

CLOSE OF THE EXHIBITION, 341.

FINE ART DEPARTMENT.

ARCHITECTURE:—
 Art-Designs for Manufactures, 328; English Designs and Models, 327.
ETCHINGS AND ENGRAVINGS:—
 English, 331; Lithography and Wood Engraving, 333.

PAINTING:—
 Austrian School, 335; Belgium, 336; Brazil, 337; Denmark, 336; English School —Oil, 324—327; Water-colours, 327; French School, 333; German School, 334; Greece,

337; Holland, 335; Italy, Portugal, and Rome, 337; Russia, 336; Spain, 337; Sweden and Norway, 336; Switzerland, Turkey, and United States, 337.

SCULPTURE:—
Belgium, 337; Denmark, 336; English, 330; French, 334; German School, 334; Rome, 337; Sweden and Norway, 336.

FOREIGN COUNTRIES.

AFRICA, CENTRAL AND WESTERN:— Cotton Cloths and Culture, and Leather dyeing, 320, 321.

AUSTRIA:— Beet-root Sugar, 297; Bohemian Glass, 298; Chemical products, 296; Clocks, 300; Coal, 296; Crystals, series of, 296; Fabrics, printed, 298; Flax, 297; Furniture, 298; Hops, 297; Hydraulic Forge-hammer, 300; Insect-destroying powder, 297; Leather goods, 297; Lithography, 298; Locomotives, 297; Merino fleeces, 297; Maize, 299; Mineral productions, 296; Musical Instruments, 298; Oil-seeds, 297; Pipes, Meerschaum, 299; Porcelain, 297; Petrified Figures, 299; Prague Iron Manufacture, 296; Printing, 298; Stearic Candles, Tin process, 297; Viennese bookbinding, 298; Wheat Flour and Wines, 297; Wood-work, 299.

BELGIUM:— Brussels Lace, 295, Candle Trophy, 296; Coal field, 295; Food products, 296; Glass and Leather, 295; Machines and Tools, 296; Mineral products, 295; Printing Fabrics, 296; Silk and Velvet, 295; Wood Carving 296; Woollen and Mixed Fabrics, 295.

BRAZIL:— Bees, 24 kinds of, 317; Coffee, Cotton, Minerals, Sugar, Teas and Tobacco; Gems and Gold, 316, 317; Manufactures, miscellaneous, 317; Photographs, 317.

CHINA:— Autograph, Confucius's skull, Vases, &c., 320.

EGYPTIAN COLLECTION, THE:— Cotton, Silk, and Woollen Goods, 321; Arms, Domestic Utensils, and Musical Instruments, Wheat, &c., 323; ancient Egyptian Jewellery, deities, enamel, &c., 323.

FRANCE AND HER COLONIES:— Algerian, or Onyx Marble, 286; Animals, acclimatized, 289; Aubusson, Beauvais, and Gobelin Tapestry, 281; Birds, small, 289; Bronzes, 286, 287; Carriages, tasteful, 288; Céladon porcelain, 282; Chiné Silk, 284; Chromo-lithography printed on porcelain, 283; Church Plate, 288; Cigars, Tobacco, and Snuff, 290; Court, best arranged, 280; Diamond-setting, 287; Double-bass improvement, 289; Dyes, improved, 285; Electro, bronze, 288; Flora of France, 289; Furniture, sumptuous, 288; Galvanoplastic process, 291; Glass, Emerald and Ruby and Stained for Windows, 285; Imitative Jewels, 288; Ironwork, ornamental, 291; Lace and Shawls, 285; Limoges, 283; Machinery and Manufactures in Metals, 290; Majolica and Enamels, 282; Manure, fabrication of, 290; Mechanics and Metallurgy, 290; Moiré Antique, 284; Oak for Shipbuilding, 287; Padded Straps, 289; Palissy Ware, 282; Paper-hangings, 281; Pianoforte, improved, 289; Plate and Jewellery, 288; Ribands, 284; Satins and Velvets, 284; Sèvres porcelain, 281, 282; Silks from Lyons, 283; Vines, Wines, and Brandies, 289.

ALGERIA:—Carpets, 293; Cereals, Provender, and Vegetables, 291; Conserves and Fruits, 292; Cotton Cultivation, 292; Cotton Fabrics, 292; Fibres, 293; Hides of Wild Beasts, 293; Minerals, 293; Paper, 293; Pottery, 293; Silk Culture, 292; Snuff and Tobacco, 293; Wines, 292; Woods, fancy, 293; Wool, 293.

COCHIN CHINA:—Edible Birds'-Nests, 295.

GUADALOUPE:—Cotton Dyes, Liqueurs, Spices, Sugar, and Woods, 294.

GUIANA:—Coffee, Cotton, Cocoa, Costume, Gold, and Woods, 294.

MARTINIQUE:—Coffee and Coffee-Cherry, Cotton, Plants, Rum, Sugar, and Woods, 294.

NEW CALEDONIA:—Turtle and Wool, 295.

REUNION:—Medical Plants, Sugars, and Woods, 294.

ST. PIERRE AND MIQUELON:— Dried Fish and Tea, 295.

SENEGAL:—Coffee, Cotton, Gold, Gems, Marabout and Ostrich Feathers, Weapons, 294.

TAHITI:—Fibres, Oils, Turtle, and Woods, 295.

GREECE:— Agricultural Produce, Carvings, Champagne, Cotton-silk, Dye-woods,

Marbles, Sculpture, Steam-engine, Stones, 315, 316.

HAYTI :—
Harness, Iron ores, Pottery, Saddlery, Sea-weed, 321.

HOLLAND :—
Carpets, and Carriages, 310; Carved Pulpit, 309; Cork Hats, 310; Furniture, 309; Implements, Agricultural, and Lace and Linen, 310; Lacquer-ware, and Photographs, 309; Preserved Meats and Vegetables, Teaching Machine, Saddles, and Sweetmeats, 310.

HUNGARY :—
Costumes, Grain, Flax, Hemp, Silk, Timber, Tobacco, Wheat, Wine, and Minerals, 303; Porcelain, Herénd, 304.

JAPAN :—
Arms and Armour, 319; Bronsework, 318; Buckles, Metal, 318; Coinage, Drugs and Surgical Instruments, and Egg-shell porcelain, 319; Ivory Carvings, 318; Lacquer-ware, Paper and Printing, 319; Porcelain, Japanese, 318; Straw-work, 320; Window-blind of Gelatine, 318.

ITALY :—
Castellani's ancient Trinkets, 306; Doccia Porcelain, 306; Genoa Silver-work, 305; Minerals, 306; Mosaic Tables of Florence and Rome, and Pietra-dura inlaying, 307; Roman Courts, and Sculpture, 308; Sword, royal State, 308.

MADAGASCAR :—
Cloths, Manufactures, and Ores, Gold and Silver work, Iron chair, &c., 321.

NORWAY :—
Carioles and Sledges, Cereals, Clothing, and Fire-arms, 312; Iron and Silver, 311; Lines and Fish-books, Mechanical contrivances, Wood-carvings, and Steam-pumps, 312.

PERU, COSTA RICA, AND URUGUAY :—
Costa Rica Mining and Chemical Substances, Skins and Furs; Peruvian Silver and Mercury, Cotton and Wools; Uruguay Roots, Skins, Wheat, Wine, Wools, &c., 316.

PORTUGAL :—
Fabrics, Mixed, Lace, Silks, and Woollen Goods, Wines, &c., 313.

RUSSIA :—
Alpaca Goods, 305; Brocades, 305; Bronzes, 305; Calico-printing, 305; Camel and Goats' Hair Cloth, 305; Church Plate, 305; Furs and Skins, 305; Cotton from the Caucasus, 305; Glass, Imperial, 305; Graphite and Malachite, 304; Jasper and Porphyry Vases, 304; Leather-work, 305; Nephrite Vase, 304; Pietra-dura Mosaic, 304; Worsted Goods, 305.

SPAIN :—
Carvings, Food, Furniture, Lace and Embroidery, Minerals, Malaga figures, Pianos, Rifle-gun, Tobacco and Snuff, Toledo swords, Wines, 312, 313.

SWEDEN :—
Agricultural Implements, 311; Carpentry, 311; Chain Cables and Anchors, 311; Runic duel, 311.

SWITZERLAND :—
Embroidery and Tambour-work, 309, Manganese, 309; Rifles, 309; Silk and Ribands, 309; Watches, 308; Woollen and Cotton Goods, 309.

TURKEY :—
Agriculture, 314; Arms, 315; Broussa Silks, 313; Cotton culture, 313; Embroidery, 314; Musical Instruments 314; Pipes, 314; Pottery, 315; Prayer Carpets, 314; Saddle-cloth, 314; Silk culture, 314; Smyrna figs, 314; Tobacco, 315; Turkey carpets, 313; Woods and Wool, 315.

UNITED STATES :—
Minerals, 317; Petroleum, or Earth oil, 317; Washoe Silver mines, 318.

ZOLLVEREIN, THE :—
Bavarian Hops, 302; Berlin Porcelain, 301; Bremen Silver-work and Lace, 302; Clocks, 302; Coronation Sword, Prussian, 301; Cutlery and Ironwork, 302; Glass Chandeliers, 302; Gold and Jewellery, 302; Meissen Porcelain, 301; Mining Products, 303; Munich Seals, 302; Musical Instruments, 303; Photographs, 302; Ploughs, 303; Prints, oil-coloured, 302; Saxon Porcelain, 300; Silver Vase, Table, and Candelabra, 301; Stag-horn Furniture, 301; State-coach, 301; Toys, 302.

MANUFACTURES.

BOOKBINDING :—
Belgian and French, 196; Cloth-binding, 196; Illuminated Gift-books, 196; Tooled books, 195; Vienna, 195.

CARPET MANUFACTURE :—
Axminster, 170, 173; Axminster wall-carpet, 172; border-carpet, 170; Brussels, 172; China, two Carpets from, 174; Floorcloths and Kamptulicon, 176; India Carpet manufactory, 170; India and Turkey, 173, 174; Kidderminster, 169, 172; Engs. by Palmers, 169; Thugs, Car-

pets made by, 174; Velvet-pile, 171; Wilton, Lapworth's, 172; Wilton or Scoto-Axminster, 169; Whytock's Edinburgh, 169.

CLOTHING, ARTICLES OF:—
Bonnets, 187; Boots and Shoes, 187; Corset, Crinoline, and Leglets, 187; Gloves, 187; Hats and Caps, 186; Nottingham and Scotch Hosiery, 187; Robes, Academical, Ecclesiastical, and Civil, 187; Trousers, reversible, 187; Umbrellas, 187.

COTTON FABRICS:—
Austrian, 166; Belgian, 166; Cotton Damasks, 163; French contributions, Ginghams, Quilts and Quiltings, Tambour-work, Threads, and Yarns, 164, 165; Glasgow contributions, 164; Improvements since 1851, 162; Milan Chamber, 166; New South Wales Cotton, 166; Paisley Threads, 163; Skirting Welts and Sateens, 164; Saxony, 166; Sewing Threads, 163; Swiss, 166; Turkish bath Towel, 163; United States, 166; Velvets, imitation, 164; Zollverein, 166.

EDUCATIONAL WORKS AND APPLIANCES:—
Austrian Collection, 198; Belgian School of Industry, 199; Bible Society, Bibles, and Prayer-books, 200; Blind, Schools for, 199; British collection, 199; Fine Art branch, 198; French contributions, 199; Globes, 197; Italy, Prussia, Russia, and Switzerland contributions, 199; Kinder-garten system, 197; Realistic Schools, 199; Reformatory and Ragged Schools, 197; School Furniture, 197; School-list, 197; Shorthand, 198; Tonic Sol-Fa method, 198; Toys and Games, 197.

FLAX AND HEMP:—
Barnsley, Belfast, Leeds, and Scotch, 167; Flax-machines, 167; Foreign productions, 167.

FURNITURE AND UPHOLSTERY:—
Buffet, oak, 202; Bullfinch, singing, 201; Cabinets, with Wedgwood plaques, 203; Carton-pierre, 201; Carved oak, walnut, &c., 201; Carvings in Wood, 204; Chintzes, new, 201; Decoration for rooms, 201; Dining-tables, circular, 201; Ebony and Ivory Furniture, 203; French Renaissance, 203; Machinery for Wood carving, 204; Ottoman, central, 201; Paperhangings, 203; Papier-maché, 204; Pianoforte, Amboyna case, 203; Pyrography, 204; Sideboard Book-case and Robinson Crusoe, 200; Sideboards, Italian, 202; Table and Cabinets, Louis XVI. and Reisnér, 202; Varnished Deal, 201; Wardrobe, walnut, 202.

FURS, FEATHERS, AND HAIR:—
Arctic Fox, 182; Down Mantle, 182; Eider-down, 182; Ermine, 182; Fur Carpet, 182; Hair, Artificial, 162; Hair, human, long, 182; Ostrich and Marabout Feathers, 182; Sable and Fox, 181.

GLASS, FOR DECORATIVE AND HOUSEHOLD PURPOSES:—
Bohemian Fancy Glass, 240; Candelabra, colossal Glass, 240; Chandelier, vast, 240; Claret-jugs, Raffaelesque, 239; Crystal Table, 239; Cut Glass, jewelled, 240; Dessert-services, superb Glass, 239, 240; Doncaster church Window, 237; Embossed Glass, 239; English and Foreign Painted Windows, 237, 238; Engraved Glass, 238, 239; Household and Fancy Glass, 238; Koh-i-noor in Crystal Glass, 239; Old Glass, imitated, 237; Painted Windows, 237; Prismatic Mirrors for the Sultan, 240; Vases, new Glass, 240; Venetian chandelier, 239.

INDIA-RUBBER MANUFACTURES:—
Bath-towel, Campticon, Ebonite Tubes, Globe, and Gutta Percha Goods, 183; Hamburg Goods, 184; Junction Rubber, and Kamptulicon, 183; Pump-valves, Perreaux's, 184; Railway Gas tubing, and Shoes, 183; Statue of Vulcanized India-Rubber, 185; Telegraph wire coating, Vegetable Leather, Vulcanized, and Waterproof Cloths, 183.

INDIAN PRODUCTS:—
Arrack and Whisky, 95; Arrow-roots, 94; Behchandee, 94; Caoutchouc and Gutta-percha, 94; Cotton and Muslins, 95; Cotton, Tobacco, and Tea, 93; Cutlery and Weapons, 96; Dye-stuffs and Tanning-substances, new, 95; Food curiosities, 95; Furniture, 96; Ginger, wild, 94; Grains and Pulses, 95; Gums and Resins, 94; Jewellery, and Gold and Silver-work, 96; Oil-seeds and Oils, 95; Opium manufacture, 95; Pianoforte, 96; Prayer-cylinders, 96; Printing-blocks, 96; Raw Materials, 96; Shawls, 96; Soils, 95; Textile fabrics, 96; Woods, 95.

IRON MANUFACTURES:—
Armour-plates for Ships, 209; Armour-plate, vast, 207; Austrian Society of State Railways, 209; Bars, Rails, and Girders, 208; Barrow-in-Furness Works, 208; Bedsteads, 217; Birmingham Buttons, 219; Birmingham Wares, 214; Brass-Toy trade, 219; Bridge-links for Suspension bridges, 209; Building Contrivances, French, 209; Canadian Iron, 210; Chandeliers, Gaseliers, and Lamps, 218; Charcoal Pig-iron,

Austrian, 206; Cooking-Apparatus, Ranges, and Stoves, 217, 218; Forged Iron, 206; French improvements, 207; Galvanized Metals, 212; Hardman and Hart's Courts, 216; Hereford Screen, the, described, 215; Indian Iron, 211; Iron Paints, 213; Kirkstall and Mersey Companies, 207; Locks and Safes, 219—221; Locks for the Exhibition Building, 221; Lowmoor and Monkbridge Works, 206; Malleable Cast-Iron, 213; Mediæval Metal-work, 216; Norwich Gates, 216; Paddle-steamer Plate, 212; Rolled Iron, Butterley and Shelton, 208; Rolled Iron Wire, French, 209; Russian Furnaces, 206; Sheet-iron, Austrian, Belgian, and Russian, 208; Swedish Boat-plates, 211; Welding, 207; Wheel, wrought-iron, French, 207; Wire-working, 214, 215; Wolverhampton Goods, 217; Yield of Cast-Iron, 205; Zinc Manufactures, 213; Zinc Roofing, 213.

JEWELLERY :—
Amethysts, Brilliants, Emeralds, Opals, Pearls, Sapphires, and Topazes, 232, 233; Ancient Jewellery, imitative, 235; Arcot and Nassuck Diamonds, 233; Cameo-cutting, 235, 236; Castellani's Jewellery, 235; Coral Ornaments, 234; Crystal Intaglios, 234; Devonshire Emerald and Jewels, 233; Diadem, diamond, 235; Diamonds, large, 232, 233; Diamond portrait of the Queen, 233; Imitation Diamonds and Pearls, 236; Imitative Jewellery, 236; Masonic Insignia, 234; Norwegian Bridal Ornaments, 235; Opals, fine, 233, 234; Pearls, fine, 233, 235; Pompeian Bracelet, 235; Rubies, large and fine, 233; Scotch Jewellery, 234—236; Sidmonth Pebbles, 236; Tennant, Prof., Illustrative Specimens from, 234; Theatrical Costume Jewels, 235.

LACE-MAKING :—
Belgian Lace, 180; British Lace, 181; French Guipure, 180; Saxony, 181; Spanish Blondes, 181.

LEATHER-SADDLERY AND HARNESS:—
Black Enamelled Leather, 185; Cape Leathers, 186; Leather Trophy, 186; Potichomanie and Embossed Leather, 186; Saddles and Harness, State, 185; Seal-skins, 186; Sole-butts, 185; Tanning Materials, 185; Whips, costly, 185.

MEDIÆVAL ART :—
Ecclesiological Society, 72, 205; Effigies, Fonts, and Monuments, 205; Frontal, 205; Hereford Screen, 215; Metal-work, 205, 216; Reredos, 205.

PAPER-MAKING AND STATIONERY :—
Account-books, 190; Bank of England Note Paper, 110—112; Copying-books, 190; Copying Machine, 190; Drawing-paper and Cardboard, 190; Fancy Papers, 191; French and English Paper, 188; Index, 190; Paper Collars, 191; Paper Materials, 188; Pencils, 191; Printing-paper, 188; Sealing-wax, 190; Straw Paper, 189; Watermarks, 189; Writing-paper, 190; Zopissa, 189.

POTTERY :—
Ceramic Marble, 243; Coalport Works, the, 243; Egg-shell China, 243; Jet-ware, new, 242; Majolica Fountain, Minton's, 241; Palissy, Limoges, Sèvres, Bleu de Roi, Rose de Barry, 241; Parian Busts and Statuettes, 242; Parian Dessert-service, long, 242; Paul Potter Tray, 243; Sèvres, imitative, 243; Vase, very large, 242; Wedgwood Collection, the, 242; Worcester Dessert-service for the Queen, 242.

PRECIOUS METALS, WORKS IN :—
Alhambresque Table Ornament, 227; Aluminium Articles, 231; Aluminium Bronze, 231; Chalices, Sacramental, jewelled, 230; Cups, Enamelled and Enamelled, the Queen's, 227; Electro-plate Dinner-service, large, 231; Elkington's Silver and Gold Work, 228; Great Seal and Dishes, 228; Imitations of the Precious Metals, 231; Improvement since 1851, 220; Kean and Manchester, Outram, and Pakington Testimonials, 229; Koh-i-noor Diamond, 226; Orders of the Garter, Bath, and Thistle, insignia, 227; Presentation Plate, 228; Race Prizes, 229; Reponssé Silver Table, Ewer, and Dessert-service, 228; Reponssé Silver Vases, 230; Rubies, Her Majesty's, 227; Silver, Frosted and Oxydized, 229; Toilet-glass and Stereoscope for the Sultan, 231; Topaz Cup, 230; Vases, oxydized Silver, by Vechte, 227.

PRINTING :—
Austrian Printing, 192; Colour-printing, 194; Electro-block Printing, 194; Glasgow Printing, 192; Kerography, 194; Lithographs and Chromo-lithographs, 194, 195; Newspaper-printing not shown, 191; Oriental Books, 192; Pencils and Crayons, 193; Playing Cards, 193; Printing Types, 191; Russian publications, 192; Steel Pens, 193; Victoria Press, 192; Whittingham, 192; Wood-engraving Printing, 192; Writing-inks, 192.

INDEX. 351

PRINTED AND DYED FABRICS:—
  Belfast and Glasgow, 179; Chemistry of Calico-printing and Dyeing, 177; Dyes, New, 178; Dyeing, English and French, 179; Electrograph Engraving Machine, 179; Engraved Cylinders, 178; French Printing, 177; Furniture Chintz, 179; Madder styles, 178; Muslins, 178; Printed Fabrics improved since 1851, 177; Russian specimens, 179; Table-covers and Felts, 179.
PROCESS COURT, THE:—
  Albion Printing-press, 244; Chromo-lithography and Steel-plate Printing, 243, 244; Clay-pipe making, 244; Coinage-press, 244; Colour-printing of the *Master-pieces of Art*, 244; Copying Lathe, 244; Lead Pencil-making, 244; Mosaics in the Roman Court, 247; Mosaic wall-pictures, 245; Needle-making, 244; Plaster-cast, colossal, 245; Salviati's Mosaics, 247; Sewing Machines, 245; Siliceous gas-burners and taps, 246; Silk Velvet Loom, 245.
STEEL MANUFACTURES:—
  Axles and Bells, Boiler, Ship and Bridge Plates, Railway Tires and Wheels, Rolls, Shafts, Wire, 224, 225, 226; Bessemer Steel, 222, 225; British and Foreign Manufactures compared, 223; Cast-steel, Swedish, 223; Cutlery and Edge Tools, 223; Foreign cutlery, 223, 224; Improvements since 1851, 222; Krupp's Cast-steel, 224; London Cutlery, 224; Malleable Steel Phaeton, 223; Mayr's Furnaces, 223; Needle-making, 224; Sheffield cutlery, 223, 225; Testing Machine, 223; Trophy of Bessemer's Steel, 225; Uchatius's process, 222; Wolfram Steel, 223.
SILK AND VELVET:—
  Coventry Ribbons, Manchester and Spitalfields Silks and Velvets, 168.
WOOLLEN AND WORSTED AND MIXED FABRICS:—
  Glasgow and Paisley goods, 169; Dublin and Norwich Merinoes, 169; Poplins, 169; West of England Cloth, 169; Woollens, 169; Yorkshire Goods, 169.
TAPESTRIES:—
  Beauvais, 176; Gobelins, 175.
SUBSTANCES USED IN MANUFACTURES:—
  Aberdeen Combs, 249; Aloe and Cocoanut fibre, 219; coloured Candles, 248; Cork, Hard Woods, and Veneers, 249; Cotton, Flax, and Silk, 249; Dressing-cases and Travelling-bags, 250; Fountains of Perfumed Waters, 250; Glycerine, 248; Ivory Carvings, 249; Lard, compressed, 250; Leather and Wax Flowers, 249; Oils for Machinery, 251; Palm Oil, 248; Paraffin Candles, 248; Paraffin and Stearic Acid, 248; Pastiles and Incense, 250; Perfumery, 249; Perfumes, how obtained from Flowers, 249, 250; Petroleum, 251; Railway Greases, 248; Soaps, 248; Sperm Oil and Spermaceti, 249; Tapers, Mediæval, 248; Vegetable Ivory, 249; Wools and Hairs, 249.

ORIGIN AND PROGRESS OF THE EXHIBITION.—THE BUILDING.

Address, by Mr. M. Milnes, 64—66.
Advice Committee, General, 54.
Albert, Prince, and the Society of Arts, 1; Exhibition of 1851, 4, 5, 6; foretels the success of the Exhibition, 20, 21; International Exhibition planned by, 13; anticipated Results of the Exhibition, 65, 66.
ART-MANUFACTURES EXEMPLIFIED IN THE EXHIBITION:—
  Architectural Drawings, English, 72, 73; Brazil, the United States, 70; English Industrial Art, 71; France, 70; Furniture, Glass-painting, and Porcelain, English, 71; Glass and Metal Work, Mediæval Art, Gold and Silver Work and Jewellery, English, 72; India and Turkey, 67; Minton's Majolica Fountain, 73; Prussia, Bavaria, Frankfort, Hamburg, Belgium, Sweden and Norway, Denmark, Greece, and the Ionian Islands, 69; Russia, 67;
Skidmore's Hereford Screen, 73; Spain and Portugal, Italy and Rome, the Zollverein, 68.
Barry, Sir Charles, and the Crystal Palace, 2.
Birmingham Exposition of Industry, 2.
Buccleuch, Duke of, and the Exhibition, 18.
BUILDING FOR THE INTERNATIONAL EXHIBITION:—
  Annexes, the, 49, 50; "Battle of the Domes," 35; cost of the Building, 50; Crace, Mr., Decoration by, 41—46, 49; Critical opinions, 46; Curiosities of Construction, 80, 81, 82; Decoration, by Mr. Crace, 41—46; Domes, construction of, 35; Domes, views of, 36, 37; Engineering certificate, 33; Exterior described, 33—37; General Description, 33; Granville, Earl, on the structure, 47, 48; Hollingshead, Mr., his *Concise Description*, 51;

Insurance from fire, 39, 40; Interior described, 37—41; Lighting of, 39; Materials, 28; Mottoes, various, 45; Progress of, 26, 27, 28; Proposed, 23; Strength of the Building, 32, 33; Vastness of the Works, 29; Works, 25.
Building for the Exhibition of 1851, 7.
Building, Exhibition, Works, and Materials of, 25, 26.
Building for the International Exhibition, proposed, 23.
Cambridge, Duke of, replies to the Commissioners' Address, 61.
Classification of the Exhibition, 54—57.
Cole, Mr. Henry, and the Great Exhibition of 1851, 3, 4.
Colonial Improvement since 1851, 19, 20.
Commissioners' Address at the Opening, 60.
Commissioners, Royal, of the Exhibition, 16.
Cork Exhibition of 1852, 12.
Crystal Palace in Hyde Park designed, 7, 8, 9, 10.
Crystal Palace, Sydenham, 12.
Cubitt, Sir W., the Engineer, 7.
Dublin Exhibition of 1853, 12.
Edinburgh Art Exhibition of 1861, 12.
Exhibition of 1851 opened, 10, 11.
Exhibition of 1851 proposed, 3, 5, 6.
Exhibition of 1851, results of, 13.
Exhibitions resulting from that of 1851, 11.
Exhibitions, National and International, 1.
Exhibition, Opening of the, 58.
Exhibition of 1862 organised, 51.
Felix Summerly's Art-Manufactures, 3.
Fowke, Capt., designs the Exhibition Building, 23, 24.
Fox, Henderson, and Co., and the Crystal Palace, 8.
Free-Trade Bazaar, 2.
French Exhibitions, various, 2.
French International Exhibition, first, 12.
Gore House Estate, the, 13.
Granville, Earl, on the Prospects of the Exhibition, 20.

Guarantors of the Exhibition Fund, 16.
Hawes, Mr. W., on national improvement since 1851, 17.
Horticultural Society and the Exhibition, 21, 22, 23.
Horticultural Society's New Garden, South Kensington, 14.
Industrial Exhibitions, our, 1.
International Exhibition of 1862 proposed, 15.
Italian National Exhibition of 1861, 12.
Jones, Mr. Owen, and Crystal Palace, 10.
Kelk and Lucas, Messrs. Building Contractors, 25.
Kensington, South, Museum at, 14.
Manchester Fine Art Exhibition of 1857, 12.
Manufactures, Exhibition of, at the Society of Arts, 4.
Medal, the Prize, 57.
Milnes, Mr. M., on the Exhibition, 64—66.
Munich Exhibition of 1854, 12.
Music at the Opening of the Exhibition, 63.
National Repository, the, 1.
New York Exhibition of 1853, 12.
Odd Applications to exhibit, 51, 52, 53.
Ode on the Opening of the Exhibition, by Tennyson, 62.
Opening of the Exhibition, 58—64.
Organization of the Exhibition, 51.
Paris Exposition of 1849, 4.
Paxton, Sir J., designs the Great Exhibition Building of 1851, 7.
Practical Mechanics' Journal quoted, 12.
Progress of Art-Manufactures exemplified in the Exhibition, 67—74.
Quarterly Review quoted, 67—74.
Railway Extension since 1851, 18.
Russell, Mr. John Scott, and the Great Exhibition of 1851, 3.
Society of Arts and Industrial Exhibitions, 1, 2.
Society of Arts and the International Exhibition Arrangements, 16, 22.
State Opening of the Exhibition, 58.
Thackeray, Mr., his May-Day Ode, 10.
Whishaw, Mr. Francis, and the Great Exhibition of 1851, 3.

RAW MATERIALS, MACHINERY, AND IMPLEMENTS.

AGRICULTURAL MACHINES AND IMPLEMENTS:—
Australian Reapers, 117; Austrian, Italian, and Prussian Implements, 116; Belgian Implements, 116; British Implements, superiority of, 117; Clod-crushers, 115; Danish Iron Milk-pans, 116; French Portable Steam-engines, 116; Locomotive, new, 115; Norwegian and Swedish Implements, 116; Ploughs, various, 115; Reapers, 114, 115; Russian, Swiss, and Turkish Implements, 116; Revolving Rakes, 114; Steam-engines, 115; Steam-ploughs, 114; Thrashing-Machines and Traction-tillage, 115; United States Implements, 117.

CHEMICAL SUBSTANCES AND PHARMACEUTICAL PROCESSES:—
Acetic Acid, 87, 88; Alkalies, 85; Alkaloids, 88; Alum, 85; Bile Pro-

INDEX. 353

ducts, 88; Borax and Boracic Acid, 89; Chemicals, rare, 88; Chlorate of Potash and Amorphous Phosphorus, 89; Coal-tar Dyes, 85, 86; Colours, 85; Dyes, new, 90, 91; Ethers, including Chloroform, 88; Graphite or Plumbago, 89; Iodine and Iodides, 88; Lichen Dyes, 91; Lucifer Matches and Laundry Starch, 86; Madder, 86; Mauve and Magenta Dyes, 91; Paraffine, 88; Parksine and Perfumery, 90; Permanganate of Potash, 87; Pharmaceutical Society's Drugs, 86; Pigments and Printing Inks, 89; Prussiate of Potash, 87; Silicate of Alumina, 87; Soap, new, 89; Soluble Glass, 90; Varnishes, 89.

CIVIL ENGINEERING, ARCHITECTURE, AND BUILDING CONTRIVANCES:—
Bridges and Graving Docks, French, 120; Architectural Productions, 122; Bridges, Iron, 118; Cement and Artificial Stone, 120; Channel Railway between England and France, 119; Chepstow and Saltash Bridges, 118; Coal-field of Shropshire, 120; Creosoted Woods, 121; Cylindrical Projectiles for Smooth-bore Guns, 123; Diving-Apparatus, 120; Draining Materials, Fire-bricks, &c., 123; Engineering Models, 117; Hydraulic-Lift Graving-Dock, 119; Niagara Suspension Bridge, 119; Cherbourg and Marseilles Harbour, 120; Paving Materials and Mosaics, 122; Piers, compressed air, 118; Pipe-making, Clay and Metal, 122, 123; Portable Gas Apparatus, 120; Railway Bridge, Rhine, 118; Railway Viaducts, 117; Raising Vessels, 119; Ransome's Indurated Stone, 121; Roofing Materials, 122; Suspension Bridge, Models and Photographs of, 119; Szerelmey's Zopissa, 121; Tudela and Bilboa Railway Bridge, 119.

CLOCKS AND WATCHES:—
Astronomical and Geographical Clock, 140; Bennett's Large Clock, 139; Benson's "Great Exhibition Clock," 139; Chronograph Watches, 140; Clerkenwell Clocks and Watches, 139; Coventry Watches, 139; Cruciform Watches, 141; Crystal and Jewel Watches, 140, 141; Curious Watches, 139, 140; Dent's Great Dial, 138; Nuremberg Watches, 140; Switzerland Watches, 139; Watch ornamentation, 139.

COAL IN VARIOUS PARTS OF THE WORLD:—
Austria, 254; Belgium, 253; Boring Wells, 256; British Supply in one year, and Cannel Coal, 253; Coke, examples of, 256; France, 254; Frog in block of Coal, 256; New Brunswick, 255; Newcastle, 252; New South Wales, 255; New Zealand, 250; Nova Scotia, 255; Safety Cages and Lamps, 256; Seam, the thickest, in England, 255; South Wales, 252; Spain and Portugal, 254; Tasmania, 256; Victoria, 256; Yorkshire, 252; Zollverein, 254.

ELECTRIC TELEGRAPHS AND ELECTRICAL APPARATUS:—
Acoustic Telegraph, 144; Automatic System, 143; Clocks, controlling, 143; Electrometers and Voltaic Piles, 144; Graphite Battery, 144; Gutta Percha Appliances, 142; Magnetic Tell-tale, 141; Printing Telegraphs, 143; Signal-train Bells, 144; Telegraph Companies, 142; Telegraphs, Domestic, 142; Telegraphs, various, 142; Train Telegraph, 143; Transmitting Relay, 144.

FOOD, SUBSTANCES USED FOR:—
Alum Crystals, 92; Biscuits and Confectionery, 92; Isinglass, 93; Manure, Fish, 93; Meat, Preserved, 93; Pedigree Wheat, 93; Poisons, 92; Sugars, 91, 92; Wine, Ale, and Beer, 92.

GAS ENGINEERING:—
Magneto-Electric Light, 132; Meters and Retorts, 131; Oxyhydrogen Lime Lamp, 132; Paraffine Candle, 132; Whistling Chandelier, 132.

MACHINERY, GENERAL:—
Bank-note Printing, 110, 111; Carpet-looms, 153; Cotton-spinning Machinery, 132; Centrifugal Pumping Machinery, 102; Diving Apparatus, 106; Drills and Planing Machines, 100; File-cutting Machine, 100; Fire-engines, 103, 251, 252; Fire-escapes, 105; Folding, Pressing, and Stitching Machine, 112; Ice-making Machine, 104; Life-boats, 105; Life-preserving Apparatus, 105; Machine-tools, 100; Paper-making Machinery, 107; Railway Plant—Locomotive Engines, 97; Railway Waggon, 98; Safety Cage and Hoist, 105; Shaping-machine, 100; Steam-carriage, 98; Steam-hammers, 101; Sugar Machinery, 106; Surface Decoration by Block-printing, 113; Type-casting Machine, Besley's, 109; Type-composing Machine, Young's, 109; Washing Machines, 134; Wheel Carriages, 98; Whitworth's Machines, 100; Traction Engines, by Bray and Taplin, 99; Universal Joiner, 103; Zimmermann's Tools, 101.

MACHINERY, AMERICAN:—
Bag-making, 159; Boot-making Ma-

A A

chines, 158; California Pump, 157;
Caloric Engine, 160; Cork-cutter,
156; Cotton, Corn, and Bean
Planters, 157; Drying Machines,
160; Hand-labour-saving Machine,
159; Life-boat, 159; Machinery
Belts, 157; Newspaper-addressing
Machine, 159; Pianofortes, 159;
Power-loom, Carpet, 157; Presses,
Eckell's, 157; Rope-making, 157;
Sewing Machines—Howe's, 160;
Wheeler and Wilson's, 161; Wilcox
and Gibbs', 161; Signal Lanterns,
158; Wringing Machine, 159.
MACHINERY, FOREIGN :—
Blowing Engines, 155; Bolting Apparatus, 155; Locomotive Engines,
155; Marine Engines, 154; Paddlewheel Engines, 155; Railway Carriage, 156; Railway Tank Truck,
156; Refrigerating Apparatus, 156;
Swiss Ribbon-looms, 156; Saw-mill,
portable, 155; Textile Machines,156.
MARINE STEAM ENGINES :—
Floating Dock, 129; Humphrey and
Tennant, 128, 129; Mandslay, 128;
Penn, 128, 130; Pumping-engines
for Waterworks, 130; Rennie, 128,
129; Richardson and Sons, 130.
MINING, QUARRYING, METALLURGY:—
Aluminium, 75; Antimony, 75;
Arsenic, 78; Cadmium, 79; Cinnabar, 79; Clays, 80; Cobalt, 78;
Copper, 76, 77; Geological Maps of
France, 84; German Silver, 76;
Gold, 75, 80; Granites, 80; Graphite from Siberia, 82; Iron, Cast
and Wrought, 76; Iron Ores, 76;
Iron Works, Low Moor, 76; Iron
Works, Round Oak, 76; Lead, 78;
Marbles, 82; Mercury, 78, 79;
Millstone Grit, 81; Mineral Wealth
of France, 83; Nephrite, 83; Nickel,
78; Platinum, 75; Serpentine, 82;
Shropshire Minerals, 75; Silver, 75;
Slate, 82; Stone, varieties of, 80;
Sulphide of Silver, 80; Tin, 78;
Zinc, 77; Zollverein Minerals, 84.
MUSICAL INSTRUMENTS :—
American Tension Instrument, 150;
Cottage Pianos, 150; Folding Piano,
150; Oblique Piano, 150; Organs,
151; Pianofortes, English and
Foreign, 149, 151; Piping Bullfinch,
the, 151; Sax-Horns and Violins,
151; Tuning Apparatus, 150.
NAVAL AND MILITARY MODELS, AND
WEAPONS :—
Armstrong Gun, the, 124; Armstrong Shell, 125; Armstrong Percussion-shell, 126; Boat-building by
Steam, 124; Cartridge, New Skin,
128; Gun-carriages and Ambulances,

127; Krupp's Steel Gun-barrels,
127; Lancaster Cannon, 127; Lighthouses, Models of, 124; Mersey
Works Gun, 126; Monster Mortar
Shells, 126; Russian Gun, 127; Ships,
Great, Models of, 124; Storm's
Breech-loading Apparatus, 126;
Whitworth and Blakeley Guns, 126;
Whitworth Guns and Projectiles,127.
PHILOSOPHICAL INSTRUMENTS :—
Babbage's Calculating Machine, 133;
Balance, wonderfully-adjusted, 134;
Calculating Machine, Babbage's,
133; Thomas's, 135; Electric Lamp,
134; Galactoscope, 132; Glassblowing, 135; Meteorological Instruments, French, 134; Micrometer
Gauges, 134; Microscopes, 132;
Microscopic Writing-machine, 133;
Ozonometer, 132; Pentographs, 135;
Photographs, instantaneous, 135;
Solar Spectrum, 134; Solidification
of Carbonic Acid, 135; Sound its
own printer, 134; Spectacles without Glass, 132; Spheres and Prisms,
135; Spherometer, 135; Stereotrope,
132; Stereoscopic Microscope, 134;
Thermometer, delicate, 134.
PHOTOGRAPHY AND PHOTOGRAPHIC
APPARATUS :—
Eclipse of the Sun, total, 136; Improvements since 1851, 136; Landscapes and Portraits, 136; Lenses,
137; London Stereoscopic Company's Photographs, 137; PhotoZincography, 136; Pictures burnt
in on Glass, 136.
SANITARY APPLIANCES :—
Concentric Ventilator, 148; Filtering Apparatus, 148; Heating Contrivances, 148; Iron Staircase, Shutters, and Sashes, 148; Main Drainage of London, 147; Reflection for
dark places, 149; Shutters and Window-fastenings, 148; Silicated Carbon Filters,148; Water, London, 147.
SURGICAL INSTRUMENTS AND APPLIANCES :—
American sticking-plaster, 147;
Arm, artificial, 146; Artificial Limbs,
145; Bath, protracted, 146; Ecraseur, 145; English and Continental
makers, 144; Laryngoscope, 147;
Leg and Eye, artificial, 146; Medicine Chests and Cases, 145; Orthopædic Instruments, 145; Osseous
system, 147; Pavia, instruments
from,147; Pulsation of an Artery,146;
Pulverization of Liquids, 146; Resuscitation instrument, 145; Stammering, treatment of, 147; Stretcher,
145; Tracheotomy, 146; Trephine,
145; Vaccination Instrument, 145.

THE END.

Advertisements.

CHUBB & SON.

"For perfection of workmanship and construction of Locks, also for the manufacture of Iron Safes."

PRIZE MEDAL AWARDED,

International Exhibition, 1862.

CHUBB'S PATENT DETECTOR LOCKS.

The most secure from pick-locks and false keys, are strong, simple, and durable, and made of all sizes and for every purpose to which a lock can be applied.

Cash, Deed, and Paper Boxes of all sizes, Travelling Bags, Letter Bags, Writing Boxes, and Desks, all with the DETECTOR LOCKS.

It will be observed that no locks or safes of inferior quality are made by Chubb and Son. The whole of their locks and safes sold to the public at large are exactly the same in security and excellence of workmanship as those supplied to her Majesty, the Government offices, the Bank of England, Stock Exchange, and other public establishments.

CHUBB'S PATENT FIREPROOF SAFES

Afford the greatest security from fire or burglars. They are constructed in the best manner of strong wrought iron, and lined with the best-known fire-resisting and non-conducting composition.

The doors are all secured by CHUBB'S PATENT DRILL-PREVENTIVE, and their Patent

GUNPOWDER-PROOF LOCKS.

ILLUSTRATED PRICE LIST GRATIS AND POST FREE.

CHUBB & SON,

No. 57, St. PAUL'S CHURCHYARD, LONDON;

28, Lord Street, Liverpool; 16, Market Street, Manchester; and Horseley Fields, Wolverhampton.

BENSON'S WATCHES AND CLOCKS.

"PERFECTION OF MECHANISM."—*MORNING POST.*

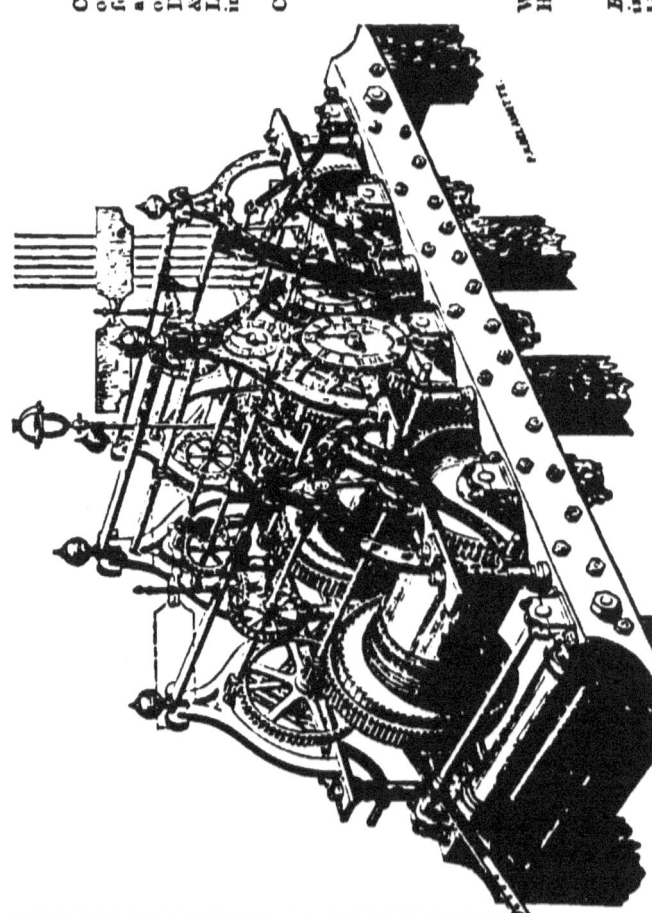

BENSON'S
ILLUSTRATED WATCH CATALOGUE,

Sent Post Free for Two Stamps,

Contains numerous designs and patterns, a description of the various Escapements at present in use, with other interesting matter, and a copious Price List of every construction of Watch, including—

Vertical Watches.
Horizontal Watches.
Lever Watches.
Duplex Watches.
Chronometers.
Chronographs.
Astronomical Watches.
Blind Men's Watches.
Repeaters.
Centre Seconds' Watches.
Reversible Watches.
Enamelled Watches.
Presentation Watches.
Keyless Watches.

ESTIMATES GIVEN FOR CHURCH AND TURRET CLOCKS.

BENSON'S
ILLUSTRATED CLOCK CATALOGUE,

Sent Post Free for Two Stamps,

Contains a great number of very handsome Designs for clocks of various kinds, a short History of the Art of Watchmaking, with Drawings of Escapements, &c., and a very full Price List of Clocks of all kinds, including—

Church and Turret Clocks.
Public Clocks.
Carriage Clocks.
Bracket Clocks.
Dining-Room Clocks.
Musical Clocks.
Drawing-Room Clocks.
Chime Clocks.
Regulators.
Library Clocks.
Hall and Staircase Clocks.
Astronomical Clocks.
Dials for the Hall, Shop, Warehouse, or Counting-House.

The above cut represents BENSON'S Great Clock in the International Exhibition. See "Times," June 11, 1862.

33 & 34. LUDGATE HILL, E.C.

BENNETT'S PATENT CLOCKS WITH ILLUMINATED HANDS.

BENNETT'S MODEL CLOCK at £10. An 8-day striking Clock, of his own best Manufacture, combining Simplicity, Durability, and Finish, and Warranted to keep Perfect Time.

WATCHES FREE & SAFE PER POST.

BENNETT'S MODEL WATCH, 65, CHEAPSIDE LONDON

SILVER FROM 5 GUINEAS — GOLD FROM 2 GUINEAS

BENNETT'S MODEL BAROMETER, For One Guinea. Warranted Scientifically accurate, and entirely free from the defects of the old Wheel Instrument. It is Portable, Neat, and Trustworthy, and adapted for every climate and purpose.

IN THE GREAT EXHIBITION, No. 3225, CLASS XV.

Manufacturer to the Admiralty, the Ordnance, the Royal Observatory, and the Queen.

Every Watch in the latest Style, and most carefully Finished.

Gold Cases and Jewelled.	Quality.			Silver Cases and Jewelled.	Quality.		
	A Gs.	B Gs.	C Gs.		A Gs.	B Gs.	C Gs.
GENTLEMEN'S.				**GENTLEMEN'S.**			
Horizontal construction, enamel dial, 4 holes jewelled............	10	8	6	Horizontal construction, sound and serviceable	5	4	3
Ditto, gold dial and strong case............................	12	10	7	Superior Lever (Geneva), 10 jewels	7	6	5
Bennett's superior London-made patent Lever, jewelled	17	14	12	Bennett's London-made Levers	8	6	5
LADIES'.				**LADIES'.**			
Horizontal construction, gold dial......................	10	8	6	Horizontal construction, neat and flat, beautifully-engraved cases	5	4	3
Patent Lever (Geneva)............	12	10	8	Superior Geneva Lever	6	5	4
Ditto (English), highly finished	16	14	12	*Elegant silver dials*, 10s. 6d. *extra*. Small London-made Levers ...	7	6	5

FOR MEDICAL MEN, DEAD SECONDS; GOLD, 20 Gs.; SILVER, 12 Gs.

Superior Lever with Chronometer Balance.   Bennett's Pocket Chronometer.
Gold, 27, 23, and 19 Gs.   Gold, 50 Gs.; Silver, 40 Gs.

EVERY WATCH SKILFULLY EXAMINED, TIMED, AND ITS PERFORMANCE GUARANTEED.

Post Office Orders, payable as under, will receive prompt attention.

JOHN BENNETT, 65 & 64, Cheapside, London
AND CITY OBSERVATORY, 62, CORNHILL.

BY ROYAL COMMAND.

METALLIC PEN MAKER TO THE QUEEN:

JOSEPH GILLOTT

Respectfully invites the attention of the Public to the following Numbers of his

PATENT METALLIC PENS,

Which, for QUALITY OF MATERIAL, EASY ACTION, and GREAT DURABILITY, will ensure universal preference.

FOR LADIES' USE
For fine neat writing, especially on thick and highly-finished papers.
Nos. 1, 173, 303, 604. In EXTRA-FINE POINTS.

FOR GENERAL USE
Nos. 2, 164, 166, 168, 604. In FINE POINTS.

FOR BOLD FREE WRITING
Nos. 3, 164, 166, 168, 604. In MEDIUM POINTS.

FOR GENTLEMEN'S USE
FOR LARGE, FREE, BOLD WRITING.
The Black Swan Quill, Large Barrel Pen, No. 808.
The Patent Magnum Bonum, No. 263. In MEDIUM and BROAD POINTS.

FOR GENERAL WRITING
No. 263. In EXTRA-FINE and FINE POINTS. No. 810. New Bank Pen.
No. 262. In FINE POINTS; Small Barrel. No. 840. The Autograph Pen.

FOR COMMERCIAL PURPOSES
The celebrated Three-hole Correspondence Pen, No. 382.
 " Four-hole " " No. 202.
The Public Pen, No. 292.
 " " With Bead, No. 404.
Small Barrel Pens, fine and free, Nos. 392, 405, 603.

TO BE HAD OF EVERY RESPECTABLE STATIONER IN THE WORLD.

WHOLESALE AND FOR EXPORTATION—
AT THE
Manufactory, Victoria Works, Graham Street, and at *96, New Street, Birmingham;* 91, *John Street, New York;*
AND OF
WILLIAM DAVIS, at the London Depot, 37, Gracechurch St., E.C.

MEMORIALS
OF THE
GREAT EXHIBITION, 1862.

A Set of 100 Selected Stereographs,
CONTAINING THE MASTERPIECES OF SCULPTURE AND ALL THE FINEST VIEWS OF THE EXHIBITION AND ITS COURTS,
£7.

A SMALL SET OF SEVEN
LARGE PHOTOGRAPHS,
10s.

A Fine Series at Five Shillings each.
- READING GIRL.
- SLEEP OF SORROW.
- TINTED VENUS.
- SIBYL.
- ROMAN COURT, &c. &c.

MICROSCOPIC.
A Series of Three Dozen of the above subjects, including Microscope, at 2s. 6d. each.

POST-OFFICE ORDERS to GEORGE SWAN NOTTAGE

London Stereoscopic and Photographic Company,

54, Cheapside (corner of Bow Church-yard); 110, Regent Street (opposite Vigo Street).

A LIST OF NEW WORKS.

Routledge's Illustrated Natural History.
By the Rev. J. G. WOOD. With upwards of 1500 Illustrations. 3 vols. super royal, cloth, 2l. 14s.

Routledge's Illustrated Shakespeare.
Edited by HOWARD STAUNTON. With 1200 Illustrations from designs by JOHN GILBERT, Engraved by the Brothers DALZIEL, with a Steel Portrait. 3 vols. super royal, cloth, 2l. 16s.

The Manual of Dates.
A Dictionary of Reference to all the most important events in the History of Mankind to be found in Authentic Records. By GEO. H. TOWNSEND. Post 8vo, half bound (960 pp.), 12s. 6d.

Men of the Time.
A Biographical Dictionary of Eminent Living Characters (including Women). Edited by EDWARD WALFORD, M.A. Post 8vo, half bound (840 pp.), 10s. 6d.

Birket Foster's Pictures of English Landscape.
Engraved by the Brothers DALZIEL; accompanied by Pictures in Words by TOM TAYLOR. Demy 4to, cloth gilt, 21s.

Routledge's Every Boy's Annual.
A Miscellany of Entertaining Literature. With an Illuminated Frontispiece and Vignette, and 100 Illustrations. Edited by EDMUND ROUTLEDGE. Post 8vo, cloth, gilt edges, 6s.

The Playbook of Metals.
By J. H. PEPPER, Author of the "Boy's Playbook of Science." With upwards of 300 Illustrations. Post 8vo, cloth, 7s. 6d.

The Boy's Playbook of Science.
By J. H. PEPPER. With 470 Illustrations. Post 8vo, cloth, 6s.

The History of England.
From the Earliest Times to the year Eighteen Hundred and Fifty-eight. By the Rev. JAMES WHITE, Author of "Landmarks of the History of England," etc. Post 8vo, cloth, 7s. 6d.

The Fall of Rome; and the Rise of the New Nationalities.
By JOHN G. SHEPPARD, D.C.L., sometime Fellow of Wadham College, Oxford, and Head Master of Kidderminster School. Post 8vo, cloth, 7s. 6d.

Fish Culture, and the Modern System of Breeding and Rearing Fish in Inland Waters.
By FRANCIS FRANCIS. Post 8vo, cloth, 5s.

London: How the Great City Grew.
By G. R. EMERSON. 2s. 6d.

Reminiscences of the late Thomas Assheton Smith.
By Sir JOHN E. EARDLEY WILMOT, Bart. A New and Revised Edition, with a Portrait and other Illustrations. Post 8vo, cloth, 2s. 6d.

A Guide to London and its Suburbs.
By GEORGE F. PARDON. With a Map and 16 Illustrations. Fcap. 8vo, boards, 1s.

Geological Gossip on the Earth and Ocean.
By Professor ANSTED. Fcap. 8vo, cloth, 2s. 6d.

LONDON: ROUTLEDGE, WARNE, & ROUTLEDGE, 2, Farringdon-street, E.C.

THE ENCYCLOPÆDIA BRITANNICA,
EIGHTH EDITION.

Now complete, in 21 vols. 4to, and Index, price £25 12s. in cloth boards, and £33 2s. 6d. in half russia,

THE EIGHTH EDITION
OF
THE ENCYCLOPÆDIA BRITANNICA;
A Dictionary of Arts, Sciences, and General Literature,
Illustrated with upwards of 5000 *Engravings on Wood and Steel.*

Edinburgh: A. and C. BLACK. London: SIMPKIN, MARSHALL, and Co.

In foolscap 8vo, Illustrated. Price 8s. cloth.

ILLUSTRATIONS OF ARTS AND MANUFACTURES; being a Series of Papers on Pottery, Limestone, and Calcareous Cements, Gypsum and its uses, Furs and the Fur Trade, Felting and Hat-making. Bone and its uses, Tortoiseshell and Whalebone, Antiquarian and Metallurgical History of Iron, Engraving and Etching, and on Paper. Read before the Society for the Encouragement of Arts, Manufactures, &c. By ARTHUR AIKIN, F.L.S., F.G.S., &c., late Secretary to that Institution.

JOHN VAN VOORST, 1, Paternoster Row.

THE USEFUL KNOWLEDGE SOCIETY'S
ATLASES.

From the Series of Maps designed by the Society for the Diffusion of Useful Knowledge.

** *They are all elegantly bound, and the Maps well coloured. The Maps (size 17 by 14 inches) may be had separately, price 6d. each plain, 9d. coloured.*

Cyclopædian Atlas, 39 selected Maps, 1 Guinea.
Family Atlas, 80 selected Maps, 3 Guineas.
Atlas of Modern Geography, the entire series of 150 Modern Maps, 5 Guineas.
General Atlas, the entire series of 174 Ancient and Modern Maps, 7 Guineas.
Complete Atlas, with the addition of 50 Plans of Celebrated Cities, 9 Guineas.

THE HARROW EDUCATIONAL ATLASES, VIZ.:—

Senior Modern, 30 Maps, 12s. 6d.	Senior Classical, 23 Maps, 12s. 6d.
Junior Modern, 14 Maps, 7s.	Junior Classical, 14 Maps, 7s.

A Specimen Map gratis on application.

GENERAL ADVERTISEMENT.

The Low PRICE of THE USEFUL KNOWLEDGE SOCIETY's extensive Series of Maps, induces the Publisher to state, that they are in every respect of the highest character, whether as to beauty of execution, scale, or accuracy of engraving. The latest discoveries and alterations are inserted on the plates, as soon as fully authenticated, and several of the Maps have been repeatedly re-engraved—the whole series being thus rendered a faithful delineation of the current state of Geographical Knowledge. Detailed Catalogues gratis, and post free.

LONDON: EDWARD STANFORD, 6, Charing Cross, S.W.

Educational Works. By Dr. Cornwell, F.R.G.S.

"Dr. Cornwell ranks among our very best editors of educational treatises. We have for many years used his 'English School Grammar,' his 'Young Composer,' and his 'School Geography,' as text-books, and can testify, from daily experience, that, in practical utility to private students, and in perfect adaptation to the purposes of public instruction, they cannot be surpassed. The four latest contributions to the Editor's Educational Series fully maintain his high reputation. The 'Geography for Beginners' furnishes an admirable initiation into the Author's more elaborate manual of 'School Geography;' the 'Map-Book for Beginners' is equal in point of execution to any atlas of its size which we have seen; while the 'Book of Blank Maps' and the 'Book of Map Projections' at once suggest and supply the true and only data for the rational and effective teaching of geography. On the whole, we can, with the utmost confidence, recommend these and other works of Dr. Cornwell to all who are engaged in the education of youth.'—*Macphail's Literary Review.*

Recently published, 1s. 6d.; 2s. 6d. coloured,

A MAP-BOOK FOR BEGINNERS:
Being a companion atlas to the "Geography for Beginners."

Also, for Map Drawing, 1s.,

BOOK OF BLANK MAPS.
The Maps, above seventy large and small, complete in everything but the names, to be filled in by the learner.

Also, price 1s.,

BOOK OF MAP PROJECTIONS.

Also, 11th Edition, price 1s.,

GEOGRAPHY FOR BEGINNERS.

31st Edition, 3s. 6d., or with thirty Maps on steel, 5s. 6d.,

A SCHOOL GEOGRAPHY.

2s. 6d. plain; 4s. coloured,

A SCHOOL ATLAS.
This Atlas consists of thirty beautifully executed small maps on steel, in which is found every place mentioned in the Author's "School Geography." It also contains a list of several hundred places, with their latitude and longitude. These names are accentuated; and, in cases of difficulty, the pronunciation is also given.

*** Current editions of the above works are corrected to the present time.

25th Edition, price 1s. 6d.,

THE YOUNG COMPOSER; or, PROGRESSIVE EXERCISES in ENGLISH COMPOSITION.   KEY. Price 3s.

4th Edition, price 3s., cloth,

DR. ALLEN'S EUTROPIUS, with a complete dictionary for Schools.

33rd Edition, price 2s., red leather; 1s. 9d. cloth,

ALLEN AND CORNWELL'S SCHOOL GRAMMAR.

39th Edition, 1s.,

GRAMMAR FOR BEGINNERS.

12th Edition, price 4s.,

SELECT ENGLISH POETRY.
For the use of schools and young persons in general. Edited by the late Dr. ALLEN.

*** This Edition is got up in a superior manner, and the book is considered to be well adapted for prizes or presents.

6th Edition, price 1s. 6d.,

SCHOOL ARITHMETIC; formerly called "Arithmetic for Beginners."

Just published, price 4s. 6d.,

KEY TO THE SCHOOL ARITHMETIC.
Every question is worked in full, practical directions accompanying each rule, and a short Introduction gives general hints on teaching Arithmetic.

8th Edition, price 4s. 6d.,

THE SCIENCE OF ARITHMETIC:
A Systematic Course of Numerical Reasoning and Computation, with very numerous Exercises. By JAMES CORNWELL, Ph.D., and JOSHUA G. FITCH, M.A.

London: SIMPKIN and Co., HAMILTON and Co. Edinburgh: OLIVER and BOYD.

PUBLISHED MONTHLY, PRICE ONE SHILLING,
Illustrated with Full-page Plates in Colours and Tints,

THE

INTELLECTUAL OBSERVER.
Review of Natural History, Microscopic Research,

AND

RECREATIVE SCIENCE.

MORRIS'S BIRDS.
CHEAP EDITION, to be completed in EIGHT VOLUMES.
Now ready, Cr. 8vo. cloth gilt, Illustrated with 43 coloured plates,
The First Volume, price 7s. 6d.;

A HISTORY OF BRITISH BIRDS.
BY THE REV. F. O. MORRIS, B.A.,
Author of "The Nests and Eggs of British Birds," "British Butterflies," &c.

Post 8vo, cloth, price 5s. Illustrated.

MARVELS OF POND LIFE.
A year's Microscopic Recreations among the Polyps, Infusoria, Rotifers,
Water Bears, and Polyzoa.
BY HENRY J. SLACK, F.G.S.

Fcap. 8vo, cloth, price 4s.

A DICTIONARY OF BOTANICAL TERMS.
ILLUSTRATED WITH FIVE HUNDRED WOODCUTS.
BY THE REV. J. S. HENSLOW, M.A.,
Late Professor of Botany in the University of Cambridge.

Imp. 16mo, cloth gilt, price 7s. 6d. With Illustrations in Colours.

TELESCOPE TEACHINGS.
A Familiar sketch of Astronomical Discovery, combining a special notice of objects
coming within the range of a Small Telescope.

BY THE HON. MRS. WARD.
Dedicated, by permission, to the Earl of Rosse.

Cr. 8vo, cloth, price 5s. Illustrated.

FIRST TRACES OF LIFE ON THE EARTH:
OR,
THE FOSSILS OF THE BOTTOM ROCKS.
BY S. J. MACKIE, F.G.S.

LONDON: GROOMBRIDGE AND SONS, 5, Paternoster Row.

THE ENGLISH CYCLOPÆDIA.
Conducted by CHARLES KNIGHT.

The ENGLISH CYCLOPÆDIA is published in FOUR DIVISIONS, *each Division being complete in itself and sold separately.*

THE CYCLOPÆDIA OF GEOGRAPHY.
Four Volumes, price 2l. 2s., or bound in 2 Vols., half-morocco, 2l. 10s.

This Cyclopædia embraces the Physical Features of every country, the Statistics of its department, and its Cities and Marts of Commerce; as well as recording its history to the most recent period.

THE CYCLOPÆDIA OF BIOGRAPHY.
Six Volumes, price 3l., or bound in 3 Vols., half-morocco, 3l. 12s.

The Cyclopædia of Biography may, without presumption, be stated to be the most complete Biographical Dictionary extant; unequalled in any language for the universality of its range, its fulness without verbosity, its accuracy, and its completeness to the present time. It possesses the new and important feature of giving notices of living persons, English and foreign, of contemporary celebrity. No work of a similar nature approaches the English Cyclopædia of Biography in cheapness.

THE CYCLOPÆDIA OF NATURAL HISTORY.
In Four Volumes, price 2l. 2s., or bound in 2 Vols., half-morocco, 2l. 10s.

The Cyclopædia of Natural History includes the contributions of the most eminent Naturalists. In BOTANY, those by Dr. Lankester, Dr. Lindley, and Dr. Royle; in GEOLOGY, those of Sir Henry de la Beche, Mr. Horner, and Professor Phillips; in MINERALOGY, those of Mr. R. Phillips and Professor W. Turner; in ZOOLOGY, those of Mr. Broderip, Professor Forbes, Mr. Ogilby, and Mr. Waterhouse; in COMPARATIVE ANATOMY and PHYSIOLOGY, those of Mr. Day, Professor Paget, and Dr. Southwood Smith.

THE CYCLOPÆDIA OF ARTS AND SCIENCES.
Eight Volumes, price 4l. 16s., or bound in 4 Vols., half-morocco, 5l. 12s.

The Cyclopædia of Arts and Sciences, embracing as it does all subjects not belonging to either of the above Divisions, is necessarily the most important and comprehensive. The following List mentions the principal subjects comprised in it:—

Mathematics and Astronomy.
Physical Sciences; Optics; Acoustics; Dynamics; Electricity; Magnetism; Meteorology.
Chemistry.
Navigation and Military Sciences.
Materia Medica; Medicine; Surgery.
Architecture; Civil Engineering.

Manufactures and Machinery.
Painting; Sculpture; Antiquities.
Engraving; Music, &c.
Rural Economy.
Philology; Mental Philosophy.
Government and Political Economy.
Law and Jurisprudence.

Also, in 1 Vol. 4to, uniform with the Work, price 6s. cloth, or 9s. half-bound, morocco.

A SYNOPTICAL INDEX TO THE FOUR DIVISIONS.

LONDON: BRADBURY AND EVANS, 11, BOUVERIE STREET, E.C.

BY THE AUTHOR OF "THINGS NOT GENERALLY KNOWN."

Now ready, with a Coloured Title, 5s. cloth, pp. 320.

SOMETHING FOR EVERYBODY;
AND
A GARLAND FOR THE YEAR.
BY JOHN TIMBS, F.S.A.

This work will form an acceptable *Companion to every Almanack*, since it contains Notices of the *most* MEMORABLE DAYS OF THE YEAR; its FASTS and FESTIVALS, and PICTURESQUE EVENTS, such as are usually *named* in Almanacks, but are here popularly explained and illustrated, under more than One Hundred and Fifty Articles. The Work also contains papers on Pall Mall; the Game and Street—Brambletye House—Whitebait—Domestic Arts and Customs—Gardening and Rural Life.

"A collection made by a diligent scholar in a long life of literature, and imparting information in such a manner as to be pleasing to the young, and welcome to the old. Mr. Timbs has published many good books, but none better or more deserving of popularity than that to which he has given the appropriate title of 'Something for Everybody.'"—*London Review.*

"In this volume the author certainly maintains the position he has won for himself as a most indefatigable collector and compiler of useful information, in a form at once clear, accurate, and vastly entertaining."—*English Churchman.*

"Mr. Timbs' charming volume, 'Something for Everybody.'"—*Notes and Queries.*

LONDON: LOCKWOOD & CO., Stationers' Hall Court.

This day, with Frontispiece, 5s.,

PREDICTIONS REALIZED IN MODERN TIMES.
Now first collected by HORACE WELBY.

CONTENTS:—Days and Numbers—Prophesying Almanacks—Omens—Historical Predictions—The French Revolutions—The Bonaparte Family and Revival of the French Emperorship—Discoveries and Inventions Anticipated—Scriptural Prophecies, &c., in more than 250 Narratives, with Original Communications.

"There is nothing in this book calculated to alarm the nicest feeling, or to repel the most serious reader."—*Illustrated London News.*

"An odd but attractive volume, full of amusing reading."—*The Critic.*

"Contains a variety of curious and startling narratives on many points of supernaturalism, well calculated to gratify that love of the marvellous which is more or less inherent in us all."—*Notes and Queries.*

By the same Author, with Frontispiece, 5s.,

MYSTERIES OF LIFE, DEATH, AND FUTURITY.
Illustrated from the Best and Latest Authorities.

CONTENTS:—Life and Time—Nature of the Soul—Spiritual Life—Mental Operations—Belief and Scepticism—Premature Interment—Phenomena of Death—Sin and Punishment—The Crucifixion of Our Lord—The End of the World Foretold.—Man after Death—The Intermediate State—The Great Resurrection—Recognition of the Blessed—The Day of Judgment—The Future States—New Heavens and Earth, &c.

"A pleasant, dreamy, charming, startling volume, every page of which sparkles like a gem in an antique setting."—*Dispatch.*

"Not inferior as an interesting literary curiosity to the famous 'Anatomy of Melancholy.'"—*Oriental Budget.*

"Nothing but what is orthodox."—*Spectator.*

"The pious believer must be charmed with these pages. Burton's 'Anatomy of Melancholy' is a fine suggestive book, and full of learning; and of the volume before us we are inclined to speak in the same terms."—*Era.*

LONDON: KENT & CO., Paternoster Row; and LOCKWOOD & CO., Stationers' Hall Court.

POPULAR FRENCH SCHOOL BOOKS.

The attention of Schoolmasters and Heads of Colleges is respectfully requested to the following eminently useful series of French class books, which have enjoyed an unprecedented popularity. A detailed prospectus will be sent on application.

De Fivas' French Grammar; or, "Grammaire des Grammaires." 20th Edition, price 3s. 6d. handsomely bound.

"At once the simplest and most complete Grammar of the French language. To the pupil the effect is almost as if he looked into a map, so well-defined is the course of study as explained by M. de Fivas."—*Literary Gazette.*

*** A KEY to the above, price 3s. 6d.

De Fivas' New Guide to Modern French Conversation. 12th Edition, 18mo, 2s. 6d. half-bound.

"Voulez-vous un guide aussi sûr qu'infaillible pour apprendre la langue Française, prenez le Guide de M. de Fivas : c'est l'indispensable manuel de tout étranger."
L'Impartial.

De Fivas, Beautés des Ecrivains Français, Anciens et Modernes. 9th Edition, 12mo, 3s. 6d. strongly bound.

"A convenient reading book for the student of the French language, and at the same time a pleasing and interesting view of French literature."—*Observer.*

De Fivas, Introduction à la Langue Française; ou, Fables et Contes Choisis. 13th Edition, 12mo, 2s. 6d. strongly bound.

"By far the best first French reading-book, whether for schools or adult pupils."
Tait's Magazine.

De Fivas, Le Trésor National; or, Guide to the Translation of English into French at sight. 2nd Edition, 12mo, 2s. 6d. strongly bound.

*** A KEY to the above. 12mo, 2s. cloth.

LOCKWOOD AND CO., 7, STATIONERS' HALL COURT, E.C.

International Exhibition, 1862. Class XIII.
Only Prize Medal Awarded
FOR "EXCELLENCE OF CONSTRUCTION OF MATHEMATICAL INSTRUMENTS."

W. F. STANLEY begs to call the attention of the Public to the excellent quality and many improvements of his Mathematical Instruments, his Engine-made Scales and Rules, and every article for the Draughtsman or Scientific Use; also to the Low Prices. A List will be sent Post Free on application.

W. F. STANLEY,
3, GREAT TURNSTILE, HOLBORN, LONDON, W.C.

WHISHAW'S
REGISTERED IMPROVED
TELEKOUPHONON,
FOR SPEAKING-PIPES.

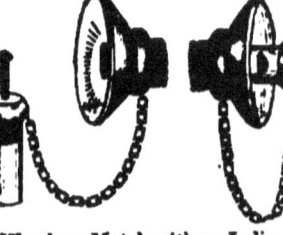

BY means of this invention, Speaking-Pipes may be rendered more generally available for Public Buildings, Club Houses, Noblemen's Mansions, City Warehouses, Offices, &c. It consists of a Whistle-mouthpiece of Ivory, Wood, or Metal, with an Indicator attached, by means of which, in case of two or more speaking-tubes being carried into one room, the mouthpiece from which a whistle proceeds is readily ascertained. Also, Zinc and Copper Speaking-Pipes of all sizes. Manufactured solely by

BENHAMS AND FROUD,
40, 41, AND 42, CHANDOS STREET, CHARING CROSS.

And to be had Retail of all respectable Ironmongers. Mr. Whishaw was formerly Secretary of the Society of Arts (*see page 3*).

LOCKS, FIRE-PROOF SAFES, AND IRON DOORS.

GEORGE PRICE'S DOUBLE-PATENT
"NE PLUS ULTRA"
PRIZE-MEDAL BANK LOCK,
UNPICKABLE AND GUNPOWDER PROOF.

Specially constructed for the outer doors of Banking Establishments, Warehouses, Mills, Ecclesiastical Buildings, Prisons, Asylums, &c. It is a Rim Lock, 10 by 7 inches; has two strong bolts, and the key is so small that it may be carried in the waistcoat-pocket, or on the key-ring.

GEORGE PRICE'S PATENT PRIZE-MEDAL
"NE PLUS ULTRA" LOCK
IS MADE OF ALL SIZES, AND SUITABLE FOR ALL PURPOSES.

GEORGE PRICE'S PATENT PRIZE-MEDAL
IRON DOORS AND FRAMES
FOR BANKERS' STRONG ROOMS,
ARE THE BEST CONSTRUCTED AND CHEAPEST IN THE TRADE.

FIRE-PROOF SAFES.
GEORGE PRICE'S
TREBLE-PATENT PRIZE-MEDAL CHAMPION SAFES,
FITTED WITH HIS DOUBLE-PATENT
"NE PLUS ULTRA" UNPICKABLE AND GUNPOWDER-PROOF SOLID PIN-KEY LOCK,

With hardened Steel "Nosle," Drill-proof Packing and Covering Plates, and Patent Case-hardened Drill Proof Doors, with Safety Spindle, &c., are the only Safes that should ever be trusted with valuable property against Fire and the modern burglar.

Illustrated Price Lists, Post Free, from

GEORGE PRICE,
Cleveland Safe and Lock Works, Wolverhampton.

CONSUMPTION IN ALL ITS STAGES.

Coughs, Whooping Cough, Asthma, Bronchitis, Fever, Ague, Diphtheria, Hysteria, Rheumatism, Diarrhœa, Spasms, Cholic, Renal and Uterine Diseases,

ARE IMMEDIATELY RELIEVED BY A DOSE OF

CHLORODYNE,

(*Trade Mark,*)

DISCOVERED AND NAMED BY

DR. J. COLLIS BROWNE, M.R.C.S.L., Ex-Army Medical Staff.

The question asked by invalids, families, and households, is—What is the *best* medicine to give in the above diseases, and what to have always ready? Medical testimony, the reply of thousands of sufferers and invalids, is confirmatory of the invaluable relief afforded by this remedy above all others.

CHLORODYNE is a liquid taken in drops according to age. It invariably *relieves pain* of whatever kind; *creates* a calm, refreshing sleep; *allays* irritation of the nervous system when *all other remedies fail*; leaving no bad effects like opium or landanum, and can be taken when none other can be tolerated. Its value in saving life in infancy is not easily estimated; a few drops will subdue the irritation of Teething, prevent and arrest Convulsions, cure Whooping Cough, Spasms, and Flatus at once.

Among Invalids it *allays* the pain of Neuralgia, Rheumatism, Gout, &c. It *soothes* the weary achings of Consumption, *relieves* the Soreness of the Chest, Cough, and Expectoration; and *cures* all Chest Affections, such as Asthma, Bronchitis, Palpitation, &c. It checks Diarrhœa, Alvine Discharges, or Spasms and Cholics of the Intestines, &c.

The extensive demand for this remedy, known as DR. J. COLLIS BROWNE'S CHLORODYNE, by the Medical Profession, Hospitals, Dispensaries—Civil, Military, and Naval—and Families especially, guarantees that this statement of its extreme importance and value is a *bonâ fide* one, and worthy the attention of all.

EXTRACTS OF MEDICAL OPINIONS.

From W. VESALIUS PETTIGREW, M.D.—"I have no hesitation in stating that I have never met with any medicine so efficacious as an anti-spasmodic and sedative. I have used it in Consumption, Asthma, Diarrhœa, and other diseases, and am most perfectly satisfied with the results."

From Dr. M'MILLAN, of New Galway, Scotland.—"I consider it the most valuable medicine known."

G. HAYWARD, Esq., Surgeon, Stow-on-the-Wold.—"I am now using Dr. J. COLLIS BROWNE'S CHLORODYNE with marvellous good effect in allaying inveterate sickness in pregnancy."

Dr. M'GRIGOR CROFT, late Army Staff, says: "It is a most valuable medicine."

Dr. GIBBON, Army Medical Staff, Calcutta: "Two doses completely cured me of Diarrhœa."

From JOHN C. BAKER, Esq., M.D., Littleham, Bideford, Devon.—"It is without doubt the most *certain* and *valuable Anodyne* we have."

From G. V. RIDEOUT, Esq., Surgeon, Egham.—"As an astringent in severe Diarrhœa, and an anti-spasmodic in Cholic, with Cramps in the abdomen, the relief is instantaneous. As a sedative in Neuralgia and Tic-Douloureux, its effects were very remarkable. In Uterine Affections I have found it extremely valuable."

CAUTION.—*Beware of Spurious Imitations or substitutes. Each bottle of the Genuine bears a Red Stamp, with the words Dr. J. Collis Browne's Chlorodyne engraved thereon in White Letters, and never buy it without, as Compounds called after it are too often vended.*

Sold only in Bottles, at 2s. 9d. and 4s. 6d. by the sole Agent and Manufacturer,

J. T. DAVENPORT,

33, GREAT RUSSELL STREET, BLOOMSBURY SQUARE, LONDON,

With Professional Testimonials Enclosed.

INTERNATIONAL EXHIBITION.

NEWTON, WILSON, & CO.'S
PATENT SEWING MACHINES.

Twelve Prize Medals and Fourteen Honourable Mentions Awarded to Exhibitors using these Machines.

The work produced by these Machines includes everything that can possibly be required in a family:—The stitch is stronger and more elastic than that of any other machines; can be applied to the finest plain sewing or the heaviest embroidery; and, in addition, are the only machines that will make a braid in cotton, silk, or Berlin wool, and stitch it on, without basting, to any pattern, at the same moment. In use by the Queen, the Empress of the French, and most of the nobility and clergy. Every machine warranted. Machines of all the different stitches produced by the sewing machine kept in stock; and purchasers are secured from the possibility of mistake by the option of exchange after a month's trial, without charge, for any other. Samples of the work in any of the different stitches in running, hemming, felling, tucking, binding, gathering, quilting, braiding, or embroidering, with Illustrated Catalogue, free, from the

GREAT CENTRAL DEPÔT,
144, HIGH HOLBORN, LONDON.

NEWTON, WILSON, & CO.'S
PATENT CARPET SCRAPER

Cleans a carpet thoroughly without any labour, without damping, and without raising a grain of dust. Prospectuses from the

GREAT CENTRAL DEPÔT,
144, HIGH HOLBORN.

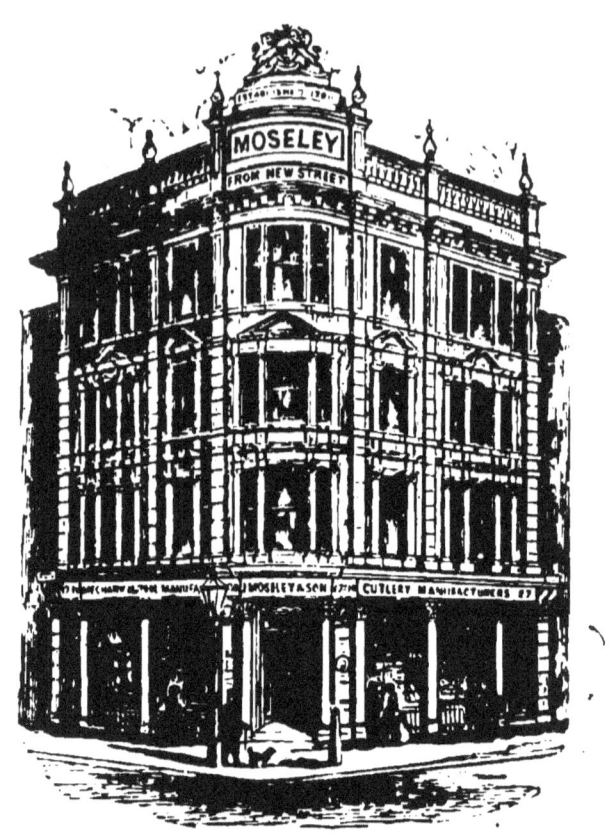

JOHN MOSELEY & SON,
CUTLERY AND TOOL MANUFACTURERS,
(*See page 224,*)
ESTABLISHED IN NEW STREET, COVENT GARDEN, A.D. 1730.
REMOVED TO
17 and 18, King Street, and 27, Bedford Street, Covent Garden,
LONDON,
(FACING THE END OF THE NEW STREET.)

PRICED & ILLUSTRATED CATALOGUES
Of Table Cutlery, Pocket Knives, Scissors, &c. and all kinds of Tools,
To be had Gratis on application, or free by post.

Every improvement in Design and Manufacture promptly introduced. Illustrated Price-list of Ladies' Carving Tools, free by post. Also, Lithograph Patterns sent for selection to all parts of the Country.

AMATEUR TOOL CHESTS
For Gentlemen, fitted with every requisite, at Moderate Charges.

Post Office Orders to be made payable at Charing Cross.

F. RANSOME'S
NEW PATENT
CONCRETE STONE,
MADE WITHOUT BURNING,

FOR WHICH

The Commissioners of the Exhibition of 1862 have

Awarded the Prize Medal,

AND WHICH FOR

SHARPNESS of OUTLINE, BEAUTY of APPEARANCE, DURABILITY, and CHEAPNESS, stands unrivalled.

Manufactured in BLOCKS of any dimensions, suitable for the construction of

SEA WALLS, DOCKS, ETC.,

As well as for the construction of Buildings generally. It surpasses every other material in its applicability to every description of

ARCHITECTURAL EMBELLISHMENTS,
CAPITALS FOR COLUMNS AND PILASTERS,
CHIMNEY-PIECES, TRUSSES, &c., &c., &c.

ALSO FOR

PARKS, GARDENS, CONSERVATORIES, &c.

AND ESPECIALLY FOR

Fountains, Vases, Jardinets, Statues,
BALUSTRADES FOR TERRACES, GATE PIERS, CAPS, AND TERMINALS,
EDGING FOR GARDEN BORDERS, &c.

MONUMENTS, TOMBS, AND ALL KINDS OF CEMETERY REQUIREMENTS.

Ransome's Patented Process for
PRESERVING STONE, BRICKS, CEMENT, STUCCO, &c.,
By which the Softest and most friable Stone, &c., can be rendered Impervious and Imperishable; decay at once arrested and prevented.

For Prices, Specimens, Illustrations, and Licences, apply to

Mr. FREDK. RANSOME,

36, Parliament Street, Westminster; or Patent Stone Works, Ipswich.

CLAYTON, SHUTTLEWORTH, & Co.,
LINCOLN,
Also at 78, LOMBARD STREET, LONDON;
125, *Marzergasse Weisgärber, Vienna;* and *Gegenüber Dem Bahnhof, Pesth;*

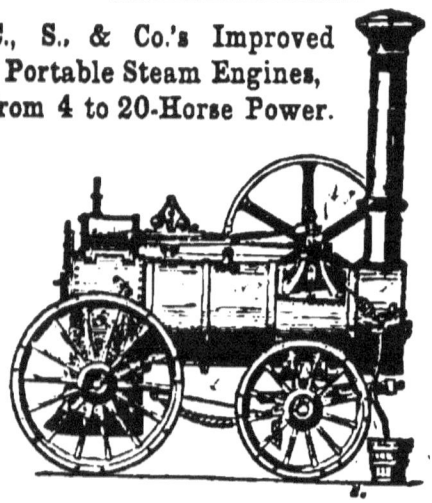

C., S., & Co.'s Improved Portable Steam Engines, from 4 to 20-Horse Power.

ENGINEERS, MANUFACTURERS OF PORTABLE AND FIXED STEAM ENGINES,

MACHINERY FOR PUMPING, HOISTING, GRINDING, SAWING, AND AGRICULTURAL PURPOSES.

INTERNATIONAL EXHIBITION, 1862.
CLASS IX.—Prize Medal for Agricultural Portable Steam Engines and Machinery.
CLASS VIII.—Prize Medal for Horizontal High-Pressure Steam Engines.
For "Good Arrangement — Good Workmanship — and Practical Success."

CLAYTON, SHUTTLEWORTH, & Co.'s HIGH-PRESSURE HORIZONTAL FIXED STEAM ENGINE
Has been awarded the Medal in Class VIII. International Exhibition, 1862.

CLAYTON, SHUTTLEWORTH, & Co.'s SELF-PROPELLING (or TRACTION) ENGINE FOR COMMON ROADS,
With their late Improvements, is most successful in work, and thoroughly under control.

CLAYTON, SHUTTLEWORTH, & Co.'s DOUBLE CYLINDER STEAM ENGINES, &c.,
for Steam Cultivating and Ploughing. Descriptive particulars and prices on application.

CLAYTON, SHUTTLEWORTH, & Co.'s COMBINED THRASHING, WINNOWING, AND DRESSING MACHINE.
These Machines will Thrash and Dress a larger quantity, and in a better manner, with a given power, than any other.

IMPROVED STRAW ELEVATORS,
For conveying Straw from the Machine to the top of the stack.

IMPROVED IRON FRAMED CORN MILLS, FLOUR DRESSING MACHINES, LIQUID MANURE PUMPS, &c.

Plans and Estimates for complete fixed Barn Machinery furnished on application to
CLAYTON, SHUTTLEWORTH, & CO.,
Lincoln; or 78, *Lombard Street, London.*

HAMILTON AND CO.'S
PATENT UNPICKABLE LOCKS,
ALSO
LEVER AND ALL OTHER KINDS OF LOCKS,
FIRE-PROOF SAFES,
DEED AND CASH BOXES, &c.
3, ROYAL EXCHANGE,
LONDON, E.C.

IMPORTANT TO ENGINEERS, ARCHITECTS AND BUILDERS.

ORNAMENTAL STAMPED ZINC,
IN RICH DESIGNS,
AND
DEVAUX'S VIEILLE MONTAGNE
THICK ROOFING ZINC.

This invaluable pure metal, if laid by Mr. TYLER, on the entire new principle introduced by J. EDMISTON, Esq., F.I.B.A., will last as long as lead, at one-third the cost.

For Prospectuses, Samples, Models, and Estimates of Works to be done with the Roofing Zinc, in large or small quantities, in Town or Country, apply to

MR. J. W. TYLER,
4, WOOD STREET, WESTMINSTER, S.W.

If the Metal be laid by Mr. TYLER, who has become so well known among Architects and Builders, superior and careful workmanship may be depended upon, and a guarantee given for its durability, if the woodwork be prepared according to directions given.

The Stamped Zinc comprises Richly-Ornamented Dormers, Mansards, Curbs, Ridges, Vanes, Finials, &c.

N.B.—There is more importance to be attached to Mr. TYLER'S Improvements than is generally known. A trial will convince judges of Metal Work.

GWYNNE AND COMPANY,
Hydraulic and Mechanical Engineers,
ESSEX STREET WHARVES, STRAND, LONDON, W.C.,
IRON FOUNDRY AT 12, WHARF, CITY ROAD BASIN, N.,

MANUFACTURE and SUPPLY EVERY DESCRIPTION OF MACHINERY for LIFTING, FORCING, and EXHAUSTING WATER and other FLUIDS and GASES.

MARINE, LOCOMOTIVE, STATIONARY, AND PORTABLE ENGINES, AND BOILERS OF EVERY VARIETY.

Patented Machinery for the Manufacture of Peat and Coal Fuels.

Blowing and Exhausting Machinery for Iron Works, Mines, &c.

PATENT STONE-BREAKING MACHINES.

THEIR UNEQUALLED PATENTED CENTRIFUGAL PUMPS, FAN BLOWERS, AND HYDRAULIC MACHINERY IN GENERAL.

Steam and Water Valves, Hydraulic and Screw Presses, Double and Single Purchase Crabs, Hydraulic and Screw Jacks, Hydraulic Lifts, &c.

General Machinery for Mines, Breweries, Distilleries, Tanneries, Dye Houses, Chemical Works.

Designs, Drawings, and Estimates for Engineering Works and Machinery Executed with Promptness and Dispatch.

Exhibition Prize Medal awarded
For "**GOOD WORK AND PRACTICAL SUCCESS.**"
(For description see page 102 in this book.)

Illustrated Catalogues forwarded on receipt of Six Stamps.

HART & SON 53 TO 58 WYCH ST. STRAND, LONDON.

And 20, Cockspur Street, Pall Mall.

Altar Desks and Vases — Communion Plate — Locks, Latches — Standards — Brackets and Coronæ for Gas — Oil and Candle.

Prize Medal, 1862, For "Great Beauty and Variety of Design and Perfection of Workmanship."

NO HOME COMPLETE WITHOUT A
WILLCOX & GIBBS'
SEWING MACHINE.

The distinguishing feature of this "MECHANICAL MARVEL AND HOUSEHOLD NECESSITY" is its REMARKABLE SIMPLICITY. Any one, however deficient in mechanical tact, can use it with success; at the same time, it is so faithfully constructed, that there is no fear of its being deranged in the hands of the most inexperienced operator. Unlike the more complicated Machines, *it never gets out of order "unaccountably,"* or otherwise, thus causing it to be set aside at a moment, perhaps, when it is most needed; hence its popularity as A FAMILY MACHINE, wherever introduced. It may, indeed, be truly characterized as "THE PERFECTION OF MECHANISM," and every Housewife may now, therefore, justly claim "EMANCIPATION FROM THE DRUDGERY OF THE NEEDLE."

WILLCOX & GIBBS, Sewing Machine Company,
No. 1, LUDGATE HILL (Corner of New Bridge Street).

PATENT PRIZE MEDAL.
ARTIFICIAL LEGS, ARMS, HANDS, EYES, NOSES, &c.

THE highest Medal in the Paris and London Universal Exhibitions, and *special notices* in the Jury Reports for valuable improvements in the above articles, have been awarded to W. R. GROSSMITH, 175, *Fleet-street*, London, Anatomical Mechanist to Her Majesty's Surgeons, the Surgeons of the London Hospitals, the Officers of Her Majesty's Army and Navy, &c.; to whom was also awarded the *Prize Medal* of the London Exhibition, 1851 and 1862.

GROSSMITH'S New ARTIFICIAL LEG, with patent-action knee and ankle joints, enables the patient to walk, sit, or ride with ease and comfort, wherever amputated. It is much lighter, and little more than *half the expense* of the old style of cork leg, will last a lifetime, and is the only leg yet invented that ladies and children can wear with safety.

The ARTIFICIAL EYES are fitted in a few hours, without pain or operation, in every case where sight has been lost: they effect a *perfect movement in* accordance with the action of the natural eye, and the colours of the iris are closely matched.—Sent by post to all parts of the world.

The prices and every information to be obtained at
THE MANUFACTORY,
175, FLEET STREET.

HOBBS'
CHANGEABLE KEY BANK LOCK.
Price £10 and upwards.

HOBBS'
PATENT PROTECTOR LOCKS.
8s. and upwards.

HOBBS'
MACHINE-MADE LEVER LOCKS.
2s. and upwards.

Prize Medal Awarded
For " EXCELLENCE OF WORKMANSHIP IN LOCKS AND SAFES."

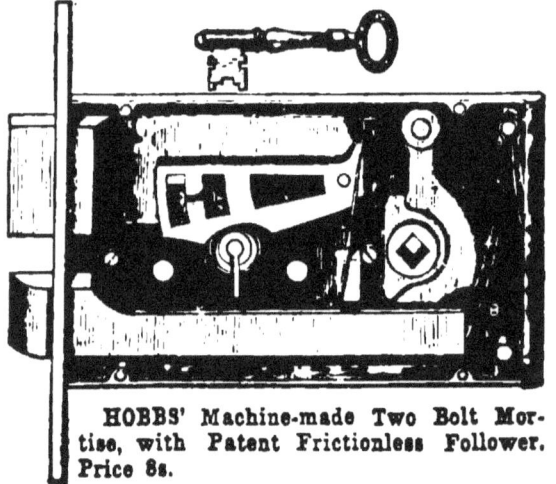

HOBBS' Machine-made Two Bolt Mortise, with Patent Frictionless Follower. Price 8s.

The Machine-made Locks are adapted for every purpose for which Locks are required, at prices that defy competition.

May be had of all respectable Ironmongers in Town and Country.

Illustrated Lists of Locks, Iron Safes, and Doors, Cash Boxes, &c., sent free on application to

HOBBS & CO.,
76, CHEAPSIDE, LONDON, E.C.

A CATALOGUE
OF
POPULAR WORKS
PUBLISHED, OR SOLD, BY
LOCKWOOD & CO.
7 STATIONERS'-HALL COURT, LONDON, E.C.

The Boy's Own Book: A Complete Encyclopædia of all the Diversions, Athletic, Scientific, and Recreative, of Boyhood and Youth. With many Hundred Woodcuts, and Ten Vignette Titles, beautifully printed in Gold. New Edition, greatly enlarged and improved, price 8s. 6d. handsomely bound in cloth.

N.B.—This is the original and genuine 'Boy's Own Book,' formerly published by Mr. Bogue, and more recently by Messrs. Kent and Co. Care should be taken, in ordering the above, to give the name of either the former or present publishers, otherwise some inferior book, with a nearly similar title, may be supplied.

The Little Boy's Own Book of Sports and Pastimes. With numerous Engravings. Abridged from the above. 16mo. price 3s. 6d. cloth.

'Many Happy Returns of the Day!' A Birthday Book. By CHARLES and MARY COWDEN CLARKE, Authors of 'The Concordance to Shakespeare,' &c. Beautifully illustrated by the Brothers Dalziel. Small post 8vo. price 6s. cloth elegant, gilt edges.

'Since the renowned volumes of "Peter Parley," we know of no book more likely to become popular among the young.'—CRITIC.

'It will be as acceptable to the young as "Sandford and Merton" was wont to be half a century since. The authors will henceforth share the affections of the young with Hans Andersen, Peter Parley, and the Brothers Grimm.'—PLYMOUTH JOURNAL.

'Sure to be a favourite with the boys.'—LEADER.

'The best book that can be found for a birthday present.'—COURT JOURNAL.

'An unobjectionable child's book is the rarest of all books. "Many Happy Returns of the Day" is not only this, but may rely, without shrinking, upon its positive excellencies for a long and deserved popularity.'—WESTMINSTER REVIEW.

Victorian Enigmas; being a Series of Enigmatical Acrostics on Historical, Biographical, Geographical, and Miscellaneous Subjects; combining Amusement with Exercise in the Attainment of Knowledge. Promoted and encouraged by Royal Example. By CHARLOTTE ELIZA CAPEL. Royal 16mo. cloth, elegantly printed, price 2s. 6d.

☞ The idea for this entirely original style of Enigmas is taken from one said to have been written by Her Majesty for the Royal children, which, with its Solution, is given.

'A capital game, and one of the very best of those commendable mental exercises which test knowledge and stimulate study. To the Queen's loyal subjects it comes, moreover, additionally recommended by the hint in the title-page and the statement in the preface, that it is a game practised by Her Majesty and the Royal children, if, indeed, it were not invented by the Queen herself.'—CRITIC.

'A good book for family circles in the long and dreary winter evenings, inasmuch as it will enable the young to pass them away both pleasantly and profitably.'
CITY PRESS.

JOHN TIMBS'S POPULAR WORKS.

Any one who reads and remembers Mr. Timbs's encyclopædic varieties should ever after be a good table talker, an excellent companion for children, a "well-read person," and a proficient lecturer; for Mr. Timbs has stored up in this little volume ("Things Not Generally Known") more knowledge than is to be found in a hundred books that might be named.'—ATHENÆUM.

Things Not Generally Known Familiarly Explained.

A Book for Old and Young. By JOHN TIMBS, F.S.A. First Series. Twenty-sixth Thousand. Fcap. 2s. 6d. cloth.

'A remarkably pleasant and instructive little book; a book as full of information as a pomegranate is full of seed.'—PUNCH.
'A very amusing miscellany.'—GENTLEMAN'S MAGAZINE.
'And as instructive as it is amusing.'—NOTES AND QUERIES.

Things Not Generally Known Familiarly Explained.

By JOHN TIMBS, F.S.A. Second Series. Tenth Thousand. Fcap. 2s. 6d. cloth. Contents:—Old English Manners, Ceremonies, and Customs; Meals and Housewifery; Herbs and Fruit; Punch and Judy, Old Plays, Pageants, and Music; Laws, Legal Customs, Privileges, and Dignities; Money, Weights, and Measures; Home Proverbs, Sayings, and Phrases; Phenomena of Life and Death; Funeral Ceremonies; A Chapter of Weather-Wisdom, Pictures, and the Care of them; Domestic Science, &c.

'The Second Series is quite as good as the first.'—CRITIC.

Curiosities of Science, Past and Present.

By JOHN TIMBS, F.S.A. First Series. Second Edition ('Things Not Generally Known' in Science.) Fcap. 2s. 6d. cloth.

Curiosities of Science, Past and Present.

By JOHN TIMBS, F.S.A. Second Series. ('Things Not Generally Known' in Science.) Fcap. 2s. 6d. cloth.

'Marked by the tact, care, and usefulness which characterise all Mr. Timbs's books.'—NOTES AND QUERIES.
'"Curiosities of Science" contains as much information in 250 pages as could otherwise be gleaned from reading elaborate treatises on physical phenomena, acoustics, optics, astronomy, geology, and palæontology, meteorology, nautical geography, magnetism, the electric telegraph, &c.'—MINING JOURNAL.

Curiosities of History. A Book for Old and Young.

('Things Not Generally Known' in History.) By JOHN TIMBS, F.S.A. Tenth Thousand. Fcap. 2s. 6d. cloth.

This book is an extension of the design of its predecessor to 'Things Not Generally Known in History;' or, where known, but imperfectly understood: as, in the salient points of history; such historic incidents and classical quotations as are often employed by public writers; and the Popular Errors of History, in the section of 'Historic Doubts.' By these means the work presents, in picturesque form, many hundred Events and Incidents, Sayings and Origins, and noteworthy instances of Human Action.

'We can conceive no more amusing book for the drawing-room, or one more useful for the school-room.'—ART JOURNAL.

Popular Errors Explained and Illustrated.

By JOHN TIMBS, F.S.A. Sixth Thousand. Fcap. 2s. 6d. cloth.

'We know of few better books for young persons; it is instructive, entertaining, and reliable. This book cannot but enhance the author's repute for curious research, and entertaining as well as instructive writing.'—BUILDER.
'A work which ninety-nine persons out of every hundred would take up whenever it came in their way, and would always learn something from.'
ENGLISH CHURCHMAN.

JOHN TIMBS'S POPULAR WORKS—*continued.*

School-days of Eminent Men. Containing Sketches of the Progress of Education in England, from the reign of King Alfred to that of Queen Victoria; and School and College Lives of the most Celebrated British Authors, Poets, and Philosophers; Inventors and Discoverers; Divines, Heroes, Statesmen, and Legislators. By JOHN TIMBS, F.S.A. Second Edition, entirely Revised and partly Re-written. With a Frontispiece by John Gilbert, 13 Views of Public Schools, and 20 Portraits by Harvey. Fcap. 5s. handsomely bound in cloth.

☞ This book is extensively used, and specially adapted for a Prize-Book at Schools.

'This is altogether a most amusing volume, and will be a most acceptable present to any school-boy ambitious of figuring in a future edition as one of England's "Eminent Men."'—GENTLEMAN'S MAGAZINE.

'The idea is a happy one, and its execution equally so. It is a book to interest all boys, but more especially those of Westminster, Eton, Harrow, Rugby, and Winchester; for of these, as of many other schools of high repute, the accounts are full and interesting.'—NOTES AND QUERIES.

Stories of Inventors and Discoverers in Science and Useful Arts. By JOHN TIMBS, F.S.A. With numerous Illustrations. Fcap. 5s. cloth.

'Another interesting and well-collected book, ranging from Archimedes and Roger Bacon to the Stephensons.'—ATHENÆUM.

'This last book is, we think, Mr. Timbs's best book.'—NATIONAL MAGAZINE.

'These stories by Mr. Timbs are as marvellous as the *Arabian Nights' Entertainments*, and are wrought into a volume of great interest and worth.'—ATLAS.

Painting Popularly Explained, with Historical Sketches of the Progress of the Art. By THOMAS JOHN GULLICK, Painter, and JOHN TIMBS, F.S.A. With a Frontispiece and Vignette, in small 8vo. pp. 336, price 6s. cloth.

☞ This work has been adopted as a text-book in the Schools of Art at South Kensington, in connection with the Science and Art Department of the Committee of Council on Education.

'This volume is one that we can heartily recommend to all who are desirous of understanding what they admire in a good painting.'—DAILY NEWS.

'This popular Manual of the Art of Painting deserves very wide diffusion. Many young men and women will find in it valuable aid to their efforts at self-education. Every school library ought to contain it.'—EXAMINER.

'This is a book which all lovers of art will rejoice in, as containing, in small compass, the very information which Exhibitions and Art Unions must have made so many thousands sensible of their want of.'—NATIONAL MAGAZINE.

The Year-Book of Facts in Science and Art. Exhibiting the most important Improvements and Discoveries of the Past Year in Mechanics and the Useful Arts, Natural Philosophy, Electricity, Chemistry, Zoology and Botany, Geology and Mineralogy, Meteorology and Astronomy. By JOHN TIMBS, F.S.A. With fine Engraved Frontispiece and Vignette, fcap. 5s. cloth.

☞ This work, published annually, records the proceedings of the principal Scientific Societies, and is indispensable for such as wish to possess a faithful picture of the latest novelties of Science and the Arts.

'Ably and honestly compiled.'—ATHENÆUM.

Just published, with a Coloured Title, post 8vo. 5s. cloth, pp. 320,

Something for Everybody; and a Garland for the Year. By JOHN TIMBS, F.S.A., Author of 'Things Not Generally Known,' 'Curiosities of London,' &c.

A SERIES OF ELEGANT GIFT-BOOKS.

Truths Illustrated by Great Authors; A Dictionary of nearly Four Thousand Aids to Reflection, Quotations of Maxims, Metaphors, Counsels, Cautions, Proverbs, Aphorisms, &c. &c. In Prose and Verse. Compiled from the Great Writers of all Ages and Countries. Eleventh Edition, fcap. 8vo. cloth, gilt edges, 568 pp. 6s.

'The quotations are perfect gems; their selection evinces sound judgment and an excellent taste.'—DISPATCH.
'We accept the treasure with profound gratitude—it should find its way to every home.'—ERA.
'We know of no better book of its kind.'—EXAMINER.

The Philosophy of William Shakespeare; delineating, in Seven Hundred and Fifty Passages selected from his Plays, the Multiform Phases of the Human Mind. With Index and References. Collated, Elucidated, and Alphabetically arranged, by the Editors of 'Truths Illustrated by Great Authors.' Second Edition, fcap. 8vo. cloth, gilt edges, nearly 700 pages, with beautiful Vignette Title, price 6s.

☞ A glance at this volume will at once show its superiority to Dodd's 'Beauties,' or any other volume of Shakespearian selections.

Songs of the Soul during its Pilgrimage Heavenward: being a New Collection of Poetry, illustrative of the Power of the Christian Faith; selected from the Works of the most eminent British, Foreign, and American Writers, Ancient and Modern, Original and Translated. By the Editors of 'Truths Illustrated by Great Authors,' &c. Second Edition, fcap. 8vo. cloth, gilt edges, 638 pages, with beautiful Frontispiece and Title, price 6s.

☞ This elegant volume will be appreciated by the admirers of 'The Christian Year.'

The Beauty of Holiness; or, The Practical Christian's Daily Companion: being a Collection of upwards of Two Thousand Reflective and Spiritual Passages, remarkable for their Sublimity, Beauty, and Practicability; selected from the Sacred Writings, and arranged in Eighty-two Sections, each comprising a different theme for meditation. By the Editors of 'Truths Illustrated by Great Authors.' Third Edition, fcap. 8vo. cloth, gilt edges, 536 pp., 6s.

'Every part of the Sacred Writings deserves our deepest attention and research, but all, perhaps, may not be equally adapted to the purposes of meditation and reflection. Those, therefore, who are in the constant habit of consulting the Bible will not object to a selection of some of its most sublime and impressive passages, arranged and classed ready at once to meet the eye.'—EXTRACT FROM PREFACE.

Events to be Remembered in the History of England. Forming a Series of interesting Narratives, extracted from the Pages of Contemporary Chronicles or Modern Historians, of the most Remarkable Occurrences in each Reign; with Reviews of the Manners, Domestic Habits, Amusements, Costumes, &c. &c., of the People, Chronological Table, &c. By CHARLES SELBY. Twenty-fifth Edition, 12mo. fine paper, with Nine Beautiful Illustrations by Anelay, price 3s. 6d. cloth, elegant, gilt edges.

N.B.—A SCHOOL EDITION, without the Illustrations, 2s. 6d. cloth.

☞ Great care has been taken to render this book unobjectionable to the most fastidious, by excluding everything that could not be read aloud in schools and families, and by abstinence from all party spirit, alike in politics as in religion.

WORKS BY THE AUTHOR OF 'A TRAP TO CATCH A SUNBEAM.'

'In telling a simple story, and in the management of dialogue, the Author is excelled by few writers of the present day.'—LITERARY GAZETTE.

A Trap to Catch a Sunbeam. Thirty-fifth Edition, price 1s.

'The whimsical wish, expressed by a friend on a dark and wintry day, that it were possible to set a trap to catch a sunbeam, originated the idea for this story.'
AUTHOR'S PREFACE.

'*Aide toi, et le ciel t'aidera*, is the moral of this pleasant and interesting story, to which we assign in this Gazette a place immediately after Charles Dickens, as its due, for many passages not unworthy of him, and for a general scheme quite in unison with his best feelings towards the lowly and depressed.'—LITERARY GAZETTE.

Also, by the same Author,

'COMING HOME;' a New Tale for all Readers, price 1s.
OLD JOLLIFFE; not a Goblin Story. 1s.
The SEQUEL to OLD JOLLIFFE. 1s.
The HOUSE on the ROCK. 1s.
'ONLY;' a Tale for Young and Old. 1s.
The CLOUD with the SILVER LINING. 1s.
The STAR in the DESERT. 1s.
AMY'S KITCHEN, A VILLAGE ROMANCE; a New Story. 1s.
The DREAM CHINTZ. With Illustrations by James Godwin. 2s. 6d. with a beautiful fancy cover.
'A MERRY CHRISTMAS.' 6d.
SIBERT'S WOLD. Second Edition, 3s. 6d. cloth.

Sunbeam Stories. A Selection of the Tales by the

Author of 'A Trap to Catch a Sunbeam,' &c. &c. In one volume, price 5s. cloth elegant, or 5s. 6d. gilt edges. Illustrated by John Absolon and Henry Anelay.

CONTENTS:

A Trap to Catch a Sunbeam.
Old Jolliffe.
The Sequel to Old Jolliffe.
The Star in the Desert.
'Only.'
'A Merry Christmas.'

Minnie's Love: a Novel. By the Author of 'A Trap

to Catch a Sunbeam.' In 1 vol. post 8vo. 10s. 6d. cloth.

'An extremely pleasant sunshiny volume.'—CRITIC.
'"Minnie's Love" adds to the reputation of the author of "A Trap to Catch a Sunbeam."'—ATLAS.
'We were first surprised, then pleased, next delighted, and finally enthralled by the story.'—MORNING HERALD.

Little Sunshine: a Tale to be Read to very Young

Children. By the Author of 'A Trap to Catch a Sunbeam.' In square 16mo. coloured borders, engraved Frontispiece and Vignette, fancy boards, price 2s.

'Young people will read it with avidity.'—CHRISTIAN WITNESS.
'Just the thing to rivet the attention of children."—STAMFORD MERCURY.
'Printed in the sumptuous manner that children like best.'—BRADFORD OBSERVER.
'As pleasing a child's book as we recollect seeing.'—PLYMOUTH HERALD.

BOOKS FOR NURSERY OR MATERNAL TUITION.

La Bagatelle: Intended to introduce Children of Five or Six Years old to some knowledge of the French Language. Revised by Madame N. L. New and Cheaper Edition, much improved, and embellished with entirely new cuts. 18mo. bound and lettered, price 2s. 6d.

'A well-known little book, revised, improved, and adorned with some very pretty new pictures. It is, indeed, French made very easy for very little children.'
— THE SCHOOL AND THE TEACHER.

'A very nice book to be placed in the hands of children; likely to command their attention by its beautiful embellishments.'—PAPERS FOR THE SCHOOLMASTER.

Chickseed without Chickweed: being very Easy and Entertaining Lessons for Little Children. A book for every Mother. New Edition, with Frontispiece by Anelay, 12mo. cloth, 1s.

Peter Parley's Book of Poetry. With numerous Engravings. New Edition, 16mo. cloth, 1s. 6d.

Cobwebs to Catch Flies: or, Dialogues and Short Sentences adapted for Children from Three to Eight Years of Age. With Woodcuts. New Edition, 12mo. cloth, 2s.; or in Two Parts, 1s. each.

PART I. For Children from Three to Five Years of Age.
PART II. For Children from Five to Eight Years of Age.

CHEAP AND ENTERTAINING BOOKS FOR CHILDREN.

The Story of the Three Bears. 17th Edition. With Illustrations, oblong, 6d. sewed.

The Great Bear's Story; or, The Vizier and the Woodman. With Illustrations, oblong, 6d. sewed.

An Hour at Bearwood; or, The Wolf and the Seven Kids. With Illustrations, oblong, 6d. sewed.

The Three Bears and their Stories; being the above Stories in 1 vol. With numerous Illustrations, oblong, 2s. cloth, lettered.

The Ugly Duck. By HANS ANDERSEN. Versified; and dedicated to the Readers of 'The Three Bears.' Four Illustrations by Weigall, oblong, 6d. sewed.

Little Sunshine: a Tale to be read to very Young Children. By the Author of 'A Trap to Catch a Sunbeam.' In square 16mo. coloured borders, engraved Frontispiece and Vignette, fancy boards, price 2s.

'Young people will read it with avidity.'—CHRISTIAN WITNESS.
'Just the thing to rivet the attention of children.'—STAMFORD MERCURY.
'Printed in the sumptuous manner that children like best.'—BRADFORD OBSERVER.
'As pleasing a child's book as we recollect seeing.'—PLYMOUTH HERALD.

The Lessons of My Farm: A Book for Amateur Agriculturists; being an Introduction to Farm Practice in the Culture of Crops, the Feeding of Cattle, Management of the Dairy, Poultry, Pigs, and in the Keeping of Farm-work Records. By ROBERT SCOTT BURN, one of the Authors of 'Book of Farm Buildings.' With numerous Illustrations, fcap. 6s. cloth.

The Fables of Babrius. Translated into English Verse from the Text of Sir G. Cornewall Lewis. By the Rev. JAMES DAVIES, some time Scholar of Lincoln Coll. Oxford. Fcap. cloth, antique, elegantly printed, price 6s.

'"Who was Babrius?" The reply may not improbably startle the reader. Babrius was the real, original Æsop. Nothing is so fabulous about the fables of our childhood as their reputed authorship. . . Mr. Davies has succeeded, to a very remarkable degree, in retaining the simplicity and terseness which are requisite to enforce the point of an apologue.'—DAILY NEWS.

'The Æsop of our boyhood is dethroned, and his sceptre taken from him, by no less a disenchanter than Her Majesty's Secretary of State for the Home Department. . . Here stands the fact that Æsop was not the author of the world-famed fables, but that the real fabricator was one Babrius. . . So Babrius has been finally set up to rule over the realm of early fables, and Æsop passes into the category of myths or plagiarists, according to the evidence.'—ILLUSTRATED LONDON NEWS.

'A fable-book which is admirably adapted to take the place of the imperfect collections of Æsopian wisdom which have hitherto held the first place in our juvenile libraries.'—HEREFORD TIMES.

'Mr. Davies' version is close and faithful.'—EDINBURGH REVIEW.

The Shadow in the House: a Novel. By JOHN SAUNDERS, late Editor of the 'People's Journal,' Author of 'Love's Martyrdom,' &c. One vol. post 8vo. 400 pages, price 10s. 6d. cloth.

'Refinement of taste, purity of moral tone, and poetical and dramatic talent in the conception and working out of character, are conspicuous throughout.'—GLOBE.
'Where properly appreciated, must achieve a success.'—MORNING CHRONICLE.
'Cook is a character as well worth studying as Mrs. Poyser.'—DIAL.
'This story will remain as one of the gems of English fiction.'—CITY PRESS.
'Mr. Saunders is destined ere long to assume a high position among the novelists of the day.'—LEADER.

⁎ By the same Author, will be published immediately,

Abel Drake's Wife: a Tale. 1 vol. post 8vo. 10s. 6d.

Mysteries of Life, Death, and Futurity; Illustrated from the best and latest Authorities. By HORACE WELBY. With an Emblematic Frontispiece, fcap. 5s. cloth.

Contents:—Life and Time; Nature of the Soul; Spiritual Life; Mental Operations; Belief and Scepticism; Premature Interment; Phenomena of Death; Sin and Punishment; The Crucifixion of Our Lord; The End of the World; Man after Death; The Intermediate State; The Great Resurrection; Recognition of the Blessed; The Day of Judgment; The Future States, &c.

The Historical Finger-Post: a Handy Book of Terms, Phrases, Epithets, Cognomens, Allusions, &c., in connection with Universal History. By EDWARD SHELTON, Assistant Editor of 'The Dictionary of Daily Wants,' &c. &c. 1 vol. crown 8vo. pp. 384, 3s. 6d. cloth.

'A handy little volume, which will supply the place of "Haydn's Dictionary of Dates" to many persons who cannot afford that work. Moreover, it contains some things that Haydn's book does not.'—BOOKSELLER.

'It is to the historical student and antiquarian what "Enquire Within" is to the practical housewife.—VOLUNTEER SERVICE GAZETTE.

WORKS BY THE REV. WM. HARRISON,
RECTOR OF BIRCH.

The Tongue of Time; or, The Language of a Church Clock. By WILLIAM HARRISON, A.M. of Brazenose College, Oxford; Domestic Chaplain to H. R. H. the Duke of Cambridge; Rector of Birch, Essex. Sixth Edition, with beautiful Frontispiece, fcp. 3s. cloth, gilt edges.

The Shepherd and his Sheep; An Exposition of the Twenty-third Psalm. Second Edition, enlarged, fcp. 2s. 6d. cloth.

Consecrated Thoughts; or, A Few Notes from a Christian Harp. Second Edition, corrected, fcp. 2s. 6d. cloth.

Sermons on the Commandments; Preached in the Chapel of the Magdalen Hospital. Second Edition, fcp. 4s. cloth.

Hours of Sadness; or, Instruction and Comfort for the Mourner: Consisting of a Selection of Devotional Meditations, Instructive and Consolatory Reflections, Letters, Prayers, Poetry, &c., from various Authors, suitable for the bereaved Christian. Second Edition, fcp. 4s. 6d. cloth.

Sidney Grey; a Tale of School Life. By the Author of 'Mia and Charlie.' Second Edition, with Six beautiful Illustrations. Fcap. 4s. 6d. cloth.

Do you Give it Up? A Collection of the most Amusing Conundrums, Riddles, &c., of the day. Fcap. price 1s. cloth limp.

The Instant Reckoner. Showing the Value of any Quantity of Goods, including Fractional Parts of a Pound Weight, at any price from One Farthing to Twenty Shillings; with an Introduction, embracing Copious Notes of Coins, Weights, Measures, and other Commercial and Useful Information; and an Appendix, containing Tables of Interest, Salaries, Commission, &c. 24mo. 1s. 6d. cloth, or 2s. strongly bound in leather.

☛ Indispensable to every housekeeper.

CHEAP AND PORTABLE LITERATURE.

The Pocket English Classics. 32mo. neatly printed, in Illuminated Wrappers, price Sixpence each.

The following are now ready:—

THE VICAR OF WAKEFIELD.
GOLDSMITH'S POETICAL WORKS.
FALCONER'S SHIPWRECK.
RASSELAS.
STERNE'S SENTIMENTAL JOURNEY.
LOCKE ON THE UNDERSTANDING.
THOMSON'S SEASONS.
INCHBALD'S NATURE AND ART.
BLOOMFIELD'S FARMER'S BOY.
SCOTT'S LADY OF THE LAKE.
SCOTT'S LAY.
COLERIDGE'S ANCIENT MARINER.
WALTON'S COMPLETE ANGLER, PART I.
WALTON'S COMPLETE ANGLER, PART II.
ELIZABETH: OR, THE EXILES.
COWPER'S TASK.
POPE'S ESSAY AND BLAIR'S GRAVE.
GRAY AND COLLINS.
GAY'S FABLES.
PAUL AND VIRGINIA.

EDUCATIONAL WORKS.

DR. CORNWELL'S POPULAR SERIES OF SCHOOL-BOOKS.

'A very useful series of Educational Works, of which Dr. Cornwell is author or editor. It (the "Geography for Beginners") is an admirable introduction. There is vast difficulty in writing a good elementary book, and Dr. Cornwell has shown himself possessed of that rare combination of faculties which is required for the task.'—JOHN BULL.

Allen and Cornwell's School Grammar. 31st Edition, 2s. red; 1s. 9d. cloth.

Grammar for Beginners. 36th Edit. 1s. cloth; 9d. swd.

Select English Poetry. Edited by the late Dr. ALLEN. 11th Edition, 4s.

The Young Composer; or, Progressive Exercises in English Composition. By J. CORNWELL, Ph.D. 23rd Edition, 1s. 6d.

Key to the Young Composer. 3s.

Dr. Allen's Eutropius. With a *complete* Dictionary, an Index of Proper Names, and Chronological Tables, 3s.

Science of Arithmetic. By J. CORNWELL, Ph.D., and J. G. FITCH, M.A. 7th Edition, 4s. 6d.

Arithmetic for Beginners. A First Book of Practical Arithmetic, with an Inductive Explanation of each Rule, and numerous Questions for Mental Calculation. By the Authors of the above. 4th Edition, 1s. 6d.

GEOGRAPHICAL WORKS BY JAMES CORNWELL, PH.D.

School Geography. 29th Edition, 3s. 6d.; or with Thirty Maps on Steel, 5s. 6d.

Geography for Beginners. 7th Edition, 1s.

School Atlas. Consisting of Thirty Maps on Steel. 2s. 6d. plain, or 4s. coloured.

Map Book for Beginners. Consisting of Twelve Plates of Maps, being a Companion Atlas to the 'Geography for Beginners.' On Steel, 1s. 6d. plain; 2s. 6d. coloured.

Book of Blank Maps. The above Maps, complete in everything except the names, which are to be filled in by the learner. 1s.

Book of Map Projections. Twelve Plates, consisting of the Lines of Latitude and Longitude only to the above Maps. 1s.

THE FRENCH LANGUAGE.

M. de Fivas' Works for the Use of Colleges, Schools, and Private Students.

The attention of Schoolmasters and Heads of Colleges is respectfully requested to the following eminently useful series of French class books, which have enjoyed an unprecedented popularity. A detailed prospectus will be sent on application.

De Fivas' New Grammar of French Grammars; comprising the substance of all the most approved French Grammars extant, but more especially of the standard work 'La Grammaire des Grammaires,' sanctioned by the French Academy and the University of Paris. With numerous Exercises and Examples illustrative of every Rule. By Dr. V. DE FIVAS, M.A., F.E.I.S., Member of the Grammatical Society of Paris, &c. &c. 20th Edition, price 3s. 6d. handsomely bound.

'At once the simplest and most complete Grammar of the French language. To the pupil the effect is almost as if he looked into a map, so well-defined is the course of study as explained by M. de Fivas.'—LITERARY GAZETTE.

_{*} A KEY to the above, price 3s. 6d.

De Fivas' New Guide to Modern French Conversation; or, the Student and Tourist's French Vade-Mecum: containing a Comprehensive Vocabulary, and Phrases and Dialogues on every useful or interesting topic; together with Models of Letters, Notes, and Cards; and Comparative Tables of the British and French Coins, Weights, and Measures: the whole exhibiting, in a distinct manner, the true Pronunciation of the French Language.

'Voulez-vous un guide aussi sûr qu'infaillible pour apprendre la langue Française, prenez le Guide de M. de Fivas: c'est l'indispensable manuel de tout étranger."
L'IMPARTIAL.

De Fivas, Beautés des Écrivains Français, Anciens et Modernes. Ouvrage Classique, à l'usage des Collèges et des Institutions. Dixième Edition, augmentée de Notes Historiques, Géographiques, Philosophiques, Littéraires, Grammaticales, et Biographiques.

'An elegant volume, containing a selection of pieces both in prose and verse, which, while it furnishes a convenient reading book for the student of the French language, at the same time affords a pleasing and interesting view of French literature.'—OBSERVER.

De Fivas, Introduction à la Langue Française; ou, Fables et Contes Choisis; Anecdotes Instructives, Faits Mémorables, &c. Avec un Dictionnaire de tous les Mots traduits en Anglais. A l'usage de la jeunesse, et de ceux qui commencent à apprendre la langue Française.

'By far the best first French reading-book, whether for schools or adult pupils.'
TAIT'S MAGAZINE.

De Fivas, Le Trésor National; or, Guide to the Translation of English into French at sight.

☞ Le 'Trésor National' consists of idiomatical and conversational phrases, anecdotes told and untold, and scraps from various English writers, and is especially intended to produce by practice, in those who learn French, a facility of expressing themselves in that language.

_{*} A KEY to the above, 12mo. 2s. cloth.

THE FRENCH LANGUAGE—*continued.*

La Bagatelle: Intended to Introduce Children of Five or Six Years old to some Knowledge of the French Language. Revised by MADAME N. L. New and cheaper Edition, much improved, and embellished with entirely new cuts, 18mo. price 2s. 6d. bound and lettered.

This little work is recommended to parents and others engaged in the education of young children, as well adapted for familiarising their pupils with the construction and sounds of the French language, conveying at the same time excellent moral lessons.

'An easy and familiar French book for children of tender years—so attractive as to create in their young minds a liking for the language—prepares them by slow and easy advances for the higher work of the grammar—and gives them an inductive faculty for discerning French idioms and peculiarities of construction.'
— EDUCATIONAL GAZETTE.

'A very nice book to be placed in the hands of children; likely to command their attention by its beautiful embellishments.'—PAPERS FOR THE SCHOOLMASTER.

'A well-known little book, revised, improved, and adorned with some very pretty new pictures. It is, indeed, French made very easy for very little children.'
— THE SCHOOL AND THE TEACHER.

Le Brethon's French Grammar: A Guide to the French Language. By J. J. P. LE BRETHON. Revised and Corrected by L. SANDIER, Professor of Languages. Twelfth Edition, 8vo. 432 pages, 7s. 6d. cloth.

VOCABULAIRE SYMBOLIQUE ANGLO-FRANÇAIS.'
Pour les Elèves de tout Âge et de tout Degré; dans lequel les Mots les plus utiles sont enseignés par des Illustrations. Par L. C. RAGONOT, Professeur de la Langue Française.

A Symbolic French and English Vocabulary. For Students of every Age, in all Classes; in which the most Useful and Common Words are taught by Illustrations. By L. C. RAGONOT, Professor of the French Language. The Illustrations comprise, embodied in the text, accurate representations of upwards of 850 different objects, besides nine whole-page copper-plates, beautifully executed, each conveying, through the eye, a large amount of instruction in the French Language. Eighth Edition, considerably improved, with new plates substituted, 4to. 5s. cloth.

☞ This work in the Anglo-French form having been extensively adopted, not only in Great Britain and on the Continent, but also in America, the publishers have determined to adapt it to other languages, and, by producing it in a more portable form, to render it equally suitable to the Tourist and the General Scholar. A German and English Edition is now ready, price 6s. cloth.

THE GERMAN LANGUAGE.

Tuchmann—A Practical Grammar of the German Language, for School and Self-Tuition; with an Appendix, containing Commercial Letters, &c. By L. M. TUCHMANN, formerly Teacher at the City Commercial and Scientific School, &c. &c. 12mo. 3s. 6d. cloth.

Symbolisches Englisch-Deutsches Wörterbuch: the Symbolic Anglo-German Vocabulary; adapted from RAGONOT's 'Vocabulaire Symbolique Anglo-Français.' Edited and Revised by FALCK LEBAHN, Ph. Dr., Author of 'German in One Volume,' 'The German Self-Instructor,' &c. With 850 woodcuts, and eight full-page lithographic plates. 8vo. 6s. red cloth, lettered.

THE GERMAN LANGUAGE—*continued.*

Dr. Falck Lebahn's Popular Series of German School-Books.

'As an educational writer in the German tongue, Dr. Lebahn stands alone; none other has made even a distant approach to him. The magnitude and value of his services have been acknowledged by the Public Press to an extent and with a unanimity of which there is no example.'—BRITISH STANDARD.

Lebahn's First German Course. Second Edition. Crown 8vo. 2s. 6d. cloth.

'It is hardly possible to have a simpler or better book for beginners in German.' ATHENÆUM.

'It is really what it professes to be—a simple, clear, and concise introduction to the German language; one, too, which will be equally useful to the self-instructing student and the member of a German class.'—CRITIC.

Lebahn's German Language in One Volume. Sixth Edition, containing—I. A Practical Grammar, with Exercises to every Rule. II. Undine; a Tale: by DE LA MOTTE FOUQUÉ, with Explanatory Notes of all difficult words and phrases. III. A Vocabulary of 4500 Words, synonymous in English and German. Crown 8vo. 8s. cloth. With Key, 10s. 6d. Key separate, 2s. 6d.

'This is the best German grammar that has yet been published.' MORNING POST.

'Had we to re commence the study of German, of all the German grammars which we have examined—and they are not a few—we should unhesitatingly say, Falck Lebahn's is the book for us.'—EDUCATIONAL TIMES.

Lebahn's Edition of Schmid's Henry Von Eichenfels. With Vocabulary and Familiar Dialogues. Sixth Edition. Crown 8vo. 3s. 6d. cloth.

'Equally with Mr. Lebahn's previous publications, excellently adapted to assist self-exercise in the German language.'—SPECTATOR.

'Mr. Lebahn has done his work in his usual clever, painstaking, and (to the student) profitable style.'—CHURCH AND STATE GAZETTE.

Lebahn's First German Reader. Fourth Edition. Crown 8vo. 3s. 6d. cloth.

'An excellent elementary work.'—SUNDAY TIMES.
'Like all Lebahn's works, most thoroughly practical.'—BRITANNIA.
'An admirable book for beginners, which indeed may be used without a master.' LEADER.

Lebahn's German Classics; with Notes and Complete Vocabularies. Crown 8vo. price 3s. 6d. each, cloth:—

PETER SCHLEMIHL, the Shadowless Man. By CHAMISSO.
EGMONT. A Tragedy, in Five Acts, by GOETHE.
WILHELM TELL. A Drama, in Five Acts, by SCHILLER.
GOETZ VON BERLICHINGEN. A Drama. By GOETHE.
PAGENSTREICHE, a Page's Frolics. A Comedy, by KOTZEBUE.
EMILIA GALOTTI. A Tragedy, in Five Acts, by LESSING.
UNDINE. A Tale, by FOUQUÉ.
SELECTIONS from the GERMAN POETS.

'These editions are prepared for the use of learners who read without a master; and they will be found convenient for that purpose. In each, the text is followed by a glossary, wherein not only the sense of every particular phrase, but also the dictionary meaning of most of the several words, is given in good English. With such aids, a student will find no difficulty in these masterpieces.'—ATHENÆUM.

Lebahn's German Copy-Book: being a Series of Exercises in German Penmanship, beautifully engraved on Steel. 4to. 2s. 6d. sewed.

THE GERMAN LANGUAGE—*continued.*

Lebahn's Exercises in German. Crown 8vo. 3s. 6d. cloth.

'A volume of "Exercises in German," including in itself all the vocabularies they require. The book is well planned; the selections for translation from German into English, or from English into German, being sometimes curiously well suited to the purpose for which they are taken.'—EXAMINER.

Lebahn's Self-Instructor in German. Crown 8vo. 6s. 6d. cloth.

'One of the most amusing elementary reading-books that ever passed under our hands.'—JOHN BULL.

'The student could have no guide superior to Mr. Lebahn.'
LITERARY GAZETTE.

Nicholson and Rowbotham's Practical System of Algebra. Designed for the use of Schools and Private Students. Seventh Edition, 12mo. 300 pages, 3s. 0d. bound.

Technical Memory. The Historical Lines of Dr. GREY's Technical Memory. With various additions, chiefly as they apply to Modern History. Sixth Edition, 1s. sewed.

O'Gorman's Intuitive Calculations; the most Concise Methods ever published. Designed for the use of all classes—Bankers, Brewers, Engineers, Land Surveyors, Manufacturers, Merchants, Wine and Spirit Merchants, Timber Merchants, Professors, Teachers, &c. With an Appendix on Decimal Computation, Coins, and Currency. By DANIEL O'GORMAN. 22nd Edition, revised. 30th thousand, crown 8vo. 3s. 6d. cloth.

O'Gorman's Original and Comprehensive System of Self-Instructing Book-keeping by Single and Double Entry. New Edition, 8vo. price 5s. cloth.

O'Gorman's Prince of Wales's New Table-Book, compiled from the 'Intuitive Calculations;' embracing all the Tables in Money, Weights, and Measures, necessary for the Arithmetician; with Tables of Decimal Coins. New Edition, 8d. stitched.

Marcus' Latin Grammar.—A Latin Grammar. By the Rev. LEWIS MARCUS, M.A., Queen's College, Cambridge, Incumbent of St. Paul's, Finsbury, and formerly Head Master of the Grammar School, Holbeach. 12mo. 2s. 6d. cloth.

Chronological Tables of Contemporary Sovereigns, Dates, Battles, Treaties, &c. Forming an easy Artificial Memory for the Study of Universal History, from the Christian Era to the Present Time. By S. M. RUFFIN. 2d Edition, 4to. 3s. 6d. cloth limp.

Events to be Remembered in the History of England. By CHARLES SELBY. Twenty-fifth (School) Edition. 12mo. 2s. 6d. cloth.

N.B.—A fine paper Edition, with nine beautiful Illustrations by Anelay (suitable for Prize or Gift Book). 12mo. 3s. 6d. cloth elegant, gilt edges.

WORKS IN ENGINEERING, ARCHITECTURE, AGRICULTURE, SCIENCE, &c.

THE YEAR-BOOK of FACTS in SCIENCE and ART.
Exhibiting the most important Improvements and Discoveries of the past year in Mechanics and the Useful Arts, Natural Philosophy, Electricity, Chemistry, Zoology and Botany, Geology and Mineralogy, Meteorology and Astronomy. By JOHN TIMBS, F.S.A. (Published Annually.)
☞ This work records the proceedings of the principal scientific societies, and is indispensable for such as wish to possess a faithful picture of the latest novelties of science and the arts.

AIDE-MEMOIRE to the MILITARY SCIENCES; framed from Contributions of Officers of the different Services, and edited by a Committee of the Corps of Royal Engineers. 3 vols. royal 8vo. upwards of 500 Engravings and Woodcuts, in extra cloth boards, and lettered, £4. 10s.; or may be had in six separate parts, paper boards.

THE HIGH-PRESSURE STEAM-ENGINE. By Dr. ERNST ALBAN, Practical Machine Maker, Plan, Mecklenburg. Translated from the German, by WILLIAM POLE, C.E., F.R.A.S., Assoc. Inst. C.E. 8vo. with 28 fine Plates, 16s. 6d. cloth.

A PRACTICAL and THEORETICAL ESSAY on OBLIQUE BRIDGES. With 13 large Folding Plates. By GEORGE W. BUCK, M. Inst. C.E. Second Edition, corrected by W. H. BARLOW, M. Inst. C.E. Imperial 8vo. 12s. cloth.

THE PRACTICAL RAILWAY ENGINEER. By G. DRYSDALE DEMPSEY, Civil Engineer. Fourth Edition, revised and greatly extended. With 71 double quarto Plates, 72 Woodcuts, and Portrait of G. STEPHENSON. One large vol. 4to. £2. 12s. 6d. cloth.

ON IRON SHIP-BUILDING; with Practical Examples and Details, in Twenty-four Plates, together with Text containing Descriptions, Explanations, and General Remarks. By JOHN GRANTHAM, C.E., Consulting Engineer, and Naval Architect. Second Edition, Atlas of Plates, with separate Text, £1. 5s.

A TREATISE on the PRINCIPLES and PRACTICE of LEVELLING. By FREDERICK W. SIMMS, M. Inst. C.E. Fourth Edition, with the Addition of Mr. Law's Practical Examples for setting out Railway Curves, and Mr. Trautwine's Field Practice of Laying out Circular Curves. With 7 Plates and numerous Woodcuts, 8vo. 8s. 6d. cloth.
☞ Trautwine on Laying out Circular Curves is also sold separately, price 5s. sewed.

PRACTICAL TUNNELLING. By FREDERICK W. SIMMS, M. Inst. C.E. Second Edition, with Additions by W. DAVIS HASKOLL, C.E. Imperial 8vo., numerous Woodcuts and 16 Folding Plates, £1. 1s. cloth.

TABLES for the PURCHASING of ESTATES, Annuities, Advowsons, &c., and for the Renewing of Leases; also for Valuing Reversionary Estates, Deferred Annuities, next Presentations, &c. By WILLIAM INWOOD, Architect. Seventeenth Edition, with considerable additions. 12mo. cloth, 7s.

THE STUDENT'S GUIDE to the PRACTICE of DESIGNING, MEASURING, and VALUING ARTIFICERS' WORK; with 43 Plates and Woodcuts. Edited by EDWARD DOBSON, Architect and Surveyor. Second Edition, with Additions on Design, by E. LACY GARBETT, Architect. One Vol. 8vo. extra cloth, 9s.

A GENERAL TEXT-BOOK, for the Constant Use and Reference of Architects, Engineers, Surveyors, Solicitors, Auctioneers, Land Agents, and Stewards. By EDWARD RYDE, Civil Engineer and Land Surveyor; to which are added several Chapters on Agriculture and Landed Property. By Professor DONALDSON. One large thick vol. 8vo. with numerous Engravings, £1. 8s. cloth.

THE ELEMENTARY PRINCIPLES of CARPENTRY. By THOMAS TREDGOLD, Civil Engineer. Illustrated by Fifty-three Engravings, a Portrait of the Author, and several Woodcuts. Fourth Edition. Edited by PETER BARLOW, F.R.S. One large Volume, 4to. £1. 1s. in extra cloth.

HINTS to YOUNG ARCHITECTS. By GEORGE WIGHTWICK, Architect, Author of "The Palace of Architecture," &c. Second Edition, with numerous Woodcuts, 8vo. extra cloth, 7s.

WORKS IN ENGINEERING, &c.—*continued.*

THE OPERATIVE MECHANIC'S WORKSHOP COMPANION; comprising a great variety of the most useful Rules in Mechanical Science, with numerous Tables of Practical Data and Calculated Results. By W. Templeton, Author of 'The Engineer's Common-Place Book,' &c. Seventh Edition, with 11 Plates. 12mo. price 5s. bound and lettered.

THEORY of COMPOUND INTEREST and ANNUITIES, with TABLES of LOGARITHMS for the more difficult computations of Interest, Discount, Annuities, &c., in all their Applications and Uses for Mercantile and State Purposes. By F. Thoman, of the Société Crédit Mobilier, Paris. 12mo. cloth, price 5s.

THE ENGINEER'S, ARCHITECT'S, and CONTRACTOR'S POCKET BOOK (Lockwood and Co.'s, formerly Weale's), published Annually. With Diary of Events and Data connected with Engineering, Architecture, and the kindred Sciences. The present year's Volume is much improved by the addition of various useful articles. With 8 Copperplates, and numerous Woodcuts, in roan tuck, gilt edges, 6s.

THE BUILDER'S and CONTRACTOR'S PRICE BOOK (Lockwood and Co.'s, formerly Weale's), published Annually. Containing the latest prices for work in all branches of the Building Trade, with items numbered for easy reference. 12mo. cloth boards, lettered, 4s.

THE TIMBER MERCHANT'S and BUILDER'S COMPANION. Containing new and copious TABLES, &c. By William Dowsing, Timber Merchant, Hull. Second Edition, revised. Crown 8vo. 3s. cloth.

A SYNOPSIS of PRACTICAL PHILOSOPHY. Alphabetically Arranged. Designed as a Manual for Travellers, Architects, Surveyors, Engineers, Students, Naval Officers, and other Scientific Men. By the Rev. John Carr, M.A., late Fellow of Trinity College, Cambridge. Second Edition, 18mo. cloth, 5s.

THE CARPENTER'S NEW GUIDE; or, Book of Lines for Carpenters, founded on the late Peter Nicholson's standard work. A New Edition, revised by Arthur Ashpitel, Arch. F.S.A.; together with Practical Rules on Drawing, by George Pyne, Artist. With 74 Plates, 4to. price £1. 1s. cloth.

TREATISE on the STRENGTH of TIMBER, CAST IRON, MALLEABLE IRON, and other Materials. By Peter Barlow, F.R.S., V.S., Hon. Mem. Inst. C.E., &c. A New Edition, by J. F. Heather, M.A., of the Royal Military Academy, Woolwich, with Additions by Prof. Willis, of Cambridge. With Nine Illustrations, 8vo. 16s. cloth.

THE COMPLETE GRAZIER, and Farmer's and Cattle Breeder's Assistant. A Compendium of Husbandry. By William Youatt, Esq., V.S., Member of the Royal Agricultural Society of England; Author of 'The Horse,' 'Cattle,' &c. Tenth Edition, much enlarged, with numerous Engravings, 8vo. price 12s. cloth lettered.

THE LAND VALUER'S BEST ASSISTANT, being Tables, on a very much improved Plan, for Calculating the Value of Estates. By R. Hudson, Civil Engineer. New Edition, with Additions and Corrections, 4s. bound.

A MANUAL of ELECTRICITY. Including Galvanism, Magnetism, Dia-Magnetism, Electro-Dynamics, Magno-Electricity, and the Electric Telegraph. By Henry M. Noad, Ph.D., F.C.S., Lecturer on Chemistry at St. George's Hospital. Fourth Edition, entirely re-written, illustrated by 500 Woodcuts, 8vo. £1. 4s. cloth. Sold also in Two Parts; Part I. Electricity and Galvanism, 8vo. 16s. cloth. Part II. Magnetism and the Electric Telegraph, 8vo. 10s. 6d. cloth.

DESIGNS and EXAMPLES of COTTAGES, VILLAS, and COUNTRY HOUSES. Being the Studies of Eminent Architects and Builders, consisting of Plans, Elevations, and Perspective Views; with approximate Estimates of the cost of each. 4to. 67 Plates, £1. 1s. cloth.

THE APPRAISER, AUCTIONEER, and HOUSE-AGENT'S POCKET ASSISTANT. By John Wheeler, Valuer. 24mo. cloth boards, 2s. 6d.

PRACTICAL RULES on DRAWING, for the Operative Builder and Young Student in Architecture. By George Pyne, Author of 'A Rudimentary Treatise on Perspective for Beginners.' With 14 Plates, 4to. 7s. 6d. boards.

New Book by one of the Contributors to 'The Reason Why' Series, and Assistant Editor of 'The Dictionary of Daily Wants.'

Now ready, 1 vol. crown 8vo. pp. 384, 3s. 6d. cloth.

The Historical Finger-Post: A Handy Book of Terms, Phrases, Epithets, Cognomens, Allusions, &c., in connection with Universal History. By EDWARD SHELTON, Assistant Editor of 'The Dictionary of Daily Wants,' &c. &c.

☞ This book will be found to contain nearly three thousand explanatory articles, some idea of the varied nature of which may be gathered from the following list of its sections:—

SECTION 1. Wars, Battles, Naval and Military Expeditions, &c. 2. Conspiracies, Plots, Revolts, Tumults, Riots, Insurrections, &c. 3. Factions, Political Parties, Secret Societies, Cliques, Coteries, &c. 4. Dynasties, Royal Houses, Noble and Illustrious Families, &c. 5. Empires, Territories, Divisions, Form of Government, &c. 6. Dignities, Titles, Officers of State and Honour, &c. 7. Treaties, Conventions, Leagues, Convocations, Councils, Deliberative Assemblies, &c. 8. Religious Sects and Denominations, Ecclesiastical Orders, Divisions, &c. 9. Philosophies, Systems, Doctrines, &c. 10. Laws, Enactments, Codes, Constitutions, &c. 11. Places, Provinces, Districts, Territories, &c. 12. Races, Peoples, Classes, Tribes, &c. 13. Military Organisations. 14. Superstitions, Fables, Traditions, &c. 15. Romance, Legend, Imaginary and Mysterious Personages. 16. Personal Epithets, Surnames, Distinguishing Titles, &c. 17. National Epithets: Political, Classical, and Social Allusions. 18. Memorable Sayings, Mottoes, Party Cries, National Songs, Hymns, &c. 19. Books of Faith, Records, Remarkable Publications, &c. 20. Literature, Art, Science, Discoveries, Inventions, &c. 21. Insignia, Emblems, Orders of Knighthood, &c. 22. National Institutions, Customs, &c. 23. Objects of Curiosity, Interest, and Wonder. 24. Epochs, Anniversaries, Sports, &c. 25. Prisons, Punishments, Penalties, Taxes, &c. 26. Parliamentary Terms, Legal and Commercial Phrases, &c. (*The whole rendered available for instant reference by the addition of a copious Index.*)

Opinions of the Press.

'A handy little volume, which will supply the place of "Haydn's Dictionary of Dates" to many persons who cannot afford that work. Moreover, it contains some things that Haydn's book does not.'—BOOKSELLER.

'It is to the historical student and antiquarian what "Enquire Within" is to the practical housewife—not dispensing with stores of hard-acquired and well-digested knowledge, but giving that little aid which, in moments of hurry and business, is the true economiser of time.'—VOLUNTEER SERVICE GAZETTE.

'The idlest reader would find it convenient to have it within reach.'
PUBLISHER'S CIRCULAR.

'Really a very useful work; and, at the present day, when everybody is expected to be up in everything, as good a handy-book for cramming on the current subjects of conversation as any that we know. About 3000 subjects have all their place in this extraordinary collection, and although tersely given, the account of each is sufficient for ordinary purposes.'—ERA.

'A very desirable companion, as containing a variety of information, much of which could only be got by diligent inquiry and research. . . . Deserves a place as a book of reference on the shelves of the study or library.'
NAVAL AND MILITARY GAZETTE.

'This is a most useful book, but its title does not do it justice. A finger-post only points to what you want to arrive at, but in these pages are contained the very objects themselves. It is a very excellent collection, and we strongly recommend it to our readers as a cheap mine of useful information.'
JOURNAL OF HORTICULTURE.

'The scope of the work is comprehensive; its compilation must have required immense care; and to persons who in miscellaneous reading stumble on references to historical events, the details of which they would be glad to understand, it will prove a book always ready for use, and so arranged as to be turned to account without the slightest difficulty.'—SUNDAY TIMES.

'Mr. Shelton deserves well of those who really wish to understand what they read.'—SPECTATOR.

'Mr. Shelton's idea is good, and exceedingly well carried out. . . . The "Historical Finger-Post" must be seen to be appreciated.'—ART JOURNAL.

'This most useful and admirably arranged handy-book will in most cases greatly lighten the labour of investigation, and obviate a long and tedious search through voluminous publications.'—WEEKLY TIMES.